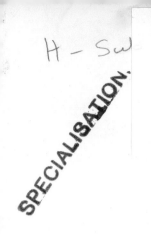

THE WESTERN HEMISPHERE

*Its Influence on United States Policies
to the End of World War II*

THE
WESTERN HEMISPHERE

Its Influence on United States Policies
to the End of World War II

Wilfrid Hardy Callcott

UNIVERSITY OF TEXAS PRESS, AUSTIN & LONDON

Published with the assistance of a grant from the Ford Foundation under its program for the support of publications in the humanities and social sciences.

Standard Book Number 292-78390-6
Library of Congress Catalog Card No. 68-55058
Copyright © 1968 by Wilfrid Hardy Callcott
All Rights Reserved

Printed in the United States of America by
The University of Texas Printing Division, Austin
Bound by Universal Bookbindery, Inc., San Antonio

TO MY STUDENTS
WHO TAUGHT ME TO STUDY
DIPLOMATIC HISTORY

PREFACE

A hemisphere policy for the United States was a matter of slow and almost unobserved growth. A number of early statesmen considered the idea as an intellectual problem but generally applied their efforts to areas immediately adjacent to their own nation. Emergent tendencies to range further afield, especially after 1850, were interrupted by the Civil War. Then followed a third of a century so devoted to domestic problems that foreign policy became largely an exercise in trial and error. Slowly, however, precedents accumulated regardless of the party in power, and national practices appeared that could be dignified by the term "policies."

During this first century and a quarter of its national existence the New World foreign policies of the United States were channeled in two quite different streams. One comprised relations with Anglo-Saxon-dominated Canada on the north, behind which stood the stable and powerful British Empire, whose trade with the United States was of primary importance. The other dealt with politically weaker states and colonies of Latin origin to the south. At the end of the century the growing young nation clashed with Spain in the Caribbean over its remaining colonies, especially Cuba. Then it worked out a policy with Great Britain by which it assumed recognized priority in Caribbean affairs. Meanwhile the Latin republics grew both economically and politically, and their significance in world affairs took on commensurate stature. Canada, too, had emerged from a colony into a dominion with increasing attributes of nationhood.

The first half of the twentieth century saw the sub-Arctic exploited for valuable raw materials, from gold to iron, petroleum, and fissionable products. Yet these new commodities found themselves in competition with products coming from Mexico, Brazil, Colombia, Ecuador, and Chile. Strategic raw materials, such as vanadium and petroleum, were of compelling importance. Whether in the Peruvian Andes or in the Arctic wastes, they had become essential to the industrial machine of the continent. At this point appeared a new problem—that industrial machine was no longer restricted to the area between the Rio Grande and the 49th parallel.

Finally, for the first time in nearly a century the imminent threat of European aggression arose. President Franklin D. Roosevelt, realizing the significance of this threat, undertook to guarantee the integrity of the whole hemisphere. Trade had already made the integration of the thinking of New World nations advisable; now defense of the hemisphere raised the problem to primary ranking among the objectives of policy makers. Economic dominance and even military control no longer provided an adequate foundation, however, for what had now become an essential program. In other words, the cooperation of the peoples whose raw material resources and whose actual numbers exceeded those of the United States had become fundamental. Yet that cooperation would be forthcoming only when based on mutual understanding. Political realists accordingly supported new programs of cultural relations. At this point World War II was both hastening the desired process and bringing forth spectacular growth of new nationalism and complications.

The Western Hemisphere was not allowed to develop its own policies in a vacuum. The two world wars forced it out of its essential isolation into the mainstream of world events. In the process the New World nations from the Arctic to the Antarctic found they had developed an essential unity in outlook and objectives in spite of bitter local rivalries and some deep-seated suspicions. Whether individual leaders liked it or not the national welfare of twenty-two nation-states had made them a unit in world affairs. The following study is an effort to sketch the frequently erratic steps that led in the direction of a hemisphere policy for the United States as it attempted to meet the changing conditions that developed by the middle of the twentieth century.

A brief statement about the procedure followed by the author may be in order. Two approaches were possible. The first is known as "shredding," the other as "chopping" the subject. In the first case an effort is made to show how a given policy is applied to each of the various chains of events that transpired. The method has obvious merits but has been discarded in the present study in favor of chopping. The reason is simple: This was the way events actually transpired. The action taken at any one time was likely to be determined by events that formed the context in which the policy was to be applied. A procedure that might have been ideal for Cuban or Argentine relations on a given occasion was occasionally wholly impractical at another date because of events transpiring elsewhere. As a result the narrative becomes a series of "stills"; it is hoped they will become a moving picture when passed in review. This procedure interrupts interesting stories (to the annoyance of the reader at times) but helps to make the emergence of policy evident. And the emergence of policy, rather than the narration of the history of events, is the primary purpose of this study.

In attempting my interpretation I have made a special effort to investigate the private papers of the chief American actors and policy makers. Also I paid attention to the keenly observant reports of British diplomatic agents in the New World. Of course these men watched Canadian-United States relations carefully. With misgivings many of them saw Great Britain recognize United States spokesmanship of the New World in the two Venezuela disputes. Next their country gave up its partial control of the Panama Canal route and withdrew its Caribbean fleet. Their observations on these matters are reasonably well known and so are only briefly reviewed here. Less well known, however, are the valuable reports of British diplomats for the significant quarter of a century following 1890 as they watched the inroads being made into their trade preserves in Canada and South America by the on-rushing United States competition.

ACKNOWLEDGMENTS

In preparing the manuscript I have incurred many obligations. Sincere thanks are extended to the librarians and custodians of manuscripts who aided me in collecting my material. At the Library of Congress, Professor St. George L. Sioussat and Miss Katherine Brand some years ago, and Dr. Paul T. Heffron more recently, aided the author in using the manuscripts in their care. The late Mrs. Woodrow Wilson gave permission to use her husband's papers. At Yale University, Miss Judith A. Schiff guided the author in the use of the Henry L. Stimson and E. M. House diaries and checked references for accuracy. The same greatly appreciated service was rendered by Miss Elizabeth B. Drewry for the extensive Franklin D. Roosevelt Papers at Hyde Park. On-the-ground reports from skilled British observers throughout the Western Hemisphere were also used as source material. This unpublished Crown-copyright material in the Public Records Office, London, has been reproduced by permission of the Comptroller of H. M. Stationery Office. The Rhodes House Collection of the Bodleian Library at Oxford supplied much difficult-to-secure Canadian material. The University of Texas Library at Austin and the National Library in Mexico City provided important Latin American materials not available elsewhere.

The Johns Hopkins University Press has most courteously given permission to use material originally published by them in the author's *The Caribbean Policy of The United States, 1890–1920* (Baltimore, 1942; reprint by Octagon Books, 1966). Thanks are also extended to the Macmillan Company for permission to quote from Cordell Hull, *The Memoirs of Cordell Hull* (New York, The Macmillan Company, 1948. 2 vols. Copyright 1948 by Cordell Hull); and from *The Memoirs of Herbert Hoover: Years of Adventure, 1874–1920* (Vol. I. The Macmillan Company, New York, 1951. Copyright 1951 by Herbert Hoover) and *The Memoirs of Herbert Hoover: The Cabinet and the Presidency, 1920–1933* (Vol. II. The Macmillan Company, New York, 1952. Copyright 1951, 1952 by Herbert Hoover). The Foreign Policy Association kindly granted permission to use material from their *Foreign Policy Association Reports*.

The University of South Carolina provided a sabbatical leave of absence, and later some travel funds, to enable me to secure manuscript material in the United States. The Fulbright international exchange program made possible a year as a senior lecturer at Oxford University. The Oxford authorities, in turn, were most generous in allowing time for substantial research in the Rhodes Collection of the Bodleian Library and in the Public Records Office. To all of these, sincere thanks are extended.

CONTENTS

THE WESTERN HEMISPHERE

*Its Influence on United States Policies
to the End of World War II*

CHAPTER I

BEGINNINGS OF HEMISPHERE THINKING

The Conception

HAS THE WESTERN HEMISPHERE lost its significance for a United States caught up in broader world policies and obligations? The present author does not think so. Any foreign policy is inevitably the product of the national needs and interests of the country concerned. From its earliest days as a nation of three million people the United States maintained a sentimental interest in the whole Western Hemisphere, but for over a century this interest could be little more than sentimental. Leaders could express objectives as ideals, but applications of policy could be made only to regions within the reach of the tools at hand. Those tools were population strength, trade, naval power, and intellectual leadership; and all but the last of these had a limited range of influence for the new nation.

Both transcontinental expansion and penetration into the adjacent Caribbean lands were part of the thinking of the colonial entrepreneurs from whom the new national leaders sprang. Enthusiasts of the time engaged in oratorical flights about vague, great ambitions that were later to be conveniently associated together in what became known as a policy under the master phrase, "Monroe Doctrine." But what did this mean? Monroe used hemispheric terms, but the most successful expansionist of the middle of the nineteenth century, James K. Polk, restricted his dicta to North America. Then, after the Civil War, the very idea appeared to lapse for a time.

By the end of the century a new school of expansionists seized the term and loosely applied it to that part of the continental area south of the United States. Indeed, it came as something of a shock to many people when President William H. Taft claimed that Canadian conduct was of vital concern to the United States. A third of a century later President Franklin D. Roosevelt implemented a program from the Arctic to the Antarctic—a genuine hemisphere policy. By this time, however, it was obvious that other nations of the hemisphere, from entirely different viewpoints and for quite different reasons, had also reached the conclusion that a hemisphere program was an essential feature in any world organization.

The question here faced is: Can we now, taking advantage of perspective, find logic and a certain amount of consistency in the emergence of a significant theme of hemisphere policy? In spite of its numerous garbled interpretations, the Monroe Doctrine does provide a key. Between the eras of isolation and world responsibility the sphere of influence of the United States expanded steadily to encompass the Western world.

Colonial Bases of Early Policies

The ideas of the colonial founders were relatively straightforward and simple. In the swashbuckling, privateering days of the Spanish Main each nation seized what it could. Tropical islands were occupied or captured as occasion offered. Scant attention was paid to the claims or even the rights of other nations, much less to claims or rights of the native heathen. If the native could be used a place was made for him; otherwise he was conveniently pushed out of the way. In the process the conquerors sincerely hoped that he would be Christianized, and the Spaniards in particular paid special attention to this task. Gold, piracy, glamour, missionary zeal, and a tropical haze of beauty and violence merged with the miasmas of tropical disease and depravity. So much for the islands.

On the mainland of North America where England established the "original thirteen" colonies the tale was not quite so violent but was founded on the same general principles. Indian relations were cultivated where the native could be used to advantage for either trade or imperial plans. This was notably the case with the Iroquois Indians, who served the double purpose of providing a supply of valuable furs, and even more important, of acting as a buffer against rival French colonies to the north.

For the most part the unstable Indians had such vague conceptions of private ownership of land that the English readily secured huge grants by means of treaties of cession. These cessions, forced and otherwise, followed hard on the heels of land hunger of insatiable colonists, and were implemented by imperial planners. A sweeping and over-all view shows that territories from the seaboard to the Alleghenies, then to the Ohio Valley, next to the Mississippi, and southward to Florida were successively occupied. Texas was next in line, and soon California followed. Meanwhile the boundary was rounded out to the northwest. All this expansion was simply the continuation of the established habits of colonial thinking (policy). Impelled by domestic interests, a reasonably consistent practice, if not a policy, had emerged in handling relations with adjacent land areas.

Whenever foreign nations stood in the way of the new nation's mainland advance they were to be swept aside just as they had been in the Caribbean islands, where the English, French, and Dutch had invaded the Spanish domain. The first mainland victims had been the Dutch in New York (and through them the Swedes in New Jersey); then fell the French in successive wars from the middle of the seventeenth to the middle of the eighteenth century. Pressures on the Spaniards in Florida culminated in temporary cession of the peninsula to the English at the close of the Seven Years' War. When Spain regained Florida in 1783 the new independent nation of the United States considered the acquisition of Florida as unfinished business.

Remnants of the old colonial rivalries were seen as the nineteenth century opened when Napoleon threatened the infant nation's hopes. Using pressure on the now impotent Spain, France reacquired the Louisiana area. Before the French threat could be implemented, however, European pressures on Napoleon fortunately enabled the United States to pick up a bargain in the Louisiana Purchase, thus eliminating a danger.

Next, border frictions and disputes along the Florida line culminated in successive occupations of West Florida in 1810 and 1812, and of East Florida in 1819. The treaty with Spain confirming the Florida cession, known as the Adams-Onís Treaty, also determined the southwestern boundary (from southeastern Texas to the Pacific Ocean) and included favorable navigation rights on boundary rivers. Recently the Lewis and Clark Expedition had held out prospects of Far Eastern trade via Oregon. Secretary of State John Quincy Adams accordingly pressed for cession of Spanish claims to the coveted area north of the 42nd parallel—and he got it. In the negotiations Adams found that the Spaniards could be pushed only so far; accordingly he acquiesced in Spanish claims to the territory west of the Sabine River (the eastern boundary of Texas, beyond which Adams really felt his country had sound claims through the Louisiana Purchase). In a sense, then, the treaty represented an exchange of what were considered less valuable claims in East Texas for more valuable claims in Oregon.

Strangely enough there was very little interest in expansion northward during this whole period. It was the West that provided gold, glamour, and adventure. Certainly the north provided enough of adventure but only the fur trader or gold hunter braved the rigors of the northern climate—and for the time the rewards of the former were meager and the efforts of the latter were in vain. For a full century after independence the population flow was southwestward or westward, not northward. Hostilities with the powerful old Mother Country over wild and useless Canadian territory were simply not worthwhile. Further, there were repeated suggestions that Canada would like to join the United States anyway. Thus, after the experience of the inconclusive War of 1812 Washington was pleased to enter into the Rush-Bagot Agreement for the nonfortification of the Great Lakes area. For its part also the Mother Country was fully engaged elsewhere and ceased to threaten the United States from Canada. In recurrent bickering of frontiersmen over timber rights and river transport along the border both Downing Street and Washington tried to keep relations as peaceful as possible.

Modus Operandi

Before going into the details of the new policies that developed, it might be well to note the machinery used in carrying on foreign relations. The Constitution placed control of foreign affairs in the hands of the President. He, in turn, selected his Cabinet, headed by the Secretary of State. This officer, through the years, slowly farmed out or eliminated many of his domestic duties, which originally varied from responsibility for taking the census, administering copyright laws, and operating the government book depository (Library of Congress), to efforts to control interstate rivalries and bickerings. In the process his major duty emerged as that of minister of foreign affairs.

Treaties entered into were to be approved by a two-thirds vote of the Senate, which, under the Constitution, had the right to give advice to the President and to consent to the treaties negotiated by him. In practice, treaties were negotiated through the State Department and then sent to the Senate by the President. In addition the Chief Executive had the right, acting either through or in disregard of the Secretary of State, to enter into executive agreements. These had no standing, except as national interests might dictate their continuance, beyond the termination of the administration of the President who negotiated them. Requiring no senatorial approval, they might be secretly entered into, though in practice they were usually a matter of public knowledge and for the most part were used for matters scarcely worthy of treaty status.

As time passed, the number and significance of these agreements increased. Indeed, from the time when the first was entered into in 1792 (to make arrangement for the exchange of mails between the United States and foreign countries) until the outbreak of World War II some 1,182 such agreements were negotiated. In the same period only some 799 treaties had been negotiated; and of these about 200 were neglected, rejected, or so modified by the Senate that they lapsed without ratification.[1] Furthermore, the President had the right—and strong Presidents exercised it—of stamping their personalities on foreign relations through the power of appointment of special negotiators, whose nominations were usually not submitted to the Senate for approval.[2] One writer has summarized the surprising range of nontreaty international agreements of the United States thus:

. . . the United States annexed Texas and Hawaii, ended the first world war, joined the International Labor Organization, the Universal Postal Union, settled over ten billion dollars worth of post-World-War-I debts, acquired Atlantic naval bases in British territory during World War II, acquired all financial claims of the Soviet Union in the United States, joined the United Nations pledging itself not to make separate peace in World War II and to

[1] Kenneth Colegrove, *The American Senate and World Peace,* pp. 95–96; Quincy Wright, "The United States in International Agreements," *International Concilia tion Documents,* No. 411 (May, 1945), p. 384.

[2] Benjamin H. Williams, *American Diplomacy: Policies and Practice,* pp. 421–422; Henry Merritt Wriston, *Executive Agents in American Foreign Relations,* pp. 220–225.

accept the Atlantic Charter, submitted over a score of cases to international arbitration, and modified the tariff in numerous reciprocal trade agreements, by means other than the treaty-making process.[3]

Foreign observers of the United States were little concerned with the machinery of operation but they were keenly alert to the policies applied that resulted in continued expansionism. A critical interpretation has been given by a Peruvian writer who insisted that mercantilist utilitarianism, the cradle and creed of the English colonist in America, became the inspiration and dominant force of the new nation.[4] He might well have observed that this influence was hardly new, for it had been active in European history since the days of the merchandising activities of the Crusaders and of the Low Country merchants in the Hanseatic League, to mention only two well-known illustrations. The Yankee trader had worthy ancestors. For his part, wherever possible he included the most-favored-nation commercial provision in his international conventions. This appeared in some twenty-one agreements with sixteen foreign states before 1870.[5]

With the isolationist sentiment (toward Europe) that arose after the War of 1812 successive administrations in Washington centered attention on domestic rather than foreign relations. Expansion into adjacent land areas was considered a domestic matter. Thanks in part to the safety derived from distance, this emphasis on home matters received such priority that, as Lord Bryce commented toward the end of the century, there was serious carelessness in the choice of persons to represent the country abroad.[6] Sir Cecil Spring-Rice commented: "In a happy country like this where politics don't affect great questions, or the happiness of the nation, the people who run them are apt to be a pretty poor lot."[7] When foreign problems emerged, therefore, Washington as a matter of course tended to follow European practices in interpreting international law.

A careful scrutiny of the machinery of international relations, how-

---

[3] Wright, "U. S. in International Agreements," *International Conciliation Documents*, No. 411 (May, 1945), pp. 381–382.   ,

[4] Felipe Barreda Laos, *La segunda emancipación de la América Hispaña*, pp. 25, 66.

[5] See Tariff Commission, *Reciprocity and Commercial Treaties*, p. 399.

[6] James Bryce, *The American Commonwealth*, II, 568.

[7] Stephen Gwynn, ed., *The Letters and Friendships of Sir Cecil Spring-Rice*. I, 104.

ever, reveals an interesting continuity of able practitioners of the art of diplomacy. William Hunter, chief clerk of the Department of State from 1829 to 1886; Alvey A. Adee, Assistant Secretary from 1882 to 1924; and John Bassett Moore, who held key positions in the Department from 1885 to 1925, were masters of both the language and practices of diplomacy. Politicians came and went but these men carried on and developed reasonably consistent policies. The political opportunist and innovator was thus held in partial restraint by career men. The net results were substantial, albeit at times unorthodox. One foreign scholar has commented: "The North American [was] brilliant at times, audacious as befits the agent of a democracy, a stranger to the beaten paths of international politics, easily vanquished in routine matters but capable of smashing all the rules of form and convention and winning success in a day, almost violent when confronted with an obstacle which the skill of others had put in his way."[8]

Contacts Prior to 1800

In the early days of the Republic only a long-range view envisioned more than occasional trade contacts with the southern half of the hemisphere. In the late 1780's Thomas Jefferson expressed a kindly, but largely academic, interest in a proposed revolution in Brazil. About the same time, Alexander Hamilton let his nationalistic dreams range somewhat further when he said: "By a steady adherence to the Union, we may hope, ere long, to become the arbiter of Europe in America, and to be able to incline the balance of European competitions in this part of the world as our interest may dictate." After 1784 Hamilton maintained contact with the revolutionist Francisco de Miranda and by the late 1790's was ready to consider the use of United States manpower in conjunction with British sea power to revolutionize the northern part of the continent. But nothing came of these interests.[9]

On our immediate borders was an entirely different situation. The

[8] Orestes Ferrara, *The Last Spanish War: Revelations in "Diplomacy,"* pp. 10–11. For a British comment see R. B. Mowat, *Diplomatic Relations of Great Britain and the United States*, p. 4.

[9] For early interest in the idea behind the Monroe Doctrine see: Albert Bushnell Hart, *The Monroe Doctrine: An Interpretation*, p. 14; John Halladay Latané, *The United States and Latin America*, p. 17; Joseph Byrne Lockey, *Pan-Americanism: Its Beginnings*, p. 264; William Spence Robertson, *Hispanic American Relations with the United States*, p. 61.

explorers, adventurers, and homeseekers pressing westward paid scant attention to unmarked boundaries; so international complications inevitably arose. This was the case whether they went to the north, the south, or the west. And from colonial days Cuba was considered to be directly associated with the adjacent mainland.

Florida early became the contact point. In the colonial period, France had failed in an effort to establish a Florida base; but from Cuba, Spain established a firm foothold in the peninsula to protect its trade route to the north and its flank on the route to the gold fields of Mexico. The English, too, saw the importance of Cuba to the southern mainland. The Scotchman William Patterson advised William III, some eighty years before the Declaration of Independence, that it would be wise to seize Cuba as an adjunct to the other British colonies.[10] Benjamin Franklin is also reported to have given similar advice, and certainly the British did occupy Cuba during the Seven Years' War. Soon after independence, in 1781, the new republic despatched consular agents to Cuba. Jefferson, too, found his interests attracted southward. While minister in France in 1787–1788 he expressed concern over rumors of European efforts to control transportation across Panama.[11] By the opening of the new century he watched with quick concern the rebellion of Toussaint L'Ouverture in Santo Domingo. He may have been influenced by his Virginia background and fear of slave rebellion, but he was also concerned about cultivating relations with France. The Negro rebels were not encouraged.

Northward the situation was somewhat different. During the closing days of the American Revolution the Allen brothers (Ethan, Ira, and Levi) revealed the uncertain loyalties of the New England frontier when they proposed neutrality in the Revolution itself and even suggested aid to the British in exchange for recognition of certain land claims. This attitude passed, however, and Vermont became a new state in the Union in 1791. When one realizes the significance of such an attitude, Franklin's "passion" to acquire Canada for the new nation has more meaning. But truth to tell, the new nation had more land than it could occupy and felt that these New England-Canadian snow-filled swamp bogs were worth little attention anyway. The west, the southwest, and the south held greater promise.

[10] Russell H. Fitzgibbon, *Cuba and the United States, 1900–1935*, p. 68.
[11] Miles P. DuVal, *Cadiz to Cathay: The Story of the Long Struggle for a Waterway across the American Isthmus*, pp. 18–19.

Accordingly the treaty of peace in 1783 outlined the northern boundary across New England (vaguely it is true) to the St. Lawrence River, thence westward through the Great Lakes to the Lake of the Woods. However, Canadian ambitions for fertile lands south of the Great Lakes and north of the Ohio River died slowly and provided food for suspicions. These feelings were aggravated by an incident that arose soon after Washington became President. A British fur-trading post on Nootka Sound on the Vancouver coast was captured by a Spanish expedition from Mexico.[12] The action could easily have led to war between Great Britain and Spain. In such a case Britain would be tempted to move southward from Canada through the Ohio and Mississippi valleys to attack Spanish holdings on the Gulf Coast. At once arose the old fear entertained by English colonies when France held Canada and the mouth of the Mississippi. Such a move would penetrate their soft back door and hem them in on the Atlantic, or even drive them into the Atlantic. Before their fears could be realized the Spaniards returned the fur-trading post and preserved the peace. Though the danger was averted, Secretary of State Jefferson had become greatly perturbed.

The War of 1812 brought early American defeats on the Canadian border. Later these were offset by the victory of Commodore Matthew C. Perry on Lake Erie to leave Upper Canada (the region around the Great Lakes) largely at the mercy of the United States. The negotiations at Ghent were between representatives of Great Britain, a tired nation anxious for peace, and their counterparts from the United States, who represented a country properly fearful now that their associate Napoleon had been overthrown. Both wanted peace more than territory. If peace could be secured both delegations were willing to avoid additional questions and awkward answers.

The next decade showed a continuation of this desire for peaceful settlement. The Rush-Bagot Agreement of 1817 limited naval vessels to be used by either power on the Great Lakes to those which might be necessary to control smuggling. "The Myth of the Unguarded Frontier" was something of an exaggeration, and periodically Canadians suffered from waves of excitement over possible conquest from the south,[13] but

---

[12] For the Nootka Sound controversy see W. R. Manning, "The Nootka Sound Controversy," American Historical Association, *Annual Report, 1904*, pp. 279 ff.

[13] C. P. Stacey, "The Myth of the Unguarded Frontier, 1815–1871," *Amer. Hist. Rev.*, LVI, No. 1 (October, 1950), 1–18; Paul Knaplund, "Armaments on the Great

the United States government remained uninterested. In 1818 the boundary from the Lake of the Woods to the Rocky Mountains was established along the 49th parallel to delimit the northern boundary of the Louisiana Purchase with no particular objection from either side of the line.

Southward

Late in 1807 Napoleon moved his troops into the Hispanic peninsula. He placed his brother on the Spanish throne and drove the Portuguese court into exile in Brazil. Washington quickly expressed a kindly interest in the fate of the Spanish and Portuguese colonies in South America. It sent stormy Thomas Sumter to Brazil, and others usually denominated as seamen's agents elsewhere, to make periodic reports of local developments. New England traders, quick to take advantage of the opening of Brazilian trade, in 1809 sold $900,000 worth of products to the new nation, but political leaders remained cautious and avoided any commercial treaty with Brazil until 1830.[14] A somewhat more positive attitude was shown when Joel R. Poinsett was sent in 1810 to Argentina and Chile. His instructions read:

You will make it your object whenever it may be proper, to diffuse the impression that the United States cherish the sincerest good will towards the people of South America as neighbors, as belonging to the same portion of the globe, and as having a mutual interest in cultivating friendly intercourse; that this disposition will exist whatever may be their internal system or European relations, with respect to which no interference of any sort is pretended; and that in the event of a political separation from the parent country . . . it will coincide with the sentiments and policy of the United States to promote the most liberal intercourse between the inhabitants of this Hemisphere.[15]

Specifically, Washington wished to avoid complications with either France or Spain. When word came that thirty-six American filibusterers were imprisoned in Caracas, a vigorous congressional debate defeated

---

Lakes," *ibid.*, XL, No. 3 (April, 1935), 474–476. The second item gives interesting correspondence of 1844.

[14] Lawrence F. Hill, *Diplomatic Relations between the United States and Brazil*, pp. 3–7.

[15] Quoted in Frederick L. Paxson, *The Independence of the South American Republics* .., p. 111.

a resolution to send an agent to secure their release. The determining factor in the decision apparently was that sending an agent might constitute recognition of local independence and be considered an unfriendly act by the Mother Country. Finally an agent was sent to Caracas, but he was carefully instructed that there existed "no intent to recognize the governments at this time, and the administration was not sure that the juntas would give public recognition to United States consuls who could not give reciprocal recognition to them."[16] Such instructions left him in the position of an unofficial but accredited representative.

Poinsett's career in Buenos Aires and later in Chile has been frequently discussed. In general it may be said that he found Buenos Aires an area worthy of independence, but its leaders still professed loyalty to the old Spanish royal family. In Chile on the other hand, there was an independence movement, though local thinking may have been confused as to whether it was independence from Peru or from Spain that was wanted. Poinsett, once he reached Chile, became quite enthusiastic about his new friends and cooperated freely with the rebels even though his ultimate influence on the independence movement was probably negligible. At the outbreak of the War of 1812 between the United States and Great Britain, Poinsett, à la Citizen Genêt, arranged for the use of the Chilean ports by United States commerce raiders. When a British naval squadron reached the coast its commander suggested that the Chileans advise the American commissioner, Poinsett, to "make immediate use of his passport." Interestingly enough, José Miguel Carrera, who followed the British suggestion and advised Poinsett to leave, was the same man who came to the United States early in 1816 to secure vessels to aid the Chilean rebels. He made arrangements to acquire four vessels on credit from private sources. One of these, the *Clifton,* carried almost a thousand muskets, and six of the thirty officers on board seem to have been "North Americans."[17]

If these contacts were tenuous it is not surprising. After all, points south of the shoulder of Brazil (Pernambuco) on the east coast and the whole of the west coast of South America were as far away from the United States as from Europe when it came to ocean distances and

---

[16] *Ibid,* p. 114.

[17] Robertson, *Hispanic American Relations with the United States,* p. 63. See also Henry Clay Evans, *Chile and Its Relations with the United States,* pp. 15–20.

trade. The northern republic itself was yet an infant nation, and few could envisage the future. Even so, in 1813 Jefferson wrote that governments to be formed in the New World, whatever their form, "will be American governments, no longer to be involved in the never-ceasing broils of Europe. The European nations constitute a separate division of the globe; their localities make them part of a distinct system. . . . America has a hemisphere to itself. It must have a separate system of interest which must not be subordinated to those of Europe." Arthur P. Whitaker quotes this statement and then comments that here appears "the first flowering of the Western Hemisphere idea in the American system."[18]

Even after the War of 1812 the consistent policy of Washington was to observe neutrality obligations strictly. Privateering out of Baltimore and New Orleans might have been good sport and profitable to the participants but the government sought to restrain such activities and President Monroe undertook to tighten neutrality laws through federal enactments in 1817 and 1818.[19] Soon word arrived that a United States consul, Joseph Ray, had supported local rebels at Pernambuco against the Brazilian government. He had been arrested and imprisoned together with United States citizens in other Brazilian ports. Still the attitude of Washington was restrained, and in the summer of 1819 Secretary Adams smoothed matters over. True, Henry Clay took advantage of his lack of official responsibility and made political hay by espousing the cause of South American patriots after 1817, but the government consistently refused to commit itself.[20] Possibly the most emphatic statement on the subject was that of President Monroe himself. When word came in 1818 that one Mr. Worthington, sent as a special agent, had negotiated a treaty with authorities in Buenos Aires, Monroe burst out "with quick and irritated tone. 'Dismiss him instantly. Recall him! Dismiss him! Now to think what recommendations that man had!

[18] Arthur P. Whitaker, *The Western Hemisphere Idea: Its Rise and Decline*, p. 29.

[19] Lockey, *Pan-Americanism*, pp. 155–175; Paxson, *Independence of the South American Republics*, pp. 119–120.

[20] Dexter Perkins, *The Monroe Doctrine, 1823–1826*, pp. 45–47; H. L. Hoskins, "Hispanic American Policy of Henry Clay," *Hisp. Amer. Hist. Rev.* VII, No. 4 (November, 1927), 461–462; Hill, *Diplomatic Relations between the U.S. and Brazil*, pp. 24–25.

Dismiss him at once, and send the notice of his dismission by every possible channel'."[21]

One way to buy time had been to send an investigating commission to look into conditions in South America and to report. Such a group, potentially of real significance, was composed of Theodoric Bland, John Graham, and Caesar A. Rodney. With divergent original interests and attitudes, members of the commission, as might have been expected, made inconclusive reports that were "without much influence" on policy making. Indeed the result may have been negative, though time had been bought and the Clay agitation stalled at least temporarily.[22]

Before the end of the Jefferson administration in 1809 there had been rumors of formal revolution in the Spanish colonies. The President was convinced that Cuba should come under the control of the United States but had addressed himself to a broader theme when he said: "If they [the rebels] succeed, we shall be well satisfied to see Cuba and Mexico remain in their dependence; but very unwilling to see them in that of either France or England, politically or commercially. We consider their interests and ours as the same, and that the object of both must be to exclude all European influence from this hemisphere."[23] Like John Q. Adams and other men of the time, the President felt that Cuba was important strategically and, so far as Spain was concerned, was almost sure to gravitate to the United States ultimately. Therefore, let nature take its course. On the other hand, control by a strong European power must be definitely opposed.

Soon after the Committee of Three had delivered its inconclusive report, the Florida controversy reached a crisis that culminated in the Adams-Onís Treaty of 1819. Spain was in no hurry to ratify the agreement and so Secretary Adams was left on tenterhooks for several months. One writer calls the cession of the Floridas Spain's "sop to Cerberus"[24] to forestall United States aid to Spain's restless colonies.

[21] Charles Francis Adams, ed., *Memoirs of John Quincy Adams . . .*, IV, 70. (Hereafter cited as Adams, *Memoirs*).

[22] Watt Stewart, "The South American Commission," *Hisp. Amer. Hist. Rev.*, IX, No. 1 (February, 1929), 36–37; Paxson, *Independence of South American Republics*, pp. 139 ff. See also Adams, *Memoirs*, V, 56.

[23] Quoted by Hart, *The Monroe Doctrine*, p. 28.

[24] Paxson, *Independence of South American Republics*, p. 195. See also Perkins, *Monroe Doctrine, 1823–1826*, pp. 47–48; W. F. Craven, "The Risk of the Monroe Doctrine," *Hisp. Amer. Hist. Rev.*, VII, No. 3 (August, 1927), 327 ff.

Indeed in Washington the Cabinet was considering a request for twenty thousand stand of arms for Colombian rebels. "There was a strong wish expressed by Calhoun and Thompson that we might furnish the arms if we could. Crawford was less explicit and more shy." Adams argued that the United States must avoid any act that might tend toward involvement in the endless Europeans wars. "There was thenceforth not a word said in its favor. . . . The decision was unanimous that the proposal could not be complied with."[25]

Once the treaty of 1819 was safely ratified—even though Clay, the great advocate of the young republics, was out of Congress in 1821— the tempo of Latin American relations quickened. On June 19, 1822, Adams presented Mr. Manuel Torres, chargé d'affaires from Colombia, as "the first formal act of recognition of an independent South American Government." By January of the next year the President was ready to send to the Senate nominations for ministers to Mexico, Colombia, Buenos Aires, and Chile, as well as that of a chargé to Peru. On May 26, 1824, Adams presented a chargé from Brazil to the President.[26]

Potential territorial acquisitions by the United States were not lost sight of in the flurry of recognitions and good will. On April 29, 1823, Secretary of State Adams notified Special Agent Randall in Cuba that if he was asked about the attitude of his government toward political conditions in the island he was to state that it "would be altogether averse to the transfer of the island to any other power."[27]

---

[25] Adams, *Memoirs*, V, 47.

[26] *Ibid.*, VI, 23, 122, 358.

In this same year there was an effort by Emperor Agustín Iturbide to force El Salvador to join his new Mexican empire. Fearful, the Congress of the little Central American country passed an act providing for annexation to the United States and sent three commissioners to Washington with full powers to make the necessary arrangements. Apparently the northern republic showed little interest; so as soon as Iturbide was overthrown the affair was forgotten. Apparently the new nation of the north had so much unoccupied territory that distant acquisitions were unattractive (Lockey, *Pan-Americanism*, pp. 76–77).

Another interesting commentary on the times is seen in the report that Consul Raguet in Rio de Janeiro could not live on his fees, which amounted to only $700 per year. Accordingly he was appointed "agent of the United States for commercial affairs" at a salary of $4,500. After the Brazilian chargé had been formally received in Washington, Raguet became chargé at Rio de Janeiro in March, 1825 (Hill, *Diplomatic Relations between the U.S. and Brazil*, pp. 27 ff.).

[27] Pertinent excerpts from communications of Adams to his ministers in Spain

Interestingly enough, the United States played a lone hand in these steps. Secretary Adams carefully refrained from satisfying the curiosity of the British Minister Stratford Canning, who enquired about the intention of the United States toward recognizing colonies that had revolted. Dexter Perkins comments that the action showed "striking independence," ignoring pertinent conditions in Spain. "It [the United States] consulted with no European power" and acted "from a purely American point of view."[28]

A year or so later, when Clay had become Secretary of State under President John Q. Adams, the question of transportation across the Isthmus of Panama was raised. Clay immediately instructed his chargé in Central America to send all possible data on the subject. The next year he instructed the United States' delegates to the Panama Conference that a canal across the Isthmus would be of substantial interest to this country. Quickly, northern capitalists, including Aaron Palmer and DeWitt Clinton, builder of the Erie Canal, awoke to the possibilities. They secured a concession to build a Nicaraguan canal under date of June 14, 1826. When they were unable to raise an adequate sum privately they appealed to the national government. In vain; the concession lapsed. Again, in the middle 1830's a canal proposal was made to Washington by the Federal Congress of the United Provinces of Central America. Once more the matter lapsed when both the United States Congress and President Martin Van Buren considered the suggestion premature.[29]

The Monroe Doctrine

By the end of 1823 incidents with the new southern republics were arising with such frequency that it behooved the President to make some kind of statement to his Congress on the subject. The Yankee trader had proved the importance of the new markets with annual purchases of nearly $2 million in Brazil and sales to that country of nearly $2.3 million. Sales to Chile were only $183,000, but purchases were in excess of $830,000. Peru, likewise on the back of the continent, also

---

and his agent in Cuba have been collected by John Bassett Moore, *A Digest of International Law*, VI, 379 ff.

[28] Perkins, *Monroe Doctrine, 1823–1826*, pp. 51 ff.; Adams, *Memoirs*, VI, 13.

[29] Adams, *Memoirs*, IX, 471 ff. For secondary accounts see Harmodio Arias, *The Panama Canal: A Study in International Law and Diplomacy*; Lockey, *Pan-Americanism*, pp. 358 ff.; J. Fred Rippy, *The Caribbean Danger Zone*, p. 83.

bought little but shipped the United States over $734,000 worth, while trade with the near-by countries of Colombia and Mexico was proportionately high. Colonization in the New World had regularly connoted more or less complete commercial monopoly; independence would inevitably stimulate trade. From this standpoint alone it is obvious that the Monroe Doctrine carried a distinct economic connotation, even though political considerations might have been dominant.[30]

Whatever the primary factors, when British Foreign Minister George Canning proposed a joint pronouncement discouraging attempts to reconquer revolted colonies in the New World, the authorities in Washington were in a sympathetic frame of mind. After consultation with living former Presidents and his local advisers, the President in 1823 sent to Congress his later famous message. Deploring any extension of the European system in the Americas, he called for two spheres of influence, with the United States asserting the right to priority of consideration in the New World. At the same time he left the door open to future expansion for his own country. In spite of the shrewd exclusion of British expansion along with that of other European countries (an idea not found in the Canning proposal), the British Foreign Office was almost sure to "go along" with the proposal. Britain had an adequate colonial empire at the time and its New World trade did need protection. Perkins reports that sixteen out of nineteen newspapers that commented on the message made no comment at all on the no-colonization idea, though two enthusiastically approved the proposal. As it happened, one in New York, the *Albion* (edited by an Englishman), referred to the "preposterous notion of regulating matters in South American States" or of limiting the "extension of the British settlements in Canada."[31]

South American governments received the friendly expression of interest gratefully. Francisco de Paulo Santander and Simón Bolívar praised it, the administration at Buenos Aires lauded it and sent a copy by Bernardino Rivadavia to Chile, Colombia, and Peru. Perhaps Chileans were most outspoken of all, but the entire continent seemed to approve. Yet Latin American leaders were realists. They knew full well that the British Navy provided a far stronger shield than that offered by the United States against possible activities of Spain and the Holy

---

[30] Robertson, *Hispanic American Relations* p. 197; Perkins, *Monroe Doctrine, 1823–1826*, p. 17.

[31] Perkins, *Monroe Doctrine, 1823–1826*, p. 16.

Alliance.[32] Not to miss any bets, however, Brazil and Colombia suggested implementing the Monroe proposal as a hemisphere doctrine by formal alliances with the United States.

By this time Henry Clay had entered the administration as Secretary of State under the statesman-President, John Q. Adams. Saddled with the responsibilities of office, Clay was a far more conservative individual than when he was merely a member of a congressional "factious opposition." Any entangling alliance he now found to be inadvisable. Further, to the proposals for an alliance with Brazil or Colombia, he answered that such agreements could quite possibly lead to war—and only Congress could declare war. Hence, especially now that there was no imminent danger of European aggression, the matter could properly be postponed until an emergency arose.[33]

On December 10, 1824, Richard C. Anderson had signed with Colombia the first treaty negotiated by the United States with a Latin American republic. Congress was still fearful of involvement; so the Senate declined to approve the convention (the first such exercise of the senatorial right of review),[34] even though the treaty contained essentially the same terms as those recently approved in a treaty with Great Britain. Another test for Clay came when war erupted between Argentina and Brazil over the Uruguayan region. Clay insisted that his country had recognized Brazil as independent. This meant that no question of European expansionism was involved and consequently that the Monroe Doctrine was not applicable. Argentines were not too happy with the interpretation, for the Brazilian monarch was the heir to the Portuguese throne and Brazilian independence might well be an ephemeral thing.[35]

Against this background came the conference called by Bolívar to consider New World problems. The Liberator was reluctant to invite the

[32] For reception of the document in Latin America see Robertson, *Hispanic American Relations*, pp. 45–49; Perkins, *Monroe Doctrine, 1823–1826*, p. 159; Lockey, *Pan-Americanism*, p. 260; Graham H. Stuart, *Latin America and the United States*, p. 298.

[33] Adams, *Memoirs*, VI, 480–481. For numerous references see Perkins' studies on the Monroe Doctrine; Alejandro Álvarez, *The Monroe Doctrine: Its Importance in the International Life*, pp. 127–129, and H. L. Hoskins, "Hispanic American Policy of Clay," *Hisp. Amer. Hist. Rev.*, VII, No. 4 (November, 1927), 471.

[34] W. Stull Holt, *Treaties Defeated by the Senate . . .* , p. 50. The Anderson diary was printed by Duke University Press in 1964.

[35] Álvarez, *The Monroe Doctrine* pp. 11, 129–130; Lockey, *Pan-Americanism*, pp. 459–460; Perkins, *Monroe Doctrine, 1826–1867*, p. 38.

United States to participate in the conference because it had recently rejected the proposed alliance and because the Senate had failed to agree to the recently negotiated treaty. Only after the specific request of Mexico and Central America did he forward an invitation. At this point, that lack of common purpose among the Latin republics emerged that has been so significant throughout the century and a half of their independence. Buenos Aires was not interested in the conference, and others, including Brazil, took no part. In fact, in spite of Bolívar's dreams of continental influence, only Peru (including Bolivia), Mexico, Colombia (including Venezuela, Ecuador, and Panama), and Central America (including its subsequently formed five states) were represented.[36]

While Canning and the British watched jealously lest the United States seize the leadership of the new nations, Washington muffed its opportunities. The Adams' proposal to send delegates became snarled in congressional political maneuvering. Final approval for the sending of delegates was given too late to be effective. The Bolívar Conference met briefly at Panama, then adjourned to reassemble at Tacubaya, Mexico. Little or nothing was accomplished at either place. Whitaker notes that the long-range effect on United States foreign policy of the fiasco of the Conference was that the Jacksonian party, which was to be the party in power essentially from 1829 to 1861, became isolationist toward Latin America.[37]

Contemporary Problems

Now the Cuban question arose in a different context. Mexico and Colombia entertained the idea of revolutionizing the island to place it under their own control. At once Secretary Henry Clay protested through Joel R. Poinsett, minister in Mexico. Europeans, including even Russians, were interested in the pre-emptive move of the United States and considered it a forerunner of hegemony in the area.[38] Neither of the Latin sponsors of the proposal was powerful or stable enough to make an issue of the matter; so the question of the control of Cuba remained quiescent for another decade. Then in 1849 rumor had it that

[36] James Brown Scott, ed., *The International Conferences of the American States, 1889–1928*, p. ix.

[37] Whitaker, *The Western Hemisphere Idea*, pp. 46–47. See also Frances L. Reinhold, "New Research on the First Pan-American Conference," *Hisp. Amer. Hist. Rev.*, XVIII, No. 3 (August, 1938), 255; Lockey, *Pan-Americanism*, p. 420.

[38] Adams, *Memoirs*, VII, 9–10, 95.

Great Britain was becoming interested in Cuba. Forthwith Secretary John Forsyth sent word to his minister in Madrid that if Spain considered any transfer of the island title "to Great Britain, or any other power, you [the United States minister] will distinctly state that the United States will prevent it, at all hazards." Further, in case any foreign power sought to seize Cuba, Spain "may [might] securely depend upon the military and naval resources of the United States to aid her in preserving or recovering it."[39]

By this time the Texas question had become an overriding issue. Early commissioners from the Texan rebels against Mexico had been given a cordial reception in Washington, while both tidewater and frontier had rung with praises of the hero-martyrs of the Alamo and Goliad, who were lamented as having been sacrificed in a struggle against the degenerate and mixed-blood offspring of the disliked Spaniard. Recognition of Texan independence in 1837 was followed by vigorous propaganda for annexation. This was temporarily counterbalanced by problems of the panic of 1840 and by sectional politics. As a result a treaty of annexation failed to secure the two-thirds approval of the Senate. Then came the election of 1844. The ebullient James K. Polk ("re-annexation of Texas and reoccupation of Oregon") carried the country, but before he could be inaugurated the repudiated President John Tyler seized his opportunity. He had long urged the annexation and now in obedience to the popular expression of opinion, he recommended annexation by a simple joint resolution which could be enacted by a majority vote in each house. This was done, and expansion was resumed toward the southwest. By 1848 the Mexican War ensued, resulting in Mexico's recognition of the loss of Texas and of the rest of its trans-desert territory in the direction of Utah, New Mexico, and California.

Beyond the Rockies in Oregon was a region desired by both Great Britain and the United States more for its trade potential in furs and its contact with the Orient than as a home for settlers. The British had trading posts in the area and had established their contacts by land and sea. The United States had established later claims by both routes and had shown increasing interest, especially after the Lewis and Clark Expedition of 1805 reported that Oregon provided the best trade route from the eastern states to China. At the time of the northern boundary

---

[39] Arnold Bennett Hall, *The Monroe Doctrine and the Great War*, p. 48. A particularly detailed study of this period is found in John A. Logan, Jr., *No Transfer: An American Security Principle*.

settlement in 1818 neither nation wished to force a decision; so they decided that for ten years each could develop its holdings. Thereafter either nation could call for a settlement by giving due notice. Thus the matter had rested for a time.

Polk, in his campaign in 1844, had called for "54–40 or fight" and had followed up his campaign with a strong statement in his inaugural address. But Mexico was demanding attention—and Great Britain was strong. Accordingly the negotiations that followed were conducted in peculiarly moderate tones. Bombast was forgotten and courteous negotiations led, in 1846, to an agreement to extend the 49th parallel (the boundary east of the Rocky Mountains) as the international boundary from the mountains to the coast, though British settlers retained trade rights on the Columbia River. The agreement was to the distinct advantage of the United States, because many British settlers actually lived south of the line agreed upon. Later writers, however, are inclined to offset the advantages gained in Oregon by the advantages that Britain gained in the settlement of the Maine boundary in 1842. In the latter agreement between Lord Ashburton and Secretary Daniel Webster, Canada acquired lands to which historians are generally agreed it had scant claims. In any case the two northern boundaries were settled on a basis of genuine negotiation and compromise.

As the years passed, it became obvious that in many ways "Canada represents politics at war with geography."[40] Trade increasingly followed a north-south pattern while politics maintained an east-west orientation. From time to time Canadian dissidents talked of annexation to the southern republic, but this was usually when they were disgruntled over some domestic issue. This very talk tended to generate a national cohesion; a recent writer has commented that "Canadian life can almost be said to take its rise in the negative will to resist absorption in the American Republic."[41] Occasionally agitators on both sides of the boundary made political capital of local unrest and friction aroused by overlapping timber grants in disputed areas in northern

[40] John MacCormac, *Canada: America's Problem*, p. 215.
[41] S. Delbert Clark, "Canadian National Sentiment and Imperial Sentiment," in H. F. Angus *et al., Canada and Her Great Neighbor* . . ., p. 243. See also John Foster Dulles, "A North American Contribution to World Order," *Conference on Canadian-American Affairs, 1939*, p. 96.

New York and Vermont.[42] But the stubborn fact was that Canadian assets were still not attractive enough to justify Washington in impairing relations with the powerful and trade-valuable Mother Country.

Canada During the Civil War and After

By the middle 1850's international trade brought about a new situation. The British corn laws had given preference to Canadian grain in the British market. Since these laws were now repealed, Canadians sought a new outlet for their surplus. At the same time they applied pressure on the United States by laying restrictions on its fishers on the off-shore fishing grounds. A swap in the way of trade privileges was arranged in the reciprocity treaty (the first of its kind for the United States) in 1854. The treaty was to last for ten years, after which it might be extended for a year at a time. In 1865 it was discontinued both because of new conditions created by the Civil War and because the United States felt that the old *quid pro quo* was inadequate now that its increased volume of manufactured goods clamored for access to Canadian markets.[43]

During the Civil War itself Canadians had maintained a strict official neutrality. Runaway slaves had created some pro-Northern sympathy, but the friends of the Confederate sympathizer C. L. Vallandigham provided a counterbalance. Then just as the war closed, conditions in Canada changed rapidly. The old expansionist slogan of the American nationalists, "From the Arctic to the Isthmus," still brought repercussions. The Fenians (later known as the Clan-na-Gael society) agitated for annexation to the southern republic and attracted support on both sides of the border. For its part, Washington responded with a perfectly correct attitude, much like that shown by Ottawa during the Civil War. Arms shipments to the Fenians from the United States were stopped and filibusters returning from raids were arrested.

Agitation in the United States for cancellation of the reciprocity treaty created resentment in Canada and a call for a stronger Canadian union. Great Britain, too, became alerted. The result was the Quebec Conference of 1864, which led to a more effective confederation organized on July 1, 1867. William A. Dunning notes that fear of the

[42] Albert K. Weinberg, *Manifest Destiny: A Study in Nationalist Expansionism,* p. 359.
[43] Tariff Commission, *Reciprocity and Commercial Treaties,* pp. 22–23. 89. Also Benjamin H. Williams, *Economic Foreign Policy of the United States,* pp. 280–281.

United States had contributed substantially to the outcome, but also comments that in formulating the new instrument of government "American history and institutions were as sedulously searched as those of the Mother Country for precedent and for warning."[44] On March 27, 1867, the House of Representatives in Washington passed a resolution vaguely protesting this expansion of the European monarchical system across the continent when, presumably, residents of British Columbia did not want to be included in the new organization.[45] But no one paid much attention to this.

Canadian fears, in some cases hopes, of annexation remained latent but still existed. The Alaska Purchase from Russia in 1867 gave Canadians real pause. More alarming was the Sumner suggestion that Britain might settle the Civil War damage claims, generally known as the Alabama Claims, by the cession of Canada.[46] The Alaska Purchase and the Sumner suggestion, however, were merely the dying flickers of the old fire of expansionism. Alaska was so large and the price so modest that the gambling instinct of almost any congressman could be aroused to take the chance. As for Sumner's proposal, the Treaty of Washington laid that to rest when the Alabama Claims were submitted to arbitration and when trade rights on boundary rivers were more clearly defined. In the process the Fenian claims of Canada were dropped —but only after the Mother Country saw to it that Canada lost nothing in the process.[47] This protection took the form of aid in building a transcontinental railroad and reminds one of the way in which the United States mollified Maine and Massachusetts at the time of the Webster-Ashburton Treaty.

For the next decade, then, Canadian-American relations proceeded quietly. The new Dominion broom (under the Dominion Act of 1867) was sweeping rather clean north of the line; and south of the border Reconstruction was fully occupying the American people. The fears aroused by the Alaska Purchase slowly subsided. New tensions arising

---

[44] W. A. Robinson, "Sixty Years of Canadian Confederation," *Pol. Sc. Quar.*, XLIII, No. 1 (March, 1928), 91–92; William Archibald Dunning, *The British Empire and the United States . . .*, pp. 270–271. See also Wriston, *Executive Agents in American Foreign Relations*, pp. 738 ff.

[45] Hart, *Monroe Doctrine*, pp. 154–155.

[46] For interesting views see Henry Adams, *Education of Henry Adams*, p. 275.

[47] Allan Nevins, *Hamilton Fish: The Inner History of the Grant Administration*, pp. 479–480.

from trade and the migration of peoples within Canada did arise but most of the disgruntled ones simply moved to the kinder climate of the south and eased their feelings. This was done without fanfare and it was some years before the tendency received governmental consideration in Ottawa. For its part, the United States entered the chaotic political period when the successive presidential elections of 1880, 1884, 1888, 1892, 1896 all saw party changes in Washington. Under such circumstances political leaders were too busy mending home political fences to do much in the way of formulating foreign policies. These would have to emerge through trial and error or as the result of accumulating precedents emerging from the application of common sense to incidents as they arose.

Overseas Expansion Southward

Polk had been able to preside over the consummation of the slogan "From the Atlantic to the Pacific." But what about that other slogan, "From the Arctic to the Isthmus"? True, as just noted, expansion to the north had been stymied both because of the power of Great Britain in Canada and because of the unattractive climate. But the tropics had no such handicaps.

In 1846 a treaty was signed with New Granada (later known as Colombia) which gave the United States freedom of transit across Panama in return for a United States guarantee of Colombian rights therein, and of the neutrality of the Isthmus. President Polk was at great pains to explain to his Congress that the no-entangling alliance idea did not apply to this special case. No wonder British agents in Central America became obsessed with a fear of the Yankee bogeyman.[48]

In Washington itself those responsible were beginning to realize that they might have encouraged the public to want to assume excessive territorial responsibilities. Polk, who certainly did little to delay the outbreak of the Mexican War and who was by no means modest in demanding cessions at the end of that war, was now to show another side of his nature. As the war with Mexico closed there was a rousing demand to "take all Mexico," and members of Congress indicated that they might respond favorably to the demand. The President forthwith asked for immediate approval of the pending treaty (before the expansionists could

---

[48] For further information see Arias, *The Panama Canal*, p. 16; Perkins, *Monroe Doctrine, 1867–1907*, p. 161; R. W. Van Alstyne, "The Central American Policy of Lord Palmerston," *Hisp. Amer. Hist. Rev.*, XVI, No. 3 (August, 1936), 347.

organize their forces). The expenses of a war in the heart of Mexico and problems of administering a people who were not readily assimilable into Anglo-Saxon traditions (as just shown in Texas), and who were not suitable as slaves, gave cause for sober second thoughts. Especially was this the case when the difficulty of transit north and south across the desert of north Mexico was taken into consideration.

Another indication of Mr. Polk's new moderation was seen in his redefinition of Monroe's dictum. He clearly assumed responsibilities for North America, but at least by inference indicated that South America was quite another matter. True, he flatly stated that the United States would never agree that an European power could deny the right of any people of this continent to join their destinies with those of the United States. Further, he reasserted that European powers had no right to transfer New World possessions among themselves and even went so far as to proclaim that New World countries (in particular Yucatán) could not alienate their own territory to an European power. The London *Times* might protest vociferously at this caveat, but such was Polk's pronouncement.[49]

Once having defined his position, the President avoided putting it to the test. Instead, he even authorized his consular agents in Central America to secure exequaturs through Belize (British) rather than from Honduras authorities for service in the area disputed by the two. But if Polk refrained from pressing matters in Central America the issue of expansionism was kept alive by interested agents on the ground. British activities conducted by the vigorous Frederick Chatfield were ably countered by United States agents such as Ephraim George Squier. The result was the negotiation of the Clayton-Bulwer Treaty of 1850. Britain, with its Crimean complications, and the United States, with its readjustments after the Mexican War, were both in a frame of mind to reach a mutual self-denying agreement on expansionism in Central America. The other major consideration was transportation rights and control of a possible isthmian canal. Great Britain had a powerful navy for protection of such a canal; it had cash reserves seeking investment; and it had available near-by bases in the West Indies. The United States countered with its location in the New World and its recently acquired interests in California that clamored for a transportation route to elimi-

---

[49] For a discussion of the Polk Doctrine see Perkins, *Monroe Doctrine, 1826–1867*.

nate the long trip around South America. The result was an agreement that if either country undertook a canal program across the Isthmus the other would have equal rights therein. All in all it was a proud day for the new nation when the Queen of the Seas agreed to such an arrangement. In fact, John Bassett Moore commented that this agreement, not the Monroe Doctrine, placed the first actual restriction upon the extension by an European power of its dominion in this hemisphere.[50] At the same time partnership with Britain in control of a great world trade route seemed to be within reach.

During the boisterous fifties expansionism at full tide seized upon the imagination of the people. Repercussions were heard in Central America as Cornelius Vanderbilt, J. P. Morgan, and others connived at filibustering through such adventurers as William Walker. President Franklin Pierce (inaugurated in 1853), who had "no timid forebodings of the evils of expansionism," refrained from discouraging such moves, but soberer counsels prevailed and nothing came of them. When troops were landed in Panama to protect the transit for the first time in 1856 they were withdrawn in due course in accordance with the treaty of 1846. Again in 1862 a similar situation developed when Secretary of State William H. Seward wrote: "This government has no interest in the matter (Panama transit) different from that of other maritime powers. It is willing to interpose its aid in execution of its treaty and for the benefit of all nations." The same stand was taken four years later.[51]

The British were stubbornly holding their ground but were content to let matters rest at that. In the words of Palmerston to Clarendon:

These Yankees are most disagreeable Fellows to have to do with about any American Question; They are on the spot, strong, deeply interested in the matter, totally unscrupulous and dishonest and determined somehow or other to carry their Point; We are far away, weak from Distance, controlled by the Indifference of the Nation as to the Question discussed, and by its Strong commercial interest in maintaining Peace with the United States.[52]

[50] John Bassett Moore, "The Monroe Doctrine," *Pol. Sci. Quar.*, XI, No. 1 (March, 1896), 25.

[51] John Holladay Latané, *Diplomatic Relations of the United States and Latin America*, p. 184. See also *Use by the United States of a Military Force in the Internal Affairs of Columbia* (Sen. Doc. No. 143, 58th Cong., 2d Sess.), p. 27.

[52] Van Alstyne, "Anglo-American Relations," *Amer. Hist. Rev.*, XLII, No. 3 (April, 1937), 500. For British Activity in Central America see Mario Rodríguez, *A Palmerstonian Diplomat in Central America, Frederick Chatfield, Esq.*

He might well have added that once the Clayton-Bulwer Treaty terminated the expansionist threats in the region his government was more interested in other areas that held greater promise.

When the expansionists turned their attention to the Caribbean islands there was greater danger of international complications. Because of the endemic revolutionary conditions in Santo Domingo and Haiti, and the restlessness in Cuba, there were repeated suggestions that Washington should work through or encourage filibusterers such as the Cuban General Narciso López. Fearing just this, France and Great Britain suggested a triple understanding with the United States to guarantee continued Spanish control of the island. Secretary of State Edward Everett skillfully stated his country's position. He suggested that the geographical location of Cuba in relation to the United States was of such significance as to require a national policy of a unilateral nature, just as an island in the mouth of the Seine River would presuppose a unilateral French policy. Hence, with European rivalries offsetting each other, and expansionists in this country restrained by domestic conditions and politics, the islands remained *in statu quo* until the Civil War put an end to the expansionist era.

The Far South

While Washington was busy with the Texas-Mexican imbroglio, the Canadian problems, and Central American affairs, South America received scant attention. When Great Britain reoccupied the Falkland Islands, off the southern Argentine coast, and when Great Britain and France intervened in the La Plata region, Washington avoided commitment. Even nearer at hand, when complications arose in the Caribbean, Britain was more likely to assert a strong policy than was the United States.[53]

During its war with the United States, Mexico endeavored to arouse sympathy in South America. As early as 1843 John Q. Adams noted that a Mexican commissioner had arrived at "Caraccas" on his way to attend a conference at Lima "said to be to form a league of defense against the grasping designs of the United States upon Mexico."[54] President Polk

[53] Gastón Nerval, *Autopsy of the Monroe Doctrine . . .*, pp. 155–181, lists ten violations of the Monroe Doctrine, as he interprets it, between 1833 and 1861 in none of which, he says, the United States showed any interest. Perkins also discusses most of these cases in his *Monroe Doctrine, 1826–1867.*

[54] Adams, *Memoirs*, XI, 367; Perkins, *Monroe Doctrine, 1826–1867*, pp. 155–156.

gave scant heed. Once more Latin American diversities prevented significant action.

When William Walker became active in Central America and Narciso López led his adventurers into Cuba, South American fears of United States expansionism took on a more active form. The northern republic had leaped across the continent to California and was now threatening the Isthmus. Where would the amazing Yankee stop? These incidents may have been more the result of opportunism than of policy but the South Americans could hardly be expected to appreciate this. West coast countries wondered if their mineral riches would next attract the Yankee gold hunter. Minister Starkweather in Chile reported in 1855: "The press here teems with lampoons against the United States." Something of an antidote to these fears was the rising grain trade of Chile with California gold hunters, and the work of such railroad builders as William Wheelwright and Henry Meiggs. By 1850 Chilean trade with the northern republic (mostly with California) reached over $3.7 million. On the other side of the continent Brazilian trade with the United States was worth more than $17 million. Probably the whole situation is not unfairly reflected in the equation: political fear versus economic satisfaction; result, nothing done.

The commercial leven in the lump of South American relations developed some interesting sidelights. Efforts of the United States to secure the opening of Amazon trade about 1850 aroused some suspicions in Brazil. Also an expedition under Lieutenant Thomas J. Page in the *Water Witch* between 1853 and 1856 was reported to have explored some 3,600 miles of the river systems of the La Plata basin, and to have conducted land explorations over an addition 4,000 miles. Friction with local authorities, involving the death of at least one man, excited awkward accusations, but the facts seem to be that the energetic explorer was simply looking around to see what he could find. Continued interest in the Amazon resulted in the opening of that stream in the late 1860's to trade, due partly to the scientific work of Professor Louis F. Agassiz of Harvard University in the river valley. These incidents, after all, represented surplus energy of individuals rather than government policy as such.[55]

[55] On the west coast situation see Perkins, *Monroe Doctrine, 1826–1867*, p. 250 n; Evans, *Chile and the United States*, pp. 59, 76–78. For detailed trade statistics see Robertson, *Hispanic American Relations with the United States*, pp. 204, 210. On the Amazon question see Hill, *The United States and Brazil*, pp. 221 ff. On the

Expansionism Quiescent

As might have been expected, as soon as the Civil War was over certain political leaders refurbished their old popular slogans of expansionism. Secretary of State William H. Seward was clearly one of these. His hopes for the acquisition of Alaska were fulfilled but his ambitious schemes for canal rights and political footholds in Spanish islands off Central America failed, and his treaties with Honduras, Nicaragua, and Colombia fell on deaf congressional ears, or amounted to nothing in the first place. When he negotiated a treaty for the acquisition of the Danish West Indies even nature turned against him, and successive catastrophes in the form of earthquake, tidal wave, and hurricane turned his proposal into a laughing matter.[56]

In a number of ways Seward's most successful diplomatic maneuver was his mixture of diplomatic pressure in Paris and military pressure on the Mexican border to aid Benito Juárez in 1867 in overthrowing the French puppet, Maximilian. Seward's moves were reinforced by disappointment among the French people at the heavy continuing costs of the Mexican intervention with resultant excessive taxation throughout France and with ominous threats of the oncoming Franco-Prussian complications. In the face of the combined foreign and domestic situations Napoleon III withdrew his support from Maximilian, and Juárez proceeded to reoccupy his capital. At the same time Seward vigorously discouraged a proposal to raise Austrian volunteers to aid Maximilian's failing empire. Thus the Secretary can be said to have vindicated the spirit of the Monroe proposal, which proclaimed that the New World should not be subject to further colonization—or reconquest. Even so, it is peculiarly noteworthy that, expansionist though he was, Seward made no significant gesture toward annexation of any Mexican territory. Southwestward the desert remained a natural barrier.[57]

---

activities of Page see Robertson, *Hispanic American Relations*, p. 337, and Stuart, *Latin America and the United States.*

[56] Charles Callan Tansill, *The Purchase of the Danish West Indies.*

[57] Detailed references may be found in the author's *Liberalism in Mexico, 1857–1929.* Significant discussion is found in Frederick Bancroft, *The Life of William H. Seward* (2 vols., New York: Harper, 1900); also in the personal memoirs of P. H. Sheridan (2 vols., New York: C. L. Webster and Co., 1888), William T. Sherman (2 vols., New York: C. L. Webster and Co., 1892), and Antonio López de Santa Anna, "Mis Memorias, Escritas de mi puña y letra sin ayude de nadie . . . (MS in University of Texas Library).

Next, President Ulysses S. Grant, the nation's savior, as President aspired to be the nation's builder. He also turned to the once popular issue of expansionism. His maneuvers to secure recognition of Cuban rebels were aborted by a conservative Secretary of State, Hamilton Fish; while his more aggressive efforts to acquire a naval base and essential control of Santo Domingo were defeated by an economy-minded and isolationist Senate. When he pressed the issue Senator Charles Sumner by his famous Naboth's Vineyard address, led the opposition that killed the proposal. And it should be noted that this was the case in spite of the fact that the island authorities were willing to deal with England, France, or Spain if they could not secure an arrangement with the United States. Thereafter sporadic calls for expansionism were heard, but the old idea had lost its glamour as the nation suffered through Reconstruction. Even schemes for acquisition of immediately adjacent Mexican territory, by war or otherwise, were dropped as the new strong man of that country, Porfirio Díaz, cemented his grip on the nation.[58]

The one situation that carried the most danger to the United States' sphere of influence was on the Isthmus of Panama. In 1865 Secretary Seward had asserted "perfect neutrality" with regard to domestic matters on the Isthmus but reaffirmed that the United States would protect the transit trade against invasion by either "domestic or foreign disturbers of the peace."[59] Five years later Secretary Fish expressed fear of a joint protectorate and appeared to favor multiple rather than unilateral control of the waterway.[60] But just at this point Ferdinand de Lesseps, successful builder of the Suez Canal, secured a concession from Colombia to construct a canal across Panama. Unfortunately for him, he was familiar with neither the American tropics nor American labor. Also he was badly handicapped by distance and inadequate local supervision. The result was a disastrous failure. Meanwhile Washington became increasingly restless. Congress considered resolutions and Secretary of State William M. Evarts sought in vain to secure a new transit convention from Colombia. President Hayes was seriously concerned. His last message to Congress stated that the protection extended by the

[58] Sumner Welles, *Naboth's Vineyard: The Dominican Republic, 1844–1924*, I, 346 ff. John Watson Foster, *Diplomatic Memoirs*, I, 89 ff.

[59] Chester Lloyd Jones, *The Caribbean since 1900*, p. 319.

[60] H. S. Knapp, "The real status of the Panama Canal as regards neutrality," *Amer. Jour. Internat. Law*, IV, No. 2 (April, 1910), 333–336.

United States to the isthmian region gave it a vital interest in any canal project. He advised that the whole question be reviewed and a proper legal basis be agreed upon for future action with both Great Britain and Colombia. Slowly the issue became less urgent as the French company encountered increasing complications and finally faced bankruptcy. But here was unfinished business.[61]

Latin America in general felt that the Civil War had effected a temporary, if not permanent, eclipse of the northern republic. Brazilian sympathies were extended to the Confederacy, though Brazil maintained good relations with the United States. Argentina continued the lone-wolf role for which it was to become increasingly famous. It had shown little interest in the Bolívar Conference of the 1820's. Now its Calvo Doctrine asserted that foreigners had no right to appeal to their home governments to enforce contracts in other countries. True, many features of the Argentine constitution (some scholars have identified sixty-three articles) resembled those of the United States' organic act. Also many of its *gaucho* leaders protested that the various Argentine provinces were separate and "could never constitute a single political entity."[62] Even so, few were the leaders who looked to the north for guidance.

When the Paraguayan War allied Argentina with Brazil and Uruguay against Paraguay from 1865 to 1870 the United States offered its services as mediator. The allies immediately declined. Obviously the United States did not have too much influence, much less hegemony, in the far south.[63]

Trade developed apace with both coasts but the similarity of products available for sale, plus trade controls exercised by United States tariffs, restrained substantial growth except for the early wheat trade of Chile with California. Comparative figures are striking. British trade with the Argentine rose from $15.5 million to $51 million (234%) in the decade following 1878; that of Germany rose from $3 million to $22 million

---

[61] Charles Richard Williams, *The Life of Rutherford Birchard Hayes* . . ., pp. 218 ff. See also Arias, *The Panama Canal*, p. 40, and Perkins, *The Monroe Doctrine, 1867–1907*, pp. 70 ff.

[62] Nicholas John Spykman, *America's Strategy in World Politics* . . ., p. 352; Robertson, *Hispanic American Relations*, p. 92; Marcel Roussin, *Le Canada et le système interaméricain*, p. 67.

[63] H. F. Peterson, "Efforts of the United States to Mediate in the Paraguayan War," *Hisp. Amer. Hist. Rev.*, XII, No. 1 (February, 1932), 15–17.

(580%), and that of the United States from $5.5 million to only $22 million (205%). There was little encouragement there. One serious obstacle lay in the wool trade of the Argentine, whose production increased 1,500 per cent between 1860 and the end of the century. Yet the 1867 tariff of the United States resulted in reduced imports from Argentina, from 37,000,000 pounds in 1867 to 2,000,000 pounds in 1882. The Department of State wished to reconsider possibilities but national legislation[64] was not forthcoming and private interests of domestic wool growers were successful in maintaining restrictions.

When the initiative of Peru brought about a conference on the codification of international law in 1847 (followed by later meetings in 1861, 1867, and 1878) the United States showed little interest. In fact, in response to an invitation to participate in 1875 the reply was that since United States law was based on the English common law and not on the Roman law, there was little ground for common consideration of such matters. Thereupon ten Latin American states adhered to certain agreements of their own in 1878.

If any suggestion remained that the United States would protect the southern part of the continent from European aggression this was quickly dispelled. The old lack of effective protest at European aggression in the Falkland Islands and in Uruguay now took a new turn in an even more serious matter. In 1865 a Spanish fleet was despatched to reoccupy Peru. On the way north from the Straits of Magellan the vessels stopped on the Chilean coast at the port of Valparaíso. Local authorities asked that a squadron of the United States, then in the harbor, provide protection in the name of the Monroe Doctrine. The commanding officer was keenly aware of critical financial and political conditions at home as the Civil War was drawing to its painful end. Accordingly, he strictly followed his instructions to avoid complications with foreign powers. He sailed about his business and left the port city to its fate, that is, bombardment. In view of this action it is surprising that the west coast countries (Chile, Peru, Bolivia, and Ecuador) did agree for the United States to mediate between themselves and the invaders toward the end of the controversy in 1869. By the agreement

[64] Gaillard Hunt, *The Department of State of the United States* . . . , pp. 148–150. For relations with Argentina see Stuart, *Latin America and the United States*, pp. 400 ff., and Harold F. Peterson, *Argentina and the United States, 1810–1960*, pp. 224 ff. For west coast affairs see Robertson, *Hispanic American Relations*, pp. 236 ff.

reached, Spain gave up its expansionist hopes and after some delays treaties were negotiated for which the United States can claim some credit.[65]

Thus the first century of hemisphere relations of the United States reflected a theoretical and idealistic interest in the whole New World that was paralleled by an imperial and practical program of expansion to its natural boundaries to the south and west. Rising interests in the Caribbean and even farther afield were effectively interrupted by the Civil War. After that followed a quarter of a century of diplomatic doldrums while the nation recuperated from its wounds and gathered strength for a new outward surge of interest and policy making. Intellectual interest in and encouragement for New World democracies remained a constant factor, but either effective aid or interference had to be restricted to a much smaller sphere of influence.

[65] Robertson, *Hispanic American Relations*, p. 149. Seward's warning to Spain on the occupation of the Chincha Islands (see Moore, *Digest*, VI, 508) could have had little or no influence on west coast thinking when compared with the fact that Valparaíso had recently been left to its fate.

CHAPTER II

PANDORA'S BOX: COMPLICATIONS AND RESPONSIBILITIES

The New Era

A NEW ERA WAS AT HAND though not immediately obvious. Rapid economic growth after the Civil War precipitated serious domestic political problems. Once these showed signs of solution, however, the old spirit of expansionism reasserted itself. In short order the United States became embroiled in war with Spain. The combined results of victory and a newly acquired colonial empire were to open a veritable Pandora's Box of complications. Mixed with the problems of administering new possessions were endless complications with sensitive neighbor nations. Genuine altruistic efforts became confused with activities on behalf of national defense and the needs of financial investors. To complicate the matter further there arose Latin American fears of absorption and international differences between the nations that precluded the adoption of any single policy to meet the varying needs.

To begin with, the domestic scene in the United States gave little indication of the impending developments. Fluctuations in political party control of the Presidency in each of the four elections following 1884 were simply an indication that both people and parties were fumbling to adjust to new conditions. The resulting uncertainty caused each temporarily successful party to use diplomatic issues for political capital in electoral campaigns; then, once in office, to reward loyal party workers by appointment to diplomatic posts. Inevitably the system produced inefficiency, but fortunately the blunders of these appointees (with some notorious exceptions) resulted from ignorance, rather than from viciousness or venality. In spite of the uncertainty and the political changes in the Secretaryship, the stability of tenure among career men in the upper levels of the State Department was reassuring. These men were aware of foreign conditions and also grasped the international significance of the rapidly rising new commercial and industrial activities of their countrymen. They saw Western Europe and Japan in vigorous competition for colonies which would guarantee markets. Did it not behoove the United States to bestir itself?

Surprisingly, the portion of United States trade from and to Latin America, when compared with the total foreign trade of the country, actually declined in the last quarter of the nineteenth century. Even so, the total was impressive. More important was the fact that the growth of manufacturing capital in the United States soon found the home market relatively well supplied. This created a demand for new markets. The capital involved increased from a modest $1.7 billion in 1870 to $9.8 billion in 1900, and to $18.4 billion in 1910.[1] Looking abroad, these manufacturers were ready to endorse some kind of inter-American customs union to guarantee their rising interests.[2]

Another group which became much interested in Latin America was composed of humanitarians imbued with the Kipling type of imperialism. They were anxious to spread the benefits of their civilization and their interpretation of Christianity to the less fortunate, their "little brown brothers." With obvious pride they seized upon the Darwinian idea of the survival of the fittest as an expression of the Divine will—and of course their own Teutonic kind was the world's "fittest." Finally, standing behind both businessmen and humanitarians were the old supporters of manifest destiny. Businessmen might be cautious about precipitating war—as in the case of the war with Spain—but the new imperialist felt no such compunction. Even the humanitarian soon rationalized approval of the war with the argument that it would lead to improvement of the lot of the unfortunate. Soaring forth on the wings of eloquence, Senator Albert J. Beveridge could declaim:

---

[1] Scott Nearing and Joseph Freeman, *Dollar Diplomacy: A Study in American Imperialism*, p. 3. See also Chester Lloyd Jones, *The Caribbean since 1900*, p. 7.

[2] Arthur P. Whitaker, *The Western Hemisphere Idea*, pp. 82–83.

. . . the trade of the world must and shall be ours. And we will get it as our mother [England] has told us how. We will establish trading posts throughout the world as distributing points for American products. We will cover the ocean with our merchant marine. We will build a navy to the measure of our greatness. Great colonies governing themselves, flying our flag and trading with us, will grow about our posts of trade. Our institutions will follow our flag on the wings of commerce. And American law, American order, American civilization, and the American flag will plant themselves on shores hitherto bloody and benighted, but by those agencies of God henceforth to be made beautiful and bright.[3]

A more prosaic but very real diplomatic contribution emerged from the interest of the businessman in politics in the form of regular publication of *Consular Reports*, which appeared for the first time in 1880.

Active among the imperialists were the members of the Big Navy League, who rallied those interested in international strategy and sea power. The evolution in the thinking of the group's chief spokesman, Captain (later Admiral) A. T. Mahan, has been carefully charted by scholars. In 1885 he was still an antiexpansionist, but he modified his position in the next five years to endorse expansion in the Caribbean as proper for national welfare.[4] Throughout his career he ardently supported the active development of the Navy and was delighted when the federal government implemented his recommendations. The early caution of this group may be seen in the statement of Henry Cabot Lodge, who commented that "neither the population nor the lands" of Central and South America "would be desirable additions to the United States." However, he also said that "when the Nicaraguan canal is built, the island of Cuba . . . will become to us a necessity." The more exuberant Theodore Roosevelt could joyously write in 1893: ". . . I personally feel very strong about . . . hauling down the flag at Hawaii. I am a bit of a believer in the manifest destiny doctrine. . . . I believe in ultimately driving every European power off this continent . . ." By 1897 Mahan had modified his thinking to the point that he could write with regard to Hawaii: "Do nothing unrighteous, but as regards the problem, take the islands first and solve the problem afterwards."[5]

---

[3] Julius W. Pratt, *The Expansionists of 1898*, p. 228. See also pp. 3 ff. and 233 ff.

[4] Captain W. D. Puleston, *Mahan: The Life and Work of Captain Alfred Thayer Mahan, U.S.N.*, pp. 129–131.

[5] These points of view may be found in Pratt, *Expansionists of 1898*, p. 207; Elting E. Morison and Jno. M. Blum, eds., *The Letters of Theodore Roosevelt*, I,

Of course the jingoes joined in the concert. One careful historian of the period concludes: "The need of American business for colonial markets and fields for investment was discovered not by business men but by historians and other intellectuals, by journalists and politicians."[6] This may be a correct evaluation, but it must be admitted that the businessman learned fast. At least one recent scholar is convinced that the businessman's role was primary when it came to policy making. The industrialists' periodicals *Iron Age*, the Chattanooga *Tradesman, American Manufacturer and Iron World*, and the *Dry Goods Economist* followed the lead of the *Age of Steel* in calling for reciprocity by which the United States could "annex territories and markets from under the muzzles of its competitors' guns."[7] The fact seems to be that the expansionist sentiment was arising from varied sources. Realizing this, a skillful politician (such as the ambitious Governor William McKinley of Ohio) could give the keynote address to the first meeting of the significant National Association of Manufacturers in 1895 calling for markets, high tariffs, and reciprocity.[8]

Grover Cleveland, President from 1885 to 1889 and again from 1893 to 1897, opposed this trend. He was basically an isolationist, as evidenced by his efforts to avoid both the Hawaiian and Cuban imbroglios. Even he, however, became involved in the Venezuelan boundary dispute and vigorously asserted United States priority in the New World. In the Pacific he was more cautious. Hawaii, long a crossroads of the Pacific, had developed increasingly close commercial ties with America after the early days of the nineteeth century. Efforts by British and French agents to secure colonial rights had been successfully forestalled by Washington prior to the Civil War. Now, when Cleveland returned to power in 1893, he found an annexation treaty before the Senate that had been negotiated by his predecessor, Benjamin Harrison. Rumors of improper pressure by business interests and strategists caused Cleveland to withdraw the treaty from the Senate before that body had acted upon it. Later he reported that such unethical procedures had been used in the negotiations

---

313; Puleston, *Mahan,* p. 182; and Allan Nevins, *Grover Cleveland: A Study in Courage,* p. 608.

[6] Pratt, *Expansionists of 1898,* p. 22.

[7] Walter LaFeber, *The New Empire: An Interpretation of American Expansion, 1860–1898,* p. 118.

[8] *Ibid.,* pp. 192–194.

that he would not resubmit the treaty for consideration. In simple language, Cleveland preferred to steer clear of overseas responsibilities.

This action was directly in line with his conduct during his first administration when he withdrew a treaty then before the Senate for canal rights in Nicaragua. The reason given on this earlier occasion was that he did not consider the terms of the convention consistent with existing obligations of the United States under the Clayton-Bulwer Treaty with Great Britain. Once more Cleveland showed he was primarily interested in domestic problems and sought to avoid foreign complications. In spite of all he could do, however, he found the Cuban complications during his second term a severe strain on his isolationism. The jingoes and yellow journals seized every opportunity for propaganda. The country had resources and energy—especially energy—for new things. It was hard to sit on the lid.

Apparently Germany respected the position and power of the United States in the Caribbean, but it was certainly surveying possibilities for naval bases in such likely areas as Santo Domingo and Costa Rica. Also rumors of a possible German-French deal by which the holdings of a bankrupt French company would be transferred to German control gave State Department officials concern.[9] Still, Cleveland remained calm. He did favor strengthening the Navy[10] for general purposes, but that was about all. German ambitions farther south appeared to be a matter of more concern to the British than to the President of the United States.

But in spite of an isolationist President, the era of the "diplomatic doldrums" was drawing to a close. Presidents from Johnson to Cleveland had shown little aptitude for or interest in diplomacy; but from Cleveland to Franklin D. Roosevelt, inclusive, only two Presidents could be classed as showing "ignorance of or unfitness for the control of foreign affairs."[11]

The Sphere of Influence Asserted

President Rutherford B. Hayes had expressed concern at French efforts to construct a canal across Panama, but it was left for James G. Blaine,

[9] Count Otto zu Stolberg-Wernigerode, *Germany and the United States during the Era of Bismarck*, pp. 210–211, 304–310.

[10] For a sample of Roosevelt's argument see Theodore Roosevelt, Jr., *American Naval Policy as Outlined in Messages of the Presidents*, p. 11.

[11] Harold J. Laski, *The American Presidency: An Interpretation*, pp. 175–176.

who became Secretary of State under President James A. Garfield in 1881, to formulate a policy about the matter, even though it was not to be effectively applied for some years. When the French needed a base of operations for canal construction they acquired the island of St. Bartholomew from Sweden in 1877. In spite of previous general endorsement of Polk's no-transfer doctrine, the United States had paid little or no attention to the deal.[12] Blaine, however, was to take a more positive position on all New World matters. He asserted that any significant detail of Western Hemisphere relations was of interest to his country. He even went so far as to insist that a dispute between Colombia and Costa Rica was not a fit subject for arbitration by an Old World ruler. (At the time he was referring to the sovereigns of Belgium and Spain.) When he felt that irresponsible financial conduct in Venezuela might invite foreign intervention he suggested that a United States customs collector be selected to forestall the danger[13]—an interesting forerunner of the policy later adopted.

Blaine's successor, F. T. Frelinghuysen, also felt that the settlement of American problems should be arranged by New World countries. For his own country he declined a Haitian offer of a naval base in 1882–1883 and again the next year, but he let it be known without hesitation that the United States would look askance at French occupation of such a base. France promptly responded: "We are very far from seeking in the New World advantages of any sort which would expose us to confront the redoubtable Monroe Doctrine." At the same time the Secretary put forth unusual efforts to encourage Mexico and Guatemala to solve a nagging boundary dispute.[14] Then, returning to quasi-expansion-

---

[12] Dexter Perkins, *The Monroe Doctrine, 1867–1907*, p. 33. See also Charles Callan Tansill, *The Purchase of the Danish West Indies*, pp. 180–181.

[13] Secondary accounts of the Blaine era may be found in Alice Felt Tyler, *The Foreign Policy of James G. Blaine*; David Saville Muzzey, *James G. Blaine, A Political Idol of Other Days*; Perkins, *Monroe Doctrine, 1867–1907*; Rayford W. Logan, *The Diplomatic Relations of the United States and Haiti, 1776–1891*; D. Y. Thomas, *One Hundred Years of the Monroe Doctrine*.

[14] For Frelinghuysen and Central America see Tyler, *Foreign Policy of Blaine*; Perkins, *Monroe Doctrine, 1867–1907*; John Holladay Latané, *The United States and Latin America*; John Bassett Moore, *Digest of International Law*; and Graham H. Stuart, *Latin America and the United States*. Two special studies are Samuel Pasco, "Isthmian Canal Question," *The Annals*, XIX (January, 1901), and George T. Weitzel, *The American Policy in Nicaragua* (Sen. Doc. No. 334, 64th Cong., 1st Sess).

ism, he negotiated a treaty with Nicaragua, looking to the possible construction of a transisthmian canal. When Cleveland returned to office in 1893 he continued his old isolationist tendencies and his desire to avoid foreign complications. He withdrew the Hawaiian treaty from the Senate and declined to become interested in a naval base in Samaná Bay.[15] As a positive approach to the troubled Central American area he reiterated the United States' suggestions, made repeatedly between 1863 and 1888, encouraging the unification of the discordant states.

The rising tide of United States influence was obvious a full decade before the outbreak of the war with Spain. An Englishman observed that the feeling in Cuba "was that the United States was, and is, the residuary legatee of all the islands, Spanish and English equally, and that she will be forced to take charge of them whether she likes it or not." He insisted that Spain had misgoverned its possessions and that the English had allowed their islands to drift in a fashion that invited disaster.[16]

Meanwhile the isthmian transit question was growing in importance as the French company undertook construction in Panama. As early as 1880 the United States minister at Bogotá was instructed to enquire if Colombia would approve acquisition by the United States of a naval station and a coaling base accessible to the increasingly valuable Panama transit route.[17] Bogotá promptly declined any suggestion of a bilateral defense agreement. Obviously it preferred general international guarantees for the neutrality of the Isthmus, but Blaine feared that anything of the kind would "partake of the nature of an alliance" against the United States.[18] Congress meanwhile was restless about the French activities. The Committee on Interoceanic Canals and the Foreign Affairs Committee both called for the repeal or reconsideration of the Clayton-Bulwer Treaty. On April 16, 1880, both House and Senate passed a resolution to this effect, and President Hayes endorsed the suggestion in his message to Congress on March 8, 1880.[19] The next year the new Secretary of State Blaine seized the idea and impulsively asserted that Great Britain had failed to fulfill its implied obligations under the Clayon-Bulwer Treaty. It followed, argued the Secretary, that the United States should not be bound by the obsolete convention. Downing Street

---

[15] Sumner Welles, *Naboth's Vineyard*, I, 468–469.

[16] James Anthony Froude, *The English in the West Indies* . . ., p. 333.

[17] Moore, *Digest*, III, p. 28.

[18] *Ibid.*, p. 189; Tyler, *Foreign Policy of Blaine*, pp. 30–32.

[19] Miles P. Duval, *Cadiz to Cathay*, p. 96.

stood firmly on its treaty rights. Evidently the new Secretary was making an effort to face new conditions, though his blunt methods were open to serious question. Once Blaine was out of office the active phase of the controversy lapsed though an executive agent was sent to Nicaragua to see what could be done toward securing a naval station on Lake Nicaragua.[20]

When civil war broke out in Colombia in 1885 the United States again fulfilled its treaty obligations to protect the transit[21] and temporarily landed troops. Yet this was the very time at which Cleveland had withdrawn the Frelinghuysen-Zavala treaty with Nicaragua from the Senate. He feared that such transit rights as provided in the treaty might infringe the Clayton-Bulwer agreement.[22]

Looking Further Afield

In many ways Blaine was the first foreign-policy maker after John Q. Adams to encompass the whole New World in his thinking. He grasped the significance of an agreement among the emergent states, which were rapidly developing their own individualities. Positivism had a strong appeal to the rising Latin American intellectual who applied its theories to varied local conditions.[23] And among these conditions were increasingly complex economic interests. For instance, in 1870 Chile had no significant export of nitrates. Ten years later it was shipping 250,000 metric tons.[24] Here was the stuff of modern Chilean history and international relations, and Chilean leaders had to allow for it in their planning. On the east coast of the continent was Brazil, of which Blaine said: "Brazil holds, in the south, much the same relationship to the other countries that the United States does in the north."[25] And the Brazilian foreign trade had shown a favorable balance that had risen from £17 mil-

[20] Henry Merritt Wriston, *Executive Agents in American Foreign Relations*, p. 794.

[21] *Use by the United States of a Military Force in the Internal Affairs of Colombia* (Sen. Doc. No. 143, 58th Cong., 2d Sess.), pp. 53, 103–104; Moore, *Digest*, III, 40–41.

[22] Weitzel, *American Policy in Nicaragua* (Sen. Doc. No. 334, 64th Cong., 1st Sess.), p. 7; Moore, *Digest*, III, 198–199.

[23] Whitaker, *The Western Hemisphere Idea*, pp. 64–70.

[24] C. C. Griffin, "States of Latin America," *New Cambridge Modern History*, XI, 522.

[25] Quoted in Moore, *Digest*, VI, 483.

lion gold (about $85 million) in 1860 to more than double that figure by the end of the century.[26]

Between Chile and Brazil lay Argentina, whose pride and whose commodities were directly competitive with those of the United States. Great Britain and Europe had need of Argentine raw materials but the United States did not. As a result, trade between the two New World republics was erratic. In 1880 the Argentines exported over $6 million of commodities to the United States in exchange for less than $1.9 million, but by 1900 the figures had become $8.1 million to over $11.5 million. Argentina had to make up the balance from profits on trade to Europe, especially to Great Britain.[27] Less than friendly with its immediate neighbors and having an adverse trade balance with the United States, Argentina had felt little urge to change from its isolationist practices at the time of the Latin American conferences of 1826, 1847, or 1864. It had even declined to adhere to a continental security treaty in 1856.[28]

Blaine turned both his personal charm and his ruthless energy toward the south. As Secretary of State he has been aptly described by the old statement, originally used in another connection, "genius is in him, but there's a journalist at his elbow." He sincerely sought a foreign policy that would "bring about peace and prevent futile wars in North and South America," the while he hoped to cultivate such friendly ties as would lead to a substantial increase of exports from his own country.[29] With these mixed motives he issued his call for a conference of the American states to meet in Washington. At this point Garfield was assassinated and Blaine was dropped from the Cabinet. The invitations were recalled[30] but the seed here sown was to bear fruit later.

More immediate was an event transpiring on the west coast of South America. In 1879 Chile had taken advantage of long-standing border friction to precipitate the four-year War of the Pacific against its northern neighbors Bolivia and Peru. Unfortunately the United States ministers sent to the respective capitals were political appointees for the most part, poorly selected and diplomatically untrained. Their inept conduct

[26] Henry William Speigel, *The Brazilian Economy . . .*, p. 118.

[27] Treasury Department, *Statistical Abstract of the United States, 1906*, p. 217.

[28] Arthur P. Whitaker, *The United States and Argentina*, pp. 86–87.

[29] James G. Blaine, *The Foreign Policy of the Garfield Administration*, pp. 1–8.

[30] James Brown Scott, ed., *The International Conferences of the American States*, p. 449.

of difficult negotiations led to confusion that was further compounded
when Frelinghuysen became Secretary of State. Washington obviously
desired peace in the southern continent, but confusing instructions and
ludicrous blundering by agents prevented the emergence of any consistent policy. Finally Great Britain and Germany suggested that the
United States cooperate with them in an effort to bring about peace.
On July 19, 1879, Washington declined to participate in the joint move
lest it smack of "coercion in disparagement of belligerent rights."[31]

Just before Blaine left office late in 1881 he sent to Chile as minister
the veteran diplomat William H. Trescot, accompanied by the Secretary's son, Walker Blaine.[32] Trescot initiated tentative mediation arrangements. At that point, when Trescot repaired to the Foreign Office
to deliver the invitation to attend the announced inter-American conference, he was astounded to find that the Foreign Office had heard that
the invitations were to be recalled, though the Minister himself had not
been informed of the fact. The President of Chile naturally concluded
that the Minister had been repudiated. Inevitably the peace efforts he
had started collapsed. Possibly they were already hopelessly deadlocked
but certainly Chilean feelings toward the United States became less
cordial. Blaine himself had been trying to force the hand of Chile in the
negotiations, even to the point of threatening to break diplomatic relations if Santiago failed to make concessions. Now Washington was not
supporting the Minister who had exerted its earlier pressures. In due
course Bolivia and Peru were defeated and despoiled of their nitrate
fields. Frelinghuysen, Blaine's successor, sympathized with the victims
but did not feel that he could use the kind of pressure to which Blaine
and Trescot had resorted. He let matters rest.

In a somewhat parallel situation on the east coast of South America,
Secretary Frelinghuysen was more assertive. Uruguay was about to cede
certain lands to Brazil after mediation efforts from Europe. The Secretary wrote: "The Department of State will not sanction an intervention
of European states in South American difficulties, *even with the consent*

[31] Moore, *Digest*, VI, 34; Tyler, *Foreign Policy of Blaine*, p. 114.

[32] For this Chilean episode see John Watson Foster, *Diplomatic Memoirs*, II;
E. M. Borchard, "The Tacna-Arica Controversy," *For. Affs.* I, No. 1 (September 15,
1922) pp. 29–48; P. M. Brown, "Frelinghuysen," in Samuel Flagg Bemis, ed., *The
American Secretaries of State and Their Diplomacy*, VIII; Moore, *Digest*, VI;
and Henry Clay Evans, *Chile and Its Relations with the United States*.

of the parties. The decision of American questions pertains to America itself."[33]

In the rest of Latin America the United States played little part during the 1880's. Blaine may have hoped for possible acquisitions on the west coast but he left office before anything could materialize. Likewise, when Argentina protested British ownership of the Falkland Islands, Secretary of State Thomas F. Bayard repeated the old stock answer in 1886. Since the British claim to the Islands predated the Monroe Doctrine, the United States did not consider the said claim to be an extension of the European system to the New World.[34] Even with the increasing unrest in near-by Cuba, Cleveland's public record gave no indication of a change in his policy of nonintervention, even though he was known to be increasingly concerned over developments. He did withdraw from the Senate treaties negotiated with Spain on behalf of its colonies, Cuba and Puerto Rico, and for Santo Domingo,[35] but both he and the Secretary of State sternly rebuffed all requests of Cuban revolutionaries for help.

Reciprocity and the Pan-American Conference

Meanwhile Congress took up Blaine's idea of a meeting of the New World nations. The first Cleveland Administration was lukewarm to the suggestion originated by its Republican predecessor, but the idea would not down. Proposals for such a meeting varied slightly from time to time, but one author lists at least five bills introduced in the House and Senate in the three years following February, 1883. In general these called for some kind of a commercial conference. Finally, on May 24, 1888, the President was "requested and authorized" to invite the Latin American republics to send delegates to such a meeting.[36] This was the more unusual because the recent defeat of the Democrats in the elections of 1888 left it to the Republicans to serve as hosts for the convention. Blaine, with poetic justice, had once more been named Secretary of State.

[33] Quoted in Gastón Nerval, *Autopsy of the Monroe Doctrine*, p. 222.
[34] Perkins, *Monroe Doctrine, 1867–1907*, pp. 61 ff.
[35] Herminio Portell Vilá, *História de Cuba en sus relaciones con los Estados Unidos y Espana*, III, 87; Tariff Commission, *Reciprocity and Commercial Treaties*, pp. 140–141.
[36] Scott, *International Conferences*, pp. 3–4; Tyler, *Foreign Policy of Blaine*, pp. 174–175. Joseph Byrne Lockey, *Pan-Americanism*, gives credit to the New York *Evening Post* for introducing the term "Pan-Americanism" in 1882.

The conference should be considered in light of the economic program of the Secretary. For some time there had been talk of reciprocity treaties with the Latin American republics. In 1884–1885 a commission of three members and a secretary visited the leading South and Central American countries. It recommended trade concessions, emphasing sugar and wool as items on which tariffs should be adjusted, while listing coffee and hides as demanding consideration. Latin American nations were much interested in the possibilities raised.[37]

Blaine was a much older and more cautious man when he resumed the office of Secretary of State in 1889 than he had been eight years earlier. In general he was still an expansionist, although, in writing to President-elect Harrison in 1889, after calmly reviewing the whole field of possible overseas acquisitions, he concluded that only Hawaii was "imminent."[38] In other areas he simply remained alert to commercial possibilities. To secure reciprocity treaties he openly endorsed high tariffs to be used as diplomatic weapons with which to pry reciprocal concessions from foreign countries.[39]

With congressional approval the agreements were forthcoming. The first treaty was signed with Brazil on January 31, 1891. It was followed by others, with the Dominican Republic, Spain (for the islands of Cuba

[37] Tariff Commission, *Reciprocity and Commercial Treaties*, pp. 141–142; H. Parker Willis, "Reciprocity with Cuba," *The Annals*, XIII (July, 1903), 134; William E. Curtis. "A Brief History of the Reciprocity Policy," *The Annals*, XXIX (January–June, 1906), 17–18.

A convention with Mexico lapsed without Senate approval (see William Spence Robertson, *Hispanic American Relations with the United States*, pp. 214–216) and a minor treaty with Spain on behalf of Cuba and Puerto Rico did not go into effect (see Tariff Commission, *Reciprocity and Commercial Treaties*, p. 21).

Interestingly enough Jacques Kulp notes that the first American railroad reached the Mexican border in 1883 to herald the economic penetration of Latin America that proceeded with "the suddenness and force of an elementary phenomenon" ("La Pénétration des États-Unis en Amérique Latine," *Revue des Deux Mondes*, 7th period, LIX [October, 15, 1930], 840 ff.). Also Walter LaFeber comments that in three years American capitalists received subsidies from the Mexican government worth $32 million and concessions for five roads to extend some 2,500 miles (*The New Empire*, p. 42).

[38] Albert T. Volweiler, ed., *The Correspondence between Benjamin Harrison and James G. Blaine, 1882–1893*, p. 174.

[39] Foster, *Diplomatic Memoirs*, II, 2–6. In connection with the reciprocal trade program, Foster tells of Blaine's interview wtih a Senate committee. In his enthusiasm for his program Blaine smashd a fine silk top hat with his vigorous gestures.

and Puerto Rico), El Salvador, Great Britain (for its West Indian islands), Nicaragua, and Honduras, during the next two years. One feature of the policy was the retaliatory rates that the Administration was authorized to impose on nations that refused to cooperate. Critics have suggested that the reciprocal trade program "simply meant the obtaining of concessions by threats of tariff discrimination."[40] And such discrimination was actually applied in the cases of Colombia, Venezuela, and Haiti. As a result of the increased rates applied especially on sugar, molasses, coffee, tea, and hides the combined shipments of the three countries to the United States in 1894 showed a 72.73 per cent decline from the figures for the three-year average from 1888 to 1890, inclusive.[41] In the Caribbean as a whole the results were quite noteworthy. United States flour almost displaced Spanish flour in the Cuban market and sugar imports to the United States practically doubled between 1891 and 1893.[42] By and large the positive results of the policy on South American nations, however, had little significance except in the case of Brazil, where a substantial trade increase ensued.

In the background remained the imperialists. The sensation-hungry Theodore Roosevelt wrote Henry Cabot Lodge in 1886 that he had offered to raise some companies of horse riflemen in case war developed with Mexico. He added: "I haven't the least idea there will be any trouble; but as my chance of doing anything in the future worth doing seems to grow continually smaller I intend to grasp at every opportunity that turns up."[43] President Harrison, when he entered office in 1889, advocated acquisition of coaling stations and dock and harbor privileges where they could be obtained without coercion.[44] The naval historian Mahan likewise added his endorsement and added the imperial note by quoting Secretary Blaine: "It is not an ambitious destiny for so

[40] Lincoln Hutchinson, "Results of Reciprocity with Brazil," *Pol. Sci. Quar.*, XVIII (No. 2 (June, 1903), 284–285; Tariff Commission, *Reciprocity and Commercial Treaties*, pp. 153–155.

[41] Benjamin H. Williams, *Economic Foreign Policy of the United States*, p. 271.

[42] John Ball Osborne, "Reciprocity in the American Tariff System," *The Annals*, XXIII (January, 1904), 65–66; Robertson, *Hispanic American Relations*, pp. 218–219.

[43] Henry Cabot Lodge, ed., *Selections from the Correspondence of Theodore Roosevelt and Henry Cabot Lodge, 1884–1918*, I, 44–45.

[44] James D. Richardson, ed., *A Compilation of the Messages and Papers of the Presidents, 1789–1897*, IX, 10; Theodore Roosevelt, Jr., *American Naval Policy*, p. 12.

great a country as ours to manufacture only what we can consume, or produce only what we can eat."[45] The strategists were making their bid for the support of the commercial interests—and Blaine frankly hoped to use the approaching Pan-American Conference in 1889 to lead the way to the desired objectives.

Latin American historians have been inclined to conclude that economic advantage, so evident a factor in the matter, was Washington's only objective in calling the conference.[46] Conversely, they have insisted that Latin American interests were broader in scope. They recall that as late as 1888 a conference of Latin American states assembled in Montevideo to consider questions of international private law. Here the leadership of Argentina was clear. One of their recent scholars has noted the differing points of emphasis, saying that while the United States sought a continental tariff system, including standardization of products, port duties, moneys, maritime communications, and the like in the interest of economic commercialism, the Hispanic republics were primarily interested in such questions as international law, obligatory arbitration, and principles of civil and criminal legislation.[47]

In opening the Conference in 1889 the United States followed the businessman's approach and suggested a kind of a *Zollverein*, or customs union, for the New World. At once Argentina objected.[48] Further, its delegates opposed the selection of Blaine as presiding officer and declined to attend the session in which his selection was consummated. Also they declined to accept many of the hospitalities offered. On firmer ground they insisted that the minutes of all sessions of the Conference be read in Spanish and in English. At the same time they openly asserted that they preferred their established European trade to uncertain New World markets.[49] Then, after the Conference agreed to establish the Bureau of American Republics, Argentina did not pay its share (a mere $1,462.50) of the first year's expenses. The United States paid it for

[45] Alfred Thayer Mahan, *The Interest of America in Sea Power* . . ., p. 5.

[46] For examples see Manuel Medina Castro, *EE. UU. y la independencia de la América Latina* . . ., pp. 69–79; Clarence H. Haring, *South America Looks at the United States*, pp. 111–113.

[47] Felipe Barreda Laos, *La segunda emancipación de América Hispana*, p. 98. See also Thomas F. McGann, *Argentina and the United States* . . ., pp. 74–79.

[48] Juan José Arévalo, *Fábula del tiburón y las sardinas* . . ., p. 93; Benjamin H. Williams, *American Diplomacy*, pp. 117–118.

[49] McGann, *Argentina and the U.S.*, pp. 132–161.

her. Actually, it was not until 1898 that Argentina began regular payment of dues.[50]

Thus the meeting of the seventeen American republics passed into history. Santo Domingo, miffed that its reciprocity treaty of 1884 had never been ratified, had not accepted the invitation to attend; and Hawaii, though invited, had not gotten its delegates to Washington in time. Of course, Cuba and Panama were not in existence as nations, and Canada was still considered a part of the British Empire.

Chile had been fearful of any discussion involving arbitration because of its preoccupation with Tacna-Arica (territory occupied by victorious Chile at the close of the War of the Pacific) and had sidetracked this noncommercial proposal of Blaine. Direct concrete results of the Conference, therefore, were severely limited. The chief item was the establishment of the continuing organization, the Bureau of the American States. Some significant resolutions were passed and some questions of genuine import were raised; and mutual acquaintance and understanding, even if not immediate agreement, were established. Further, all the republics came to realize that in such sessions their delegates could frankly talk over needs and possibilities. Contacts meant improved business relations and held out the promise of new markets. Also, there was general approval of the declaration that "acts of conquest, whether the object or the consequence of war" were in violation of the public law of America.[51]

While Western Europe watched jealously[52] the movement seemed to lose momentum. Blaine died, the imperialists turned to other interests, and the public was not yet awake to possibilities. However, in the broader field of inter-American relations one detail should be noted. The Bureau of the American Republics was operating on a budget of approximately $25,000 per year by 1895.[53]

---

[50] *Ibid.*, pp. 182–183. See significant letter of M. García Merou, November 2, 1896, in Richard Olney Papers, LC.

[51] Discussion of the Conference may be found in Scott, *International Conferences*, pp. 11 ff.; Moore, *Digest*, I, 292 ff., VI, 600 ff., and VII, 72; and in Joseph B. Lockey, "Blaine," in Bemis, *Amer. Secs. of St.*, VIII, 166–181. For two accounts in Spanish see José Joaquín Caicedo Castillo, *El panamericanismo*, pp. 235–236, and Enrique Gil, *Evolución del panamericanismo . . .*, pp. 66–67.

[52] Orestes Ferrara, *El panamericanismo y la opinión europea*, pp. 35–37.

[53] An itemized copy of the budget may be found in the Olney Papers, LC, dated October 1, 1895. For work being done see Department of State, *Papers Re-*

Ecuador proposed another general session or conference to take place in Mexico City in 1896. Secretary of State Richard Olney frowned on the suggestion, and at the appointed time only the five Central American Republics, together with Venezuela and Mexico, had representatives in attendance. The American minister at Mexico City stood by to attend if advisable but he did not see fit to grace a failing movement when his own government was unenthusiastic. Those present would express concern at the implications of the Monroe Doctrine but would have only themselves as an audience for their remarks. Probably the varying attitudes of different officials in Brazil were typical of general thinking in Latin America. Its minister in Washington informed Olney confidentially and unofficially of the interest of his government in the meeting. Then he hastened to add that he felt the preliminaries should be conducted secretly and confidentially "so that no European government will know what is going on until the congress meets and in a few sessions signs the treaty."[54] At the same time the British minister in Rio de Janeiro wrote the Marquis of Salisbury on February 2, 1896, that the Brazilian Minister of Foreign Affairs was lukewarm about the conference, had expressed doubts that Ecuador was a proper country to promote such a meeting, and had asserted that "in any case Brazil would not participate in any collective action whatever of an anti-European character." The result of such varying points of view was that Brazil declined the invitation to send delegates to the conference, implying that Cleveland's recent action in the Venezuelan boundary dispute (see below, this chapter, "Closer Home Once More") made any meeting at the time inadvisable. The Brazilian action was interpreted to imply that at the time the United States would act as it pleased in the area and that it would be of little service for Latin America to protest.[55]

On the other hand, it is interesting to note that in the index of a work by an eminent historian discussing United States expansionism of

---

lating to the Foreign Relations of the United States, 1898, p. lxxxiv. (This set is hereinafter cited as For. Rels).

[54] Mendoza (sic) to Olney, June 20, 1896, Olney Papers, LC. For pertinent material see Genaro Estrada, ed., La doctrina de Monroe, pp. v–xv; and Moore, Digest, VI, 602.

[55] Phipps to Salisbury, February 2, 1896, F.O. 13 (Brazil), 1896, Vol. 757. (All Foreign Office [F.O.] materials cited are found in the Public Records Office in London.)

the 1890's Venezuela is the only South American country listed.[56] From this negative background South American events were soon to force their attention on the State Department.

Chile

Even at the time of the Pan-American Conference complications were arising in the shoestring republic of Chile on the west coast of South America. For some years an orderly succession of Chilean presidents had encouraged foreign investments, especially those of British and other European capitalists, in the nitrate fields. The new Harrison Administration sent one Patrick Egan, a naturalized Irish immigrant, as minister to Santiago. Before coming to the United States Egan had found Ireland "uncomfortable" because of his anti-British activities.[57] After reaching the United States he became an ardent Republican Party worker in the Middle West, where he amassed a fortune in the grain business. When he arrived in Chile it was to find an administration controlled by José Manuel Balmaceda. Actually a dictator, Balmaceda had bypassed his Congress and appealed for popular support by agitation for sanitation and health and welfare programs. These were to be financed, the masses expected and the conservatives feared, largely from new taxes to be levied on foreign holdings. Egan liked the dictator's program and assisted him in establishing a grain marketing program. Meanwhile he sent enthusiastic reports to Washington.

The old Constitutionalists, from whom the dictator had seized control, soon took the field with the active encouragement of certain foreign investors. They sent a ship, the *Itata*, to San Diego, California, for military supplies. There the captain submitted a false manifest to customs officials. Then, fearing detention, he sailed southward carrying with him a United States marshal who had been placed on board to watch the situation. This official was landed farther down the coast and drops out of the story. Meanwhile orders were issued for a United States squadron in southern waters to intercept the vessel. This was done. Forthwith, the Constitutionalists asked that only the captain, with the ship's papers,

---

[56] Pratt, *The Expansionists of 1898.*

[57] The further story of Minister Egan in Chile and the *Itata* case may be followed in Hardy Osgood, "Was Patrick Egan a 'blundering minister'?" *Hisp. Amer. Hist. Rev.*, VIII, No. 1 (February, 1928), 80–81; Evans, *Chile and the United States*, p. 138; and Tyler, *Foreign Policy of Blaine*, pp. 132 ff.

be returned to the United States to face trial, while the *Itata* and cargo were held in Chilean waters in the custody of the United States Navy. This arrangement would allow for prompt release of the supplies if the court so authorized. Urged by Egan, however, the State Department insisted that the vessel itself be returned for the investigation. At the hearing it became evident that the conduct of the captain of the *Itata* had been both suspicious and unwise, but not sufficiently illegal to justify confiscation of the cargo. However, after release the supplies could not be returned to Chilean waters in time to aid the already victorious Constitutionalists. They had succeeded thanks in part at least to aid and encouragement from German and British interests in the country.[58] Egan naturally was now most unpopular with the reinstated Constitutionalists. Additional irritation arose when it became known that the United States legation and its naval vessels, especially the *U.S.S. Baltimore*, had aided fallen Balmaceda leaders to escape.[59]

A short time later, on October 16, 1891, Captain W. S. Schley of the *Baltimore* allowed some 150 of his men shore leave in Valparaíso. Trouble soon broke out between the sailors and a hostile populace in the tenderloin district of the port city. In the ensuing melee one sailor was killed and others emerged considerably the worse for wear.[60] Secretary Blaine was an ill man, so President Harrison assumed responsibility for demanding a full apology and substantial financial reparations for the injuries suffered. Before Chile had a chance to respond to the ultimatum, President Harrison sent his Congress the correspondence exchanged with Chilean authorities. His reference to the "dignity as well as the prestige and influence" of the United States was bellicose to say the least. The President's haste in the matter was described by later President W. H. Taft in writing to Theodore Roosevelt in 1906. He said that Harrison's action was similar to that of the old workman running from the hayfield to the barn to get out of the rain. When asked why he was running so hard he answered, "I am afraid the storm will be over before I

---

[58] The question of the amount of Balmaceda support derived from wealthy Chileans apparently needs further study. See Harold Blakemore, "The Chilean Revolution of 1891 . . .," *Hisp. Amer. Hist. Rev.*, XLV, No. 3 (August, 1965), 393 ff., especially pp. 417–418.

[59] *For. Rels., 1891*, pp. 161–162, 194.

[60] Moore, *Digest*, VI, 856–857; Tyler, *Foreign Policy of Blaine*, pp. 159–161; Evans, *Chile and the United States*, pp. 146 ff.

get to the barn."[61] Whatever the motives of the President, the fact is that Chile was forced to apologize and to send reparations for injuries. Chileans remained convinced that their government had been imposed on only because their country could not face the naval might of the United States. Sir Cecil Spring-Rice, of the British legation in Washington, commented: "We are on the verge of a war here, which is owing to inconceivable stupidity on our (that is, the American) side and trickery on the other." Referring to Blaine as conservative and as an influence for peace, he placed primary responsibility on the President.[62]

When Cleveland returned to office in 1893 Latin America breathed a sigh of relief and its official representatives in Washington welcomed him enthusiastically.[63] The new President promptly instructed Egan in Chile to cease to grant asylum to refugees of the old regime. He also reported to Congress that United States representatives can "under no circumstances be permitted to interrupt criminal justice in other countries." If more assurance was needed it was forthcoming when the United States minister in Quito proved overly generous in extending the right of asylum to overthrow Ecuadorian officials. His action, too, was at once disapproved in Washington.[64]

Thereafter relations with the west coast countries settled down for the time. When there were rumors that Great Britain sought control of the Galápagos Islands, off the coast of Ecuador, in 1892, Minister Roland B. Mahaney informed Ecuadorian officials of the concern of the United States. The President and other high officials readily gave assurances that they would oppose such a cession.[65]

Rather typical of the wild financial speculations and resulting rumors prevalent on the west coast was the case of German claims against Chile arising from the Balmaceda era. British Minister E. C. Phipps from Brazil informed his Foreign Office in 1895 he had just heard that the

[61] Taft to Roosevelt, September 17, 1906, William Howard Taft Papers, LC.

[62] Stephen Gwynn, ed., *The Letters and Friendships of Sir Cecil Spring-Rice*, I, 118.

[63] Nevins, *Grover Cleveland*, pp. 549–550.

[64] For the attitude of Cleveland on the right of asylum see *For. Rels., 1893*, p. iv, and Moore, *Digest*, II, 798–807. The President's repudiation of Egan was promptly noted in other capitals. British Ambassador Pauncefote sent a report on it to the Earl of Rosebery on December 7, 1893, F.O. 5 (America), 1893, Vol. 2188.

[65] J. Fred Rippy, *The Caribbean Danger Zone*, pp. 129–130.

Germans were presenting claims for "about five million marks (£250,-000) but had recently stated that, on receipt of a lump sum of £25,000, they would . . . desist from further demands."[66] British policy kept in rather close step with that of the United States, and when relations were broken between Britain and Bolivia the United States chargé was asked to take charge of British interests in that country.

Brazil and the East Coast

Brazil, too, was having its troubles in 1889. In the last months of the year the Braganza monarchy was overthrown. A year later Harrison informed his Congress that as soon as Washington had ascertained that the new Brazilian administration had popular support and approval "no time was lost in extending . . . a full and cordial welcome into the family of American Commonwealths." The next word that reached Washington was that a movement was afoot to restore the old royal line. Blaine, on November 9, expressed "friendly solicitude" for the republic and then added a word of advice: "This Government's counsel would favor a wise moderation; for retaliation too certainly follows bloodshed, while enemies will be made friends by a firm yet merciful defense of the just prerogatives of a free government."[67]

In September, 1893, several units of the Brazilian Navy led a movement to restore the monarchy. The commander of the United States squadron on the scene announced that the rebels would not be permitted to shell areas where foreign properties might be endangered. Since the rebels had no land base this limitation severely curtailed their prospects of success.[68] Naturally enough the monarchies of Western Europe were much interested in the events. Britain had long been friendly to the Braganzas, but on this occasion went out of its way to keep in step with the United States. As early as February 3, 1894, Germany and Italy sounded out Downing Street about its intentions concerning the Brazilian unrest. On February 9 in Washington the British Ambassador Sir Julian Pauncefote answered a "very secret" telegram from his Foreign

[66] Minister E. C. Phipps to Foreign Office, April 18, 1895, F.O. 13 (Brazil), 1895, Vol. 742.

[67] Message to Congress, December 1, 1890. *For. Rels., 1890*, pp. iv–v; *1891*, p. 42.

[68] Lawrence F. Hill, *Diplomatic Relations between the United States and Brazil*, pp. 280–281; Moore, *Digest*, II, 1117–1118; Schuyler, "Gresham," in Bemis, *Amer. Secs. of St.*, VIII, 252–253; *New York Times*, editorial, March 15, 1894, 4.2, and December 30, 1894, 17.1.

Office. He stated that he had called on Secretary of State Walter Q.
Gresham to ask what were the United States' intentions. The answer was
that the matter had been "most carefully considered"; that the United
States had not extended recognition to the rebels as belligerents and as
yet "could see no reason to depart from that decision."[69] One midnight
shortly thereafter word reached Gresham that the revolt had failed and
that a British warship had taken the defeated rebel leader on board. At
2:00 A.M. the Secretary was calling on the British Ambassador to say
"Sir Julian, I have word from Brazil that your flagship has taken Da
Gama [the rebel leader] aboard. Of course that is not true. You and I
know it is not true, but I must be able to tell the President and Cabinet
when we meet this morning that it is not true." The account continues
that when the Cabinet met at eleven o'clock Sir Julian had already called
at the State Department to say he had cabled the Foreign Office, which
reported from the Admiralty that it had communicated with its flagship
at Rio de Janeiro and that Da Gama had been put back on his own ship.[70]

This incident did not mean that the United States was seeking every
occasion to make its weight felt in the area. Cleveland still preferred
isolationism. When the somewhat ridiculous case of claims to the island
of Trinidad, in the mid-Atlantic, arose between Brazil and Great Britain
the United States stood aloof. The island was apparently unoccupied
and was of use only as a potential point for a trans-Atlantic cable landing. An adventurer claimed it, adopting the title of "Baron" Hardin-
Hickey. For the sake of his own pretensions he urged the State Department to support the Brazilian claim. In response to repeated requests
from the "Baron," Acting Secretary of State A. A. Adee merely called
for a report on the matter but carefully side-stepped any definite stand.[71]
Apparently this was too similar to the Falkland Islands case for the
United States to become involved.

As the century closed, Europe continued to dominate trade of the
Atlantic coast of South America, but American interests were making
an increasingly substantial bid. A major handicap was the lack of American emigrants to serve as a connecting link. Europe, on the contrary,

[69] Pauncefote to Rosebery, February 9, 1894, F.O. 5 (America), 1894, Vol. 2234.
[70] Matilda Gresham, *Life of Walter Quintin Gresham, 1832–1895*, II, 780–781.
[71] The Olney Papers, LC, contain much correspondence in the latter part of 1895
on the "Baron" Hardin-Hickey claims to Trinidad. The comic-opera aspects of the
case were obvious but certain principles were involved. See *For. Rels., 1895*, pp.
63 ff.

sent out some 500,000 settlers to Latin America between 1870 and 1879, and then increased the number to over, 2,000,000 in the decade following 1890.[72] Another serious handicap to United States trade was the lack of steamship connections. In 1892 the quite excellent service of the United States and Brazil Mail Steamship Company went into receivership. Thereafter for twenty years connection from New York to Brazilian ports was via steamships carrying foreign flags,[73] and much freight had to be routed through European ports. Similarly, the only banking facilities were those of European origin. Inevitably European banks used their influence in favor of European trade. In spite of these handicaps, the reciprocal trade treaty with Brazil brought substantial results.[74] Even in Argentina, the special British preserve for so long, British exports increased only 12.2 per cent in the five-year periods between 1885–1889 and 1900–1904. At the same time United States exports were increasing 108 per cent and amounted to a third of the British total. Imports to all South America from Great Britain in the same period increased only 4.6 per cent. Those of the United States increased 46.3 per cent.[75]

Even so, it was the Germans in South America who commanded the most jealous attention of the Foreign Offices. At the time of the overthrow of monarchy in Brazil there was discussion in Germany and in the United States concerning the probable position that the already substantial German colony in South Brazil would take. Bismarck, like the British Foreign Office, watched Washington carefully. He instructed his chargé in Washington to declare officially that his country had no intentions of interfering with events in Brazil.[76] Still the German migration to Brazil continued. Indeed, as early as 1859 the German prohibition on emigration of its citizens was rescinded. By the fall of 1896 the *New York Times* remarked editorially that three German companies had secured

---

[72] *New Cambridge Modern History*, XI, 518.

[73] Robertson, *Hispanic American Relations*, p. 238.

[74] Lincoln Hutchinson, "Results of Reciprocity with Brazil," *Pol. Sc. Quar.*, XVIII, No. 2 (March, 1903), 300–303. For power of the British banks see Hill, *Diplomatic Relations*, p. 272.

[75] "Exports to China and South America," *Accounts and Papers, 1906*, CX, 4–5.

[76] Stolberg-Wernigerode, *Germany and the U.S.*, pp. 192–193. For German migration to Brazil see Loreta Baum, "German Political Designs," *Hisp. Amer. Hist. Rev.*, II, No. 4 (November, 1919), 592–594.

large tracts of land in Santa Catarina province, Brazil, for colonization. It then raised the question of the applicability of the Monroe Doctrine.[77] By the next year the *New York Tribune* was so concerned that the British chargé in Washington reported the matter to his Foreign Office: "As your Lordship [Marquis of Salisbury] is already aware, the 'Tribune' is the leading Republican Organ in New York, and its views may generally be considered to reflect the attitude of the present administration especially in regard to foreign politics."[78] At the same time the British ministers in Brazil were regularly reporting on the local situation and on local opposition to Germanization of the country. Just at the turn of the century and at the close of the Spanish-American War, the British chargé at Rio gleefully reported that on April 29, 1900, Secretary of War Elihu Root had stated in the United States that "the United States will soon either have to abandon the Monroe Doctrine or to fight in its defense." This, the chargé continued, was interpreted in Brazil as a clear reference to the German settlers in that country.[79] (see below, this chapter, "Closer Home Once More").

Diplomatic correspondence of the period reveals some queer details about foreign conduct in Latin American affairs. The German menace to Brazil was clearly recognized in London as much more serious than that of the Italians, who were also migrating to South America in large numbers. The tone of reports on Italians in the New World was more like that of Minister E. Constantine Phipps, who reported that the Italian legation at Rio was having difficulties in collecting certain damage claims. He commented, "curiously enough amongst the claims, whilst murders of a wife and of a son are respectively estimated at £200 [$1,000], the attempted rape of a wife at £80, the loss of a hand at £200," it was damages to property for which "enormous demands" were made.[80] The fact was that British ministers in all South America reported in great detail on every conceivable type of subject; the refunding of the provincial debt of Buenos Aires, annual revenues of each country, and local fears of Chilean influences on a local Uruguayan revolution were all covered

[77] *New York Times*, September 12, 1896, 4.4.
[78] Chargé C. F. Frederick Adam to Salisbury, July 19, 1897, F.O. 5 (America), 1897, Vol. 2321.
[79] Minister Phipps [unsigned] to Foreign Office, June 22, 1899, F.O. 13 (Brazil), 1899, Vol. 793.
[80] Letter of June 29, 1895, *ibid.*, Vol. 743.

carefully.[81] The United States, however, paid much less attention to the southern part of the continent. It wanted no part of the Falkland Islands dispute, and the *New York Times* openly supported the British claims to the islands.[82]

In spite of these contretemps, the United States was exercising increased diplomatic influence, illustrated by its services as arbitrator of significant Argentine boundary disputes. In 1876 Argentina and Paraguay signed a treaty requesting the President of the United States to arbitrate a serious boundary dispute on the Pilcomayo River. The award of President Hayes, announced in November, 1878, favored the Paraguayan contention. In the 1890's came two more awards. A long-standing dispute between Brazil and Argentina over the Missiones area was submitted in 1892 to the United States President for settlement. The British minister in Brazil noted that "It cannot be doubted that the solution will contribute strongly to enhance the influence of the United States in this country."[83] The award, announced in February, 1895, generally favored Brazil. There were a number of rather formal expressions of friendship on the occasion though the Argentines were clearly chagrined at this second loss of territory through a United States arbitral award. The third award was in connection with the long and mountainous boundary between Argentina and Chile. For the two disputed sections of the line the King of Great Britain and the minister of the United States in Argentina, William I. Buchanan, were selected as arbitrators.[84] Buchanan made his award on the Puna de Atacama region in northwestern Argentina in 1899. This time the greater part of the disputed territory fell to Argentina.

Closer Home Once More[85]

Meanwhile, closer at hand arose the Venezuela boundary dispute. The

[81] Numerous manuscript reports from Minister A. C. Barrington to Lord Salisbury are typical. See F.O. 6, Vol. 451.

[82] *New York Times*, January, 26, 1896, 4.4.

[83] Phipps to Foreign Office, February 14, 1895, F.O. 13 (Brazil), 1895, Vol. 742; *For. Rels., 1892*, pp. 1, 18; *British and Foreign State Papers*, LXXXVII, 701–702.

[84] *For. Rels., 1898*, p. 4.

[85] Details of incidents occurring in the Caribbean are largely omitted here since they have been fully treated by the author in his *Caribbean Policy of the United States, 1890–1920*. For an excellent later study, conservative in approach, using new source materials see Dana G. Munro, *Intervention and Dollar Diplomacy in the Caribbean, 1900–1921*.

swampy district between Venezuela and British Guiana had remained in dispute ever since Venezuela gained its independence. Various British efforts to delimit the frontier had met with obstructionist tactics from its weak antagonist. In time British trade and settlement began to invade the disputed area. Next, gold was discovered. As early as 1876 Venezuela asked the United States to support its claims.[86] Time passed and Venezuela became more insistent. Before leaving office at the end of his first term Cleveland sent a despatch urging Lord Salisbury to lighten British pressure in the case. In view of Cleveland's recent defeat at the polls this despatch was not delivered by Minister Thomas F. Bayard though the President apparently was unaware of his minister's action. Four years later Cleveland therefore resumed the Presidency apparently thinking that the British had ignored his previous expression of interest and was using its strength to take unfair advantage of a weak New World power. Cleveland's new Secretary of State, Walter Q. Gresham, however, apparently remained far from excited or aggressive on the subject. Moreover, Cleveland's message to Congress on December 3, 1894, expressed hope for a solution of the matter by arbitration, "a resort which Britain so conspicuously favors in principle and respects in practice and which is earnestly sought by her weaker adversary." Upon Gresham's death Richard Olney became Secretary of State. A hard-working, flinty Yankee, he aspired to the Presidency but was already unpopular because of the role he had played as Attorney General in the Pullman Car strike and his other conservative associations. Allowing no grass to grow under his feet, Olney drafted a vigorous communication with a gratuitously forceful overstatement of United States domination in the New World.

The draft was sent to Cleveland while he was on vacation in Buzzard's Bay, Massachusetts. On July 7, 1895, the President responded. First he announced the birth of a baby daughter; next he thanked the Secretary for the thoughtful gift of rubber gloves to wear while fishing. Finally he acknowledged the Venezuelan note, calling it "quite the best thing of

[86] Grover Cleveland, *Presidential Problems*, pp. 228 ff.

Suggestive material on the well-researched Venezuela boundary dispute may be found in *For. Rels. The New York Times* and the *Times* (London) gave it full coverage. The Olney Papers, LC, contain significant material. For Lord Pauncefote's reports to the Foreign Office see F.O. 5 (America), 1896, Vol. 2290. Secondary accounts include Tansill, *Foreign Policy of Bayard, 1885–1897*; Nevins, *Grover Cleveland*; Robert McElroy, *Grover Ceveand*; Schuyer, "Gresham," in Bemis, *Amer. Secs. of St.*, VIII; Henry James, *Richard Olney and his Public Service*; and R. B. Mowat, *The Life of Lord Pauncefote*.

the kind I have ever read." Then he suggested "a little more softened verbiage" and proposed that the two of them "go over it together." Olney took the approval and seized the initiative by despatching the note. The famous statement that the United States' "fiat is law" in the New World caught the American people by surprise. A few demurred but most applauded. On general principles Uncle Sam's American eagle enjoyed the sport of tweaking John Bull's British lion's tail. The President, thus committed, did not turn back, but sent a message to Congress in which he called for an investigation and demanded that arbitration be accepted. Congress approved and appropriated $100,000 to meet the expenses of an investigation commission.

Roosevelt was enthusiastic, Lodge vociferous; the *New York Times* approved, and Venezuela seized the opportunity to employ a press agent while it hastened to make land grants in the disputed area to United States citizens. The story of the ensuing negotiations has been told so often that it is not repeated here. Soberer views emerged on both sides of the Atlantic. An overly simple statement is that arbitration was agreed upon, carrying a preemption provision that assured Britain against loss of much of the territory it had policed for so many years. The United States agreed to serve as representative of Venezuela in presenting the case of that country to the court.[87] Reasons for the conciliatory British attitude are well known and included the dangerous conditions on the continent of Europe and heavy Empire obligations in the Far East and Africa. Olney himself later admitted that his words had been "bumptious" but felt that they were excusable because "only words the equivalent of blows" would be effective to penetrate the supercilious British self-confidence.[88] Lord Pauncefote, writing to the Foreign Office, commented: "I am convinced that Olney is far from wishing to give offense. But the main characteristics of American Diplomatic Notes are vulgarity and verbosity."[89] For his part, Cleveland had a real respect for Lord Salisbury and, in 1908, regretfully stated that he no longer desired to

[87] The treaty was signed at Washington, February 2, 1897. See *British and Foreign State Papers*, LXXXIX, 57–65.

[88] Olney to Knox, January 29, 1912. Philander Chase Knox Papers, LC. Also quoted in Wilfrid H. Callcott, *Caribbean Policy of the United States*, p. 90.

[89] Pauncefote to "My dear Bertie," June 26, 1896, F.O. 5 (America), 1896, Vol. 2290.

make a trip to Europe. Once he would have liked to do so to meet two men—Bismarck and Lord Salisbury.[90]

And what of the results of the whole affair? Great Britain had clearly recognized the priority position of the United States. Continental powers in Europe were not too happy about such recognition but it had become a fact "in practice if not in theory."[91] The later severe critic of the United States, Blanco Fombona, commented: "The truth is that without the Monroe Doctrine . . . England would have been planted on the banks of the Orinoco River, soon to become its Mistress."[92] Other Latin Americans joined in the praise with strikingly few unfavorable comments. Careful students among them might be inclined to squirm at the implications of the "fiat is law" statement, but for the time being the Yankee peril was not too obvious. As one writer has put it, this was "one of the great turning points" in the relations of the United States both in the Old World and in the New.[93]

In the neighboring republic of Colombia a careful watch was kept on revolutionary disturbances and on filibustering, as well as on any disorders on the Isthmus of Panama that might involve the freedom of transit. Routine questions arose in 1885, 1893, and 1902 in such matters as the use of good offices on behalf of Chinese citizens since the Celestial Empire had no diplomatic representation at hand. Also in routine fashion efforts were made to eliminate troublesome boundary disputes. In one case Cleveland reversed the Blaine position when he encouraged arbitration by Spain of the Colombia-Costa Rican boundary dispute. Also he agreed to serve as arbitrator in a dispute arising between Colombia and Italy.[94]

[90] Howard to Foreign Office, July 8, 1908, F.O. 371 (U.S.), 1908, Vol. 567.

[91] Perkins, *Monroe Doctrine, 1867–1907*, p. 223; John W. Foster, *A Century of American Diplomacy*, pp. 474–475; *New York Times*, December, 24, 1895, 4.4.

[92] Quoted by W. S. Robertson, "Appreciations of the Monroe Doctrine," *Hisp. Amer. Hist. Rev.*, III, No. 1 (February, 1920), 15. See also Perkins, *Monroe Doctrine, 1867–1907*, pp. 210 ff.

[93] Arthur P. Whitaker, *The United States and South America: The Northern Republics*, pp. 159–160.

[94] On troop landings see *Use by the United States of a Military Force* (Sen. Doc. No. 143, 58th Cong., 2d Sess.), pp. 160 ff., and the Olney Papers, LC. For protection of Chinese interests see *For. Rels., 1885, 1893,* and *1902*. For Colombian-Italian dispute see *For. Rels., 1898*, and Moore, *Digest*, VII, 42–43. For Colombian-Costa Rican dispute see Moore, *Digest*, III, 32–33.

Still nearer at hand was Mexico. During the long administration of Porfirio Díaz (1876–1910) relations had become increasingly cordial even though Díaz sought to use German trade and influence to counterbalance those of the United States. During the 1890's appeared a series of agreements concerning such problems as bandit chasing across the international line,[95] and business agreements and questions arising from Chinese and Syrian migration to the United States via Mexico to avoid immigration restrictions. Rising Mexican nationalism was fearful of the imperialism of Harrison and Blaine but the fears proved groundless. Yankee investments developed fast in Mexican mines, railroads, and real estate but they were thought to provide more of blessings than of menace. True, the dictator was restless at the efforts of the United States to settle Mexican boundary disputes with its southern neighbor, Guatemala, but this attitude too was classed as offiicious rather than dangerous.

The effort to create a United States of Central America to include Nicaragua, Honduras, and El Salvador was chiefly interesting because Great Britain immediately consulted Washington on procedure.[96] Unfortunately the proposal was to have no greater success than earlier efforts in the same direction and it collapsed by 1898.[97]

A more important matter from the standpoint of policy arose in connection with the expansion of British interests from British Honduras at the expense of neighboring areas. In 1894 British and American citizens in the coastal districts took matters into their own hands and asked support from Washington. This eventuated in the landing of United States troops whose leader simultaneously protested against British aggression and against Nicaraguan abuses of local rights. Public opinion became somewhat exited. An earlier effort at arbitration by the Emperor of Austria had been ineffective. Now Nicaragua appealed to Secretary of State Olney "as the natural protector of all the small republics of America." Britain proved conciliatory but insisted that it had

[95] For Mexican relations see *For. Rels.*; *British and Foreign State Papers*; Moore, *Digest*; and Foster, *Diplomatic Memoirs*. A detailed study is found in James Morton Callahan, *American Foreign Policy in Mexican Relations*. See also Estrada, *La doctrina de Monroe*; W. R. Castle, "Foster," in Bemis, *Amer. Secs. of St.*, VIII; and Robert D. Gregg, *The Influence of Border Troubles* . . . .

[96] Pauncefote to Olney, December 1, 1896, Olney Papers, LC; Gough to Lord Salisbury, October 20, 1896, F.O. 5 (America), 1896, Vol. 2291.

[97] *For. Rels., 1898*, pp. lxix–lxx, 175–176; *British and Foreign State Papers*, XCII, 241–242; James Brown Scott, "Central American Peace Conference of 1907," *Amer. Jour. Internat. Law*, II, No. 1 (January, 1908), 124–125.

the right to protect the Indians against oppression by Nicaraguan authorities. In an interview the Secretary of State assured Sir Julian Pauncefote that "We will see that she [Nicaragua] does not [oppress them]."[98]

Meanwhile increased attention was being paid to the Caribbean as such. Mahan had recognized the importance of isthmian transit and now characterized the Caribbean as "the very domain of sea power," which, together with Hawaii, must be controlled in connection with "such a maritime highway as a canal." He likened the area to Aden and Malta, which were vital outposts of the Suez Canal.[99] In view of this type of thinking British writers were urging that the fifteen British islands and possessions in the Caribbean be confederated, even though some frankly said that absorption by the United States might have distinct advantages.[100]

Naturally enough the United States became interested again in the Danish West Indies, which Seward had once sought to acquire. The proposal of acquisition was broached in early 1893 but the change in administrations ended the matter for the time. After the Republican victories in 1896 Senator Lodge introduced a resolution from the Senate Foreign Relations Committee calling for the acquisition of a naval base in the islands at a recommended cost of $5 million.[101] Nothing came of the proposal at the time, but in the fall of 1898 a German commercial company became interested in the islands, apparently with the encouragement of the German Foreign Office. About the same time, the notorious Captain Lee (Leon Whitfield) Christmas declared that the real purpose of the company was to acquire territory to place under German control. Secretary of War Elihu Root, in a dinner address, on April 27, 1900, commented that" no man who carefully watches the signs of the times can fail to see that the American people will within a few years either have to abandon the Monroe Doctrine, or fight for it, and we are

[98] Gresham, *Life of Gresham*, p. 782. See also Guzmán to Olney, June 27, 1895, Olney Papers, LC; L. M. Keasby, "The Nicaraguan Canal and the Monroe Doctrine," *The Annals*, VII (January–June, 1896), 24–25; Tansill, *The Foreign Policy of Bayard*, pp. 689–690; Moore, *Digest*, III, 244–246.

[99] Mahan, *The Interest of America in Sea Power*, pp. 99–100, 260 ff.

[100] C. S. Salmon, *The Caribbean Confederation . . . A Plan of Union of Fifteen British . . . Colonies . . .*, pp. 129–141.

[101] Pauncefote to Salisbury, April 1, 1898, F.O. 5 (America), 1898, Vol. 2361. See also Tansill, *The Purchase of the Danish West Indies*, pp. 194 ff.

not going to abandon it."[102] Maybe Root also had the situation in Brazil in mind (see above, this chapter, "Brazil and the East Coast"). If so, he apparently was aiming at two birds with one stone.

Another perennial question was that of bases in Haiti and Santo Domingo. Blaine was actively interested in possibilities. Visiting United States war vessels repeatedly aroused local suspicions and certainly the Navy was awake to possibilities. On January 22, 1890, Admiral Bancroft Gerardi reported that "The strategic value of this island from a naval point of view is invaluable."[103] Either the Môle Saint Nicholas or Samaná Bay would be desirable. Soundings and suggestions flew back and forth. Local political factions in the island were irresponsible. European chancelleries had long looked askance at United States expansionism; but party control was changing so frequently in Washington that no consistent policy on the islands had yet appeared. The result was that nothing was done. Minister Julian Pauncefote was convinced "that President Harrison and Mr. Blaine and General Foster directed their best efforts up to a very recent period to obtain a lease of the Bay of Samana." With Cleveland back in office in 1893, however, the minister felt that the idea was abandoned.[104]

The War with Spain

A recent writer has commented on the "aggressive self-assertion" which found enthusiastic expression in the Republican Party platform of 1896. In spite of the depression of the early 1890's the nation had recovered from Reconstruction. Now a rising tide of immigration had occupied most of the available free lands and a new generation financed by a vigorous industrial system was clamoring for new adventures and a new domain. Such an electorate turned from the siren call of Bryan and free silver to the self-confident platform and promises of the industrialists. As the new President William McKinley took office there ensued a struggle for power as the easy-going President found himself tugged in various directions by his obstreperous followers. Among the most vociferous was Theodore Roosevelt, who trumpeted that "No triumph of

[102] Quoted by Dexter Perkins, *Hands Off: A History of the Monroe Doctrine*, p. 209.

[103] Logan, *Diplomatic Relations with Haiti*, pp. 432–433; Welles, *Naboth's Vineyard*, I, 478 ff., and II, 505–506.

[104] Pauncefote to Rosebery, March 13, 1893, F.O. 5 (America), 1893, Vol. 2187.

peace is quite so great as the supreme triumphs of war."[105] Lodge, Mahan, and others joyously intoned a chorus of expansionism. As for the New World, Roosevelt again sounded the note: "I should myself like to shape our foreign policy with a purpose ultimately of driving off this continent every European power."[106]

When Cleveland left office in 1897 conditions in Cuba were serious. Early filibustering expeditions from the United States had had tacit encouragement from many port authorities and even from some of the lower federal courts before which suspects had been arraigned. Then the Supreme Court took a hand and the nuisance subsided.[107] Many businessmen feared war would disrupt trade, and even the steel industry felt that such a contest would not last long enough to enable it to recoup the expense of retooling expensive plants. Strategists, humanitarians, and imperialists, egged on by surplus national energies and agitated by sensation-hunting newspapers, and a few industries with special interests joined hands in a stampede for action. McKinley, responsive as always to popular pressures, was led, cajoled, or driven into exerting steadily mounting pressures on Spain even though his own inclinations favored peace.

The Spanish government, with the sympathy of most of the Western European powers and the Papacy, was in no condition for war. Yet its own grip on political power was so tenuous that it did not dare risk public criticism by taking hasty and unpopular steps in granting United States demands. War might be a better alternative than the risk of political overthrow by an already disgruntled people. The one significant friend of the United States in Europe was Great Britain—and even there Queen Victoria personally sympathized with the adopted country of her daughter, the Queen of Spain. Under considerable stress from its Empire commitments in the Far East and Africa, British policy was to let its Yankee offspring assume responsibility for the chaotic Caribbean. These

[105] For comment on the Republican Party platform see Pratt, *Expansionists of 1898*, p. 213. For Roosevelt's exuberant comment see Morison, *The Letters of Theodore Roosevelt*, I, 621 n.

[106] Quoted in Joseph Bucklin Bishop, *Theodore Roosevelt and His Time*, I, 79.

[107] French Ensor Chadwick, *The Relations of the United States and Spain*, pp. 414 ff.; Elbert J. Benton, *International Law and Diplomacy of the Spanish-American War*, p. 58.

relations are scarcely a part of the present story and so are merely referred to here.

The pertinent fact is that McKinley, who had favored a peaceful solution of the Cuban problem, apparently lost his nerve just as his minister in Madrid thought a solution was in sight. McKinley's weakening may have been due in part to the pressure of family complications (his wife's serious illness), to an awareness of political expediency, or to conviction arising from arguments of the yellow journals and imperialists. Whatever the cause for his change in attitude, on April 11, 1898, he sent a message to Congress in which he reviewed recent relations with Spain. He indicated that he had done his best to secure an adjustment of the Cuban problem but had failed. He only casually referred to late conciliatory reports from Spain and left matters to that Congress of which the *Times* (London) had said less than two weeks previously: "Congress is trying, first of all, to provoke a war, careless whether Cuba can be freed by peace."[108] On April 17 the Senate by a vote of 67 to 21 passed a resolution to the effect that Cuba was independent. Two days later an amended resolution to the same effect was approved in the House of Representatives by a vote of 310 to 6, and again in the Senate by 42 to 35. The final form left out one significant provision of the earlier proposal which read: "And that the Government of the United States hereby recognizes the Republic of Cuba as the true and lawful government of that island."[109] This omission freed the United States from any obligation to recognize the rebel administration, whose stability was uncertain and whose conduct of the rebellion had been irregular.

The "glorious little war" was over in a matter of weeks. A Spanish fleet was cut to pieces in the Philippines; a second fleet was sunk off Cuba; and the United States expeditionary forces advanced at will through Cuba and Puerto Rico. Now, what should be done about it all? Detailed reports in the Olney Papers (MS) show that the Cleveland Administration had been fully aware of conditions in Cuba. Business interests in the island had once wanted self-determination under Spain.[110] Now that war had come anyway they wanted as firm a govern-

108 The *Times* (London), March 31, 1898, 5b.

109 *For. Rels., 1898*, p. 762.

110 Edwin F. Atkins, *Sixty Years in Cuba*, pp. 235 ff. A recent study of the activities of the U.S. consul in Havana in the two years preceding the war may be found in Gerald G. Eggert, "Our Man in Havana: Fitzhugh Lee," *Hisp. Amer. Hist.*

ment as possible and feared for their security under an inexperienced Cuban administration. However, the word of the United States was pledged that Cuba should be independent. Accordingly the peace protocol provided that Cuba should become a separate nation, but that Puerto Rico should be ceded outright by Spain to the United States. Also, one of the Ladrone Islands (Guam) was to be ceded while control of the Philippines was to be determined by the peace conference.[111]

Latin American reaction to the war was based on sincere misgivings. Mexico remained strictly neutral. Colombia rationed the sale of coal to belligerent vessels during the contest to prevent violations of neutrality. The far-away Argentines were entertained by a cartoon showing Uncle Sam in the guise of a fat hog engaged in besmirching the fair garments of the Queen of Spain in his violent efforts to gobble up her few remaining American possessions.[112] Officially Argentina recognized the war as a rather logical development, yet one of its former Presidents wrote that he understood a United States senator had just said that "the Yankee empire will have as its bounds the *aurora borealis* in the north, the equator in the south, the rising sun in the east, and the immensity of the west. Lucky for us they are stopping for the present at the equator."[113]

Inevitably the southern nations paid increasing attention to this expansionism. Their fears found expression in what was known as Pan-Hispanism. On the four-hundredth anniversary of the discovery of America the idea was popularized that there should be closer ties between the mother countries of Spain and Portugal and their New World offspring. The existing cultural affinity was to be supported by the exchange of European products for those of the New World.[114] The

---

Rev., XLVIII, No. 4 (November, 1967), 463–485. This article shows Lee seeking annexation, but not war with Spain, while he was desirous of street-railway concessions for himself and for his United States friends.

[111] Benton, *International Law and Diplomacy*, pp. 225 ff. See also Alfred L. P. Dennis, *Adventures in American Diplomacy, 1896–1906*, p. 99.

[112] For Mexico see *British and Foreign State Papers*, XC, 370. For Colombia see Benton, *International Law and Diplomacy*, pp. 191 ff. For Argentina see Hiram Bingham, "The Monroe Doctrine, an Obsolete Shibboleth," *Atlantic Monthly*, III (1913), 724.

[113] Quoted by McGann, *Argentina and the U.S.*, p. 187.

[114] Clarence H. Haring, *South America Looks at the United States*, pp. 180–181.

suggestion was patently impractical, for the mother countries could neither provide the goods needed by the ex-colonies nor consume the products of Latin America. As the facts became obvious, a modification of the idea, known as Pan-Latinism, appeared. This called for the addition of France and Italy to the European producers and consumers in the arrangement. As will be seen, however, even this expansion of the concept was inadequate in the face of economic realities.

By and large Manuel Ugarte was to express the more critical Latin American viewpoint rather well:

Oh, the country of democracy, of puritanism, and of liberty! The United States are great, powerful, prosperous, astonishingly progressive, supreme masters of energy and creative life, healthy and comfortable; but they have developed in an atmosphere essentially practical and proud, and their principles are almost always sacrificed to their interests or to social superstitions.

He then continued that the position of the harassed Negro, subject to lynch law and other abuses, showed the insincerity of the disliked northerner. Further, the Yankee disdain for things foreign, especially if of Latin origin, was coupled with an infatuation with getting results. All this, said Ugarte, resulted in a rough and brutal tendency to surpass all other races and in a certain exclusiveness that sought to humiliate others.[115]

In Europe Bismarck might characterize the Monroe Doctrine and its recent applications as "extraordinary insolence." The British, however, were more concerned with any event affecting their trade with the Latin American republics and lacked that compelling drive for new colonial possessions that beset Germany. E. Constantine Phipps, British minister in Brazil, was little concerned with the Spanish-American War but reported in great detail about claims of United States citizens in the Acre region of interior Brazil.[116] At the same time he kept a close watch on all European trade rivals.

Meanwhile Washington found its hands full with its new obligations in the Caribbean and in the Far East. Trade with the temperate part of South America was largely forgotten. In fact a trade treaty with Argentina was shelved in the United States when opposition was expressed

[115] Manuel Ugarte, *El destino de un continente*, pp. 18–19.

[116] Numerous letters from Minister Phipps include those of June 9, June 20, July 4, and July 9, 1899, and of March 31, 1900, F.O. 13 (Brazil), 1899, Vol. 783.

by the wool growers of the West.[117] Some United States scholars even favored outright British control of the Argentine.[118] Trade with Brazil was pleasingly good, but even this received little attention.

Canada

Canada throughout this period continued to command a separate niche in United States diplomatic history. One student of Canadian-American relations has commented that from the close of the Civil War to the end of the century "at least seven overtures for reciprocity" were made by Canada to its southern neighbor. One reason for the general indifference with which these were received was the fact that for twenty years after 1874 United States trade with Canada constituted only 4 to 6 per cent of its total international trade.[119] For Canada the question was much more important. Exports from Canada to the Mother Country increased from 37 per cent of the total exports of Canada to 56.1 per cent in 1900. Between 1868 and 1900 imports from the United Kingdom declined from 50.9 per cent to 24.7 per cent. Conversely, exports to the United States dropped from 47.9 per cent to 35.7 per cent, but imports rose from 36.6 per cent to 60.7 per cent.[120] Repeated neglect or declination of the Canadian approaches generated a reaction in that country against the idea of reciprocity. The reaction reached a peak after the passage of the McKinley tariff. The Canadians retaliated with their tariff of 1897 favoring Empire trade. In spite of this it became evident that the flow of trade was continuing its previous course regardless of the new rates, and imports continued to flow into Canada from the south.[121]

One troublesome area on both sides of the border was politics, which

[117] McGann, *Argentina and the U.S.*, p. 177; Barrington to Salisbury from Buenos Aires, May 5, 1900, F.O. 6, Vol. 464, foll. 45–48.

[118] J. W. Burgess, "The Recent Pseudo-Monroeism," *Pol. Sc. Quar.*, XI, No. 1 (March, 1896), 60.

[119] Edward Porritt, "Canada's National Policy," *ibid.*, XXXII, No. 2 (June, 1917), 192; Tariff Commission, *Reciprocity with Canada*, p. 27.

[120] Osborne, "Commercial Relations of the United States with Canada," *The Annals*, XXXII (September, 1908), 332–333.

[121] See "Canada," *Edinburgh Review*, CXCIII, No. 396 (April, 1901), 313; Tansill, *Canadian-American Relations*, pp. 458 ff.; Callahan, *American Policy in Canadian Relations*, pp. 420 ff.; John Bartlet Brebner, *North Atlantic Triangle*, pp. 256–257; Porritt, "Canada's National Policy," *Pol. Sc. Quar.*, XXXII, No. 2 (June, 1917), 190.

were at least partly responsible in 1888 for the defeat of a treaty with Canada that Cleveland sent to the Senate. Involved in the matter were problems of the long-standing fisheries disputes. When the Senate defeated the treaty, Cleveland interpreted its action as an instruction for the Administration to apply restrictions to Canadian trade. Forthwith the Senate disapproved the restrictions and thus tacitly admitted that its action had been essentially political and inspired by domestic considerations.

Canadian claims to the fishing grounds of the North Atlantic had a distinct advantage over those of the United States. After the United States lost its "privilege" to use the grounds in the War of 1812, both nations resorted to a succession of stopgap, or temporary, agreements. These authorized various arrangements for securing supplies and bait, and for drying fish on lands adjacent to the grounds. The result was a succession of petty annoyances: violations of local regulations by Americans and extortion by Canadians.[122] Each invited retaliation. When the Chamberlain-Bayard Treaty of 1888 failed, another *modus vivendi* merely postponed a settlement until the new century. Meanwhile, as a cooperative step, the two governments appointed a joint commission to recommend methods by which to control fishing and to preserve the fish supply. The ensuing investigations had few or no concrete results but may have led to a better understanding in general.

Another irritating problem was the fur-seal controversy in the Bering Sea area. The seal herds had long used the Pribilof Islands and the neighboring mainland shoreline on which to establish their rookeries. These came under the jurisdiction of the United States after the purchase of Alaska in 1867. Promiscuous killing of the seals resulted in a tragic depletion of the herds. In 1874 a survey ordered by an act of Congress indicated that some 4,700,000 animals were in the herds. In 1890 another survey showed that the number had been reduced to an estimated 959,655, and in 1900 the United States Fish Commission reported that a mere 360,000 remained.[123] Cleveland became thoroughly exasperated over the matter and Blaine plunged into the controversy.

[122] Extracts from pertinent documents may be found in Moore, *Digest*, I, 865 ff. See also Tansill, *Canadian-American Relations*, pp. 78 ff.; Nevins, *Grover Cleveland*, pp. 412–413; and J. L. Garvin, *Life of Joseph Chamberlain*, II, 329–330.

[123] Enclosure sent by Hay to Herbert, July 27, 1903, F.O. 5 (America), 1903, Vol. 2546. For official correspondence see *For. Rels., 1903*, and *British and Foreign State Papers*, LXXXVII, 1120 ff., and LXXXIX, 776 ff.

He threatened to treat all intruders in the Bering Sea as trespassers. Canadians stood squarely on their rights and insisted that the British flag protected them since their operations were conducted on the high seas and outside territorial waters. For its part, the United States wanted Great Britain to help police the grounds and to protect the herds. The British position was an awkward one. Lord Salisbury commented that "Great Britain stood as a broker between the United States and Canada, and had great difficulty in managing their Canadian clients." At one point in 1888 Lord Salisbury was ready to recommend a closed season (Russia having agreed to this) and the United States wanted it; but Canada continued to stand on its technical rights.[124]

In 1892 it was agreed to submit the question to arbitration. Both sides prepared their cases.[125] The commission met in Paris on February 23, 1893, and announced its decision on August 15. It repudiated the United States' contention that the Bering Sea was a "closed sea" and merely recommended cooperative measures to protect the herds. Canada had won its point, but the seals were rapidly disappearing, so the victory was an empty one. Since no one was really happy at the lack of a definitive solution, the principals quarreled along—London and Washington more or less amicably; Ottawa and Washington with increasing irritation.[126]

Latent in the minds of thinking people on both sides of the border was the old question of annexation. The Tariff Commission frankly considered the value of commercial union;[127] as early as 1888 Senator John Sherman bluntly commented that our whole history since Britain secured Canada in 1763 "has been a continuous warning that we cannot

---

[124] A detailed study of the controversy is found in Tansill, *Canadian-American Relations*, pp. 43 ff., 304 ff. See also Tyler, *Foreign Policy of Blaine*, pp. 307 ff.; Lady Gwendolyn Cecil, *Life of Robert, Marquis of Salisbury*, IV, 349 ff.; and Allan Nevins, *Henry White*, pp. 63–64.

[125] Foster relates the interesting case of fraudulent translations of documents submitted to the court by the United States, then later withdrawn with apologies (*Diplomatic Memoirs*, II, 40–41). For notes on interviews of Olney and Pauncefote see Olney Papers, LC, for December, 1894.

[126] The subsequent history is interesting. When a recalcitrant Congress failed to appropriate the sum of $425,000 to pay for the seized vessels, the matter was referred to a special commission. Under this arrangement the United States then paid $473,151.26 on June 16, 1898 (Tansill, *Canadian-American Relations*, p. 347).

[127] Tariff Commission, *Reciprocity and Commercial Treaties*, pp. 98 ff. ,

be at peace with each other except by political as well as commercial union. . . . This union is one of the inevitable events that must inevitably come in the future . . . and no politician or combination of politicians can prevent it."[128] In Canada itself the commercial interests still wanted reciprocity but the powerful French Canadians feared anything that savored of annexation. They felt that their peculiar institutions were far safer in a weak Canada than in the powerful United States.[129] As noted above, political alignments were still at war with geography and economics. The one positive fact was that goods flowed to logical markets and migrants blandly ignored an invisible line across western prairies when they sought a more prosperous future.[130]

Canadians were definitely concerned by the sweeping terms of the Olney pronouncement on Venezuela. Olney's reference to "unnatural" ties across three thousand miles of intervening ocean was especially irritating. However, Britain was so involved with other Empire problems in the Far East and Africa that it was anxious to cultivate good relations with the United States. Canadians could merely seek to take advantage of any opportunity to play the Mother Country off against the United States as they became increasingly convinced that the Mother Country was callous to their needs. On the other hand Senator Lodge wrote Henry White on January 31, 1898, saying Canada was thumbing its nose at the United States from behind its Mother Country's skirts.[131]

Slowly Canada had been acquiring stature in British eyes. In 1871 it was officially represented in the negotiation and signing of the Treaty of Washington. Also, in the 1800's and again in 1893 it had a voice in the

[128] Edgar W. McInnis, *The Unguarded Frontier*, pp. 279–280.

[129] F. R. Scott, *Canada and the United States*, p. 29.

[130] For figures on Canadian migration to the United States see G. E. Jackson, "Emigrations of Canadians to the United States," *The Annals*, CVII (May, 1903), 28.

[131] The question of attitudes has been widely commented on. See Brebner, *North Atlantic Triangle*, pp. 253 ff.; an article by Brebner in Stanley Pargellis, *The Quest for Political Unity in World History*, pp. 198–199; Tansill, *Canadian-American Relations*, p. 360; James, *Richard Olney*, pp. 240 ff.

Other significant Canadian and British points of view are seen in Pierre Sibelleau, *Le Canada et la Doctrine de Monroe*, pp. 112–117; Thomas Hodgins, *British and American Diplomacy Affecting Canada, 1782–1899*, pp. 98–99; and "The Growth of American Foreign Policy," *Edinburgh Review*, CCIII, No. 415 (January, 1906), 259 ff.

negotiation of treaties with France and Spain.[132] Now at the end of the century Sir Wilfrid Laurier and John W. Foster proposed reference of Canadian-United States issues to a joint high commission. Twelve issues were listed for investigation. These included two questions on fisheries; the Alaska and other international boundary problems; four topics concerning trade and tariffs; and others dealing with labor laws, mining, and the conveyance of prisoners, as well as the modernization of the Rush-Bagot Agreement. A few years later five more issues were listed, including the use of boundary streams, taxes on temporary immigrants, requirements for health inspections of vessels, and pecuniary claims.[133] Viewed together, both groups are peculiarly intranational, rather than international, in character. Did they portend that union so long talked of, so sought after, and so feared? Outside of the fish and the seal problems the issues bore scant resemblance to contemporary complications arising with the southern republics. Even Mexico, sharing a border with the United States along the Rio Grande and being governed by a strong dictator, was on an entirely different footing with its neighbor than Canada. Irritations with Canada were more bitterly contested in some ways and less so in others. On the one hand was the feeling in the United States that Canadians were like us and ought to know better; on the other hand, in relation to Mexico there was a recognized difference of cultures that included both language and racial dissimilarities.

[132] N. A. M. MacKenzie, "Treaty Making Power in Canada," *Amer. Jour. Internat. Law*, XIX, No. 3 (July, 1925), 490–491.
[133] Callahan, *American Policy in Canadian Relations*, pp. 457–458, 494.

CHAPTER III

READJUSTMENTS*

The New Possessions

THE END OF THE Spanish-American War left its heritage of worldwide responsibilities. The result was a rapid change in the tone of United States foreign policy. In the Pacific were new possessions, Guam and the Philippines. These were rapidly increased by the division of the Samoan Islands with Germany, and the annexation of Hawaii. In the Atlantic, Puerto Rico was acquired, and Cuba became a protectorate. Next came Panama and increasing Caribbean complications. Also, the political picture in Washington changed fast. In spite of the wishes of the pliant McKinley, Theodore Roosevelt was nominated as Vice President in 1900. Soon after the election an assassin's bullet removed McKinley, and Roosevelt ascended to the Presidency in 1901.

The ebullient archimperialist at once took charge and was determined that the public should be aware of the fact. The new President had inherited a confirmed Kipling imperialist, John Hay, the scholar in politics, as Secretary of State. Truth to tell, Hay had little patience with

---

* Note to the reader: Attention is called to the fact that events arising in the Caribbean area are summarized in Chapters Two, Four, and Five only to provide the reader with perspective in the larger field of hemisphere relations. More detailed discussion of these events may be found in the author's *The Caribbean Policy of the United States, 1890–1920* (The Johns Hopkins Press, 1942, and Octagon Books, Inc., 1966).

politics and political management but he had a genuine admiration for the British style of diplomacy; and in this he was no amateur. He looked upon Latin Americans with an aloof superiority and would apply to them the term "dagoes" with a kind of amused disdain. He wished them well but his condescension was most irritating.[1]

Nor should it be forgotten that there was a side to the new President other than mere showmanship and supernationalism. He had a genuine interest in the development of those who were less fortunate, and especially for those who were in the new empire of which he was so proud. Further, he was blessed with initiative and no small amount of ability. He persuaded the remarkably able Elihu Root to become Secretary of War for the special purpose of setting up colonial governments in the new dependencies. Then, when the ailing John Hay retired as Secretary of State, Root was asked to head the Cabinet. John Hay had ably negotiated with the British for a canal treaty and over the Canadian boundary, but had commanded only irritated respect from Latin Americans. Root secured equal respect from the British and Canadians and also displayed a kindly feeling for Latin Americans that generated both respect and personal liking in the southern republics.

Root's immediate problem on entering the Cabinet was the establishment of governments in Puerto Rico and Cuba. Since Puerto Rico was ceded outright to the United States further arrangements between the two ceased to be a matter of international relations. It is sufficient to say that the rest of Latin America for the next two-thirds of a century saw peace and prosperity in the island. Potential foreign critics saw little to complain of.

Cuba was a different matter. The immediate problem was how to make it independent and at the same time provide safety of property, prosperity, and reasonable democracy for the people. Cuban rebels against Spain resented the fact that the United States had refused to recognize them. The reports of General Leonard Wood, in charge of the occupation troops in Cuba, to Secretary Root detailed numbers of complications. A broad sanitation program was launched and a number of Cuban teachers were sent to Harvard University for special training programs. Locally, Wood attempted to reform Cuban prisons and advised a tighter control of Cuban politics. He reported that radicals dominated the elections and the newly elected constitutional conven-

[1] Tyler Dennett, *John Hay, from Poetry to Politics*, p. 264.

tion. In line with his fears the convention drafted a new instrument of government that largely ignored the United States and what it had done for the island. To offset this, Root and senatorial leaders drafted the Platt Amendment, which was adopted March 2, 1901.[2]

Convention leaders were then informed that unless they acquiesced in the changes to their proposed constitution, also to be negotiated in the form of an international treaty, United States military occupation would continue indefinitely. One of Root's despatches to Wood explained clearly: "The Platt Amendment is of course final."[3] This guaranteed to the United States the right of intervention to protect democratic forms of government, the right to supervise the contracting of new Cuban loans, and the right to lease such naval bases on Cuban coasts as it might find needful. From this last provision arose the arrangements by which the United States developed Guantánamo Bay.

The President now showed a genuine interest in Cuban prosperity. When Congress failed to approve a reciprocal trade treaty guaranteeing the island a market for its sugar, he cracked the executive whip and called that body back in special session. In December, 1903, the treaty was approved. After 1900 sugar imports from Cuba steadily rose from 308,000 tons to approximately 1,000,000 tons. Under the new treaty the figure reached 1,425,000 tons in 1907.[4]

So far so good, but the end of the first presidential term in the island brought trouble in 1904. Stuffed ballot boxes and general unrest precipitated a crisis in which the Cuban President-elect resigned. While militarists chortled "I told you so" and while Secretary of State Root was on his way to South America on his famous good-will tour, Secretary of War William H. Taft was hastily sent to Cuba as a trouble shooter. Behind a temporary military administration he conferred with all

[2] An extensive supply of material on this subject is in the Elihu Root Papers, LC. See also David F. Healy, *The United States in Cuba, 1898–1902*; Russell H. Fitzgibbon, *Cuba and the United States, 1900–1935*; Philip C. Jessup, *Elihu Root, I*; and Louis A. Coolidge, *An Old-Fashioned Senator: Orville H. Platt of Connecticut.*

[3] Root to Wood (telegram), March 20, 1901, Root Papers, LC.

[4] For passage of the bill see Tariff Commission, *Reciprocity and Commercial Treaties*, pp. 319 ff.; C. E. Chapman, *A History of the Cuban Republic*, pp. 155 ff.; and Howard C. Hill, *Roosevelt and the Caribbean*, pp. 80 ff. On the sugar interests in Cuba see Edwin F. Atkins, "Tariff Relations with Cuba," *The Annals*, XXXII (September, 1908), 327.

factions and as rapidly as possible organized a new civil administration.[5] He repudiated the idea of permanent United States control and instructed temporary Governor C. E. Magoon: "I have your letter of January sixteenth about the protectorate. It is simply out of the question, and you must not give any encouragement to it."[6] This interregnum lacked the effective leadership of the early military control. Spoilmanship, of which the Cuban was a past master and the Yankee a not too poor practitioner, marred the record. In spite of Roosevelt's impatience,[7] Taft, with Root's cordial support, was able to "sit on the lid." Cuba was given another chance at self-government.

From this date to the outbreak of World War I conditions remained reasonably quiet in Cuba. When unrest developed, especially among certain Negro groups in 1912, Secretary of State Philander C. Knox undertook what has become known as preventive intervention.[8] This was a forthright but successful threat to send in troops unless order was maintained. During the same period much was said of the application of dollar diplomacy to the island economy. Investigation shows, however, that only about one third of the new foreign capital entering Cuba was from the United States, and of the total foreign investments in the island only about half were from this country. In few cases were restraints exercised on foreign investments unless there was some question of strategic significance involved (as in the case of the widely advertised Zapata Swamp controversy).[9]

Strategic Needs of an Empire

The war with Spain awakened the United States to the naval needs of

[5] *For. Rels., 1906,* Pt. I, p. 479; Hill, *Roosevelt and the Caribbean,* pp. 88–89. The British ambassador in Washington wrote the Foreign Office that Roosevelt had informed Congress: "If the elections [in Cuba] become a farce, and the insurrectionary habit becomes confirmed in the island, it is absolutely out of the question that Cuba should continue independent" (F.O. 371 [America], 1906, Vol. 160).

[6] Taft to Magoon, January, 23, 1907, William Howard Taft Papers, LC, letter book p. 222.

[7] Fitzgibbon, *Cuba and the U.S.,* p. 120. For a critical view see Leland H. Jenks, *Our Cuban Colony: A Study in Sugar,* pp. 96–97.

[8] *For. Rels., 1912,* pp. 264 ff.; Harry F. Guggenheim. *The United States and Cuba,* pp. 210–211.

[9] *For. Rels., 1912,* pp. 309 ff.; Jenks, *Our Cuban Colony,* pp. 108 ff.

an empire located in two oceans. Hawaii, the Philippines, Samoa, and Guam were in the Pacific; the coasts of the United States itself faced both the Atlantic and the Pacific; and now the new Caribbean possessions called for attention. Naval costs and estimates soared. A canal through the Panama-Central American region became a compelling need. Once constructed, it would greatly reduce maintenance costs and add to the strategic effectiveness of naval units that could reinforce each other in case of emergency. But the Clayton-Bulwer Treaty provided for joint ownership of any interoceanic canal that might be built by either Great Britain or the United States. In view of the complications being faced by Britain in the rest of its Empire and of its current rivalry with Germany there was little probability that Downing Street would be inclined to venture into additional New World responsibilities. A further deterrent lay in the fact that the rest of the Western European powers had been irritated by recent British acquisition of control of the Suez Canal. They would not take kindly to its substantial control of a second interoceanic transit route.

This was the kind of problem that appealed greatly to Secretary John Hay. He loved to deal with world affairs and he liked to negotiate with the British. They were "proper" people and worthy of his mettle. Strategists, scholars, and businessmen considered the canal a necessary adjunct of empire. Did it not follow that construction by the United States was a new but primary demand upon his country? In December, 1898, President McKinley had told Congress that "the construction of such a maritime highway is now more than ever indispensable."[10] On February 5, 1900, a convention was signed by Secretary Hay and Ambassador Pauncefote providing simply that the United States might construct the canal singlehandedly and should retain the right of managing it. The canal was to be neutralized and other powers were to be invited to subscribe to the agreement. Lodge immediately protested that Britain still held joint rights under the Clayton-Bulwer Treaty and that "The American people will never permit a canal which they do not control." Roosevelt agreed that joint control was not to be tolerated. Though Hay might characterize a leading opponent as a "frantic little

[10] *For. Rels., 1898*, pp. lxxi–lxxii; L. M. Keasby, "Terms and Tenor of the Clayton-Bulwer Treaty," *The Annals*, XIV (November, 1899), 22–23; G. L. Rives, "Problems of an Inter-Oceanic Canal," *Pol. Sc. Quar.*, XIV, No. 2 (June, 1899), 201–202.

lunatic,"[11] the Senate retorted to his disdain by rejecting the treaty by a vote of fifty-five to eighteen. The London *Times'* correspondent somewhat bitterly summed up the opposition. He said it was dominated by a gratuituous desire to make the treaty objectionable to Britain, and was composed of certain railroad interests who sought to block the construction, and a political opposition of Democrats who wished to defeat a Republican treaty.[12]

Reluctantly Hay returned to the bargaining table. The result was a new draft which clearly abrogated the old Clayton-Bulwer Treaty. Construction and control by the United States was approved for a neutralized canal, but the joint-guarantee feature was eliminated. Likewise the question of fortification was passed over in silence with the tacit understanding that a nation could defend its own property. Of course the British feared indiscriminate expansion of United States power in Central America, but they were pragmatists. They remembered the threat of De Lesseps and preferred United States control of the Isthmus to that of some rival European power. In December, 1901, the new President informed his Senate that the new treaty was ready for consideration.[13] This time it was approved without difficulty.

It had been generally taken for granted that the canal would be constructed via the Nicaraguan route. Hay himself commented: "I think it hardly conceivable that any other route than Nicaragua will be chosen."[14] On the other hand the French company was about to lose its latest lease renewal at Panama and was anxious to save something from its expensive debacle. If the United States acquired the French holdings for a nominal figure, completion of the Panama venture might cost less than building the whole Nicaraguan enterprise. With such a possibility in mind Hay undertook negotiations with Colombia, which culminated in an agreement for the lease of a six-mile canal zone across Panama on a

[11] Allan Nevins, *Henry White*, p. 151. Also Dennett, *John Hay*, pp. 250–251; William Roscoe Thayer, *The Life and Letters of John Hay*, II, 339 ff.; Alfred L. P. Dennis, *Adventures in American Diplomacy, 1896–9106*, pp. 159–160.

[12] The *Times* (London), December 21, 1901, 3a. Other comments on adjacent dates.

[13] Roosevelt to Congress, December 3, 1901, *For. Rels., 1901*, p. xxxv; "Correspondence respecting a convention . . . relative to . . . a . . . ship canal," *Accounts and Papers*, XCI (1901), 1051. Also Thayer, *John Hay*, II, 259 ff.

[14] Hay to Choate, September 29, 1901, in *Diplomatic History of the Panama Canal . . .* (Sen. Doc. No. 474, 63rd Cong., 2d Sess.), p. 45.

ninety-nine-year basis. There was to be a cash payment of $10,000,000 and an annual rental of $250,000. But the Colombian President who had negotiated the treaty could not control his Congress. That body sought to foreclose on the French works, then sell them to the United States, and still be in a position to lease the canal strip.[15] They refused to approve the treaty.

Roosevelt had never been convinced that patience was a virtue. He wrote Senator Mark Hanna: "I feel we are certainly justified in morals, and therefore, justified in law, under the treaty of 1846 [providing for transit across the isthmus], in interfering summarily and saying that the canal is to be built and that they must not stop it." Later he commented that a report had reached him that Colombia was seeking to have either Great Britain or Germany undertake construction of the canal, but there is no indication that this possibility was taken seriously.[16] It was enough that Colombia had flouted the United States. There was little further consideration of the Nicaraguan route. Colombian politicos had become "contemptible little creatures," "foolish and homicidal corruptionists," "jack rabbits," etc.[17]

In such an atmosphere Felipe Bunau-Varilla, chief engineer of the old French company, reached Washington. In interviews with key men he encountered openly expressed sympathy.[18] It was easy for him to encourage disappointed Panamanians—who feared a disgruntled United States would transfer its interest back to Nicaragua—to revolt. Their movement duly started on November 3, 1903; United States warships appeared at the terminals of the transit route on the Isthmus; Colombian troops were not allowed to suppress the rebels; and the United States forthwith extended recognition to the newly declared republic of Panama. Now Bunau-Varilla appeared in a new role as minister from the new republic. He signed a treaty on November 18 ceding a canal strip ten miles wide to the United States under terms similar to those rejected by Colombia.

[15] For correspondence and documents see *For. Rels., 1903*, pp. 133 ff.; and *Diplomatic History of the Panama Canal*, pp. 379 ff. Also Dennett, *John Hay*, p. 376; Miles P. DuVal, *Cadiz to Cathay*, p. 157; Dwight Carroll Miner. *The Fight for the Panama Route*, various.

[16] Joseph Bucklin Bishop, *Theodore Roosevelt and His Time*, I, 278. Also Theodore Roosevelt, *Fear God and Take Your Own Part*, p. 324.

[17] Henry F. Pringle, *Theodore Roosevelt: A Biography*, p. 311.

[18] Valuable correspondence is found in the Philippe Bunau-Varilla Papers, LC, especially for the months of November and December, 1903.

France, China, Austria, and Germany extended recognition before the end of November. Then followed Denmark, Russia, Sweden and Norway, and Belgium by the ninth of December. Be it noted that all of these countries acted before recognition was extended by any New World country. By the end of December, Great Britain, Italy, Switzerland, and Japan had joined the procession, but even then only Nicaragua, Peru, Cuba, and Costa Rica represented Latin America. However, the Panamanians' independence was a *fait accompli* and slowly other nations recognized the fact.[19] The realistic nations of Western Europe had long been accustomed to such shot-gun weddings and divorce procedures. As Root admitted in a public address early in 1904 there was probably more heart-searching over the matter in the United States than elsewhere.[20]

Colombia quickly realized that its efforts had backfired. Hastily it offered to accept the recently rejected treaty. Too late. On the other hand, President Roosevelt strictly enjoined all naval personnel to avoid hostilities with Colombia.[21] Fortunately, even hotheads in that country realized that a war was out of the question. In an effort at a dignified retreat the Colombian government insisted that the action of the United States constituted a violation of the Treaty of 1846 and offered to submit the validity of its stand to the Hague Court. The United States in response suggested a plebiscite in Panama and arbitration of claims of "material order" that had arisen between Panama and Colombia.[22] Here the story rested for the time being. The United States had acquired its strategic canal strip across the Isthmus.

Again, Great Britain in the New World

At the opening of the new century three negotiations involving hemisphere policies of the United States and Great Britain took place almost simultaneously. One already discussed was the Hay-Pauncefort Treaty. Then came the Alaska boundary dispute, and finally there was the Venezuela debt controversy. The Joint High Commission had discussed the Alaska boundary in 1898 and 1899 but had been unable to agree on

[19] For recognition dates see list in John Hay to Root, February 15, 1904, in Root Papers, LC.

[20] DuVal, *Cadiz to Cathay*, pp. 439–440.

[21] *Ibid.*, pp. 371 ff. For Colombia offer see *For. Rels., 1903*, pp. 224–225, and *Diplomatic History of the Panama Canal*, pp. 474–475.

[22] *For. Rels., 1903*, pp. 229, 313–314.

a solution.[23] At this point the question was aggravated by the discovery of gold in Alaska. The *Edinburgh Review* commented: "So long as the hinterland was believed to be valueless no one cared how it was reached, but with the announcement of gold discoveries in the Klondike region the means of access thereto became at once an object of actual and pressing concern."[24] Numerous legal technicalities and geographical details, of course, were involved, though apparently John Hay and Lord Paunceforte both felt that a quick agreement could have been reached except for Canadian sensibilities and the "narrowness and prejudice" of certain members of the American Senate. Lord Salisbury compared Canada to a coquettish girl playing off her two suitors against each other. Hay rejoined by describing Canada as "a married flirt, ready to betray John Bull on any occasion, but holding him responsible for her follies."[25]

Britain wished to settle the Clayton-Bulwer and Alaskan matters simultaneously. Washington objected that there was always a tendency to offset two issues against each other. These two cases were totally unrelated and each should be determined on its own merits. Britain, involved in the Boer War, and fearing European complications, was conciliatory and reluctantly agreed. After careful planning an odd arbitral tribunal was established, to be composed of three representatives from each side. Meanwhile Roosevelt had quietly reinforced the few troops stationed along the Alaskan boundary. He then named as his arbitrators two active partisans of the United States' contention, and Secretary of War Root.[26] Two Canadians (also partisans) and Lord Chief Justice Alverstone were selected by the British.

The basic convention involved was an old agreement between Russia and Great Britain which defined the boundary between Canada and Russian Alaska. This called for a line at a certain distance from the windings of the coastline. The essential question was whether this line should be drawn at the given distance from the headlands, or from the tidewater bays. In addition, some other details and transit rights were involved at special points. In general, the four partisans on the tribunal divided two to two. This left the real work to be done by the two chiefs.

---

[23] Charles Callan Tansill, *Canadian-American Relations*, pp. 169 ff.

[24] *Edinburgh Review*, CXCI, No. 392 (April, 1900), 280.

[25] Quoted in Tansill, *Canadian-American Relations*, pp. 163, 213.

[26] *Ibid.*, pp. 223–224; Howard K. Beale, *Theodore Roosevelt and the Rise of America to World Power*, p. 121.

To the laymen the decision reached was logical. The bays were considered as seacoast and the line drawn from them as a base. Roosevelt's "so-secret" bluster about sending more troops if the decision was adverse is merely an interesting personal sidelight and can scarcely be said to have affected the decision.[27]

Raucous headlines in the Canadian jingo press immediately clamored that as usual the Mother Country was buying United States favor by a sacrifice of Canadian rights.[28] Once more annexation was talked of and feared, while half-expected, in parts of Canada. And the Pacific Coast did seem to be in danger. Sir Wilfrid Laurier was even concerned about United States expansion into northern Canada, and noted that his government had sent an expedition to the mouth of the Mackenzie River and to Hudson's Bay to secure a better control of those unoccupied lands.[29] The United States remained strangely uninterested, but would naturally have been receptive if a good opportunity offered. An article in the *Edinburgh Review* quoted and apparently endorsed President Roosevelt's statement: "The Englishman at bottom looks down on the Canadian, as he does on anyone who admits inferiority, and quite properly too. The American, on the other hand, with equal propriety, regards the Canadian with the good-natured condescension always felt by the freeman for the man who is not free."[30] Galling indeed to Canadians! All knew that Roosevelt was right when he stated that in case of war between the Anglo-Saxon nations, Great Britain might take over Puerto Rico and the Philippines "but they would be a very poor offset for the loss of Canada" which could not be defended against the United States.[31]

[27] Interesting letters on the subject are found in Henry Cabot Lodge, ed., *Selections from the Correspondence of Theodore Roosevelt and Henry Cabot Lodge, 1884–1918*, II, 1–50. See also John W. Foster, *Diplomatic Memoirs*, II, 203; Tansill, *Canadian-American Relations*, pp. 243 ff.; and Beale, *Theodore Roosevelt and the Rise of America*, p. 130.

[28] J. A. Stevenson, "The Alaska Boundary Arbitration," in H. F. Angus, *et al.*, *Canada and Her Great Neighbor*, quotes many of these including: "sacrificed on the altar of diplomacy," "Robbed of our Rights," "tricked," "Canadian independence may . . . be arbitrated away," "surrenders our rights," "like a lamb to the slaughter," "Canada robbed of the fruits of victory."

[29] "Secret" report of the Earl of Minto of conversation with Sir Wilfrid Laurier, December 3, 1903, F.O. 5 (America), 1903, Vol. 2538.

[30] *Edinburgh Review*, CCIII, No. 415 (January, 1906), 240.

[31] Elting E. Morison, ed., *The Letters of Theodore Roosevelt*, III, 97.

The third of the issues arising was also of substantial significance. In 1899 Cipriano Castro had come to power in Venezuela. Corrupt and a thorough despot, he sat on his plateau "cracking his knuckles" in contempt of creditors who could not reach him. British and German claimants became increasingly restless. In 1901 the German embassy notified the State Department of its citizens' dilemma but eschewed any intention of "permanent occupation of Venezuelan territory." London also kept Washington informed of the problem. Italy soon joined its protests to those of other European creditors. Washington responded that it had no objection to proper pressures to insure collection of debts due. However, it advised arbitration and indicated disapproval of any possible territorial occupation.[32] In due course the protestants established a blockade (December, 1902) to restrain Venezuelan trade. Some small ships were captured. Then came word that the German squadran had been unnecessarily harsh in destroying the vessels captured.

Immediately there was a clamor in the press, especially against the long-suspect Germany. The Teuton had showed similar ruthless tactics in Samoa and when Dewey was besieging Manila. More important, Germany could scarcely maintain a blockade in the Caribbean for any appreciable length of time without a land base—and it had none in the neighborhood. This made occupation of a Venezuelan port all the more likely.[33] If such a base were occupied would it not *ipso facto* constitute a violation of the Monroe Doctrine? Thus ran popular comment.

The much-debated Roosevelt "ultimatum" to Germany presumably was given in early February, 1903. Certainly Dewey's fleet was peculiarly intact and available for use in case of need. The blockading powers carefully denied any intentions of asking territorial acquisitions

---

[32] *The Venezuela Arbitration before the Hague Tribunal* . . . (Sen. Doc. No. 119, 58th Cong., 3d Sess.); *For. Rels., 1903*; and Francis B. Loomis, "Position of the United States in the American Continent," *The Annals*, XXII (July, 1903), give the American point of view. For the British approach see "Correspondence respecting the affairs of Venezuela," *Accounts and Papers*, CXXX (1902) and LXXXVII (1903); and *British and Foreign State Papers*, XLVI. See also Count Bernstorff, *My Three Years in America*, pp. 16 ff.

For interpretations see Dexter Perkins, *The Monroe Doctrine, 1867–1907*, pp. 338 ff.; Hill, *Roosevelt and the Caribbean*, p. 110; Chester Lloyd Jones, *Caribbean Interests of the United States*, p. 220; and Dana G. Munro, *Intervention and Dollar Diplomacy in the Caribbean, 1900–1921*, p. 71 ff.

[33] A. L. P. Dennis, "John Hay," in Samuel Flagg Bemis, ed., *The American Secretaries of State and Their Diplomacy*, IX, 174–175.

and finally suggested that Roosevelt settle the dispute as arbitrator. Although this probably appealed to Roosevelt's vanity, the tempting suggestion was declined, possibly at the suggestion of John Hay. Instead, Washington advised that the issue be referred to the Hague tribunal. The blockading powers agreed provided they were to receive preferential treatment in the debt payments that were anticipated. For a second time the United States had assumed the position of spokesman for Venezuela[34]—and for a second time Venezuela found itself required to meet its international obligations. In the boundary dispute it had lost much of the controverted territory. Now, on the second occasion, it had to pay its debts. Wherein lay the vaunted protection of its new friend?

Once more Great Britain pursued a consistent course in retiring from New World responsibilities. It specifically recognized the Monroe Doctrine; Lord Balfour went so far as to remark, "The Monroe Doctrine has no enemies in this country that I know of."[35] Then on March 22, 1904, the Earl of Shelbourne, First Lord of the Admiralty, notified the House of Commons that expansion of West Indian fortifications of the Empire was unnecessary. Thereafter the old Empire left patrol duty in the Caribbean largely to the United States.[36] In general, European recognition of the priority of the United States in the area was little short of remarkable. The exception was Germany, whose new industrial plants sought outlets, whose Navy clamored for bases, and whose unsatisfied ambitions sought an empire.

The Big Stick

Economic pressures by the Roosevelt Administration were seldom obvious officially and certainly were not admitted by the President, even to himself. He preferred the rare atmosphere of grand planning and strategy and paid little attention to the humdrum activities of the

[34] See collections of documents and references cited in the last two footnotes; also *British and Foreign State Papers*, XCV, and G. P. Gooch and Harold Temperly, *British Documents on the Origins of the War, 1898–1914*, II. For additional secondary references see Thayer, *John Hay*, II, 288–289; Bishop, *Roosevelt and His Time*, I, 221 ff.; John Holladay Latané, *The United States and Latin America*, pp. 252 ff.; *Rev. of Revs.*, XXV (January, 1902), 12.

[35] Quoted in Alejandro Álvarez, *The Monroe Doctrine*, p. 92.

[36] Apparently Canada was too concerned with internal affairs to pay much attention to all this. Anyway, "Where the Royal Navy was less disposed to patrol the Monroe Doctrine would protect," said Lionel M. Gelber (*The Rise of Anglo-American Friendship*, p. 132).

market place. He could send word to Root to "skin these wretched creatures" (naming four prominent political leaders of the day) as "minor vermin."[37] He was likely to apply similar terms to any opposition that arose, but his enthusiasms were usually reserved for political issues or abuses of humanity, and seldom applied to economic issues as such.

The President advised Secretary of War Root to send one or more of the best officers of the Army to gather information concerning the coasts of South America that might be of strategic value in the Caribbean area.[38] For him "national defense was a passion; it was, indeed, almost a religion." Construction of the canal carried with it a need for substantial control of the water approaches thereto. And all steps in this connection were immediately sanctified in the name of the Monroe Doctrine, though it must be noted that the responsibilities entailed were freely assumed and the usual vigorous contempt expressed for those who thought the action unnecessary. Flagrant cases of "wrong doing or impotence"—both equally contemptible—by small countries were held to justify intervention by foreign nations to protect the rights of their endangered nationals. From this position it was but a step to the idea that the United States should intervene in areas of primary significance to itself, lest other foreign nations do so.[39]

At this point a word of caution is needed. Aggressive and hasty though the President might have been, he always had a keen awareness of that which was possible. In spite of his great pride in his new empire, he soon reached the conclusion that the Philippines were the Achilles Heel of that empire. He tended to endorse the advice of Mahan and others that the United States "should not undertake to keep Europe out of South America below the Caribbean Sea . . . Northern South America and Central America are enough for us to protect."[40] Whitelaw

---

[37] Roosevelt to Root, December 29, 1902, Root Papers, LC.

[38] Roosevelt to Root, March 14, 1903, *ibid*.

[39] The annual messages of the Presidents are regularly found in *For. Rels.* for the appropriate year. See also Theodore Roosevelt, *Theodore Roosevlt: An Autobiography*, p. 543.

Public opinion may be interpreted from Hiram Bingham, *The Monroe Doctrine, an Obsolete Shibboleth*, pp. 47–48; W. V. Judson, "Strategic Value of the West Indies to the United States," *The Annals*, XIX (May, 1902), 61; W. W. Pierson, "Political Influences of an Inter-Oceanic Canal," *Hisp. Amer. Hist. Rev.*, VI, No. 4 (November, 1926), 226; and Hill, *Roosevelt and the Caribbean*, pp. 198–212.

[40] Quoted in Beale, *Roosevelt and the Rise of America*, p. 393 n. Also *Rev. of Revs.*, XXXI (April, 1905). 398–399.

Reid had publicly referred to the Caribbean as the "legitimate sphere of our national interest," adding that beyond that sphere the doctrine should be modified. Roosevelt wrote him, "I am nearer your view than you would think as regards to Monroe Doctrine," but added that he could not say so publicly for fear the statement would invite European aggression. On other occasions he was not so discreet, and he told the German diplomat H. von Sternberg that he was "inclined to see the best guarantee of improvement down there [in the South American area] in the expansion of German influence." Then he enlarged upon establishment of an independent state by Germans in Brazil as the best solution.[41] On January 18, 1906, the *New York Times* commented editorially that if Berlin could persuade Brazil to convey to Germany "freely and of its own free will" part of its territory, "the United States will not undertake in any way to prevent the transaction."[42]

Roosevelt always conceived of diplomacy as high-level administrative action. In appointing young Joseph Grew to the diplomatic service he frankly said, "I can't recommend it [diplomacy] as a permanent career. There is no career; it's all politics."[43] Panama, Alaska, and Venezuela marked the high tide of the President's personalism—and they formed a pattern. From here on out a broader basis than presidential inclinations was to be used. And the immediate spokesman of the broader approach was the new Secretary of State, Elihu Root.

The broader base soon became apparent in Venezuela, where the dictator Castro got into more trouble—this time with the United States. Roosevelt confessed later that he would have intervened in Venezuela as he had done in Cuba, Santo Domingo, and Panama, but the people of the United States would not have gone along with him on what he considered a "reasonable and intelligent foreign policy which would put a stop to crying disorders at our very doors." Instead, after he worried along with the situation for a time, relations were broken for some months until a new administration in Venezuela improved matters temporarily.[44]

[41] Morison, *Letters of Theodore Roosevelt*, III, 527; Dennis, *Adventures*, pp. 296–297.

[42] *New York Times*, January 18, 1900, 6.3.

[43] Joseph C. Grew, *Turbulent Era . . . 1904–1945*, I, 13.,

[44] *For. Rels., 1908* and *1909*. Also, Jessup, *Elihu Root*, I, 497–498; Chester Lloyd Jones, *The Caribbean since 1900*, pp. 264 ff.; Henry Merritt Wriston, *Executive Agents in American Foreign Relations*, pp. 375–376.

Another effort of the expansionists and strategists was to secure a naval base in the Danish West Indies. To this end Secretary Hay negotiated a treaty for the cession of the islands through a cash sale to the United States. The convention was signed in Washington on January 24, 1902, providing for a price of five million dollars. A favorable report of the Foreign Relations Committee on February 5 was followed on the seventeenth by senatorial approval. Denmark, however, had mixed feelings on the matter. The islands had long been an economic liability but they were a symbol of empire. After an acrimonious struggle between the two houses of the Danish national congress the measure was defeated on October 22, 1902. Some saw the cloven hoof of German imperialism in the rejection but careful students have reached the conclusion that the Danish decision was not materially influenced by Germany. Whatever the reason, United States expansionists had suffered another rebuff. Now they tended to be less vociferous, though Senator Lodge still insisted that the United States should take over both Greenland and the Danish West Indies as part of its proper sphere of influence.[45]

An even more obvious case showing the change in public sentiment arose in Santo Domingo. Before discussion of this it should be said that the change in policy was not the result of a simple waning of enthusiasm for expansion, but it also involved disillusionment arising from multiple experiences. In the name of self-government the Filipinos had revolted against the new masters who had intervened in the islands; a second Cuban intervention had been necessary; and the public was dissatisfied with the Panama intervention. All these incidents played a part. The Dominican Republic, cursed by endemic revolution, occupied a strategic position long coveted by major naval powers.[46] At least seventeen constitutions were promulgated in the country between 1844 and 1908. Both Germany and France were keenly alive to possibilities and could

[45] For a scholarly study see Charles Callan Tansill, *Purchase of the Danish West Indies*. For the interest of Lodge in Greenland see Lodge, *Correspondence of Roosevelt and Lodge*, II, 119 ff.

[46] *For. Rels., 1905*, pp. 306 ff.; Sumner Welles, *Naboth's Vineyard*, II, 620 ff.; Otto Schoenrich, *Santo Domingo*, p. 304; Dana G. Munro, *The United States and the Caribbean Area*, pp. 104 ff.; Wriston, *Executive Agents*, p. 755; J. Fred Rippy, "Initiation of Custom's Receivership in Santo Domingo," *Hisp. Amer. Hist. Rev.*, XVII, No. 4 (November, 1937), 430 ff.

Pertinent correspondence is found in both Taft Papers, LC, and the Root Papers, LC.

readily find financial grounds for intervention. Even though the African crisis had temporarily tied the hands of Western European powers Roosevelt determined to put an end to the danger. If they (the small American republics), don't behave themselves, spank them (intervene) before someone else does.

On December 30, 1904, Secretary Hay confidentially instructed his minister in Santo Domingo, T. C. Dawson, to find out if the island President would be inclined to ask the United States to collect the Dominican customs duties and distribute the same. While naval vessels stood by, Minister Dawson was joined by Commander A. C. Dillingham and later by Professor J. H. Hollander. They soon secured a treaty giving the United States the right to collect the customs and to divide the proceeds between the local government and foreign claimants. On February 7, 1905, the President asked the Senate to approve the new convention. He reminded the senators that the Monroe Doctrine carried with it certain responsibilities—and here was one of them.

But the reaction was on. The Senate declined to approve the treaty in spite of a second admonition from the President on March 6. Indignant at the rebuff, the President acted on his own responsibility, claiming that the Constitution did not forbid his doing so. He instructed Admiral Bradford to keep the island quiet: ". . . I shall treat any revolutionary movement as an effort to upset the *modus vivendi*. That this is ethically right, I am dead sure, even though there may be some technical or red tape difficulty."[47] Next he established a customs collection system by executive order and distributed the funds received. In this connection it must be noted that a reasonably efficient, even though inexperienced, administration gave the Dominicans more revenue from the limited portion allotted to local uses than they had been able to collect themselves from all sources. In addition, the island enjoyed peace at home and security from European intervention—albeit at the expense of United States control. Exports and imports mounted steadily with a substantial trade balance. The later distressing controversy about fees paid,[48] as well as the details of the administration of the local government, is beside the question here. The essential fact is that the President had

[47] Quoted in Hill, *Roosevelt and the Caribbean*, p. 164.
[48] For the much disputed Hollander fee see Jessup, *Elihu Root*, I, 551–552. For foreign trade in Santo Domingo see F. F. Fairchild, "Public Finance in Santo Domingo," *Pol. Sc. Quar.*, XXXIII, No. 4 (December, 1918), 465–466.

been able once more to force through a program, but the American people and the Senate were restless at methods employed and were demanding a modification of policy.

The Senate hand had written on the wall in the defeat of the Dominican treaty. Roosevelt, a master politician, responded to the ground wave of public opinion and replaced the ailing John Hay with Elihu Root in the State Department. Where Hay had been inclined to dismiss Latin American diplomatic agents with the generic term "dagoes," Root sought to cultivate them. He wrote: "I really like them and intend to show it. I think their friendship is really important to the United States, and that the best way to secure it is by treating them like gentlemen." He replaced social snubs by invitations to his personal table as honored guests. Later, Roosevelt was to write generously that the work on Latin American affairs was "entirely Root's." Perkins concludes: "In 1906, moreover, the administration embarked upon a studied policy of courting" the southern republics.[49]

The new Secretary had already expressed grave concern at the extralegal position in which his government found itself, saying: "If the Senate refuses to give the President the legal right to act officially in regard to Dominican finances, I do not think we should go on as we are now."[50] He proceeded to pour oil on wounded senatorial feelings while he tried to conciliate Dominicans. Both responded reasonably. A modified treaty was negotiated and ratified in 1907. By this agreement the United States continued to collect the customs but far more attention was paid to Dominican sensibilities. Truth to tell, the Senate was probably relieved to have a way to save its face. The President had saved his also. The Dominicans were having their customs collected but their debts were being liquidated and they were enjoying peace and improved trade. True, they had officially lost certain rights of self-government, but it should be remembered that this was among a people who had endured nineteen revolutions and fifty-three Presidents in seventy years of national life.[51]

A final demonstration of the new nationalism is seen in the decision

[49] Perkins, *Monroe Doctrine, 1867–1907*, p. 458; Jessup, *Elihu Root*, I, 468 ff. 560.

[50] Root to Taft, November 16, 1905, Taft Papers, LC. See also Welles, *Naboth's Vineyard*, II, 647 ff.; Hill, *Roosevelt and the Caribbean*, pp. 166–167.

[51] Carl Kelsey, "American Intervention in Haiti and the Dominican Republic," *The Annals*, C (March, 1922), 175.

of the United States to be known thereafter as "America." On August 3, 1904, the Acting Secretary of State notified all "American" diplomatic and consular officers "that hereafter in correspondence and in printing official stationery and in cutting new seals for the diplomatic and consular service the adjective used shall be 'American' instead of 'United States'."[52]

Root's Program

The background of Elihu Root was that of an intensely practical and successful lawyer connected with leading business and industrial concerns. He had accepted service as Secretary of War primarily to administer the new colonial empire but also to clean up the War Department after the Spanish-American War scandals. In both jobs he was eminently successful. He showed a personal sympathy for less-developed areas but was by no means a "starry-eyed" dreamer. He firmly believed in a tariff program by which the trade of dependent areas would be channeled to the United States (as in the case of the Philippines). He applied the same idea as Secretary of State to develop the mutual welfare of the New World countries. He addressed business conferences and wrote articles to advocate better steamship connections with the south and to improve trade conditions. President Roosevelt endorsed Root's suggestions cordially. As early as 1905 Root had undertaken steps to reorganize the diplomatic service by providing for merit promotions and a better selective process. The next year he tackled the consular service to bring it under the civil service regulations.[53] This launched a program which further curtailed the old "political" appointment system that had long been open to criticism.

One topic demanding consideration was the Drago Doctrine. The Argentine Minister of Foreign Affairs, Luis M. Drago, took advantage of the Venezuela debt controversy to assume spokesmanship of the Latin American group. On December 12, 1902, he wrote the United States asserting that "The collection of loans by military means implies

[52] *For. Rels., 1904*, p. 7.

[53] See address of Root to a commercial conference at Kansas City, November 20, 1906, in Elihu Root, *Latin America and the United States*; and "Development of the Foreign Trade of the United States," *The Annals*, XXIX (January, 1906), 443. See also Roosevelt to Congress, December 3, 1907, *For. Rels., 1907*, I, xlix ff.

For reorganization of the Foreign Service see James Brown Scott, "Elihu Root," in Bemis, *Amer. Secs. of St.*, IX, 239 ff.

territorial occupation to make them effective." Then he added: "Such a situation seems obviously at variance with the principles many times proclaimed by the nations of America, and particularly with the Monroe Doctrine."[54] This naming of the Monroe Doctrine was patently calculated to secure United States endorsement, while the first assertion skillfully appealed to the other nations of the continent.

How could Washington reject this apparent endorsement of the very program it was espousing in its efforts to prevent the forcible collection of debts due in Venezuela? Yet Washington leaders were keenly aware that American investors were at the moment seeking foreign markets in which to place their funds. Certainly the investors expected the customary governmental protection. Also the fact was that in many cases the investments were made "at the direct instance of the American Government."[55] The leaders in Washington argued that it was simply common sense to support American investments in the New World in order to forestall the extension of foreign loans under the protection of European governments. To them, preventive financial investments were as logical as preventive military intervention. Yet how could more such investors be found if the government refused to protect those whose money was already at risk on governmental recommendation?

The answer sent to Drago was skillful: The United States would be pleased to refer the matter to the Second Hague Conference (to meet in 1907) for consideration. After all, no such proposal could be effective unless endorsed by the major lending nations of Europe. Further, since the Conference would be controlled by the major creditor nations the holdings of all investors would be reasonably safe. The result was the endorsement of the idea of no forcible collection of debts unless the debtor had first refused reference of the dispute to a recognized international tribunal. Since the First Hague Conference had established such a court the result was reasonably satisfactory to all except a few unscrupulous borrowers and lenders.

In many ways the high point of Root's hemisphere policy was his trip

[54] *For. Rels., 1903*, p. 3; John Bassett Moore, *Digest of International Law*, VI, 593–594.

[55] Quoted from speech of A. A. Berle to Academy of Political Science, New York City, May 3, 1939, in Samuel Flagg Bemis, *The Latin American Policy of the United States*, p. 167. See H. E. Nettles, "The Drago Doctrine," *Hisp. Amer. Hist. Rev.*, VIII, No. 2 (May, 1928), 217–218. For the British view see Gooch and Temperly, *British Documents*, VIII, 242 ff.

to the Third Pan-American Conference at Rio de Janeiro in 1906. The *Times* (London) had watched the planning jealously. President Roosevelt reviewed the prospects in detail with the Secretary of State. It appeared that the chief item for discussion at the Conference was likely to be that of arbitration of international disputes. This was to be accepted in principle but there was a great variety of opinions as to methods of reference and as to items to be referred. In drafting instructions for delegates to the Third Conference, Root endorsed further development of arbitral agreements and also recommended enlargement of the functions of the Pan-American Union. The delegation selected was an able one, but overshadowing all else was the fact that the Secretary of State proposed to visit the Conference in person. True, Root was somewhat suspect because he had served as Secretary of War under an aggressive President, but it was hoped that his position and personality would counterbalance the handicap.

All spadework possible for the Conference was carefully done. The United States legation in Rio de Janeiro had recently been raised to an embassy and a number of controversial items were removed from the agenda. Next Root sought to reach accord on items mutually helpful, hoping to proceed from them to the more difficult. He was aware that reciprocal trade treaties were of little significance to countries whose exports were noncompetitive with our own. Yet he knew the indirect values of international good will. Indeed, later the United States Ambassador at Rio de Janeiro could report a preferential rate proposed on Brazilian imports from the United States as "The first practical results of your visit."[56]

[56] For instructions to United States delegates see *For. Rels., 1906*, II, 1966 ff. Also Moore, *Digest*, VII, 94–95. The *Times* (London) carried scattered articles from March 20, 1900, to July 27, 1901, on the subject.

Root was well aware of Latin American fears and rivalries. His papers (LC) contain a clipping from *El Diario de la Mañana* (Paraguay), July 12, 1905, which refers to him as "a decided partisan of the imperialistic policy" and as a man whose declarations had caused "sensation and alarm in the Latin American countries." Also, *For. Rels., 1905*, p. 102; Barnes to Root, July 27, 1903. Root Papers, LC.

Reports of British observers are found in the Public Records Office (MS). See particularly; Barrington to Marquis of Lansdowne, April 19, 1902 (F.O. 6, Vol. 474, fol. 78); Harford to Grey, February 12, 1904 (F.O. 371, Vol. 4 [1906]); Haggard to Grey, September 30, 1906 (F.O. 371, Vol. 5 [1906]); Haggard to Lansdowne, August 24, 1904 (F.O. 6, Vol. 485). These refer to international rival-

At Rio internal difficulties in Latin America had to be watched. Included were the long-standing rivalries between Argentina and Brazil which involved Brazilian territorial ambitions at the expense of its neighbors as well as the budding naval rivalry among the ABC powers. At the same time, Uruguay feared Argentine expansionism and there was the long-standing Peruvian-Bolivian-Chilean dispute over the Tacna-Arica boundary.[57]

Brazil recognized that the precedent-making visit was calculated to put Latin America on the map. The reception alone given the Secretary in Rio de Janeiro was reported to have cost about $700,000. He was carried ashore in the sixty-four-oared barge of royalty and then ate his way through eight days of elaborate luncheons and dinners.[58] The high-water mark of the visit was the Secretary's address to the Conference in which he pledged, "We wish for no victories but those of peace; for no territory but our own." This statement the President himself reaffirmed and quoted in his message to Congress the following December.[59] In addition to the good will engendered by Root's trip, probably the most important act of the Conferenc was the reorganization of the Pan-American Union.[60] This was calculated to strengthen the organization and to simplify its procedures.

From Rio the Secretary went southward to Argentina.[61] Here every effort was made to eclipse the reception given in Brazil. As the British

---

ries in Latin America. For the general Argentine position see Thomas F. McGann, *Argentina and the United States* . . ., p. 255.

[57] *For. Rels., 1906,* I, 134.

[58] For the Root visit to Rio de Janeiro see Lloyd C. Griscom, *Diplomatically Speaking,* pp. 266 ff.; and Jessup, *Elihu Root,* I, 478. Also, *For. Rels., 1906,* I, xlvii–xlviii, and various.

The British representatives kept the Foreign Office fully informed, noting behind-the-scenes rivalries, incidental items such as the appearance of yellow fever and reports of entertainment expenses. Chargé Barclay, for instance, noted that the reported exclusion of the gentlemen of the press from the Conference was due in no small degree to their "extraordinary appetite" at the buffet where each bona fide delegate was reported to have consumed three bottles of champagne and forty-five cigars daily (Dering to Grey, July 16, 1906, F.O. 371 [Brazil], 1906, Vol. 13).

[59] *For. Rels., 1906,* I, xlvii ff.

[60] *Ibid.,* II, 1578 ff.

[61] For the Argentine visit see *For. Rels., 1906,* I, 23 ff.; Haggard to Grey, August 20, 1906, F.O. 371 [Argentina], 1906, Vol. 5. Also Root, *Latin America and the U.S.,* p. 80.

minister put it, "Part . . . was doubtless pure Argentine ostentation," but he felt that Argentina wanted to prove that it, not Brazil, "was the horse to back" in South America. Later the minister in a confidential report to Sir Edward Grey abstracted a message of the Argentine President to his Congress in which he alluded "to Mr. Root's visit as the most important political event of the year." The round of entertainments brought the regular spate of speeches and expressions of respect. Again Argentines professed approval of the Monroe Doctrine, and the newspapers of the city poured out their adulation and enthusiasm.

From Argentina Root visited Uruguay, then crossed to the west coast and made his way via the Isthmus to Cartagena, where he quietly met General Vásquez Cobo, Acting Colombian Minister of Foreign Affairs. This meeting led to the abortive tripartite treaty between Panama, Colombia, and the United States.[62] The ice of the frozen relations between the two republics was slowly beginning to thaw. Not to play favorites, Root the next year made a similar trip to Mexico to visit the aging Porfirio Díaz. On the personal side, the Secretary carefully followed up his trips with suitable presents to his hosts.

Similarly the State Department lent its full support to the resolutions passed at the Third Pan-American Conference and urged its diplomatic agents in Latin America to encourage ratification of the acts by careless or reluctant governments.[63] Then the President on December 8, 1908, recommended that Congress pay "careful attention" to the commercial and material progress of the Latin American republics. He commented that no other area of the world had shown a "greater proportionate development of its foreign trade" in the preceding decade and that it probably offered "larger opportunities for legitimate expansion of our commerce than any other group of countries."[64] On the other hand, the realist British ambassador in Washington H. M. Durand, reported that the latent suspicions of Latin America still existed and that it was doubtful if Root's efforts to allay them had been too successful.[65]

And this view of Latin American opinion had considerable justification. That brilliant polemic by José Enrique Rodó, *Ariel* (published in

[62] For visit to Peru see *For. Rels., 1906*, II, 1228 ff., 1420. For visit to Colombia see *ibid.*, I, 286, and *Diplomatic History of the Panama Canal*, pp. 128 ff.

[63] *For. Rels., 1908*, pp. 2–3.

[64] *Ibid.*, p. xliv.

[65] Annual Report to Foreign Office, December 28, 1906, F.O. 371 (America), 1907.

1900), insisted that democratic degeneration had set in with the migration of the British to America. Many of the fine old characteristics of the race had been lost and the new folk had become the impersonation of utilitarianism.[66] Manoel de Oliveira Lima of Brazil said that the Monroe Doctrine was "from the very beginning an egoistic" doctrine.[67] The *Gaceta Comercial* of Lima claimed that the only interest of the United States in Peru was commercial.[68] Manuel Ugarte still felt that the United States was synonymous with power, progress, and brutality.[69] Rufino Blanco Fombona warned that if Latin Americans did not mend their ways they were lost, for one certain fact was that the Yankees were at the door.[70]

The German Menace

One of the most intriguing areas for scholarly speculation is that of German influence and its threat to the integrity and independence of Latin America. As early as October 25, 1901, the American embassy in Berlin warned the State Department of repeated efforts to direct the flow of German migration from Canada and the United States to South America, "where it may remain German, nationally and economically, to the greatest possible extent."[71] Vice Admiral Valois in *Deutsche Revue* (Stuttgart) denounced the Monroe Doctrine as an effort to monopolize an area at the possible expense of Germany.[72] Dr. A. Hettner in *Geographische Zeitschrift* of November, 1902, called for a colony to which Germany could send its emigrants just as Britain had Canada. The writer felt that there was no likelihood of the area being annexed[73] but annexation, too, was desirable if a proper opportunity appeared. On the other hand, the *Mercurio*, perhaps the most influential newspaper in Chile, was speculating in 1904 whether there was a possibility of a German protectorate over Colombia to serve as an offset to the United States.[74] Others wondered if Germany might move into the Dutch possessions of Curaçao,

[66] See pp. 61–96 in particular.

[67] Quoted by Álvarez, *The Monroe Doctrine*, p. 284.

[68] Quoted by *Rev. of Revs.*, XXXIV (August, 1906), 244.

[69] See *The Destiny of a Continent*, pp. 11–12. (This is the English version of *El destino de un continente*.)

[70] *El hombre de hierro*, pp. 213–214.

[71] Jackson to Hay, October 25, 1901, *For. Rels., 1901*, p. 191.

[72] Quoted in *Rev. of Revs.*, XXX (September, 1904), 351.

[73] Précis in Public Records Office, F.O. 13 (Brazil), 1902, Vol. 831.

[74] *Rev. of Revs.*, XXX (August, 1904), 230.

Saint Eustatius, or Dutch Guiana, or into the Galápagos on the west coast; while von Tirpitz was suggesting to the German budget commission that the empire should have a naval base on the south coast of Brazil.[75]

Hay was inclined to feel that "If a big German speaking community in a South American state could not stand mis-government, and set up for itself. . . there would be in that act by itself nothing to which I should object."[76] But what about possible annexation to the empire? On February 28, 1903, the German ambassador assured President Roosevelt that his country had no idea of "acquiring territory in South and Central America."[77] Interestingly enough, other Western European nations were as concerned as the United States about the situation. In 1906 British Minister Reginald Lister reported from Paris that the political director of Foreign Affairs suspected that Germany was behind the definance of Cipriano Castro in Venezuela.[78] Later this was denied, but the suspicion was there. From Buenos Aires came repeated reports to the British Foreign Office of German military and naval efforts to monopolize Argentine military purchases, and to train young officers in Germany for the Argentine and Uruguayan forces.[79] In May, Secretary of War W. H. Taft discounted the rumor that the German government was sending "one thousand soldiers into Brazil a month."[80] For its part, Germany was trying to suppress the excitement, and one Dr. Scharlach, presiding at a meeting of the Hanseatic Colonial Society on March 3, 1903, "spoke strongly against the transmaritime aspirations of the Pan-German party, which, he said, imperiled the interests of Germany, especially in Brazil, where such German bombast was published by the newspapers and created the greatest suspicion of German policy."[81] Fears, then, remained latent in

[75] Dexter Perkins, *Hands Off*, p. 210.

[76] Quoted in Beale, *Theodore Roosevelt*, p. 393.

[77] J. Fred Rippy, *Latin America in World Politics*, p. 152.

[78] Report of January 26, 1906, F.O. 371 (Venezuela), 1906, Vol. 163.

[79] Harford to Grey, May 29, 1906, also "Very confidential," January 17, 1906, F.O. 371 [Argentina], 1906, Vol. 4. For rumors of German penetration in Mexico see Warren Schiff, "German Military Penetration . . .," *Hisp. Amer. Hist. Rev.*, XXXIX, No. 4 (November, 1959), 570 ff.

[80] Taft to Shoemaker, May 9, 1905, Taft Papers, LC.

[81] *Times* (London), March 6, 1903, 3c. On the question of German activities in the New World students should consult Alfred Vagts, *Deutschland und die Vereinigten Staaten in der Weltpolitik* (2 vols., The Macmillan Co., New York), and Count Otto zu Stolberg-Wernigerode, *Germany and the United States during the Era of Bismarck*.

Washington but evidently it would have taken very little to have aroused public excitement.

British Influence

British influence in the New World south of the equator remained predominant. On the east coast it was firmly based on long-established contacts, investments, and trade. In Brazil there was the Portuguese-English association and treaties dating back to the fifteenth century. In Argentina British purchases of wheat and meat dominated trade. In 1908 an article in the *Edinburgh Review* noted that the British imports of wheat and wheat products from the United States had declined from 55 per cent of the total in 1892–1894 to 23.05 per cent in 1904–1906. At the same time the imports from the Argentine had increased from 8.21 to 21.80 per cent.[82]

United States emigrants to Argentina and Brazil remained insignificant in number and as late as 1910 less than 3,000 of them were in Argentina. Yet in the preceding year newcomers into the nation of 5,410,000 amounted to:

Italians	88,984
Spaniards	52,856
Russians	10,100
Syrians	7,099
Austrians	5,347
French	3,524
Germans	1,853

The total was over 3 per cent of the domestic population, and in a population of 200,000,000 (approximate population of the United States in 1968) would have amounted to over 6,000,000 per year.[83] Evidently, British, United States, and even German influence had to derive primarily from investments, trade, and sea power, not from citizens in residence.

Root noted that foreign vessels entering the harbor of Rio de Janeiro in the year ending June 30, 1906, carried the following flags:

---

[82] *Edinburgh Review,* CCVIII, No. 425 (July, 1908), 244.

[83] For American figures see William Spence Robertson, *Hispanic American Relations with the United States,* p. 281. For European immigrants see Harford to Grey, January 1, 1906, F.O. 371 [Argentina], Vol. 4, No. 3407.

Austria-Hungary	120
Norway	142
Italy	165
Argentina	264
France	349
Germany	657
Great Britain	1,785
United States	7 (two being in distress).[84]

No wonder Roosevelt endorsed the need for a larger mechant marine in his annual message to Congress in 1905. When money was needed London banks were asked for credit. If the credit arrangement was abused in local communities the Argentina government was quick to render assistance to the creditors. Similarly, almost in routine fashion, British Chargé W. Haggard could report in 1906 that the Brazilian Minister of Foreign Relations had told him "that the key-note of his policy would be the fostering of good relations with England." The Minister added that the President of the Republic "completely agreed with him in that line of policy." Maybe contradictory was another report from the same source six months later commenting that the New World foreign policy of Brazil might be said to "revolve around the United States and the Argentine Republic."[85] This obviously referred to neighborhood problems in the one case, and to satisfactory trade relations arising from the reciprocal trade agreements with the United States reinforced by the good effects of the Root visit.[86] In Argentina, the British minister reported a waning of United States influence due to its "unnatural" trade situation. Of all American exports, he said, only agricultural implements were of significant value to Argentina.[87]

The multiple intra-Latin American international relations were carefully evaluated by the British agents in reports to the Foreign Office from the various capitals. Revolution in Paraguay, Argentine suspicions of Chile, Argentine and Brazilian ambitions to annex Uruguay, French adventurers on the upper Amazon—all were reported. At the same

[84] Address of November 20, 1906, in Root, *Latin America*, p. 257.

[85] "Very confidential," June 28, 1906, F. O. 371 [Argentina], 1906, Vol. 5; and Annual Report, F.O. 371 (Brazil), 1907, Vol. 221.

[86] Tariff Commission, *Reciprocity*, pp. 32–33; *For. Rels.*, *1906*, I, 112–113.

[87] Townley from Buenos Aires to Grey, February 6, 1908, F.O. 371 [Argentina], Vol. 397. *For. Rels.*, *1905*, pp. 45 ff., gives correspondence from United States Minister A. M. Beaupré on similar subjects.

time arms races were discouraged when British debts were still to be paid. However, if armaments were to be bought every effort was to be made to insure that they were purchased in Britain.[88]

Careful attention was paid to United States activities. Its ministers were characterized with frankness and shrewdness: "Mr. Barett is sentential [sic], bumptious & advertising like all American journalist-diplomatists. Not a bad sort of man, however, by any means, & a gentleman."[89] Roosevelt's indiscretions as reported in the south were gleefully recorded, as on the occasion when he was said to have told the Argentine minister in Washington that the similar progress of the two countries was clearly due to the purity of their white blood as contrasted with the mixed-blooded peoples of Brazil and the Caribbean.[90] Rumors of Latin American cooperation against the United States were immediately reported. One such report of action in Colombia, Chile, and Ecuador came from the British legation in Washington.[91] Another came from Argentina with regard to a movement including Argentina, Bolivia, Brazil, Chile, Colombia, and Ecuador. On the other hand, suggestions of a United States-Peruvian alliance were discounted.[92]

In spite of the critical appraisals of United States policy, it was obvious to those who hoped Germany might challenge the northern republic that Britain and the United States were working together. One critic wryly commented: "The United States, once more, owed their salvation to that providence which, according to the proverb, watches over drunks and the North Americans."[93]

Brazilian friendship for the United States was seen when the good offices of the United States were requested in the dispute with Bolivia over the Acre region. When Washington declined to act, the two nations

[88] See Dering to Grey, June 11, 1904, and July 25, 1906, F.O. 13 (Brazil), 1904, Vol. 841; and F.O. 371 (Brazil), 1906, Vol. 13. See also Arthur P. Whitaker, *The Western Hemisphere Idea,* p. 86.

[89] Harford to "Larcom," March 15, 1904, F.O. 6 [Argentina], Vol. 485, foll. 109–111.

[90] Harford to Grey, April 20, 1906, F.O. 371 [Argentina], Vol. 5.

[91] Herbert to Marquis of Lansdowne, October 24, 1902, F.O. 5 (America), 1902, Vol. 2488.

[92] Haggard to Marquis of Lansdowne, March 21, 1904, F.O. 6 [Argentina], Vol. 485, foll. 114–116. See also Chargé Clarke to Marquis of Lansdowne, October 30, 1902, F.O. 6 [Argentina], Vol. 474, foll. 182–183.

[93] Carlos Pereya, *El mito de Monroe,* p. 343.

turned to Great Britain.[94] On the west coast the United States was more consistently influential. The United States legation at La Paz took over British interests when that country was not represented in Bolivia.[95] When it became a question of recognizing a new Ecuadorian government, nearly all foreign legations waited for the United States to act before extending recognition. Also, it was the United States that undertook the sanitation of that pesthole of the tropics, Guayaquil.[96]

By way of a more general appeal in January, 1906, word went out to Mexico and to Central and South American states that the War Department had agreed to receive trainees from those countries at the Infantry and Cavalry School at Fort Leavenworth, at the School of Application for Cavalry and Field Artillery, and at the Army Medical School. An even broader contact arose from the sending of students to American institutions of higher learning. By April, 1905, the Argentine minister in Washington reported that in the preceding four years he had supervised twenty-five young Argentines studying in this country. Other young Latin Americans were also beginning to awake to the possibilities of training in the north, especially in technical courses, agriculture, commerce, medicine, and engineering.[97]

Closer Home

Relations with Mexico continued satisfactory. José Ives Limantour, that able Mexican financier, might begin to fear the sheer quantity of northern money flooding south of the border, but both countries were prospering.[98] President Díaz himself was extremely cautious in his statements on the Panama affair, and diplomatic correspondence centered largely on business details or on border matters. One such was the question of Japanese who, after the Russo-Japanese War, were attempting to enter the United States in increasing numbers via a short stay in Mexico. But hemisphere policy was scarcely involved in such matters. One event of note occurred in 1907. In that year the old dictator told an American

---

[94] Dering (telegram) to Foreign Office, February 25, 1903, F.O. 13 (Brazil), 1903, Vol. 834. On Acre dispute see Lewis A. Tambs, "Rubber, Rebels and Rio Branco . . . ," *Hisp. Amer. Hist. Rev.*, XLVI, No. 3 (August, 1966), 254–273.

[95] *For. Rels., 1899*, pp. 107–108; *1902*, pp. 101–102.

[96] *Ibid., 1906*, I, 624 ff.; *1904*, p. 296.

[97] *Ibid.. 1906*, I, 2–3; Robertson, *Hispanic American Relations*, pp. 296 ff.

[98] James Morton Callahan, *American Policy in Mexican Relations*, pp. 521 ff.; *Report of the Secretary of Commerce and Labor, 1907*, p. 148.

journalist, James Creelman, that he was tired and would not be a candidate for re-election in 1910.[99] For many years he had successfully "discouraged" presidential rivals. Now the door was opened to passionate presidential ambitions, if not to potential revolution. The Taft Administration was to inherit a restless situation.

In Central America Root performed another *demarche* on behalf of cooperation and peace.[100] On invitation of President Roosevelt, with the endorsement of President Díaz of Mexico, the five quarreling republics agreed to send delegates to Washington in 1907 to discuss their problems. They were welcomed by Root for sessions which lasted from November 14 to December 20. The result was to establish a Central American Peace Court and an International Bureau, which were to function for a preliminary period of ten years. During this time it was hoped that pending international disputes would be settled and steps taken to bring about essential economic and political union of the small republics. The idea so appealed to Andrew Carnegie that he provided funds for a handsome peace palace to house the tribunal.

A watchful eye was kept on Panama.[101] Here, as in Cuba, the economic provisions of international relations were somewhat ineffectively expressed by negotiators having little experience in such matters. Much of the credit for the details of the arrangement with the isthmian republic must be given to Secretary of War Taft, who personally supervised the matter. Questions of strategic significance were carefully supervised: Steps were taken to control the stock of the Panama Railroad; order was maintained both in the Canal Zone and in the neighboring republic; the standing army of Panama was effectively demobilized; and exclusive control of telegraph and cable connections was established. Health measures were promoted in neighboring areas of the Republic of Panama

[99]Francisco Bulnes, *The Whole Truth about Mexico*, pp. 152–153.

[100] *For. Rels., 1907*, II, 637 ff.; *1908*, pp. 222–223, 421, 674 ff.; James Brown Scott, "Central American Peace Conference of 1907," *Amer. Jour. Internat. Law*, II, No. 1 (January, 1908), 125 ff.; Carnegie to Root, June 9, 1908, Root Papers, LC.

[101] An outstanding source of information for material on this period of relations with Panama is the Taft Papers, LC, for 1904 to 1907. See also Hay to Choate in London, December 5, 1904, F.O. 5 (America), 1904, Vol. 2562; *Diplomatic History of the Panama Canal*, pp. 112 ff.; William D. McCain, *The United States and the Republic of Panama*, pp. 57 ff.; Munro, *The U.S. and the Caribbean*, pp. 81–82; Chester Lloyd Jones, "Loan Controls in the Caribbean," *Hisp. Amer. Hist. Rev.*, XIV, No. 2 (May, 1934), 144–145.

and the cooperation of British authorities was sought to secure laborers from Jamaica for canal construction. When criticism arose about some of the contracts awarded Taft kept his equanimity and sense of humor. He simply reported to his brother that "All we ask is that the hogs should take their hind feet out of the trough."

On the other hand, Washington did not allow its protegé to abuse its position. When a suggestion was made that neighboring provinces of Colombia would like to join the revolted area and share in the largesse of the Yankee, Root curtly cabled, "The United States does not approve any such movement."[102] When the old boundary dispute with Costa Rica on the north was revived, the matter was referred to the United States for arbitration. Ultimately the decision favored Costa Rica, to the great chagrin of Panama. By 1907 this steady policy was beginning to have effects even in Colombia. British agents in Bogotá reported in 1906 and 1908 that the feeling of hostility toward the United States was disappearing steadily, though they cautiously added that it could be revived easily.[103]

Root felt that the inevitable result of construction of the Panama Canal was that the United States would have to police the surrounding premises, which included much of the Caribbean. In line with his program of trade integration, he favored placing states near the Canal under the financial control of Americans rather than permit the alternative of having them financed from Europe. In his own words:

I think the key of our attitude to these countries can be put in three sentences:

(1) We do not want to take them for ourselves;
(2) We do not want any foreign nation to take them for themselves;
(3) We want to help them.[104]

---

[102] Jessup, *Elihu Root,* I, 519.

[103] Dickson to Grey, January 14, 1906, F.O. 371 (Colombia), 1906, Vol. 42. Also Annual Report for 1907, F.O. 371 (Colombia), 1908, Vol. 437.

[104] Elihu Root, "Development of the Foreign Trade of the United States," *The Annals,* XXIX, (January–June, 1906), 444–445.

CHAPTER IV

DOLLARS AND IDEALISM

Canada

DURING THE FOUR YEARS before 1909, Secretary of State Root and Ambassador James Bryce made special efforts to cultivate friendly relations with Canada. Dominion pride wanted control of its own foreign relations but made no special issue of the matter so long as the friendly and considerate Bryce was in Washington. The Canadian Premier, Sir Wilfrid Laurier, was outspoken on this matter.[1] In 1905 and 1906 Great Britain withdrew imperial troops and Canada assumed responsibility for defense of Halifax and Esquimault. Then in 1905 an International Waterways Commission of Canadians and Americans assumed supervision of boundary waters and international streams. From this increased responsibility Canadians pressed their claims more forcefully. Fortunately Sir Wilfrid was a realist. In 1902 he admitted that the Canadian militia must not be taken too seriously for anything except suppressing internal disorders. The fact was, he said, "the Monroe Doctrine protects us against enemy aggression."[2]

[1] James Morton Callahan, *American Policy in Canadian Relations*, pp. 488–489; Philip C. Jessup, *Elihu Root*, II, 97 ff. For opinion of Sir Edward Grey on address of Sir Wilfrid Laurier to Canadian Parliament on December 15, 1909, see F.O. 371 (U.S), 1910, Vol. 1020.

[2] John Bartlet Brebner, *North Atlantic Triangle*, p. 271. Also Sir Edward Porritt, "Sir Wilfrid Laurier," *Quar. Rev.*, CCXXXV, No. 466 (January, 1921), 35; R. A.

The southward migration of Canadians had become alarming. An estimated 70,000 were expected to leave in 1910, according to preliminary Canadian estimates, but the actual figures reached 103,798. There was much justification for the statement that it was in vain for Canadians to declare they would never become Americans—"they were already Americans without knowing it."[3] It was at this time than an element appeared in the situation that many political analysts overlook. This was the development of new strains of rapid-maturing wheat which could be grown as far north as 56° north latitude. True, the effects were hardly noted at the time, but they should not be ignored. The actual wheat production of the Dominion rose from 42 million bushels in 1891 to three times that figure twenty years later. By 1916 the output was approximately 250 million bushels, and it reached 400 million in 1922.[4]

The three statesmen—Root, Bryce, and Laurier—exchanged visits and discussed pending issues freely. A treaty of April 11, 1908, provided for ironing out remaining difficulties along the northern boundary line of the United States, and the century-old Atlantic fisheries dispute was settled by an arbitral award rendered on September 7, 1910. This award also eased relations between Newfoundland and Canada, for since 1890 Canada had been suspicious of Newfoundland fisheries agreements with the United States.[5]

Only the stubborn question of the fast-diminishing seal herds remained unsolved. The onslaught of Japanese and Canadian pelagic sealers threatened the complete extinction of the animals. Washington prodded London for action, and London, in turn, prodded Ottawa. The

---

MacKay and E. B. Rogers, *Canada Looks Abroad*, pp. 127–128. The *Times* (London) carried regular dispatches from Canada.

[3] Brebner, *North Atlantic Triangle*, pp. 216–217, 231–232.

[4] Bryce to Grey, August 15, 1910, F.O. 371 (U.S.), 1910, Vol. 1020. Also Samuel E. Moffett, *The Americanization of Canada*, p. 119.

[5] On the boundary question see James Brown Scott, "Elihu Root," in Samuel Flagg Bemis, ed., *The American Secretaries of State and their Diplomacy*, IX, 270 ff.

On the fisheries question see Robert Lansing, "North Atlantic Coast Fisheries Arbitration," *Amer. Jour. Internat. Law*, V, No. 1 (January, 1911), 31; Charles Callan Tansill, *Canadian-American Relations, 1875–1911*, p. 113; *British and Foreign State Papers*, C, 588 ff.

On Canadian-United States-Newfoundland relations see Tansill, *Canadian-American Relations*, pp. 424 ff.; and Tariff Commission, *Reciprocity and Commercial Treaties*, pp. 359–360. ,

Canadian Foreign Office professed to fear Russian and Japanese competition and so continued to "drag its feet." When Russia proposed a protocol for control of sealing which would have included Japan as well as the Western powers a notation on the document in the British Foreign Office read: "We are still awaiting as usual Canadian views, and have pressed for them."[6] Similar comments were made on communications in the Foreign Office under dates of March 20, 1909, April 5, 1909, and June 11, 1909. The critical nature of the situation appeared in the annual report of the United States Secretary of Labor in 1907. He estimated that the pelagic fleet was composed of thirty-five Japanese and fifteen British Colombian schooners. He added that the total estimated number of breeding females in the Pribilof seal heard had dwindled to 50,000. It was so obvious that all parties were losing everything that in 1911 it was agreed that 15 per cent of the skins taken on the Pribilof Islands would go to Japan and the same amount to Great Britain, with the slaughtering of the animals to be done under the United States' supervision.[7]

In the election of 1908 Taft, as a candidate, had advocated tariff adjustments understood to mean general revision downward. Once in office, however, he left tariff legislation largely to Congress on the theory that it was the business of Congress to legislate. As a result, Congress gave him a tariff bill that was a revision upward, the Payne-Aldrich bill. To keep faith with his campaign promise, Taft then sought to offset the increased protection by a reciprocal trade agreement with Canada to allow importation of substantial quantities of Canadian raw materials at cheap rates.

At once the reciprocity debate was revived. In 1905 the *Review of Reviews* had discussed the idea but had discounted it because of Senate opposition. That same year President Roosevelt had written Senator Lodge that he approved the suggestion but had added that he felt Canada was not interested.[8] It is true that an increasing number of Canadians

6 F.O. 371 (U.S.), 1909, Vol. 782.

7 *Report of the Secretary of Commerce and Labor, 1907*, p. 52. Also Tansill, *Canadian-American Relations*, pp. 368 ff.

8 *Rev. of Revs.* XXXI (February, 1905), 136; Henry Cabot Lodge, *Selections from the Correspondence of Theodore Roosevelt and Henry Cabot Lodge, 1884–1918*, II, 207–208. Also *Edinburgh Review*, CCXV, No. 440 (April, 1912), 459 ff.; Edward Porritt, "Iron and Steel Bounties in Canada," *Pol. Sc. Quar.*, XXII, No. 2 (June, 1907), 200–201.   ,

wished to monopolize their own markets by keeping out the manufactured goods which a reciprocity treaty could be expected to admit freely. In spite of this, a treaty was negotiated and in due course was submitted to the Senate. There, with the vigorous support of President Taft, it was approved. In Canada Sir Wilfrid Laurier gave wholehearted endorsement. He reported that seven million Canadians had secured "peace and good relations" with their ninety-million-strong neighbor, and added, "We have made concessions that amount to nothing, so far as I can see."[9] Unfortunately for the fate of the treaty, the Hearst papers and other imperialists undertook an active campaign on behalf of the treaty as the forerunner of annexation. Taft added fuel to the flames by a letter to Roosevelt in which he commented that the treaty would make Canada, especially western Canada, "only an adjunct of the United States."[10] Canadians rejoined with a clamor to prevent national suicide.[11]

The United States Tariff Commission, in its laconic style, commented: "It is not likely that the agreement would have been defeated in Canada upon economic grounds alone." After pointing out the benefits accruing to Canadians under the proposal, it added that the opposition, "unable to deal with it [the proposal] upon its merits, 'beat the big drum of imperialism'."[12]

The *Quarterly Review* (British) noted that at great cost Canada had built its east-west railroads and that if reciprocity became a fact, these would wither away as trade flowed along natural north-south lines. Its logic seemed to agree with Taft that the whole of western Canada might well be absorbed.[13] In addition there was the hostility of the manufacturing and financial interests of Ontario and Quebec, plus the fears of the French Canadians that their power, great in the Dominion, would be lost in the United States. A further argument was that the convention was an executive agreement, dependent upon legislation in the two countries for its fulfillment. Hence, there could be no guarantee of permanence once the existing administrations were out of office. Rudyard Kipling, the apostle of empire (chiefly British), warned the Dominion

[9] *Edinburgh Review*, CCXV, No. 440 (April, 1912), 470.

[10] *Rev. of Revs.*, XLV (June, 1912), 667.

[11] Pierre Sibelleau, *Le Canada et la Doctrine de Monroe . . .*, pp. 143 ff.

[12] Tariff Commission, *Reciprocity and Commercial Treaties*, p. 380.

[13] *Quar. Rev.*, CCXIV (October, 1911), 491 ff. Also speech of G. H. Bradbury, April 5, 1911, *Official Report of the Debates of the House of Commons of the Dominion of Canada, 1911*, p. 6686.

of its peril in making an agreement between nine million and ninety million. For Canada he could visualize in it nothing "except a little money, which she does not need, and a very long repentence."[14]

Britain watched with bated breath. Would Empire preference in Canadian trade be lost? Would Canada itself be lost? The *Quarterly Review* considered the trade loss at least inevitable.[15] Taft might deny the political implications of the treaty and try to offset blundering talk of annexation but the big drums beat on. Canada would be its own mistress. Nationalism won the day. The treaty was defeated.

Next Canada sought to foster trade in other quarters. Efforts for a reciprocal trade agreement with the British West Indies proved a sad disappointment when a decline instead of an increase of trade ensued.[16]

At the same time a volume appeared in London under the title *Confederation of the British West Indies versus annexation to the United States.* From the standpoint of the islands the study concluded that Canada could neither take their produce nor send the supplies needed. Since the islanders feared color prejudice in the United States, the conclusion was reached that only federation in the Empire could meet the islands' needs, but union with Canada was dismissed as impractical.[17]

As early as 1909, Canada sought to build a navy of its own. Now a proposal was made in the Canadian Parliament for the Dominion to contribute $35 million to construct three major naval vessels for the Royal Navy. The debate lasted for six months and the proposal was finally rejected.[18] Another gesture at nationalism was seen in the prosecution of the new program of exploration of unoccupied lands in the far north, which the Foreign Office in London suggested proceed apace. It was deemed inadvisable to stress that these lands might not be British. The King accordingly authorized the work to proceed with the understanding that when the results of the proposed expedition were known, the home government would stand prepared to issue a new Order in

[14] *Rev. of Revs.*, XLIV (October, 1911), 402 ff. See also Tariff Commission, *Reciprocity with Canada*, pp. 79 ff.; Hugh L. Keenleyside, *Canada and the United States*, pp. 268 ff.

[15] *Quar. Rev.*, CCXIV (October, 1911), 507. Also the *Times* (London), February 16, 1911, 8d, and February 23, 1911, 5a.

[16] *New York Times*, May 18, 1914, 8.1.

[17] Louis S. Meikle, *Confederation of the British West Indies versus Annexation to the United States of America*.

[18] *Rev. of Revs.*, XLVII (January, 1913), 279–280, and XLVIII (July, 1913), 21–22; *New York Times*, editorial, April 11, 1913, 8.1.

Council to cover the findings.[19] Here Dominion and Mother Country interests coincided.

Even so, trade trends would not be denied. After the reciprocity agreement had been rejected, an article in the *Edinburgh Review* pointed out regretfully that a listing of comparable classes of Canadian imports from Britain and from the United States gave an increase of 138 per cent for the former and 280 per cent for the latter.[20] Portentious. And closely associated with this was a new factor—the imminent opening of the Panama Canal, which would reduce the distance from Vancouver to Liverpool by an estimated 40 per cent. It meant a saving of from twenty-three to twenty-five days, and a reduction of existing transportation costs by one third.[21] But by the same route distance, time and rates on shipments between the Canadian ports on the west coast and the east coast of the United States were similarly reduced. Rail freight rates to eastern United States markets had been prohibitive, but the Canal opened up new United States markets for the Canadian northwest.

Problems and Personalities

As the imperial era gave place to a businessman's approach, and that in turn to a greater emphasis on local self-government in the underdeveloped countries, four hemisphere centers of interest to Washington diplomats were to be noted. One of these was Canada. Another was the complex of problems associated with the Panama Canal. A third was a rising consciousness of South America below the Canal environs. Finally, there was the quite distinct problem of the next-door neighbor, Mexico.

The new administration in 1909 enjoyed an immediate heritage of good will derived from the cooperative program of Root. Taft himself was a kindly man, and one who had considerable experience with undeveloped areas. He had established the civil government of the Philippine Islands, had supervised the re-establishment of order and constitutional government in Cuba, and had negotiated the executive agreement with Panama under which the Canal Zone had been administered. It

[19] Harcourt for Colonial Office to "Officer Administering the Government of Canada," May 10, 1913, F.O. 371 (U.S.), 1913, Vol. 1858.

[20] *Edinburgh Review*, CCXVII, No. 444 (April, 1913), 443.

[21] E. R. Gosnell, "British Columbia and British International Relations," *The Annals*, XLV (January, 1913), 15. Also O. D. Skelton, "Canadian Capital Requirements," *ibid.*, LXVIII (November, 1916), 219; John Ball Osborne, "Commercial Relations . . .," *ibid.*, XXXII (September, 1908), 331.

should be noted, however, that all of these experiences were with peoples unfamiliar with the technicalities of constitutional government. Taft himself was a legalist through and through. His thinking was based on precedent—and these peoples had just broken all precedents and were establishing new ones. Also it should be remembered that in domestic affairs the Administration was engaged in a series of efforts to control the burgeoning business life of a prosperous people. This resulted in a series of legislative acts and numerous lawsuits in which the country's finest lawyers honed their wits to razor edge in striving for legal decisions and in legal maneuverings that would yet remain within a given law. All those involved took for granted the basic "rightness" of business success, and assumed that "first-class" recognition presupposed "first-class" business and legal skill.

The new Secretary of State was Philander C. Knox. He had spent twenty-five years as a practicing attorney, followed by six years in the Senate and a period as Attorney General. A skilled lawyer, he was eminently fitted to represent his country in a technical negotiation. His approach has been described as that of an attorney for the defense rather than that of a statesman. Also his disposition was unfitted to cope with the Latin American temperament. Root commented that the Knox association with Latins reminded him of mixing a Seidlitz powder. An English writer referred to him as a "clever corporation lawyer" who considered Latin American states as "a group of commercial vassals who should obey the nod of a Protecting Power." Yet he was an efficient administrator and began by reorganizing the State Department to emphasize expert knowledge and professional training.[22] He had almost a contempt for "do-gooders" and became vitriolic in writing to Taft on the "ignorance, mendacity and impudence" of the philanthropist Andrew Carnegie.[23] Although written in connection with British relations, it is indicative of the man's attitude. Ambassador Bryce commented that the Secretary's policy on Latin America appeared "to any impartial observer to have been guided by none of the lofty principles of which he is so proud, but by the fixed determination to push U.S. financial and

[22] Jessup, *Elihu Root*, II, 251. Also H. F. Wright, "Philander Chase Knox," in Bemis, *Amer. Secs. of St.*. IX, 303–304, 355–356; Gaillard Hunt, *The Department of State . . .*, pp. 244 ff.; *For. Rels., 1912*, pp. viii–ix.

[23] Knox to Taft, March 3, 1913, Philander Chase Knox Papers, LC.

commercial interests without regard for the feelings of any other country."[24]

Taft himself consistently supported the idea of a strong merchant marine and was pleased to preside at a session in April, 1912, representing some 1,100 commercial organizations that organized the Chamber of Commerce of the United States. He believed that "There is nothing inconsistent in the promotion of peaceful relations, and the promotion of trade relations." After nearly four years in office, he informed Congress that "The diplomacy of the present administration has sought to respond to modern ideas of commercial intercourse." The same doctrine was preached by members of the State Department until there appeared to be some justification for the London *Times'* comment that Taft's message to Congress was based on the "paramount necessity of perpetuating a diplomacy calculated to help American commercial interests the world over."[25]

The Canal Area

Commercial policy alone is inadequate to explain all phases of policy in the Caribbean area. Taft told his Congress: "It is obvious that the Monroe Doctrine is more vital in the neighborhood of the Panama Canal and the zone of the Caribbean than anywhere else."[26] In fact there was a general feeling in the public mind that the Canal constituted a part of the coastline of the United States. Knox put the whole matter more bluntly when speaking before the American Society for Judicial Settlement of International Disputes on November 8, 1911: The Monroe Doctrine, he said, "does not depend upon technical legal right, but upon policy and power."[27]

A cardinal tenet of the Administration was that peace was fundamental to trade and progress. In 1912 Secretary Knox made a trip

[24] Bryce to Foreign Office, June 15, 1910, F.O. 371 (U.S.), 1910, Vol. 1023.

[25] The *Times* (London), December 4, 1912, 5d. See annual messages of Taft as follows: *For. Rels., 1909*, pp. xxxiv–xxxv; *1911*, pp. xxvi–xxvii; *1912*, p. x. *Report of the Secretary of Commerce and Labor, 1912*, pp. 75–76, and *1913*, p. 169, show the work of the Department. Also Assistant Secretary of State Huntington Wilson cordially endorsed "dollar diplomacy" in an address at Baltimore, May 4, 1916. For copy of this see Knox Papers. LC.

[26] *For. Rels., 1912*, p. xii.

[27] Quoted by Joshua Reuben Clark, *Memorandum on the Monroe Doctrine*, (Sen. Doc. No. 114, 71st Cong., 2d Sess.), p. 176.

through the Caribbean somewhat similar to the Root journey through
South America six years before. On this trip he commented: "It be-
hooves them [nations which hope to benefit from the Canal] to be
cooperative, not obstructive."[28] A Latin American critic observed that
the United States policy offered "The choice between dignity and a
future," and provided a hope of "peace at the cost of liberty." As he
saw it there was little to choose between the methods of Germany and
the United States.[29] The more excitable repeated a rumor that Taft had
once boasted that the Stars and Stripes would fly from the North Pole,
the Isthmus of Panama, and the South Pole.[30] Others claimed that Root
had once stated that it was only a matter of time until his country would
place its flag over all territory north of the Canal.[31] Of little avail were
categorical denials by Taft and Root that they had ever made the statements attributed to them. For cerain young intellectuals in "the Antilles
and in Central America hostility against the Anglo-Saxon invaders [as-
sumed] the character of a Latin crusade."[32]

Europe watched with interest. Count von Bernstorff, the German
ambassador, sought to make German hay while the opportunity offered.
He again sought to lay the ghost of German expansionism in an address
before the American Academy of Political and Social Science, saying,
"there is not the slightest intention on our part to get a territorial foothold in the Western Hemisphere."[33] But he carefully avoided giving
approval of United States hegemony and did not endorse the beloved
Monroe Doctrine. Sir Edward Grey did just that with the proviso that
application of the doctrine should not disturb British possessions.[34] His
only demurrer was on a rumor that Washington might use the forthcoming Pan-American conference to secure an agreement restricting
debt-collection efforts by Europe. He wrote: "The U.S. cannot have it
both ways; if they expect (?) the right to protect the South American

[28] Philander Chase Knox, *Speeches* . . ., p. 151.

[29] Francisco García Calderón, *Latin America: Its Rise and Progress*, pp. 292, 322.

[30] Gerardo Falconi R., *Hispanoamérica para los Hispanoamericanos*, p. 19.

[31] Manuel Ugarte, *El destino de un continente*, pp. 193–194.

[32] García Calderón, *Latin America*, p. 298.

[33] As quoted in the *Washington Star* and sent by Bryce to Sir Edward Grey,
November 17, 1909, F.O. 135 (Colombia), 1909, Vol. 329. Also *Rev. of Revs.*, XL
(December, 1909), 660 ff.

[34] G. P. Gooch and Harold Temperley, eds., *British Documents on the Origins
of the War, 1898–1914*, VI, 786.

republics they must in some degree undertake responsibility for their [the said republics'] good conduct."[35]

The Administration for its part was busy with specific problems. President Taft's private papers bear ample evidence of his continued interest in Panamanian affairs. One letter sent to Root, dated September 16, 1908, is interesting:

My dear Athos: Obaldia is to be inaugurated in October. He will be in a pliable condition for the first month or two of his administration. *Verbum sap.* Sincerely yours, Porthos.[36]

Two years later he was still interested. This time he wrote to Acting Secretary of State Huntington Wilson:

I have the following telegram from Pablo Arosmena . . .: quote My nomination first Vice President adopted Panama Assembly. Hope will have sympathy of Government you worthily preside. Have been, am, and will be friendly to American people. end quote. I would have no objection to Pablo Arosmena's election. I believe he is a good man.[37]

At the same time careful supervision was continued over railroad construction and wireless installations. The following opinion of the United States solicitor was sent for the use of the minister in residence in Panama:

. . . it is submitted that if this Government is prepared to say, as it is understood it is, that the erection of wireless telegraph stations on the zone or anywhere within the territory of Panama is necessary either for the maintenance, the operation, or the protection of the canal, or if it is prepared to say that such wireless stations are necessary for the successful completion of other works, which works in themselves are necessary or convenient for the maintenance, operation or protection of the canal, that then the Government of the United States has a complete and indefeasible right to erect such station.[38]

[35] Endorsement by "E.G." on report of Minister Lowther from Rio de Janeiro, March 26. 1906, F.O. 371 (Brazil), 1906, Vol. 13.

[36] Taft to Root, September 16, 1908, William Howard Taft Papers, LC, letter book 26. See also Jessup, *Elihu Root*, I, 525–526, and Callcott, *Caribbean Policy*, pp. 264–266.

[37] Taft to Wilson, September 7, 1910, Taft Papers, LC, letter book 285.

[38] *For. Rels., 1912*, p. 1232. For supervision of railway construction see *ibid., 1912*, pp. 1198 ff., and *1913*, pp. 1081 ff.; William D. McCain, *The United States and the Republic of Panama*, pp. 167 ff.; and Benjamin H. Williams, *American Diplomacy: Policies and Practice*, pp. 200–201.

Ineffectiveness of the Panamanian Army and police brought increasing restriction imposed by the Canal Zone authorities, until the Army was disbanded entirely. In protest the Panamanian President blurted out to the Latin American firebrand Ugarte: "If a political insurrection were to break out tomorrow on Panamanian territory, I could not suppress it unless the United States authorized me to equip troops and transport them from one division of our country to another."[39]

Yet in Panama, too, the joint objectives were efficiency and peace. Taft and Knox went "all out" to mend relations with Colombia. Tripartite treaties negotiated by Root to re-establish relations were promptly approved in Panama and in Washington.[40] In Bogotá they ran into a roadblock and were indefinitely postponed.[41] Now Taft and Knox made another attempt to cultivate Colombia. In 1910 the British minister reported that his United States colleague Elliott Northcott "has always conducted himself with remarkable probity and tact." The next year he commented that the United States Chargé Arthur Hugh Frazier showed "considerably more than ordinary courtesy and attention" to his British colleague. He concluded that "The feeling of hostility to the United States has certainly diminished during the last few months."[42]

As a background for a settlement Great Britain somewhat reluctantly agreed to arrangements by which Colombia might be extended special privileges for use of the Canal.[43] The new tripartite convention negotiated provided that Colombia would cede to the United States two coaling stations and the right to construct a new canal through the Atrato route, located in Colombia and substantially south of the Panama installation. In return Colombian vessels would have transit privileges across Panama, and that country would receive $10 million in cash and would be authorized to present claims arising from damages to the Panama Rail-

---

[39] Manuel Ugarte, *Destiny of a Continent*, p. 146.

[40] *For. Rels., 1910*, pp. 361 ff.

[41] *Ibid., 1910*, pp. 378 ff.; *Diplomatic History of the Panama Canal* (Sen. Doc. No. 474, 63rd Cong., 2d Sess.), pp. 193 ff.

[42] Francis Strange to Sir Edward Grey, April 6, 1910, F.O. 371 (Colombia), 1910, Vol. 876, and February 18, 1911, F.O. 135 (Colombia), 1911, Vol. 340; Douglas Young to Grey, June 12, 1911, F.O. 371 (Colombia), 1911, Vol. 1101, and November 9, 1911, F.O. 135 (Colombia), 1911, Vol. 340.

[43] The British ambassador in Washington was informed on July 5, 1911: "You can give note stating that H[is] M[ajesty's] Gov[ernment] do not consider that Hay-Pauncefote Treaty inhibits fortification of Panama Canal" (Gooch and Temperley, *British Documents*, VIII, 578 ff.).

road to an artibral court. But all to no avail. Colombian pride still stood in the way and Taft regretfully informed Congress in his last annual message that he had been unable to reach a definite settlement.[44] As a matter of fact, Colombians were determined to wait until after the election of 1912, which they hoped would unseat the Taft-Knox Administration.

In Central America a less savory situation developed under the dollar diplomats. In Nicaragua there was an especially confused situation. An unscrupulous dictator, José Santos Zelaya, had emerged from endemic revolution. In the preceding few years substantial investments had been made in the country by United States capitalists, some of whom had close relations with the Taft Administration. Now their companies became involved in revolutionary disturbances.[45] In the disorders two American citizens were killed. Quickly marines were landed and the "right" faction was soon victorious—the dictator was eliminated. Smedley Butler of the Marine Corps, that bull in a china closet, commented on the situation:

The troops of [Adolfo] Diaz were losing heart. Something had to be done at once, so I took unofficial command of the government of four thousand men. I had absolutely no authority for this step, but the government could not win without our support, and I knew which way the wind blew. Our State Department certainly wanted the Diaz government then in power to win, even if it didn't say so in a red sealed document.[46]

Two comments taken from the British Foreign Office are illuminating. The first is a "minute," or commentary, on a copy of Taft's annual message of December, 1910:

Nicaraguan Revolution (p. 13). But for U.S. intervention that revolution would have been crushed early in the year. Thanks to U.S. help it was suc-

---

[44] House of Representatives Document No. 1444, February 20, 1913. J. Fred Rippy refers to this as an effort to "appease" Colombia (*The Capitalists and Colombia*, p. 105). Viscount Bryce referred to it as "virtually a bribe," in a letter to Sir Edward Grey, March 3, 1913 (F.O. 135 [Colombia], 1913, Vol. 350).

[45] Financial conditions are illustrated by the fact that in fifteen years from 1896 to 1910, values of local currency in terms of the stable British pence had dropped from 22¾ to 2⅞ in Guatemala, and from 15 to 3⅞ in Nicaragua (Carden to Gray, May 30, 1912, F.O. 371 [Central America], 1912, Vol. 1308).

[46] Lowell Thomas, *Old Gimlet Eye: The Adventures of Smedley D. Butler as told to Lowell Thomas*, pp. 139–140. This should be compared with the careful discussion of Dana G. Munro, *Intervention and Dollar Diplomacy in the Carib-*

cessful but only after months of fighting. Among the first actions of the U.S. candidate for the Presidency was the cancellation of important tobacco and liquor contracts previously held by British firms. An association of planters, chiefly British was also prevented from resuming work unless it would become a U.S. concern.[47]

Another is in a letter from Sir Edward Grey to Ambassador Bryce in Washington:

In Central and South America we have great difficulties in making commercial treaties with the countries there, though the treaties include no special favour and are merely open door treaties. We are constantly finding that the difficulty is caused by a belief among Central and South Americans that the United States are not favourable to the open door.

I do not suggest that Mr. Knox has instigated this belief . . . though I think it possible that some of his representatives may have encouraged it.[48]

Ambassador Bryce expressed his opinion thus: ". . . if they [the American public] knew the facts [concerning Nicaragua] more fully a stronger disapprobation of the policy Mr. Knox has followed there, would probably before now have been expressed."[49]

Out of the complicated situation in Nicaragua Minister Thomas C. Dawson secured what became known as the Dawson Pact, signed on October 27, 1910, by leaders of the chief Nicaraguan factions. This contained provisions for a claims commission dominated by two United States members.[50] Also a treaty known as the Knox-Castrillo Convention

bean, 1900–1921, pp. 167 ff. Also For. Rels., 1912, pp. xii–xiii; James W. Angell, Financial Foreign Policy of the United States, pp. 29 ff.; Williams, American Diplomacy, p. 191. For severe criticism see Rufino Blanco-Fombona, Crímenes del imperialismo Norte-Americano, pp. 5–7; Rafael de Nogales, The Looting of Nicaragua, pp. 7–8.

[47] F.O. 371 (U.S.), 1910, Vol. 1023.

[48] Letter of January 7, 1911, F.O. 371 (Central America), 1911, Vol. 1057.

[49] Letter of July 28, 1910, to Grey, F.O. 371 (U.S.), 1910, Vol. 1020.

[50] For negotiation of the agreement see Department of State, The United States and Nicaragua, pp. 10 ff.; Scott Nearing and Joseph Freeman, Dollar Diplomacy, pp. 155 ff.; and Dana G. Munro, The United States and the Caribbean Area, p. 229. The British manuscript records in the Public Records Office show that the British resisted the idea that a United States-dominated commission might have compulsory jurisdiction over claims of British citizens (F.O. 371 [Central America], 1911, Vol. 1058, and 1913, Vol. 1584).

For defeat of the treaty see For. Rels., 1912, pp. 1077 ff.; Department of State,

was signed. It provided for a loan to be advanced by New York bankers, for a customs collectorship and for other details. In spite of a special message from the President to the Senate, the reaction anticipated by Bryce had set in. After long debate and delay the Senate finally defeated the treaty on May 9, 1912.

A similar reaction was shown toward a treaty signed with Honduras to refinance the debt of that country. This also provided for a customs collector. But the Senate was not inclined to act and the treaty was ultimately rejected in Honduras.[51]

In Guatemala was another such situation, but one that had European connotations. Here, too, Knox endeavored to put the situation "under bonds" by means of a loan. The British minister on the ground, Sir Lionel Carden, a gentleman whose attitude was strongly critical of the United States both at the time and later in Mexico, reported that this scheme was arranged to force Guatemalans to convert their "public debt with American financiers, in order that they may [might] obtain a right of intervention in their finances."[52] On one of Sir Lionel's vigorous reports calm Sir Edward Grey wrote: "But to oppose United States influence in these small States & to back them against the United States will only precipitate an aggressive policy on the part of the latter towards the former & provide an excuse for it. We can never back these distant & worthless little States effectively against the United States."[53] Yet substantial British investments were at stake, and German investments in Guatemala were greater still. Berlin soon proposed joint action with London to secure consideration of claims. The Foreign Office followed Grey's line and responded that Britain had no claims against Guatemala justifying joint action.[54]

U.S. and Nicaragua, p. 13; and Dana G. Munro, *The Five Republics of Central America*, pp. 240 ff.

[51] Munro, *The Five Republics of Central America*, pp. 217 ff.; Wright, "Knox," in Bemis, *Amer. Secs. of St.*, IX, 336 ff. In the Knox Papers, LC, may be found a detailed comparison of the Nicaraguan and Honduran treaties showing similarities. It appears logical to conclude that Knox considered them together as part of a single program or policy.

[52] Carden to Grey, November 3, 1911, F.O. 371 (Central America), 1911, Vol. 1056.

[53] Carden to Grey, November 30, 1911, with memorandum of Grey, *ibid.*

[54] Memorandum of Luis Mallett, January 26, 1911. *ibid.*, Vol. 1057.

In 1901 united protests of Great Britain, France, Germany, and Italy had secured results when the United States was "indisposed to join" in coercive pres-

Manuel Estrada Cabrera, the Guatemalan dictator, showed consider-able skill in playing off the varied interests against each other. Britain, increasingly restless about its investments, was asked by Washington to allow more time. For his part, Cabrera assured London that only minor details remained to be settled with Washington. Time dragged on—and on. At last Britain apparently realized that Knox was stymied and sent one of its own cruisers to visit Puerto Barrios. At once a satis-factory agreement was forthcoming. Just possibly Knox was not too unhappy at this concrete demonstration of the fact that European inter-vention was still a possibility. It proved that if the United States did not act even friendly Britain would take matters into its own hands.

In the Caribbean island republics matters were worrying along. The question of the Danish West Indies remained quiescent and Cuba and Puerto Rico were peaceful. Knox made efforts to protect Cuba from its own politician adventurers in the malodorous Cuban Ports Bill and also in the Zapata Swamp controversy. He informed his minister in Cuba: "The Department considers that besides the direct protection of Ameri-an interests, you are to endeavor, by friendly representations and advice, to deter the Cuban Government from enacting legislation which appears to you to be of undesirable or improvident character, even though it seem improvident or ill-advised purely from the Cuban standpoint."[55] By the end of 1912 Cuban resentment at State Department tutelage had become quite serious but all tended to wait for the new Democratic administration to take office.

Unfortunately the Haiti-Santo Domingo combination gave cause for more concern as the major nations suspiciously eyed each other's activi-ties in the Negro republics. United States naval units "visited" Haiti in 1902, 1903, 1904, 1905, 1906, 1907, 1908, 1909, 1911, 1912, and 1913, but actual troop landings were usually avoided.[56]

To forestall foreign investments with strategic connotations Taft and Knox turned to efforts to persuade Wall Street bankers to make loans

sures (Munro, *Intervention and Dollar Diplomacy*, p. 143).

For British pressure exerted in 1912 see *ibid.*, pp. 243 ff.; Rippy, *Caribbean Danger Zone*, pp. 217 ff.; Chester Lloyd Jones, *Guatemala, Past and Present*, pp. 84–85.

[55] Munro, *Intervention and Dollar Diplomacy*, p. 472.

[56] *Inquiry into the Occupation and Administration of Haiti and Santo Domingo* (Report of the Navy Department in Hearings on Senate Resolution 112, 67th Cong., 1st and 2d Sess.), I, 63; Jessup, *Elihu Root*. I, 554–555.

to the improvident nations. A recent scholar concludes that in each case involving bank controls in Haiti and Santo Domingo, American financiers had proceeded "unwillingly, at the direct urging of the Department of State; and that the Department of State urged American financial moves as a means of eliminating European financial moves."[57]

Changes in Personalities

In the election of 1912 the Republican Party was split by the Roosevelt, or Progressive, revolt. Taft with his methodical nature could not compete with the glamour and romance radiated by the scintillating Teddy. Taft, however, controlled the party machinery and insured his own renomination. The Democrats rose to the opportunity. They reversed their conservative position of 1908 and nominated Governor Woodrow Wilson of New Jersey, who was also former president of Princeton University. From a Presbyterian-minister father the nominee derived a dominating sense of moral integrity and of "right" versus "wrong." As a professor of political science he had come to the conclusion that the President of the United States had the legal right to be as powerful as his ability permitted. As a governor of a state he had been associated with conservative interests but had sponsored a striking array of antimonopoly legislation. Accordingly, though he had had no experience in national administration or international affairs, Wilson was handily elected, thanks in part to the Republican split and to the powerful support of the liberal William Jennings Bryan.

For Secretary of State, Wilson named Bryan, the strong man of the party since 1896. Three times Bryan had been the presidential nominee and at the party convention in 1912 had been a determining factor in securing Wilson's nomination. After his own repeated personal disappointments the old war horse was convinced that elections were won by party organization. His profound moral convictions and Christian principles were thus likely to be strained by his efforts to reward party workers whose political ethics were open to serious question. As a counterbalance

[57] Munro, *Intervention and Dollar Diplomacy*, p. 378. See also Department of State, *Press Releases*, XX, No. 501 (May 6, 1939), 378; Raymond Leslie Buell, "American Occupation of Haiti," *For. Pol. Assn. Reports*, V, Nos. 19–20 (December 12. 1929), 333 ff.; Kelsey, "American Intervention in Haiti and the Dominican Republic," *The Annals*, C (March, 1922), 134 ff.; P. H. Douglas, "American Occupation of Haiti," *Pol. Sc. Quar.*, XLII, No. 2 (June, 1927), 229 ff.; Sumner Welles, *Naboth's Vineyard*, II, 674 ff.

to the diplomatically untried and inexperienced Secretary of State, a thoroughly trained international lawyer, Robert Lansing, was named as Assistant Secretary. Also on hand was the widely experienced John Bassett Moore as counselor of the Department. The *Review of Reviews* commented that Moore would "provide broad conceptions, as well as technical and legal knowledge" to balance the fact that Bryan in the State Department "was bound to keep the emotional newspapers in a state of more or less controlled hysterics for a number of days."[58]

According to expectation Bryan rewarded the faithful with diplomatic appointments.[59] At the same time he made efforts to eliminate earlier appointees who might have been tainted by Republican dollar diplomacy, as in the case of the arbitrator Henry L. Janes, who was on a board considering claims between Ecuador and the Guayaquil Railway Company.[60] It soon became evident, however, that Wilson intended to retain personal control of critical matters and to leave routine questions of foreign relations to the State Department. Matters to be termed critical in 1913 included relations with Colombia, with their annoying implications of moral turpitude, and those with Mexico.

The President lost no time in outlining his Latin American policy. Under date of March 11, 1913, he issued a statement which was sent to all diplomatic officers in the New World republics that asserted: "Cooperation is possible only when supported at every turn by the orderly processes of just government based upon law, not up arbitrary or irregular force." "As friends . . . we shall prefer those who act in the interest of peace and honor, who protect private rights, and respect the restraints of constitutional provision."[61] On October 27, 1913, he delivered an address before the Southern Commercial Congress at Mobile, Alabama, in which he expressed sympathy for Latin American nations that had been abused by foreign money-lenders. He insisted that morality and not expediency must guide his nation's policy.[62] Specifically he

[58] *Rev. of Revs.*, XLVII (April, 1913), 402.

[59] For Bryan's attitude toward the faithful see Bryan to Wilson, May 24, 1913, William Jennings Bryan Papers, LC, and Ray Stannard Baker, *Woodrow Wilson: Life and Letters*, IV, 40. For typical current criticism see *Rev. of Revs.*. XLIX (March, 1914), 349.

[60] Selig Adler, "Bryan and Wilsonian Caribbean Penetration," *Hisp. Amer. Hist. Rev.*, XX, No. 2 (May, 1940), 205–206 n.

[61] *For. Rels., 1913*, p. 7.

[62] Harley Notter, *Origins of the Foreign Policy of Woodrow Wilson*, p. 272.

stated: "I want to take this occasion to say that the United States will never again seek one additional foot of territory by conquest."[63] Yet the assurances were coupled with a disconcerting insistence on democratic self-government: "So long as the power of recognition rests with me the Government of the United States will refuse to extend the hand of welcome to anyone who obtains power in a sister republic by treachery or violence."[64]

In spite of discouraging experiences in the meantime the President in his annual message at the end of 1915 was able to tell Congress that the role of guardianship so properly applied by the United States in the past was "always difficult to maintain . . . without offense to the pride of the peoples whose freedom of action we sought to protect. . . . All the governments of America stand, so far as we are concerned, upon a footing of genuine equality and unquestioned independence."[65] As might have been expected, these statements precipitated an active discussion of the nature of the Monroe Doctrine on the part of both diplomats and scholars.

Bryan, like his predecessors, feared European investments in Latin America. He had never had cordial relations with banks and bankers and the latter were not eager to risk their funds in uncertain ventures abroad with his erratic backing from the State Department. Instead Bryan advised Wilson to make United States credit or moneys available for loans to Latin American countries in need. He suggested floating bonds at 3 per cent interest in the United States, with the loans carrying 4.5 per cent to the borrowers; the profits were to be used to hasten the repayment date. Wilson declined the idea as too "novel and radical."[66] Yet in May, 1915, the President was to tell the Pan-American Financial

[63] Quoted by David F. Houston, *Eight Years with Wilson's Cabinet*, I, 77.

[64] Edgar Eugene Robinson and Victor J. West, *The Foreign Policy of Woodrow Wilson*, p. 346.

[65] *For. Rels., 1915*, pp. ix–x.
For discussion at the time see Elting E. Morison, *Letters of Theodore Roosevelt*, VII, 75, and VIII, 852; *The Lansing Papers, 1914–1920*, II, 462 ff.; *New York Times*, May 31, 1914, V, 8.1; George H. Blakeslee, *The Recent Foreign Policy of the United States*, p. 83.

[66] For Bryan proposals, specifically for Ecuador and Panama, see Bryan to Wilson, August 6, 1913, and February 21, 1914, in Bryan Papers, LC. For Wilson's response see Wilson to Bryan, March 20, 1914, *ibid*. For discussion see Notter, *Origins of the Foreign Policy of Wilson*, p. 287; Link, *Wilson: The New Freedom*, pp. 329 ff.

Conference that if private capital could not meet the needs of physical communication "the Government must undertake to do so."[67] Bryan, having received a negative answer to his proposal, returned to the old and tried procedures of dollar diplomacy in conducting foreign affairs.

The President himself was busy with a far-reaching program of domestic reform which included organization of the Federal Reserve banking system, tariffs, and other matters. Two congressional enactments from the new programs affected foreign relations. By one of them banks which could meet certain qualifications were authorized to open overseas branches. In addition, commercial houses could combine for foreign sales when in competition with overseas competition, even though such combination was forbidden in domestic trade. Both acts had substantial effects in Latin America. The Wilsonian idealism, feared by many as unrealistic, was showing a practical side.[68]

Fear of Foreign Investors

The complex of issues arising from the new Canal enterprise was basic in formulating foreign policy. During the 1912 campaign, candidate Wilson had favored exemption of United States ships from tolls payments on the nearly completed Canal. This thinking was in line with Taft's position and rested on reasonable precedents. More important during the campaign was the argument that free transit for United States ships would provide needed competition for the monopolistically inclined transcontinental railroads. Once in office, however, Wilson received forceful British protests that this interpretation was contrary to the understanding at the time of the signature of the Hay-Paunceforte Treaty. The British had surrendered joint ownership rights with the United States in the Canal but absolutely insisted on full equality of transit charges for their shipping. Sir Edward Grey told Wilson's personal emissary, E. M. House, that his government would be reasonable as to timing but would insist on arbitration if its understanding were not accepted.[69] Most of the negotiators of the Hay-Paunceforte convention were dead, but Root confirmed the British position. Wilson, convinced, reversed his campaign position and argued that a first-class power could

[67] This was promptly noted abroad. See the *Times* (London), May 25, 1915, 5e.

[68] For a typical European reaction see Walter Allison Phillips, "The New Monroeism," *Edinburgh Review*, CCXIX, No. 447 (January, 1914), 225 ff.

[69] Diary, July 3, 1913, Edward M. House Papers, Yale.

not afford to interpret a treaty too technically merely because it was in a position to do so. He asked Congress to repeal the original tolls act and accept the British contention. It was done.[70]

Less than two months after the new administration took office, the Colombian minister requested that the controversy over the Panama revolt be referred to the Hague tribunal. Wilson countered with a proposal for direct negotiations. After a false start in which United States plans were prematurely leaked to the press,[71] negotiations settled down. The result was a convention in which the United States expressed regret that friendly relations had been interrupted, and agreed for Colombia to have free use of the Canal for military needs; equality of rights with United States citizens for intra-Colombian trade; special rates on the Panama Railroad; and a $25 million gold payment from the United States. Colombia, for its part, was to recognize the independence of Panama.[72] The terms of the treaty aroused a storm of criticism among the old Theodore Roosevelt faction. A single example of the criticism is the editorial of the *Review of Reviews* which insisted that the success of the Canal enterprise had "prospectively doubled the value of all the resources of Colombia. The whole tone of this treaty is unfortunate, and its proposals would seem impossible."[73] By this time the European war had broken out and attention quickly centered on the rights of neutrals in the crisis. The Colombian treaty remained unratified.

But the Canal question had another interesting ramification. In his message asking approval of the repeal of the tolls act, Wilson stated that if Congress declined his request he would not know how to handle other matters of grave import. This obviously referred to the maneuvers of foreign capitalists to secure canal rights in the Atrato area; to the control of potential oil reserves and a canal route through Nicaragua; and to foreign support of Victoriano Huerta, a new Mexican dictator whom Wilson vigorously opposed. As early as 1908 reports had circulated in Buenos Aires, Bogotá, London, and Washington of efforts of a Chilean engineer-adventurer who was said to be seeking British or German support for a rival canal venture in Colombia. Sir Edward Grey had sent a confidential note to his foreign agents on July 29, 1908,

[70] *Ibid.*, June 17, 1914; Baker, *Woodrow Wilson*, IV, 410 n; Elihu Root, *Addresses on International Subjects*, pp. 238 ff., and 299 ff.

[71] Link, *Wilson: The New Freedom*, p. 322.

[72] *For. Rels., 1914*, pp. 163–164.

[73] *Rev. of Revs.*, XLIX (June, 1914), 683.

indicating that any such action would surely create "a very acute" political situation and that His Majesty's government would have nothing to do with it.[74] At about the same time reports had appeared that one Mr. Tregellis had been employed by Messrs. Pearson, "the well-known contractors [British]," with extensive engineering and petroleum experience in Mexico and the New World, to secure petroleum concessions in Colombia.[75] For the next year and a half, however, the Foreign Office had continued to assure all inquirers, either British or American, that it would not endorse or touch such a proposal.

The recrudescense of Yankeephobia following the Nicaraguan intervention was felt throughout the Caribbean and included both Venezuela and Colombia. It was accompanied by a carefully nurtured pro-Germanism for which there were plenty of ambitious and eager local agents. True, the German Foreign Office does not seem to have actively fostered the pro-German movement,[76] even though it had employed men of this type as agents in the first place. Not surprisingly, Latin American leaders such as the notorious President Castro of Venezuela, easily convinced themselves that German support would be available in case of a clash with the Monroe Doctrine. "Like another Ajax, President Castro is ready to defy the lightning. He has said that he is confident of success, 'for,' he says, 'the Kaiser is with me'."[77] Throughout 1912 Germany watched developments in Panama jealously. The Albingia Company, closely connected with the Hamburg-American Steamship Company, planted some 2,500 acres of land in bananas and secured extensive railroad and wharf rights directly in the area of the proposed Atrato canal route. Other reports indicated that Germans were trying to secure grants on the Pacific coast of Colombia.[78]

[74] Extensive correspondence on the subject is found in the Public Records Office. For 1908 see F.O. 371 (Colombia), Vol. 397, and for 1909 see Vol. 643. See also F.O. 135 (Colombia), 1909, Vol. 329.

[75] Stronge to Grey, July 24, 1908, F.O. 371 (Colombia), 1908, Vol. 437.

[76] Minister Corbett to Grey, March 16, 1909, F.O. 371 (Venezuela), 1909, Vol. 793; Corbett's Annual Report, March 28, 1910, F.O. 371 (Venezuela), 1910, Vol. 1026. Also, Munro, *Intervention and Dollar Diplomacy*, pp. 6–7.

[77] Corbett to Grey, June 27, 1908, F.O. 371 (Venezuela), 1908, Vol. 569. On December 12, 1908, Corbett reported that Castro was boasting that with the Kaiser's support "I shall make them [the Dutch] cede it [Curaçao] to Venezuela" (Corbett to Grey, *ibid.*).

[78] Minister Wyndham to Grey, June 11, 1912, F.O. 135 (Colombia), Vol. 345; Wyndham to Mallett, June 12, 1912, F.O. 371 (Colombia), Vol. 1350.

Meanwhile Mr. Weetman Pearson (Lord Cowdray), in spite of the professions of the British Foreign Office, had been operating quietly to secure concessions. In addition to lending support to the Mexican dictator, Huerta, he turned to "petroleum" concessions in Colombia and elsewhere. A report from Bogotá to London indicated that Pearson and Son "now have a fair chance of coming in." The report ended "I think we should endeavour to consolidate our interests as far as possible before the Panama settlement is concluded." On August 11, 1913, Sir Edward minuted on this report:

It is time that the question of these contracts came before me. . . . Nor have I seen any papers about the Pearson contract except one individual reference to it in a telegram.

I must know what the Pearson & other contracts referred to in this telegram & what we have done about them & what we propose to do before I can decide any action.[79]

The British Embassy in Bogotá reported that five British firms were said to be interested in Colombia, but emphasized that the Pearsons were particularly important. Evidently the United States was quietly using its influence to block concessions having strategic significance. The Foreign Office continued to refuse support, so on November 24, 1913, the British minister at Bogotá reported that the Pearson contract had been formally withdrawn.[80] That the threat was serious appears from the fact that the proposed contract carried bases on both the Atlantic and Pacific Oceans with the right to build communications [a canal (?)] between the two. Rumors and facts are difficult to disentangle, but it appears that the seasoned international fisherman, Lord Cowdray, was simply casting baited hooks in troubled waters, and hoping for a favorable strike.

But the ramifications went even further. The Pearson syndicate had secured substantial holdings on the Costa Rican side of the possible Nicaraguan canal route. Were these banana lands, or did the whole affair amount to strategically placed concessions looking to future and rival canal construction by an experienced engineering corporation

[79] Telegram, Wyndham to Sperling, October 1, 1913, F.O. 371 (Colombia), 1913, Vol. 1631.
[80] Wyndham to Grey, November 24, 1913, F.O. 135 (Colombia), Vol. 351.

with ample financial resources?[81] Wilson's fears of foreign concession hunters were not unfounded. Such schemes in the "grand days" of the previous century had eventuated in "glorious" empire building. Now the Foreign Office frowned and the Pearson house of cards crumbled. A writer in the *Edinburgh Review* might grumble that while Wilson professed disinterest his government "was throwing all its weight on the side of the Standard Oil Company in its contest with the Cowdray group" in Colombia and Ecuador. Possibly, but the major players knew full well that the real game had larger stakes than mere oil concessions. Fortunately the British government was content when the trade rights of its nationals on the canal were protected; while the United States was involved in strategic considerations as well as trade.

Next the new administration had to consider Nicaragua, recently the crux of the Central American problem. Bryan undertook to replace the convention recently rejected by the Senate, as well as a still-later agreement of February 8, 1913, that had reached Washington too late for action under the Taft Administration. The later agreement, had authorized naval bases for the United States in Fonesca Bay and in the Corn Islands. Bryan's new convention, known as the Bryan-Chamorro Treaty, was similar to the one unacted upon. It provided for a $3 million cash advance to Nicaragua. In return the United States was to acquire a naval base in Fonseca Bay on the northwest coast of Nicaragua, rights to the Corn Islands off the Atlantic coast, as well as an option on Nicaraguan interests in a canal route via the San Juan River and Lake Nicaragua.[82] These stipulations would prevent foreign control of both the canal route and of a potentially dangerous base on the west coast approach to the canal. At the same time the country would be financed. To make security double certain the convention included the Platt Amendment provision, giving the United States the right of intervention. The Foreign Relations Committee of the Senate, however, was so sensitive on the subject that the right of intervention was omitted from the treaty as actually signed on August 5, 1914.[83]

[81] *Edinburgh Review*, CCXLV, No. 499 (January, 1927), 16. See the *Times* (London), September 24, 1913, 5f, and January 12, 1914, 7f.

[82] Munro, *Intervention and Dollar Diplomacy*, p. 213; Isaac Joslin Cox, *Nicaragua and the United States*, pp. 731–732.

[83] For discussion of the Platt Amendment idea in Nicaraguan treaty see Bryan to Wilson, June 16, 1913, and Wilson to Bryan, June 19, 1913, in Wilson Papers, LC; and Bryan to Wilson, June 12, 1914, in Bryan Papers, LC.

A chorus of protest greeted news of the new accord. The *New York Times* commented that the treaty made the old dollar diplomacy look like activity of the "ten-cent" variety.[84] Even more severe were the criticisms from Central American countries which feared the proposed Fonseca Bay naval base. They appealed to the Central American Peace Court to invalidate the cession, claiming that the bay was jointly owned by the three countries bordering on it and that unilateral cession by Nicaragua constituted sale of property by one of three equal owners. By a strictly partisan vote the Court condemned the treaty, even though the protestants themselves had spotted records with regard to attempted concessions in the area. The United States had sponsored the establishment of the Court in 1907 but was in no sense subject to its jurisdiction. Therefore, in spite of the Court decision, the treaty stood. The subsequent history of the bay is not only interesting but significant in indicating national policy. Once it was under control no effort was made in either World War I or World War II to develop the base. The objective was to preclude foreign control.[85]

Once more, in the case of Nicaragua as in those of Ecuador and Panama, Bryan proposed extension of United States credit to its minion. Again Wilson disapproved.[86]

Just at this time Panama was protesting the White award in its quarrel with Costa Rica over the boundary.[87] But the State Department remained consistent in its policy. It brooked no delay and insisted on application of the award.

The Islands

In Santo Domingo and Haiti, Wilson found a new testing ground for his principles. He was truly desirous of showing "the paths of freedom to all the world."[88] Unfortunately, many of the agents chosen for the work, largely at the instance of Secretary Bryan, were peculiarly ill-

---

For printed materials see *For. Rels., 1914*, pp. 953–954; *1916*, p. 850; Department of State, *The U.S. and Nicaragua*, p. 26

[84] Quoted by T. A. Bailey, "Interest in the Nicaragua Canal," *Hisp. Amer. Hist. Rev.*, XVI, No. 1 (February, 1936), 4.

[85] *For. Rels., 1916*, p. 886.

[86] Notter, *Origins of the Foreign Policy of Wilson*, p. 256.

[87] *For Rels., 1914*, pp. 994–995; *1915*, pp. 1147 ff.,

[88] Notter, *Origins of the Foreign Policy of Wilson*, p. 303. Also Welles, *Naboth's Vineyard*, II, 717 ff.; and *For. Rels., 1914*, pp. 232 ff.

fitted for tasks in the island republics. Misuse of funds, local disorders, and general dissatisfaction culminated in intervention in Santo Domingo in December, 1913. This in turn led to the appointment of a financial adviser the next year. But still the disorders continued until more drastic steps became necessary.

In Haiti fear of German intervention continued though French financial interests provided the major threat. Bryan frankly sought a naval base in Haiti[89] and Rear Admiral Colby N. Chester referred to Haiti as "practically part of the shore line of our republic."[90] During the endemic local disorders periodic landings of foreign marines had been made to protect foreign interests. Whenever such steps were taken by Great Britain, France, or Germany, Washington experienced premonitions of occupation, and rumors spread. Dollar diplomats invoked the old remedy of encouraging American investments in the Haitian National Bank.

In January, 1914, a new Haitian President emerged but by the end of October he had fled the capital. In the face of renewed disorders, the *U.S.S. Machias* was used to transfer some $500,000 (about half the gold then held by the bank) to safety in New York City in the late fall.[91] The new victor went through the maneuver of a so-called election but early in January, 1915, he too had been displaced. By March 4, 1915, a third occupant had been "regularly and constitutionally" elected. Indeed, it has been estimated that in the seventy years prior to 1916 the country had suffered forty-three Presidents, only three of whom had completed the terms which they had begun.[92] Thus Wilson and Bryan, handicapped by ineffective agents, were muddling along to almost in-

[89] Letter of Lansing to Chairman of Committee of U.S. Senate quoted by Harold Palmer Davis, *Black Democracy*, p. 312.

The House Diary (Yale) entry for June 24, 1915, carries the statement: "He [Wilson] said that while Mr. Bryan was always using the 'soft pedal' in negotiations with Germany, he had to restrain him when he was dealing with Santo Domingo, Haiti and such small republics." Also see Bryan to Wilson, June 14, 1914, Bryan Papers, LC.

[90] Colby N. Chester, "Present Status of the Monroe Doctrine," *The Annals*, LIV (July, 1914), 36.

[91] *For. Rels., 1914*, pp. 365 ff.; Buell, "American Occupation of Haiti," *For. Pol. Assn. Reports*, V, Nos. 19–20 (December 12, 1929), 337; Wilfrid Hardy Callcott, *The Caribbean Policy of the United States, 1890–1920*, pp. 277 ff.

[92] Otto Schoenrich, *Santo Domingo*, p. 306.

evitable forcible intervention when the European war added its confusions to the tangled situation.

Mexico

Sui generis was the situation in Mexico and its resulting effects on
United States policy. The long-continued peace of the Díaz Administration had resulted in spectacular economic developments south of the
Rio Grande. Here was a happy hunting ground for dollar diplomats.
By 1910, it has been estimated, United States citizens owned approximately 43 per cent of all property values in Mexico, while Mexicans
owned a mere 33 per cent—the remainder being controlled by British
or other European nationals.[93] The Knox-Taft Administration had sent
the well-trained scion of a western mining and timber family, Henry
Lane Wilson, as ambassador to Mexico. The British were represented
by Sir Lionel Carden, also thoroughly experienced in imperial problems
and Latin American affairs. Although Carden was suspicious of Yankee
dollar diplomats, his correspondence shows an appreciation of the values
of dollar diplomacy itself.[94]

Many Mexicans were increasingly fearful of United States investments and even Díaz sought to offset their larger European credits. This
was evident in the efforts of José Ives Limantour to promote a Mexican
railway system at the expense of northern capitalists. Ambassador Wilson did his best to counteract the plan.[95] Just as the Díaz dictatorship
weakened, Taft was losing control of his party. His chief desire for
Mexico, then, was to keep Díaz in power until after the election. As a
good-will gesture a meeting of the two Presidents was arranged to take
place on the Texas border in 1909.[96] All proceeded on schedule but the
days of the dictatorship were numbered.

Francisco I. Madero, grandson of a friend of Díaz, had been educated
in the United States and in France. He returned to Mexico and soon
launched his candidacy to succeed Díaz in the election of 1910. His
"pronouncement" included demands of lands for the landless and for a
Mexico controlled by Mexicans. To discourage his candidacy, the

[93] *Investigation of Mexican Affairs* (Sen. Doc. 285, 66th Cong., 2d Sess.), pp.
3321–3322.
[94] Charles Seymour, *The Intimate Papers of Colonel House,* I, 199–200; Burton J. Hendrick, *The Life and Letters of Walter Hines Page,* I, 219 ff., 196–197.
[95] *For. Rels., 1911,* pp. 363 ff.
[96] *Ibid., 1909,* pp. 425 ff.

government arrested him, but he escaped north of the border and continued his campaign. The once-efficient Díaz military machine had become sadly ineffective; the idealistic young leader gained widespread support and the dictatorship collapsed. Apparently some northern money helped the rebels but certainly Ambassador Wilson and most of the American colony in Mexico deplored the successful revolution which they were convinced was thoroughly antagonistic to the United States.

The Cuban minister in Mexico reported that from the early days of the new regime the American ambassador had sought its overthrow.[97] But Taft was in the midst of his own desperate campaign for re-election and about all that he could do was to police the border heavily, warn the Navy to be ready for eventualities, and hope that the crisis would subside. He did embargo arms shipments to Mexico on March 14, 1912, and then continued a strictly neutral policy. After his defeat in the November elections, feeling that he should not commit his successor in office to a specific program, he continued his hands-off policy in spite of strident calls for action by his ambassador in Mexico City.[98]

Meanwhile foreign and domestic moneyed interests in Mexico rallied against the twin Madero slogans. The first, "Lands for the landless," could be manifested only at the expense of landlords; and the second, "Mexico for the Mexicans," clearly envisioned reduction of the investments and influence of foreigners. A new revolution was organized by friends of the old dictator. The general in charge of Madero's troops retained his command but secretly headed the revolt which was plotted at least in part at the United States legation. Madero was overthrown, and then shot while being transported through the streets under guard. A cowed and obedient Congress duly "elected" the victor, Victoriano Huerta, as President ad interim in February, 1913.[99]

Here was a direct challenge to the newly announced Wilsonian idealism. He had pledged that his administration would not recognize

[97] M. Márquez Sterling, Los últimos días del Presidente Madero, pp. 336–339.

[98] For United States policy see For. Rels., 1912, pp. 733–738, 863; 1911, xi–xiii. Also Taft to Wood, March 12, 1911, Taft Papers, LC, letter book 142. For H. L. Wilson's point of view see "Errors with reference to Mexico," The Annals, LIV (July, 1914), 150–151. For Madero's opinion see José Vasconcelos, Ulises Criollo, pp. 302–303.

[99] For. Rels., 1913, pp. 698 ff.; Henry Lane Wilson, Diplomatic Episodes in Mexico, Belgium and Chile, p. 286; Márquez Sterling, Los últimos días del Presidente Madero, p. 472; Pedro González-Blanco, De Porfirio Díaz a Carranza, pp. 98–99.

any government in the New World that had secured office by treachery or violence. Yet Huerta headed a *de facto* government guilty of both. To add complications, it had the apparent endorsement of the British under their comfortable *de facto* recognition policy, as well as that of the United States ambassador on the ground. Also backing the same new dictator were the Pearson interests (so active in Central America), which held extensive Mexican properties. Ambassador Wilson was recalled and then asked to resign while a number of presidential agents were despatched from Washington to report. Active revolts soon broke out under the leadership of Pancho Villa (Doroteo Arango) and Venustiano Carranza, while the Zapata brothers led Indian protests in the south.[100] Huerta had a strong army and scouted the United States' suggestion of financial aid in exchange for a free election in which he would not be a candidate for the supreme office.

An irritating episode at Tampico involving United States sailors and local police brought a demand for an apology from Washington. Huerta refused. At this point reports reached Washington that Krupp arms were en route to the dictator by sea. Wilson seriously considered a declaration of war to justify a formal blockade but settled for a military occupation of Veracruz in which a reported two hundred Mexicans were killed.[101] Huerta was defiant, Carranza was sullen and refused to cooperate, and only the unscrupulous Villa was willing to work with the Yankees.[102] One interesting proposal was made for administration

---

[100] For further information on the Pearson interests see J. A. Spender, *Weetman Pearson*, and Desmond Young, *Member for Mexico: A Biography of Weetman Pearson*. Also J. Fred Rippy, "The United States and Colombian Oil," *For. Pol. Assn. Reports*, V, No. 2 (April 3, 1929), 23.

For special agents sent to Mexico by Wilson see Henry Merritt Wriston, *Executive Agents in American Foreign Relations*, pp. 492 ff.

The significance of the Indian element in Mexico is seen in the estimate by Clarence Senior, *Land Reform and Democracy*, p. 39, which classifies the Mexican population of 1910 as follows:

Whites	. . . . .	1,150,000. or 7.5%
Mestizos	. . . .	8,000,000, or 53.5%
Indians	. . . . .	6,000,000, or 39.0%

[101] For a running commentary on Wilson policy see the diary of E. M. House (Yale), entries for October 14, 28, 30; November 3, 5, and 12, 1913. On January 16 and 21, 1914, follow-up estimates are given.

[102] Clarence C. Clendenen, *The United States and Pancho Villa*, pp. 102–103, 155 ff.; Isidro Fabela, ed., *Documentos históricos de la Revolución Mexicana*.

of Mexico by a commission composed of representatives from each of the ABC powers and the United States. Bryan was not enthusiastic and Wilson turned to other solutions. The House Diary bears ample evidence that the policy followed was that of the President, and that only McAdoo of the President's Cabinet was in his confidence. The puzzled British were assured by Ambassador W. H. Page in London that the purpose of Wilson was to make the Mexicans be democrats, even if it was necessary to shoot them into self-government.[103]

But how turn loose of the bull's tail? An offer of Argentina, Brazil, and Chile to serve as mediators was gladly accepted by Washington. Villa approved, Huerta shouted defiance, and Carranza refused to admit that such a group had any right to discuss the internal affairs of Mexico but was careful not to repudiate the entire idea. At the ensuing Niagara Falls Conference the Wilson dictum was that "Huerta must go." Beyond that, he little cared what happened. Villa was fast losing support and only the stubborn Carranza appeared able to handle the siutation. Huerta could no longer stand the pressure and left for exile. The United States withdrew its forces from Veracruz, Carranza was installed in Mexico City, and formal *de facto* recognition was authorized on October 19, 1915.[104]

Throughout the disturbances the United States had tried to protect the interests of foreigners in the southern republic. The volumes of *Foreign Relations* for 1913 show efforts to protect French, Chinese, Germans, Spaniards, and Turks.[105] Wilson evidently meant it when he told his private secretary Joseph Tumulty that "there won't be any war with Mexico if I can prevent it." Further, "were I considering the matter from the standpoint of my own political fortunes, and its influence upon the result of the next election, I should at once grasp this opportunity and invade Mexico, for it would mean the triumph of my administra-

[103] Hendrick, *Life and Letters of Page*, I, 188–189.

[104] *For. Rels., 1914* and *1915* contain multiple references. Also Edgar Eugene Robinson and Victor J. West, *The Foreign Policy of Woodrow Wilson*, p. 207; Baker, *Woodrow Wilson*, IV, 293, 336 ff.; Arthur S. Link, *Wilson: The Struggle for Neutrality* . . ., p. 491.

An interesting proposal by House for the administration of Mexico by means of a commission composed of representatives from the United States and the ABC powers may be found in his Diary (Yale), entries for January 24 and 25, 1915. It apparently attracted Wilson's interest, but Bryan was "not [as] enthusiastic as the President."

[105] *For. Rels., 1913*, pp. 912 ff.; *1915*, pp. 1030 ff.

tion."[106] True, his energies were being rapidly diverted to World War I, but his policy seems clear. He believed that he was training a people for democracy.

Beyond the Caribbean: The East Coast

The glow of good fellowship arising from the Root visit to South America in 1906 suffused the thinking of many east coast residents. They hailed the Secretary's comment in his address at Rio de Janeiro concerning the acceptance of Latin American nations at the forthcoming Hague Conference as indicative that "for the first time the recognized possessors of every foot of soil upon the American continents will be represented with the acknowledged rights of equal Sovereign States in the Great World Congress [*sic*]—this will be the formal and final acceptance of the declaration that no part of the American Continents is to be deemed subject to colonization." The British chargé at Rio de Janeiro considered this by "far the most important statement" of the address.[107] The Secretary's trip paved the way for American publicists to urge better nominees in the diplomatic services, as well as better trade connections, banking facilities, and mail connections.[108] At the same time imperialism was deplored and Latin American criticism of the United States given increasing attention.[109]

Some Latin Americans were modifying their criticisms of the United States. Ugarte still complained but noted that the tyrannical conduct of the United States was more the fault of the conquered than of the conqueror. Francisco García Calderón feared that the northern districts and the west coast were inevitably lost to the Latins unless they secured Japanese aid, or learned to cooperate among themselves with active support from England, France, and Italy. Manoel de Oliveira Lima felt that the mixing of races in Latin America made the people inferior, even if their original races were not. A later writer was to emphasize the

[106] Joseph P. Tumulty, *Woodrow Wilson as I Know Him*, p. 158.

[107] Chargé Barclay to Grey, August 4, 1906, F.O. 371 (Brazil), 1906, Vol. 13.

[108] Report of Bureau of Navigation in *Report of the Secretary of Commerce and Labor, 1908*, p. 397; John Barrett, "South America—our . . . greatest opportunity," *The Annals*, XXXIV (November, 1909), 529 ff; Elihu Root in *Columbian Magazine*, March, 1910 (summary in Pan-American Union, *Bulletin*, XXX (April, 1910), 530–531.

[109] Hiram Bingham, "The Monroe Doctrine, an Obsolete Shibboleth," *Atlantic Monthly*, III (1913), 728–729; George W. Critchfield, *American Supremacy*, II, 582.

constructive efforts of the United States electorate—whose work had only been interrupted by one civil war—as contrasted with the endless parade of Latin American revolutions. He continued that dollar diplomacy had built the Canal and had sanitized pestholes, and had created wealth that was being transformed into universities, fine arts, and happiness for those enjoying a new peace and prosperity. They still had qualms about United States activities in the Caribbean but the southern part of the continent felt little responsibility in the matter.[110] And increasing numbers of South Americans did not especially want to abolish the Monroe Doctrine. It existed; they were protected; why assume unpleasant involvements and responsibilities such as Drago had proposed in the Venezuelan debt collection affair?

On the other hand many felt that the facts of international life were such that treaties between Latin American republics and their northern neighbor were often similar to agreements that might be made between the sardine and the whale when the latter's natural and proper food was the sardine.[111] An Englishman added the observation that "The political master-passion of the Latin American peoples is not the love of personal liberty, but patriotic pride; and they would rather suffer any wrongs at the hands of the compatriots than have these wrongs redressed by the intervention of foreigners."[112] Such quotations posed the problem of how to devise a policy that would satisfy such disparate needs and peoples. The redoubtable Dr. Marcial Martínez, of Chile, in addressing Theodore Roosevelt, had openly stated what many Latin Americans now agreed to, that is, Pan-Americanism really did not exist in South America.[113] Lord Bryce, in reporting on his trip to South America, commented that South Americans felt self-reliant: "Since there are no longer rain clouds coming up from the east, why should a friend, how-

[110] Ugarte, *Destino de un continente*, pp. 177 f.; García Calderón, *Latin America: Its Rise and Progress*, p. 392; M. de Oliveira Lima, *La evolución histórica de la América Latina*, pp. 258–259; Juan José Arévalo, *Fábula del tiburón . . .*, pp. 29, 78–79; Roberto Kurtz, *La Argentina ante Estados Unidos*, pp. 121, 253.

[111] Walter Allison Phillips, "The New Monroeism," *Edinburgh Review*, CCXIX, No. 447 (January, 1914), 229–230.

[112] Paxton Hibben, "The South American View," *The Annals*, LIV (July, 1914), 63–64. Also Blakeslee, *Recent Foreign Policy of the U.S.*, pp. 134–135.

[113] James Bryce, *South America*, p. 509. Also Enrique Gil, *Evolución del panamericanismo*, pp. 346–347.

ever well-intentioned, insist on holding an umbrella over us?"[114] A Chilean expressed the same idea with "We don't want any papa."[115]

Even so, the dollar diplomats were not always denounced. The Argentines were enjoying a golden era of prosperity[116] and looked confidently to a future in which they would copy United States procedures to become the recognized spokesman of the neighboring countries. To this end a number of their leaders sought to cooperate with the United States to counteract dominant European influences. To the dismay of British and Germans who felt they had a vested right in such matters, Buenos Aires awarded contracts to United States shipyards for two battleships costing some $23 million. Taft was so delighted that he reported the incident to Congress.

This item was only a detail in a serious naval rivalry that was brewing. Brazilian trade with the United States had long been satisfactory. Now the powerful Baron Rio Branco hoped to induce the United States to support Brazil in its contest for leadership of the southern continent. Britain had been building vessels for the Brazilian Navy, and as a kind of international chore had accepted Brazilian sailors on board British ships for training. Next it appeared that Germany might also accept such trainees. At this point the United States awoke. Realistically Sir Edward Grey noted on one despatch concerning the matter: "If the Americans really desire the [training] mission for themselves they will prevent anyone else getting it. There will be either an American mission or no mission. If the Americans do not much care about it for themselves their influence will send it our way."[117] Brazil had launched a naval

---

[114] Quoted by Blakeslee, "New Basis Needed . . .," *North Amer. Rev.*, CXCVIII (1913), 779.

[115] Frank Tannenbaum, "Argentina, the Recalcitrant American State," *For. Affs.*, XXIII, No. 2 (January, 1945), 279; Thomas F. McGann, *Argentina and the United States . . .*, pp. 260 ff.

[116] *For. Rels., 1910*, p. xv; McGann, Argentina and the U.S., p. 268; Walter Scholes, "Philander C. Knox," in Norman A. Graebner, ed., *An Uncertain Tradition*, pp. 65–66; Henry F. Pringle, *The Life and Times of William Howard Taft*, II, 699.

[117] See Report No. 41690 of October 3, 1911, F.O. (Brazil), 1911, Vol. 1051. For other British reports see Haggard to Grey, March 19, 1910, *ibid.*, 1910, Vol. 832; Haggard to Grey, February 14, 1912, *ibid.*, 1912, Vol. 1302; Captain Marcus R. Hill to Admiralty, October 7, 1911, *ibid.*, 1912, Vol. 1302. Also *Rev. of Revs.*, XXXIX (February, 1909), 243.

building program and let a contract with a British firm for a super-dreadnought of 32,000 tons displacement, mounting fourteen-inch guns and eighteen-inch torpedo tubes. (The largest British vessel then under construction only displaced 26,000 tons.) No wonder the construction and subsequent discussion of the possible resale of this vessel to some other country greatly perturbed Argentina.[118]

Another feature of the situation was the vigorous German drive in Brazil which undertook to challenge United States trade. Maybe leaping to conclusions in 1910 the German economist von Schmoller wrote in his *Handels und Machtpolitik*:

We must desire that at any cost a German country containing some twenty or thirty million Germans may grow up in the coming century in South Brazil—and that, too, no matter whether it remains a portion of Brazil or becomes an independent state or enters into close relationship with our empire. Unless our connection with Brazil is always secured by ships of war, and unless Germany is able to exercise pressure there, our future development is threatened.[119]

On the same subject it is interesting to note that on January 22, 1913, E. M. House confided to his diary that he thought Wilson, the British Minister of Foreign Affairs, and the German Emperor might "encourage Germany to exploit South America in a legitimate way, that is by development of its resources and by sending her surplus population there . . ."[120]

When the United States applied its antitrust laws to coffee owned by Brazilian government and stored in this country, Brazilian officials were so perturbed that their Foreign Minister made a special journey to the United States to settle the trouble. The importance of the trip is attested by the fact that the British minister at Rio, Sir William Haggard, filed at least thirteen reports with the Foreign Office between February 10 and July 14, 1912, concerning details of the trip.[121] Local newspapers in

---

[118] Pan-American Union, *Bulletin*, XXXI (September, 1910), 515; the *Times* (London), August 20, 1910, 5c. Also Milne Cheetam to Grey, July 18, 1908, F.O. 371 (Brazil), 1908, Vol. 403.

[119] Quoted by P. A. Martin, "Brazil," in A. Curtis Wilgus, ed., *Argentina, Brazil and Chile . . .*, pp. 254–255. Also Cheetam to Grey, September 22, 1908, F.O. 371 (Brazil), 1908, Vol. 403.

[120] Diary, January 22, 1913, and October 15, 1915, House Papers, Yale.

[121] For the coffee question see *For. Rels., 1913*, pp. 59 ff., and F.O. 371 (Brazil), 1913, Vol. 1580. For general trade conditions in Brazil see *For. Rels., 1908*, p. 48;

Rio might give the United States a bad press, reporting rarely on their northern neighbor and then only on "accidents, robberies and administrative scandals,"[122] but a study of trade conditions submitted to the British Parliament commented that the *Bulletin* of the Pan-American Union was "undoubtedly the best available source of information regarding current developments in Latin America published in the English language."[123]

In Argentina as well as in Brazil frequent reports of German activities circulated, though Minister Haggard in 1907 tended to discount their significance. The hopes of ardent German nationalists were expressed in 1911 by Otto Richard Tannenberg, *Grossdeutschland*. This book went far beyond von Schmoller and included a sketch map of South America with United States, English, and German spheres of influence clearly indicated. The United States was to extend south to Colombia; Britain was to take over the Brazilian-Bolivian-Peruvian tropics, and Germany was to dominate from South Brazil through Paraguay, Uruguay, Argentina, and Chile. The German drive took many directions, including contracts secured by the Krupp works for field artillery equipment and an invitation for an Argentine training ship to visit the Kiel Week festivities. As a result, said an observer, "it is not unlikely that German trade" would benefit substantially.[124] This proved to be the case. The percentages of Argentine imports from major countries from 1909 to 1911 were reported as showing a decline for the United Kingdom from 32.8 per cent of the total to 29.6 per cent; those from the United States held steady at about 14.2 per cent to 14.3 per cent; while those from Germany rose from 14.7 per cent to 18 per cent.[125]

The game was being played from both ends. The German minister in Buenos Aires after 1910 was Baron von dem Bussche Haddenhausen, who married an Argentine lady. His brother-in-law was German-educated and represented German firms holding extensive Argentine con-

1909, p. 40; *1910*, p. 121; *1911*, p. 30; Tariff Commission, *Reciprocity and Commercial Treaties*, pp. 286 ff.

[122] Cheetam to Foreign Office, Annual Report of February 25, 1909, F.O. 371 (Brazil), 1909, Vol. 604.

[123] G. T. Milne, "Trade with Central America . . .," *Accounts and Papers: Commercial and General Interests*, LXVIII (1913), 25.

[124] Townley to Grey, April 30, 1907, F.O. 371 (Argentina), Vol. 194; Russell to Grey, December 31, 1908, *ibid.*, Vol. 598.

[125] Pan-American Union, *Bulletin*, XXXV (July, 1912), 142. Also Bryce to Grey, Annual Report of April 30, 1908, F.O. 371 (U.S.), 1908, Vol. 566.

tracts. New German helmets had just been issued in 1913 to the entire Argentine Army; its field artillery had been entirely rearmed with Krupp equipment and the first consignment of 1909 Mauser rifles had just been received for the Army. Clemenceau reported on his South American visit that the Germans had reorganized the Argentine Army, not hesitating to send out their skilled officers for the purpose.[126] When an Argentine trade commission visited Berlin the entertainment was lavish in the extreme. The *New York Times* commented that apparently the German Emperor was out to prove that German "hospitality, like German goods, is the finest in the world."[127] Proud and sensitive Argentines basked in this unwonted red-carpet attention.

Periodically the Argentines threatened retaliation against the United States' wheat and grain trade with Brazil.[128] At the same time Washington had difficulty securing good men for diplomatic service in Buenos Aires. Costs of living were high and the prestige was not equal to that of European posts. In 1914 Secretary Bryan recommended one active party supporter and listed among his qualifications the fact that "I think he is rich enough to afford it."[129]

The little sociological experiment station, Uruguay, had received scant attention from Washington. One writer has noted that to 1906 Uruguay was the "only independent country in America with which the United States had never had a treaty."[130] In 1909 it was observed that the local United States minister "knows no French [and his] Spanish is execrable and accent so odd his English is almost unintelligible," yet his general bonhommie and extravagant bachelor hospitality helped him greatly. Under critical conditions he was reported as showing "firmness and courage." Probably such a man was able to contribute somewhat to the increased interest of Yankee meatpackers, if not of bankers and railroad builders in the little republic.[131] To

---

[126] Tower to Grey, January 1, 1913, F.O. 371 (Argentina), 1913, Vol. 1573; Georges Clemenceau, *South America To-Day*, pp. 106–107.

[127] *New York Times*, June 5, 1913, 3.5.

[128] *For. Rels., 1911*, pp. 30 ff.

[129] Bryan to Wilson, August 19, 1914, Bryan Papers, LC.

[130] John Bassett Moore, *Digest of International Law . . .*, V, 867.

[131] Almost three times the space devoted to any other diplomat in the annual report of the British minister on foreign diplomatic agents in Uruguay was assigned to the agent of the United States. F.O. 135 (Colombia), 1909, Vol. 329. Also Scott to Grey, Annual Report of January 3, 1910, F.O. 371 (Uruguay-Venezuela), 1910, Vol. 1024.

Argentines and to the dominant British investors all new American activity was of concern.

Inter-Latin American Relations

Argentina had long aspired to leadership of Latin America. It capitalized on its slogan "America for Humanity" as broader and more significant than the Pan-Americanism sponsored by the United States. As early as the Pan-American meetings held at Washington and Mexico City, the rivalry of the two temperate-zone republics for hemisphere leadership had been more or less avowed. Now the disconcerting Argentine practice of nonratification of agreements that had been carefully negotiated became annoying. Its delegates attended the conferences and participated in the deliberations. Yet of the seventeen Pan-American treaties sponsored at the Second, Third, and Fourth Conferences only three were ever ratified by Buenos Aires.[132] It retained the privileges of membership and a chance for leadership without assuming responsibility for action.

After the love feast at Rio de Janeiro in 1906 careful preparations were made for the Fourth Conference. The plan was to emphasize economic questions such as communications, copyrights, trademarks, and arbitration of pecuniary claims. Knox wisely instructed his delegates to be unobtrusive and to cultivate solidarity. The head of the delegation was the experienced Henry White, recent ambassador to Paris. Before leaving Washington, he told Ambassador Bryce "that the 'business' of the meeting would virtually be dinners, lunches, and complimentary speeches." Whenever a conflict threatened at the sessions, the United States gave way as White skillfully guided his delegation. A few items of business did touch on deeper feelings. Brazil proposed a formal endorsement of the Monroe Doctrine by name. This precipitated a plethora of interpretations and complications. The subject was dropped. Finally, a proposal was introduced to authorize a country, not formally represented in Washington, to send a separate delegate to sit on the board of the Union. This was rejected though it was agreed that an unrepresented country could authorize some other regular member of the board to vote as its temporary representative.[133] In general, negative

[132] McGann, *Argentina and the U.S.*, p. 283. Also Oliveira Lima, *Evolución de la América Latina*, p. 279; Peterson, *Argentina and the U.S.*, p. 287.

[133] For official reports see *For. Rels., 1910*, pp. xiii, 13–18; *British and Foreign State Papers, 1913*, pp. 829 ff., 1158 ff. For British field officers' reports on the

results. Clearly, the meeting did not dare to face controversial issues.

Up to 1913 Lord Bryce felt that Pan-Americanism had made little progress under the Taft Administration. He felt that the terms "dagoes" and "gringos" characterized the real opinion the two respective peoples held of each other. Yet he admitted that even dollar diplomacy was "based on the desire to advance the cause of decent government as well as the commercial interests of the United States."[134]

At this point appeared the Wilson Administration. The Argentines were not too favorably impressed. *La Prensa* found the Wilson policy of nonrecognition of disorderly governments "essentially offensive," and gave no favorable notice to the Mobile speech. Mexico, as expressed in *La Nación*, found the new policy "bumbling and offensive."[135]

Against this background emerged the ABC Aliance. By 1910 rumors of such an accord were widespread. The pro-German press of Brazil cordially endorsed the suggestion as a move "put in practice by South American nations . . . [to] tear all the countries of that part of the continent from the economic dependence of the great trusts of the United States."[136] The *Quarterly Review* saw it as a countermove against United States hegemony.[137] In the United States the *Review of Reviews* commented that this move was "for common protection against the Yankees."[138] A further boost was provided when the ABC powers were accepted as mediators in the Mexican troubles of the Wilson Administration. But built into any association of these three powers was a fatal element of rivalry. Brazil had just ordered the world's largest battleship; Argentina was following suit, and Chile was determined not to be left behind. In addition, the long-established boundary and trade

---

Conference see Bryce to Grey, July 18, 1910, F.O. 371 (U.S.), 1910, Vol. 1020; and Townley to Grey, August 31, 1910, F.O. 371 (Argentina), 1910, Vol. 825.

For secondary accounts see Alejandro Álvarez, "The Monroe Doctrine at the Fourth Pan-American Conference," *The Annals*, XXXVII (May, 1911), 607 ff.; C. B. Casey, "Creation and Development of the Pan-American Union," *Hisp. Amer. Hist. Rev.*, XIII, No. 4 (November, 1933), 449–450; Allan Nevins, *Henry White*, pp. 309–310; Clemenceau, *South America To-Day*, pp. 66–67; Charles Evans Hughes, *Pan-American Peace Plans*, p. 22. The *New York Times* and the *Times* (London) gave regular coverage.

[134] Annual Report, May 16, 1913, F.O. 371 (U.S.), 1913, Vol. 1859.

[135] McGann, *Argentina and the U.S.*, p. 306.

[136] Haggard to Grey, April 12, 1910, F.O. 371 (Brazil), 1910, Vol. 832.

[137] *Quar. Rev.*, CCXIII, (February, 1913), 461–462.

[138] *Rev. of Revs*, XLVII (February, 1913), 151.

rivalries could not be conjured away by the distant menace of the northern republic.

At this point the Wilson-Bryan Administration launched its new program. It is difficult to tell how much of it was due to the rising pressures out of Europe and how much would have developed if conditions had remained peaceful. The impression received from the multiple contacts established is that there was a ground swell of activity. The contacts were too numerous and too varied to have arisen from the war pressures alone. The Bryan Peace Treaties (cooling-off treaties) made a distinct appeal.[139] The Pan-American Scientific Conferences (the first had met in 1908) were continued. In the period including 1915 and 1916 six Pan-American public and private sessions took place: the Panama-Pacific International Exposition; the Panama-California International Exposition; the First Pan-American Financial Conference; and the International Conference on Education; the Second Pan-American Scientific Congress, and the Christian Congress.[140]

The meeting of the Pan-American Financial Congress, originally scheduled to meet in Buenos Aires, was an outgrowth of the fourth general conference. Now it took on added significance because of the collapse of financing from the old banking centers. Latin America had long complained of United States lack of interest in the recodification of international law[141] but now it tended to forget irritation and to welcome any new port in the existing financial storm. It accordingly welcomed a call for a financial conference at Washington. Eighteen republics (Mexico not included) accepted invitations to send delegations to Washington on March 12, 1915, to consider emergency needs. Wilson greeted them, saying: "We are not ... trying to make use of each other, but we are trying to be of use to one another."[142]

More significant was the Pan-American Pact idea, which Wilson developed through House and later through Lansing. Secretary of State

[139] *For. Rels., 1915*, p. 35; Fletcher to House, July 23, 1915, House Papers, Yale.

[140] *For. Rels., 1915*, p. 1310; James Brown Scott, *Wilson's Foreign Policy*, pp. 159 ff.; Robertson, *Hispanic American Relations*, p. 403.

[141] Samuel Flagg Bemis, *The Latin American Policy of the United States*, pp. 226 ff.

[142] James Brown Scott, *Wilson's Foreign Policy*, p. 103. Also *For. Rels., 1915*, pp. 20 ff.; W. G. McAdoo. "International High Commission and Pan-American Cooperation," *Amer. Jour. Internat. Law*, XI, No. 4 (October, 1917), 772–773; Arthur Welles Dunn, "Pan-American Financial Conference," *Rev. of Revs.*, LI (June, 1915), 728 ff.

Bryan apparently vaguely approved of the suggestion but was too busy with his peace treaties to pay much attention. In his diary Colonel House clearly claims credit for originating this proposal but states that Wilson seized upon it eagerly.[143] It was first proposed to the ABC powers. After refinement the pact provided for a solemn covenant and agreement for the New World republics to join one another "in a common and mutual guarantee of territorial integrity and of political independence under republican forms of government"; for efforts to settle existing boundary disputes by submission to arbitration; and for a one-year cooling-off period to elapse between the arising of a dispute and recourse to war. During this interim, investigation by a commission might, if necessary, be supplemented by arbitration. On December 26, 1914, House wrote the President that he thought the pact negotiations should have more consideration even than existing European problems. On September 11, 1915, Wilson urged action on his Secretary of State, saying, "I regard it [the pact] as of the utmost importance." A month later House summarized negotiations up to that time, concluding his statement thus: "Of course you understand that one of the President's purpose is to broaden the Monroe Doctrine so that it may be upheld by all the American Republics instead of by the United States alone as now."[144] Marginal notes on a copy of this in the House Papers indicate that "one of" was eliminated in the copy sent to Lansing. Another marginal comment is that "I asked L. to eliminate this entire paragraph." In any case, the thinking of the policy makers of the day seems clear.

Wilson and House wished to get the endorsement of the ABC powers before approaching the smaller republics. Argentina supported the idea and Brazil gave its endorsement with some qualifications. Chile proved the stumblingblock. It remained fearful of any move to stimulate recourse to arbitration of disputes so long as the Tacna-Arica question

---

[143] House Papers (Yale), Diary entries for December 16 and 19, 1914, January 13, June 3, June 18, July 24, and December 15, 1915. Also for February 21, March 28 and 31, April 11, May 26, September 18, and December 28, 1916.

Valuable material on the pact is found in Seymour, *Intimate Papers of Colonel House*, I, 231 ff.; *The Lansing Papers*, II, 485 ff.; and Link, *Wilson: The New Freedom*, pp. 325–326.

[144] House to Secretary of State, October 15, 1915, *The Lansing Papers*, II, 488. For a more extended discussion of the pact see Callcott, *The Caribbean Policy, 1890–1920*, pp. 322 ff.

was unsolved. Later, in 1916, it was suggested that Canada be brought into the agreement. Accordingly a change in wording from "republican forms of government" to "existing forms of government" was introduced into the document.[145] To try to get the proposal off the ground, Ambassador Henry P. Fletcher was called from Chile to head the efforts. Fletcher was thought to be able to handle Chile if anyone could. Incidentally, the legations in all the ABC powers had recently been raised to embassies with appreciation expressed by all of them.

Just at this point, unfortunately, the exigencies of war generated serious controversies between the United States and Chile over excess profits in the nitrate trade; House was called on for service in Europe; Bryan had never been much interested in the pact; Fletcher did not have the prestige necessary to push the matter; Wilson became increasingly involved in European problems; and the pact idea grew stale. When Bryan resigned as Secretary of State, Lansing knew little of what had happened and the whole matter lapsed.[146] Given peace it might have developed, but under the circumstances, Wilson transferred his energies and enthusiasm to his newly conceived idea of a world-wide league of nations. In the famous Article X of the Covenant of the League reappeared the central idea of the pact. This provided an undertaking "to respect and preserve as against external agression the territorial integrity and existing political independence of all Members of the League."[147]

The West Coast of South America

United States relations with the west coast countries arose largely from developing conditions, rather than from calculated policy. The advance guard of American businessmen had appeared as successors of such sporadic early builders as William Wheelwright. Boliva was still so isolated that Britain neglected to maintain a regular representative at La Paz, asking the United States to care for its interests.[148] United States investments there and in Ecuador remained nominal. In Peru, however, new vanadium and other mines had swelled United States investments to some $63 million,[149] and in Chile they had advanced to

[145] House to Wilson, June 18, 1916, House Papers, Yale.
[146] Seymour, *Intimate Papers of Colonel House*, I, 231–232.
[147] Edward H. Buehrig, ed., *Wilson's Foreign Policy in Perspective*, p. 51.
[148] Moore, *Digest*, IV, 592; *For. Rels.*, *1902*, p. 102.
[149] *The U.S. and Latin American Relations* (Sen. Doc. 125, 86th Cong., 2d Sess.),

about $181 million. Henry Ford and others had realized the significance of vanadium, copper, nitrates, and other minerals of the region.

In all four of the west coast countries there was only one domestic situation that attracted attention outside of the continent—the intolerable hardships imposed on the Indian rubber gatherers in the Putamayo area of the Ecuadorian and Peruvian frontiers. The abuses were partly attributable to callousness and cupidity of local authorities, though certain foreign, especially British, interests were involved. Secretary Knox showed little interest when inquiries were made about possible United States efforts on behalf of the unfortunates. A British investigator, Sir Roger Casement, in January, 1911, submitted a scathing report on "tortures that baffle description" suffered by quasi slaves in the interior. American travelers confirmed his statements and the press began to call for action. Peru, meanwhile, tried to prevent outside inspection of the areas involved,[150] though the rising foreign protests seem to have brought some relief to the abused people.

Complicating the matter were the uncertain boundary lines through the jungles on the eastern slopes of the Andes. From 1904 onward the United States had periodically urged peaceful negotiation but to no avail. When in 1910 it offered to mediate, the President of Brazil commented to his Congress: "The initiation of this policy was due entirely to the United States of America, while Brazil and Argentina gladly accepted the invitation extended to them by the American Government to take joint and friendly action in the interests of peace." It was suggested that King Alfonso XIII of Spain act as arbitrator. He declined lest an award precipitate hostilities. Then it was proposed that the dispute be submitted to the Permanent Tribunal at The Hague. Ecuador declined the suggestion, saying its vital interests were involved because two-thirds of its national territory was in dispute.[151] Thus another problem was carried over to the future.

Efforts of United States philanthropy to improve sanitary conditions in Guayaquil, Iquitos, and other Ecuadorian ports were cordially en-

---

p. 296. Also Cleona Lewis and Karl T. Schlotterbeck, *America's Stake in International Investments*, p. 258.

[150] *For. Rels., 1910*, pp. 449 ff.; *1911*, pp. 29, 176; *1913*, pp. 521 ff., 1148 ff. Also Jerome to Grey, June 20, 1911, F.O. 135 (Colombia), 1911, Vol. 339; *Rev. of Revs.*, XLVI (September, 1912), 325 ff.; Robertson, *Hispanic American Relations*, pp. 368 ff.

[151] For peace efforts see *For Rels., 1904*, p. 683; *1910*, pp. 449 ff., 492 ff.

dorsed. A further good impression was made when the Wilson Administration removed two of its officials in Ecuador who were tainted with unfortunate business connections.[152] Then complications arose when a question of payment of some disputed railroad bonds held by the British was submitted to an arbitral board on which a United States citizen served. Disagreements ensued between the arbitrators. Britain prodded Washington, which did its best to reason with an obstreperous Ecuador. Slowly the air cleared somewhat.[153]

Another item involved the Galápagos Islands, off the coasts of Ecuador. Of little intrinsic value, they were significant outposts of the Panama Canal. Periodically strategists had cast jealous eyes on them. In 1899 Secretary Hay had sought a coaling station there, and in 1909 and 1911 rumors of German overtures were heard. Alvey A. Adee in 1906 apparently expressed the current official opinion in the words: "We don't want them ourselves and won't allow any European (or extra-American) power to acquire control of them."[154]

In 1908 Augusto B. Leguía was elected President of Peru. Overtures to secure a naval base and business contracts apparently met with his approval. However, by 1913 he had run his course and was overthrown. Minister H. Clay Howard was instructed to remain aloof from events but to use his influence to protect the life of the former President. The next year came another change in administrations. Wilson had enough complications in the Caribbean and in Mexico, so Bryan simply telegraphed that since the new junta was in "uncontested exercise of executive power," and since the people acquiesced, the United States minister was instructed to extend recognition to the provisional government.[155] It was difficult to apply too strictly the principles enunciated in Washington and Mobile in far-distant Peru.

With Chile relations had been essentially normal. The long-standing Alsop claim against Chile was at last settled. It dated back to 1876 and involved properties originally under the jurisdiction of Bolivia but

---

[152] *Ibid.*, *1908*, pp. 285–286; *1912*, pp. 429 ff., 1282 ff.; Notter, *Origins of the Foreign Policy of Wilson*, pp. 244–245; Ray Stannard, Baker, *Woodrow Wilson*, IV, 431–432.

[153] *For. Rels.*, *1913*, pp. 471 ff.; *1914*, p. 276; *1915*, pp. 344 ff.

[154] Quoted by J. Fred Rippy, *The Caribbean Danger Zone*, p. 131.

[155] *For. Rels.*, *1908*, pp. 684–685; *1913*, pp. 1142 ff.; *1914*, pp. 284, 1061 ff. Also Pringle, *Life and Times of Taft*, II, 679–680, for comment on naval base negotiations.

located in territory which was seized by Chile in the War of the Pacific. Finally, in 1909 the case was submitted to arbitration by the King of England. His award was handed down two years later in favor of the claimants.[156]

In Chile, however, the overriding problem of foreign relations was the Tacna-Arica dispute. When relations were ruptured between Peru and Chile in 1910 the United States was asked to represent Peru in the southern republic but it found Chilean feelings so bitter against Peru that such action was felt unwise. Fortunately relations remained cordial with the United States, which agreed to send a Coast Artillery officer to help train Chilean defence forces.[157]

No over-all policy for the west coast countries is obvious. Local factors were so varied that no one policy was applicable. Local fear of United States dominance was expressed from time to time and in 1911 representatives of Ecuador and Peru met with delegates from Venezuela and Colombia (the old Bolivarian countries) to condemn recent happenings in the Caribbean. Once more it was a British observer who summed up local feelings when he commented: "Divided by burning feuds, the Republics are one only in their dislike and fear of the United States, and even were this fear insistent enough to drive them into some form of union, it is hard to see that they would gain appreciably thereby."[158] As for the conference itself, a local newspaper, *El Tiempo* (promptly suppressed for *lèse-majesté*), aptly summed up its results thus: "0 plus 0000 equals 0."

---

[156] *For. Rels., 1910*, pp. 186 ff.; *British and Foreign State Papers*, CIV, 867. Also Henry Lake Wilson. *Diplomatic Episodes, in Mexico, Belgium and Chile*, pp. 103 ff.

[157] *For. Rels., 1913*, pp. 1188 ff., and in general pp. 1175–1224; *1912*, pp. 44–45; Pringle, *Life and Times of Taft*, II, 680.

[158] O'Reilly to Grey, March 15, 1911, F.O. 135 (Colombia), 1911, Vol. 339.

CHAPTER V

WAR AND PEACE, 1914–1920

The Canadian Position

WORLD WAR I CREATED new issues in the relations of the United States with Canada. Force of circumstances increased feelings of irritation at the same time it emphasized the closeness of the two countries. Replenishment of the Canadian population by immigration, especially from the Old Country, continued satisfactorily until the war broke out. Then immigration dropped alarmingly. At the same time, climate, industry, and good farm lands in the United States combined to drain Canada of its new citizens as soon as they had become acclimated to the New World. The number of these southward migrants remained at an alarming 100,000 or more per year until 1916. Though desperately needing occupants for its vacant lands, Canada had to face the fact that well over a million of its local-born citizens were residing south of the border.[1] Of course in some ways the migration did much to foster understanding and to lead the way to a convention signed on June 3, 1918, providing that males of either country resident in the other could serve

---

[1] For Canadian migration see F. H. Soward *et al.*, *Canada in World Affairs: The Pre-War Years*, pp. 9, 165–166 n; G. E. Jackson, "Emigration of Canadians to the United States," *The Annals*, CVII (May, 1923), 27; Hugh L. Keenleyside, *Canada and the United States*, pp. 306, 331.

in the military forces of either.[2] This arrangement satisfied local military obligations without resultant loss of citizenship.

When foreign shipping was curtailed during the war, Canadian trade southward rose to an estimated 69 per cent of total Canadian exports.[3] In addition, nearly all new Canadian stock and bond issues were floated in the United States. By 1923, it was estimated that approximately $2.5 billion of American money was invested north of the border. This figure included investments in some seven hundred branches of United States factories.[4] The dollar was replacing the pound on all sides. Once more the question of reciprocity arose. On March 25, 1919, a bill in the Dominion House of Commons on reciprocity was defeated by a party vote of 115 to 61[5]—but the ghost still walked.

Internationally, the position of Canada was changing. Heretofore Canadians had looked to Britain for defense—and by implication it was defense against the United States that was needed.[6] On the other hand, Taft commented that in case Canada were attacked the United States would be drawn into the contest.[7] Also the European war stimulated new thinking in the Dominion. One historian concludes that "Before 1919 there was no Canadian foreign policy in the accepted sense."[8] Yet, early in the war the home government asked Dominion leaders to help bring pressure on the United States in connection with embargo matters.[9] By December 1, 1918, Sir Robert L. Borden, Laurier's successor, recorded in his diary: "I am beginning to feel that in the end and perhaps sooner, Canada must assume full sovereignty."[10] In recognition of the changed conditions, a British order in council dated April

[2] *British and Foreign State Papers, 1917–1918,* pp. 573–574.

[3] Hugh G. J. Aitken *et al., The American Economic Impact on Canada,* p. 155.

[4] Harvey E. Fisk, "The Flow of Capital—Canada," *The Annals,* CVII (May, 1923), 175. Also O. D. Skelton, "Canadian Capital Requirements," *ibid.,* LXVIII (November, 1916), 221–222; John Bartlet Brebner, *The North Atlantic Triangle,* p. 238.

[5] Tariff Commission, *Reciprocity with Canada,* p. 88.

[6] G. P. de T. Glazebrook, *A History of Canadian External Relations,* pp. 256–257.

[7] Dexter Perkins, *Hands Off,* pp. 358–359.

[8] Glazebrook, *History of Canadian External Relations,* p. v.

[9] Gaddis Smith, "Canadian External Affairs in World War I," in Hugh L. Keenleyside *et al., The Growth of Canadian Policies in External Affairs,* p. 51.

[10] *Ibid.,* p. 57. Also Sir Robert Borden, "Imperial Conference," *International Affairs,* VI, No. 4 (July, 1927), 200 ff.

10, 1919, authorized the Dominion to send its own delegates to the Peace Conference at Versailles. Neither Wilson nor House was enthusiastic, but the Mother Country had agreed and Canadian pride rebelled at the idea that their delegates should occupy a lower position than that accorded "Liberia or Cuba, Panama or Hedjaz."[11]

War enthusiasm in the United States was met with mixed emotions in the Dominion. Canadian casualties were serious (about 105,000 out of 650,000 Canadians engaged in France), and the country's financial contribution in proportion to its wealth had been heavy indeed. Now the United States' assumption of spokesmanship for the West—to say nothing of its pretentions to moral leadership—aggravated sensitive Canadians. The boast "We won the war," they felt to be "slightly exaggerated."[12] Later a Canadian could remark philosophically on the "amusingly obvious" "national feminine attitude" of Canada to its southern neighbor, saying: "the Canadians have enjoyed United States [boasting and noisy vigor] much as a good wife enjoys the spectacle of a robust husband being himself."[13] This, however, was written in 1949. Feelings were not ready for philosophical and detached analysis in 1920.

An Emergency Program for Latin America

Before World War I only four colleges in the United States offered courses in Latin American history. The public had occasionally become excited about abused Cubans, revolutionary Mexico, or chaotic Haiti, but real understanding of the southern peoples was seldom encountered. Efforts were made to develop an American Institute of International Law, but progress had been slow and unimpressive.[14] More promising were substantial efforts to bring about settlement of international disputes by arbitration. Twenty-nine decisions against Hispanic-American

[11] Edgar W. McInnis, *The Unguarded Frontier*, p. 339. Also N. A. M. MacKenzie, "The Treaty Making Power in Canada," *Amer. Jour. Internat. Law*, XIX, No. 3 (July, 1925), 493–494. Even so, any idea of Canadian association with the British West Indies was looked at askance. See Sir Patrick Thomas McGrath, "Canada and the West Indies," *Rev. of Revs.*, LXII (July, 1920), 69–70.

[12] Keenleyside, *Canada and the U.S.*, pp. 346 ff.; Pierre Silbelleau, *Le Canada et la Doctrine de Monroe*, p. 154.

[13] Hugh MacLennan, "Psychology of Canadian Nationalism," *For. Affs.*, XXVII, No. 3 (April, 1949), 415.

[14] Address of Sumner Welles, January 17, 1935, in Department of State, *Inter-American Series*, No. 9, p. 11; Alejandro Álvarez in *Hisp. Amer. Hist. Rev.*, I, No. 3 (August, 1918), 334.

nations and in favor of the United States had been rendered for a total of slightly less than $18.5 million. In return, seven decisions against the United States had awarded those states about $3.5 million.[15]

A puzzled administration now had to adjust its paternalistic control of the New World to meet totally unexpected contingencies. It was one thing to patrol borders and coasts to give Mexicans time to find their own way to democracy. It was quite another matter to contemplate the possibility that a strategic center might fall into chaos and in turn open the way to establishment of a new submarine base so located as to threaten either the United States itself or the Panama Canal.

Fortunately official interest had exceeded and preceded that of the public. Just after the United States entered the war a group of scholars and experts, known as The Inquiry, was established to study needs and possibilities of world peace and conditions precedent thereto. It was generally understood that European and Far Eastern problems would dominate the considerations. Strangely, 246 of the reports (13 per cent) prepared by The Inquiry dealt with the Americas. These could be expected to include careful studies "of all South American boundary disputes," but actually they went much further. Even for far-distant Argentina, 20 out of 36 reports were devoted to economic topics. In fact, the Latin American Division of The Inquiry became "an essential research auxiliary of the State Department." One scholar concludes that "There is evidence to support the view that the Latin American project received the benefit of more extensive planning than did any other area considered by the Inquiry."[16]

Slowly the confused thinking of years began to clear. Critics had pointed out that on no less than twenty occasions United States marines had landed as interventionists in Latin America.[17] Panicky thinking culminated in such charges as those that the real objective of World War I was to enable Great Britain to victimize Belgium and France; and then to enable the United States to victimize Great Britain especially at the expense of Latin America. Critics were gravely concerned about events

[15] William Spence Robertson, *Hispanic American Relations with the United States*, p. 166. Also Charles Evans Hughes, *Our Relations to the Nations of the Western Hemisphere*, pp. 85–86.

[16] Lawrence E. Gelfand, *The Inquiry: American Preparations for Peace, 1917–1919*, p. 277.

[17] Bryce Wood, *The Making of the Good Neighbor Policy*, p. 5.

in the Caribbean and felt that Wilson's idealism had become confused by imperialism.[18] The scholar is given pause, however, when he notes that all of the interventions complained of took place in militarily strategic areas and the later ones occurred at the very time that special emphasis was being placed on a cooperative hemisphere program. The more logical conclusion would seem to be that there were two policies: an emergency one based on strategic needs, and a general policy that was aspired to and applied when possible.

The New World nations were developing fast. The simple *caudillo*-led revolt practically disappeared with World War I. Unfortunately this did not mean that local peoples had become satisfied. Instead, aroused peoples who were untrained in self-government clamored for economic and social rights while they insisted on political freedom. The result was bitter factionalism.[19]

No one expected twenty nations in Europe to follow identical policies with regard to any one foreign issue. Yet Lansing piously welcomed the Second Pan-American Scientific Congress in December 27, 1915, calling for "One for all; all for one." In addition Rear Admiral Colby N. Chester stated in 1914 that many Latin American nations were strong enough to share in the common defense of the continent.[20] But, did they want either to follow the motto of Lansing or to assume the obligations implied by Chester? An analysis shows that only eight of the Latin American countries (and seven of these were in the Caribbean) declared war on the Central Powers; five more (including Santo Domingo) broke relations with Germany; and seven remained neutral (including Mexico and El Salvador).[21] This variety of action demands consideration. No one single program out of Washington could meet all these types of thinking. A weary Woodrow Wilson on September 12, 1919, admitted: "I will confide to you in confidence that when I tried to define it [the Monroe Doctrine] I found that it escaped analysis." Obviously

---

[18] Manuel Ugarte, *El destino de un continente*, pp. 376–377; Gastón Nerval, *Autopsy of the Monroe Doctrine*, p. 281. Also Gerardo Falconi R., *Hispanoamérica para los Hispanoamericanos*, p. 166.

[19] Edwin Lieuwen, *Arms and Politics in Latin America*, pp. 30–31; John P. Humphrey, *The Inter-American System: A Canadian View*, pp. 73–74.

[20] Alejandro Álvarez, *The Monroe Doctrine*, p. 472; Colby N. Chester, "The Present Status of the Monroe Doctrine," *The Annals*, LIV (July, 1914), 24.

[21] Percy Alvin Martin, *Latin America and the War*, pp. 1–2.

projecting his past policy toward the future and attempting to reconcile the Monroe Doctrine and the League, he stated:

. . . the United States means to play big brother to the Western Hemisphere in any circumstances where it thinks it wise to play big brother. Therefore, inasmuch as you could not, or would not, define the Monroe Doctrine—at least I would not, because I do not know how much we may want to extend it—what more could you say than that nothing in the instrument [covenant of the League] shall impair the validity of the Monroe Doctrine?[22]

To amass trade statistics for the war period would be easy but relatively fruitless. They simply reflect the fact that since foreign competition was impossible hungry peoples bought and sold in the only market available. The totals, then, during the war period meant little more than would the score obtained by a basketball player calmly standing on the foul line and tossing balls into the basket without the distractions of nine other players on the court. In a single statement it may be said that United States exports to the rest of North America rose from approximately $529 million in 1914 to some $1,288 million in 1919. In the same period, exports to South America rose from less than $125 million to over $400 million. Imports from North America increased from about $427 million to over $1,052 million; and from South America from less than $223 million to over $568 million.[23]

After the middle of 1917 Wilson became immersed in world problems and lifted his sight for international cooperation from the Pan-American Pact to that of a global pact.[24] The Covenant of the League of Nations as originally drafted had a great appeal to Latin America as a whole. In addition, the sincerity of Wilson began to generate substantial respect. Indeed, it was an Argentine who admitted that the war had cost the United States far more than the profits it had derived therefrom—contrary to much Latin American publicity.[25] Such new friends were nonplussed when Wilson, after his interim visit to Washington during the Peace Conference, insisted on amending the Covenant by adding a guarantee of the Monroe Doctrine. This was not included in his original thinking but arose from the realities of domestic politics. When Sir

[22] Quoted by Philip Marshall Brown, "The Monroe Doctrine and the League of Nations," *Amer. Jour. Internat. Law*, XIV, No. 1 (January, 1920), 207.

[23] Simon Litman, "Foreign Trade of the United States since the Signing of the Armistice," *The Annals*, XCIV (March, 1921), 5.

[24] Arthur P. Whitaker, *The Western Hemisphere Idea*, p. 124.

[25] Roberto Kurtz, *La Argentina ante Estados Unidos*, pp. 215–216.

Robert Cecil was asked in Paris by a representative of *La Nación* (Buenos Aires) what he thought of the relation of the Monroe Doctrine to the new League of Nations, he proved too skillful a diplomat to disturb his colleague's (Wilson's) walk along the tight-rope of political expediency. He blandly responded that the doctrine had worked in practice and should be able to continue to do so; the League would naturally authorize New World nations to handle local matters and European nations would simply be in a position to protect themselves against unjust injury.[26]

Obviously, in the clamor of war the voices of Latin America were seldom heard. Yet the fact remained that their voices were growing in strength. And they were now asking with insistence that the apparent contradictions between war practices and announced policies be explained.

Now the story turns to wartime problems of specific areas.

Mexico

Following the Niagara Falls Conference the United States had recognized the *de facto* administration of Venustiano Carranza in October, 1915. Thereafter relations stumbled along until February 24, 1917, when Washington received word of the Zimmermann note. This was a proposal of Germany to tie down United States energies in a war with Mexico. Spoils of United States territory were to be made available to Mexico and to Japan if they would become allies of the Central Powers. To enquiries about the note the First Chief (Carranza) was "extremely cautious."[27] As late as October 20, 1917, a resolution of "benevolent neutrality toward the Entente nations" was defeated in secret session of the Mexican Senate by a vote of thirty-five to thirteen. And this was subsequent to repeated reports of German dabbling in Mexican affairs.[28]

[26] The *Times* (London), January 30, 1919, 10f.

[27] Alfred Zimmerman was German Secretary of State for Foreign Affairs. See Burton J. Hendrick, *The Life and Letters of Walter Hines Page*, III, 332 ff.; *For. Rels., 1917*, Sup. I, pp. 238–239; Barbara W. Tuchman, *The Zimmermann Telegram*. Most of the ensuing negotiations were handled by the experienced Henry P. Fletcher, who presented his credentials as ambassador on March 3, 1917 (*For. Rels., 1917*, p. 910).

[28] *Ibid.*, Sup. I, pp. 349, 392. Also *Investigation of Mexican Affairs* (Sen. Doc. 285, 66th Cong., 2d Sess.), pp. 2898 ff., 3212 ff.; Auchincloss to Secretary of State, June 4, 1918, Edward M. House Papers, Yale; *New York Times*, August 31, 1917, 11.3.

The anti-United States feelings had arisen from old fears that had been aggravated by the Veracruz occupation and the pursuit of the bandit Pancho Villa onto Mexican soil. Earlier Villa had been inclined to cooperate with the United States (see above, "Mexico," Chapter Four). However, his erratic conduct and questionable activities as cattle rustler and ore-train robber, together with his penchant for summary "justice" administered to his opponents and his amoral social conduct, all militated against him. At the same time he proved unable to command the continued confidence of Mexican leaders. Disappointed, he now made an effort to recoup his local popularity by assaulting American citizens in Mexico. When these activities brought meager results he crossed the border and attacked Columbus, New Mexico. Promptly, General J. J. Pershing was despatched with an expeditionary force on the "hot trail" across the border. The bandits scattered into the chaparral and scrub growth of the Mexican hills and deserts. Soon Carranza asked that the United States withdraw its forces. He, too, could send troops before whom the bandits would retire—and apparently the proud Yankee was accomplishing no more than that.

North of the Rio Grande a real clamor for war against Mexico arose. Why not clean up the Mexican chaos and acquire mineral-rich territory in the process?[29] Wilson steadfastly vetoed the suggestion, insisting that the only purpose of the expeditionary force was to suppress marauders. Whether Wilson's stand was because of his fear of possible war with Germany is uncertain, but slowly the clamor for intervention faded. There ensued painful negotiations with an obstreperous Mexican national government over the expedition itself and over additional border incidents involving casualties on both sides of the line. Now that the bandits were dispersed it was agreed the troops would withdraw. The last of them crossed the border on February 6, 1917.[30]

In Martín Luis Guzmán, *Memoirs of Pancho Villa*, Villa states that about January or February, 1915, a captain of a Japanese warship asked what his attitude would be "when our war with the United States breaks out." Villa asserts that he gave a categorical answer that the United States would have the full support of Mexico in such a case. See also, Tuchman, *The Zimmermann Telegram*, pp. 59, 159.

[29] James Morton Callahan, *American Foreign Policy in Mexican Relations*, pp. 564 ff.; Harley Notter, *The Origins of the Foreign Policy of Woodrow Wilson*, pp. 532 ff.

[30] For a renewed expression of annexationist sentiment see A. S. Burleson to Lansing, July 13, 1916, with enclosure, Robert Lansing Papers, LC.

For the Pershing expedition see *For. Rels., 1917*; Ray Stannard Baker, *Woodrow*

During the war Mexico found itself the producer of two raw materials greatly needed by its northern neighbor. One of these was henequen (a fiber used in the making of binder-twine and an essential both in United States grain fields and for cordage in general). The Yucatán growers of the fiber organized a monopoly control of the product, for they grew 75 per cent of the world's supply. They next raised the price of henequen from about a cent and a half to over nineteen cents a pound, and demanded a further increase to twenty-three cents. Diplomatic pressure on Carranza to remedy the situation merely aroused resentment. Interventionists again wanted to land troops, this time to control a price situation. The State Department responded that the result would be war that would cut off all the supply. Instead, the Food Administration managed to hold the price in the neighborhood of nineteen cents by a combination of diplomatic representations, the latent threat of military action, and pressures brought through application of clearance controls in United States ports to vessels engaged in the henequen trade.[31]

The other critically needed raw material was petroleum. In spite of political unrest south of the border actual petroleum production rose from approximately 26 million barrels in 1913 and 1914, to over 87 million barrels in 1919 and to 156 million barrels the next year.[32] But the First Chief was unable to police the lands adjacent to the oil fields. The companies were thus faced with a fantastic demand for their product at a time when they were in dire need of adequate police protection. Accordingly they employed a local bandit with a reputation for efficiency. His new duties were to protect the companies from whom he had recently been collecting tribute. The oil companies through Mr.

Wilson: Life and Letters, VI, 76; Edgar Eugene Robinson and Victor J. West, *The Foreign Policy of Woodrow Wilson*, pp. 313–314; Clarence C. Clendenen, *The United States and Pancho Villa*, pp. 230 ff. Arthur S. Link indicates that at one stage Wilson lost his nerve and was ready for war. Fortunately, Mexico made conciliatory gestures just in time. Strong public sentiment in the United States favored peace (*Wilson: Confusions and Crisis, 1915–1916*, pp. 310–316).

[31] For letters of Bryan to Silliman and Canada, February 24, 1915, and March 13, 1915, see William Jennings Bryan Papers, LC. For discussion see Benjamin H. Williams, *Economic Foreign Policy of the United States*, pp. 392–393; Thomas A. Bailey, *The Policy of the United States toward Neutrals, 1917–1918*, pp. 327 ff. For the feeling in Yucatán see Salvador Alvarado. *Mi actuación revolucionario en Yucatán*, pp. 90 ff.

[32] Guy Stevens, *Current Controversies with Mexico*, p. 280.

Chandler P. Anderson elicited the information that the State Department would not be averse to shipments of military supplies from the United States to the ex-bandit now protecting the oil fields, even though in the eyes of Mexico he was a bandit still.[33] The vital oil shipments continued.

Involved in the question of oil production were the provisions of the Mexican Constitution of 1917. Typical of the Mexican point of view was the statement that the Mexican Eagle Petroleum Company, organized in 1907 with a capital of thirty million pesos, between 1911 and 1920 earned net profits of 164,248,000 pesos, or five times the amount of the original capital.[34] *Ergo*, said the Mexican, such profits should go to the nation. The new constitution provided for national ownership of subsoil rights, though the document was to go into effect only after it had been "applied," either by an enforcing decree of the President or by legislation of the Congress. Now Carranza initiated a series of tax decrees. Britain, involved in war, agreed to be guided by United States action in the matter. The companies themselves placed their interests in the hands of Mr. James R. Garfield as spokesman.[35] He worked steadily with United States Ambassador Fletcher and, supported by the State Department, secured a *modus operandi* by the fall of 1918.[36] This agreement postponed complications for a few more years.

Another disconcerting incident arose from the efforts of Mexico to call a conference of neutrals in 1917. It was proposed that the neutrals should ask for a definition of war aims by each group of belligerents. Then, if the neutrals disapproved the expressed objectives of either group they would presumably apply trade restrictions to enforce their own views. Trade with the Central Powers was nonexistent, and that to Western Europe was severely curtailed already. Only that with the United States was especially vulnerable, so the call for the meeting could be interpreted in Washington only as a potentially hostile act.

[33] *For. Rels., 1917*, p. 1062; *1918*, pp. 688 ff.; Diary, March 10 and April 13, 1917, Chandler Parsons Anderson Papers, LC; *Investigation of Mexican Affairs*, pp. 289–290; George H. Blakeslee, ed., *Mexico and the Caribbean*, pp. 63–64.

[34] Paul Boracres, "Mexican Petroleum," in T. H. Reynolds, trans. and ed., *The Progress of Pan-Americanism*, pp. 262–263.

[35] Diary, May 16, 1918, states: "We now represent fifty million of the fifty-five million [barrel] production of last year" (James R. Garfield Papers, LC, Box 110).

[36] Frederick Sherwood Dunn, *The Diplomatic Protection of Americans in Mexico* p. 340; Blakeslee, *Mexico and the Caribbean*, pp. 60–61; Diary, November 7, 1918, Anderson Papers, LC; *For. Rels., 1918*, pp. 771–772.

On February 12, 1917, President Carranza made his proposal. Tentative arrangements were for the conference to assemble in Buenos Aires; the question, therefore, is discussed further in connection with that country[37] (see below, "South America—The East Coast," this chapter). Here it is sufficient to say that the move fell into the pattern of quasi hostility that characterized Mexican official conduct throughout the war.

Just before Carranza completed his presidential term in 1920, he selected as his successor a man whom people felt to be little more than a puppet. Mexico wanted none of this. It had suffered too much from *continuismo* of administrations. At the same time friction with Washington revived and interventionists again became vocal. The oil companies were alarmed and bankers wanted action. Once more began the old round of arms embargoes and controls while the Wilson Administration centered its attention on world problems and was most reluctant to be involved in new complications next door. Finally, on April 20, 1920, Álvaro Obregón rose in rebellion, denouncing Carranza for not allowing fair and free elections. The Carranza house of cards collapsed. The First Chief himself sought to flee but was shot on his way to Veracruz.[38]

Obregón was evidently the strong man of the day, but the Wilson Administration, itself facing quadrennial elections, delayed action on Mexico. After the Democratic defeat in November the question of recognition was left to the Republicans under President Warren Gamaliel Harding.[39] Thus at the cost of much worry and the loss of substantial properties, not to mention prestige, Wilson had avoided in Mexican relations the more serious acts connoted by the ugly words "intervention" and "war." Indeed, though even Wilson himself could hardly have hoped that such would be the case, a pattern of nonintervention had been set for the future.

The Strategic Center in War Time

Relations with Panama naturally became closer and controls became

---

[37] *For. Rels., 1917*, Sup. I, pp. 308, 367 ff.; Martin, *Latin America and the War*, pp. 255 ff., 532.

[38] *For. Rels., 1918*, pp. 548 ff., 806 ff.; *1919*, II, 551 ff., 633 ff., and III, 234 ff. Also see *Investigation of Mexican Affairs*, pp. 189–190, 333, for propaganda in the United States; Pratt, "Robert Lansing," in Samuel Flagg Bemis, ed., *Amer. Secs. of St.*, X, 169; J. Fred Rippy, *The United States and Mexico*, pp. 359 ff.

[39] *For. Rels., 1920*, III, 180 ff.; Callahan, *American Policy in Mexican Relations*, p. 582.

more rigid during the war. Highway construction was watched carefully by the War Department and railway construction was supervised while wireless communications were controlled under a Panamanian decree of April 29, 1914. Detailed regulations were issued for the neutrality of the Canal itself and preparations were made in earnest for defense of the transit. Defense, in turn, involved new land acquisitions adjacent to the Canal strip and even of part of Taboga Island.[40]

Now arose the question of defense in a broader sense. Roland G. Usher, a popular writer on imperial expansion, stated that the maintenance of the Canal would demand "at least a protectorate over the States immediately around the Canal" including land approaches through Mexico and Central America, and control of strategic defense of the Bahamas, the Bermudas, the Windward Islands, and Jamaica. He admitted that a protectorate would practically annihilate sovereignty in the neighboring states.[41]

Just as the Taft Administration had left office, an incident of the kind anticipated by Usher caused some excitement. Senator Henry Cabot Lodge, possibly to stimulate support for a naval building program, reacted to rumors that Japanese interests were seeking control of Magdalena Bay on the coast of Lower California. He introduced a resolution in the Senate which became known as the Lodge Corollary of the Monroe Doctrine. Approved by a vote of fifty-one to four, it provided that any harbor or other place in the American continents whose occupation for military or naval purposes might threaten the communications or safety of the country, when occupied by a country not American, would be viewed by the United States as a matter of grave concern. Japan quickly sent assurances that it had no interest in the area and the matter was dropped. Popular support for the resolution, however, was widespread. Again, as late as March, 1919, Senator Phelan of California repeated the old threat of Japanese acquisition of territory in Lower California.[42]

Closely akin to this agitation was the feeling reflected in the Bryan-

---

[40] *For. Rels., 1916*, pp. 1–2, 942–943; *1917*, pp. 1180 ff.; *British and Foreign State Papers* (1914), CVIII, Pt. 2, pp. 834–835, and III, 926 ff.; *Department of State Bulletin*, X, No. 240 (January 29, 1944), 128.

[41] Roland G. Usher, *The Challenge of the Future*, pp. 38–39.

[42] T. A. Bailey, "The Lodge Corollary and the Monroe Doctrine," *Pol. Sc. Quar.*, XLVIII, No. 2 (June, 1933); H. F. Wright, "Philander Chase Knox," in Bemis, *Amer. Secs. of St.*, IX, 340–341.

Chamorro Treaty, which ceded rights to a naval base in Fonseca Bay. Protests[43] of neighboring states to the Central American Peace Court were brushed aside as the United States stood on its treaty rights. The action sounded the death knell for the court which had been instituted in 1907 for an initial period of ten years, but to foreign countries it meant that a potential enemy had been frozen out of another strategic point.[44]

Close supervision of Nicaragua continued without any particular change in practices or policies.

Guatemala found that Secretary of State Lansing was willing to use personal pressure to force it to declare war on the Central Powers. Its minister was told that ships for transport of its vital banana trade would be available only to countries that had entered the war.[45] The little country responded as expected and even placed the extensive German holdings in Guatemala under an enemy-property custodian who was a United States citizen approved by Washington. When the war was over Lansing saw to it that American citizens had ample opportunity to bid on the ex-German properties now offered for sale at bargain prices— though probably Woodrow Wilson knew little or nothing about this.[46]

At the close of the war unrest increased in Guatemala in connection with the termination of dictator Estrada Cabrera's control. Through 1919 Washington vainly urged the dictator to practice the principles of democracy. Finally in the spring of 1920 a conference on board a United States warship decided that a change was essential.[47] Constitutional forms were reasonably observed and Estrada Cabrera retired to obscurity.

El Salvador, picqued by the Fonseca Bay affair and not in need of financial assistance, maintained a benevolent neutrality but only that. When the Peace Conference at Versailles agreed to the amendment to the Covenant guaranteeing the Monroe Doctrine, El Salvador persistently tried to secure a definition of "the authentic idea" of that doctrine. The formal answer was a reference to Wilson's address to the

---

[43] *For. Rels., 1916*, pp. 811 ff. See also the Anderson Papers, LC, Dairy, October 15 and 17, 1917, on the uselessness of the Central American Peace Court.

[44] *For. Rels., 1917*, pp. 30 ff.

[45] Aro Sanso, *Policarpo Bonilla*, pp. 409 ff.

[46] *For. Rels., 1918*, Sup. II, pp. 365 ff.; *1919*, II, 288 ff.; *1920*, pp. 757–758.

[47] *Ibid., 1919*, II, 263 ff.; *1920*, II, 744 ff.

Second Pan-American Scientific Conference. This answer El Salvador considered a "run-around."[48]

It was in Costa Rica, however, that the most interesting situation developed, representing a definite clash between the idealism of Wilson, who had declared that his administration would not recognize New World governments acquiring power by treachery or violence and "practical" policy. On May 23, 1917, Secretary Lansing frankly admitted to the President that the new Federico A. Tinoco government in Costa Rica was founded on "unprincipled revolution." Still it evidently wished to cooperate with Washington in the war while the ousted administration had been openly accused of being pro-German. Therefore, from the standpoint of expediency, "it would seem as if the recognition of Tinoco, was . . . probably the better policy." London and Paris lent their support. Wilson was convinced that such advice ran counter to a matter of principle.[49] To make matters worse, Tinoco was probably supported by foreign financial interests—and Wilson had little sympathy for such. Accordingly the instructions went out: "No recognition," not even if the new regime did have popular support. Now pro-allied revolutionaries proposed to overthrow Tinoco, but again the consistent answer was "No revolution." This stalemate continued until finally Joaquín Tinoco was assasinated and his brother Federico fled to Kingston, Jamaica, on August 12, 1919. The chapter was closed and in due course a new group held elections and received the coveted recognition. Wilson's stubborn attitude reminds the reader of the comment of J. M. Keynes on the President: "It was harder to de-bamboozle this old Presbyterian than to bamboozle him."[50]

[48] *Ibid.*, *1917*, Sup. I, p. 251; *1920*, I, 223; Sanso, *Policarpo Bonilla*, p. 522.

[49] Lansing to Wilson, May 23, 1917, *The Lansing Papers*, II, 519–520. The story of the Tinocos is found in *For. Rels.*, *1917*, pp. 301 ff., and Sup. I, p. 274; *1918*, pp. 230, 270; *1919*, I, 810 ff. See also the Anderson Papers, LC, Dairy, February 15 and April 6, 1917; Wilson to Ransdell, March 5, 1918, Woodrow Wilson Papers, LC; Dana G. Munro, *Intervention and Dollar Diplomacy*, pp. 429–430; Theodore Paul Wright, Jr., *American Support of Free Elections Abroad*, pp. 97 ff.

[50] An item of minor but significant interest appeared in the periodic reports of petroleum deposits and of activities by British oil companies in Costa Rica (*For. Pol. Assn. Reports*, VII, No. 9 (July 8, 1931), 179 ff.; Parker Thomas Moon, *Imperialism and World Politics*, pp. 428–429; *For. Rels.*, *1919*, I, 872 ff.). The involved Amory concession was granted by Tinoco in 1918 to a company purported to be American but suspected of being British (Munro, *Intervention and Dollar*

More or less systematic attempts were also made to moderate feelings and to secure settlement of the numerous boundary disputes that plagued the area. The precedent of forcing Panama to accept the White award[51] had good effects. A dispute between Honduras and Nicaragua was carefully watched and good offices were offered in 1918. But as late as 1940 the quarrel continued.[52] Good offices were also offered in the Guatemala-Honduras dispute, and relief was felt only when the King of Spain handed down an award that settled the line between Honduras and British Honduras.[53] As any one of these issues threatened to become acute, the role of the United States was composed of a mixture of cajolery and pleading to try to keep the peace. The injunctions became an odd mixture of "Be good—or else," and "Be good—please."[54]

One noteworthy procedure was consistently employed by the Wilson Administrations throughout Central America. This was the sending of financial advisers, said to have been patterned largely on the British system used with the independent princes of India. By these arrangements a United States citizen, with the approval of the State Department, was to be appointed with salary paid by the local government of a small country. He could be dismissed at will and had no administrative power and no legislative functions. He was simply to advise on the budget and on expenditures and finances in general. That the system was considered effective is seen from the fact that such advisers were sent to Panama, Nicaragua, Guatemala, and Honduras.[55]

The Caribbean Islands—The Land Screen

Florida, Cuba, Haiti, Santo Domingo, Puerto Rico, and the Danish West Indies—these were located in an arc north and east of the Canal and stood guard over the trade routes approaching it. Florida and Puerto Rico as United States territory gave no concern, but the inde-

---

Diplomacy, pp. 438, 445; Woodrow Llewellyn, "A British View . . .," in Edward H. Buehrig, ed., *Wilson's Foreign Policy in Perspective*, p. 147.

[51] *For. Rels., 1914*, pp. 994, 999; *1915*, p. 1147.

[52] *Ibid., 1918*, pp. 23 ff.; *1919*, I, 119 ff.; *1940*, V, 444 ff.

[53] *Ibid., 1917*, pp. 765 ff.; *1919*, I, 95 ff.; *British and Foreign State Papers, 1925*, Pt. I, pp. 784 ff.

[54] *For. Rels., 1920*, II, 855 ff., and III, 732 ff.

[55] See *For. Rels.* for advisers: in Panama, *1919*, pp. 679 ff.; in Nicaragua, *1917*, p. 1098; in Honduras, *1920*, pp. 872 ff.; in Guatemala, *ibid., 1919*, II, 276 ff.

pendent countries were a different matter. William E. González, scion of a Cuban patriot family of the 1850's, was the able American minister sent to Cuba. As soon as Wilson was convinced that a Cuban declaration of war would not precipitate German attack on the island, the minister passed on the word. Forthwith both houses of the Congress unanimously authorized the Cuban President to declare war on Germany.[56] Very soon disorders developed in the sugar-growing districts. This could be a serious situation. President Mario García Menocal worked smoothly with González and new arrangements were soon completed. Marines were dispatched on Cuban invitation for training for war purposes in the kindly climate of a war partner. The rebellion soon dissipated.[57]

Meanwhile, uncontrolled prosperity cursed the island. Foreign trade skyrocketed from $305 million in 1913 to over $1,351 million in 1920. Of these totals exports rose from $165 million to $794 million. The price of sugar delivered in New York by 1920 gyrated from $9\frac{1}{8}\phi$ per pound on February 18, 1920 to $22\frac{1}{2}\phi$ on May 19, and then collapsed below 4ϕ in mid-December.[58]

Gross election frauds had been revealed in 1918 but the matter had been kept quiet. Now with the financial collapse and a general atmosphere of panic came political unrest. But, as in Mexico, the Wilson Administration did not want to intervene in 1920. Instead it sent General E. H. Crowder as a special representative to engage in what has become known as preventive intervention.[59] His effort was to reorganize the budget, re-establish confidence and credit, and get the island back on its financial feet. The work was so well done that the incoming Republican administration in Washington kept Crowder on the job and confirmed his procedures.

Immediately to the east of Cuba lay Haiti-Santo Domingo. The protectorate established in the Dominican Republic was administered by the ineffective Bryan appointees starting in 1913. Revolts broke out and

[56] *The Lansing Papers*, I, 594 ff.; *For. Rels., 1917*, Sup. I, pp. 221–222, 246.

[57] *For. Rels., 1917*, pp. 354 ff.; William E. González, "Concerning Dollar Diplomacy . . .," pp. 27 ff.; J. L. Meyer, "The United States and the Cuban Revolt of 1917." *Hisp. Amer. Hist. Rev.*, X, No. 2 (May, 1930), 159 ff.; Milton Offutt, *The Protection of Citizens Abroad . . .*, pp. 134 ff.

[58] Raymond Leslie Buell *et al.*, *Problems of the New Cuba*, pp. 44, 49; Leland H. Jenks, *Our Cuban Colony: A Study in Sugar*, pp. 218–219.

[59] *For. Rels., 1919*, II, 3 ff., 43 ff.; 79 ff.; *1920*, II, 41–43; Harry F. Guggenheim, *The United States and Cuba*, p. 213; Russell H. Fitzgibbon, *Cuba and the United States, 1900–1935*, pp. 168 ff.

Bryan had become seriously concerned by March, 1915. Such disorders had always invited intervention but the dangers inherent in the world situation gave less time than usual for consideration. In May, 1916, marines were landed and on June 20, Admiral W. B. Caperton announced that he would remain until the revolution was stamped out. When conditions continued to deteriorate, Lansing advised the President that essential governmental control should be vested in the United States authorities. Wilson, now awake to the alarming situation (he had apparently been preoccupied with the European complications), "with the deepest reluctance" acquiesced on November 26, 1916.[60] On the twenty-ninth Captain H. S. Knapp formally proclaimed military occupation of the republic. This essentially stabilized conditions for the war period, but obviously Washington had little in the way of a carefully planned policy in the matter. It was fighting a world war and was playing this "by ear." Blunders and mistakes appear to have been made by inexperienced administrators and Dominican reaction was understandably resentful. Hindsight indicates that many of the blunders arose from the fact that Santo Domingo tended to fall between the two stools of the State Department and military administrations.[61] Neither knew just what to do or what the other was attempting at a time when both were preoccupied with more important matters.

At the close of the war the old Wilsonian idealism again reasserted itself. The President had never liked military government and on December 23, 1920, he abruptly announced that the United States was ready to withdraw its troops from Santo Domingo, allowing scant time indeed to make adequate plans for the transfer.[62] Whether the sudden announcement was one of the vagaries of a sick man, or whether it would have been undertaken regardless of the President's health and was simply in line with his passion for self-government, may long be debated. The stark narrative of facts can be listed thus: In time of war the country was occupied; and when hostilities ceased in Europe orders were issued to discontinue the occupation.

[60] Sumner Welles, *Naboth's Vineyard*, II, 792. Also *ibid.*, pp. 771 ff.; *For. Rels., 1915*, pp. 279 ff.; *1916*, pp. 231 ff.

[61] *For. Rels., 1916*, p. 247; Welles, *Naboth's Vineyard*, II, 827; Carl Kelsey, "American Intervention in Haiti and Santo Domingo," *The Annals*, C (March, 1922), 178 ff.

[62] Kelsey, "American Intervention," *The Annals*, C (March, 1922), 192; *For. Rels., 1920*, II, 145 ff.

Conditions in the neighboring country of Haiti were even more lamentable. Back in the days of dollar diplomacy Root had declined to take action in Haiti and thus add "a black pearl" to his "crown of glory." Even in peace time political conditions had been tragic. In the twenty years from 1896 to 1915 nine presidents had served the so-called republic—and every one of them had been either overthrown or killed in office.[63] And such a situation could be peculiarly dangerous in time of war, when Germany was eagerly seeking submarine bases.[64] Lansing especially feared German penetration. As early as January, 1914, a report reached Washington that the Haitian President had taken refuge on a German vessel and that landing of a German legation guard was imminent. Amid the disorders financial interests were clamoring for protection and bankers sought to have their reserves removed to safety.[65] Bryan tried to keep Wilson informed of conditions but a distrait President paid him scant attention. Later Lansing was to state that the aims of the intervention were: 1) to terminate the appalling conditions of anarchy and savagery, and 2) to forestall any foreign effort to seize the customs control or a coaling station.[66]

After removal of the gold reserves (see above, "The Islands," Chapter Four) conditions rapidly deteriorated. France and the United States landed marines to try to stabilize conditions. Then occurred a peculiarly heinous episode, even for chaotic Haiti. In July, 1915, the government collapsed completely. The President, Vilbrun Gillaume Sam, who in his last days was attempting to rule by terrorization, was seized in the French legation to which he had fled. Thereupon he was torn to pieces by the mob and portions of his body paraded around the capital.[67] What might have been done under peacetime conditions is a matter for speculation. In time of war there was little hesitation. Wilson expressed it: "I suppose there is nothing for it but to take the bull by the horns

[63] For a list of these men and their fates see *For. Rels., 1916,* p. 311.

[64] *For. Rels., 1914,* pp. 334 ff.

[65] James W. Angell, *Financial Foreign Policy of the United States,* pp. 25–26; Douglas, "The American Occupation of Haiti," *Pol. Sc. Quar.,* XLII, No. 2 (June, 1927), 236–238.

[66] A six-page report of Bryan to Wilson, April 2, 1914 is found in the Bryan Papers, LC. See also *The Lansing Papers,* II, 526; and Lansing to McCormick, May 4, 1922, in *Inquiry into the Occupation and Administration of Haiti and the Dominican Republic* . . . (Sen. Report No. 794, 67th Cong., 2d Sess.), p. 37.

[67] *For. Rels., 1915,* p. 475.

and restore order."[68] Admiral W. B. Caperton was instructed to take charge of the administration of both government and finances. He announced that no revolutionary activity of any kind would be "tolerated."[69] Another country was occupied.

In the pacification of the Haitian countryside, casualties occurred as follows: 212 for 1915, 50 for 1916, and 2 for 1917.[70] Unfortunately, either the occupying forces became stale or a people accustomed to relatively free marauding returned to their old ways at this point. Trouble arose over the *corvée*, or roadwork, required of the natives, and soon the vicious Caco rebellion broke out. Casualties in 1919 rose to 1,861, then declined to 90 the next year as the marines repacified the country. Recriminations as to the conduct of the marines were apparently due to the action of only a small number of the troops who were located in a restricted area. In fact, most of the occupation forces were praised by investigators for effective service. Discussions of the internal administration of education, finances, and the like for the nation of upwards of 2,500,000 are beside the question here. Essential peace was restored and exports rose rapidly.[71] There is reason to think that in the press of world events Wilson knew little of what was happening.[72] Abuses were probably traceable largely to the lack of experience of the "colonial" administrators and to a rapid and constant turnover of administrative officials.[73] From the "practical" standpoint, this was war time and, strategically speaking, another vital link in the land screen was under control. The Caco revolt in particular gave the Republican party ammunition in the election of 1920, but the question of what long-range policy was to be followed remained to be solved.

East of Santo Domingo lay United States-owned Puerto Rico; then off to the southeast were the Danish West Indies. The Civil War had

[68] Link, *Wilson: The Struggle for Neutrality*, p. 536.

[69] On Caperton in Haiti see *For. Rels., 1915*, p. 522. Also *Inquiry into the Occupation and Administration of Haiti and Santo Domingo* (Hearings before select committee, 67th Cong., 1st and 2d Sess.), I, 327 ff.; *Inquiry into Haiti and Dominican Republic*, p. 7.

[70] *Report of the Secretary of the Navy, 1920.* p. 178.

[71] The essential facts of the occupation are revealed in *Inquiry into Haiti and Santo Domingo*. Good secondary accounts are those of Kelsey, "American Intervention," *The Annals*, C (March, 1922), and Arthur C. Millspaugh, *Haiti under American Control, 1915–1930*. See also *Inquiry into Haiti and Dominican Republic*.

[72] *Inquiry into Haiti and Santo Domingo*, I, 128.

[73] Harold Palmer Davis, *Black Democracy*, p. 236.

revealed the strategic value of the Danish islands and their importance had been underlined by periodic subsequent efforts of the United States to acquire them. The popular writer T. Lathrop Stoddard referred to St. Thomas as the Gibraltar of America. With the German advance in Western Europe, it became evident that Denmark might be occupied at any time. In such a case the islands might easily fall into German hands and become a serious danger. Rumors of this possibility were current in Washington.[74] These, in turn, generated the suggestion that the United States might occupy the islands. When the Danish minister raised the question with Lansing, the Secretary responded frankly that preventive occupation was a possibility. With Wilson's approval Lansing and the Dane proceeded with arrangements for a transfer of the islands by means of a sale. A treaty of cession was signed on August 4, 1916; Senate approval followed and ratifications were exchanged on January 17, 1917. For $25 million the United States had forestalled (as in the case of Magdalena Bay and Fonseca Bay) a potential enemy base. This time, however, it was at the expense of assuming an economic liability. By 1919 an annual islands' deficit in governmental expenses had to be made good by the United States.[75] The population declined steadily. In 1835 the islands had boasted 43,178 inhabitants. By 1911 the figure was down to 27,086; in 1917 it had declined another thousand; and in spite of the prosperity of the 1920's only 22,012 people could be counted in 1930.[76] "Uncle Sam's poor house" the islands were called. But the acquisition completed the land screen in front of the Panama Canal.[77]

With some justification the Caribbean could be described as an American lake.

[74] T. Lathrop Stoddard, "The Danish West Indies . . .," *Rev. of Revs.*, LIV (September, 1916), 292. See *For. Rels., 1917*, pp. 457, 516 ff., and the *Times* (London), February 15, 1916, 8d.

[75] A good account of the acquisition is found in Charles Callan Tansill, *The Purchase of the Danish West Indies*, while *The Lansing Papers*, II, 501 ff., gives much information on the negotiations. See also *Report of the Secretary of the Navy, 1919*. p. 140.

[76] L. H. Evans, "Unrest in the Virgin Islands," *For. Pol. Assn. Reports*, XI, No. 2 (March 27, 1935), 15.

[77] Chester Lloyd Jones, *Caribbean Interests of the United States*, pp. 274–275; Oswald Garrison Villard, "Rights of Small Nations in America," *The Annals* LXXII (July, 1917), 165 ff.; Blakeslee, *Mexico and the Caribbean*, pp. 322 ff.; L. S. Rowe, "Scope and Limits of our Obligations." *The Annals*, LIV (July, 1914), 220 ff.; Usher, *The Challenge of the Future*, pp. 291 ff.

South America—The North Coast

The territory farther south, too, was coming into the picture with increasing frequency, and with increasing emphasis. Occasional rumors of German activity in Colombia seem to have given Wilson little concern, though the United States, prodded by Britain, did use its good offices to persuade Bogotá to remove German employees from a Cartagena radio station.[78] The treaty of April 6, 1914, for reopening relations after the Panama affair left the Colombian administration in a cooperative frame of mind toward Washington. True, misgivings arose when the treaty was not ratified, and some newspaper propaganda critical of the United States appeared. Even so the Colombian response to the proposed Conference of Neutrals was a prompt rejection. Thus matters rocked along to the end of the war.[79]

By that time a new element had been added. Substantial deposits of petroleum had been discovered in Colombia. Bogotá first suspended action on applications for exploration rights and then in December, 1919, authorized private concessions in preference to nationalization of oil deposits.[80] But now it appeared that applications of United States companies for concessions would be rejected so long as the international treaty was unratified. The State Department made it clear that it would not attempt "to force concessions for American nationals" in return for treaty approval,[81] but Colombia knew that it now had a potent weapon in its hands. Yet, even though Colombia was maneuvering to secure approval of a treaty that tacitly recognized the independence of Panama, it carefully specified when it adhered to the League of Nations that acceptance of Article X of the pact did not "imply on the part of Colombia the recognition of Panama as an independent nation."[82]

In Venezuela General Juan Vicente Gómez bestrode the country with an absolute dictatorship. Foreign capital had been favored but the dictator found the German system more congenial to his nature than that

[78] *The Lansing Papers*, II, 514–515; Martin, *Latin America and the War*, pp. 413 ff.

[79] Martin, *Latin America and the War*, pp. 424 ff.; *For. Rels.*, *1919*, I, 724 ff.; I. J. Cox, "Yankee Imperialism," *Hisp. Amer. Hist. Rev.*, IV, No. 2 (May, 1921), 264 ff.

[80] *For. Rels.*, *1919*, I, 763 ff.; *1920*, I, 826–827.

[81] *Ibid.*, *1920*, I, 824.

[82] *Ibid.*, p. 825.

of the United States.[83] Throughout the war Venezuela remained strictly neutral while the dictatorship waxed fat on war profits. One communication of Wilson to Secretary Lansing is illuminating. On February 16, 1918, he wrote: "I have read this Memorandum with the greatest concern, as I have also the many recent communcations from our Minister in Venezuela. This scoundral [Gómez] ought to be put out. Can you think of any way in which we can do it that would not upset the peace of Latin America more than letting him alone will?"[84] Wilson did not want a repetition, this time on an inaccessible plateau on the far side of the Caribbean, of the situation which had given so much trouble in near-by Mexico.

South America—The East Coast

The four east coast countries (Brazil, Argentina, Uruguay, and Paraguay) felt the impact of World War I with peculiar intensity. Brazil declared war on the Central Powers; Uruguay severed relations with them; and Argentina and Paraguay remained neutral. The effects of the war were first apparent in trade relations with the old markets in Germany, Great Britain, and France. Strangely Spanish trade was of minor significance and even the "romantic" appeal of Spanish culture was admitted to have little influence in stimulating it.[85] More significant was the substantial pro-Italian sentiment that was especially evident in the large Italian population of Argentina. The anti-Yankee propagandists, such as Blanco Fombona, Carlos Pereya, and Manuel Ugarte continued to shout their accusations against the northern colossus, but detached observers were increasingly inclined to make certain distinctions. They conceded that few of the northern republics, including Mexico and those in Central America, had more than nominal independence but agreed that "no policy of this sort was possible to the United States in South America."[86]

Further, with the possible exception of the formation of a locally autonomous German state in south Brazil, there was little actual fear of

[83] Martin, *Latin America and the War*, pp. 462–463. See also Cleona Lewis and Karl T. Schlotterbeck, *America's Stake in International Investments*, pp. 223 ff.

[84] Quoted by Baker, *Wilson: Life and Letters*, VII, 550.

[85] J. Fred Rippy, "Pan-Hispanic Propaganda . . .," *Pol. Sc. Quar.*, XXXVII, No. 3 (September, 1922), 398 ff.; *Rev. of Revs.*, LXIV (September, 1921), 331.

[86] *Survey of Int. Affs.*, 1925, II, 401. Also Clarence H. Haring, *South America Looks at the United States*, pp. 156 ff.

aggression on the South American continent. As a result, discussions and inclinations were largely based on: 1) racial ties and cultural sympathies; 2) trade contacts with Great Britain versus Germany, and 3) some rising fear of the power of the United States versus the now surprising value of trade with the northern republic.

As early as 1918 both Britain and Germany were actively looking to the future. Britain sent an able trade mission that summer headed by Sir Maurice de Bunsen to strengthen its trade fences. And in Parliament the Undersecretary for Foreign Affairs answered a question about United States film and periodical propaganda in Argentina by saying that the situation was being watched with an eye to the use of proper British counterpropaganda.[87] Even before this, in November, 1916, Germany organized a special institute to promote postwar trade. It included publication of periodicals such as *El Heraldo de Hamburg* and *La Cultura Latino-Americano* to further its cause.[88]

Meanwhile the rising tide of trade with the United States was supported by a new merchant marine that commanded respect. Tonnage available for foreign trade rose from 783,000 tons in 1910 to 1,863,000 in 1915 and to over 9,900,000 tons in 1920.[89] Propaganda support in the form of substantial news despatches came from the Associated Press. On January 1, 1919, the AP initiated cable despatches to two newspapers in Buenos Aires, four in Lima, two in Chile, three in Panama, and one in Ecuador. By the end of March two outlets were opened in Rio de Janeiro and contacts with Uruguay were planned.[90]

On April 7, 1917, the United States declared war on Germany. Four days later President Wenceslau Braz of Brazil severed diplomatic relations with Germany and left it to his Congress to take the next step. Soon, on the advice of President Wilson, Brazil took over German vessels interned in Brazilian ports to carry local products to market at a time when foreign cargo vessels were largely unavailable. Other steps

[87] For the Bunsen mission see "Correspondence of . . . British Mission to South America," *Accounts and Papers*, LIII (1919), and the *Times* (London), May 10, 6a; May 16, 5e; June 5, 5a; and September 10, 1918, 5b. For the *Times'* view of United States competition see issues for November 22, 1918, 7a, and February 21, 1919, 15b.

[88] Lewis Melville, "German Propagandist Societies," *Quar. Rev.*, CCXXX, No. 456 (July, 1918), 83 ff.

[89] Treasury Department, *Statistical Abstract of the United States, 1955*, p. 605.

[90] *New York Times*, January 2, 1919, 13.1; March 30, 1919, 11.4.

followed until on October 26 the Brazilian Senate unanimously recognized that a state of war existed with Germany.[91] At once Brazilian naval units were employed in coastal patrol duty. Soon they were asked by the British to help protect the "principal maritime routes between the two continents." Next two Brazilian cruisers and four destroyers were based on Gibraltar to serve in cooperation with the United States Navy.[92] Of all this participation Brazilians were very proud.

Germany had been providing about 17.5 per cent of Brazilian imports and taking 14 per cent of their exports in 1913. By 1919 these had faded to 0.26 and 0.54 per cent, respectively. In the same years British exports to Brazil had dropped from 24.5 per cent of the total to 16.3 per cent; and imports from Brazil had declined from 13.2 to 7.3 per cent. The decline let the United States step into the gap and increase its exports to Brazil from 15.7 to 47.9 per cent of their total. At the same time its purchases increased from 32.2 to 41.6 per cent of Brazilian exports.[93] Such figures tell their own story. One commodity of great value to Brazil was rubber, which reached its peak production in 1912. Unfortunately for South America, the Asiatic plantations were coming into production backed by an ample cheap labor supply. Once the seaways were again open Brazil could not compete.[94] A new commodity, manganese, however, found an eager market in the United States and offset the loss. Brazilian exports of the mineral rose from 245,000 tons in 1914 to 432,000 tons in 1916.[95]

As the war drew to its close the United States' near monopoloy of the Brazilian markets was sharply challenged by the British. In one case Western Union secured cable bases in Brazil over British competition,[96] but more significant rivalry arouse over construction of steel and armaments production in Brazil. It was not probable that any British firm could start construction before the end of the war, but Lansing was fearful. He confidentially cabled his ambassador at Rio de Janeiro that "it is of the utmost importance to our interests in Brazil that no other than

[91] *For. Rels., 1917*, Sup. I, p. 352; Martin, *Latin America and the War*, p. 57.

[92] *For. Rels., 1918*, p. 80; *1918*, Sup. I, p. 663.

[93] Quoted from *Anuario estatistica do Brazil*, 1939–1940, pp. 1365 ff., by Henry William Speigel, *The Brazilian Economy . . .*, p. 127.

[94] M.W.D., "The Search for Rubber," *For. Affs.*, IV, No. 2 (January, 1926), 335.

[95] Pan-American Union, *Bulletin*, XLIV, No. 5 (May, 1917), 666.

[96] *For. Rels., 1918*, pp. 65 ff.; *1919*, I, 200 ff. See also Williams, *American Diplomacy*, p. 190.

an American company should eventually secure it [the concession] and the vast amount of trade it would control."[97] Efforts were made to unite the offers of the two groups into an Anglo-American combine, but the maneuvering was to continue until well after the war closed. Evidently Uncle Sam was keeping his eyes open, and it was equally obvious that John Bull had not lost his cunning. Italy, too, made some effort to build new fences and sent an ambassador to Rio who was regarded as one of the ablest and most active of Italian representatives. His critics even called him "a great intriguer."[98]

At the Peace Conference at Versailles the United States felt that it would automatically represent the New World republics. Pending more formal representation, the republics were advised simply to send one or two delegates to be on the ground. As it turned out, Wilson was asked to name a New World country whose delegate would serve with the representatives (after the Big Five) of the secondary powers (Belgium and Serbia). He named Brazil for the honor. Then on January 13, 1918, the Supreme Council authorized three official delegates for Brazil.[99]

During the Conference Brazil was concerned about its stocks of coffee which had been seized in Germany at the outbreak of hostilities; and also about the forty-three interned German vessels it had taken over (thirty of which had been released to France). Arrangements were made for payment for the coffee, but a long wrangle ensued with France over the ship question. In the debate France lost much of the capital of good will it had built up in the New World republic. Finally Brazil secured the vessels.[100]

As a final gracious gesture Secretary of State Colby made a good-will tour to Brazil, Uruguay, and Argentina where his "peculiarly graceful oratory" was put to good use.[101] But this was a farewell gesture of a repudiated administration and did little to affect policy.

With the proud and sensitive Argentines relations had not been so smooth. Skeptical of the Mexican situation, uncooperative in the International High Commission, and little inclined to ratify Pan-American conventions (as late as 1933 they had only ratified four out of fifty-six

[97] *For. Rels., 1919*, I, 205. Also *ibid.*, pp. 204–218.
[98] Page to Lansing, "Very Confidential," January 30, 1919, Lansing Papers, LC.
[99] *For. Rels., The Paris Peace Conference, 1919*, I, 223 ff.; XI, 7.
[100] Martin, *Latin America and the War*, p. 105.
[101] Spargo, "Bainbridge Colby," in Bemis, *Amer. Secs. of St.*, X, 213–214; *For. Rels., 1920*, I, 228 ff.

such conventions signed since 1890),[102] they retained their sympathy for Italy and enjoyed the huge profits to be made on exports of their vital foodstuffs. Value of farm lands skyrocketed once shipping to the Western Powers was reasonably available.[103] British shipping tonnage in the Argentine trade dropped from about 4,100,000 tons in 1913 to 1,114,000 in 1917, and then rose to over 2,125,000 in 1919. At the same time United States tonnage took up part of the slack, reaching some 800,000 tons for goods flowing to the new northern market. The balance of trade in favor of Argentina was a novelty in the relations of the two countries. For the period from 1913 to 1918 it was estimated at more than a billion dollars for the little nation of approximately eight million people.[104] Argentine realists were delighted and could see no reason to disturb such happy conditions by entering the war with its attendant war taxation.

When the United States declared war, President Hipólito Irigoyen expressed appreciation of the action but insisted that he could only lead Argentina into war because of "concrete injury"—and Germany had not committed such against his country. Soon a small Argentine vessel or two were sunk, but Germany tended to "explain" the incidents. Exasperated, the State Department sent to Buenos Aires copies of intercepted German telegrams showing complete disregard for Argentine rights. In one of these the Acting Minister of Foreign Affairs was referred to as "a notorious ass and an Anglophile." Another telegram revealed that on one occasion the resident German minister in Buenos Aires recommended stern treatment instead of "easy-going good nature" in communications, adding, "This [good nature] is dangerous in South America, where the people under a thin veneer are Indians." On receiving the revelations, the government handed the German minister his passports on September 12, 1917. The Senate overwhelmingly voted to break relations with Germany and before the end of the month the lower house agreed. Still the President would not be moved from his profitable neutrality.[105]

[102] Samuel Flagg Bemis, *The Latin American Policy of the United States*, p. 261 n.

[103] Ysabel F. Rennie, *The Argentine Republic*, pp. 219–220.

[104] H. O. Chalkley, "Report on the Economic and Industrial Situation of the Argentine Republic," *Accounts and Papers, 1920*, XLIII, 36, 42.

[105] Harold F. Peterson, *Argentina and the United States, 1810–1960*, p. 308; *For. Rels., 1917*, Sup. I, pp. 322 ff.; *For. Rels., 1918*, Sup. I, Vol. I, pp. 673–674; Martin, *Latin America and the War*, pp. 215 ff., 246–247.

It was against this background that the Secretary of Foreign Relations of Mexico proposed a meeting of neutral powers. On April 20, 1917, the American ambassador in Buenos Aires stated he had been asked if his country would look with sympathy on such a conference, to which it (being a belligerent) would not be invited. It was apparent that the proposed sessions were to meet in Buenos Aires. Lansing sent word to American diplomatic agents throughout Latin America (Argentina, Mexico, Panama, Cuba, Brazil, and the Dominican Republic being excepted): "For your own information and discreet use should occasion arise, the Department after careful consideration, does not consider that such a conference would serve any useful purpose at this time."[106] Presumably "discreet uses" were found. The New World nations began to make their excuses. Panama, Guatemala, Venezuela, Costa Rica, and Colombia sent their regrets; and Peru, Bolivia, Ecuador, and Uruguay reported that they would attend a conference only if "it were called for the avowed purpose of breaking relations with Germany." Only Mexico and El Salvador were understood to have accepted outright.[107] The movement collapsed.

Thus Argentina maintained the form of strict neutrality. Later scholars have pointed out that the policy followed was pro-Argentine rather than pro-German, but in the heat of war time the distinction was difficult to appreciate. When Secretary Colby planned his South American tour an invitation to visit Buenos Aires was slow indeed in forthcoming, though when he did arrive the reception was cordial enough.[108] As a recent writer has said, Irigoyen was determined not to become a tail to the United States–Pan-American kite. He had endorsed the Conference of Neutrals, and, in spite of the recommendations of his ambassador in Washington, had helped to defeat the Pan-American Pact idea. When his country joined the League of Nations it was with the determination that it should enjoy equal status with "the greatest powers."[109]

An interesting footnote to Argentine policy and thinking was Argentina's reflection of the excitement in the United States known as the "Red Scare" in 1919. On January 26 the *New York Times* reported that the previous day 1,400 prisoners were on board a cruiser in Buenos Aires

[106] *For. Rels., 1917*, Sup. I, pp. 260 ff. See also pp. 45–46, 235 ff.

[107] *Ibid.*, pp. 364 ff.

[108] *Ibid., 1920*, I, 231 ff.

[109] Arthur P. Whitaker, *The United States and Argentina*, pp. 100–101. Also the *New York Times*, May 26, 1919, 3.6.

awaiting exportation. A majority were said to be Russian Jews, though some Spaniards were reported to be in the number.[110]

Throughout the war Paraguay remained neutral. Its expressions of sympathy with the United States were apparently real, and generally in line with the statement of former President Cecilio Báez, who wrote on July 17, 1917, on the eve of a visit to his country by an American fleet: "Our republics began their existence as independent nations protected by the United States and England."[111] Given his country's inland position, this was about as much as could be expected.

Uruguay was in a somewhat different position. It had long feared its powerful and ambitious neighbor, Argentina. Also it had a valuable port in Montevideo. On November 9, 1917, relations were broken with Germany and in due order eight German interned steamers were leased to the Emergency Fleet Corporation of the United States.[112] On June 19, 1917, word was sent to the State Department that Uruguayan ports would be open for use by any American country finding itself in a state of war in defense of its own rights against a non-American power. Indeed, feelings were so exuberant that the *New York Times* reported editorially that Uruguay had just made July 4 a national holiday in honor of the United States.[113] Colby was given an enthusiastic reception on his trip. Uruguayan leaders did not hesistate to laud the Monroe Doctrine, which had faced the German threat to Latin America "already planned in 1914 and 1917 . . . [and] accentuated in 1918."[114]

South America—The West Coast

The transit of the first ship through the Panama Canal, in August, 1914, induced visions of wealth in the mineral-rich west coast countries. Of these Chile in particular found itself in an almost surprising position of world significance because of its enormous deposits of available nitrates, to say nothing of the rapidly rising importance of its copper reserves.[115]

---

[110] *Ibid.*, January 26, 1919, 3.6.

[111] Martin, *Latin America and the War*, pp. 481–482; *For. Rels., 1917*, Sup. I, pp. 254, 292.

[112] Martin, *Latin America and the War*, pp. 373–374.

[113] *New York Times*, July 5, 1918, 10.5. For official attitude see *For. Rels., 1917*, Sup. I, pp. 302 ff., 340.

[114] Baltasar Brum, *The Peace of America*, p. 18. For a report on the Colby visit see the *New York Times*, December 30, 1916, 15.6.

[115] Henry Clay Evans, *Chile and Its Relations with the United States*, pp. 179–180.

For such a position it was ill prepared. Unfortunately its relations with the United States, now the chief market for its produce, had included quite serious friction in the last quarter of the nineteenth century.

Also Chilean rivalries with Argentina were always to be considered. The boundary settlements at the end of the century had helped relations somewhat but recent rivalries over naval building were acute. The ABC Alliance seemed to hold real promise when it served as mediator in the case of the Mexican imbroglio with the United States, but the fact remained that the basic interests of the three allies were entirely different. Wheat and beef exports of Argentina called for one foreign policy; the coffee of Brazil for another; and the nitrate and copper of Chile for entirely different procedures. It is not surprising, therefore, that each of the three chose different courses during the war.

Germany had long been popular in Chile. German investments were heavy and the local army used German drillmasters. In 1913 Germany provided 24.6 per cent of Chilean imports and took 21.5 per cent of its exports.[116] Allied disruption of this trade brought recriminations. To make matters worse, early in 1915 a British squadron violated Chilean sovereignty by capturing the German vessel *Dresden* in the harbor at Cumberland Bay in the Juan Fernández Islands. Prompt apologies were forthcoming and Britain tried to cultivate Chilean good will by transferring title to submarines under construction in the United States to compensate for delays in construction of Chilean vessels in British shipyards.[117] For its part the United States, too, paid court to Santiago when it raised its legation to an embassy.[118] In addition, Wilson recalled Ambassador Fletcher from Santiago to take charge of the Pan-American Pact negotiations.

Nitrates, so essential for maintaining troops on the Western Front, now demanded increasing attention. Sales to Germany were eliminated

[116] Frederick Alexander Kirkpatrick relates an interesting maneuver as follows: "The Chilean Government bought the nitrate, and paid the German owners by drafts on Berlin, which were met out of Chilean money deposits in Germany. Thus Germany received Chilean gold in exchange for inaccessible nitrate, while the Chilean Government received the nitrate in exchange for its inaccessible gold" (*South America and the War* . . ., p. 37). Chile then sold the nitrate to the United States. See also Galvarino Gallardo Nieto, *Panamericanismo*, pp. 97 ff.; Martin, *Latin America and the War*, pp. 346–347.

[117] *British and Foreign State Papers, 1915*, pp. 670–671; *For. Rels., 1916*, Sup. Pt. III, pp. 712 ff.

[118] *For. Rels., 1914*, p. 36; *1915*, p. 35.

and those to Great Britain were curtailed. These losses were recouped by sales to the United States, which increased from 5,722,000 tons in 1913 to 8,641,000 tons in 1915.[119] As the war continued, the situation became increasingly acute. Britain entered agreements to buy guaranteed amounts of the product at excessively high prices. In the United States the feeling developed that prices were so high that Chile was guilty of gross profiteering.[120]

During the war Chile maintained strict neutrality, though pro-Allied sentiment in 1918 caused it to decline to represent the Imperial German Government in South American republics where Germany was not represented. Also it eliminated a number of German consuls by cancelling the exequaturs of all members of foreign consular services in Chile who were not of Chilean nationality. Meanwhile the *Dresden* incident had made Chileans conscious of the danger of violations of their country's neutrality. Accordingly Chile took special steps to prevent belligerent use of Chilean ports as supply bases for potential raiders. It forbade the sale of coal to any foreign belligerent vessel beyond the amount needed to enable the vessel to reach the next neutral port in the direction of its proposed destination.[121]

In spite of special assurances, profits derived from war trade, the raising of the United States legation to embassy rank, and the fact that the Ambassador to Chile was placed in charge of the Pan-American Pact negotiations, Chile declined all blandishments. It refused to enter any agreement that implied that arbitration should be employed to settle all international disputes. This doomed the Pan-American Pact.[122]

As the war was drawing to a close Peru and Chile resumed their quarreling over the border. Consuls were withdrawn and troops on the frontier were reinforced. The United States was greatly concerned. It

[119] Pan-American Union, *Bulletin*, XLIII, No. 6 (December, 1916), 740.

[120] For British purchases see *Britain and Foreign State Papers, 1918*, III, 236–237.

For the relationship between oil purchases and nitrate shipments see Anderson Papers, LC, Diary, July 11, 1918. See also Martin, *Latin America and the War*, pp. 345–346; and Arthur Kapper, "The American Farmer and Foreign Policy," *For. Affs.*, I, No. 4 (June, 1915), 132–133. For general pressures on Chile see *For. Rels., 1918*, Sup. I, Vol. I, pp. 715 ff.

[121] *British and Foreign State Papers*, 1914, II, 805 ff.; *1915*, pp. 883–884; Martin, *Latin America and the War*, pp. 281 ff.

[122] Frederick B. Pike, *Chile and the United States, 1880–1962*, pp. 150 ff.

pleaded against mobilization and urged reconsideration. Then it asked the neighboring countries of Argentina, Brazil, Colombia, Ecuador, Paraguay, and Uruguay to support efforts for peace.[123] When Peru proposed to refer the matter to the Versailles Conference, Lansing advised that this was not a good idea since Chile was not a member of the Conference. Among the procedures proposed were: 1) the United States to act as sole arbiter; 2) the United States to act as arbiter in connection with some European nations; 3) the question to be submitted to the Peace Conference; 4) the question to be submitted to the future League of Nations. Wilson personally preferred the second proposal, though he thought arbitration under the auspices of the League might be advisable.[124]

Once the question of the entrance of the United States into the League of Nations was joined in the Senate another phase of the matter emerged. Bolivia asked the League to take cognizance of the Tacna-Arica controversey and to enable Bolivia to secure an outlet to the Pacific. On May 6, 1920, Secretary of State Bainbridge Colby asked the Brazilian ambassador at London to transmit to the Council of the League the suggestion that it refrain from action in the matter. Like its numerous predecessors, the Wilson Administration preferred that New World questions be settled in the Western Hemisphere if possible.

Disconcerting, however, were the reports that Chile was using its new-found wealth to plunge into the naval race in South America by buying the battleship *Canada* and four light cruisers from Great Britain; also that it was considering the acquisition of six additional light destroyers.[125] Already no west coast country in South America could challenge Chile on the seas, and now its balance of power with Brazil and Argentina was endangered.

Bolivia, landlocked since the close of the War of the Pacific, had been repeatedly victimized in a series of boundary disputes. In 1903 Brazil had secured a boundary adjustment to the extent of nearly 73,000 square miles; the next year Chile had occupied nearly 35,000 square miles; and in 1909 Peru had settled for an acquisition of over 96,500 square miles

[123] *For. Rels., 1919*, I, 126 ff.; *1920*, I, 331–332. For a narrative account see Evans, *Chile and the U.S.*, p. 206.

[124] *For. Rels., 1919*, I, 123 ff.; *1920*, I, 341; *For. Rels., The Paris Peace Conference, 1919*, I, 553 ff.

[125] *New York Times*, August 24, 1920, 15.5.

that Bolivia had once claimed.[126] These were all undeveloped lands but the area involved was four times that of New York state. During the world war Bolivia had broken relations with Germany and had vigorously condemned German submarine warfare, urging a collective protest by all the South American republics.[127]

Now Bolivia grasped at the straw of the Tacna-Arica controversy. Since the region in dispute was relatively valueless, why not separate the quarreling powers (Peru and Chile) by assigning the coveted strip to Bolivia? Such thinking was behind its effort to secure League action. Washington and the South American nations, however, sought to keep the dispute as simple as possible. They were inclined to ignore the pleas of the impotent Bolivia, responding merely with the injunction: "Keep quiet."[128] When a governmental overturn in Bolivia occurred in the summer of 1920 the United States consulted with the ABC powers to reach agreement that recognition by the four should await the outcome of impending Bolivian elections. By December the elections had been held, and the United States, urged on by Argentina, led the way in extending recognition.[129]

Peru, too, was tasting the fruits of mineral wealth, especially vanadium, which now had ready access to United States markets through the Panama Canal. From the beginning, Peru had expressed sympathy with Wilson's protests at submarine warfare and in early August the Peruvian Senate passed a special resolution endorsing a continent-wide adoption of rules for united action.[130] On October 6 it had severed relations with the Central Powers.

Just as the Tacna-Arica quarrel was becoming acute, a confused election situation arose in which Augusto B. Leguía may actually have been elected. Before the air had cleared the old President was accused of trying to prevent his successor's installation and the impatient Leguía seized control through a military revolt on July 4, 1919. The next month elections for members of both houses of Congress and on a number of consitutional amendments passed off quietly. Thereupon, on August 28,

[126] Arthur P. Whitaker, *The United States and South America: The Northern Republics*, p. 18.

[127] *For. Rels., 1917*, Sup. I, p. 273; Martin, *Latin America and the War*, pp. 476 ff.

[128] *For. Rels., 1920*, I, 328 ff.

[129] *Ibid.*, pp. 376 ff.

[130] *Ibid., 1917*, Sup. I, p. 311; Martin, *Latin America and the War*, pp. 389 ff.

1919, the United States extended *de facto* recognition. In the next ten days Belgium, Bolivia, Ecuador, France, Italy, Uruguay, and Great Britain also recognized the new government.[131] By the end of October a request reached the State Department for Washington to send a naval mission to reorganize the Peruvian Navy. Details were worked out and three men were sent down about a year later.[132]

In its involved border controversies Peru was largely on the defensive except in the case of Ecuador. In addition to the confused southern border there was another involved controversy over the Amazon jungles. There Brazilian, Colombian, Venezuelan, and Peruvian territory converged. As the dispute waxed bitter between Peru and Venezuela, Washington instructed its diplomatic agents to use their good offices orally and informally to encourage direct negotiations.[133] Here was another New World problem Washington preferred to have settled locally rather than by the League of Nations.

Ecuador seems to have been relatively little affected by the war. On December 7, 1917, it had severed relations with Germany,[134] but the small country was never really brought into the current world events. Washington contented itself with the occasional use of its good offices on behalf of Chinese citizens (China had no diplomatic agents in the country) or with efforts to persuade the Ecuadorian administration to pay interest on foreign debts due.[135]

Imperceptibly a new day was dawning in hemisphere relations. Argentina and Brazil had emerged as national "personalities" on the east coast, each with its distinct tendencies and interests. Yet, oddly enough, it was on the west coast that a more coordinated policy was emerging. Nitrates, copper, tin, and vanadium, located in three different countries, had each attracted large investments of United States money. In addition to the sums involved there was the fact that these products were now recognized as strategic raw materials. The United States might turn to isolation in regard to the League. On the other hand, its manufacturers had no intention of being "caught short" of essential products and fully expected their government to protect their South American

---

[131] *For. Rels., 1919*, II, 720 ff.

[132] *Ibid., 1920*, III, 367 ff.

[133] *Ibid., 1919*, I, 82.

[134] *Ibid., 1917*, Sup. I, pp. 383–384.

[135] For aid to Chinese see *ibid., 1916*, pp. 259–260. For finances see *ibid., 1917*, pp. 730 ff.; *1919*, II, 171 ff.; *1920*, II, 179 ff., 204 ff.

ventures, which were becoming of fundamental importance to both the business life and the very safety of the nation. In the past Bolivia might have lost three major boundary settlements in a decade. Who in Washinton cared? By 1920 such disregard was a thing of the past. Now the Chaco, Tacna-Arica, and Leticia disputes were seen as involving areas where similar raw materials might possibly be at state.

At this same time additional billions were being invested and additional strategic raw materials were being revealed north of the United States boundary. The new businessman's program had to encompass the hemisphere.

CHAPTER VI

1921–1929: CONDITIONS

Personalities

THE YEAR 1921 SAW multiple changes in politics, personalities, and programs as the United States moved from war to peace. In the preceding thirty years Grover Cleveland, at first a convinced isolationist, was driven by events to assume increased responsibilities. James G. Blaine dreamed of a hemisphere policy which would combine imperial expansion with economic advantages. Theodore Roosevelt, the adolescent imperialist, was associated with the aristorcatic and poetic John Hay, and both dreamed of world power which would control undeveloped areas for their own good. Then appeared Elihu Root and W. H. Taft as practical statesmen who sought to replace the old imperialism with economic controls to induce mutual prosperity. Finally, the idealistic Woodrow Wilson, handicapped by war, sought to apply paternalistic pressure to impel backward peoples to develop themselves. Viewed in perspective, a strange but very real continuity becomes evident.

Then came the reaction. Major attention centered on world relationships but the American people were wearied of these. The new President, Warren Gamaliel Harding, longed for the "good old days" of isolation from Europe, Asia, and Africa. Nor did he have much interest in a positive program for Latin America. Neither his special message to Congress on April 12, 1921, nor his annual message on December 6, 1921, discussed Latin America; and his second annual message only contained a single paragraph of 124 words in which he rather casually expressed the hope that pending boundary disputes would be settled and that the delegates of the Central American countries who were then meeting in Washington would reach an agreement.[1] Calvin Coolidge, too, was equally uninterested. His annual message of December 6, 1923, said nothing at all of Latin America, while his second message, in 1924, simply professed a "special interest in the peace of this hemisphere" and hoped that all disputes therein would be settled while the countries concerned enjoyed "increased prosperity"—all of which was in eight lines of type. The 1925 message contained a similarly innocuous statement; that of 1926 said nothing; in 1927 the President was concerned about injuries to properties of United States citizens in Nicaraguan disorders; and in 1928 he merely mentioned the Sixth Pan-American Conference and endorsed the Inter-American Highway and better communications in general.[2] Policy making for Latin America, therefore, obviously did not reside in the Presidency at the time. Was anyone else more awake to possibilities?

This was the era of the businessman who had successfully carried the nation through the war. The new Cabinet was an odd mixture of personalities and interests. In it were some of President Harding's old political cronies, such as Albert B. Fall and the petroleum magnates Edward L. Doheny and Harry F. Sinclair. These members, soon discredited by scandals, could be expected to advocate a policy of vigorous exploitation of the economic resources of adjacent countries. Fortunately, they soon passed from the scene leaving behind two Cabinet members who were the real architects of the new New World foreign policy—Secretary of State Charles Evans Hughes and Secretary of Commerce Herbert Hoover. Both of them were able men who earnestly sought a constructive international policy in spite of a nationwide wave of isolationism. Hughes' broad legal training and his humanitarian instincts led him in the direction of the general program initiated by Root. Hoover was an experienced engineer with extensive European contacts. His professional experience in undeveloped countries convinced him that prosperity for the peoples of such areas lay primarily in the development of local resources by huge outside financial concerns.

Hughes considered the Caribbean a strategic center[3]—the old idea—

[1] For presidential messages see *For. Rels., 1921* and *1922*.
[2] *Ibid., 1924*, I. xxii; *1925*, I, xiv; *1927*, I, xxiv; *1928*, I, ix, xviii.
[3] Dexter Perkins, *Hands Off*, p. 335.

but hastened to say: "I utterly disclaim, as unwarranted, the observations that have occasionally been made implying a claim on our part to superintend the affairs of our sister Republics, to assert an overlordship ... and to make our power the test of right in this hemisphere."[4] Hoover, however, as Secretary of Commerce, became increasingly involved in problems of guaranteeing an adequate supply of strategic raw materials to American industry. The fact should be borne in mind, however, that the competition for control of raw materials was world-wide. The Secretary of Commerce reported that government-controlled combinations dominated nine major items of United States imports, including Egyptian long staple cotton, coffee, iodine, nitrates, potash, mercury, rubber, and sisal.[5] The Caribbean was not an adequate source of supply and many of the new needs had to be met from farther south. The result has been described as a policy "to keep business Europe rather than political Europe out of Latin America."[6]

A writer in the British *Quarterly Review* represented the European reaction when he commented that the policy of the United States reminded one of the frame of mind in which Voltaire wrote D'Alembert: "My compliments to the devil, for it is he who governs the world."[7] The Frenchman Jules Cambon put it another way when he referred to the United States' program as "a policy of shooting preserves."[8] Still another writer commented that the Associated Press, the United Press, the United States cinema monopoly, and the Pan-American Union all gave the United States control over the "Empty Continent" through its ambassadors, ministers, and counsuls.[9] To sum up: In the eyes of crippled Europe "The United States pursues the most illiberal commercial policy of any nation in the world."[10]

In December, 1920, Hoover outlined his conception of a proper loan

[4] Quoted by Alejandro Álvarez, *The Monroe Doctrine*, p. 423.

[5] Parker T. Moon, "Raw Materials and Imperialism," *International Conciliation Documents*, No. 226 (January, 1927), p. 38.

[6] Julius Klein, "The Monroe Doctrine as a Regional Understanding," *Hisp.* CCXXXVIII, No. 472 (July, 1927), 162.

[7] Quoted by E. J. Dillon, "Mexico and World Reconstruction," *Quar. Rev., Amer. Hist. Rev.*, IV, No. 2 (May, 1921), 254.

[8] *Rev. of Revs.*, LXXVIII (October, 1928), 422.

[9] Ignatius Phayre, "America's Sovereignty," *Quar. Rev.*, CCL, No. 495 (January, 1928), 43–44.

[10] W. A. Hirst, "British Influence in South America," *Edinburgh Review,* CCXLVII, No. 504 (April, 1928), 328.

policy in an address to the American Bankers' Association. He said two major qualifications should be borne in mind: Loans should be made only for economically productive purposes (no loans for military equipment), and should be extended through private channels. He insisted that the world "needs to get away from the notion of governmental help . . . and get back to work and business."[11] The American Academy of Political and Social Science fell in with this interpretation and devoted its entire issue of the March, 1924, session of *The Annals* (Vol. CXII) to some three hundred pages of articles on "Raw Materials and Foodstuffs in the Commercial Policies of Nations."

When Coolidge (who became President on the death of Harding in August, 1923) did wake up to foreign affairs it was to emphasize this same economic interpretation. Speaking to the United Press Association April 25, 1927, he said:

. . . there is a distinct and binding obligation on the part of self-respecting governments to afford protection to the persons and property of their citizens, wherever they may be . . . if it is wrong to murder and pillage within the confines of the United States, it is equally wrong outside our borders. . . . These rights go with the citizen. Wherever he goes these duties of our Government must follow him.[12]

A British scholar wondered where this policy would lead. He commented on the dominance of the United States north of the Canal, then remarked that its trade with Colombia-Venezuela had increased from $10 million per year in 1910–1914 to $89 million in 1926, while the export of its capital to Colombia and Venezuela since 1912 had been reported as increasing by 6,000 and 5,300 per cent, respectively.[13] Would all South America be engulfed—and what about Canada?

A forthright Latin American scholar viewing the situation and knowing his fellow countrymen commented that "It has been maliciously observed that the administration of these republics consists of tyranny tempered by treason."[14] Unfortunately, in spite of itself therefore, the United States was frequently lending its money for the perpetuation of tryanny. The dictators were the ones who held out promises of peace and

[11] Joseph Brandes, *Herbert Hoover and Economic Diplomacy*, p. 152.
[12] *For. Rels., 1927*, III, 213.
[13] *Survey of Int. Affs., 1927*, p. 420.
[14] F. García Calderón, "Dictatorship and Democracy in Latin America," *For. Affs.*, III, No. 3 (April, 1925), 474.

guarantees of property. Hoover sought such guarantees and Hughes endorsed the economists' search for "Constitutional stability, electoral orderliness, internal and external peace."[15]

Hughes recognized the peculiar responsiblities of his country. He sought to liquidate the Wilsonian interventions and to withdraw marines from Caribbean countries, but admitted that this must be done slowly to prevent the growth of "conditions prejudicial to the United States." He wanted none of Wilson's mutual approach as seen in the Pan-American Pact. Instead he insisted that the Monroe Doctrine was a unilateral policy while he limited its application solely to defense. He recognized the equality of the American republics; respected their territorial integrity; sought to eliminate disputes between them; sponsored international conferences and unconditional most-favored-nation treaties. At the same time he asserted that the United States would not apply its policies unilaterally merely to advance its own peculiar interests. Herbert Feis noted that incorporated in this program were contradictions in practice. Private interests concerned in the very development the Secretary sought to foster did not always cooperate in the abstemious and supposedly cooperative features of the program.[16]

When Frank B. Kellogg took over as Secretary of State in 1925 he, too, had a business and industrial background. Yet he had neither the "training, experience, nor temperament" to handle many of the delicate Latin American problems then pending. Fortunately, he still leaned on Hughes for advice and when the critical Havana Conference was to assemble in 1928, it was Hughes who headed the United States delegation and who spoke for his country. As a matter of fact, by that time the administration policy was already changing. Hughes still preached the right of intervention though he practiced abstention. Kellogg was not to be so careful—this was notoriously true in Nicaragua.[17] Also Coolidge's inclinations leaned toward the Kellogg position rather than to-

[15] William Hard, "Charles Evans Hughes," *Rev. of Revs.*, LXXVII (January, 1928), 40. See also H. W. Dodds, "The United States and Nicaragua," *The Annals*, CXXXII (July, 1927), 136–137.

[16] Merlo J. Pusey, *Charles Evans Hughes*, II, 530 ff.; Herbert Feis, *The Diplomacy of the Dollar*, pp. 26 ff. See also John Chalmers Vinson, "Charles Evans Hughes," in Norman A. Graebner, ed., *An Uncertain Tradition*, p. 147.

[17] Ethan Ellis, "Frank B. Kellogg," in Graebner, *An Uncertain Tradition*, pp. 158 ff.; David Bryn-Jones, *Frank B. Kellogg: A Biography*, pp. 34, 38, 52 (Kellogg's business connections); Graham H. Stuart, *Latin America and the United States*, p. 7.

ward that of Hoover when it came to the matter of armaments. Loans for military equipment were actually made to Nicaragua under Kellogg, and Coolidge admitted that under "no circumstances" would he make Hoover Secretary of State.[18]

Economic Policies

At the close of the war Western Europe rushed its products into New World markets, whose warehouses were full of United States products but had long been empty of European supplies. United States exports fell alarmingly.[19] The result was an almost panicky response by a businessman's administration and Congress, both essentially untrained in foreign policy making. The almost ludicrous result has been described thus: "Except in a few instances, American economic policy was not dictated by international consideration . . . Balance-of-payments analysis and the complications of the transfer problem, though familiar to the academic economists, had not penetrated the thinking of most government officials and congressmen of the Coolidge era."[20] Specifically, this meant panic-inspired legislation to raise tariffs and prevent dumping of European goods in the United States; demands for most-favored-nation treaties to prevent foreign nations from establishing high tariffs against United States exports; penalty tariffs for countries discriminating against American trade; and national supervision of private foreign investments.[21]

Except in the case of Argentine products, 80 to 90 per cent of the raw-material exports of the major Latin American republics to the United States were on the free lists. Also over the years many Latin Americans had learned to like United States products. Logically, therefore, after an initial recession in 1921 trade tended to resume a more normal flow. The value of trade of the ten South American republics with the United States increased 160 per cent from 1913 to 1927; while that of the ten northern republics rose nearly 82 per cent.[22] Canada, too, was affected.

[18] The *Times* (London), May 3, 1927, 15c.

[19] *Report of the Secretary of Commerce, 1921*, p. 50, notes that the 1920 exports of $7,950 million declined to $6,386 million in 1921.

[20] Raymond F. Mikesell, *United States Economic Policy and International Relations*, p. 11.

[21] Benjamin H. Williams, *American Diplomacy*, p. 171.

[22] Max Winkler, *Investments of United States Capital in Latin America*, p. 284; Treasury Department, *Statistical Abstract of the United States, 1920*, p. 411; *1930*, p. 491; *1936*, p. 454.

In the five years at the end of the nineteenth century Canada took less than 7 per cent of United States exports and sent only 5 per cent of its own exports south of the line. Yet in the five years from 1926 through 1930 Canada consumed 17.4 per cent of United States exports and shipped 11.9 per cent of United States imports.[23]

"In South America trade is the breath of life." "Inability to export is the bugaboo of South American governments." At the peak of postwar prosperity in 1929 an estimated 36.7 per cent of the foreign trade of Latin America was with its northern neighbor.[24] In spite of this fact the American manufacturer and salesman were home-trained and home-oriented. They all too often tended to neglect the niceties of intercourse and minor accommodations with which Europeans were so ready to oblige. The result was a substantial weakness in what might have been an exceedingly firm economic front.[25] With its "breath of life" dependent on foreign trade Latin America was less than happy when word reached all United States diplomatic officers under date of August 18, 1923, that their government was adopting the *unconditional* most-favored-nation basis for future trade treaties.[26]

This idea was incorporated in the German trade treaty signed by the United States on December 8 and which read:

Any advantage of whatsoever kind which either High Contracting Party may extend to any article, the growth, produce or manufacture of any foreign country shall simultaneously and unconditionally without request and without compensation, be extended to the like article, the growth, produce, or manufacture of the other High Contracting Party.[27]

Another fact to be remembered was that Latin American trade was peculiarly dependent on the European money markets which had been largely destroyed by World War I. Thus Toynbee was to state that in the eight years prior to 1927 Latin America had been able to borrow only $200 million from its old creditors but had secured over six times that

[23] Lewis M. Hacker, *American Problems of Today*, pp. 142, 144. See also *Report of the Secretary of Commerce, 1927*, p. xxiv; *1930*, p. xxi; *1931*, p. xxii; *1932*, p. 54.

[24] J. F. Normano, *The Struggle for South America*, p. 21; Williams, *American Diplomacy*, p. 89.

[25] Nicholas John Spykman, *America's Strategy in World Politics*, p. 324.

[26] *For. Rels., 1923*, pp. 131 ff.

[27] Quoted by Williams with pertinent comments, *American Diplomacy*, p. 172. See also Benjamin H. Williams, *Economic Foreign Policy of the United States*, pp. 289–290.

sum from the United States.[28] Another estimate had it that American private investment in Canada increased from $150 million in 1900 to $1,960 million in 1929; while the figures for South America were $35 million and $1,548 million.[29] As the booming 1920's advanced, the American investor found himself with more available capital than he knew how to use. His home plant, his office buildings, his housing developments, and even his country clubs were seriously overbuilt. Not surprisingly, he poured his money into increasingly speculative markets abroad. The Commerce Department might warn that "several Latin American countries 'were going wild on borrowing' " but the money continued to flow southward.[30] At the same time a striking change was taking place in the type of investment being made. In the early days it was the European who invested in Latin American government bonds; the Yankee preferred mining and industrial enterprises in which men *made* things. In 1914 less than $15 million of Latin American government securities were offered on the United States market. From 1915 to 1920 this figure had increased to $125 million, and from 1921 to 1927 it rose to a spectacular $1,400 million.[31]

From this background came a demand for some kind of supervision of loans made by private investors. Secretary Hoover felt that the Commerce Department should exercise the controls. Hughes rejoined that such investments involved the policy making of the State Department —and Harding agreed with Hughes. On March 3, 1922, the State Department issued a press release indicating the "desirability of cooperation" between bankers and the Department. It carefully explained that its disapproval of any proposed loan did not prevent a banker from proceeding on his own responsibility, but the fact remained that the advice was usually effective.[32] True, on occasion Wall Street bankers beat the

[28] *Survey of Int. Affs.*, 1927, p. 411.

[29] Charles A. Beard, *The Idea of National Interest*, p. 209. See also Herbert Feis, "The Export of American Capital," *For. Affs.*, III, No. 4 (July, 1925), 669.

[30] Committee on Finance, *Sale of Foreign Bonds or Securities in the United States* (Hearings before Senate Committee on Finance, 72d Cong., 1st. Sess.), Pt. 2, pp. 845 ff. See also Brandes, *Hoover and Economic Diplomacy*, p. 48.

[31] Charles Evans Hughes, *Our Relations to the Nations of the Western Hemisphere*, p. 58; W. O. Scroggs, "American Investment in Latin America," *For. Affs.*, X, No 2 (January, 1932), 502–503.

[32] *For. Rels.*, 1922, pp. 557–558; Feis, *Diplomacy of the Dollar*, p. 11; Williams, *Economic Foreign Policy*, pp. 87–88.

devil around the stump and invested in disapproved securities via European houses,[33] but still disapproval remained a powerful deterrent. One writer comments that "nominally a request . . . the request in fact became a command."[34] Disapproval of loans to Guatemala, Honduras, and Haiti (for a bank sale) were all effective.[35] And a loan to the Brazilian Coffee Institute to stabilize coffee prices was blocked by Secretary Hoover. (The money was later secured in London.) Inevitably criticism of such supervision arose, but so long as Hoover remained Secretary of Commerce and while he was President, no official change could be expected.

South America

On the west coast of South America was an especially tempting field for the new type of competition. Hughes continued the Wilsonian idea of financial advisers[36] and steps were taken to provide such an agent in Ecuador though that country cannily insisted that a loan should be negotiated before the adviser was selected.[37] The next year, 1924, Ecuador sought to dissolve the cacao-growers association without providing for the liquidation of the association's debts due to the Mercantile Bank of the Americas. Strong diplomatic protests ensued.

More significant was the influence of American investments in Peru, which doubled between the prewar period and 1925. These moneys came from a variety of corporations, including New Jersey Standard Oil (through International Petroleum, Ltd.), the Cerro de Pasco Copper Corporation, the American Smelting and Refining Company, and the Vanadium Corporation of America. They practically dominated copper, vanadium, and petroleum production while the construction of roads and sanitation projects was largely in the hands of the Foundation Company of New York.[38] When a new loan was negotiated, a collection agency was established to insure proper handling of the government-pledged revenues.

[33] Charles P. Howland, in *Amer. For. Rels., 1928*, pp. 193–194.

[34] J. F. Dulles, "Our Foreign Policy," *For. Affs.*, V (October, 1926), 33.

[35] Feis, *Diplomacy of the Dollar*, p. 28. See also James W. Angell, *Financial Foreign Policy of the United States*, pp. 100–102.

[36] Hughes, *Our Relations to . . . the Western Hemisphere*, pp. 71–72. See also *For. Rels., 1921*, II, 656 ff.

[37] *Ibid., 1923*, I, 924 ff.; *1924*, I, 692 ff.

[38] Parker Thomas Moon, *Imperialism and World Politics*, pp. 454–455; James C. Malin, *The United States after the World War*, pp. 433–434.

In Bolivia there were even more striking developments. In 1922 a $33 million loan, guaranteed by a substantial part of the national revenue, was negotiated through New York bankers.[39] The lenders also had the right to approve future bond issues. Using this power they "discouraged" new loans from British and French sources, even though the terms proposed were attractive indeed as compared with offers termed acceptable when presented by the original lenders.

The crux of the Bolivian economy was tin. By the mid-1920's the Federated Malay States produced some 46,000 tons, the Dutch East Indies some 3,000 tons, and Bolivia about 36,600 tons.[40] The United States was the world's largest consumer of the metal, though its home production was relatively insignificant, and American capital dominated the Bolivian tin mines. Another product attracting attention was petroleum. In 1921 the Standard Oil of Bolivia was organized to develop the industry. An idea of conditions is seen in the fact that to ship the product via Buenos Aires would have required a five-hundred-mile pipeline costing some $12 million plus a barge haul of seven hundred miles. To begin explorations two hundred carts and eight hundred mules were needed to get material to the concessions. By 1927 oil had been discovered but the output was a meager seventy-one barrels per day after an investment of over eleven million dollars.[41] Possibly this report was exaggerated, but the fact is that the Bolivian government began to fear that their oil fields would be monopolized. It therefore passed a law that only European capital could secure new concessions. Hughes protested that the legislation was discriminatory and contrary to the existing Treaty of Friendship, Peace, Commerce and Navigation between the two countries. The objectionable action was canceled.[42]

In Chile came another quite spectacular development in spite of the decline of the nitrate trade, which was suffering twofold ills arising from heavily curtailed consumption once the war closed and the rapid rise of synthetic production. In 1912 the total United States investment in the shoestring republic amounted to a scant $15 million. Then appeared the Guggenheim interests, Bethlehem Steel, Grace and Com-

[39] *For. Rels., 1922*, I, 640 ff. For a critical interpretation see Margaret Alexander Marsh, *The Bankers in Bolivia*, pp. 104–105.

[40] *Ibid.*, p. 36.

[41] George Sweet Gibb and Evelyn H. Knowlton, *History of Standard Oil Company of New Jersey: The Resurgent Years . . .*, pp. 382–383.

[42] *For. Rels., 1926*, I, 564 ff.

pany, the National City Bank, and others to push loans and investments to $100 million in the early 1920's and up to an estimated $800 million by the time of the Wall Street crash in 1929.[43] Much of this new money was in the new bonanza, copper. Some bankers were learning caution, but general competition for Chilean investments was keen indeed.[44] Prior to the war Chile had sent to and bought from the United States a mere 6 per cent of its foreign trade, but by the end of the 1920's both exports and imports with the northern country exceeded 30 per cent of the Chilean totals. Even more interesting was the fact that 96 per cent of the Chilean exports to the United States was duty free while 98 per cent of what the United States sold to Chile carried import duties of approximately 20 percent.[45]

In some ways the economic policies of the day were seen in their most typical form in Brazilian relations. In 1925 an organization of coffee producers in São Paulo sought a loan to stabilize badly depressed coffee prices. Secretary of Commerce Hoover felt that the loan "would simply bolster up the extravagant prices to the American consumer." Thereupon the State Department notified the bankers concerned that it could not view this $15 million loan "with favor." Again in 1928 a similar notice was sent to interested bankers.[46] As a further step the Department of Commerce helped to organize the United States importers, roasters, jobbers, and distributers of coffee, noting with apparent pride that Brazilians seemed to be impressed with the fact that the "conservation campaign" of the United States had recently been able to force reduction of prices charged by the great rubber monopoly "by more than 50 per cent."[47] The disapproval of the coffee loan did not represent antagonism to Brazil itself but reflected the basic economic foreign policy of the time. Actually the relations between the two countries remained quite good and a loan to São Paulo for refunding purposes and for a new water supply and for railroad construction was approved. When a protest was made that the new loan was not sound the State Department responded that it never endorsed the soundness of investments but re-

[43] S. G. Inman in Carleton Beals *et al.*, *What South Americans Think of Us*, p. 354. See also Frederick B. Pike, *Chile and the United States . . .*, p. 161.

[44] *Sale of Foreign Bonds*, Pt. II, pp. 742 ff.

[45] Carlos G. Dávila, *North American Imperialism*, p. 12.

[46] *For. Rels.*, *1925*, I, 533 ff.; *1928*, III, 1020; Malin, *The U.S. after the World War*, p. 329.

[47] Brandes, *Hoover and Economic Diplomacy*, pp. 131–135.

stricted itself to clearance of any proposal from the standpoint of national policy.[48]

As part of a program to revive Brazilian rubber production, Secretary Kellogg inquired on December 12, 1925, through Ambassador Morgan in Rio de Janeiro if Brazil would be interested in development of Brazilian rubber resources through use of United States money. If so, would it guarantee not to restrict free export of the product. The answer was an "emphatic 'yes' " to the first question though note was made of the fact that Brazilian states exercised certain export rights. In short order assurance of state interest was also forwarded to the Department.[49] Unfortunately for Brazil, its labor conditions did not enable it to compete with the flood of higher-grade plantation rubber coming on the market from the East Indies. The "dance of the millions" seen on the west coast and in the oil fields of the Caribbean was not so obvious in Brazil, but the policies applied were similar.

A small east coast country that did feel the effects of the new United States money in substantial quantities was Uruguay. A $5 million investment in 1912 had burgeoned to $77 million in 1927. The investment was found in packing plants, telegraphs, telephones, cables, power plants, and sewer systems, as well as in bonds of government agencies.[50]

In next-door Argentina an anomalous situation developed. United States money poured into that market also, increasing some 1,400 per cent from 1913 to the onset of the depression.[51] Yet the strange and alarming fact remained that the per capita wealth of the country was falling. Before the war the two countries were essentially on a par in this respect, but by the mid-1920's United States per capita wealth had more than doubled while that of Argentina had decreased slightly.[52] Trade flow had been materially readjusted. Imports from Great Britain (the old supply house) had remained essentially the same, but those from the United States had more than doubled. A special complication lay in the fact that the Argentine meat trade was seriously declining and the United States was severely restricting imports in competition with its

[48] *For. Rels., 1928*, III, 1027–1028.

[49] *Ibid., 1926*, I, 575 ff.

[50] H. A. Gibbons, "Uruguay Comes of Age," *Rev. of Revs.*, LXXVIII (September, 1928), 292.

[51] Arthur P. Whitaker, *The United States and Argentina*, p. 103.

[52] Roberto Kurtz, *La Argentina ante Estados Unidos*, p. 38.

domestic interests.[53] In 1929 American imports from Argentina were less than $118 million but exports to that country were over $210 million. How pay the balance, to say nothing of interest on the new investments that had been made? And this problem was added to numerous other strains of the postwar period. Not surprisingly, the Argentines showed little interest in an unconditional most-favored-nation trade treaty, but strove manfully to rechannel their trade back to Great Britain.[54]

One portent of the future lay in the petroleum situation. The Standard Oil Company of New Jersey entered the Argentine fields and by 1927 reported that its payrolls showed two thousand workmen employed though as yet production was a disappointing 765 barrels daily.[55] When the Argentines considered granting monopoly rights in the fields, the State Department carefully instructed its chargé in Buenos Aires. He was to call attention to the restrictive and unwise tendencies arising from monopolies but to admit that a country had a perfect right to grant such to its own citizens. If foreigners were to be the beneficiaries the Department dared hope that United States citizens would be given equal consideration with those from other countries.[56]

Caribbean Policies

The Caribbean area, long the center of United States New World policy, was rapidly being outgrown in importance but still demanded careful consideration. Essential control of the area was not challenged, so the chief question was simply how to proceed. Two programs emerged. One was concerned with key raw materials and the new type of supervision of loans involved; and the other with the general rise of economic prosperity and new political ambitions.

Bankers' loans as an instrument of government policy were familiar but the new contract with El Salvador needs to be mentioned. After negotiations lasting over a couple of years and involving Mr. Minor C. Keith, of the United Fruit Company and New York Bankers, it was

---

[53] *Rev. of Revs.,* LXV (April, 1922), 429–430. For trade with Great Britain see W. A. Hirst, "British Trade in South America," *Quar. Rev.,* CCLI, No. 498 (October, 1928), 316–320, and J. B. Condliffe, *The Reconstruction of World Trade,* pp. 320–321.

[54] *For. Rels., 1927,* I, 421–422.

[55] Gibb and Knowlton, *Standard Oil of New Jersey,* pp. 381–382.

[56] *For. Rels., 1920,* I, 369–370.

agreed that new bonds would be sold at 88 per cent of their face value of $21.5 million. They would carry interest of from 6 to 8 per cent and were guaranteed by a substantial part of the import and export taxes of El Salvador. In case of default the bankers were to name a customs collector for the little country. One of the most interesting features of the arrangement was that in case of disagreement as to the terms of the contract, the dispute was to be settled by the Chief Justice of the United States Supreme Court. In view of the enforcement of the Panama-Costa Rica boundary award by the United States, any decision by the Chief Justice would be considered definitive.[57] With this built-in interest it is not surprising that El Salvador was among the early nations to subscribe to one of the new most-favored-nation treaties. After some delays ratifications were exchanged on September 5, 1930.[58]

Economic development in Colombia resembled that in the west coast countries. The two special points of consideration were Colombian interest in the unratified treaty negotiated by Wilson and the rapid growth of Colombian oil fields. These were all the more important in view of feared exhaustion of American reserves and the uncertainties of the Mexican fields. Colombia calmly pressed its advantage and informed would-be American concessionaires that they could expect few contracts until the treaty was signed. One writer laconically remarks: "By 1919, petroleum had thrown a new light upon the discussions." On April 20, 1921, the Senate changed its mind and recommended approval of the treaty by a vote of 69 to 19. Ratifications were exchanged January 1, 1922.[59]

This opened the door for another "dance of the millions" as United States money flowed into Colombia. Less than $4 million in 1913, it amounted to some $30 million in 1920, then leaped to the unbelievable figure of $280 million by 1929.[60] In spite of malaria, amoebic dysentery, and other ailments causing an annual hospital admission rate of 750 per 1,000 among employees of the Standard Oil Company of New Jersey, the profits piled up after an initial slow start. By the end of 1927 that

[57] *Ibid., 1922*, II, 886 ff.; *1923*, II, 24 ff.

[58] *Ibid., 1926*, II, 933 ff. For comment see Moon, *Imperialism and World Politics*, pp. 431–432.

[59] *For. Rels., 1921*, I, 639 ff.; *1922*, I, 976. For comment see Williams, *Economic Foreign Policy*, pp. 75–76; J. Fred Rippy, "The United States and Colombian Oil," *For. Pol. Assn. Reports*, V, (1929–1930), 28–29.

[60] J. Fred Rippy, *The Capitalists and Colombia*, pp. 152, 176.

company could report that it had expended $23.5 million on its development efforts, but listed total assets as slightly in excess of $92 million, with a net profit from all branches of operation of $6,943,000.[61]

Inevitably there were complications that arose in the process. Colombia, restless at seeing so much wealth leave the country considered ways by which to staunch the flow. A restrictive decree in 1928 met with diplomatic pressures until relief from the courts could be secured. Meanwhile, bankers had extended their investments to bonds of various national, as well as state and local, issues. Rippy concludes that thirty-two loans for a total of $173.8 million brought bankers "nearly six per cent on the actual investment."[62] Again the program had tended to broaden as it developed. In 1923 it was agreed that Professor E. W. Kemmerer of Princeton University, together with four other gentlemen, would survey and make recommendations to the Colombian government on banking and monetary matters.[63] Many Latin Americans felt that the old dollar diplomacy had become a new dollar domination.

Next door, in Venezuela, was another petroleum field. Here, too, the game was a ruthless one among exploiters who were not too nice in methods employed. By and large the Yankee held his own in the competition. But Venezuela played its game coolly and no critical situation developed for some time. Efforts at a most-favored-nation treaty collapsed as the local administration riveted its control on its people but carefully observed its international obligations.

President Coolidge's biographer may have somewhat overstated his case when he said that in Nicaragua "Actually Collidge had no object except to restore tranquility as soon as possible."[64] Yet there was a distinct element of truth in the statement when it is applied to much of the Caribbean area in the decade following the war. The European imperial menace was gone; hence there was no need to re-emphasize the old Monroe Doctrine. Likewise, European economic competition had become relatively insignificant. The question that remained was how would the United States exercise the hegemony that rested so completely in its hands?

[61] Gibb and Knowlton, *Standard Oil of New Jersey*, pp. 371, 397.

[62] Rippy, *Capitalists and Colombia*, p. 155. See also *Sale of Foreign Bonds*, Pt. 2, pp. 723 ff., 825–826; *For. Rels., 1928*, II, 594 ff.; Rippy, *Capitalists and Colombia*, pp. 31–33.

[63] *For. Rels., 1923*, I, 831–833.

[64] Claude M. Fuess, *Calvin Coolidge: The Man from Vermont*, p. 414.   ,

Mexico

Relations with Mexico fall naturally into two periods: first, that while Hughes was Secretary of State, and second, that under his successor, Kellogg. When Carranza was overthrown and General Alvaro Obregón became President of Mexico the administration in Washington naturally wondered if its neighbor was again descending into anarchy. Following Republican precedents, established under Taft, and prodded by alarmist agitations of the Fall Committee, Washington sought economic guarantees prior to the extension of recognition. Obregón insisted that such guarantees were inconsistent with sovereignity. In response the State Department continued to frown on bankers' loans to the new regime[65] —but Obregón grew stronger.

After substantial delays agreement was made for a commission to discuss pending claims. The United States appointed Charles Beecher Warren, former ambassador to Japan, and former Secretary of the Interior John Barton Payne as its representatives. It was agreed that Mexico would respect subsoil rights (the heart of the petroleum issue) in all cases where positive acts of exploitation had taken place prior to the passage of the new laws, and that it would extend preferential treatment in certain other cases. Likewise a claims commission was established to consider damages suffered by United States citizens during the revolutionary disturbances. Though the work of this commission was not to prove too successful,[66] the establishment of the commission did improve relations. Finally, on August 28, 1923, an *aide-mémoire* was sent to representatives in Belgium, Cuba, France, Great Britain, and Poland (who had asked for guidance in their own handling of Mexican relations) stating that recognition would be extended to Mexico at noon on September 3, 1923.[67]

In short order the revolutionary habit reasserted itself and Obregón was faced by a serious rebellion, headed by 20 per cent of the 508

---

[65] *Investigation of Mexican Affairs* (Sen. Doc. 285, 66th Cong., 2d. Sess.), pp. 3369 ff.; *For. Rels., 1922*, II, 697 ff.; F. J. Dillon, "Mexico and World Reconstruction," *Quar. Rev.*, CCXXXVIII, No. 472 (July, 1922), 159–160.

[66] Pusey, *Charles Evans Hughes*, II, 54 ff.; Frederick Sherwood Dunn, *The Diplomatic Protection of Americans in Mexico*, pp. 405–406, 418–420; *Survey of Int. Affs., 1927*, p. 468; James Morton Callahan, *American Foreign Policy in Mexican Relations*, pp. 592 ff.

[67] *For. Rels., 1923*, II, 554.

generals of the Army, and troops to the number of more than 23,000. Involved was the bitterness invoked by rebellious and fanatical Roman Catholics who resented new and stringent anti-Church laws. During the controversy, the apostolic delegate was driven out of the country.[68] In spite of excited propaganda, Hughes staunchly supported the Obregón Administration. A request for the sale of warships to Mexico was declined but arms shipments were permitted[69] and Obregón triumphed. After Plutarco Elías Calles was elected as regular successor to Obregón in 1924 he was cordially entertained in Washington. Meanwhile extra war vessels had been withdrawn from Mexican waters and in 1925 a coaling station which had been maintained in Pichilingue Bay in Lower California since 1861 was relinquished at the request of Mexico City.[70]

Secretary of State Kellogg apparently thought he knew his Latin America after his attendance at the International Conference of States at Santiago, Chile, and after something of a tourist-type trip to neighboring states. But the fact was that by nature he was not *simpático* with either their culture or their intellectual processes. To make matters worse in the case of Mexico, his ambassador was James R. Sheffield, a man who did not like the altitude of the Mexican capital or the customs of the people. He considered firmness as absolutely essential in dealing with a Mexican Cabinet composed of mixed breeds. His critical reports probably added to his chief's already critical predisposition. In 1925 Mexico undertook to regulate the constitutional provisions of the petroleum laws. Under any circumstances this was likely to precipitate controversy, so it was not surprising that under the direction of Sheffield and Kellogg the existing controversy became acute. Further, it should be remembered that President Coolidge insisted on full protection of United States economic interests abroad and gave solid and sympathetic support to the oil companies in their protests.[71] An additional problem

[68] Álvaro Obregón, *Informes rendidos . . . ante el H. Congreso . . .*, p. 58; Luis C. Balderrama, *El clero y el gobierno de México*, I, 158–160.

[69] *For. Rels., 1923*, II, 567 ff.; Callahan, *American Foreign Policy in Mexican Relations*, p. 595.

[70] *For. Rels., 1924*, II, 436 ff.; *1925*, II, 584 ff.; C. C. Hyde, "Charles Evans Hughes," in Bemis, *Amer. Secs. of St.*, X, 308–309.

[71] Charles Wilson Hackett in *Mexico: Lectures before Inter-American Institute . . .*, pp. 85 ff.; Robert H. Ferrell, *Amer. Secs. of St.*, XI, 30 ff.; Bryn-Jones, *Frank B. Kellogg*, pp. 174 ff.

arose from Mexican expropriation of holdings of large landholders in its new economic and sociological program.[72]

Obviously nervous over the situation, on January 12, 1927, Kellogg informed the Foreign Relations Committee of the United States Senate that the Bolshevik menace in Mexico was serious and was calculated to bring about "the destruction of what they term American imperialism." At once many Americans became alarmed, and Mexicans felt outraged. The correspondent of the *Times* (London) had anticipated the rising agitation two months earlier, saying that a drastic policy on the part of Washington in connection with the oil and land situations was to be expected. The *New York Times* editorially expressed no doubts of the sincerity of the Secretary's fears, but felt that Bolshevik activities in Mexico and Central America were "only one of their [the Communists] glittering though futile plans of campaign."[73]

At this point Washington appeared to doubt the wisdom of its own approach. Kellogg's biographer thinks the Secretary wished to name Dwight Morrow to replace Sheffield; others say the inspiration for the appointment came from the President himself.[74] Be that as it may, the name of the J. P. Morgan partner was sent to the Senate and approved. The new appointee liked Mexico, its food, its atmosphere, and its culture. He invested his own money in a home in beautiful Cuernavaca and became a part of Mexican life in spite of his background in the citadel of finance, Wall Street.

Though his wife had mixed feelings and though Kellogg was almost cynical, the new ambassador tackled his job with an enthusiasm that was contagious. He suggested to President Calles, who truly wished to establish cordial relations with the United States, that the Mexican Supreme Court could do much to clear away obstacles. The hint was acted on and the Court at once defined and interpreted the laws both for petroleum and landowners. Then, on the heels of the Court action, Calles submitted an amendment to the petroleum act to his Congress.

[72] *For. Rels., 1926*, II, 605 ff.; Hackett in *Mexico: Lectures*, pp. 76 ff.; Stuart, *Latin America and the U.S.*, pp. 168–170.

[73] *New York Times*, editorial, January 13, 1927, 24.1; *For. Rels., 1927*, I, 356–357. See also the *Times* (London), November 20, 1926, 12c; November 25, 14c; November 27, 12c; and December 8, 15e.

[74] On the Morrow appointment see Ferrell, *Amer. Secs. of St.*, XI, 34, 54; Bryn-Jones. *Frank B. Kellogg*, pp. 181–182; Fuess, *Calvin Coolidge*, pp. 411–412; Harold Nicholson, *Dwight Morrow*, p. 291.

The amendment was quietly approved and the worst of the current storm was over. The hysteria of interventionism died.[75] The oil companies themselves were circumspect, but the long-existing talk of a "stern" policy had not been forgotten in the United States. Even worse, the spirit of the Mexican Constitution of 1917 called for nationalization of petroleum deposits. This meant that the threat of expropriation (to be implemented a few years later) remained.

With much justification the first application of the Good Neighbor policy may well be attributed to Dwight Morrow.[76] Acting extraofficially he brought about a solution of the delicate Church-state problem. Himself a Protestant, he felt it essential to eliminate the papal interdict and reopen the churches for the people. A British historian considers that this was Morrow's greatest triumph and comments that it was an "extraordinarily delicate enterprise for a citizen of the United States, who did not happen to be a Catholic himself, to undertake in a country where he was his own Government's official representative."[77] By the agreement negotiated, the clergy acknowledged the new Mexican property laws and agreed to abide by regulations of the individual Mexican states as to numbers of clergymen to be allowed within their borders.

An indication of the increasing stability of the Mexican government was a steady reduction in military expenditures from 107 million pesos in 1924 to 70 million in 1930. At the same time the Army itself was reduced from 75,000 to 50,000 men.[78] Relations with the United States became increasingly cordial and the Presidents of the two countries could exchange congratulatory telegrams on the opening of the first regular air-mail service between the two nations on October 1, 1928.[79]

[75] *For. Rels., 1928*, III, 306 ff.; Plutarco Elías Calles, *Informe . . . al H. Congreso . . . Educación Pública*, XVIII, No. 19 (1928), 89.

For secondary accounts see Hackett in *Mexico: Lectures*, pp. 90–91; Guy Stevens, *Current Controversies with Mexico* (Foreign Policy Association addresses, March 13, 1926, and April 29, 1927), pp. 34–35, 190–191; J. Reuben Clark, "Oil Settlement with Mexico," *For. Affs.*, VI, No. 4 (July, 1928), 614; Dunn, *Diplomatic Protection of Americans in Mexico*, pp. 365–366.

[76] *Rev. of Revs.*, XCIV, No. 6 (December, 1936), 73–74; Walter Lippmann, "Church and State in Mexico," *For. Affs.*, VIII, No. 2 (January, 1930), 200–201.

[77] *Survey of Int. Affs., 1930*, pp. 384–385; *For. Rels., 1928*, III, 326 ff.; *1929*, III, 479 ff.

[78] Edwin Lieuwen, *Arms and Politics in Latin America*, p. 111.

[79] *For. Rels., 1928*, III, 325–326.

Central America

In the campaign of 1920 the Republicans inveighed against Democratic interventionism, saying that they would return to the old and tried *de facto* recognition policy. But the Central American situation soon proved the *de facto* program might not be advisable in practice. Further, the extraordinary complications arising in Nicaragua precipitated the last military intervention undertaken by the United States for more than a third of a century.

To begin with there were perennial negotiations about actual and prospective loans; an endless procession of rivals for power; questions of the maintenance of marines in the troubled areas; attempts to withdraw marines and to replace them with a satisfactory local constabulary; periodic sending of warships to protect threatened interests; and efforts to satisfy fearful minorities who wanted continued intervention. All these added up to a constant headache which involved the recurring problem of whether to hold supervised elections or not. No wonder an interviewer on December 16, 1924, found Secretary Hughes "in a frightfully bad humor" on the subject of Nicaragua.[80] The Secretary's wrath had been aroused over an election in which an incumbent President had secured 48,000 votes over opponents who received 28,000 and 7,000, but an election in which "Many of the customary abuses seem to have occurred."[81] Making the best of a bad situation, the United States extended recognition though all knew the lid was likely to blow off because the man who had received 28,000 votes was almost sure to take matters into his own hands.[82] Nevertheless the United States continued its plans to withdraw its marines even when the legally (?) elected President blandly stated that he had no plans for a constabulary and that the withdrawal would mean serious disorders.[83] It was easier, once he had secured recognition, to have the United States police the country than to do it himself. In spite of his protests, the last of the

[80] Diary, December 17, 1924, Chandler P. Anderson Papers, LC. See also entries for March 12 and December 20, 1921; February 7, May 17, and June 21, 1922; *For. Rels., 1921*, II, 557 ff.; *1922*, II, 748–749; *1923*, II, 605 ff.; *1924*, III, 487; Department of State, *The United States and Nicaragua*, pp. 43 ff. For a critical view see Rafael de Nogales, *The Looting of Nicaragua*, pp. 86–87, 204–205.

[81] Dana G. Munro, *The United States and the Caribbean Area*, p. 245.

[82] Department of State, *The Right to Protect Citizens in Foreign Countries . . .*, p. 123.

[83] Department of State, *U.S. and Nicaragua*, p. 53.

legation guard of about a hundred men withdrew in 1925. Within a month a revolt was launched; the President was persuaded to resign; the Vice President fled the country; and General Emiliano Chamorro seized power via a procedure which *he* pronounced to have been constitutional. After a number of maneuvers one Juan B. Sacasa claimed the chief office in opposition to a Washington-endorsed candidate, Adolfo Díaz.[84] Again the merry-go-round. Mexico recognized Sacasa and sent him supplies, while the United States continued to support Díaz. Marines were again landed. For the most part Latin Americans on general principles sympathized with those who were resisting the intervention.[85]

Exasperated, Coolidge took matters into his own hands and sent down a personal agent, Henry L. Stimson, to see what could be done. Stimson had served as Secretary of War under Taft and had had some military experience in Europe in World War I. His instructions were relatively simple: "If you find a chance to straighten the matter out, I want you to do so."[86] By the end of April, 1927, he had interviewed representatives of the contending factions and had installed a coalition government under United States auspices. This involved the surrender of arms by rebel bands to United States marines, the organization of a local constabulary, and supervision of elections to be held in 1928. A British comment was that the efforts of the United States authorities seemed to have been "Prompt, energetic, and conscientious," instrumented with a degree of success that might be "held to justify the somewhat high-handed methods" employed.[87] The fly in the ointment was the fact that Augusto Cesar Sandino refused to recognize the agreement and betook himself to the jungles to defy both the newly established regime and the United States marines supporting it. Sympathy for

[84] *For. Rels., 1926*, II, 780 ff.; Lawrence Dennis, "Nicaragua: In Again, Out Again," *For. Affs.*, IX, No. 3 (April, 1931), 498; Raymond Leslie Buell, "Reconstruction in Nicaragua," *For. Pol. Assn. Reports*, VI (1930–1931), No. 18, 319–320.

[85] For Mexican aid to Nicaragua see the Anderson Papers, LC, Diary, October 6, 1926, and *For. Rels., 1927*, III, 294–295. For troops sent see *ibid.*, pp. 312–313; Department of State, *U.S. and Nicaragua*, pp. 68–69; and Bryn-Jones, *Frank B. Kellogg*, pp. 196–197.

[86] Diary, April 1 in "Nicaragua" volume, Henry L. Stimson Papers, Yale.

[87] *Survey of Int. Affs., 1927*, p. 504; *For. Rels., 1927*, III, 318 ff.; Munro, *U.S. and the Caribbean*, pp. 255–256. Stimson's Diary, "Nicaragua" insert after entry for April 18, points out reported racial frictions arising from varying tribal origins of the factions (Stimson Papers, Yale).

Sandino ran high in Mexico and in neighboring countries which had long feared intervention. To the United States he was just a renegade swamp rat who posed as a patriot.[88]

Slowly a semblance of order was established and preparations were made for the elections of 1928. When Stimson asked a leading Nicaraguan if there was "any possibility" of "fair elections in Nicaragua at any time" the answer was "Yes," progress had already been made. "Elections many years ago [were] controlled by violence and force; now [they are] controlled by fraud."[89] Nicaraguans, tired of disorders, accommodated themselves philosophically to the new order; the rebels lost their glamour; disarmament proceeded apace; an election board was established and elections were held on November 4, 1928. Nearly 150,000 votes were recorded with no disorders of any kind. The Liberals were easily victorious under General José María Moncada, and the consensus seemed to be that this was the nearest to a fair election in the history of the republic. Now there remained the old problems of financing the new administration and then of withdrawing the intervention forces.[90]

In the background there was the question of the strategic value of a possible Nicaraguan canal. Coolidge expressed it thus: "The proprietary rights of the United States in the Nicaraguan Canal route, with the necessary implications growing out of it affecting the Panama Canal, together with the obligations flowing from the investments of all classes of citizens in Nicaragua, place us in a position of peculiar responsibility."[91] Sporadic talk of the matter was to be noted. The French

[88] *For. Rels., 1927*, III, 286 ff.; Department of State, *U.S. and Nicaragua*, p. 103. For interpretations see José Vasconcelos. *Bolivarismo y Monroismo*, p. 188; Carleton Beals, *Banana Gold*, pp. 178 ff.; Bryce Wood, *The Making of the Good Neighbor Policy*, pp. 35 ff.

[89] Diary volume for "Nicaragua," memorandum of interview of April 18, Stimson Papers, Yale.

[90] For pacification see Stimson Papers (Yale), Diary volume for "Nicaragua," II, May 15; *For. Rels., 1928*, III, 559 ff.; Department of State, *U.S. and Nicaragua*, p. 77 ff. For Nicaraguan finances see the Stimson Diary, "Nicaragua," II, May 14; *For. Rels., 1927*, III, 418–432; *1928*, III, pp. 527 ff.; Department of State, *U.S. and Nicaragua*, p. 97. For supervision of elections see *ibid.*, pp. 82 ff.; H. W. Dodds, "American Supervision of Nicaraguan Elections," *For. Affs.*, VII (April, 1929), 488; Buell, "American Supervision of Elections in Nicaragua," *For. Pol. Assn. Reports*, VI (1930–1931), 385 ff.

[91] Quoted in Department of State, *U.S. and Nicaragua*, p. 67.

Contre-Admiral Degouy considered that the fundamental motive back of the United States' actions in Nicaragua was that of naval policy and a canal.[92] It was patently incumbent on the United States to keep a guiding hand on the Nicaraguan shoulder.

The story for the rest of Central America should be considered in the context of efforts being made in the direction of peace among the neighboring republics. Realistically, García Calderón declared: "In Central America it is not the *caudillos* but the strong arm of the United States which watches over the destiny of the five republics."[93] The question now was whether the strong arm would operate singlehandedly or in cooperation with other republics of the hemisphere. H. W. Dodds, responsible for supervising the Nicaraguan elections of 1928, felt that any effort to secure Latin American endorsement for necessary intervention was "utterly visionary and impractical."[94]

After the demise of the Central American Peace Court in 1917 many still hoped that something might be salvaged from the idea involved. Early in 1921 all the Central American republics except Nicaragua took steps to enter a pact looking toward ultimate union. By October, Guatemala, El Salvador, and Honduras had actually announced such a union. But by December came word that El Salvador and Honduras had "rather broadly intimated" that they intended to intervene in Guatemala because of revolutionary conditions in that republic. The United States frowned heavily and no intervention took place. Washington then took the initiative. Arrangements were made for the Presidents of Honduras, Nicaragua, and El Salvador to meet on board the *U.S.S. Tacoma* on August 22. The meeting reaffirmed the treaty of 1907, denounced international meddling by one country in the affairs of a neighbor, and encouraged freedom of trade and the settlement of boundary disputes by arbitration. Hoping that the other two Central American countries would subscribe to the agreement, the Secretary of State of the United States

---

[92] "Le Canal de Nicaragua et la Stratégie Américaine," *Revue des Deux Mondes,* 7th period, XXXVIII (March 15, 1927), 446 ff. See also *For. Rels., 1923,* I, 834 ff.; T. A. Bailey, "Interest in Nicaraguan Canal," *Hisp. Amer. Hist. Rev.,* XVI, No. 1 (February, 1936), 13 ff.; *For. Pol. Assn. Reports,* IV (1928–1929). p. 113.

[93] "Dictatorship and Democracy in Latin America," *For. Affs.,* III, 469. It appears that there were a scant 5,000 United States citizens living in all of Central America at this time, and only 482 were in Nicaragua in 1929 (Chester Lloyd Jones *et al., The United States and the Caribbean,* pp. 69–70).

[94] Dodds, "Intervention in Central America," *The Annals,* CXLIV (July 1929), 99.

then invited all five of the republics to send representatives to a meeting at Washington. By November, 1922, all had accepted.[95]

Secretary Hughes presided over the sessions with his usual talents for organization and management. He held quarreling groups together, never "letting his dignity get thawed or his geniality get frozen."[96] The result was a mutual pledge dated February 7, 1923, to submit international difficulties to commissions of enquiry and not to recognize revolutionary governments in Central America. In spite of the recently announced return to the *de facto* recognition policy, Secretary Hughes subscribed to this *de jure* practice to be applied by his country in Central American affairs. Specifically, the statement was "that North American recognition to a new government in Central America would not be given, if the new president should have been a leader in the preceding revolution or should be related to such leader by blood or marriage, or if he should have been a cabinet officer, or held some high military command during the accomplishment of the revolution."[97]

When trade with the ten countries of the Caribbean area was increasing 81.82 per cent from 1913 to 1927 (in no single one of the countries was the increase less than 24.87 per cent)[98] investors and traders commanded increasing attention. They naturally were looking for profits but Washington gladly helped them lest European moneys re-enter the scene. In particular, rubber production was fostered, radio control secured, and airlines established in Nicaragua. With regard to government loans Dodds appropriately expressed the situation thus: "Don't blame the bankers for past Nicaraguan loans. They have acted, oftimes reluctantly, at the request of the State Department. And don't believe that

[95] *For. Rels., 1921*, various but especially p. 144; *1922*, I, 420 ff., II, 567 ff. See also Philip Marshall Brown, "The Federation of Central America," *Amer. Jour. Internat. Law*, XV, No. 2 (April, 1921), 255 ff.; James G. McDonald, "Mandates: America's Opportunity," *The Annals*, XCVI (July, 1921), 93–94.

[96] William Hard, "Charles Evans Hughes," *Rev. of Revs.*, LXXVII (January, 1928), 41; *For. Rels., 1923*, I, 320 ff.

[97] Edwin Emerson, *Hoover and His Times*, p. 401. See also Chandler P. Anderson, "Central American Policy of Non-Recognition," *Amer. Jour. Internat. Law*, XIX, No. 1 (January, 1921), 166.

[98] Winkler, *Investments in Latin America*, p. 277. See also *For. Rels., 1927*; Jones *et al.*, *U.S. and the Caribbean*, pp. 73, 185–186; Chester Lloyd Jones, *Caribbean Backgrounds and Prospects*, pp. 293 ff.; Brandes, *Hoover and Economic Diplomacy*, pp. 122–123; Samuel Crowther, *The Romance and Rise of the American Tropics*, p. 357 ff.

the United States marines are in Nicaragua to protect bankers' investments. . . . Were they [the Central American republics] thrown open to unrestricted exploitation by the armed forces of governments whose nationals had interests therein, they would readily become another arena of friction such as Africa and the Balkans have been in the past."[99]

The old boundary disputes called for periodic consideration. When Panama refused to accept the White award in its dispute with Costa Rica, the *U.S.S. Pennsylvania* took on board marines for service on the Isthmus. Panama accepted the award.[100] Another dispute was that between Guatemala and Honduras which had arisen about the middle of the nineteenth century.[101] Finally in 1930, at the insistence of Washington, negotiations were renewed and an arbitral award secured from the Central American tribunal specially functioning in this case. The award was applied and the boundary defined in 1936 by a technical commission under a United States officer as neutral member and chief. The Honduras-Nicaragua line also gave trouble. In this case efforts to find a solution in 1921, 1922, and 1923 failed chiefly because of revolutions which disrupted the governments of both countries.[102]

Early in 1922 came an election in Guatemala with returns of some 168,000 votes to 400. The United States recognized the victor and tried to protect his administration against loan sharks.[103] However, Guatemala was next door to Mexico and the Mexican influence proved to be anything but placating.[104] Honduras, too, fell on hard times politically in spite of effective work of its financial adviser. In the election of 1923 the United States refused to endorse any one presidential candidate but stated that it would recognize the candidate accepted by the other Central American republics as victor. Pleas for a visit from a warship were declined until actual rebel attacks occurred and martial law had been established. Finally, at the end of 1923 a vessel was sent.[105] The

[99] Dodds, "The U.S. and Nicaragua," *The Annals*, CXXXII (July, 1927), 141.

[100] *For. Rels., 1921*, I, 177 ff., 213 ff.; Howland in *Amer. For. Rels., 1929*, pp. 212 ff.

[101] *For. Rels., 1923*, I, 354–355; *1928*, III, 714 ff.; J. Lloyd Mecham, *The United States and Inter-American Security, 1889–1960*, pp. 170–171.

[102] Extensive correspondence is in Volume I of each year of *For. Rels.*

[103] Extensive correspondence on the topic is found in Volume II of each year of *For. Rels.*

[104] Beals, *Banana Gold*, pp. 75–76; Wallace Thompson, "The Doctrine of 'Special Interest' . . . in the Caribbean Sea," *The Annals*, CXXXII (July, 1927), 157.

[105] *For. Rels., 1921*, II, 247–248; *1923*, II, 425 ff.

next April, Sumner Welles was sent down to try to decide what was to be done in a political battle royal involving ten presidential candidates. Government had broken down and marines were landed to protect foreign holdings. Consultations, attended by representatives of other Central American countries, worked out an arrangement for a new administration which was to be recognized "unofficially as the Provisional Government of Honduras."[106] Also vital military supplies were made available and the neighboring countries (El Salvador and Guatemala) were warned to prevent non-neutral activities within their borders against Honduras. An apparent solution had been reached but arms shipments still had to be watched. Under such tutelage and with the active support of the United States Fruit Company an unconditional most-favored-nation treaty was negotiated and ratifications were exchanged on July 19, 1928.[107]

With little El Salvador all went rather smoothly under the direction of the loan agreement of 1923. The same was true of Costa Rica, which appreciated the position taken by Washington in the boundary award with Panama. The question of the Nicaraguan Canal route, however, was a difficult one. Part of the proposed route ran through the valley of the boundary river which separated Nicaragua and Costa Rica. The latter country, therefore, felt a tremor of fear whenever there were indications of rising United States interest in a new canal. Efforts to commit Costa Rica to any kind of agreement met with obstructions.[108] These arose both from fears of losing a bargain and from jealousy of United States power and influence in Nicaragua. To add to the uncertainties were recurrent rumors of petroleum deposits in or near the potential canal zone. Ever since the activities of Lord Cowdray there had been waxing dreams and waning hopes of such possibilities.[109] No solutions were reached. Here was another country with which there

---

[106] Henry Merritt Wriston, *Executive Agents in American Foreign Relations*, pp. 516–517. See also *For. Rels., 1925*, II, 316 ff.; *1928*, III, 77–79; *1931*, II, 584 ff.

[107] *Ibid., 1927*, III, 92 ff.

[108] *Ibid., 1923*, I, 834–836; Department of State, *U.S. and Nicaragua*, p. 32.

[109] *For. Rels., 1922*, I, 996 ff. In a treaty of August 5, 1914, the United States secured a ninety-nine year lease on the Corn Islands off the Nicaraguan coast (*ibid., 1923*, II, 615). When an ownership dispute arose between Colombia and Nicaragua over the islands the United States was interested but professed no desire to acquire the islands for itself (*ibid., 1928*, I, 701 ff.).

appeared no propitious time to negotiate one of the newly desired trade treaties.[110]

In Panama irritation over the White award was partly moderated by the good offices of Washington which led the way in 1924 to an agreement with Colombia over the joint boundary of the two countries.[111] Bankers' loans to the little republic were customarily approved in Washington and local financial conditions were subject to indirect oversight through a financial adviser.[112]

Another item of importance in Panamanian relations was the uncertainty arising from the Hay-Bunau-Varilla Treaty of 1903 and from the executive agreement negotiated by Taft for the management of Canal Zone affairs. After twenty years many provisions of these early arrangements had become obsolete. Both House and Senate in Washington passed a joint resolution recommending abrogation of the agreement. Panama soon let it be known that it preferred for the negotiations to proceed in Washington rather than through the "dictatorial" military authorities in the Zone. Commissions were appointed which held twenty-one sessions in the early part of 1924. Later the commissions were reconstituted and held additional sessions in July, 1925, and again a year later. Finally, on July 28, 1926, a treaty was signed. This convention carried out the spirit of the Hughes pronouncement that "We intend in all circumstances to safeguard the Panama Canal."[113] To this end the treaty gave the United States military access to all parts of the republic in case of war. It also agreed that American authorities could hold military maneuvers in Panama at any time merely on giving notice of intention. Panama declined to approve the treaty and asked to reopen negotiations. Then word came in 1928 that it would be futile to resubmit the treaty to the Panamanian assembly.[114] In the United States serious criticism had also arisen. The treaty lapsed.

[110] *Ibid., 1927*, II, 500 ff. An interesting set of British claims against Costa Rica were arbitrated by Chief Justice Taft of the United States Supreme Court (*ibid., 1921*, I, 665 ff.). Students interested can secure some delightful details by consulting the Anderson Papers, LC, Diary, May 28, 1924.

[111] *For. Rels., 1923*, I, 331 ff.; *1924*, I, 287 ff.

[112] *Ibid., 1921*, II, 600 ff.; *1923*, II, 689 ff. See also *Sale of Foreign Bonds*, Pt. 4, pp. 1934 ff.

[113] Hyde, "Charles Evans Hughes," in Bemis, *Amer. Secs. of St.*, X, 349. Also *For. Rels., 1922*, II, 751 ff.; *1923*, II, 676 ff.; *1926*, II, 828 ff.

[114] *Ibid., 1927*, III, 486 ff.

One petty item will serve to illustrate the sensitive Panamanian feeling. On November 11, 1928, President Coolidge ineptly remarked that "Our outlying possessions, with the exception of the Panama Canal Zone, are not a help to us but a hindrance." Forthwith the Panamanian minister took sharp exception to any suggestion that the Zone was a "possession."[115] He was only partly mollified when Secretary Kellogg gave assurance that both the policy of the United States and the relations existing between the two countries remained unchanged.

The Islands

Some suggested that the United States should take advantage of European postwar necessities to make generous offers to take over all remaining European colonies in the Caribbean. But even with the recent example of the Danish West Indies in mind, the United States took no formal steps in this direction.[116] Actually the United States had enough complications in the area to keep it busy.

In the first place there was Cuba. The economy of the island still rested primarily on sugar. In the early 1920's Cuba supplied some 56 per cent of the United States sugar market. Then started a decline, until in 1933 it provided a scant 25 per cent of the market. Sales of tobacco, molasses, and fresh fruits helped only to a small degree to compensate for the loss. To make matters worse a population of less than three million in 1919 became approximately four million in 1931.[117] Extracts from a wage table of a leading sugar company for prices paid for each hundred *arrobas* of cane harvested show the effects of the combined situation on the common man:

Prices Paid in Cuban Sugar Industry

Year	Cutting	Hauling	Contractor
1920	$1.20	$0.60	$0.50
1925	.80	.25	.30
1928	.60	.20	.25
1933	.20	.05	.07[118]

[115] *Ibid., 1928,* III, 680.
[116] Charles H. Sherrill, "The Front Door of America," *Rev. of Revs.,* LXXIII (February, 1926), 168–170. For Hoover's interesting effort in this direction see below, "The West Coast," Chapter Eight.
[117] Buell *et al., Problems of the New Cuba,* pp. 26, 48, 236.
[118] *Ibid.,* p. 287.

In this process large numbers of the weaker companies, and a disproportionate percentage of these were Cuban-owned, were squeezed out of the market. More and more of the production was controlled by large foreign-owned corporations.[119]

General Enoch H. Crowder was sent down as adviser to the Cuban government in January, 1921, to try to stem the tide. He sponsored drastic economies to reduce the Cuban budget from $130 million to $55 million. The reduction eliminated some fifteen thousand government employees and precipitated the resignation of seven of the nine Cabinet members.[120] Here were articulate critics. A new loan was floated by an American banking house early in 1923. The circular advertising the bond sale carried the interesting statement that it was "Issued with the acquiescence of the United States Government under the provisions of the Treaty dated May 22, 1903." In the same notice appeared a summary of the first three articles of the Platt Amendment under the caption of "Agreement with the United States."[121]

To carry through his extensive reforms Crowder submitted a series of fifteen memoranda to the Cuban administration involving numerous internal matters.[122] The following extract from a summary of one of his telephone calls to the acting chief of the Latin American Division of the State Department appears typical of the procedure followed:

General Crowder just telephoned from Habana to say that Congress last night had practically all-night session and passed loan law, including the provision of the one per cent sales tax by a vote of 86 to 12. The bill comes before the Senate today, and General Crowder expects quick action. He also expects the other reform bills to be passed this week, and that Congress will then adjourn until November.[123]

Crowder's success in reorganizing the island economy was rewarded when he was made United States ambassador to Havana. But repercussions were inevitable. The reforms had impinged on the famous Cuban National Lottery with resulting protests. True, the fiscal year 1922–1923 closed with a surprising surplus of about $12 million avail-

[119] *Survey of Int. Affs., 1933*, pp. 370 ff.; Leland H. Jenks, *Our Cuban Colony*, p. 284.

[120] Charles Edward Chapman, *A History of the Cuban Republic*, p. 438.

[121] Harry F. Guggenheim, *The United States and Cuba*, p. 228.

[122] *Ibid.*, pp. 213–215; Russell H. Fitzgibbon, *Cuba and the United States, 1900–1935*, pp. 173–174.

[123] *For. Rels., 1922*, I, 1042–1043, 1031 ff.

able for debt retirement. But the Cuban administration had "wearied of being so completely divorced from the fleshpots." Several members of the "honest cabinet" were dismissed and corruption again crept into the picture. President Alfonso Zayas on a twenty-five-thousand dollar annual salary was able to acquire a $300,000 property in a two-year period, while the expense account at the presidential palace listed $10,000 worth of chickens bought in a single month.[124]

Widespread unrest culminated in armed revolt in 1924. Washington quickly invoked an embargo on arms shipments to the rebels but allowed supplies to go to Zayas. The revolt was crushed but Zayas knew that his time had run out. He withdrew from the new electoral campaign in favor of General Gerardo Machado, who was duly elected and then inaugurated on May 20, 1925.[125] Cordial support was extended to the new strong man as the sugar crisis deepened.

In 1924 Machado had stated: "A Liberal President cannot be re-elected. This is now a noble tradition—the most noble of this party." But as 1928 approached he found his presidential appetite was still unsated, so he had the constitution amended to provide for a single presidential term of six years. Election to such a term, he insisted, was not incompatible with his previous pledges since he had only served four, not six, years.[126] He had made his own law and now controlled the ballot boxes. He was re-elected. Crowder clearly recognized that this was a serious step toward dictatorship, but Washington, faced with manifold problems, took the easy way out and announced that "this was a question for the Cuban people and their government to decide; that the United States only desired that the people of Cuba should have whatever government and constitution they themselves genuinely wanted."[127] The State Department was properly suspicious but hoped for the best.

[124] Chapman, *History of the Cuban Republic*, pp. 464–465; *For. Rels., 1923*, I, 844 ff.; Stuart, *Latin America and the U.S.*, pp. 234–236.

[125] Stuart, *Latin America and the U.S.*, pp. 236–237; Fitzgibbon, *Cuba and the U.S.*, pp. 183–184; Howland, in *Amer. For. Rels., 1929*, pp. 43 ff.; Chapman, *History of the Cuban Republic*, pp. 477–478.

At this time the ownership of the Isle of Pines (disputed since Cuba became independent) was recognized by the United States as a part of Cuba. The *Times* (London) reported this as part of a consistent program on the part of the United States to improve its New World relations (March 17, 1925, 13a).

[126] Buell, "Cuba and the Platt Amendment," *For. Pol. Assn. Reports*, V (1929–1930), No. 3, 38–39.

[127] Wood, *Making of the Good Neighbor Policy*, p. 51; *For. Rels., 1927*, II, 522.

Though the Republicans had criticized the military occupation of Haiti, Hughes proved to be a realist. When he was informed that the current President was cooperative but was faced with serious opposition, the Secretary advised that it would be satisfactory for the President to abstain from premature elections.[128] Meanwhile High Commissioner John H. Russell (recently brigadier general of the Marines) was instructed to reorganize the powers of United States treaty officials and to take steps to stabilize finances. At the same time marines were to be replaced by a local *gendarmerie*.[129] There ensued an apparently endless round of petty problems concerning the tendency of provost courts to dabble in political affairs (this Washington discouraged); the supervision of bond issues; questions of customs collections; and a multitude of others. All in all, however, events seemed to muddle along reasonably well.

In the United States the Foreign Policy Association and the Popular Government League and other protestants called for immediate withdrawal.[130] Yet the fact remained that financial efficiency had been secured and that much constructive work had been done in pacification of chaotic conditions, in addition to the construction of communications systems and public works, new agricultural development, and the improvement of public health. It was claimed that Haiti now enjoyed "a more truly representative system of government than she has ever known."[131]

An unfortunate feature of the situation was the dislike of Americans for "colonial" service in Haiti. "Between 1922 and 1928 five Financial Advisers, four sanitary engineers, three chief of *gendarmerie*, and two chief engineers for public works" held office.[132] In spite of this constant turnover of administrative officials the public debt was reduced by nearly one third between 1924 and 1930 and a substantial balance was accumulated in the treasury. These results were the more remarkable in

---

[128] *For. Rels., 1921*, II, 202.

[129] *Ibid., 1922*, II, 461–560; *1923*, II, 394–395; Arthur C. Millspaugh, *Haiti under American Control*, pp. 99 ff.; P. H. Douglas, "American Occupation of Haiti." *Pol. Sc. Quar.*, XLII, No. 3 (September, 1927), 385–387.

[130] D. Y. Thomas, *One Hundred Years of the Monroe Doctrine*, p. 266.

[131] Buell, "American Occupation of Haiti," *For. Pol. Assn. Reports*, V (1929–1930), Nos. 19–20, 357 ff.; Department of State, *Report of the President's Commission for Study and Review of Conditions in Haiti*, p. 26.

[132] *Amer. For. Rels., 1929*, p. 146.

view of an actual decline of the value of exports in the twenty years before 1929.[133]

Opinions differ widely on the amount of training in self-government provided by the intervention. The percentage of United States commissioned officers in the Haitian *garde* was the same (i.e., 10 per cent) in 1927 as in 1917. Indeed, after fourteen years of experience and when the treaty had only six more years to run, only five Haitians had reached the rank of captain. It is true that noncommissioned officers of the United States who were employed in the *garde* were reduced from 85 per cent to 54 per cent of the total, and Haitians rose from 5 to 35 per cent. The Health Service had a better record[134] in its upper ranks but an increasing number of observers were convinced that up to 1929: "We have built an airplane for a man accustomed to riding a donkey. . . . The machine runs beautifully now while we are at the controls, but how will it run when we step out in 1936 and the man who all the time has been on the donkey steps in to fly alone?"[135]

The field of public education was a peculiarly sore spot. The intervention had no direct responsibility for public schools under the treaty but it did control the finances and the distribution of moneys to the schools. Few Haitians had ever enjoyed school privileges, and those who had done so endorsed the old European prejudice against the "practical" and in favor of the "classical" type of education. When United States financial officers began to funnel moneys into the *Service Technique* for experimental farms, dairies, agricultural agents, and the like there were horrified protests.[136]

When France protested that Haiti was failing to live up to the terms of a loan agreement, the United States accepted the advice of its financial adviser in the island republic and refused to use pressure to force Haiti into an arbitration that would almost certainly have granted the French

---

[133] Millspaugh, *Haiti under American Control,* p. 125; Buell, "American Occupation," *For. Pol. Assn. Reports,* V (1929–1930), Nos. 19–20, 380–381.

[134] H. P. Fletcher, "Quo Vadis, Haiti," *For. Affs.,* VIII, No. 4 (July, 1930), 546–547; Millspaugh, *Haiti under American Control,* pp. 172 ff.; Williams, *Economic Foreign Policy,* pp. 172–173.

[135] Buell, "American Occupation of Haiti," *For. Pol. Assn. Reports,* V (1929–1930 , Nos. 19–20, 384.

[136] *Ibid.,* pp. 363–364; Millspaugh, *Haiti under American Control,* pp. 150 ff.; Douglas, "American Occupation," *Pol. Sc. Quar.,* XLII, No. 3 (September, 1927), 371; Emily Green Balch, ed., *Occupied Haiti . . .,* pp. 103–104.

demands.[137] Another irritating issue that remained unsettled, the boundary dispute with Santo Domingo, was the subject of sporadic reports and protests through the 1920's.[138]

In 1925 the new Secretary of State (Kellogg) again agreed that it appeared unwise to hold the elections scheduled for the coming January. The President of Haiti, who was a candidate to succeed himself, at once took the appropriate steps. He removed eighteen of the twenty-one members of his Council of State—the body that had the responsibility to choose the President in default of an election. The new body then re-elected him. A new unconditional most-favored-nation trade treaty was negotiated, and the Haitian constitution was revised in line with substantial recommendations from Washington. One of the changes extended the presidential term from four to six years with the proviso that the incumbent President was not to be a candidate to succeed himself. (The Machado maneuver was not to be permitted here.) When the election approached, the President evidently intended to run again. Washington frowned. Soon the commissioner reported that he had orally and unofficially pointed out to the Haitian President that an announcement from him that he would not again be a candidate for the office would add luster to his already great renown.[139] He did not run.

Efforts were made as early as June, 1921, to plan for withdrawal of marines from Santo Domingo. Negotiations proceeded through 1922 as American control was reduced step by step until it retained only the customs receivership. On June 12, 1924, a new President was inaugurated.[140] By September 18, 1924, the last of the marines embarked. Unfortunately relations between the commissioner and the new administration quickly deteriorated and a marked apathy in the prosecution of reforms became noticeable.[141] Meanwhile Santo Domingo had

[137] For French claims see *For. Rels., 1926,* II, 407 ff., and for British claims see *1928,* III, 61.

[138] *Ibid., 1920,* I, 303 ff.; *1922,* I, 439 ff.; *1923,* I, 359 ff.; *1928,* I, 711 ff.

[139] *Ibid., 1925,* II, 298–299; *1926,* II, 401 ff.; *1927,* III, 52 ff.; *1929,* III, 170 ff. For comments see Buell, *For. Pol. Assn. Reports,* V (1929–1930), Nos. 19–20, 386; and Harold Palmer Davis, *Black Democracy,* pp. 252 ff.

[140] *For. Rels., 1921,* I, 834 ff.; *1922,* II, 10 ff.: *1924,* I, 618 ff.; Sumner Welles, *Naboth's Vineyard,* II, 859 ff.; Pusey, *Charles Evans Hughes,* II, 533–534.

At this point Sumner Welles, who had recently been appointed as commissioner to Santo Domingo, began to assume importance in the Latin American policy-making field.

[141] Welles, *Naboth's Vineyard,* II, 899, 883–884. *For. Rels., 1924,* I, 662 ff.,

entered the League of Nations,[142] but its entry was to have no significant effect on its relations with the United States.

For the next year or so negotiations between the two countries centered on such problems as approval of periodic bond issues; questions concerning sugar and timber concessions; problems involved in the expenses of the customs receivership and the like.[143] In 1927 the President extended his term by two years. The opposition, through the Vice President of the republic, at once asked the United States to do something to block the procedure. The response was that if the United States intervened even the opposition would resent it. Therefore, Washington declined to act, especially since the extension was only for two years. At the same time the chief of the Latin American Division of the State Department personally warned potential protestants "that the Department would view with the greatest regret any political disturbances in the Dominican Republic."[144]

Unfortunately early satisfactory trade balances had been deceiving. The value of Dominican trade with the United States, which reached a peak in 1921, was reduced to less than half of the peak figure in 1926 and was to continue downward to reach one fifth that figure by 1931.[145] A sad situation indeed for the Hoover Administration to face.

In its outright possessions in the Caribbean the United States also faced complications. The alarming population increase in Puerto Rico caused the total to reach an estimated 396.2 persons per square mile.[146] The islanders boasted of their progress and were sure that twenty years of training should entitle them either to statehood or to some other form of self-control.[147] A more realistic view, expressed in 1930, was that "Ever since 1921 Porto Rico's financial history has been marked by rising public expenditures, increased taxes, and a mounting public debt.

---

gives terms of the new treaty, dated December 27, 1924. See also *For. Rels., 1940,* V, 804 ff.

[142] For implications see George H. Blakeslee, *The Recent Foreign Policy of the United States,* pp. 179–180.

[143] *For. Rels., 1924,* I, 654–655; *1926,* II, 40 ff. For economic developments see Williams, *Economic Foreign Policy,* p. 184; Melvin M. Knight, *The Americans in Santo Domingo,* pp. 138–139, 151.

[144] *For. Rels., 1927,* II, 553.

[145] Stuart, *Latin America and the U.S.,* p. 293.

[146] Victor S. Clark *et al., Porto Rico and Its Problems,* pp. xxiv–xxv.

[147] Pedro Capó Rodríguez in Blakeslee, *Mexico and the Caribbean,* pp. 337–360.

During recent years, indeed, Porto Rico's debt has included borrowing to cover a deficit in current funds, and, on a few occasions, the government has been unable to meet payrolls and other urgent bills when due."[148]

The Virgin Islands were in an even more perilous financial state. They had been acquired for strategic purposes and, even in 1917, had been recognized as a liability. As an observer had written to Lansing: "The purchase price of these islands was very great, and yet the islands constitute an indefinitely continuing liability. Additional millions will have to be given for sanitation, education and social ameliorations generally, and those extra millions added to the purchase price will make up a sum perhaps equal to the cost of one day of modern war."[149] Now the piper had to be paid and there was no war psychology to gloss over the unhappy economic facts. Two of the chief exports of the Islands had been rum and bay rum. The prohibition act had scuttled the one and synthetic hair tonics had ruined the sale of the other. Administration there was a thankless task. Six governors came and left between 1917 and 1925. [150]

Control of the "American Lake" remained unchallenged in the hands of Uncle Sam. Strategically he was determined to dominate it—and dominate it he did. Economically too his business was in control. But now restless local peoples were unhappy. Here was a foretaste of conditions in Africa and the Far East at the end of World War II. Suffering and unhappy peoples in the 1920's did not have the world-wide audience they later secured but their plaints were increasingly heard on the mainland from the temperate zone of the north to the temperate zone of the south. The businessman's administration in Washington was primarily interested in maintaining peace and showed scant sympathy. To it the righteous man was made prosperous by an appreciative Almighty. Feckless folk who were not prosperous evidently enjoyed little Divine favor. They should be governed for their own good. Such logic satisfied most of the governing group. Others were not so sure.

[148] Clark *et al., Porto Rico and Its Problems*, p. 288.
[149] December 31, 1917, Lansing Papers, LC.
[150] D. D. Hoover, "The Virgin Islands under American Rule, *For. Affs.*, IV, No. 3 (April, 1926), 503.

CHAPTER VII

1921–1929: RELATIONS

Canada

DOMINION PRIDE HAD RECEIVED a substantial boost during World War I and as a result of the recognition secured at the Versailles Conference. Some claimed that Canada was a confederation and not a nation,[1] yet a proud and sensitive people demanded nationalism in defiance of both politics and economics. It was still the fact that major economic ties were of a north-south variety across the border, while Canadian political ties were oriented from east to west. In 1896 Canada sent the Mother Country about three-fifths of its exports and bought there one third of its imports. By the mid-twenties these figures were down to less than two-fifths of the exports and less than one fifth of the imports. By this date the United States was buying almost as much of Canadian exports as the Old Country and was sending its neighbor goods valued at nearly four times the amount purchased from Great Britain.[2] Also, the wartime shift of the money market to Wall Street became a fixture. Canadian bond sales in Great Britain from 1916 to 1924 never exceeded $15 million per year, while an average of some $170 million went to American investors.[3] In the first thirty years of the century 70 per cent of

[1] John MacCormac, *Canada: America's Problem,* pp. 199, 215.
[2] *Survey of Int. Affs., 1928,* p. 414.
[3] Scott Nearing and Joseph Freeman, *Dollar Diplomacy,* pp. 26–27.

Canada's total immigration was lost by emigration to its southern neighbor. Sadly it was noted that the percentage of native-born Canadians in the Dominion had actually declined and that about one out of every six of the Canadian-born (and probably a third of the original Canadian stock) had moved south of the line by 1930.[4]

The *Times* (London) repeatedly commented on Canadian demands for independence or equality of status in the Empire. For instance, its Toronto correspondent reported that "There is no doubt that the Taft-Laurier agreement would now be accepted by the Canadian Parliament," if presented again in 1922.[5] Officialdom whistled bravely and reiterated that there was no danger of absorption by the United States but at the same time it eagerly sought means to forestall the possibility.

In Canada itself a new nationalism was arising. Some west Canadians resented domination by the French-Canadian, Roman Catholic group and were likewise attracted to the idea of union with the United States because of economic reasons.[6] Yet the politically powerful French Canadians continued to feel their political institutions were more secure in the Empire than they would be in an independent nation, or in the United States.[7]

Almost unconsciously Canada had become a Western power. British titles were accepted but any idea of a Canadian aristocracy was wholly incompatible with local ideas—ideas which had become strangely like those of its southern neighbor. In 1918 the Canadian House of Commons voted ninety-six to forty-two in favor of the abolition of titles.[8] The same tendency was seen in international policy. Secretary of State Hughes noted this when he said:

In 1921 the Disarmament Conference was held in Washington, and this Conference was due in a measure at least to the failure of Canada to agree to the renewal of the Anglo-Japanese Treaty that had come up for discussion at the

[4] MacCormac, *Canada: America's Problem,* pp. 201–202. See also *Survey of Int. Affs., 1924,* p. 106; J. A. Stevenson, "Political and Economic Situation in Canada," *Edinburgh Review,* CCXLI, No. 492 (April, 1925), 212–213.

[5] The *Times* (London), March 2, 1922, 11c. Also January 4, 1921, 9a; January 16, 1924, 11d; January 19, 1925, 11e; and January 27, 1925, 16–17.

[6] Stevenson, "Political and Economic Situation in Canada," *Edinburgh Review,* CCXLI, No. 492 (April, 1925), 226–227, and CCXLIV, No. 497 (July, 1926), 20.

[7] Stevenson, "Canada and Foreign Policy," *For. Affs.,* III (March 15, 1923), 114.

[8] John Gladstone Grace, "Canada as a World Power," *Rev. of Revs.,* LXXV (June, 1927), 636.

Imperial Conference which met that same year. Of this it is claimed that "the episode of the Anglo-Japanese alliance provided the first instance of the complete deflection of British foreign policy through the action of a Dominion. . . . The Foreign Office had definitely made up its mind to renew the pact. . . . But Mr. Meighen, the Canadian Premier, who had a better knowledge of American repugnance to the Alliance, took a very resolute stand against renewal."[9]

Refuting the suggestion that Canada had become a henchman of the United States, a skillful later historian has concluded that as a matter of fact: "What Mr. Meighen found in Canada and in himself was Canadianism. . . . It is not surprising the Canadian interest and policy revealed themselves to be quite similar to the interest and policy of the United States, for they sprang from a North Americanism whose roots in time and experience were of equal depth in the two nations."[10]

At the first meeting of the Assembly of the League of Nations in 1920 Canada began a four-year campaign against Article X of the Covenant. This clearly reflected the same isolationism that was so strong south of the border. One writer commented: "It is probably correct to say that on nearly every important political question that has come before the League, Canada has adopted a point of view that may be described as North American, one that would probably have been adopted by the United States herself if she had become a member of the Geneva organization."[11]

Canadian spokesmanship for the West was facilitated through the establishment of the new Canadian legation in Washington. This had been authorized by simultaneous declarations made in the British House of Commons and the Canadian Parliament in 1920. The new direct contact was implemented, so to speak, by a fisheries convention negotiated in Washington. For the purpose, the King issued full powers to a Canadian, appointed by the Canadian government, to conduct the nego-

[9] Address to American Bar Association, August 30, 1923, "Observations on the Monroe Doctrine," *Amer. Jour. Internat. Law*, XVII, No. 4 (October, 1923), 496–497.

[10] J. Bartlet Brebner, "Canada, the Anglo-Japanese Alliance and the Washington Conference," *Pol. Sc. Quar.*, L, No. 1 (March, 1935), 58.

[11] R., "Neighbors: A Canadian View," *For. Affs.*, X, No. 3 (April, 1932), 423. See also Frederick H. Seward, "Canada and the League of Nations," *International Conciliation Documents*, No. 283 (October, 1932), 38–39, Appendix; and James Frederick Green, "Canada in World Affairs," *For. Pol. Assn. Reports*, XIV, No. 8 (July 1, 1938), 92.

tiations. With great pride Canadians noted "the British Ambassador at Washington had no part in the undertaking."[12]

Over the years between 1909 and 1928 the International Joint Commission had satisfactorily disposed of fifteen cases. All but one of these had been by unanimous vote. Though the Commission had no power to enforce decisions the fact was its decisions had been implemented and troublesome problems had been laid to rest. In addition it had done much constructive work through its investigations and reports on other difficult international complications.[13] By the mid-twenties Canada sought public recognition of its status by an exchange of envoys extraordinary and ministers plenipotentiary. Coolidge was understood to consider the suggestion unnecessary.[14] However, such matters as renewed consideration of the St. Lawrence Waterway, the diversion of the waters of the Great Lakes, and solution of fisheries complications brought reconsideration of the idea.[15] In January, 1927, the British Secretary of State for Foreign Affairs was notified that Washington was sending ministers to both the Irish Free State and to Canada. Accordingly, on June 1 William Phillips presented his credentials at Ottawa while the Honourable Vincent Massey was approved as Canadian minister at Washington.[16]

Meanwhile Canada reviewed its position vis-à-vis Latin America. The opening of the Panama Canal had reduced the transportation costs of British Colombian lumber delivered to Eastern ports from $27.30 to $10.11 per thousand feet between 1920 and 1929.[17] Also the Canal opened new commercial prospects in Latin America. A step in this direction was taken in a series of trade agreements signed in 1925 between Ottawa and Britain's colonies in the Caribbean. But again the results were disappointing and new trade with South America developed slowly.

[12] N. A. M. Mackenzie, "Treaty Making Power in Canada," *Amer. Jour. Internat. Law*, XIX, No. 3 (July, 1925), 498; Charles Evans Hughes, *Our Relations to the Nations of the Western Hemisphere*, pp. 21–22; A. L. Lowell, "Treaty Making Power of Canada," *For. Affs.*, II, No. 1 (September 15, 1923), 17 ff.; *For. Rels.*, *1923*, pp. 473 ff.

[13] Hughes. *Our Relations to . . . the Western Hemisphere*, pp. 27 ff.

[14] *New York Times*, October 20, 1926, 8.2.

[15] *For. Rels.*, *1924*, I, 335 ff.

[16] *Ibid.*, *1926*, I, 578–580; *1927*, I, 482–483.

[17] Hugh L. Keenleyside, *Canada and the United States*, p. 289. Also James Quayle Dealey, *Foreign Policies of the United States*, p. 336.

Voices in Latin America called for Canada to be represented in the Pan-American conferences, and the influential James Brown Scott commented in 1931: "One day the Dominion of Canada will join the impressive procession of American States and take its place in the Governing Board" of the Pan-American Union.[18] However, few Canadian leaders dared advocate weakening the "bonds of Empire" at just this time. Thus the Fifteenth Conference of the League of Nations Society in Canada merely recommended "serious and careful" study of the questions of Canadian relations with other nations of the Western Hemisphere.[19] To many the Pan-American Union looked suspiciously like a colonial office through which to administer United States interests in the southern republics. Yet it is to be noted that Canada had been represented at more than twenty New World meetings or conferences on labor, radio broadcasting, postal affairs, international cooperation, medical problems, and the like.

Latin America and the League of Nations

While Canada was acting as a quasi spokesman of the United States before the League of Nations, the Latin American nations assumed a different position. They had received scant consideration at Versailles and were inclined to blame the United States for that.[20] When the League Covenant affirmed the rights of small powers Latin Americans applauded and eighteen of them joined the League in spite of its endorsement of the Monroe Doctrine. They hopefully felt that the spirit of the Covenant would tend to provide protection against the overweening influence of the United States. The ABC Alliance was defunct, and now the choice that remained appeared to be between the League on the one hand and the United States on the other.[21]

The League itself soon found its position to be a delicate one. It still hoped for the adherence of the United States. Further, it had all the complications on hand it could manage, and certainly did not want to acquire responsibility for the complicated New World disputes with

[18] James Brown Scott, ed., *International Conferences of the American States,* p. xiv; *New York Times,* January 14, 1923, I, Pt. 2, 8.3.

[19] Charles G. Fenwick, "Question of Canadian Participation in Inter-American Conferences," *Amer. Jour. Internat. Law,* XXXI, No. 3 (July, 1937), 475–476; John P. Humphrey, *The Inter-American System: A Canadian View,* pp. 255 ff.

[20] *For. Rels., The Paris Conference, 1919,* XI, 531–532.

[21] *Survey of Int. Affs., 1925,* II, 403.

which the United States had been wrestling. As though to give point to the problem in 1921 Bolivia, hoping to secure outside aid for its claims, besought the League to take cognizance of the violently disputed Tacna-Arica problem. Forthwith, Chile protested that this was a New World matter and came under the provision guaranteeing "regional understandings like the Monroe Doctrine" which were specifically exempted from League jurisdiction.[22] And even Panama tried to get the League to take jurisdiction over its boundary dispute with Costa Rica. Another appeal was from Nicaragua in 1926 when it asked for League good offices in a dispute with Mexico. In all these matters the League at once began to make excuse. Swiss arbitrators did settle one Colombian-Venezuelan boundary dispute but old tendencies were resumed and all other cases arising in the New World resorted to Washington, rather than to Geneva, for efforts at settlement.[23]

Latin American enthusiasm for the League declined steadily though the Geneva organization did its best to maintain its prestige in Latin America. Brazil, then Uruguay, were assigned seats on the Council in the early twenties, and the Chilean Agustín Edwards, followed by the Cuban Cosme de la Torriente Peraza, presided over the Third and Fourth Assemblies.[24] Brazil became disgruntled when its Council seat was not made permanent, and Argentina, never more than lukewarm on internationalism and having qualified its adhesion to the League by disapproving Article XXI, soon ceased to send representatives to League meetings. By 1929 only Chile of the major Latin American powers remained active at Geneva. In general the feeling became prevalent that the League was dominated by the great powers of Europe. Latin Americans did not want to be involved in European affairs and so drifted away from the League itself. From the first they wanted the League to protect them against possible aggression of the United States. Also they wanted it to help solve their problems, but always without interfering in their affairs. For its part, the League was inclined to feel with Jules Cambon: "It has become superfluous to discuss the sanction back of the

[22] The *Times* (London), September 8, 1921, 7f.

[23] *Survey of Int. Affs., 1925,* II, 405–406.

[24] *Ibid.* For waning interest see Enrique Gil, *Evolución del panamericanismo,* pp. 208–209; Royal Institute of International Affairs, *The Republics of South America,* pp. 326 ff.; A. T. Wilson, "The Monroe Doctrine and the Latin American States," *Edinburgh Review,* CCXLIX, No. 508 (April, 1929), 247.

Monroe Doctrine; the fact is the Monroe Doctrine is recognized by all the members of the League."[25]

When Costa Rica pressed for a definition of that doctrine the *Times* (London) reported that for three days the Council discussed the request and then declined the "invidious task." The official answer was a bland statement that this was a question to be decided by the states concerned; that El Salvador had asked Washington for such a definition and was presumably satisfied [!] with the answer given.[26]

All but three of the Latin American republics sent representatives to the first session of the League Assembly. Six sent no delegates to the second. Then more and more of them lost interest until the ninth session, when only five (Chile, Paraguay, Colombia, Uruguay, and Venezuela) had representatives in attendance.[27] And not one of these was from the Caribbean area, where presumably fear of the United States was at its peak. A late study has reported that of 1,545 ratifications of eighty League conventions, agreements, and protocols enacted prior to 1934, only 164 came from Latin America. Even in the case of the protocol for the Permanent Court of International Justice, five of the nine failures to ratify were those of Latin American nations.[28]

In more specific fields a few minor items might be mentioned. The League did express disapproval of the provision of the 1926 treaty of the United States with Panama which provided automatic inclusion of Panama in any war to which the United States might become a party.[29] When the treaty lapsed without ratification this ceased to be an issue. On its part, Washington protested the recommendations of the League to limit sales of arms to states not members of the Convention. In this connection it specifically mentioned the Latin American states.[30]

---

[25] Jules Cambon, "La Doctrine de Monroe," *Revue des Deux Mondes*, 7th period, XLVII (September, 1928), 91.

[26] The *Times* (London), September 3, 1928, 12a.

[27] Warren H. Kelchner, *Latin American Relations with the League of Nations*, pp. 138–139.

[28] J. Lloyd Mecham, *The United States and Inter-American Security*, p. 93.

[29] *Amer. For. Rels., 1929*, p. 218; Graham H. Stuart, *Latin America and the United States*, p. 119.

[30] *For. Rels., 1922*, I, 549 ff.; *1923*, I, 38 ff.

When Mexico sought to buy two discarded naval cruisers from the United States in 1923 the Secretary of State declined on the basis of Article XVIII of the Treaty of Limitation of Naval Armament signed with Great Britain, France, Italy, and Japan on February 6, 1922. Periodically, however, shipments of arms were

Similarly, in 1925 the United States frowned on the proposal of Brazil to invite the League of Nations to send a representative of the International Law Section of the League to the Rio meeting of the International Congress of Jurists. Secretary Hughes pointed out that this was a Pan-American meeting of regional interest and not a proper forum for European representatives.[31]

In 1924 the Geneva protocol providing for arbitration of certain types of international disputes was formulated. Five times the British explored the attitude of Washington as the proposal progressed. Ambassador Howard reported from Washington that a violent explosion could be expected if the protocol were applied to any question involving the Panama Canal or Caribbean area. Both Hughes and Kellogg regarded this agreement as a potential "Holy Alliance." They noted that if it had been in existence in 1913 it might have served as a serious handicap for the United States in the Mexican situation. Hughes fell back on the idea that American questions should be settled by American nations. On March 12, 1925, British Foreign Minister Chamberlain informed the League Council that his government could not accept the protocol. On July 3 President Coolidge praised the Locarno negotiations, which by implication were a substitute for the protocol.[32] Possible hemisphere interference by Europe had again been side-stepped.

Europe Courts South America

As has been said, the proud Spaniard, the gallant Frenchman, the passionate Italian, and the conservative but persuasive Englishman all made their offers and proposals to the fair damsel South America. In

---

authorized to Honduras, Nicaragua, Mexico, and Ecuador on the basis of existing conditions and after the exercise of due care. Similarly, in 1928, great caution was to be employed in authorizing shipments of munitions to the quarreling powers of Peru, Bolivia, and Chile. Later Stimson was to boast of his part in drafting the joint resolution of 1912 which authorized arms embargoes, saying: "By 1928 its beneficent influence was so generally recognized that at the great Pan-American Conference held in Habana in that year, all of the nations of this hemisphere embodied in the treaty of 1928 as a definite and compulsory legal obligation the same policy we had been able to initiate as a discretionary power of the American President" (Stimson, "United States and . . . Latin American Republics," *For. Affs.*, IX, No. 3, Sup. [February 6, 1931], p. xiv.)

[31] *For. Rels., 1925*, I, 302–303.

[32] David D. Burks, "The United States and the Geneva Protocol of 1924," *Amer. Hist. Rev.*, LXIV, No. 4 (July, 1959), 891 ff.

addition, "The Teuton planned to abduct her by force. The awkward lover from the United States alternates declarations of love with a big-stick policy. Even the Japanese deigns to make sheep's eyes at her."[33]

Some anti-Japanese feeling arose but the amazing development of that country inspired respect, while its trade possibilities could not be ignored. German diligence was unsurpassed but its proud military heritage was sadly crippled by recent defeat. Only Bolivia now replaced a French military mission with a German one. In itself this step was significant in providing a foundation for Nazi influence in the Second World War.[34] Of all the rivals, however, the British probably proved the most effective.

At the Brazilian Centennial Conference, the *Times* (London) boasted, the crowds were so great at the British exhibit that the doors had to be closed from time to time to reduce the crush. It enthusiastically reported on the success of Latin American visits of British battle cruisers, parliamentary delegations, and of cotton manufacturers and other agents. It also commented openly that everything possible was being done to prevent renegotiation of the Brazilian reciprocity treaty with the United States. These activities culminated in 1923 with the appointment of four British financial experts to advise Brazil on economic development.[35]

Latin American courses began to make their appearance in British universities by 1922. An Anglo-South American Association was formed in 1925 to promote British trade with the southern continent and to inform the British public of the vital urgency of recapturing the great South American market. Even the Prince of Wales was sent on a South American tour; the *New York Times* reported that the "underlying interest" in the Prince's trip was "the development of British trade in the present great and potentially, in the future, greater markets of Argentina and her neighboring republics."[36] In Chile the Prince demonstrated a "keen interest" in securing a British team of five naval and air officers to help with "matters of organization, training, gunnery, sub-

[33] J. F. Normano, *The Struggle for South America . . .*, pp. 74–75.

[34] For view of Japan see J. Fred Rippy, *Latin America in World Politics,* pp. 228–229. For view of Argentine relations with Europe see *Survey of Int. Affs., 1929,* pp. 534 ff. For view of Germans in Bolivia see Germán Arciniegas, *The State of Latin America,* pp. 126–127.

[35] The *Times* (London), October 17, 1922, 11d, with later reports on the eighteenth and twenty-fifth of the month; November 28, 1923, 12d and 19b.

[36] *New York Times,* August 23, 1925, II, 1.8. Also the *Times* (London), March 20, 1922, 8c, and October 2, 1925, 8d.

marines and aviation." It was hoped this would eventuate in British construction of several units for the Chilean Navy.[37] Thus any United States competition faced experienced, alert, aggressive, and resourceful rivals, many of whom enjoyed entrenched interests.

Soviet Russia, too, was receiving consideration for both ideological and economic reasons. In August, 1926, Uruguay extended formal diplomatic recognition to the Soviet Union—the first Latin American state to take the step. By the same date Argentine and Brazilian coffee and rubber interests were investigating the possibilities of the Russian market.[38] More serious was the fact that various restless groups were intrigued by the possibilities of Communist affiliations. These disparate groups included Brazilian anarchists, Uruguayan and Chilean socialists, Cuban syndicalists, revolutionary generals in Mexico, and middle-class reactionaries in Peru. Many of them lost interest when they became acquainted with the rigidities of the Communist system, but certain idealists remained infatuated.

In the early twenties, however, Moscow paid little attention to Latin America. Then for the tenth anniversary of the Bolshevik Revolution a number of Latin American trade unionists and Communist leaders were invited to Moscow.[39] Soon it became apparent that in New World affairs the Soviet interest was "above all else aimed at the United States, whom it is hoped to embroil in international conflicts as a result." Elimination of American imperialism was considered as a prerequisite to the development of the revolutionary movement in the New World.[40] But organized Communist progress was clearly negligible. By July 30, 1927, a despatch from Rio de Janeiro reported that the Chamber of Deputies had voted to suppress Communism by a vote of 118 to 18, and that a number of the minority had voted on the grounds of "freedom of thought, speech and the press" and not because of Communist sympathies.[41] Three years later, in the midst of the depression, the *Times* (London) reported on "a vague form of Communism" in São Paulo, but added that this did not indicate "that labour is thinking of a Communist

[37] The *Times* (London), September 22, 1925, 14c and September 26, 11e.

[38] *New York Times*, August 26, 1926, 23.6.

[39] Robert J. Alexander, *Communism in Latin America*, pp. 19–20, 33 ff.; Dorothy Dillon, "International Communism in Latin America," *Latin American Monographs*, No. 19 (1962), pp. 2–4.

[40] *For. Rels., 1927*, I, 356 ff.; *New York Times*, April 25, 1926, 1.6 and 2.4.

[41] *New York Times*, July 31, 1927, II, 4.2.

experiment." It was "rather to be regarded as a sign of increasing anger at unexpected hardship."[42]

West Coast Problems

Strategic needs were not forgotten in the decade following the war. The Secretary of the Navy reported in 1925 and in 1926 that hydrographic mapping and an aerial survey of the Gulf of Venezuela were in process. Also *Foreign Relations* for 1928 carried extensive correspondence concerning airline contracts with every one of the twenty Latin American republics as well as with British possessions in Nassau and Belize. Also the Secretary of the Navy reported in 1929: "The aviation charting program had been modified by order of the Chief of Naval Operations to give charts of the east and west coasts of South America precedence over those of the west coast of Mexico from Punta Arenas to Rosario." In addition the Department of Commerce made "very elaborate studies" of Chile, Peru, Bolivia, and Colombia.[43]

With regard to internal affairs and disorders in the more distant republics, Washington was increasingly cautious. Undersecretary of State Joseph C. Grew recorded in his diary for October 10, 1924, that the policy of Secretary Hughes provided that no *de facto* government was to be recognized as such, yet: "Lately Mr. Hughes has been less and less inclined to place ourselves in the position where we should have to decline to recognize a government if it was shown that the elections were fraudulent or not constitutionally carried out." Grew then added: "In the course of our discussion the Secretary laughed and said, 'Why we have not had a fair or constitutional election in the United States for the last forty years.' He was, of course, referring to suppression of Negro suffrage in the southern states."[44]

When a *coup d'état* occurred in Ecuador in 1925 the United States chargé was instructed to keep all communications with the new authorities on a friendly but strictly informal basis, omitting all such titles as "Minister of Foreign Affairs." Three years later, on August 13, 1928,

[42] The *Times* (London), November 29, 1930, 13c, 13d.

[43] *Report of the Secretary of the Navy, 1925*, p. 196; *1926*, p. 607; *1929*, p. 205 Also *For. Rels., 1928*, III, 775 ff.; *Sale of Foreign Bonds or Securities in the United States* (Hearings before Senate Committee on Finance, 72d Cong., 1st Sess.), Pt. 2, p. 849.

[44] Joseph C. Grew, *Turbulent Era: A Diplomatic Record of Forty Years*, I, 637–638.

Secretary of State Kellogg informed his minister in Ecuador that the progress of the country since the *coup d'état* had given the United States much satisfaction. In view of the fact that progress could be expected to continue, recognition was extended.[45] The contrast of this position with Wilson's in the Tinoco affair is obvious.

From time to time alarmists proclaimed that the United States was about to seize the Galápagos Islands. To prevent such desecration, cession of the islands to either Colombia or Peru was suggested. For its part, however, the recent conduct of the United States had been so discreet that even one of the alarmists lamented that the Ecuadorian President was so fearful of Peru that he had lost all sense of danger from the United States.[46]

President Augusto B. Leguía in Peru had been the beneficiary of much financial aid from the United States. He was amenable to reason and requested that a northern naval mission be maintained at Lima.[47] Yet when Washington supported the boundary treaty negotiated between Peru and Colombia, Peruvians took offense. They claimed the United States forced the agreement on them and had cajoled Brazil into acquiescence while Colombia took potentially valuable lands on the upper Amazon. They argued that this was done to placate and partially reimburse Colombia for the Panama affair. Local feelings became inflamed and the Peruvian Congress declined to accept the treaty in either 1926 or 1927. It was not until 1928 that ratifications were completed. To make matters worse, on March 4, 1925, President Coolidge handed down his award in the Tacna-Arica dispute. This infuriated the Peruvians.[48]

On September 8, 1924, Don Arturo Alessandri resigned as President of Chile, seeking "hospitality" at the American embassy. In granting the request, the United States made no formal reference to "asylum." Four days later Secretary Hughes stated that since constitutional forms had apparently been followed he did not wish to raise the question of recognition. When doubts arose the ambassador was instructed to avoid

---

[45] *For. Rels., 1925*, II, 64–65; *1928*, II, 742.

[46] Manuel Ugarte, *Destiny of a Continent*, pp. 178 ff.; José Vasconcelos, *Bolivarismo y Monroismo* ..., p. 207.

[47] *Report of the Secretary of the Navy, 1926*, p. 12; *1930*, p. 10.

[48] Arthur P. Whitaker, *The United States and South America: The Northern Republics*, pp. 177–178. For the official record see *For. Rels., 1923*, I, 351–352; *1924*, I, 303–304; *1925*, I, 438 ff.; *1926*, I, 538–539; *1927*, I, 333–344.

"any formal relations" with the new authorities. Then on October 9 instructions were sent to recognize the present officials as *de facto* "authorities," rather than as a *de facto* government.[49] During the uncertainties of the next year the United States carefully refrained from allowing warships to visit Chilean waters for fear of misinterpretations. Finally, all breathed a sigh of relief when Alessandri reassumed his office on March 20, 1925. This enabled the United States to maintain formal relations with no special problems of recognition.[50] The following year Professor Edwin W. Kemmerer of Princeton University was invited to make financial recommendations to the Chilean government. Under his direction a federal reserve bank was organized and a new banking law and other fiscal reforms were recommended. Following Kemmerer, an expert on sanitation was engaged from the United States for a year.[51]

Relations with Bolivia remained on an even keel. In January, 1921, there was some uncertainty over the outcome of a hard-fought election. Two weeks later, however, Washington joined with Buenos Aires, Rio de Janeiro, and Santiago in extending recognition.[52] Bolivia still sought in vain to have the United States take the initiative in trying to secure an outlet to the sea in the settlement of the Tacna-Arica dispute. President Harding softened his declination by a personal letter to the President of Bolivia but pointed out that the current discussions were between Peru and Chile; hence Bolivia could only be included in the negotiations with the concurrence of the other two countries. Secretary Hughes also wrote that: "the Government of the United States regrets that it feels unable to take any initiative in this matter." In response to further pressure from La Paz the State Department reaffirmed its stand on May 5, 1924.[53]

East Coast Problems

In the heart of the continent but facing eastward was Paraguay. Diplomatic reports from that country revealed little of direct international concern to the United States, though the rankling Chaco dispute with Bolivia was disturbing. The minister in Paraguay reported that he had

[49] *Ibid., 1924*, I, 357 ff.
[50] *Ibid., 1925*, I, 582–587.
[51] Henry Clay Evans, *Chile and Its Relations with the United States*, pp. 181–182.
[52] *For. Rels., 1921*, I, 281, 289.
[53] *Ibid., 1922*, I, 468–469; *1924*, I, 320–322.

suggested to local officials that the two countries might ask the League, of which they were both members, to handle the matter. On April 5, 1926, he was sharply informed: "As you know the United States is not a member of the League of Nations and does not desire that its representatives propose the intervention of the League in any matter."[54]

Uruguay had long maintained friendly relations with the United States, especially in view of its long-standing fear of neighboring Argentina. In 1923 its minister at Washington wrote: "In the Republic of Uruguay the Monroe Doctrine has done no harm during one hundred years and this is indeed a long enough period of time to safely test any human institution."[55]

Next door was Argentina, where European trade and investments predominated. In October, 1924, at the annual meeting of the British and Latin American Chamber of Commerce, the statement was made that 70 per cent of the beef, mutton, and lamb imported to the United Kingdom came from South America[56]—and the overwhelming portion of this came from the Argentine. When President-elect Marcelo T. de Alvear visited England he has entertained by the Lord Mayor of London. One of the toasts proposed included the statement that the speaker (an Englishman) "believed it to be strictly true that in fact and substance, in power and potency, the Argentine Republic was now one of the great Powers of the world."[57] Music to thirsty ears.

Another European contact of growing significance to Latin America was strengthened by immigration controls recently established in the United States. The controls curtailed the rate of flow of Italians coming to this country in 1921–1923 to less than one fourth of those who arrived between 1900 and 1914. The Italians flowing to the United States had numbered three times as many as those going to Argentina. Now Italian immigration to Argentina substantially exceeded that to the United States.[58]

Relations between the United States and Argentina remained friendly, but not cordial. A naval mission despatched by Washington to Brazil

[54] *Ibid., 1926,* I, 532.

[55] J. Varella, "Meaning of the Monroe Doctrine to the Republic of Uruguay," *The Annals,* CXI, Sup. (January, 1924), 21.

[56] The *Times* (London), October 17, 1924, 10e.

[57] *Ibid.,* July 22, 1922, 9d.

[58] *Survey of Int. Affs., 1924,* pp. 107–108. Also Pan-American Union, *Bulletin,* LXII, No. 10 (October, 1928), 1027.

aroused much irritation in Buenos Aires. When the Argentines initiated a new navy building program[59] the business was routed to Italy, Spain, and Great Britain. Answers to protests by United States builders were that their bids were too high and included the frank admission that Argentina naturally bought supplies where it sold its produce. A side light was thrown on the matter by a simple additional statement to the effect that the chief of the naval mission liked Italy.[60]

When President-elect Hoover planned his South American tour in 1928 Argentina failed to invite him to visit that country until cautious enquiries revealed that he would travel on a United States warship and be accorded full presidential honors. After his arrival Mr. Hoover labored hard to make a good impression and apparently met with moderate success. But on all sides was heard the boast that Argentine international policy was "America for Humanity" in contrast with the Monroe Doctrine, which was understood to mean "America for the (North) Americans."[61]

A central theme in diplomatic correspondence with Brazil was that of naval construction. Brazilians felt that their Navy had brought them international recognition in the war. In 1922 Rio de Janeiro let it be known that it was considering the selection of a foreign naval mission to advise and strengthen the Navy. In spite of the Argentine protests, the American mission mentioned above was selected and its services were extended again in 1926.[62]

Before long the head of the naval mission recommended an extensive building program for Brazil. This included sixty thousand tons for cruisers and seventy thousand tons for battleships. On hearing the news, Secretary Hughes was so perturbed that he sent word he would rather recall the mission than be in the position of sponsoring the naval race in South America that this report portended. The head of the mission hurriedly revised his recommendation and omitted any proposals as to tonnage or types to be constructed.[63] Obviously, the head of the mission was thinking logically as a navy man assigned to one country, but Secre-

[59] For. Rels., 1922, I, 655–656; New York Times, July 5, 1923, 14.7, and July 24, 13.1.

[60] For. Rels., 1927, I, 424 ff.

[61] Roberto Kurtz, La Argentina ante Estados Unidos, pp. 279–280; Edwin Emerson, Hoover and His Times . . ., pp. 47 ff.

[62] For. Rels., 1922, I, 651 ff.; 1926, I, 574 ff.

[63] Ibid., 1924, I, 323 ff.

tary Hughes had to remember international feelings in neighboring countries.

Perhaps an overstatement of Brazilian feelings, but nevertheless an indicative one, was expressed in the *Jornal do Comercio,* a government organ, on the occasion of Mr. Hoover's visit in 1928: "Brazil was the first to recognize the Monroe Doctrine as an instrument of safety. The United States was the first in recognizing the independence of Brazil and later the proclamation of the republic. We admire the North American people; but we do not fear them knowing we are as strong as they."[64]

Wars and Rumors Thereof

The oft-referred-to Tacna-Arica controversy remained the overshadowing issue in South America. The story has been told so many times that repetition of the facts is omitted here. The League of Nations sought to head off debate on the issue because it feared the implications for Silesia and other world problems and because it did not want to antagonize the United States.[65] At the same time the United States sought to avoid South American complications[66] but was determined that the League should be kept out of New World affairs if at all possible.

Hughes preferred that arbitration of the dispute be left to a commission of jurists and sought to avoid a request that President Harding be asked to serve as sole arbitrator. Only when both Chile and Peru indicated that the President alone would be acceptable to both of them did Hughes acquiesce. The protocol of arbitration was signed on July 20, 1922. It provided that the arbitrator was to decide if a plebiscite, as approved at the time of the original truce negotiations in 1883, should now be held in the disputed area. If this were to be done, the conditions for holding the plebiscite were to be specified. On January 23, 1923, Secretary Hughes, on behalf of the President, reluctantly accepted the onerous task.[67] Bolivian claims and protests were ignored.

On March 4, 1925, President Harding signed the award, which required the holding of the plebiscite under the supervision of a commission of three, one appointed by each of the South American states, and

[64] Quoted by Emerson, *Hoover and His Times,* p. 43.
[65] *New York Times,* September 8, 1921, 1.1 and 2.4; September 9, 1921, 2.7; Kelchner, *Latin American Relations with the League,* pp. 76 ff.
[66] The *Times* (London), May 16, 1922, 9b.
[67] Hyde, "Charles Evans Hughes," in Bemis, *Amer. Secs. of St.,* X, 353; *For. Rels., 1922,* I, 505 ff.; *1923,* I, 364 ff.

the third named by the arbitrator. The commission was to determine boundaries and procedures to be followed in the voting.[68]

Endless complications ensued. General John J. Pershing—his European laurels still fresh—was asked to head the commission. On his arrival in South America, the General encountered obstructionist tactics by local officials. After a few months he informed the Secretary of State that ill health compelled his return to the United States. Once more Bolivian hopes arose only to be again ignored. General William Lassiter was selected to replace Pershing. Meanwhile Chile was sharply warned about the improper conduct of its officials, and the President of Peru was cautioned to watch his statements. Again progress proved to be impossible and Stimson as a special investigator of the Department of State reached the conclusion that no fair plebiscite was possible. This, incidentally, was the opinion of that skilled internationalist Edwin M. Borchard as early as 1922, who anticipated that the President would probably reach that conclusion when the case was first submitted to him.[69] Lassiter was completely baffled and withdrew from the commission, leaving feelings even more exacerbated.[70]

Secretary Kellogg next suggested that the region be demilitarized; that the disputed areas be ceded to Bolivia for adequate compensation, and that Arica become a free port. This suggestion was categorically rejected by Peru. Lima now proposed that the area be administered by the United States but this was not to be considered. At this point a ray of hope appeared in the very fruitlessness of all previous efforts. At the Havana Conference, Secretary Kellogg had conversations with Chilean and Peruvian delegates who agreed that diplomatic relations should be resumed by their countries.[71] This was the first break.

Another serious complication was the rising Chaco issue between Bolivia and Paraguay. Various proposals looking to arbitration of ownership of the area had been considered in vain since 1907. Meanwhile

[68] For. Rels., 1925, I, 304 ff.

[69] Ibid., 1925, I, 409 ff.; 1925, I, 392 ff.; 1926, I, 284; 1926, I, 454 n.; Borchard, "The Tacna-Arica Controversy," For. Affs., I, No. 1 (September 15, 1922), 47.

The Stimson Diary (in Henry L. Stimson Papers, Yale) for May 1, 1926, carries an evaluation from the Administration's point of view. Stimson had been asked by Secretary of State Kellogg to make a special report on the problem. Apparently Kellogg leaned heavily on former Secretary Hughes for guidance in the matter.

[70] For. Rels., 1926, I, 289 ff.

[71] Ibid., pp. 504 ff.; 1928, I, 669–670; 1928, I, 647 ff.

Paraguay had sold public lands in the disputed zone to Argentine specu- lators who set about securing immigrants for their holdings. Bolivia protested in 1924 and asked if the United States would consider making suggestions in the matter.[72] The answer was that such an action would only be undertaken if both republics asked for it.[73] Argentina tried to appear as peacemaker and vainly offered its good offices. Bolivia still wanted United States arbitration, but chauvinist agitators in both coun- tries soon excited public opinion to the point that each government found itself forced to demand exclusive control of the whole area.[74]

It would appear that Bolivian legal claims, going back to colonial days, were strong. Unfortunately, for them, as in the case of Mexican claims to Texas in the 1830's, Mother Nature had not cooperated with the legalists. The lands involved were almost inaccessible from the Boliv- ian plateau but could easily be reached from Paraguay—and actual oc- cupation was now taking place. Bolivia, in part because of its desperate need of access to water navigation via the eastern rivers, especially since its loss of the Arica outlet, clamorously stood upon its legal rights. Both nations hastily began straining slender resources to purchase military equipment.

Meanwhile the Gondra Convention (see below) had come into opera- tion, but Bolivia was not a signatory; hence, she was not bound by it. Further, the Kellogg Pact was not operative.[75] Stepping into the breach, the League of Nations despatched identical notes to both parties calling attention to their obligations under the Covenant, while it informally asked what Washington considered to be the best approach to the prob- lem. The response came from the action of the International Conference of American States on Conciliation and Arbitration (Secretary Kellogg being chairman), which passed a resolution offering its good offices to promote conciliatory measures and maintain the principle of arbitration. Bolivia accepted, but Paraguay wanted a commission of enquiry of the Gondra type. This Bolivia declined and added new demands for repara- tions for outrages already committed. The League, thinking the Pan- American arbitration movement held prospects of success, was inclined to keep in the background.[76] Meanwhile, the two contestants continued

[72] David H. Zook, *The Conduct of the Chaco War*, pp. 27, 37, 56.

[73] *For. Rels., 1924*, I, 282 ff.

[74] Zook, *Conduct of the Chaco War*, p. 47.

[75] *For. Rels., 1928*, I, 680–690.

[76] *Ibid.*, pp. 686 ff.; *British and Foreign State Papers, 1929*, Pt. I, pp. 890 ff.

to snarl at each other. Thus closed 1928. (See "The East Coast: The Chaco," Chapter Eight.)

Pan-Americanism

Latin American opinion of the policy of the northern republic at the end of the war was a mixture of endorsement of Wilsonian idealism and criticism of military intervention in Haiti, Santo Domingo, Cuba (for training purposes), Nicaragua, and Panama. In addition there was confused thinking about the Mexican problem. The United States had insisted on world recognition of the Monroe Doctrine in the League Convenant but it declined to define the doctrine so recognized. To make matters worse, many writers and men in public life carelessly used the term to cover any American activity in the New World, even though the problem discussed had nothing to do with European intervention. Now renewed economic penetration supplemented and appeared to be replacing military intervention to provide a situation that some Latins considered more insidious and dangerous than the old procedures.

Pan-Americanism had long been criticised as the major tool of United States foreign policy in the Western Hemisphere. The Union had its headquarters in Washington with the American Secretary of State as the presiding officer. American policy makers have been notorious for watching over their shoulders to see what the world thinks of their conduct. So it was that Latin American fears were well known in the United States. In fact, the sheer quantity of articles in English explaining the Latin American point of view was surprising. For their part, Latin Americans, too, were vocal in both Spanish and English.[77] Crimes of

[77] Books showing typical American opinions are: George H. Blakeslee, *The Recent Foreign Policy of the United States*; Rippy. *Latin America in World Politics*; Stuart, *Latin America and the U.S.*; Arthur P. Whitaker, *The Western Hemisphere Idea*. For articles on the subject see: C. H. Haring, "South America and our Policy in the Caribbean," *The Annals*, CXXXII (July, 1927), 146–147; S. G. Inman, "The Monroe Doctrine and Hispanic America," *Hisp. Amer. Hist. Rev.*, IV, No. 4 (November, 1921), 655–657; W. R. Shepherd "The Monroe Doctrine Reconsidered," *Pol. Sc. Quar.*, XXXIX, No. 1 (March, 1924), 35; Frank H. Simonds, "Unrest in Asia and Latin America," *Rev. of Revs.*, LXXV (March, 1927), 276–277.

For Latin American opinions see Alejandro Álvarez, *The Monroe Doctrine*, p. 201; Rufino Blanco-Fombona, *Crímenes del imperialismo Norte-Americano*, pp. 33–37, 143–144; Jesús María Henao and Gerardo Arrubla, *History of Colombia*, p. 521; Arturo Capdevila, *América. Nuestras naciones ante los Estados Unidos*, pp. 118–119; Gastón Nerval, *Autopsy of the Monroe Doctrine*, pp. 4–5; Ugarte, *Destiny*

North American imperialism, the Monroe Doctrine as synonymous with the right to intermeddle, Pan-Americanism as suicidal to the Latin republics, the danger of United States bases, and the need for Latin cooperation against the Yankee menace were topics thoroughly explored. Then came the question of what Latin America could—or would—or should—do about it. In 1923 Victor Raúl Haya de la Torre, a refugee from Peru who was living in Mexico, founded what became known as the Aprismo.[78] This organization appealed to local patriotism to face both home and foreign dangers. Other groups endorsed the already mentioned Pan-Hispanism and Pan-Latinism movements, which argued that Latin nations of the Old and New Worlds should buy and sell in markets where people were culturally *simpático* and from which no interventionist menace would arise. They even plied their propaganda through Roman Catholic agencies, as opposed to United States Protestantism. For this purpose the Eucharistic Conference in Chicago in 1926 was skillfully used for propaganda.[79]

The Latin nations of Europe stood only to gain from this program. Spain showed a rising interest; French publicists lent sympathy and encouragement; and Italy "sought to share in the 'Latin Sentiment' among South Americans."[80] Naturally, the British were chary of such programs, but British Empire experience gave a basis for a reasoned evaluation. They looked upon the Pan-American Union as a most effective economic agency and recognized Pan-Latinism as a popular force. Yet the London *Times*, after recognizing Latin American fears, added: "But Pan-Americanism and the Monroe Doctrine as expounded by Mr. Hughes, are no more incompatible with them than are the British Empire and the principles it embodies. . . . it [the Monroe Doctrine] has saved South America from invasion for a hundred years. That is its abundant justification to the mind and conscience of the world."[81]

---

of a Continent, pp. 126, 288–289; Ricardo J. Alfaro, "A Century of the Monroe Doctrine," *The Annals*, CXI, Sup. (January, 1924), 24–25.

[78] Germán Arciniegas, *The State of Latin America*, pp. 86 ff.

[79] Clarence H. Haring, *South America Looks at the United States*, p. 175. Also Vasconcelos, *Bolivarismo y Monroismo*, pp. 9 ff.

[80] Haring, *South America Looks at the U.S.*, p. 186; Alfred Boudrillot, "Chez les Latins d'Amérique . . .," *Revue des Deux Mondes*, 7th period, XVIII (December, 1, 1923), 619 ff.; F. García Calderón, "Latin America, Europe and the United States," *For. Affs.*, VII, No. 2 (January, 1929), 188; *New York Times*, editorial, February 24, 1929, III, 4.3.

[81] The *Times* (London), December 1, 1923, 11c, and December 3, 1923, 12c. Also

And some Latin Americans began to attempt to see the whole situation. Even Ugarte asked his people to take stock of their own shortcomings, saying, "It would be madness to desire the ruin of the United States, since at the stage which we have reached, this ruin would be the signal of our own downfall." Another writer commented: "Distrusting himself, he [the Latin American] distrusts his fellows. . . . As a citizen, he is without morale." Normano repeated Blanco Fombona in saying that a proper obituary of the South American would be, "Here lies a soul of the sixteenth century, and a man of the twentieth century." Capdevila suggested it would be well before indulging in wholesale denunciations to decide if the United States had been responsible for civil war, anarchy, feudalism, lack of communications, clericalism, military oligarchies, fiscal rapacity, etc. in the southern republics. He admitted that the northern Yankees had not shown respect for their southern neighbors but added the biting comment that only the respectable were respected. And an Argentine, after a three-year residence in the United States, came to the conclusion that Yankee imperialism and love of money really did not dominate American life. He insisted that religious life was active and widespread throughout the northern society and that it was coupled with a love of the arts and an altruistic devotion to social and political betterment. Gil felt that the word "Pan-Americanism" (analogous to Pan-Germanism, Pan-Slavism, and Pan-Hellenism) had been unfortunate. In fact the development of United States policy had evolved quite naturally from Romantic continentalism, to imperialism, and then on to Pan-Americanism. Orestes Ferrara went so far as to suggest that the inclusion of the Monroe Doctrine in the League Covenant was to guarantee that that Covenant would not be used as a cover for European imperialism in the New World.[82]

It is just possible that feelings were improving, as Secretary Kellogg's biographer has stated.[83] On the other hand, it must be remembered that emotional masses in Latin America as elsewhere were basically uninter-

W. A. Hirst, "British Influence in South America," *Edinburgh Review*, CCXLVII, No. 504 (April, 1928), 321 ff.; Orestes Ferrara, *El panamericanismo y la opinión europea*, p. 85.

[82] Ugarte, *Destiny of a Continent*, p. 286; Waldo Frank, *America Hispana*, p. 336; Normano, *Struggle for South America*, p. 206; Capdevila, *América*, p. 119; Kurtz, *La Argentina ante EE. UU.*, p. 10; Gil, *Evolución del panamericanismo*, pp. 195–197; Ferrara, *Panamericanismo y la opinión europea*, p. 262.

[83] David Bryn-Jones, *Frank B. Kellogg*, p. 201.

ested in foreign relations until they became excited; then they commonly followed their emotions rather than logic. It was always easy to shout "Hispanoamérica para los Hispanoamericanos."[84]

Hughes as Secretary of State took advantage of the centennial of the Monroe pronouncement to try to clear the air. In a detailed exposition before the American Bar Association on August 30, 1923, at Minneapolis, and in an article in *The Annals* the following January, he made his government's position clear. He insisted that the original doctrine was unilateral, and unilateral it had remained. It was announced for the defense of the continent against aggression, and had never been a catch-all for a promiscuous series of acts and policies. Instead of standing in the way of Pan-Americanism, it provided the very basis for such cooperation. He insisted on the equality of the American republics and on his country's intention to respect the territorial integrity of its neighbors. Not flinching from responsibility, he asserted, his government would also seek to adjust differences that might arise among its neighbors, but all states had duties which included respect for the rights of others.[85]

Against this emotional background the Fifth Pan-American Conference was opened at Santiago, Chile, on March 25, 1923.[86] To the regret of Washington, Bolivia and Peru declined to send representatives to attend a meeting in Chile because of the Tacna-Arica dispute, and Mexico was unrepresented because of its irritation over lack of recognition by the United States. At the head of the United States delegation was Henry P. Fletcher, former ambassador to Chile and Mexico and recently in charge of the abortive Pan-American Pact efforts of Woodrow Wilson. Items for discussion included clarification of the meaning of the Monroe Doctrine and the problems arising from the rapidly flaring naval rivalry of the ABC powers. Haitian and Dominican delegates protested their "annexation" to the United States, and Central American delegates sought to make the presidency of the Union elective, instead of appertaining to the office of the United States Secretary of State. They also sought to reorganize the Governing Board of the Union.

The last proposal was partially accepted. The presiding office was

[84] Gerardo Falconi R., *Hispanamérica para los hispanoamericanos*, p. 208.

[85] Charles Evans Hughes, "The Centenary of the Monroe Doctrine," *The Annals*, CXI, Sup. (January, 1924), 8–18, and "Observations on the Monroe Doctrine," *Amer. Jour. Internat. Law*, XVII, No. 4 (October, 1923), 626–627. Also Álvarez, *The Monroe Doctrine*, pp. 445 ff.

[86] Bryn-Jones, *Frank B. Kellogg*, p. 129.

made elective and states not recognized by Washington were authorized to send delegates who were not diplomats accredited to Washington to attend board meetings.[87] The ABC naval rivalry proved intractible. Argentina had the largest naval tonnage, but Brazil felt it should have the largest navy because of its coastline. When Brazil sought to reduce the navies of the other two states to its own level, they refused. Feelings on the subject became even more embittered than before.[88]

At the outset of the Conference, Fletcher of the United States' delegation asserted that the Monroe Doctrine was not to be internationalized by any such procedure as a New World League of Nations. This idea had been proposed by Uruguay and had become the subject of considerable international discussion. The proposal was accordingly shunted to the Consejo Directivo for further study.[89] The bluntness of some of the exchanges at the Conference was reflected in the *New York Times* reference to the "petulance" shown by Fletcher, coupled with a reference to the fact that the Monroe Doctrine had "long been one of the sacred cows of American Diplomacy."[90] Not surprisingly the London *Times* rather gleefully reported that the Conference had adjourned on May 3 "without having come to any agreement on the naval armaments, the American League of Nations, or the Monroe Doctrine questions." Two weeks later it reiterated that the Conference had fallen "lamentably short" in its accomplishments, and that the only item of significance adopted was the modification of the Governing Board of the Union, which had been accomplished over the opposition of the United States.[91]

Such a summary omits one significant success of the Conference. The Bryan Peace Treaties had commanded considerable attention in Latin America. Now, the idea was developed in the Gondra Pact, which was approved at Santiago. This provided for the submission of all interna-

[87] For attendance see *For. Rels., 1923*, I, 289 ff.; Stuart, *Latin America and the U.S.*, p. 21.

For protests and complaints see Blanco-Fombona, *Crímenes del imperialismo*, pp. 52–53; Ugarte, *Destiny of a Continent*, p. 289 n; Isaac Joslin Cox, *Nicaragua and the United States*, p. 771; C. B. Casey, "Creation and Development of the Pan-American Union," *Hisp. Amer. Hist. Rev.*, XIII, No. 4 (November. 1933), 452.

[88] *Survey of Int. Affs., 1925*, II, 408 ff.; *New York Times*, March 21, 1923, 16.2.

[89] *For. Rels., 1922*, II, 984 ff.; Gil, *Evolución del panamericanismo*, p. 97; Baltasar Brum, *The Peace of America*, pp. 45 ff.

[90] *New York Times*, May 3, 1923, 18.4.

[91] The *Times* (London), May 5, 1923, 11a, and May 19, 1923.

tional controversies arising in the New World, including those of honor, to *ad hoc* commissions for investigation and report. To provide continuity two permanent commissions were established, one at Washington and the other at Montevideo. These had the duty of calling special fact-finding commissions into existence at the request of either party to a dispute. Meanwhile the signatories agreed not to make warlike preparations pending receipt of the reports, which were to be submitted by the special commissions within a year of the date of appointment.[92] Other minor items which were adopted by the Conference included a convention for publicity of customs documents and a convention providing for uniformity of nomenclature in the classification of merchandise.

In June, 1926, the Pan-American Centennial Conference assembled in Panama in honor of the first centenary of the congress called by Bolívar. Efforts were made to use this gathering to cultivate Pan-Hispanism, and Spain made the most of it.[93] The United States, however, insisted that its delegates consider the occasion a purely ceremonial and commemorative one. They were to eschew discussion of all matters carrying political implications. Thus, resolutions deploring aggression and on behalf of a Pan-American League of Nations were ignored. At the last session a resolution was introduced by a delegate from Nicaragua to recommend that the coming Pan-American Conference consider moving the headquarters of the Union from Washington. Behind-the-scenes opposition by the United States delegation secured the withdrawal of the proposal.[94]

Two years later when the Sixth Pan-American Conference assembled at Havana, the Latin American reaction against the United States was at its peak. It was now evident to all that it was futile to rely upon the League of Nations for effective action in New World affairs. Secretary Kellogg had professed interest in Latin America ever since the days of the Santiago Conference, but his conduct of the State Department had failed to inspire reciprocal cordiality. Too, President Coolidge's open support of financial investments abroad and Hoover's policies as Secre-

---

[92] *For. Rels., 1923*, I, 308 ff., 297 ff.; *British and Foreign State Papers, 1925*, Pt. II, p. 53; Hughes, *Our Relations to the Western Hemisphere*, pp. 97–99; Charles A. Thompson, "Toward a New Pan-Americanism," *For. Pol. Assn. Reports*, XII, No. 16 (November 1, 1936), 206; Gordon Cornell-Smith, *The Inter-American System*, p. 60.

[93] Haring, *South America Looks at the U.S.*, pp. 119–120.

[94] *For. Rels., 1926*, I, 255 ff.

tary of Commerce had brought recriminations in spite of sincere efforts to get marines out of Caribbean countries. With some justification, leading European journals, such as *Le Temps* and *Le Journal de Genève*, indicated that the current meeting might prove to be the last of the Pan-American series.[95]

In November, 1927, Cuba as prospective host indicated it would like to invite the League of Nations to send a representative to the Conference. The State Department at once sent word that such an invitation would be contrary to the original purpose of the Union. Cuba dutifully responded that no such invitation had been extended, and also that it had declined to invite a Spanish representative.[96] With aloof detachment the *Times* (London) commented in anticipation that "lofty language of idealism has served the United States badly. Everybody knows that behind the facade of democracy and representative institutions there frequently exists a parody so grotesque that the parodists have no claim to be respected, and that the case for the American interests is generally a strong case when it is stated simply on its merits."[97]

President Coolidge decided to attend the opening session by way of courtesy. At the head of the United States delegation was the highly respected and very able former Secretary of State Charles Evans Hughes, and on the delegation was the popular Dwight Morrow. After a courteous speech devoted to generalities Coolidge returned home and the Conference settled down to the tug of war. Should the Union be still further modified to restrict United States control? How eliminate the high tariffs that were keeping Latin American goods out of United States markets (a good talking point but, as has been noted above, most Latin American goods already were on the free lists)? And above all, could interventionism be restrained?[98]

The United States' delegates were instructed: to approve resolutions to respect territorial integrity provided intervention was not precluded; to avoid discussion of the Monroe Doctrine; to view with caution any formal association with non-American powers; to disapprove Spanish,

[95] Ferrara, *Panamericanismo y la opinión europea*, pp. 143–144.
[96] *For. Rels., 1928*, I, 529 ff.
[97] January 16, 1928. 13c.
[98] For significant comments see James Brown Scott in *Amer. Jour. Internat. Law*, XXII, No. 2 (April, 1928), 354–355; Walter Lippmann, "Second Thoughts on Havana," *For. Affs.*, VI, No. 4 (July, 1928), 541–543; Raymond Leslie Buell, *Isolated America*, pp. 132–133.

French, Italian, Portuguese, or any other non-American or League of Nations representation at the Conference; to discourage any American or Latin American league or permanent court of justice; to avoid active opposition to moving the Union headquarters from Washington, but to encourage friends to point out the inconveniences of such an action. With regard to Canadian membership in the Union, the delegates were to be guided by oral instructions.[99] Such was the blueprint.

Various early critical attacks were successfully turned aside thanks largely to the skill and personality of Hughes. The question of intervention was apparently shunted forward to the next conference. The Union was strengthened by making it the depository for New World treaties, conventions, and agreements signed at the conferences. States were allowed to withdraw from the Union on giving due notice, and were allowed freedom in selecting representatives who might not be diplomatic representatives at Washington.[100]

Just as the Conference was closing and it appeared that it would end on a note of harmony came the bombshell that had been side-stepped to this point. On February 18 the head of the Argentine delegation proposed a declaration: "Intervention—diplomatic or armed, permanent or temporary—is an attempt against the independence of nations, and cannot be justified on the plea of the duty of protecting the interests of citizens." The Salvadorian delegate chimed in with the statement that "The right of intervention is the right of might."[101] And thirteen states were already on record as disapproving intervention. Hughes had no alternative. So, practically "off the cuff," he rose for one of the great oratorical efforts of his career, saying in part:

We do not wish the territory of any American republic. We do not wish to intervene in the affairs of any American republic. We simply wish peace and

[99] For instructions see *For. Rels., 1928*, I, 573 ff.

[100] Humphrey, *Inter-American System*, pp. 96–97; Casey, "Creation and Development of the Pan-American Union," *Hisp. Amer. Hist. Rev.*, XIII, No. 4 (November, 1933), 454–455; *Survey of Int. Affs., 1927*, pp. 435–436.

It is interesting to note that the budget for the year ending June, 1929, carried a total sum of $227,594.86. Of this the United States was to contribute $132,256.00; Brazil, $33,767.34; and Panama only $446.10 (*Survey of Int. Affs., 1927*, p. 431).

Up to this time the secretary of the Pan-American Union had been sent to the international conferences as a member of the United States delegation. This arrangement tended to stigmatize the Union as a tool of the northern republic. After the Havana Conference, at the request of Mr. Hughes, the secretary attended the sessions in his own right, and so did not represent any one country.

[101] Bryn-Jones, *Frank B. Kellogg*, p. 198. ,

order and stability and recognition of honest rights properly acquired so that this hemisphere may not only be the hemisphere of peace but the hemisphere of international justice.

As for Nicaragua, he commented:

Now what is the real difficulty? Let us face the facts. The difficulty, if there is any, in any one of the American republics is not of any external aggression. It is an internal difficulty. . . .

What are we to do when government breaks down and American citizens are in danger of their lives? Are we to stand by and see them butchered in the jungle because a government in circumstances which it cannot control and for which it may not be responsible can no longer afford reasonable protection?[102]

The compelling persuasiveness of Hughes and the frankness of his answer brought the occupants of the galleries and many of the delegates to their feet in applause. The resolution was withdrawn. The stand of the brilliant former Secretary may have been unpopular and its argument somewhat specious,[103] but its appeal in a disordered world was clear. The skilled correspondent of the London *Times* reported that the Conference was not devoid of significance in spite of the paucity of its accomplishments. The leadership of the United States remained intact thanks to the skill of Hughes and to the divisions of opinion among the Latins. Yet the correspondent made record of the rising energies of the Latin delegates as they clamored, confused, as yet, for more recognition in hemisphere affairs.[104]

On August 27, 1928, the Kellogg Pact was signed to outlaw war and rapidly secured the adherence of nations throughout the world. Secretary Kellogg insisted that this had nothing to do with the Monroe Doctrine; but to make sure of the fact, when the Committee on Foreign Relations of the Senate approved the pact it stated that the doctrine was a factor in national security and defense, hence was not subject to the new convention.[105] Though the pact was approved by a vote of

[102] Merlo Pusey, *Charles Evans Hughes*, II, 559–560. Pusey notes that the phrase "butchered in the jungle" was modified in the official text, but one of those who heard the address insists that Hughes used the phrase.

[103] Dexter Perkins, *Charles Evans Hughes and American Democratic Statesmanship*, p. 136.

[104] The *Times* (London), February 21, 1928, 16a, and February 22, 1928, 15b.

[105] A. Lawrence Lowell, "Frontiers of the United States," *For. Affs.*, XVII, No. 4 (July, 1939), 668; Perkins, *Hands Off*, p. 309.

eighty-five to one in the Senate, various senators characterized it as a "noble gesture" and an "international kiss," but "not worth a postage stamp in the direction of accomplishment of world peace."[106] Nevertheless, one more step had been taken to stimulate the peace movement. Most of the New World nations promptly adhered to the pact, though Argentina and Brazil both refrained.

Soon another step was taken to make more specific the aspirations toward international peace in the Western Hemisphere. From December 10, 1928, to January 6, 1929, there assembled in Washington the meeting that has been characterized as the Locarno of the New World.[107] Just as the Havana Conference drew to its close, a resolution was adopted providing for two plenipotentiaries to be selected by each American republic to give definite form to a resolution calling for obligatory arbitration and for the settlement of disputes by conciliation. Argentina, disgruntled over the Havana Conference, at which the critical stand of its chief delegate had been repudiated by its president, sent no representative. The remaining delegates worked diligently and brought forth two general conventions. Their purpose was to close loopholes through which international peacemaking machinery might fail to secure the results so much desired. Though domestic questions were reserved, it was agreed that questions "juridical in nature" arising from interpretations of treaties, questions of international law, and the existence of established facts which would constitute a breach of international obligations should be acted upon. The implementation of the Commissions of Inquiry endorsed at the Fifth Pan-American Conference at Santiago was also provided for.[108]

[106] Ferrell, *Amer. Secs. of St.*, XI, 115; Robert Endicott Osgood, *Ideals and Self-Interest in America's Foreign Relations*, p. 348 .

[107] Katherine Duff, "The American Continent," in *Survey of Int. Affs.*, *1936*, pp. 815, 834; James Oliver Murdock, "Arbitration and Conciliation," *Amer. Jour. Internat. Law*, XXIII, No. 2 (April, 1929), 273; Scott, *International Conferences of American States*, pp. 256–257, 457–458; Scott, "Pan-American Conference on Conciliation . . .," *Amer. Jour. Internat. Law*, XXIII, No. 1 (January, 1929), 143–144; *For. Rels.*, *1929*, I, 653 ff.

[108] Charles Evans Hughes, *Pan-American Peace Plans*, pp. 10–11, 23 ff. Articles on the subject include: James Brown Scott "Pan-American Conference on Conciliation and Arbitration," and James Oliver Murdock, "Arbitration and Conciliation in Pan America," in *Amer. Jour. Internat. Law*, XXIII, No. 1 (October, 1936); Manley O. Hudson, "Inter-American Treaties of Pacific Settlement," *For. Affs.*, XV, No. 1 (October, 1936), 170–171.

Efforts to codify international law for New World countries had met with a cool reception from Secretary Kellogg, who preferred that all such matters be centered in the Permanent Court of International Justice at The Hague.[109] In other fields, however, substantial progress was made. A Pan-American Sanitary Convention was drafted late in 1924 with United States ratification deposited April 23, 1925.[110] Other specialized conferences followed rapidly. A single issue of the *Bulletin* of the Pan-American Union listed the following:

3rd Pan-American Conference of Architects, Buenos Aires, July 1–10, 1927.
8th Pan-American Sanitary Conference, Lima, October 12–20, 1927.
5th Pan-American Child Conference, Habana, December 8–13, 1927.
1st Pan-American Conference on Eugenics and Homoculture, Habana, December 21–23, 1927.[111]

Also the Union formed a Division of Intellectual Cooperation in 1928, which was to serve as a clearing house for information and for cultural exchanges.[112]

On the surface, the eight-year period following 1921 had brought a low point in the Pan-American movement, but even so there were promising indications that better understanding was developing and this in itself held out new hope.

For Canadian and British views see Humphrey, *Inter-American System*, pp. 107 ff., and *Survey of Int. Affs., 1930*, pp. 376 ff.

[109] Samuel Flagg Bemis, *The Latin American Policy of the United States*, p. 248.
[110] *British and Foreign State Papers, 1924*, pp. 3, 15.
[111] Pan-American Union. *Bulletin*, LXII, No. 2 (February, 1928), 122 ff.
[112] Ben M. Cherrington, "The United States and Inter-American Relations," *Department of State Bulletin*, II, No. 51 (June 15, 1940), 664.

CHAPTER VIII

THE HOOVER QUADRENNIUM, 1929–1933

Establishing Contact with Latin America

AN INTERPRETATION OF THE Monroe Doctrine to the effect that we had the right to maintain order in those states by military force, in order not to give excuse for European intervention, created antagonisms and suspicions which dominated the politics of much of the Latin area. . . . Moreover, our "dollar diplomacy," by threats and intimidation on behalf of our speculative citizens when their investments went wrong, added fuel to the fire. The policy of military intervention practiced by the Wilson administration had been continued by Harding and Coolidge. . . . The United States, to put it mildly, was not popular in the rest of the Hemisphere.[1]

Thus Hoover wrote in his *Memoirs*.

Yet Hoover, as Secretary of Commerce, had encouraged control of essential raw materials and investments in Latin America—the very stuff of which critics made so much in their denunciations. Soon after the election of 1928 the President-elect made his good-will tour, visiting Honduras, El Salvador, Nicaragua, Costa Rica, Ecuador, Peru, Argentina, Uruguay, and Brazil. Latin Americans applauded Hoover's work in Europe during and after the war but now had serious misgivings. From Chile came a cartoon showing Uncle Sam looking at an X-ray exposure of Hoover's chest. It showed his heart carrying an outline of

[1] Herbert Hoover, *The Memoirs of Herbert Hoover*, II (*The Cabinet and the Presidency*), pp. 210–211.

South America, presumably as the area most coveted.[2] In Argentina the
visitor had to exert special efforts to counteract the marked coolness that
existed, and in Brazil there was the antagonism of the coffee interests
which resented the former Secretary's efforts to block their coffee loan.[3]

In the United States, Mark Sullivan hailed the pre-inauguration trip
as one of the most important contributions to international good will in
the Americas;[4] and Frank H. Simonds commented: "What Mr. Hoover's
journey really meant was that South America, in the mind of the President-elect, has become our most important question of foreign policy."[5]
British observers took a similar attitude. An immediate result of the trip
was a systematic attempt to appoint better men to Latin American diplomatic posts. One observer commented that for the first time a "scramble
for Latin American posts began."[6] Toward the end of the administration
the chief of the Latin American Division of the State Department could
write that "we have today as Chiefs of Mission in the Capitals of Latin
America, sixteen career officers; and at the four remaining posts, one
Chief of Mission having nearly ten years' successful service in Latin
America, one having long held high office in the Department of State
and two whose command of Spanish and understanding of the peoples
of Latin America eminently qualify them for the positions they hold."[7]

The new Secretary of State was Henry L. Stimson, who had served
as a trouble shooter for Coolidge in Nicaragua and as adviser to Kellogg
on Tacna-Arica. At the time of his selection for the Cabinet he was governor general of the Philippines. It should be remembered, however, that
at heart the new Secretary was a military man who had seen active
service in World War I and who was to serve as Secretary of War in
World War II. His policies could be expected to vary therefore from
those of his Quaker Chief. Hoover's cable of invitation emphasized Stimson's value "in national and Philippine interests." Stimson's three-page

[2] *Rev. of Revs.*, XCIV. No. 6 (December, 1936), 61.

[3] Alexander DeConde, *Herbert Hoover's Latin American Policy*, pp. 20–22;
Joseph Brandes, *Herbert Hoover and Economic Diplomacy*, pp. 137–138.

[4] Mark Sullivan, "With Hoover in Latin America," *Rev. of Revs.*, LXXIX, No. 2
(February, 1929). 53–54.

[5] Frank H. Simonds, "Hoover, South Americanus," *ibid.*, pp. 68–69. For a
British view see *Survey of Int. Affs.*, *1930*, pp. 361–362.

[6] William Franklin Sands, *Our Jungle Diplomacy*, p. 194.

[7] Walter C. Thurston, "Relations with our Latin American Neighbors," *The Annals*, CLVI (July, 1931), 125. Also DeConde, *Hoover's Latin American Policy*, pp.
111 ff., and Hoover, *Memoirs*, II, 335.

letter of acceptance, dated January 31, 1929, followed a cable of the preceding day. In the letter he expressed appreciation of the offer, then referred only to Philippine problems and personal matters. Stimson's diary and letters to friends likewise show a strange omission of references to either Canadian or Latin American affairs. He showed special interest in the Far East, the Geneva Conference, War Debts, and national politics, merely recording, "My only other problem is Paraguay and Bolivia which Francis White is handling very faithfully and very satisfactorily."[8]

The new President's first draft of his inaugural address apparently included statements as to limitations he expected to apply on the use of military intervention. Hughes advised against being too specific, and so more general terms were employed for the address as actually delivered.[9] However, his first annual message to Congress pointed out that the marines in Nicaragua had been reduced to 1,600 and full withdrawal was hoped for in the near future. In uncertain Haiti only 700 marines remained.

Just as the Hoover Administration took office, the International Conciliation and Arbitration Treaties were available for ratification. Some thirty-six of these calling for submission of New World disputes to arbitration were in operation.[10] Also the Gondra Convention, which had been generally accepted, provided commissions on conciliation.[11] The United States and six other republics approved the treaty without reservations, but thirteen of the states qualified their approvals. All in all, however, the signatures came in satisfactorily. By 1938 only Bolivia, Paraguay, and Costa Rica had failed to ratify the arbitration treaty; and only Costa Rica and Bolivia had failed to ratify the conciliation treaty.[12]

On the question of investments, Undersecretary of State Joseph Cotton in July, 1929, warned the Third Pan-American Commercial Congress that five types of loans might expect disapproval by the new administration. These were:

---

[8] Diary, August 12, 1932, Henry L. Stimson Papers, Yale.

[9] Robert F. Smith, *The United States and Cuba*, pp. 134–135.

[10] W. T. Stone, "The Pan-American Arbitration Treaty," *For. Pol. Assn. Reports,* V, No. 18 (November, 1929), 313.

[11] *Survey of Int. Affs., 1930*, pp. 376 ff.

[12] Robert H. Ferrell, *The American Secretaries of State . . .*, XI, 81, 299 n; James Brown Scott, "Pan-American Conference on Conciliation," *Amer. Jour. Internat. Law*, XXIII, No. 1 (January 1929), 145–148.

1. Loans to enable governments to balance budgets when local taxation was considered inadequate.

2. Loans for military purposes.

3. Loans to assist foreign monopolies to maintain prices adverse to the United States consumer.

4. Loans to governments not recognized by the United States.

5. Loans to either governments or citizens of countries which had failed to maintain their international obligations to the United States.[13]

On his trip south the President-elect had stressed that "We have a desire to maintain not only the cordial relations of governments with each other but with the relations of *good neighbors*."[14] He pursued the same idea on April 13, 1929, when he told the Gridiron Club in Washington that "The implications that have been colored by that expression [dollar diplomacy] are not a part of my conception of international relations."[15] To a Pan-American Day audience in 1931 he emphasized the need for cultural exchanges and better understanding.[16] No wonder home and foreign observers felt that possibly a new day had dawned in inter-American relations.

How and why did these fine hopes collapse? Hoover himself later made an effort to claim substantial accomplishments in Latin American relations, but the evidence is inconclusive.[17] Welles, who knew Latin Americans and was himself active in the diplomatic service attributed much blame to the Smoot-Hawley Tariff.[18] Another observer was more perceptive, saying: "The trouble with the Hoover-Stimson policy was that it was largely negative." Secretary of State Stimson outlined the bases of United States foreign policy from 1929 to 1933, together with steps taken to implement them, but here again the negatives are strikingly evident.[19] In his diary for May 17, 1932, the Secretary probably gives about the right explanation, saying, "But the President is so ab-

[13] Herbert Feis, *The Diplomacy of the Dollar*, pp. 18–19.

[14] Hoover, *Memoirs*. II, 213–214.

[15] Quoted by William Starr Myers, *The Foreign Policies of Herbert Hoover*, p. 43.

[16] DeConde, *Hoover's Latin American Policy*, p. 119.

[17] Hoover, *Memoirs*. II, 333–334.

[18] Sumner Welles, *The Time for Decision*, pp. 190–191; Charles Wertenbaker, *A New Doctrine for the Americas*, p. 75.

[19] Arthur P. Whitaker, *The Western Hemisphere Idea*, pp. 134–135; H. L. Stimson, "Bases of Foreign Policy during the Past Four Years," *For. Affs.*, XI, No. 3 (April, 1933), 394–395.

sorbed with the Domestic situation that he told me frankly he can't think very much of foreign affairs."

What did it all add up to? A reasonable summary must include: a substantial improvement in the calibre of diplomatic representatives in Latin America; withdrawal of marines; a definition of improper types of loans; efforts to maintain peace, and generally to maintain the *status quo.* And it should be borne in mind that this last was difficult because a world-wide depression had disrupted international commerce and credit facilities. At such a time economic nationalism was rampant, and Latin America was far from immune to the contagion.[20]

One statement on foreign policy deserves more definite attention. This was what became known as the Clark Memorandum on the Monroe Doctrine. Some months before the end of the Coolidge Administration, J. Reuben Clark, of the State Department, had prepared a careful study of the applications of the doctrine over the century of its existence and then added some recommendations for future policy. It appears that Secretary Kellogg initiated the study to prove to hesitant senators that the Kellogg Pact would not endanger the doctrine. The memorandum emphasized that Monroe's pronouncement applied only to defense, hence it clearly repudiated the Roosevelt Corollary.[21] Actual publication of the memorandum was delayed. Finally it was sent to diplomatic representatives concerned, then publicly released in March, 1930.

This was reassuring but skeptics remained. Some felt that the insistence that tariffs constituted a domestic issue only undermined international cooperation.[22] Others maintained that the Monroe Doctrine was an agency of feudalism of English-speaking peoples who thought in Yankee terms.[23] The Spanish scholar Salvador Madariaga wrote in the *Times* (London):

The little Filipino schoolboy, who, taught history in spirited American manuals vibrating with liberty, was asked to write an essay on the cow, created this masterpiece: 'The cow is an animal with four legs, one in each

[20] Edwin Lieuwen, *Arms and Politics in Latin America,* pp. 41–42.

[21] Joshua Reuben Clark, *Memorandum on the Monroe Doctrine.* For comments see Graham H. Stuart, *Latin America and the United States,* p. 73; *Survey of Int. Affs., 1930,* p. 370; L. Ethan Ellis, *Frank B. Kellogg and American Foreign Relations;* Robert H. Ferrell "Repudiation of a Repudiation," *Journal of American History,* LI, No. 4 (March, 1965), 669–673.

[22] Galvarino Gallardo Nieto, *Panamericanismo,* p. 13.

[23] Gerardo Falconi R., *Hispanoamérica para los hispanamericanos,* pp. 130, 134.

corner. The cow gives milk. As for me, give me liberty or give me death.'
Every Caribbean nation is busy writing essays on the Cow of Liberty. And
Washington is much embarrassed by the genuine American style of them.[24]

On May 16, 1931, the *New York Times* commented that the heart of the
question was: To what subjects does the United States still "confine its
interposition?" "Aye, there's thee rub."[25]

Any student who plows through the mass of diplomatic correspondence from the Latin American capitals to Washington for the Hoover
period immediately notes the mounting complications of the economic
depression. Defaults on debt payments were inevitable and only vestiges
of the gold standard remained in Latin America by the end of 1932.
Markets were lost, incomes dropped or disappeared. Suffering peoples
expressed themselves in their customary manner; in other words, they
revolted against the governments which, they felt, were in some way to
blame.[26] The President, bedeviled by the world-wide situation, could do
little but watch the storm.[27] In Central America and the Caribbean the
quieting hand of the United States remained reasonably effective, but
of the ten republics of South America only Colombia, Uruguay, and
Venezuela escaped revolution between 1930 and 1932. In 1930 to 1931
alone eleven of the twenty Latin American republics experienced irregular changes of government. Interestingly enough, few of these were
caudillo-inspired. Instead, they arose from popular unrest.[28] Ultimately
success of a revolution seldom brought the relief sought. The new leaders
were untrained, and frequently were only too glad of an opportunity for
self-gain. The significant fact, however, was that would-be rebels now
found it necessary to sponsor public welfare and reforms. Unfortunately
the unrest carried militarism as a by-product. It was the military who
had access to that power through which the protestants sought to accom-
plish their purposes. In this chaotic situation it was always popular to

[24] The *Times* (London), February 6, 1929, 16a.

[25] *New York Times*, May 16, 1931, 16.3.

[26] *For. Rels., II, 1931*, various. For comments see Lippmann, *U.S. in World Affs.,
1932*, pp. 49–52; H. L. Stimson, "The United States and Other Latin American Republics," *For. Affs.*, IX No. 3, Sup. (February, 1931); i; Henry Kittredge Norton,
The Coming of South America . . ., pp. 86 ff.

[27] *For. Rels., 1930*, pp. xvii–xviii and scattered.

[28] *U.S. in World Affs., 1931*, p. 63; *1932*, p. 52; J. H. Parry, "Latin America,
1899–1949," *New Cambridge Modern History*, XII, 195.

blame the foreign creditor.[29] And this invidious position was occupied by the United States.

Rumors of Communist activity inspired a special congressional committee to investigate the matter. The President himself had been fearful of Communism ever since his European experiences at the end of World War I.[30] However, the basic trouble in Latin America was the one of long-hungry peoples who were now awakening. Bewildered by events, the Hoover Administration continued the recent Republican trend toward *de facto* recognition without asking too many questions.[31] Of course European nations were only too glad to do the same.

As an illustration of the practice, on September 17, 1930, Secretary Stimson announced that instructions had been sent to recognize new governments in Argentina, Peru, and Bolivia. This was done by the simple procedure of renewing disrupted diplomatic relations in each case. If a new administration could provide substantial evidence of popular support and had a reasonable prospect of maintaining itself, few other questions were asked. Wherever possible in extending recognition Washington endeavored to detect legal continuity of the new with the old administration; but it must be admitted that often this was little more than a polite fiction. At a time of world crisis both humanitarianism and good judgment dictated acquiescence in the new. One could only be glad if the new held reasonable promise of being able to control at least one of the multiple difficult and troublesome sets of existing problems.

Masses of statistics based on rapidly fluctuating values can be interpreted to prove almost anything during the economic gyrations from extreme prosperity to extreme depression between 1929 and 1933, but a few facts and trends may be mentioned as symptomatic. Herbert Feis reached the conclusion that the actual quantity of world trade declined by one fourth and its value by over one half.[32] Comparatively speaking,

[29] *Survey of Int. Affs., 1930*, pp. 372 ff.; Lieuwen, *Arms and Politics*, pp. 122–129.

[30] Hamilton Fish, "The Menace of Communism," *The Annals*, CLVI (July, 1931), 54 ff.

[31] *For. Rels., 1930*, I, 382–418; Myers, *Foreign Policies of Hoover*, p. 46; *Survey of Int. Affs., 1930*, pp. 366 ff.; *U.S. in World Affs., 1931*, pp. 64 ff.

It should be noted that the Washington agreement of 1923 precluded application of *de facto* recognition in Central America.

[32] Herbert Feis, *The Changing Pattern of International Economic Affairs*, p. 32. See also Feis, *The Sinews of Peace*, pp. 154, 230–231.

as seen in the following table, the United States did not do too badly in the bitter trade wars that involved Latin American markets.[33]

| | Imports to Latin America | | Exports from Latin America | |
Country	1910–1913	1932–1934	1910–1913	1932–1934
United States	24%	31%	33%	31%
United Kingdom	25	17	20	20
Germany	16	10	12	7
France	8	5	8	6

But this was cold comfort in the face of bankruptcies.

Also to be noted was the fact that the approach to the problem was different in the United States and in Latin America. The former had become a creditor nation; the latter republics were debtors. Debts owned were in terms of gold, and it now took vastly more Latin American raw materials to produce the requisite amount of the precious metal to repay moneys borrowed.

Depression measures taken by the administration in Washington were largely beside the point for Latin Americans. The American business-man desperately strove to protect his home market with the Smoot-Hawley tariff bill. Actually this did not affect too many Latin Americans whose products were mostly on the free lists, but the principle was obvi-ous and provided an excellent talking point for insolvent and suspicious peoples. Washington soon sponsored a moratorium on intergovern-mental debts. This, again, gave little help to Latin Americans, since most of their debts were to private individuals or corporations. In fact, Hoover issued a press statement denying that his government was taking any steps in the matter of South American debts.[34] Another negative.

Investments in the nearby areas of Mexico, Central America, and the Caribbean were largely in "factories, mines, sales agencies, and the like." Only about 22 per cent of the total was in portfolio investments, or securities of public or private concerns. In South America the pro-portion was about eight to seven in favor of direct investments, and in Canada the two types were almost equal. The grand totals were esti-mated to be:[35]

[33] Julian G. Zier, "Latin American Foreign Trade," Pan-American Union, *Bulle-tin*, LXXIV, No. 7 (July, 1940), 527. Also *Report of the Secretary of Commerce, 1934*, p. xviii.

[34] DeConde, *Hoover's Latin American Policy*, pp. 70 ff.

[35] Louis M. Hacker, *American Problems of Today*, pp. 134–135. Also W. O.

Mexico, Central America & the Caribbean	$2,564.9 million
South America	3,041.9 million
Canada	3,941.7 million

As a partial remedy, the Administration did refuse to endorse intervention in cases of default of payments which were based on customs collections.[36] Merely another negative that solved no problems.

One Latin American reaction to the depression was an increased economic nationalism that was expressed in high tariffs and in trade controls.[37] For this there was ample precedent in the conduct of the great nations as they grasped at any procedure that held out some prospect of aiding their own citizens. Great Britain, in spite of its proud history, withdrew from the gold basis in the fall of 1931. The United States devalued its dollar and was forced to make other painful adjustments. For instance, it was unable to meet world competition with its expensive World War I merchant marine. In 1932 alone nearly 800,000 gross tons of shipping were scrapped, and some 2,662 vessels of over 4,000,000 tons were laid up out of commission. Strenuous efforts were made to offset this, one of which was to foster the Pan-American Highway and air traffic.[38] Such programs, however, were handicapped by the money scarcity.

Unexpected complications also arose from the fact that Latin America in good times had started public works in expectation of receiving further credits to complete the projects. Now the additional moneys could not be had. The projects, in turn, were held up, with resultant hardship and increased unemployment, when interest on sums already advanced was coming due. At the same time the unemployed were becoming responsive to various forms of radicalism and to Communism.[39] Each nation, at its wits' end, whether in Europe or Latin America, strove to take care of its own and became increasingly critical of others.

Scroggs, "American Investments in Latin America," *For. Affs.*, X, No. 3 (April, 1932), 504; Max Winkler, "American Foreign Investments in 1931," *For. Pol. Assn. Reports*, VII, No. 24 (February 3, 1932), 429; Elizabeth Hannan and Willy Feuerlein, *Dollars in Latin America*, p. 16.

[36] *Survey of Int. Affs.*, 1933, p. 321.

[37] Norton, *The Coming of South America*, pp. 253–254.

[38] *Report of the Secretary of Commerce, 1933*, p. xxi; *For. Rels., 1929*, I, 542 ff.; *1930*, I, 281 ff.; *1931*, I, 709 ff.

[39] *New York Times*, May 29, 1931, 10.7.

Mexico and Central America

The day before Hoover was inaugurated a serious revolt had broken out south of the Rio Grande.[40] Promptly the new administration applied an arms embargo under the congressional resolution of 1922. The key man in the diplomatic relations of the two countries was Ambassador Dwight Morrow. When he resigned to enter the United States Senate he was succeeded by the knowledgable Latin Americanist J. Reuben Clark. Mexico quickly suppressed the revolt and international relations continued smoothly. The land reform program of the Revolution was pursued steadily. Census reports show that a mere 15,085 landlords in 1854 had increased slowly to become 47,939 by 1910, and then leaped to 858,209 by 1930.[41] Of course this involved major adjustments in the social and economic life of the Republic. Here Morrow's sympathetic reporting did much to avoid complications when properties of United States citizens were involved in the expropriations that preceded land distribution to the new owners. One particularly popular move was the announcement that questions arising in Mexico between citizens of the two countries were to be settled by the "due operations of Mexican administrative departments and the Mexican courts."[42] Direct evidence of Morrow's influence is seen in the diary of James R. Garfield for the years from 1928 to 1933. Clearly this agent of the American oil interests in Mexico had confidence in and respect for the work being done by the ambassador, and later this respect was transferred to Clark.[43] It was at about this same time that Morrow brought to a successful conclusion his unofficial mediation between the Vatican and the Mexican government after the bitterness of the Escobar rebellion.[44]

Internationally Mexico was again beginning to assert itself. It broke

[40] *For. Rels.*, 1929, III, 336 ff.; H. L. Stimson, "U.S. and other Latin American Republics," *For. Affs.*, IX, No. 3, Sup. (February 6, 1931), x–xii; Stuart, *Latin America and the U.S.*, pp. 179–180.

[41] Clarence Senior, *Land Reform and Democracy*, pp. 28, 239; Lucio Mendieta y Nuñez, "The Balance of Agrarian Reform," *The Annals*, CCVIII (March, 1940), 127.

[42] *Survey of Int. Affs.*, *1930*, pp. 362–365.

[43] Entries from March 28, 1927, to December 16, 1935, in the James R. Garfield Diary (LC) show that he had repeated interviews with leading Mexicans and United States officials.

[44] Harold Nicholson, *Dwight Morrow*, pp. 338–345. This was the rebellion led by fanatical Roman Catholic religious groups in protest against the application of new and far-reaching restrictive acts of the Revolution and the new constitution drafted in 1917.

diplomatic relations with Moscow as soon as it became convinced that the Soviet legation was being used to train local agitators and had become a "hotbed of political unrest."[45] In 1931 it was admitted to the League of Nations.[46] In the way of general principles it promulgated the Estrada Doctrine of recognition. This specified that in international contacts the Mexican government would confine itself to the maintenance or withdrawal of diplomatic agents and that in no case would it consider such action as pronouncing judgment "regarding the right of foreign nations to accept, maintain or replace their governments or authorities."[47] Needless to say, such a pronouncement was widely acclaimed in Latin America.

The *de jure* system of recognition for Central America, agreed to in 1923, continued, at least in the eyes of its protagonists, to be very successful. In the period to 1931 not a single revolutionary government had been able to maintain itself in any one of the five republics involved. Temporarily successful rebels in Nicaragua and Guatemala had fallen when they were unable to secure financial support. Other would-be revolutionists had either taken "proper" advice or had hesitated to move at all.[48]

Against this background a few special items are to be mentioned. In Nicaragua there was the sorry aftermath of the Sandino rebellion. The 5,673 sailors and marines on duty there in 1928 were reduced to 2,215 men by the fall of 1929; and to less than 1,000, including over 200 who were serving as officers in the local *guardia*, by April 1, 1932. Withdrawal of the last of these was delayed by an earthquake which shifted the work of the marines from keeping order to that of disaster service.[49] The Coolidge policy of property protection of United States citizens abroad was changed materially in 1931 as depression-invoked disorders increased. At that time the State Department notified Americans in

[45] MS memoir of Emilio Portes Gil, "Fifteen Years of Mexican Life," in the Josephus Daniels Papers, LC, Box 19.

[46] Manley O. Hudson, "Mexico's Admission to the League of Nations," *Amer. Jour. Internat. Law*, XXVI, No. 1 (January, 1932), 114–115.

[47] Genaro Estrada, "Estrada Doctrine of Recognition," *ibid.*, XXV, Supplement, 203; Philip C. Jessup, book review, *ibid.*, XXV, No. 4 (October, 1931), 805.

[48] Chandler P. Anderson, "Our Policy of Non-Recognition in Central America," *Amer. Jour. Internat. Law*, XXV, No. 2 (April, 1931), 299–301.

[49] Dana G. Munro, *The United States and the Caribbean Area*, pp. 263–264. Also *For. Rels., 1931*, II, 788 ff.; Department of State, *The United States and Nicaragua*, p. 112.

Nicaragua and Honduras that their government could not be responsible for them (much less for their property) at scattered points in disordered areas. Instead, citizens would be expected to remain in places where aid could be easily extended. If they persisted in living in danger areas they "must not expect American forces to be sent inland to their aid."[50]

American investments in Nicaragua remained relatively small—only $15 million in 1930. Strangely enough, this was less than the sum at stake in any Latin American country except Ecuador and Paraguay.[51] But a businessman's administration kept a watchful eye on possibilities for future canal construction. On June 12, 1929, the War Department, with the approval of Nicaragua and Costa Rica,[52] authorized the despatch of a battalion of troops to undertake a canal survey. A report on the findings was presented to Congress on December 10, 1931. It indicated that a new canal could be constructed for an estimated $722 million. On the other hand, the Panama Canal was reported to be operating at only half its capacity; so the logical conclusion was that no additional commitments should be made.[53]

Peace was an essential for progress, but how to secure peace in a bandit-infested region? The answer of the Hoover Administration was an increased emphasis on a local constabulary and on road building; "good roads and banditry are antagonistic." In 1929 it had been reported that the bull-cart transportation for the marines in Nicaragua had amounted to $700,000; and this was in a country where able-bodied laborers for road construction could be hired for sixty cents a day.[54]

An example of contradictory points of view is seen in two reports. Nicaraguans claimed that foreigners' profits on railroad investments were exorbitant, amounting to 1.5 per cent per month. Yet a report of the State Department showed that two New York banking firms and the managing firm in charge of the Pacific Railway had resigned because of disagreements over policies followed[55]—a situation hardly credible if earnings were at the rate of 18 per cent per year.

[50] *For. Rels., 1931*, II, 808.
[51] Department of State, *The U.S. and Nicaragua*, p. 4.
[52] *For Rels., 1929*, III, 703 ff.
[53] Department of State, *The U.S. and Nicaragua*, p. 113; T. A. Bailey, "Interest in the Nicaraguan Canal 1903–1931," *Hisp. Amer. Hist. Rev.*, XVI, No. 1 (February, 1936), 17–19.
[54] *For. Rels., 1929*, III, 697 ff.
[55] Rodolfo Huete Abella, *Los banqueros y la intervención en Nicaragua*, p. 31; Department of State, *The U.S. and Nicaragua*, p. 96.

Efforts to bring stability centered on the electoral process. Hoover personally attempted to conciliate the rival factions when he visited the country on his good-will tour. Then followed constructive suggestions advising caution against unwise political arrests, discouragement of extension of terms of incumbents in office, and modification of the rough-and-ready "dyed-finger" technique for discouraging repetitive voting. When election-law reform could not be secured in time for the election of 1930 through congressional enactment and court processes it was secured by the familiar presidential decree.[56] Meanwhile, the press was controlled and hostile papers suppressed. "American officers and marines were chairmen of local [electoral] boards"—an arrangement that called for the services of 52 officers and 597 enlisted men. The costs of the operation amounted to some $52,000 for the local government and to about $500,000 for the United States. The Liberals elected seven senators and sixteen deputies, to two senators and six deputies for the Conservatives.[57] In his message to Congress in 1931 Hoover took it for granted that supervision of the elections of 1932 would continue.[58] However, the reaction in the United States, reinforced by depression economies, caused the insertion in the Naval Appropriation Act of a prohibition against using funds for this purpose from regular sources. Stimson, thereupon, with the President's approval, used funds from other sources and employed 371 marines already in Nicaragua for the work. This time well over half the electoral boards had Nicaraguan chairmen.[59]

In the Nicaraguan-Honduran and Honduran-Guatemalan boundary disputes the United States wished to be strictly neutral. Its one desire was to get the questions settled.[60] When a revolution broke out in Honduras, Washington remained aloof and refused to allow its naval vessels to patrol local waters for fear the action might be interpreted as favoring one faction or the other. It merely agreed informally to the use of United Fruit Company vessels by local authorities. A revolt in Guatemala at the end of 1930 carefully adhered to constitutional procedures, so no prob-

[56] Hoover, *Memoirs* II, 411–412; *For. Rels., 1929*, III, 605 ff.; *1930*, III, 645, 697 ff.

[57] Department of State, *The U.S. and Nicaragua*, pp. 115 ff; *For. Rels., 1930*, III, 637 ff.; Buell, *For. Pol. Assn. Reports*, VI (1930–1931), 328 ff., 390 ff.

[58] *U.S. in World Affs., 1931*, Appendix VII, 353.

[59] Diary, June 18, 1932, Stimson Papers, Yale; Dana G. Munro, "Establishment of Peace in Nicaragua," *For. Affs.*, XI, No. 4 (July, 1933), 701–702.

[60] *For. Rels., 1929*, I, 964 ff.; *1930*, I, 344 ff., 361 ff.; *1931*, I, 795 ff.

lem of recognition arose. Stimson did make it clear that the State Department attached "imperative importance" to the fact that no person involved in the recent political revolt should become a member of the new provisional government.[61]

When a revolution displaced the President of El Salvador late in 1931 Washington followed the treaty of 1923 and refused to extend recognition.[62] Guatemala, Honduras, and Nicaragua followed the lead of the United States, though Costa Rica broke ranks and established relations with the successful rebel Maximiliano Hernández Martínez (see below, "The Chaco," Chapter Ten). At the same time it gave notice that it was denouncing the treaty of 1923. Promptly eight other Latin American states followed Costa Rica while twenty-seven European and Asiatic states also recognized the new administration. An interesting feature of the situation was the fact that under an existing understanding between El Salvador and American bankers the latter in case of default on loan payments (and such a default immediately followed the revolt) had a right to establish a customs receivership. With widespread defaults around the world, however, the State Department felt it unwise to endorse such a receivership even though it refused to extend recognition to the new Martínez Administration. In May, 1933, a negotiated agreement was reached between El Salvador and the bankers.[63]

Panama had been one spot that Hoover carefully avoided on his southern tour. Feelings there were still high over the sending of marines to enforce the White award in the Costa Rican boundary dispute. Better to let the situation rest. There had been no supervision of elections on the Isthmus since 1918, but the "outs" claimed that this had simply meant that they had no chance because the "ins" controlled the polls.[64]

[61] For revolt in Honduras see *ibid.*, *1931*, II, 559 ff. For revolt in Guatemala see *ibid.*, *1930*, III, 183 ff., and *1931*, II, 394 ff.

[62] *Ibid.*, *1931*, II, 169 ff.
Stimson confided to his diary (Yale) on December 9, 1931, that his minister on the ground had been "rather sloppy" in handling the situation. He had apparently sympathized with the rebels when he should have warned them that they would not be recognized. Subsequent entries for January 25, March 2, March 9, and March 12, 1932, indicate that a special trouble shooter, Jefferson Caffrey, had been sent down to Nicaragua. The entry for January 25, 1932, refers to Communist activity as adding an "awkward" element to the situation.

[63] C. A. Thompson, "The Caribbean Situation," *For. Pol. Assn. Reports*, IX, No. 12 (August, 1930), 147–148.

[64] Edwin Emerson, *Hoover and His Times*, p. 78; Gastón Nerval, *Autopsy of the Monroe Doctrine*, p. 273.

Unrest culminated in January, 1931, when rebels seized President Harmodio Arosemena and occupied the administrative offices. The President
considerately resigned, and the forms of legality were preserved when
the Supreme Court did its part and declared that the preceding election
of *designados* to the Presidency had been illegal. This left the *designado*
of the old administration, Ricardo Alfaro, who was then serving as minister at Washington, to succeed as Executive.[65] Fortunately, he was
persona grata both to the rebels and to Washington. The old Kellogg
dictum of no revolution on the Isthmus had been ignored.[66] A satisfactory
little revolution had been enjoyed by all.

The Islands

The Machado dictatorship in Cuba, already firmly entrenched at the time
of the Havana Conference, continued its ruthless course. There were
rising suspicions in Washington, but, after all, here was at least one
peaceful situation. Why disturb it?[67] The new administration sent Harry
F. Guggenheim as ambassador and maintained a strictly correct attitude.[68] After an abortive revolt the dictatorship became even more ruthless. An interesting memorandum of an interview of Secretary Stimson
and the Cuban ambassador in Washington reflects Machado's attitude.
The ambassador argued that any compromise would indicate weakness,
and at any sign of weakness the Cubans would jump on the opposition
band wagon. He insisted that a successful government had to operate
through either force or prestige; legality had little to do with it. Leniency
to any opposition had bad effects; when convictions could not be secured
before the courts, indefinite imprisonment had to be employed.[69]

Ambassador Guggenheim's background gave him a conservative lean-
ing, and his sympathies were with the maintenance of good order and
stability. Even so he reported: "The basic cause of the revolutionary
sentiment is poverty, especially in the cities. The immediate cause is
found in the indignant idealism of the students." He amplified his state-

[65] *For. Rels., 1931*, II, 898 ff.; DeConde, *Hoover's Latin American Policy*, pp.
60–62; William D. McCain, *The United States and the Republic of Panama*, pp.
90–91.

[66] *For. Rels., 1928*, III, 678.

[67] Smith, *The U.S. and Cuba*, pp. 117–118; Bryce Wood, *The Making of the Good
Neighbor Policy*, pp. 55–56; Carleton Beals, *The Crime of Cuba*, pp. 333–334.

[68] DeConde, *Hoover's Latin American Policy*, pp. 104 ff.; Russell H. Fitzgibbon,
Cuba and the United States, p. 193.

[69] *For. Rels., 1931*, II, 51 ff.

ment on January 21, 1931, saying that the Cuban troubles were not economic and political, but "economic and communistic."[70] By 1933 the situation had reached a crisis with bomb outrages, sugar-mill and sugar-cane burning, and increased guerrilla activity.[71] Meanwhile there occurred frequent references to Communistic activities. As yet they were not taken too seriously but later events might indicate that a groundwork was being established at this time.[72]

The underlying effects of the Depression are seen in the following figures, estimates in part, of public revenues:[73]

	Municipal	Provincial	National
1929–1930	$18,962,189	$2,912,228	$95,278,376
1932–1933	10,112,226	2,389,611	53,033,321

To make matters worse, the Cuban share of the United States' sugar market—its all-important source of cash—dropped from 49.4 per cent to 25.3 per cent in 1933. The decrease was due to the rising importance of domestic production and to increasing imports from other areas. Washington did all it could to relieve the situation. Little effort was made to press claims for financial payments due. In fact, when one Joseph E. Barlow declined to have a claim submitted to arbitration on the basis of Cuban law, claiming that such an arbitration would be unfair, the Department took the position that further effort on behalf of the claimant would be inappropriate.[74]

Cubans felt that the Platt Amendment was an indignity and a handicap to the good government of the island. Legislators sniped at it with measures designed to undermine it,[75] while on the mainland scholars

[70] *Ibid., 1930*, II, 678; *1931*, II, 44 ff., 80. Also Harry F. Guggenheim, *The United States and Cuba*, pp. 179 ff.; Stuart, *Latin America and the U.S.*, p. 238.

[71] *For. Rels., 1930*, II, 649 ff.; Guggenheim, *The U.S. and Cuba*, pp. 233–234; *Survey of Int. Affs., 1933*, pp. 373 ff.

[72] Raymond Leslie Buell et al., *Problems of the New Cuba*, pp. 195 ff.; Dorothy Dillon, "International Communism in Latin America," *Latin American Monographs*, No. 19 (1962), pp. 6–10.

[73] Buell et al., *Problems of the New Cuba*, p. 350.

[74] *For. Rels., 1930*, II, 697–698. For financial conditions, especially those related to sugar, see Fitzgibbon, *Cuba and the U.S.*, pp. 189 ff.; Guggenheim, *The U.S. and Cuba*, pp. 141 ff.; Smith, *The U.S. and Cuba*, pp. 32, 70, 165 ff.; Beals, *The Crime of Cuba*, pp. 391–392.

[75] The chief arguments may be secured from Guggenheim, *The U.S. and Cuba*, p. 236, and Guggenheim, "Amending the Platt Amendment," *For. Affs.*, XII, No. 3 (April, 1934), 449–450; Cosme de la Torriente, "The Platt Amendment," *For. Affs.*,

seriously questioned its value and asserted that in seeking to avoid disorders in the island the United States had established a virtual dictatorship. The result was violation of the very principles Washington desired to foster. Ambassador Guggenheim himself called for amending the Amendment and advocated new political and commercial treaties. At this point, on January 5, 1929, both the United States and Cuba subscribed to the Pan-American arbitration agreement which provided for arbitration of differences arising between countries from the interpretation of treaties. By implication this meant that any future intervention, undertaken under the terms of the Platt Amendment (itself a treaty), would be subject to arbitration if Cuba protested the action taken.

The passive program followed in Cuba was impossible in Haiti. Within a month after taking office the Secretary of State, on April 11, 1929, notified High Commissioner Russell that the Department considered the President ineligible for re-election. On October 10 the commissioner reported that he had strongly discouraged President Luis Borno by telling him that he was sure the United States would not recognize his re-election. Six weeks later the Secretary of State could ask Russell to congratulate Borno on his recent public statement that he would not be a candidate for re-election.[76]

But Hoover was tired of the "indefinite policies of the last administration." Early in December he asked Congress for $50,000 to enable him to send a commission of five eminent men to investigate and report. Marines were ordered to stand by and the press became quite concerned.[77] The W. Cameron Forbes Commission landed at Port-au-Prince on February 28, 1930, for a sixteen-day stay. Its report applauded much of the work that had been done, particularly that of Commissioner Russell. In addition it made a set of seven recommendations to be implemented by nine sequent steps. By these it was hoped the United States could withdraw entirely and return military and fiscal control to local authorities. This was to be accomplished by May 3, 1936, the date of the expiration of the existing treaty. Hoover promptly endorsed the report and reversed

---

VIII, No. 3 (April, 1930), 374–375; R. L. Buell, "Changes in our Latin American Policy," *The Annals*, CLVI (July, 1931), 128, and Buell, "Cuba and the Platt Amendment," *For. Pol. Assn. Reports*, V (1929–1930), No. 3, 60–61; Wood, *Making of the Good Neighbor Policy*, p. 57; *For. Rels., 1929*, II, 894 ff.

[76] *For. Rels., 1929*, III, 170 ff.

[77] *Ibid.* 188 ff.; Ernest Gruening, "The Issue in Haiti," *For. Affs.*, XI, No. 2 (January, 1933), 284–285.

the old tendency of reserving high offices for non-Haitians. At the same time a detailed study of educational conditions in the country was undertaken.[78]

More complications arose. The High Commissioner reported that he had "argued with" the President for over an hour to get him to recommend the right man as his successor. The election was to be held by the Council of State, so the members opposing the chosen candidate had to be replaced by others who would vote correctly. Still things did not work out; so "After much discussing and arguing" the Council was adjourned for eight days during which twelve of its members were replaced. The newly constituted Council then cast twenty-one unanimous votes for Mr. Eugene Roy, who was duly inaugurated on April 15, 1930.[79] One member of the Commission commented on Roy's election saying that the Commission had sought to find a man acceptable to the hostile factions at a time when representatives of both groups agreed that such a "white blackbird" did not exist.[80] Finally they had agreed upon Roy, and his election became official.

Minister Dana G. Munro now directed the Haitianization of local services.[81] On December 10, 1931, Hoover reported to his Congress: ". . . the Haitian Government on October 1 assumed definitely the administration and control of the Department of Public Works, the Sanitary Service, and the Technical Service of Agriculture, which includes the educational system." He added that to improve health conditions a scientific commission of nine naval officers and corpsmen only were left behind in Port-au-Prince and Cap Hatien.[82]

But the United States minister in Haiti continued to encounter difficulties. The local administration endeavored to avoid its financial obli-

[78] For the official report of the Commission see *For. Rels., 1930*, III, 217 ff. For additional comments see Department of State, *Report of the United States Commission on Education in Haiti*, pp. 66 ff.

[79] *For. Rels., 1930*, III 244 ff.

[80] H. P. Fletcher, "Quo Vadis, Haiti?," *For. Affs.*, VIII, No. 4 (July, 1930), 544.

[81] *For. Rels., 1931*, II, 505 ff. Secretary of State Stimson in his diary (Yale) on October 1, 1930, noted that Munro himself thought it "vitally important that we should not leave Haiti. . . . In this he is in sharp contrast with the President." Mr. Hoover insisted that "we should get out anyhow" even if a later return became necessary. "I [Stimson] am inclined to agree with Munro." See also *For. Rels., 1931*, I, xxviii.

[82] *For. Rels., 1931*, I, XXVIII.

gations and ineptly handled its funds in time of economic crisis. Finally, just before the end of the Hoover Administration a new treaty was negotiated. This left a fiscal representative, to be nominated by the President of the United States, to collect customs duties with the assistance of personnel to be named by him on recommendation of the Haitian President. This arrangement was to continue until the 1922 debt had been satisfactorily refunded.[83] Congressional opposition to the new treaty caused the Haitian President to resort to the old maneuver and apply the agreement by executive decree. The explanation has been given that this was done because of Haitian fears that the delay would enable President-elect Franklin D. Roosevelt to adopt a sterner policy.[84] Thus in spite of the complications of the times, the Hoover Administration felt that definite progress had been secured in at least one of the Caribbean republics. Credit apparently should go largely to Hoover himself. Secretary Stimson commented in his diary for April 22, 1931, that under the influence of the Forbes Commission "We are trying to give away to the Haitians gradually, but of course that is not the way to deal with Negroes, and I am afraid it is going to make trouble."

Santo Domingo, like the rest of the world, found its finances demoralized. In response to a request, General Charles G. Dawes, one of the leading financiers of the United States and architect of the Dawes Plan for European reparations payments, headed a commission that spent three weeks of careful work in the Dominican Republic planning a scientific budget for the country. The report was presented to the President of the republic on April 23, 1929. Within a month he had approved the plan and the Congress had enacted the laws proposed in the report. These included a budget law, a law of finances, a law covering projected public works, and a law reorganizing governmental departments. At the same time the President appointed appropriate officers for the work planned. The result was substantial economies that did much to soften the brunt of the depression.[85]

Next rose the perennial question of the election of a new President. The American minister reported in 1930 that finances were in deplorable

---

[83] *Survey of Int. Affs., 1933*, pp. 356 ff.; Munro, *U.S. and the Caribbean Area*, pp. 191–192.

[84] Roosevelt was reported to have boasted that as Assistant Secretary of the Navy during World War I he had written the Haitian constitution (Gruening, "The Issue in Haiti," *For. Affs.*, XI, No. 2 [January, 1933], 287–288).

[85] Charles G. Dawes *et al. Report of the Dominican Economic Commission.*

condition and that Rafael Leonidas Trujillo was likely to capture the election. The minister asked that he be authorized to state that Trujillo would not be recognized if he were elected. The answer was: "The Department regrets that it cannot authorize the statement suggested." It merely expressed the hope that in a friendly but unofficial fashion Trujillo might be persuaded not to run. If he actually secured the election he would be recognized. On May 19, 1930, Minister C. B. Curtis reported that 223,851 votes (a number greatly exceeding the number of voters in the country) had been cast for Trujillo. In due course, the United States sent a special representative to be present at the inauguration on August 17, 1930.[86] By October 13 Stimson confided to his diary that in view of the depression Trujillo was "panning out to be a very good man." On December 3 Stimson reported that Colonel Theodore Roosevelt (son of the old President) had come to deliver a message saying that Trujillo "wanted us to appoint a military commission to train his army so that he could stay in power indefinitely." No illusions there. When a hurricane devastated the country in 1931 the State Department authorized diversion of moneys due on debt amortization to current expenses and the bankers concerned were notified accordingly.[87]

In spite of economic conditions which aggravated existing problems it appears that Hoover was making substantial efforts to break the vicious circle outlined by Walter Lippmann:

. . . under the Monroe Doctrine we alone can intervene in this hemisphere; because the Central American [and Caribbean] countries are too immature to conduct elections they have chronic revolutions; because they have revolutions they have disorder; because they have disorder we are compelled to intervene; because we do not wish to intervene we have in effect forbidden revolution; to enforce our prohibition we have to intervene; because we intervene we are in the morally unpleasant position of always supporting the existing regime; because we think that some change of government must be allowed, because no change can take place peaceably, we have to intervene again to compel natives to submit to peaceable elections.[88]

[86] *For. Rels., 1930,* II, 706 ff.

[87] *Ibid., 1931,* II, 88 ff., 134–135.

[88] Walter Lippmann, "Second Thoughts on Havana," *For. Affs.,* VI, No. 4 (July, 1928), 549.

Northern South America

A successful dictatorship held conditions reasonably stable in Venezuela, so no particular issues arose in international relations.

By common consent the stormy two decades in Colombian relations following the Panama revolt in 1903 were ignored in both Bogotá and Washington. Extensive correspondence did develop over rapidly expanding petroleum fields. The Tropical Oil Company and the Barco concession were both involved but the diplomatic positions taken and the points at issue were those to be more or less expected in a rapidly developing oil field. Correspondence of the State Department on the subject reflected an essentially normal, albeit a conservative, procedure and hardly indicated any significant change of policy.[89] Arrangements were made for reciprocal landing privileges for air traffic[90] and adjustments were made on literage charges in Colombian ports.[91] In 1930 depression-inspired unrest ousted the Conservative control that had dominated the country since the turn of the century. The Liberals, to be re-elected four years later, launched a quite progressive program by the mid-thirties. Their support by radicals of various types may have given food for future concern but for the time being conditions appeared to be satisfactory.[92]

To the southeast of Colombia lay that no-man's land known as Leticia, where the Amazon jungle was claimed by Colombia, Brazil, Ecuador, and Peru. Periodically one or the other of the four countries attempted to exercise jurisdiction over Indians in the area, or attempted to exploit the sparce supply of wild rubber. Exploration or the sending of small military detachments to assert control from time to time precipitated skirmishes both military and diplomatic. Finally, just as the Hoover administration reached its close the dispute again erupted. Both Washington and the League of Nations sought to preserve the peace.[93] When diplomatic relations were broken between Colombia and Peru the United

[89] *For. Rels., 1928*, II, 588 ff.; *1931*, II, 1 ff. The Mellon interests had substantial holdings in Colombia through the Gulf Oil Company and were accused of using diplomatic pressures to aid their own investments.

[90] *Ibid., 1929*, II 882–884.

[91] *Ibid., 1930*, II, 641 ff.

[92] Stephen Naft, "Fascism and Communism in South America," *For. Pol. Assn. Reports*, XIII, No. 19 (December 15, 1937), 233.

[93] Russell M. Cooper, *American Consultation in World Affairs* . . ., pp. 310–311.

States legation took charge of Colombian interests at Lima, but to maintain strict neutrality it refused to allow use of its dry-dock facilities in the Canal Zone by either disputant.[94]

The West Coast

When Professor E. W. Kemmerer, the financial trouble shooter for small countries, returned to the United States in the fall of 1931 he reported: "At least five South American countries will maintain the gold standard as a result of the conference of five South American central banks at Lima."[95] So far so good. When the Ecuadorian President resigned in August, 1931, Colonel Larrea Alba, next in line for the presidency, promptly assumed office. In twenty-four hours Washington responded that there was no question of recognition involved. On September 1 new elections were called to take place in October. On the twenty-second of that month they were reported as having been held in an "orderly, free and fair" manner.[96] Presumably all was well.

Peru provided a more difficult problem. On his South American tour Hoover found that both Peru and Chile were willing to consider reasonable terms for the settlement of the troublesome Tacna-Arica problem.[97] Peru then requested that Hoover propose the compromise to which both had tentatively agreed. This would save their official faces. However, the new President declined the responsibility; to have taken it would have invited condemnation for interference. Instead, Washington indicated that it had used its good offices and that the agreement announced was the result of direct negotiations.

On May 17, 1929, the details of the settlement were released by the

---

[94] *For. Rels., 1933*, IV, 549 ff.; DeConde, *Hoover's Latin American Policy*, p. 44.

On October 14, 1932, Stimson confided to his diary (Yale) that after exchanging compliments with Peruvian officials on opening telegraphic communications with that country, "I took the [Peruvian] Ambassador aside . . . and I told him if I were to convey my real sentiments to his honorable chief, the Foreign Minister of Peru, I should have told him that if he didn't get his damned scoundrels out of Leticia without delay I'd string him up. . . . The Leticia incident is still on and it is perfectly indefensible on the part of Peru." The Secretary seems to have made his meaning clear.

[95] The *Times* (London), December 30, 1931, 15b.

[96] *For. Rels., 1931*, II, 139 ff.

[97] Myers, *Foreign Policies of Hoover*, pp. 44–45; DeConde, *Hoover's Latin American Policy*, pp. 28 ff.

Department of State.[98] Bolivia remained convinced that its just claims had been ignored and was unhappy, for Chile and Peru had simply agreed to divide the disputed provinces and merely promised Bolivia outlet rights to the coast without control of the routes involved. To moderate Bolivian feelings a secret provision was included in the treaty to the effect that neither of the parties would at any time in the future alienate any part of the Tacna-Arica territory without the consent of Bolivia.[99] This was cold comfort but was all that could be secured.

Peru was not to escape the epidemic of political disorders engendered by the depression. In August, 1930, the United States chargé at Lima reported that President Agusto B. Leguía had resigned. By the middle of the next month the new government appeared able to support itself and to fulfill its international obligations. Following a now familiar and easy course, the State Department instructed its legation in Lima to enter into full diplomatic relations.[100] Furthermore, the naval mission serving the Peruvian government was authorized to continue its services to the new government. Throughout the change-over Washington instructed its diplomatic agents not to take part in, or to express opinions concerning, domestic problems of Peru. The next year brought more trouble when the new Peruvian President resigned and then asked the United States ambassador to aid him in regaining power. The State Department not only refused to do so but declined to be associated with European powers, Far Eastern powers, or the League in endeavoring to mediate in the internal complications of the country. The temporary administration then proceeded with an election and by December 8, 1931, a new president, Luis M. Sánchez Cerro, assumed office.[101] The multiple changes had apparently followed legal procedures, so the United States refrained from questions.

Chile was lukewarm toward Hoover on his good-will tour, since it apparently feared he would support Bolivian demands for an outlet to the sea.[102] An even more substantial fear was connected with the price of copper. During World War I the price had risen to exorbitant heights. Next it dropped disastrously. Critics said that during the War, Wash-

[98] *For. Rels.*, *1929*, I, 803.
[99] *Ibid.*, 779 ff.
[100] *Ibid.*, *1930*, III, 724 ff. ,
[101] *Ibid.*, *1931*, II, 910 ff. Also *ibid.*, *1930*, III, 727 ff.
[102] Emerson, *Hoover and His Times*, p. 56.

ington had tried to control prices adversely to Chilean interests, but that when the disaster loomed the Department of Commerce (Hoover being Secretary) had allowed private capitalists to drive down prices as they wished.[103] In part this was the result of a 4 per cent import tax which sought to protect a remaining small market for domestic producers in the United States. To demoralize matters further, Northern Rhodesia was now flooding the depressed market with cheap ore.

An even more alarming condition existed in the nitrate fields. Synthetics had largely taken over the market. One report had it that in 1924–1925 Chilean nitrate production was valued at £23,500,000 (about $117 million) gold, but that eight years later it was down to £2,000,000 gold.[104] Since much of the national revenue derived from nitrates and copper, political unrest was to be expected. It began in May, 1931. The Cabinet resigned in July. Again the change was effected according to the constitution, so there was no question of recognition. Elections followed in early October and the new President was promptly congratulated. When he sought to buy submarines and arms he was informed that no sale of vessels was permitted under the naval armament treaty of 1922, but that arms purchases would be approved and deliveries made as soon as possible. Soon came the welcome word that the arms would not be needed. It was generally understood that social reforms could be expected in the relatively near future.[105]

Bolivia may still be considered a west coast country though it had lost its Pacific outlet. Whatever the causes—and among them mismanagement must be included—a foreign debt of less than $4 million in 1920 had mounted to over $30 million in 1925 and to more than $60 million by 1930. True, the domestic debt had been reduced from over $17 million to less than $7 million but still service on the foreign debt alone called for from 65 to 75 per cent of the income of the national government.[106] The Standard Oil Company of Bolivia was making tentative explorations for petroleum in the interior[107] but the wealth of the

[103] Juan José Arévalo, *Fábula del tiburón y las sardinas*, pp. 146–147.

[104] *Survey of Int. Affs., 1934*, pp. 53–54. Also C. A. Thompson, "Chile struggles for . . . recovery," *For. Pol. Assn. Reports*, IX, No. 25 (February 14, 1934), 288–289.

[105] *For. Rels., 1931*, I, 906 ff. Also *Rev. of Revs.*, LXXXVI, No. 2 (August, 1932), 48.

[106] *For. Pol. Assn. Reports*, VII, No. 5 (May 13. 1931), 106–109.

[107] Wood, *Making of the Good Neighbor Policy*, p. 168.

country lay in tin. Ownership of the mines technically resided in various Bolivian nationals but the managers of the Patiño mines, the Aramayo mines, and the Hochschild mines were all North Americans and control was vested in Wall Street.[108] When labor protested on wages, labor conditions, or the like, local owners quickly shifted the blame to the suspect Yankee. When the depression demoralized the tin market government income was jeopardized and bad conditions became worse. As a further complication, substantial portions of all moneys received by the government both from current income and from loans were being devoted to military expenditures to meet the threatening situation in the Gran Chaco Boreal.[109]

The East Coast—The Chaco

Hoover's "intransigent hostility to the Brazilian coffee defense policy"[110] left nationals of that country fearful indeed. From 1916 to 1925 their average annual balance of trade had mounted to a handsome figure of $80 million. Just when they had adjusted their expenditures to this level a rapid decline reduced the balance to less than $33 million in 1928.[111] The next year came the depression proper. The price of coffee dropped in the United States from 24.8 cents per pound in 1929 to 7.6 cents in 1931.[112] United States capital invested in Brazil had increased from a scant $50 million in 1918 to more than eleven times that figure in 1930.[113] Washington therefore found it increasingly difficult to ignore internal conditions in its neighboring republic.

The long story reduced to one word was "revolution." Getulio Vargas seized power in 1930. Forty-eight hours before the rebels were victorious Secretary Stimson had announced an embargo on all munitions to be sent to the rebels. The action was in line with previous conduct in the cases of disorders in Cuba and Central America but seriously irritated the immediately successful Brazilian rebels. This, in fact, was the occasion for Stimson's being dubbed by his familiars as "wrong horse Harry."[114]

---

[108] Germán Arciniegas, *The State of Latin America*, p. 152.
[109] Denna Frank Fleming, *The United States and World Organization*, p. 305.
[110] Emerson, *Hoover and His Times*, p. 152.
[111] *For. Pol. Assn. Reports*, VI (1930–1931), No. 26, 499.
[112] *Survey of Int. Affs., 1934*, p. 50.
[113] *For. Pol. Assn. Reports*, XI, No. 1 (March 13, 1935), 4.
[114] Richard N. Current, *Secretary Stimson*, p. 55.; *For. Rels., 1930*, I, 434 ff.;

Following the by now familiar policy, as soon as the new government seemed firmly established the United States ambassador was instructed to join his diplomatic colleagues in continuing with the new government "the same friendly relations as with its predecessors." Vargas was not especially impressed and in short order notified Washington that because of financial difficulties his government could not renew its contract for the United States naval mission in that country. Further, in spite of both direct and indirect pressures, Brazil declined to repeal a decree favoring Brazilian shipping over that of the United States. Probably all this had nothing to do with the declination of a Brazilian request in 1931 to purchase two light cruisers to strengthen its Navy in competition with its neighbors, for similar declinations had also been sent to Chile.[115] Whatever the reasons, there was no indication of the close friendship that had so long existed between Washington and Rio de Janeiro.

One interesting arrangement was made to exchange 1,275,000 bags of coffee for 25,000,000 bushels of northern wheat held by the Federal Grain Stabilization Corporation.[116] This forthwith evoked vigorous complaints of unfair competition on the part of Argentine grain growers.

Uruguay continued its friendly relations with the United States. It was not afraid of Yankee aggression, for worse dangers were closer at hand. Thus, its minister in Chile in 1930 expressed a general attitude when he called for the South American republics to "join themselves to the great republic of the north" to claim that position in world affairs "which of right and by nature belongs to them."[117]

In 1928 Argentina elected Hipólito Irigoyen, the country's leader in World War I, as President. His attitude toward the United States was at best reserved. Hoover's cool reception, therefore, in Buenos Aires was not surprising.[118] Argentina was not represented at the Washington meeting to consider conciliation and arbitration, did not adhere to the Kellogg-Briand Pact, and soon vacated its ambassadorial post at Washington. To make matters worse, age, personal idiosyncrasies, and hard times caused loss of Irigoyen's popularity. His overthrow in 1930, said

---

John Bassett Moore, *Candor and Common Sense*, pp. 20–21; DeConde, *Hoover's Latin American Policy*, pp. 98–99.

[115] *For. Rels., 1930*, I, 451 ff.; *1931*, I, 876 ff.

[116] *U.S. in World Affs., 1931*, pp. 88–89; *Survey of Int. Affs., 1931*, pp. 106, 397.

[117] Carlos G. Dávila, *North American Imperialism*, p. 18.

[118] Hoover, *Memoirs*, II, 413; *New York Times*, January 20, 1929, III, 6.1.

United States Ambassador Bliss Woods, was a popular movement that might be termed a "restoration rather than a revolution."[119]

In truth, Argentina stood peculiarly alone. It had a proud record of regular payments of its foreign debts, but recent payments had been continued only at the cost of increasing financial maneuvers. Also the depression reduced returns from the huge British investment in the country (estimated at over $2 billion) to the point that railway dividends were cut in half.[120] At the same time the Ottawa Agreements on Empire trade threatened to replace British purchases from Argentina with products from New Zealand, Australia, and Canada. From this vantage point Great Britain negotiated the Runciman-Roca convention which practically integrated Argentina into the British trade orbit to the substantial detriment of the small republic. Heretofore Argentina had customarily used credits derived from its trade with Great Britain to offset deficits incurred in trade with the United States. The new agreement pegged British purchases in Argentina to a percentage of previous quantities and authorized the British to use their trade balances to service existing Argentine debts in Great Britain. Argentina, therefore, could no longer spend its balances as it wished, that is, in the United States. The agreement further provided that Argentina would reduce its tariffs on many British articles while British coal was placed on the free list. Here were blocked currencies, quota systems, and trade controls with a vengeance.[121] As the depression deepened, Argentina strove vainly to peg its currency to the dollar, then to the franc, and then by the end of 1933 it resorted to wholesale exchange control. The alarming effects of the combined depression and new trade controls are seen in the United States-Argentina trade figures. Imports to the United States from the southern republic dropped from $117.6 million in 1929 to $15.8 in 1932; and exports to Argentina from the United States declined in the same years from $210.3 to less than $31.2 million.[122]

[119] Arthur P. Whitaker, *The United States and Argentina*, p. 60; Harold F. Peterson, *Argentina and the United States*, pp. 379–380; *For. Pol. Assn. Reports*, VII, No. 17 (October 28, 1931), 313 ff.

[120] Ysabel F. Rennie, *The Argentine Republic*, pp. 230 ff.; Samuel Flagg Bemis, *The Latin American Policy of the United States*, p. 335; the *Times* (London), February 5, 1931, 18a.

[121] Rennie, *The Argentine Republic*, p. 335; Nicholas John Spykman, *America's Strategy in World Politics*, p. 267.

[122] *Department of State Bulletin*, I, No. 9 (August 26, 1939), 166–167; *Survey of Int. Affs., 1934*, pp. 46 ff.

Official relations did not improve. In 1930 the chief of the Argentine delegation to the Pan-American Reciprocal Trade Conference in Sacramento bluntly said that his countrymen had learned that Hoover's promises of increased purchases of Argentine wool, linseed, and hides were false and that only at the last minute had Argentina decided to send any delegates at all to the Conference.[123] The former chancellor of the Argentine embassy in Washington told the Williamstown Institute of Politics that "as soon as a new generation gets the reins of government in its hands, or perhaps sooner," his country would withdraw from the Pan-American Union, a United States institution, just as it had withdrawn from the League of Nations because it was European-dominated.[124] After four years in Argentina a British observer commented that the Argentines were "the most genuinely neutral [people] I have ever known" as far as Europe is concerned. As for the United States, they were "not neutral"; they considered the Monroe Doctrine obsolete and feared marines would follow the dollar. As an additional complicating factor, he said, their desire for American manufactures, such as motor vehicles, radios, cameras, electric goods, cinematographs, were complicated by the Runciman-Roca controls.[125]

In the dispute between Paraguay and Bolivia over the Chaco Boreal, Washington, as early as 1924, refused to mediate except in response to a request from both parties involved. In addition to the old boundary frictions the new possibility of the control of rich oil fields was dangling before both contestants. United States money had become interested in Bolivian petroleum development, but the Argentines were seriously short of oil and felt that this disputed area was a proper field for their own exploitation.

The League of Nations sought to pacify the quarreling nations but ceased its efforts upon hearing that both of them had agreed to accept the good offices of the Pan-American Conference on Conciliation and Arbitration.[126] The findings of the Commission of Inquiry reported that fifty-two fortified border posts were held by the opposing forces. Explosive contacts were imminent. The neutral members of the Commis-

[123] New York Times, August 6, 1930, 8.4.

[124] The Times (London), August 21, 1930, 9b.

[125] Malcolm Robertson, "Economic Relations between Great Britain and the Argentine Republic," International Affairs, IX, No. 2 (March, 1930), 224, 227.

[126] For. Rels., 1924, pp. 282 ff.; Cooper, American Consultation in World Affairs, pp. 109 ff.; Survey of Int. Affs., 1930, pp. 426 ff.

sion promptly extended the good offices of their countries to search for a solution. Paraguay accepted, but Bolivia preferred direct negotiations. The Commission itself had an unhappy experience when Argentina refused to cooperate because President Irigoyen's direct offer of his nation's good offices had been declined. He took the position that the question was of primary concern to his country so if he were not allowed to take the lead he would have nothing to do with the solution. Next, the Commission of Neutrals tried direct negotiations. This quieted matters for a time.[127]

Brazil, Peru, Uruguay, Chile, and Colombia stood by more or less helpless. All Washington could do was to encourage the conversations and offer to help in any way possible.[128] Thus passed 1930 and most of 1931. On October 16, 1931, all the other Latin American states joined in asking that the belligerents sign a nonaggression pact. A month later Paraguayan delegates arrived for a conference in Buenos Aires but Bolivian delegates delayed arrival, so the opening session had to be postponed for two weeks. Just as the delegates were finally assembling, the Bolivian Congress repudiated any idea of nonaggression and called on its administration to join any such meeting only "to gain time" in which to complete military preparations. Once more the apple cart was upset.

On August 3 came another appeal signed by all the other American republics urging peace and negotiations. It added that the signatories would not recognize any territorial settlement of the controversy that had not been secured by peaceful means, nor would they recognize territorial acquisitions as a result of the use of force. Since neither of the belligerents were signers of the Kellogg-Briand Pact, nor members of the League, the only international peace organization recognized by both was the Pan-American Union. But now it developed that several South American states were jealous of the fact that the Chaco dispute

---

[127] *For. Rels., 1929*, I, 830 ff.; *Survey of Int. Affs., 1930*, pp. 432–433.

[128] *For. Rels., 1930*, I, 344. For a discussion of the involved situation that ensued see David H. Zook, Jr., *The Conduct of the Chaco War*; Cooper, *American Consultation*; R. S. Cain, "Chaco Dispute and the Peace System," *Pol. Sc. Quar.*, L, No. 3 (September, 1935); *Survey of Int. Affs., 1930*, pp. 371–372.

The general attitude of the United States government was expressed by Francis White thus: "The only interest of the United States in the matter is to have this question settled and have fighting and bloodshed cease. We are not looking for credit for ourselves . . . and we are not looking for any glory in this matter" (quoted in Bryce Wood, *The United States and Latin American Wars*, p. 27).

was a local problem and felt that the United States-dominated Union was scarcely a proper agency to take a forceful position in the matter. Yet the efforts of five neutral states in 1931, and of the ABCP (Argentina, Brazil, Chile, and Peru) group in 1933 disclosed internal rivalries among the would-be South American peacemakers that boded ill for the outcome. Argentina, in particular, was now urging the League to assume leadership to offset the influence of the United States.

In December, 1932, the Commission of Neutrals, under the chairmanship of Assistant Secretary of State Francis White, tried its hand by proposing a truce during which arbitration would be resorted to. The League and the other Latin American republics gave cordial endorsement. Paraguay, on the grounds that its national security might be endangered by this procedure, withdrew its representative from Washington as an expression of disapproval. Thereupon the Commission asked the ABCP group to resume the lead. No progress. On May 20, 1933, the League again tried its hand. At this point the Hoover Administration bequeathed the problem to its successor. (See below, "The Chaco," Chapter Ten.)

Canada

At the end of World War I Canada was convinced of the superiority of the British as compared with the American system, especially when the latter resulted in such irresponsible conduct as was demonstrated toward the League of Nations. It sympathized with the British position on the War Debts and felt that the United Sates had not played the game. This feeling resulted in a strangely bifurcated policy in foreign affairs. On the one hand was a rising Canadian nationalism and self-assertiveness,[129] which Coolidge irritated when he refused to establish an appropriate legation at Ottawa and neglected ceremonial visits.[130] A petty matter, but annoying. On the other hand there was a growing isolationism widely noted by Canadian writers. This reflected a mixture of Canadian nationalism and of the very feelings that dominated the foreign policy of their southern neighbor: Britain had not properly protected Canadian interests against the United States from the days of the Alaska boundary controversy; the Anglo-Japanese alliance was a

---

[129] H. F. Angus *et al.*, *Canada and Her Great Neighbor*, pp. 20–21, 171, 197; R., "Neighbors: A Canadian View," *For. Affs.*, X, No. 3 (April, 1932), 422.

[130] John Bartlet Brebner, *The North Atlantic Triangle*, p. 313.

mistake; interest was active in the Washington Disarmament Conference; British cooperation with European nations against the United States was all wrong; Canada courted the League of Nations, which recognized Canadian sovereignty, but did not want the League dictating to that sovereignty; Canada disapproved of Article X of the League Covenant; and Canada wanted to be assured of "freedom from the vortex of European militarism." And a final item: now that the fur-seal controversy was ended Canada pursued the same interests in the North Pacific as the United States.[131]

Canada enjoyed the prosperity of the 1920's, then suffered the depression in much the same way as its southern neighbor. A fine wheat crop in 1928 had brought Canadian farmers an estimated $612 million, but from 1931 through 1933 their wheat sales yielded a scant $170 million per year. And the fine No. 1 northern wheat, after transportation and handling charges, was yielding the farmer a meager twenty-five cents per bushel.[132] Yet, for Canada export trade was vital, and wheat was a major factor in that trade. The United States was estimated to export about 10 per cent of its total net national production, but Canada exported three times that proportion of its output.[133]

Against this background the Smoot-Hawley Tariff was enacted. Consultation of the *Statistical Abstract of the United States* shows that the percentage of Canadian exports entering the United States duty free in 1916–1920 was 87 per cent, but by 1935 the figure was down to 61 per cent.[134] That this would be the probable effect of the proposed rates was fully known to congressmen when the bill was in process. A "confidential" memorandum in the Stimson Diary under date of June 22, 1929, reports a talk with Senator William E. Borah. The Senator

[131] For discussion see George M. Wrong, "Nationalism in Canada," *International Affairs*, V, No. 4 (July, 1926), 177–178; Hugh L. Keenleyside *et al.*, *The Growth of Canadian Policies in External Affairs*, pp. 8–10; G. P. de T. Glazebrook, *A History of Canadian External Relations*, p. 353; F. H. Soward, *Canada and the Americas*, p. 21; R. MacGregor Dawson, *William Lyon Mackenzie King*, pp. 401–402; R. A. MacKay and E. B. Rogers, *Canada Looks Abroad*, pp. 94 ff.; Brebner, *North Atlantic Triangle*, p. 280; Hughes, *Our Relations to the Western Hemisphere*, pp. 22–23.

[132] Keenleyside, *Canada and the U.S.*, pp. 291.

[133] F. R. Scott, *Canada and the United States*, p. 21. Also *Survey of Int. Affs., 1934*, pp. 70 ff.

[134] Treasury Department, *Statistical Abstract of the United States, 1920*, pp. 405; *1936*, p. 454.

expressed concern at House amendments to the pending tariff measure. Rates on "feeder cattle, potatoes, cedar logs and dairy products" affected Canada alone. He felt that Canadian reaction was likely to throw that country into the hands of the Conservatives, which was "the Wet Party, the anti-American party, the anti-St. Lawrence party, and the party which desires to give a 50% preference to Great Britain."

In the Canadian election of 1930 the tariff was the major issue. As Borah feared, the result was a victory for the Conservatives, who forthwith embarked on a high protective tariff policy in retaliation.[135] The response of the British Empire to the Smoot-Hawley Tariff challenge was the Ottawa Trade Agreements. These bore out Senator Borah's fears in another way, for they fostered Empire trade and Empire preferences.[136] Canada enacted 225 changes in its tariff rates, and of these 223 represented added preferences for British goods. One Canadian indicated that the United States' share of Canadian imports dropped from 67 per cent to less than 57 per cent.[137] Later, Secretary of State Hull cited the egg trade as an example of results of the tariff war. United States import taxes on Canadian eggs were raised from eight to ten cents a dozen. Imports of the Canadian product dropped from 13,299 dozen to 7,939 dozen between 1929 and 1932. Canada reciprocated by raising its rates on United States eggs from three cents to ten cents. United States exports of eggs to Canada declined from 919,543 dozen to 13,662 dozen.[138] Whose nose and whose face?

One interesting development was the increased rush of manufacturers to open branch plants in Canada so they could be within the new tariff barriers. According to a statement of the Canadian Premier on June 1, 1931, eighty-seven new branch plants were opened in Canada in the preceding ten months. And of these, seventy-four were American.[139]

Canadian relations with Latin America remained of minor significance. Occasional trade treaties were signed, as with Cuba,[140] but most

[135] Keenleyside, *Growth of Canadian Policies*, pp. 288–289; J. B. Condliffe. *The Reconstruction of World Trade*, pp. 184–185. ,

[136] *Survey of Int. Affs., 1932*, pp. 27 ff.

[137] Keenleyside, *Growth of Canadian Policies*, p. 294. Also Herbert Feis, "A Year of the Canadian Trade Agreement," *For. Affs.*, XV, No. 4 (July, 1937), 662; Brebner, *North Atlantic Triangle*, p. 291.

[138] Cordell Hull, *The Memoirs of Cordell Hull*, I, 355–356.

[139] *Report of the Secretary of Commerce, 1931*, p. xxiii. Also *U.S. in World Affs., 1932*, pp. 99–101.

[140] *British and Foreign State Papers, 1927*, Pt. I, pp. 466–467.

of the trade of the southern republics was oriented either to the United States or to Europe. Canada could not compete. Repeatedly the question of Canadian membership in the Pan-American Union was raised. Some scholars in the United States advised the step, but political leaders feared complications that might arise from Dominion relationships in the British Empire. For their part, possibly because of the known hesitance of the United States, most Canadian leaders seemed to take the position that "Contact with that [Latin American] turmoil has the same lack of attraction for her [Canada] as participation in European questions has for certain United States Senators."[141]

In Far Eastern affairs Canada associated itself closely with United States policies. Prime Minister Richard B. Bennett sent word to Secretary Stimson in December, 1932, cordially endorsing Stimson's policy in Manchuria, saying that he wanted to have Canada "conform exactly to it."[142] Also, when asked by the League of Nations to accept membership on the commission to negotiate between China and Japan, Canada responded that it was inclined to do so provided that the United States also had a representative on the commission.[143]

President Hoover succinctly recorded in his *Memoirs* one other item of interest:

I made one other proposal to him [Ramsay MacDonald] which hitherto has not been made public. I suggested that the British consider selling to us Bermuda, British Honduras, and the island of Trinidad. I told him that I thought we could give them a credit upon the war debt that would go a long way to settle that issue. I explained that we were not interested in their West Indian possessions generally. I wanted Trinidad and Berumda for defense purposes, and I wanted to have British Honduras as an item to use in trading with Mexico for the use of the mouth of the Colorado River so as possibly to cure certain frictions between Mexico and Guatemala. He did not rise to the idea at all. He even excluded British Honduras although, aside from officials, probably fewer than 1,000 Englishmen got a living out of it. I had a hunch he did not take the payment of the debt very seriously.[144]

---

[141] For points of view see R., "Neighbors," *For. Affs.*, X. No. 3 (April 1932), 424; Scott, *International Conferences of American States*, p. xiv; John MacCormac, *Canada: America's Problem*, pp. 65–66, 82–83; Marcel Roussin, *Le Canada et le système interaméricain*, pp. 208–209.

[142] Diary, December 6, 1932, Stimson Papers, Yale.

[143] Memorandum, February 18, 1933, *ibid.*

[144] Hoover, *Memoirs*, II, 345–346.

CHAPTER IX

THE GOOD NEIGHBOR: THEORY

Reactions to World Conditions

THE OPINIONS OF LITERATE Latin Americans may be determined with a fair degree of accuracy, but, especially before the wide diffusion of the radio, it can be doubted that they always spoke for the masses. The latter remained largely ignorant and apathetic toward international affairs. Estimates of literacy in the ten South American republics indicated that Uruguay and Argentina could claim 75 to 80 per cent of their population were able to read and write; Colombia and Chile were forced to lower the figure to 45 per cent; while in the six remaining states a mere 20 to 35 per cent were literate.[1] Another classification of South American peoples divided them as follows:[2]

Nomads and wild Indians	10%
Peons	60
Relatively skilled labor	20
Intellectuals	10
	100%

[1] Royal Institute of International Affairs, *The Republics of South America.* p. 303.
[2] *International Affairs*, XII, No. 2 (March–April, 1933), 171.

It was the third group (in which were classed the small merchants) and some of the younger intellectuals who provided most of the political ferment. Many of them were attracted by the earlier accomplishments of Fascist dictatorships in Portugal and Italy and by their recent successes in Spain and Germany. Depression-suffering masses all too readily responded to suggestions from their relatively skilled and partially trained "betters" in thinking that Fascist militarism promised the way to a happier state. Lieuwen reaches the conclusion, therefore, that it was the depression that brought on the rash of militarism.[3] Patriotism was always popular, so nationalism became the theme song of a Fascistic appeal to restless masses. Who were more patriotic than army men, and who were more obvious symbols of patriotism than army men? Even more important, the army controlled the machinery by which power might be seized.

In 1929 rightist dictators controlled Cuba and Venezuela, and in the next two years Argentina, Peru, Ecuador, Bolivia, and El Salvador set up similar administrations. Attempted coups failed in Paraguay and Honduras, but the powerful Calles in Mexico turned from the Left to the Right; while Trujillo and Jorge Ubico seized military control of Santo Domingo and Guatemala. In Chile the military were "in and out" of power. Only Uruguay, Costa Rica, and Colombia could claim locally controlled civilian governments in the early 1930's, for United States marines were responsible for Nicaragua and Haiti.[4] This does not mean that a majority of the people of fifteen republics were Fascists, but Fascism had clearly become a force to be reckoned with. One observer of the scene commented: "Latin America's most formidable rampart against Fascism, in brief, lies in the fact that her hundred and twenty millions can be dictated to but not regimented."[5]

The European dictators were too busy at home to support actively sympathetic movements in Latin America on idealistic grounds, but they did want Latin American products. In addition, they were always willing to lend a hand to help their friends.[6] Under their controlled trade systems Germany, Italy, and Japan sent Latin America only 17 per cent of its imports in 1929, but by 1936 this figure had risen to

[3] Edwin Lieuwen, *Arms and Politics in Latin America*, pp. 60 ff.
[4] *Ibid.* Also *For. Pol. Assn. Reports*, XIII (1937–1938), No. 19, 228 ff.
[5] Duncan Aikman, *The All-American Front*, p. 301.
[6] *U.S. in World Affs., 1937*, pp. 139–141.

28 per cent.[7] Also, they were making special efforts to use the raw materials that Latin America was so desperately anxious to sell.

Communism as such made little appeal. Dictators readily used the term with which to belabor their opposition, but this very fact indicated its general unpopularity. Its propagandists freely damned Yankee imperialism and capitalism, but whenever a local government generated a positive program Communism faded into the background.[8]

Another factor was that Latin American republics were becoming increasingly disillusioned about Europe. Even though Nazi-Fascist trade was enthusiastically welcomed at first, the rigid controls under which it operated soon became extremely galling. Too, goods secured at barter prices in Latin America were periodically dumped on the world markets for other products more needed by Hitler and Mussolini. The result further depressed world markets and aroused a resentment in Latin America that tended to extend to Europe in general. After the failure of the London Economic Conference the President-elect of Colombia "warned the South American countries that they need expect nothing from Europe."[9]

The personality cult had always been strong in Latin America. Thus it hailed the dazzling Mussolini and the dynamic Hitler. Fortunately for the United States, by antithesis now appeared the magnetism of Franklin D. Roosevelt. Unseen leaven also working on behalf of United States prestige was the popularity of the Good Neighbor policy and the presence in the northern republic of some one thousand young Latin Americans in institutions of higher learning. Some failed to enjoy their experiences but for the most part they returned home with a better understanding of their northern neighbor. Also they helped to generate a genuine interest on the part of their host institutions. Courses in Latin American subjects in American universities increased from 435 in 1930–1931 to 981 in 1938–1939.[10]

El Peligro Yanqui ("The Yankee Peril") remained a phrase to con-

---

[7] Manuel Medina Castro, *EE. UU. y la independencia de América Latina*, p. 91.

[8] *For. Pol. Assn. Reports*, XIII (1937–1938), No. 19, 236; Robert J. Alexander, *Communism in Latin America*, pp. 5–15.

[9] Diary, July 9, 1934, Josephus Daniels Papers, LC.

[10] *Survey of Int. Affs., 1938*, I, 688–689; Stephen Duggan. "The Shuttle of Scholars," *Survey Graphic*, XXX (1941), 140; Philip Leonard Green, *Pan-American Progress*, pp. 150–151; Graham H. Stuart, *Latin America and the United States*, p. 42.

jure with[11] but no European power or the League could be relied on for defense against that peril. Successively Brazil, Chile, and Argentina resigned from League membership and the smaller nations simply lost interest in it. Its aid was periodically invoked (usually in vain) to solve difficult New World problems but there was almost as much jealousy as cooperation in any negotiations that ensued. The *Times* (London) in its lead article for December 1, 1936, remarked on the Latin American idea that the League was not adequate to meet New World problems. True, fear of the United States had declined but never since its independence had Latin America been so willing to accept United States leadership.[12]

Meanwhile, as Europe watched fearfully, aware of its own impotence, the United States reassessed its foreign policies under the New Deal.[13] On his way to the Montevideo Conference, Secretary of State Hull commented: "Europe is finished. You and I will hardly live to see the day when Europe will be able to drag itself out of the pit it is now digging. The race of political and economic nationalism which has started in Europe will have to be run to its conclusion—to the impoverishment of its inhabitants—whether or not there is actual war."[14]

Publicists in the United States freely debated questions of intervention, the Monroe Doctrine, or isolationism, but old-style interventionists were seldom heard.[15] Now demands were for redefinitions and clarifications of policies. Latin Americans, too, were awake to new possibilities. Gastón Nerval considered the Monroe Doctrine ready for an autopsy but admitted that his countrymen were "gradually drifting

[11] J. F. Normano, "Changes in Latin American Attitudes," *For. Affs.*, XI, No. 1 (October, 1932), 165–166.

[12] Warren H. Kelchner, *Latin American Relations with the League of Nations* (World Peace Foundation Pamphlets, XII, No. 6 [1929]), 5–6, 13; N. P. Macdonald, *Hitler over Latin America*, p. 130.

[13] William E., Jr., and Martha Dodd, eds.. *Ambassador Dodd's Diary, 1933–1938*, pp. 362 ff.

[14] Quoted by Harold B. Hinton, *Cordell Hull*, p. 2.

[15] *For. Rels., 1933*, IV, 23 ff.

For typical appeals see Albert Shaw, "Pan-America's Past," *Rev. of Revs.*, XCIV, No. 6 (December, 1936), 62 ff.; P. M. Brown, "Mexico and the Monroe Doctrine." *Amer. Jour. Internat. Law*, XXVI, No. 1 (January, 1932), 118 ff.; Dexter Perkins, "The Monroe Doctrine up to Date," *For. Affs.*, XX (October–July, 1942), 264–265; J. F. Normano, "Changes in Latin American Attitudes," *For. Affs.*, XI, No. 1 (October, 1932), 170; Robert Endicott Osgood, *Ideals and Self-Interest in America's Foreign Relations*, p. 408.

away from Europe" in the direction of the United States.[16] Sayan Vidaurri did not hold the United States blameless but recognized that it was both supplanting Europe as the major influence in foreign affairs and was rapidly becoming the bulwark of liberty. As a practical matter he noted that only in Washington did all New World republics have regular diplomatic representation; hence, only there could full consideration of all matters be promptly secured. After listing the withdrawal of marines from Haiti and Santo Domingo, and the cancellation of the Platt Amendment, the revision of the Panama Treaty, and the independence of the Philippines, he concluded that one could hardly envision either Britain or France taking such enlightened and progressive action. Then he noted that in Asia Japan was prohibiting Koreans from using their native language in public conversations. He concluded: "No, the Yankees are not as bad as some wish to make them appear."[17]

Economic Conditions

World trade ground to a nearly complete pause with the onset of the depression. Fortunately, Latin Americans had plenty of food. They might go naked, but they were seldom underfed; they might suffer from an unbalanced diet, but they had never known anything else. The logical reaction was an effort to industrialize. Chile, whose export loss was particularly severe, rejoiced that its industrial production rose more than 43 per cent between 1928 and 1936.[18]

First there had been the adoption of exchange controls. Then, except in the case of Argentina, there was general default on the public external debt, and the curtailment of private international debt service.[19] The following table indicates the dates of adoption of exchange controls:[20]

---

[16] Gastón Nerval, "Europe versus the United States in Latin America," *For. Affs.*, XV, No. 4 (July, 1937), 636; Gastón Nerval, *Autopsy of the Monroe Doctrine*, pp. 6–9, 314.

[17] Alberto Sayan Vidaurri, *Por la cooperación interamericana*, pp. 127–128, 281–287, 305.

[18] *For. Pol. Assn. Reports*, XIII (1937–1938), No. 13, 155.

[19] *For. Rels., 1934*, IV, 395.

[20] *For. Pol. Assn. Reports*, XIV (1938–1939), No. 23, 274–280; J. B. Condliffe, *The Reconstruction of World Trade*, p. 232 n.

Country	Date Adopted	Country	Date Adopted
Argentina	1931	Ecuador	1933
Bolivia	1931	Honduras	1934
Brazil	1931	Nicaragua	1932
Chile	1931	Paraguay	1932
Colombia	1931	Uruguay	1932
Costa Rica	1932	Venezuela	1936

Each country continued frantic efforts to help its own people. Big fish ate small fish; small fish ate minnows; and minnows ate animalculae. Great Britain moved to a protectionist policy at home and followed that with the Ottawa Trade Agreements for the Empire and the Runciman-Roca agreement with Argentina. The United States responded with all the pressure it could exert to secure "equality of opportunity."[21] It refurbished its old most-favored-nation agreements and pressed for their general acceptance. Between 1920 and the early days of the New Deal it had made such agreements on the unconditional basis with Honduras and El Salvador, and on a conditional basis with Argentina, Paraguay, Bolivia, Colombia, and Costa Rica. In addition it secured executive agreements including the most-favored-nation clause with Brazil, Chile, Nicaragua, Guatemala, Haiti, and the Dominican Republic.[22] This meant thirteen out of the twenty republics.

Germany attacked the situation with a technique that approached barter. It supplemented private initiative with the bargaining power of the state itself. Private shippers were required to consign their goods to, and receive payments through, the state, which determined purchases and sales.[23] This enabled the government to stock-pile strategic materials and to stimulate strategic industries, while it curtailed the unessential.

Japan, too, made its bid and was looked upon by some Latin Americans as a possible make-weight against United States power. It sought to use its plentiful cheap labor to penetrate the Latin American market

---

[21] *For. Pol. Assn. Reports*, XIII (1937–1938), No. 13, 164; *U.S. in World Affairs, 1933*, pp. 21–23; Herbert Feis, *The Changing Pattern of International Economic Affairs*, pp. 57 ff.

[22] James Constantine Pearson, *The Reciprocal Trade Agreements Program*, pp. 167–168 n.

[23] Feis, *Changing Pattern*, pp. 53–55; Percy W. Bidwell, *Economic Defense of Latin America*, pp. 38–39.

with exports that would bring in desperately needed cash.[24] If a person is to judge from percentages of Latin American trade expressed in dollars in 1929 and again in 1933 it appears that the United Kingdom and Japan responded to the crisis most promptly; Germany appears to have gotten a slow start but even before Hitler rose to power the Fatherland had managed to hold its own; while the United States rose to the emergency most tardily.[25]

Trade in gold dollars

Country	1929	1933	1936
United States			
% of L.A. Imports	35.9	24.5	29.4
% of L.A. Exports	35.0	24.2	25.0
United Kingdom			
% of L.A. Imports	14.3	16.4	13.7
% of L.A. Exports	21.2	27.0	25.2
Germany			
% of L.A. Imports	8.8	8.9	14.0
% of L.A. Exports	11.6	8.7	10.2
Japan			
% of L.A. Imports	0.5	1.2	2.2
% of L.A. Exports	0.2	0.3	1.8

The figures for 1936 are given to show the early results of the reciprocal-trade program which sought to moderate the disasterous Smoot-Hawley Tariff.[26]

[24] *For. Pol. Assn. Reports*, XIII (1937–1938), No. 13, 162; Gerardo Falconi R., *Hispanoamérica para los hispanamericanos*, p. 141.

[25] Taken from extensive summary by years in Howard J. Trueblood, "Trade Rivalries in Latin America," *For. Pol. Assn. Reports*, XIII, No. 8 (September 15, 1937), 157. Compiled as follows: for United States from Department of Commerce, Bureau of Foreign and Domestic Commerce, *Foreign Trade of the United States* (calendar year 1935), and *Monthly Summary of Foreign and Domestic Commerce* (December, 1936); for United Kingdom from Board of Trade, *Statistical Abstract for the United Kingdom* (No. 77, 1934), and *Accounts Relating to the Trade and Navigation of the United Kingdom* (January, 1936, and 1937); for Germany from Statisches Reichsamt, *Statisches Jahrbuch für das Deutsche Reich* (1931, 1934 and 1935), and *Wirschaft und Statistik* (February 2, 1937); for Japan from Department of Finance, *Financial and Economic Annual, 1935*, and Mitsubishi Economic Research Bureau, *Monthly Circular* (No. 161, March, 1937).

[26] See Stuart, *Latin America and the U.S.*, p. 378.

Ingredients of the Good Neighbor Pudding

It is fruitless to debate the origin of the term "Good Neighbor." One writer has traced its use to the early 1800's,[27] and certainly Hoover repeatedly employed it on his South American tour. What is important is the fact that Roosevelt skillfully used the term to describe his special brand of foreign policy. He had been thinking along this line for many years. At a later date he ascribed the formulation of his new program to his reactions at the time of the Veracruz crisis when Woodrow Wilson was President. His thinking evolved in the direction of substituting a "quarantine system for the restoration of order rather than the use of force in occupations." He resented also the use of bankers' loans so frequently associated with exorbitant interest rates and excessive commission fees.[28] In 1928 he wrote in an oft-quoted article:

It is possible that in the days to come one of our sister nations may fall upon evil days; disorder and bad government may require that a helping hand be given her citizens as a matter of temporary necessity to bring back order and stability. In that event it is not the right or the duty of the United States to intervene alone. It is rather the duty of the United States to associate with itself other American Republics, to give intelligent joint study to the problem and, if the conditions warrant, to offer it the helping hand or hands in the name of the Americas. Singlehanded intervention by us in the internal affairs of other nations must end; with the cooperation of others we shall have more order in this hemisphere and less dislike.[29]

In discussions with associates after the election of 1932 the term Good Neighbor was agreed upon. The question was whether Roosevelt could use it to rejuvenate New World relations. The Pan-American Union was moribund. Its monthly *Bulletin* was able to circulate only eight thousand copies even though it was published in three languages.[30] Unilateralism as expressed at the Santiago and Havana Conferences might be logical, but Latin America could not be made to like it. In his inaugural address the new President launched his program saying, "I dedicate this nation to the policy of the good neighbor." The idea was elaborated in his Pan-American Day address on April 14, 1933, when he called for mutual understanding.

[27] Alexander DeConde, *Herbert Hoover's Latin American Policy*, p. 126.
[28] Bryce Wood, *The Making of the Good Neighbor Policy*, pp. 130–131.
[29] *For. Affs.*, VI, No. 4 (July, 1928), 584–585.
[30] Laurence Duggan, *The Americas*, p. 193.

Sumner Welles had long been a friend of Roosevelt. Indeed, in the President's papers is found a note from Welles dated April 13, 1914. This thanked the later President for recommendation of the youthful Welles for an appointment in the diplomatic service.[31] In January, 1928, Welles cordially endorsed Roosevelt's idea of consultation with representatives of Latin American republics in case the United States needed to intervene in some Caribbean country.[32] After the election and before Roosevelt's first inauguration repeated letters from Welles filled in the President-elect on pending Latin American problems.[33]

The opportunity was great. The envious reluctantly commented: ". . . the Western Hemisphere was the most truly self-sufficient economic unit in the world—it has been said that it possessed everything but three things: Kings, Kangaroos and Kaviar."[34] The immediate question was whether its republics with their given resources could be made individually viable and collectively effective. On the foundation of Hoover's consideration for debt-laden republics in time of depression and his withdrawal of marines as occupation forces[35] Roosevelt was to build a new program with all the flair of a sparkling personality. He quickly recognized the value of the catch-phrase, "good neighbor," and kept it before the public. In 1936 he remarked: "This declaration [of his first inaugural address] represents my purpose; but it represents more than a purpose, for it stands for a practice. To a measurable degree it has succeeded. . . . We seek no conquest; we stand for peace."[36]

Domestic issues naturally had taken priority in the election of 1932 and in the early days of the new administration. Americanists claimed that only a handful of leaders gave consistent support to the Good Neighbor policy, and that surprisingly few chiefs of mission even in Latin America were enthusiastic about it.[37] Then the change began. At first the term Good Neighbor was used on a global basis, but increasingly after the twin debacles of the London Financial Conference and the

---

[31] Roosevelt to Mrs. Welles, August 12, 1942, with enclosure, Franklin D. Roosevelt Papers, Hyde Park, P.P.F. 2961.

[32] Welles to Roosevelt, January 20, 1928, *ibid.*, Welles file, 1928.

[33] Welles to "Dear Franklin," December 19, 1932, *ibid.*, O.F. 470.

[34] Quoted by D. Mitrany, "The American Continent," *Survey of Int. Affs., 1938,* I, 688.

[35] *For. Pol. Assn. Reports,* X, No. 21 (December 19, 1934), 280.

[36] *New York Times,* August 15, 1936, 4.2.

[37] Duggan, *The Americas,* pp. 74 ff., 102 ff.

Geneva Disarmament Conference the term was applied to New World relations.[38]

Further, the President himself quickly demonstrated his personal interest in both the problems and the personnel engaged in diplomatic activities. On one occasion Acting Secretary of State Phillips wrote the President saying that he had been submitting to his Chief all the names of persons representing the United States in international congresses and conferences. Since many of these meetings were of a technical nature and many of the names involved were those of men already in government service he suggested that the practice be discontinued. The President endorsed the letter: "w.p. I would rather continue the present practice as it keeps me 'au courant'! F.D.R."[39] Out in Japan, Ambassador Grew recorded in his diary for December 9, 1933, that he had received a personal letter from the President. Then he added: "We have never had a President who has taken so direct an interest in the Foreign Service; in spite of tremendous political pressure from hungry Democrats after sixteen years on the side lines, he didn't throw overboard a single career chief of mission."[40]

Roosevelt himself had a working knowledge of Spanish and had visited the mainland countries of Venezuela, Colombia, and Panama, as well as the island countries of Cuba, Haiti, and Santo Domingo. Thus his approach was based on at least some firsthand information. His understanding of the southern republics enabled him to say that "As a citizen of some other republic I might have found it difficult to believe fully in the altruism of the richest American republic."[41] By 1936 L. S. Rowe, of the Pan-American Union, reported a "marked change" in the attitude of southern countries in the preceding three years. Even Manuel Ugarte stated publicly that because of the change of the policy of the United States he felt "the Latin American nations should now welcome any plan for closer cooperation with the United States."[42]

[38] Arthur P. Whitaker, *The Western Hemisphere Idea*, pp. 144–145.

[39] Phillips to Roosevelt, November 9, 1934, Roosevelt Papers, Hyde Park, O.F. 20, 1934.

[40] Joseph C. Grew, *Ten Years in Japan*, p. 109.

[41] Quoted by Nerval, *Autopsy of the Monroe Doctrine*, p. 289. Also Sumner Welles, *The Time for Decision*, p. 192.

[42] Rowe to Roosevelt, July 31, 1936, Roosevelt Papers, Hyde Park, O.F. 480, Pan-American Union 1933–1938.

For Latin American approval see Felipe Barreda Laos, *La segunda emancipación de América Hispana*, p. 120; Isidro Fabela, *Bueno y mala vecindad*, p. 37;

More detached observers recognized a gradual process. The Royal Institute of International Affairs reported that the change began toward the end of the Coolidge Administration (with the Dwight Morrow program); that it was carried forward with the Hoover tour and the Pan-American Convention on Conciliation and Arbitration in 1929, when the United States surrendered its full freedom of action; and had finally culminated in the FDR program.[43] A more skeptical interpretation had it that the Latin American republics "were inclined to suspect that they were somewhat in the position of the lesser beasts who had entered into a partnership with the lion, even if the United States was not going to claim its share with such uncompromising directness as the lion in La Fontaine's fable." Using a similar figure of speech later a Latin American critic published his story of the whale and the sardines.[44] The businessman in the United States feared considerable embarrassment if the right of intervention were foresworn, and many Latins still feared that the whole new program would be transitory.[45] But for good or ill the program was on its way and in general was cordially received.

Tariffs and Trade

With his rallying cry that nothing was to be feared but fear itself, the President hailed the arrival of a delivery van bringing a load of beer to the White House to symbolize the end of the period of strain that looked to the past, and the return of a relaxed optimism that looked to the future. But how approach the international scene for a world in depression? The new Secretary of State, Cordell Hull, had devoted a lifetime to the study of tariffs and the industrial life of his country. His selection to head the Cabinet clearly foreshadowed a forthright low-tariff approach to depressed international trade. The first need was to prime the pump to restart the flow of goods.

Galvarino Gallardo Nieto, *Panamericanismo*, p. 27; Ricardo A. Martínez, *De Bolívar a Dulles*, pp. 145–146; Raúl Osegueda, *Operación Centroamericana*, p. 117.

[43] Royal Institute of International Affairs, *The Republics of South America*, p. 321.

[44] *Survey of Int. Affs., 1936*, p. 809; Juan José Arévalo, *Fábula del tiburón y las sardinas.*

[45] For a businessman's fears see John Hays Hammond, *The Autobiography of John Hays Hammond*, II, 730. For Latin American fears see Medina Castro, *EE. UU. y la independencia de América Latina*, pp. 95 ff.

Great Britain continued to need food and raw materials, so its share of Latin American trade tended to rise slowly. At first German trade held its own for the same reasons. Among the chief customers of the southern republics only the trade of the United States showed a serious decline (see p. 284). Increasingly the German challenge became more serious as the effects of the new trade controls and barter system brought results that were little short of startling. Vital raw materials such as linseed, wool, hides, and skins were secured from Argentina; coffee, cotton, and rubber from Brazil; wool and hides from Uruguay; saltpeter and copper from Chile—"in all cases without incurring the expenditure of foreign currency and against a corresponding rise in German exports."[46] Analysis of United States foreign commerce showed that its share of world trade had declined from 14 per cent to less than 10 per cent between 1929 and 1933. To make matters worse, world exports calculated in gold had declined 13 per cent, but those of the United States had declined 19 per cent.[47]

To make matters still worse, foreign bonds issued or guaranteed by divisions of foreign governments had an appalling record so far as Latin American republics were concerned. Outstanding bond issues for Canada, Europe, and Latin America floated in the United States were approximately $1.78, $1.59, and $1.56 billion, respectively, but the percentages in default were .08 per cent, 40.2 per cent, and a staggering 82.1 per cent, respectively.[48] To meet the critical situation two programs were sponsored: the Export-Import Bank and the Reciprocal Trade Program.

Originally chartered to finance trade with the Soviet Republic, the Export-Import Bank soon extended its facilities to the New World republics. It bought the obligations of foreign purchasers of American goods, extending credit up to 65 per cent of the amounts customarily advanced to such purchasers by American sellers. In other cases the loans were extended directly to foreign governments. At the end of

---

[46] *Documents on German Foreign Policy, 1918–1945.* Series C, III, 930 ff. See also Macdonald, *Hitler over Latin America*, pp. 22 ff., 67 ff., 203; Herbert M. Bratter, "Foreign Exchange Control in Latin America," *For. Pol. Assn. Reports*, XIV (1938–1939), No. 23, 284; Percy N. Bidwell, "Latin America, Germany, and the Hull Program," *For. Affs.*, XVII (1938–1939), 375–376.

[47] *U.S. in World Affs., 1934–1935*, pp. 100–101.

[48] *Ibid.*, pp. 84–85. See Cleona Lewis and Karl T. Schlotterbeck, *America's Stake in International Investments*, p. 414.

1935 the loans of the Bank to Latin American borrowers exceeded $4 million and by the end of 1939 amounted to more than $19 million, Brazil being the outstanding beneficiary.[49]

Another step was quietly taken by the Administration. This was in connection with the policy of passing on the diplomatic expediency of foreign bond issues by American banks. In his campaign for the Presidency, Roosevelt had stated that if elected "it will no longer be possible for international bankers or others to sell foreign securities to the investing public . . . on the implied understanding that these securities have been passed on or approved by the State Department or any other agency of the Federal Government." Now, inconspicuously and quietly the policy was discontinued by the end of 1933.[50]

Once in office Hull turned his attention to stimulation of trade by means of reciprocal trade agreements. The negotiations proceeded along new lines for the United States. Any one such agreement with a major country involved highly complicated calculations and the balancing of numerous factors. If drafted as a treaty each of these agreements would have had to run the gauntlet of Senate approval by a two-thirds vote. Even if the treaties were approved, the debates were sure to be protracted, and securing passage of an appreciable number of these would have been next to impossible. Yet the senators themselves recognized the compelling need to stimulate trade. Accordingly, both houses of Congress agreed for the Administration, within certain broad guidelines laid down by Congress, to negotiate executive agreements for trade control with specific countries for periods not in excess of three years. The measure passed the House on March 29, 1934, by a vote of 274 to 111. The Senate gave approval by a vote of 57 to 33, and the bill became law with the President's signature on the twelfth of June.

The act provided that an agreement with any one country could reduce existing tariffs by as much as 50 per cent, though it was agreed

[49] For. Pol. Assn. Reports, XVII (1941–1942), No. 7, 84 and 199–200; Lewis and Schlotterbeck, America's Stake, p. 414; Herbert Feis, The Changing Pattern of International Economic Affairs, pp. 76–77, 101.

Hoover comments in Volume III of his Memoirs that "prior to 1945 it [the Bank] was used for all kinds of political, economic and diplomatic pressures by the Office of Economic Warfare. Since 1945 it has served proper and legitimate purposes" (pp. 459–460).

[50] Herbert Feis. The Diplomacy of the Dollar, p. 14 n; Samuel Flagg Bemis. The Latin American Policy of the United States, pp. 337–338.

that the President might refuse to extend the new benefits to nations discriminating against American commerce.[51] Also in certain cases the chief-supplier principle introduced exceptions. The new enactment was variously interpreted as a resort to the European type of tariff bargaining, and as a recognition of the "glaring inability" of Congress to deal with tariff legislation.[52] Regardless of interpretation, the Administration was now free to act.

Another element in the situation was the devaluation of the dollar that followed hard upon the accession of the Democrats to power. There was an immediate rebound of prices and an improvement of business that "decided the issue between *laissez-faire* and deliberate management."[53] In foreign trade United States exporters could once more compete with the devalued British pound.

The Cuban trade agreement, signed on August 24, 1934, became the pilot project. During the first four months of the operation of the new agreement, trade increased 125 per cent over the corresponding period of the previous year, and automobile export sales were reported to have increased 300 per cent in a single month.[54] Even though such figures doubtless included sales that had been deliberately held up pending completion of the agreement, their publication naturally stimulated other negotiations.

Any general interpretation of the trade agreements acts becomes confused in statistical complications. Critics held that the net results to signatory countries were negligible and that nonsignatory countries benefited about as much as signatories. Some foreign critics feared that the new program would result in a huge customs union dominated by the United States. Others feared that through the system the United States was building up an overpowering manufacturing machine while the undeveloped countries were lowering rates on manufactured goods, hence making it ever more difficult for them to become self-sufficient.[55]

[51] *For. Rels., 1933*, IV, 186–187; *U.S. in World Affs., 1934–1935*, pp. 106, 109.

[52] Henry J. Tosca, *The Reciprocal Trade Policy of the United States*, pp. 283–284.

[53] *U.S. in World Affs., 1933*, pp. xix, xxii.

[54] Diary, January 10, 1935, Josephus Daniels Papers, LC, Box 9; Stuart, *Latin America and the U.S.*, pp. 13–14. Also Feis, *Changing Pattern*, pp. 99–100; *U.S. in World Affs., 1933*, p. 191.

[55] For endorsements see Raymond F. Mikesell, *United States Economic Foreign Policy and International Relations*, p. 309; Edward O. Guerrant, *Roosevelt's Good Neighbor Policy*, pp. 96 ff. For misgivings see Bemis, *Latin American Policy*

But regardless of criticism, this was the answer of the United States in an era of cut-throat competition among both great and small powers for trade survival.

Latin American republics negotiated thirty such agreements (by fourteen countries) in 1937 while they negotiated only sixteen trade conventions (by ten governments) of the German type.[56] By the end of 1942 agreements had been signed by the United States with all the Latin American republics except Bolivia, Chile, the Dominican Republic, Panama, and Paraguay—and negotiations were pending with Bolivia, and Panama trade was on a special basis. Also agreements were signed with France and the Netherlands on behalf of their New World colonies.[57] The Republican *New York Herald Tribune* on May 14, 1936, commented on some shortcomings of the Democratic program but added: ". . . the Hull reciprocity program remains about the only practical contribution now being made in the world toward amelioration of world entanglements, and as such its influence is of greater value than the specific concessions suggest."[58] One final post-World War II opinion may be suggestive in spite of changed conditions: "Before any trade agreements were concluded, the average ad valorum duty on dutiable goods (weighted by value of imports in 1947) was 28.4 per cent. On the same basis the average of rates effective on January 1, 1950 was 14.5 per cent, an average reduction of 49 per cent from the pre-arrangement rates."[59]

Closely associated with the question of trade was that of communications. It has been implied that the Pan-American Highway was primarily a military project developed as a result of World War II. The facts do not bear out such an interpretation. As early as 1933 the *New York Times* reported a despatch from Montevideo indicating that President Roosevelt had offered to ask Congress for funds to cover the entire cost of initial surveys for a motor transport link between the Americas. The work itself would be undertaken later on a joint basis.[60]

---

of the U.S., p. 302; Medina Castro, *EE. UU. y la independencia de la América Latina*, pp. 137–138.

[56] *U.S. in World Affs.*, *1937*, pp. 95–96; *Survey of Int. Affs.*, *1936*, pp. 806–807; *Documents on German Foreign Policy*, Series C, III, 74–75.

[57] *Department of State Bulletin*, VIII, No. 191 (February 20, 1943), 172; *U.S. in World Affs.*, *1936*, p. 255; Bemis, *Latin American Policy*, p. 440.

[58] Quoted in *U.S. in World Affs.*, *1936*, p. 161.

[59] Mikesell, *U.S. Economic Policy*, p. 309.

[60] *New York Times*, December 24, 1933, 8.5.

Thus the idea was launched in Latin America as well as in the United States long before the war. By 1935 diplomatic despatches concerning details appeared in substantial numbers[61] and the *Department of State Appropriations Bill for 1936* (p. 220) referred to a hearing before a subcommittee of the Committee on Appropriations on the Inter-American Highway. Mexico, proudly declining financial assistance, led the way and opened a 750-mile section of its road from Laredo, on the Texas border, to Mexico City.[62]

Intervention and Strategic Interests

President Wilson had proclaimed nonrecognition of Presidents who had secured office in the Americas by treachery or violence. Roosevelt's Democratic administration was to be more cautious. Welles, writing to his soon-to-be Chief on January 23, 1933, cautiously endorsed the Wilsonian dictum but pointed out that in certain situations revolution was the only means open to a people to secure needed changes in government. He therefore suggested that nonrecognition be practiced until the people of a country had been afforded an opportunity to express approval or disapproval of an existing government in national elections. In spite of objections that such a procedure would delay needed recognition and lead to controlled elections, Welles felt that it would tend to secure "constitutional government on this Continent."[63]

Early reassurance was given concerning unilateral intervention by Washington. The preview of Roosevelt policy in his *Foreign Affairs* article of 1928 was to be put into practice. At the Montevideo Conference intervention was discussed in detail. Next Roosevelt spelled out and popularized the principle involved in an address to the Woodrow Wilson Foundation dinner on December 28, 1933. In forthright words he stated that it was "the definite policy" of his country to oppose "armed intervention." "The maintenance of consitutional government in other nations is not, after all, a scared obligation devolving upon the United States alone."[64]

---

[61] *For. Rels., 1935*, IV, 243 ff.

[62] Stuart, *Latin America and the U.S.*, p. 35. Also *Department of State Appropriations Bill for 1936*, p. 220.

[63] Welles to Roosevelt, January 23, 1933, Roosevelt Papers, Hyde Park, P.P.F. 2961.

[64] Quoted in *For. Pol. Assn. Reports*, X (1934–1935), No. 21, 272. Also Department of State, *Inter-American Series*, No. 8 (December, 1934), p. 9.

Improvisation did take place to meet contingencies, but a principle was emerging. Hoover's reluctance to intervene not only was followed but slowly became recognized as policy. "Advice, warnings, and other types of tutelage" were used.[65] Even in that peculiarly difficult and near-by problem of Cuba special efforts were made to reassure Argentina, Brazil, Chile, and Mexico that marines would not be landed and that the matter would be treated as a continental responsibility if foreign interests were seriously menaced.[66] Even more significant was the about-face performed in January, 1934, in recognizing the three-year-old Martínez regime in El Salvador.[67]

It should be noted that the question of military spheres of influence had not yet arisen. When World War II forced consideration of the matter, the general aversion to unilateral action was seen in the plans for the administration of colonies that might be occupied on an emergency basis. In such a case military, as contrasted with economic or political administration, was to be carefully distinguished.[68]

In the decade following the naval limitation agreement of 1922 the United States had practically ceased naval construction. Under the agreement the British Empire laid down over 520,000 tons of new construction; the Japanese began work on more than 483,000 tons; but the United States had undertaken only 330,890 tons. President Roosevelt had always been interested in the sea and promptly initiated a substantial navy building program. Funds were allocated from the National Industrial Recovery Act of 1933 for the construction and equipment of some 989,000 tons. This was calculated to stimulate the whole national economy, though it would still leave the United States below maximum treaty authorizations.[69] Part of this slack was taken up in 1935 and 1936.[70] Inevitably the rest of the world watched with interest; and Latin America, with increasing concern.

A joint resolution of Congress under date of January 31, 1922, had authorized the President to restrict sales of arms to countries of the Western Hemisphere which were the victims of domestic violence. Such embargoes had been applied from time to time and in 1937 they were

[65] Wood, *Making of the Good Neighbor Policy*, p. 137.
[66] Duggan, *The Americas*, pp. 62–63.
[67] Raymond Leslie Buell, *Isolated America*, p. 140.
[68] Willard D. Range. *Franklin D. Roosevelt's World Order*, pp. 106–107.
[69] *Report of the Secretary of the Navy, 1932*, pp. 2–5.
[70] *Ibid., 1935*, p. 3; *1936*, p. 3.

still in effect on shipments to Cuba, Honduras, and Nicaragua.[71] These naturally helped the "ins" at the expense of the "outs." In addition, an inter-American treaty of 1928 outlined the Duties and Rights of States in the event of civil strife and called for a limitation on the traffic in arms and war materials.[72] Both of these official steps had been supplemented by President Hoover's consistent efforts to restrain excessive purchases of war equipment by New World republics. Under the New Deal a circular of the State Department indicated that it was not the policy of the United States to encourage the sale of arms and equipment of war. Diplomatic officers, therefore, were instructed not to promote such on their own initiative. If specifically requested to give aid of that type they would only extend the same kind of help they would provide other exporters and in all such cases would carefully disassociate the Department and their government from their effort.[73]

In 1937 a new angle was presented when Brazil sought to lease six decommissioned destroyers from the United States. Secretary Hull asked the Foreign Relations Committee of the Senate to study the question. He pointed out that the arrangement proposed might be better than having Brazil acquire vessels elsewhere, though he stated that if the lease were approved the same arrangements would have to be made available to all New World countries. He also sent similar notices to the chairman of the House Committee on Foreign Affairs and to the Senate and House committees on naval affairs. Within the week the Secretary informed diplomatic missions throughout Latin America that a joint resolution had been introduced in Congress to make vessels available. Argentina presented an immediate protest, and Great Britain expressed strong misgivings. Most of the Latin American republics, however, felt that the action would be unexceptionable if all of them were given equal treatment. When rumors spread that vessels had actually been leased to Brazil, the Nye Committee (which was investigating the munitions traffic) showed an interest in the matter. The Department of State promptly denied that any transaction of the kind had taken place and pointed out that such a step could only be taken after the enactment of necessary legislation. There the matter rested.[74]

[71] Joseph C. Green, "Supervising American Traffic in Arms," *For. Affs.*, XV, No. 4 (July, 1937), 739.
[72] Bemis, *Latin American Policy*, p. 283.
[73] *For. Rels., 1937*, I, 862 ff.
[74] *Ibid.*, V, 149 ff.

Here arises the question of the Nye Committee. In mid-1934 the Senate authorized a special committee, headed by Senator Gerald P. Nye of North Dakota, to investigate the activities of the munitions industry. Immediately there reappeared a succession of newspaper headlines and articles denouncing the international maneuverings of the industry as it sought to promote sales of its products. Excessive profits during World War I and after were reported, while price-fixing and excessive sales promotions were reported. The Army and Navy Departments were accused of stimulating foreign sales to maintain home production lines, while diplomatic agents were said to have lent injudicious aid. Tidbits published included such statements as that of an arms producer to a friend in Britain: "It is too bad that the pernicious activities of our State Department have put the brake on armament orders from Peru by forcing resumption of formal diplomatic relations with Chile."[75]

The long-range results of the revelations are difficult to assess. Certainly they had no adverse effects on appropriations for the Army and the Navy. Appropriations rose in the two years following the opening of the Committee hearings from $553 million to $909 million.[76] In fact, the recommendations of the Committee itself were soon lost sight of in the hectic days of the late 1930's. If the revelations affected the Latin American nations—and Mexico, Argentina, Bolivia, Peru, and Chile did protest aspersions cast on their public men—those governments apparently "feigned a good bit of their indignation."[77] When munitions were wanted they appeared to buy them with satisfactory frequency in the United States.

Mixing the Ingredients—Inter-American Conferences

Was Pan-Americanism dead and would the coming Seventh Conference bury the corpse? As will be remembered, the Argentine delegation had left the Havana Conference, thus presaging a possible disruption of the movement. By 1932, the scheduled date of the next conference, the depression presented all the republics with new complications. Thus, on June 4, 1932, the Secretary of State notified his diplomatic representa-

[75] Quoted in *U.S. in World Affs., 1936*, p. 115. Here also appears a summary of the Nye Committee's recommendations, p. 116.

[76] *Ibid.*, p. 109.

[77] John E. Wiltz, *In Search of Peace*, p. 154. This provides a full-length study of the work of the Committee.

tives that the Governing Board of the Pan-American Union had requested a series of reports and technical studies on questions of international law and comparative legislation. These would take considerable time, so with the approval of the host country, Uruguay, the Seventh Conference was postponed until December, 1933.[78] Old hands such as Undersecretary of State William Phillips and Assistant Secretary Jefferson Caffrey were reported to be very pessimistic about the prospects for any meeting at the time.[79] Hull and Roosevelt, however, agreed that the Conference should go forward with Hull to lead the United States delegation in person.

At the opening sessions in Montevideo ninety-four delegates (three being women) were in attendance. Only Costa Rica was unrepresented, and that because its Congress had failed to appropriate expense money for its delegates.[80] The Argentine Foreign Minister, Carlos Saavedra Lamas made an immediate attack on interventionism. In spite of Argentine failure to ratify the Kellogg-Briand Pact he now pressed for an antiwar pact of his own to be applied throughout the New World though adherence was to be open to all nations. Prior to presenting his proposal, the Argentine had secured support from representatives from Brazil, Chile, Mexico, Paraguay, and Uruguay. The proposal called for *ad hoc* commissions to reduce international frictions. Actually the proposed treaties were rather innocuous but did give Saavedra Lamas a substantial prominence as an architect of international peace.[81]

Hull records in his *Memoirs* (I, 328–329) that he decided to use the Argentine proposal and told Saavedra Lamas personally that he (Hull) had two resolutions prepared for the Conference, the one dealing with economic affairs and the other with international peace. He then added: "You yourself are the one person who should introduce the peace resolution. . . . I will give you my utmost support." And so it was arranged. The Conference passed a resolution to ratify the existing antiwar pacts: the Gondra Treaty of 1923, the Kellogg-Briand Pact of 1928,

[78] *For. Rels., 1932*, V, 6. For the question of codification of international law at the Conference see José Joaquín Caicedo Castillo, *El panamericanismo*, p. 282; Bemis, *Latin American Policy*, pp. 226 ff., 274.

[79] Diary, October 28. 1933, Stimson Papers, Yale.

[80] For delegations present see *For. Pol. Assn. Reports*, X (1934–1935), No. 7, 86.

[81] Manley O. Hudson, "Inter-American Treaties of Pacific Settlement," *For. Affs.*, XV, No. 1 (October, 1936), 174–175; Guerrant, *Roosevelt's Good Neighbor Policy*, pp. 60 ff.

the International Conciliation and Arbitration conventions of 1929, and the new Argentine Antiwar Treaty of 1933.[82] In the United States the President gave quick support to the Argentine proposal and Senate approval followed by June 6, 1934.[83]

Hull did a surprising job of salesmanship at the Conference. He personally paid his respects to each of the ten Foreign Ministers who headed their respective delegations, but skillfully remained in the background for most of the Conference activities.[84] Consistent with its earlier stand, the United States disapproved the presence at the sessions of "observers" from Spain, Portugal, the League of Nations, and other non-American organizations.[85] This did not reduce European interest. The *Times* (London) carried almost daily reports of Conference activities. It paid careful attention to the Hull economic program which further developed his idea of trade agreements. These, incidentally, bore some resemblance to the Open Door policy in China.[86] In spite of Roosevelt's known hesitation about stabilization of international currencies, Hull agreed to an early financial conference and to an inter-American commercial conference.[87] Saavedra Lamas exulted: "For the first time we have given economic content to Pan-Americanism; for the first time we have discussed commercial and tariff policies."[88] But worthy of note are the facts that he was using the suspect term, "Pan-Americanism," and that his exultation derived from the Hull program. Hull's efforts for bilateral trade agreements were also applauded by the Mexican Manuel Puíg Casauranc: "Pan-Americanism is a noble lie.

[82] Philip C. Jessup, "Argentina Anti-War Pact," *Amer. Jour. Internat. Law*, XXVIII (1934), 541; Cordell Hull, *The Memoirs of Cordell Hull*, I, 328–329.

[83] *For. Rels., 1933*, IV, 233 ff.

[84] Hinton, *Cordell Hull*, pp. 245 ff.

Another minor item showing the cooperative spirit of Washington is seen in the enquiry from Chargé Caffrey in El Salvador asking if embarrassments would arise from the attendance of a Salvadorian delegate to the Conference, when the existing regime in El Salvador was not recognized by Washington. The answer was: certainly not, simultaneous attendance at such meetings did not constitute recognition. Further, El Salvador had a member on the Governing Board of the Pan-American Union in Washington even though it was not officially recognized by the United States (*For. Rels., 1933*, IV, 15, 30–31).

[85] *Ibid.*, pp. 36–38; *For. Pol. Assn. Reports*, X (1934–1935), No. 7, 87–88; *New York Times*, December 7, 1933, 11.1.

[86] Lloyd C. Gardner, *Economic Aspects of New Deal Diplomacy*, p. 58.

[87] *Survey of Int. Affs., 1933*, pp. 318 ff.

[88] Quoted in *Rev. of Revs.*, XCIV, No. 6 (December, 1936), 56.

It could never exist while it has not juridical content, political scope, or economic aim. Hence I applaud Mr. Hull's proposal as laying the basis for economic cooperation."[89]

The more prickly nettle of intervention was handled with Hull's famous poker face and surprising skill. At a meeting of the Governing Board of the Union on January 4, 1933, Assistant Secretary of State Francis White, representing Secretary of State Stimson, had agreed to the Argentine proposal to place the antiwar project of Saavedra Lamas on the agenda. This in itself indicated that Hoover and Stimson were willing to abandon the "right" of intervention.[90] Ambassador Daniels in Mexico was urging Hull and Roosevelt to internationalize the Monroe Doctrine, but the Secretary appeared unconvinced of the advisability of the step.[91] Yet when the Conference was in session on December 26, 1933, Hull endorsed and voted for the provision: "No state has the right to intervene in the internal or external affairs of another."[92] Hull also stated to the Conference: "Under the Roosevelt administration the United States government is as much opposed as any other government to interference with the freedom, the sovereignty, or the internal affairs or processes of the government of other nations." "I feel safe in undertaking to say that under our support of the general principle of non-intervention as has been suggested, no government need fear any intervention on the part of the United States under the Roosevelt administration."[93] Two days later the President told a meeting of the Woodrow Wilson Foundation: "The definite policy of the United States from now on is opposed to armed intervention."[94] Next he endorsed another step: joint responsibility for re-establishing violated constitutional government in American nations.[95]

The term "continental solidarity" had begun to appear with increasing frequency. It was in the Saavedra Lamas pact and was taken up elsewhere. In this same connection Dr. Puíg Casauranc said at a dinner

[89] Quoted in Charles Wertenbaker, *A New Doctrine for the Americas*, pp. 102–103. For a Latin American view see Gallardo Nieto, *Panamericanismo*, p. 50.

[90] DeConde, *Hoover's Latin American Policy*, p. 60.

[91] E. David Cronon, *Josephus Daniels in Mexico*, p. 73. For instructions to the delegates on the Monroe Doctrine see *For. Rels., 1933*, IV, 137, 210.

[92] Department of State, *Peace and War*, p. 26.

[93] Quoted by C. A. Thompson, "The Seventh Pan-American Conference," *For. Pol. Assn. Reports*, X (1934–1935), No. 7, 95. Also *For. Rels., 1933*, IV, 201 ff.

[94] Benjamin H. Williams, *American Diplomacy*, p. 112.

[95] *Survey of Int. Affs., 1933*, p. 351.

in his honor in Mexico City that "the Montevideo Conference was a great success and that he had been to the funeral of the Monroe Doctrine, as it had been administered and understood."[96]

The new Convention on the Rights and Duties of States went far toward establishing the Latin American interpretations of "recognition, equality, inexpungibility of rights, nonintervention, the Calvo Doctrine, inviolability of territory, and refusal to recognize the fruits of force."[97] United States public acquiescence meant a revolutionary change in policy. Hull, writing to the President the following February, commented that the Conference had met under "entirely unfavorable auspices," yet the outcome marked "the beginning of a new era." "A new spirit inspired by the policy of the good neighbor was born at Montevideo."[98]

By January 30, 1936, President Roosevelt was gravely concerned over European conditions and over the Chaco affair. He wrote directly to the Chiefs of State of the New World republics citing the significance of the recent protocols between Bolivia and Paraguay and suggesting that the other republics use this opportunity for considering "their joint responsibility and their common need." All approved the idea. A committee on agenda was established and the proposal for a meeting was underway.[99] Roosevelt again moved directly with a personal letter (not sent through diplomatic channels) to President Agustín P. Justo of Argentina. He stressed the importance of the proposed session and stated that he would "value highly your Excellency's opinion" on certain matters.[100] Some years later Sumner Welles wrote that he considered the conference that ensued at Buenos Aires as "intrinsically the most important inter-American gathering" that had ever taken place.[101] This statement ranked it above the dramatic Rio de Janeiro Conference of 1906 and the even more dramatic conference in which Welles was personally responsible in 1942. The very fact that the Buenos Aires

[96] Diary, January 21 1934, Daniels Papers, LC. Also *Department of State Bulletin*, I, No. 24 (December 9, 1939), 659.

[97] Bemis, *Latin American Policy*, pp. 273–274.

[98] Department of State, *Press Release*, February 10, 1934.

[99] *For. Rels., 1936*, V, 3 ff.; *For. Pol. Assn. Reports*, XIII (1937–1938), No 8, 90.

[100] *Report of the Delegation of the United States . . . to the Inter-American Conference . . .*, p. 46.

[101] Welles, *Time for Decision*, p. 206.

Conference was called on a special basis gave it a flavor of its own.

Withdrawal of troops from Haiti and the negotiation of new treaties with Cuba, Haiti, and Panama had inspired respect for the sincerity of the United States declarations at Montevideo.[102] Then the re-election of Roosevelt in 1936 gave added assurance to the movement. The response of the other republics was both unanimous and enthusiastic. All of them were represented at Buenos Aires and eleven (Argentina, Brazil, Chile, Bolivia, Colombia, Costa Rica, Cuba, Honduras, Nicaragua, Uruguay, and the United States, and later Paraguay) sent their Ministers of Foreign Affairs or Secretaries of State as delegates. Hull would have preferred to wait for the forthcoming regular conference in 1938, but Roosevelt and Welles were insistent on the 1936 session.[103] To give a special tone to the meeting, the President, who always loved a naval voyage, determined to attend the Buenos Aires Conference in person and to sound its keynote in a personal address. In this he was following the advice of his old friend Josephus Daniels, who had written from Mexico: "It is my mature judgment that you will be wise to go to Buenos Aires . . . You called the Conference and . . . your presence would insure epoch-making declarations."[104]

The dramatic reception and the electric atmosphere created by the President's visit have been frequently recounted.[105] In his keynote address Roosevelt lamented the tragic conditions existing in Europe and called for an expression of faith in the Western World with its democratic form of constitutional representative government. He pled for a wider distribution of culture, education, free thought and expression— all coupled with greater security of life with equal opportunities for all. These, he asserted, would lead to development of commerce, the arts and sciences, with a resultant reduction of armaments and international

[102] Hudson, "The Inter-American Treaties," *For. Affs.*, XV, No. 1 (October, 1936), 165.

[103] *For. Pol. Assn. Reports*, XIII (1937–1938), No. 8, 91; Sumner Welles, *Seven Decisions that Shaped History*, p. 103.

[104] Daniels to Roosevelt, November 2, 1936, Roosevelt Papers, Hyde Park, P.P.F. 86, Josephus Daniels. The draft of this letter to be found in the Daniels Papers (LC) varies slightly from the letter as sent.

[105] *U.S. in World Affs., 1936*, pp. 200 ff.; Cordell Hull, "Foreign Policy of the United States," *International Conciliation Documents*, No. 365 (December, 1940), p. 397.

frictions. In turn, he asserted, they would lead to "peace and a more abundant life to [for] the peoples of the whole world."[106]

French and British newspapers were inclined to comment that the meeting would have little effect on European peace—their overwhelming concern at the moment. Rome and Berlin censors eliminated all references to war-minded aggressors in reporting the proceedings to their readers, but the Germans did note the skillful Roosevelt assumption of leadership on the Western continent.[107] And all of them more or less agreed with the *Times* (London) of December 12, 1936, that the President's decision to attend the Conference in person changed "what might have been a regional meeting into a gathering of world-wide importance."

The President left soon after his address. Once more the old poker player Hull and the old chess player Saavedra Lamas were left face to face. The 104 delegates worked with a will. At the heart of the discussions was Hull's beloved trade agreements program. Argentine trade was still primarily with Europe, so Saavedra Lamas would endorse no new agreement that might endanger its European contacts. Resolutions for equality of trade treatment and the elimination of discrimination met the consistent opposition of the host country, which was in the forefront in Latin America in applying trade licensing and control practices. To get an agreement, therefore, the members accepted escape clauses which provided that the signatories would act "to the extent that the several economies permit."[108] A qualified accomplishment only.

The new United States proposal for a league of neutrals, a proposal that it had strongly reprobated when proposed by Argentina and Mexico in the midst of World War I, was now vigorously rejected by Argentina, which remembered its halcyon days as a neutral in the first world contest.[109] Akin to this question was the disagreement between the pro-League of Nations Argentina and the non-League Brazil.[110] A proposal

[106] *Rev. of Revs.*, XCV, No. 1 (January, 1937), 78, gives an effective summary of this address.

[107] *U.S. in World Affs.*, *1936*, pp. 204 ff.; *For. Rels.*, *1936*, V, 32.

[108] *U.S. in World Affs.*, *1936*, pp. 211 ff.; J. Lloyd Mecham, *The United States and Inter-American Security*, pp. 127 ff.

[109] Nicholas John Spykman. *America's Strategy in World Politics*, pp. 373 ff.

[110] *U.S. in World Affs.*, *1936*, pp. 211 ff.; *For. Pol. Assn. Reports*, XIII (1937–1938), No. 8, 95–96; Harold F. Peterson, *Argentina and the United States*, pp. 390 ff.

for a New World League of Nations was sponsored by Colombia and the Dominican Republic but was side-stepped by postponement to the next regular (the Eighth) Inter-American Conference.[111]

In spite of dire warnings from the old guard about the danger of mutual pacts which would weaken the Monroe Doctrine,[112] the Conference brought forth the Convention for the Maintenance, Preservation, and Re-establishment of Peace. This was commonly referred to as the Consultative Pact, or the Convention for Collective Security. It, coupled with the convention to coordinate, extend, and assure the fulfillment of existing treaties between the American States and its additional protocol on nonintervention, Hull considered to be the chief accomplishments of the sessions.[113] The Consultative Pact simply provided that in case of a threat to the peace of the Americas there should be common consultation preliminary to the formulation of policy. Other conventions were endorsed looking toward the extension of the Pan-American Highway and the promotion of inter-American cultural relations.[114]

In the eyes of many the declaration of inter-American solidarity provided a Magna Carta for the small republics, especially those in the Caribbean. Also the steps taken to establish more firmly the machinery for the settlement and prevention of international disputes bade fair to inaugurate a new era.[115] Though Hull had suffered distinct rebuffs in presenting his program, he could take pride in reviewing the *Report* of the delegation of the United States to the Conference.[116] Truly the Monroe Doctrine had been "continentalized."[117] A Canadian view was that the United States had renounced its position as sole guardian of the

---

[111] *Survey of Int. Affs., 1936*, pp. 834–835; Max Henríquez Ureña, *La Liga de Naciones Americanas . . .*, pp. 13 ff., 87.

[112] Chandler P. Anderson, "The Monroe Doctrine distinguished . . . from mutual protective pacts," *Amer. Jour. Internat. Law*, XXX, No. 3 (July, 1936), 478–479.

[113] Cordell Hull, "Results and Significance of the Buenos Aires Conference," *For. Affs.*. XV, No. 3, Sup. (February, 1937), v–vi.

[114] *For. Rels., 1936*, V, 33–34; *For. Pol. Assn. Reports*, XIII (1937–1938), No. 8, 92 ff. Also *U.S. in World Affs., 1936*, pp. 212 ff.; *British and Foreign State Papers, 1936*, pp. 313 ff.

[115] *For. Pol. Assn. Reports*, XIII (1937–1938), No. 8, 93–94; *U.S. in World Affs., 1936*, p. 214.

[116] See pp. 83–87 of the *Report*.

[117] Charles G. Fenwick, "Inter-American Conference for the maintenance of Peace." *Amer. Jour. Internat. Law*, XXXI, No. 2 (April, 1937), 201–225.

Doctrine and had taken part in "the longest step forward that had ever been taken at a Pan American conference."[118] In general, Latin American observers too agreed with Henríquez Ureña that the result was a greater step toward the unification of the continent than had been taken at any time in the past.[119]

[118] John P. Humphrey, *The Inter-American System: A Canadian View*, p. 139.
[119] Henríquez Ureña, *La Liga de Naciones Americanas*, p. 88.

CHAPTER X

THE GOOD NEIGHBOR: PRACTICE

Conditions

AN IMMEDIATE NEED OF the new administration in 1933 was to convince neighboring states of the value to them of the Good Neighbor Policy. This was the more imperative because of the inroads made by the recent German trade campaign. The Ibero-American Institute, founded in 1930, was only one of at least four German organizations engaged in promoting better relations with Latin America. They trained business-men, diplomats, and other specialists in Ibero-American needs and opportunities.[1] Ambassador Josephus Daniels in Mexico made himself a spokesman in preaching the counteracting doctrine of the Good Neighbor. He told Mexicans that the "dominant purpose" of the ad-ministration in Washington was concentrated on restoring "fair, friend-ly, and normal trade" between the two countries. He boasted that the Big Brother idea was gone.[2] Welles added the statement that in case United States property was located in Latin American republics, it

[1] Richard F. Behrendt, "The Totalitarian Aggressors," Latin American Eco-nomic Institute, *Economic Defense of the Western Hemisphere*, p. 107. See also Alton Frye, *Nazi Germany and the American Hemisphere, 1933–1941*, for a general treatment.

[2] Daniels to Hull, September 27, 1938, Josephus Daniels Papers, LC, Box 16. For address of Daniels in Mexico City, May 9, 1933, see Franklin D. Roosevelt Papers, Hyde Park, O.F. 237, 1933. For address in Mexico City, November 29, 1934, see *ibid.* P.P.F. 86, 1933–1936 (clipping from Raleigh *News and Observer* of December 2, 1934).

should, in his opinion, "in fact as well as in theory, be subordinate to the authority of the people of the country where it was located."[3]

One member of the official family stated that as soon as the Montevideo Conference was over the Department of State set about to clear up the debris of past interventions. This involved:

1) Abandonment of the policy of nonrecognition of revolutionary governments in Central America. It recognized Martínez, 1934.

2) Withdrawal of marines from Haiti, 1933.

3) Abrogation of the Platt Amendment, 1934.

4) Signature of a new treaty with Panama, 1936.

5) Signature of a new treaty with Mexico, 1937.

6) Abrogation of financial controls in Dominican Republic, 1940.[4]

Steady work along these lines, however, was overshadowed by the immediate needs of two situations that had already involved bloodshed and threatened the peace of all South America. These were the Leticia and Chaco situations. The second involved the southeast coast and heart of the continent while the first involved the northwestern shoulder of the continent. Nine of the ten republics of South America (only Venezuela was moderately isolated) were involved in one or the other of the two controversies.

Leticia

The Leticia dispute had reached a somewhat critical stage as early as 1924 when Peru and Colombia considered a settlement. Unfortunately, the strip of territory in dispute bordered on the Ecuadorian line and the village of Leticia itself was within a mile or so of the Brazilian border.[5] Thus four nations were interested. Another complication lay in the fact that effective occupation of Leticia by either Peru or Colombia was almost certain to involve use of the Amazon River as a supply route. Again Brazil was concerned.

The simmering dispute reached an acute stage on the night of August 31, 1932, when Peruvian troops seized the village of Leticia and expelled the local Colombian authorities. Ecuador called up its military reserves while Brazil sought to mediate but sent warships up the Amazon

[3] Department of State, *Inter-American Series*, No. 9 (January 17, 1935), p. 6.

[4] Laurence Duggan, *The Americas*, pp. 65 ff.

[5] *For. Rels., 1924*, I, 304; *1933*, IV, 561 ff.; *Survey of Int. Affs., 1933*, pp. 436 ff. Bryce Wood, *The United States and Latin American Wars, 1932–1942*, provides a recent general discussion of this topic.

to protect its waterway and vested rights. Secretary of State Stimson invoked the Kellogg Pact and prodded other American republics to do the same in urging moderation on Peru. Meanwhile the League of Nations sought to mediate.[6] By early 1933 more troops were converging on the disputed territory and one Peruvian raid penetrated some two hundred miles beyond Peruvian soil. Brazil thereupon withdrew its mediation offer and determined to protect its own holdings. By the end of February the League proposed the establishment of an international police force to administer the disputed area pending a solution by way of negotiation. The United States lent its full support just as the Hoover Administration was about to leave office.[7]

This meant that within two weeks of taking office the new officials in Washington had to decide if they would accept the League invitation to cooperate in establishing a commission to supervise the disputed territory. The answer was affirmative,[8] even though it thus endorsed League activity in a New World controversy. At the same time every effort was made to insist on complete neutrality. Canal Zone facilities such as dry docks were refused to either potential belligerent except where the services were required for regular peacetime activities. Notice was given that American aviators acting as instructors of Colombian forces would have their services automatically terminated in case Colombia became involved in hostilities.[9]

The League commission, including Colonel Arthur Brown of the United States and Captain Alberto Lemos Basto of Brazil, administered Leticia through the services of Colombian troops. The commission was to serve for one year only, but the contestants failed to make effective arrangements in the time allowed. Thereupon the commission announced it would terminate its services as of June 19, 1934. Brazil now took the lead with Hull's full endorsement. It offered a compromise plan which was accepted by Colombia and Peru as a basis for a settlement that was finally agreed upon on May 24, 1934. More trouble was threatened when the Colombian Senate rejected the treaty by a tie vote. Immediately pressures from France, Great Britain, Italy, and New

---

[6] *For. Rels., 1932*, V, 285 ff.; *1933*, IV, 441 ff.; Russell M. Cooper, *American Consultation in World Affairs . . .*, pp. 307–308.

[7] Cooper, *American Consultation*, pp. 317 ff.; *For. Rels., 1933*, IV, various, especially pp. 421 ff.

[8] Cordell Hull, *The Memoirs of Cordell Hull*, I, 310–311.

[9] *For. Rels., 1933*, IV, 381 ff., 525.

World republics brought a reconsideration. The treaty was then approved on August 22, 1935. Ratifications were exchanged on September 27, 1935.[10]

Ecuador and Peru also had sent delegates to Washington to arrange arbitration of a boundary dispute in 1924, but no solution was reached for a dozen years. Finally it was agreed that direct negotiations would begin under the personal sponsorship of the President of the United States.[11] More complications erupted and relations became badly strained in mid-1941. Once more Washington gave full support to Brazil as active mediator. After six months of delicate negotiations a protocol was signed on January 29, 1942 (at the time of the Rio Conference), to end the last major boundary dispute in South America. Both countries made concessions and gains. Possibly the outbreak of World War II had had something to do with the precipitation of the quarrel, but it also lent its influence to bring about a solution. New World countries wanted no internal conflicts when they were in danger of being drawn into the world struggle.

So far as its policy was concerned, the United States steadily endorsed whatever procedure seemed most likely to lead to peace in South America. It had employed its own mediation efforts and had supported similar efforts by other New World republics, or by the League of Nations. Cooperation was the keystone of the policy here.

The Chaco

The mediation of New World neutrals had failed to secure peace in the Chaco by early 1933. Once more the League tried its hand at peacemaking. With some hesitation the United States welcomed the League efforts. Once more, no progress; so by the end of the summer the League withdrew in favor of renewed efforts of the ABCP (Argentina, Brazil, Chile, and Peru) group.[12] Neither of the small belligerents had armaments factories, so the League proposed to restrain hostilities

[10] *Ibid.*, *1934*, IV, 323 ff.; *1935*, IV, 206 ff. Also L. H. Woolsey, "The Leticia Dispute," *Amer. Jour. Internat. Law*, XXVII, No. 3 (July, 1933), 527; *U.S. in World Affs.*, *1933*, p. 194.

[11] *For. Rels.*, *1936*, V, 118 ff.; Charles G. Fenwick, "The Ecuador-Peru Boundary Controversy," *Amer. Jour. Internat. Law*, XXXI, No. 1 (January, 1937), 97–98; *Inter-American Affairs*, *1942*, p. 15.

[12] *For. Rels.*, *1932*, V, 220 ff.; *1933*, IV, 263 ff.; *Survey of Int. Affs.*, *1933*, pp. 412 :. For commentary see Arthur P. Whitaker, *The United States and South America: Northern Republics*, pp. 182–183.

through an arms embargo by the thirty-one leading arms-manufacturing nations. A resolution to cooperate was passed by both houses of the United States Congress by May 24, 1934. Support by twenty-six other governments brought substantial unanimity behind the effort. Paraguay quickly accused the United States of favoring Bolivia in enforcing the resolution, but Hull answered that a mere $615,000 of arms had been allowed to go to Bolivia, while over $2 million had been stopped.[13]

Canards were rife. In faraway Berlin there was a report that a Japanese group was trying to buy oil lands in the disputed territory on which to settle eighty thousand Japanese families.[14] Another report had it that the Standard Oil Company was aiding Bolivia with funds and with gifts of United States uniforms. In the latter case it appeared that a dealer in surplus army clothing had sold some uniforms to Bolivia without removing the old buttons; hence the rumor.[15] To further reassure Paraguay, the Secretary of State sent word that the president of Standard Oil Company had communicated with President Roosevelt: "This message affirms that none of the Company's concessions lie within the territory in dispute and that the total actual production during 1933 from the Company's concessions in Bolivia was an average of 307 barrels per day, sold locally in Bolivia."[16] Possibly this statement was somewhat disingenuous. Production was negligible, but there was the suspicion that this might be due to the lack of an outlet, and success by Bolivia in the war might be expected to provide that outlet. Another element in the confused situation was the fact that Bolivia had recently reduced Standard's concessions substantially, thus regaining Bolivian control of considerable areas. And the new government owners were as anxious for the outlet as the old private ones had been.[17]

Jealousies among the leaders of the South American neutrals continued to give trouble. For instance, British Ambassador Fred Morris Dearing wrote the President that Saavedra Lamas of Argentina so resented Chilean support of another candidate for the Nobel Prize (which Saavedra Lamas coveted) that his vanity now demanded vindication

[13] *For. Rels., 1934*, IV, 237 ff., 296. Also *Survey of Int. Affs., 1933*, pp 431 ff.; *U.S. in World Affs., 1934–1935.* pp. 132–133.

[14] William E., Jr., and Martha Dodd, eds., *Ambassador Dodd's Diary*, p. 217.

[15] Wilson to Caffrey, August 25. 1933. Roosevelt Papers, Hyde Park, O.F. 659, Bolivia.

[16] *For. Rels., 1934*, IV, 298.

[17] *Survey of Int. Affs., 1936.* pp. 838–829.

via a personal performance in settling the Chaco dispute.[18] Brazil had served as a peacemaker in the northwest (Leticia), so Argentina was the more inclined to keep Brazil out of Chaco negotiations. In early 1934 an effort was made for joint proposals to be sent to the belligerents, but somehow Brazil was not notified of the plans. Much offended, Brazil informed Washington that it could not join the proposed mediation. Secretary Hull then sent word that he had been informed from Buenos Aires that the omission was "typographical." Unmollified, Brazil rejoined that the omission had been called to the attention of both Chile and Argentina "several weeks ago" but had elicited no response. On April 26, 1935, the Secretary sent his chargé in Rio de Janeiro a copy of an invitation which was being sent to Brazil from Buenos Aires, Santiago, Lima, and Washington asking Brazil to cooperate. On May 2 Brazil agreed to do so.[19]

At the Montevideo Conference, Secretary Hull appealed to the assembled delegates to use their individual and unofficial efforts for peace, cooperating with the League in the process.[20] The Governing Board of the Pan-American Union on July 30, 1934, lent support and called on the neutral American governments to use their united efforts to end the fighting. Four months later, on November 24, the League, in extraordinary session, called for the immediate cessation of hostilities; demobilization under a neutral commission composed of representatives from Chile, Argentina, Uruguay, and Peru, as well as Brazil and the United States; and the convocation of a peace conference at Buenos Aires. When Paraguay refused the proposal, the League designated it as an aggressor and recommended lifting the arms embargo on Bolivia while retaining it on Paraguay. The United States Congress, reluctant to apply an arms embargo on one belligerent only, retained its restrictions on both. Hull pointed out in his *Memoirs* that to have raised it for both would have handicapped the League effort seriously, so in default of congressional action (which was extremely unlikely) this was the best the Administration could do to cooperate.[21]

[18] Dearing to Roosevelt, March 4, 1935, Roosevelt Papers, Hyde Park, P.S.F. Peru, 1935.

[19] *For. Rels., 1935*, IV, 20 ff.,

[20] Cooper, *American Consultation in World Affairs*, pp. 182 ff. Also *For. Rels., 1935*, IV, 95 ff.

[21] Hull, *Memoirs*, I, 347; *U.S. in World Affs., 1934–1935*, pp. 135 ff.; Graham H. Stuart, *Latin America and the United States*, pp. 413–414.

Both little countries were feeling the pressures of the conflict. After three years of fighting Bolivia had lost over 52,000 killed and some 10,000 deserters. Of over 21,000 of its men who had been captured more than 20 per cent were reported to have died. In addition, the financial costs of the war were estimated at more than $228 million. Paraguay, with a much smaller population, had lost about 36,000 men (3.5 per cent of its population) at a financial cost of about $124 million.[22] The stalemate in the fighting was complicated by the fact that each belligerent government feared domestic overthrow. Under the circumstances, it was more popular to bury soldiers than to negotiate.

The League embargo on Paraguay was unpopular among Latin American nations. None of them were arms producers and they did not like the idea that their own supply might be cut off at some future date. Anyway, they had been losing confidence in the League. Finally, after careful discussion of details the old ABCP group was reorganized in association with Uruguay and the United States in a new mediation effort. This was accepted by both contestants, and on June 12 an armistice was signed. A neutral commission assumed control of the disputed area within which the forces of each belligerent were reduced to five thousand men. Meanwhile direct negotiations were to take place to arrange arbitration of specific issues.[23]

Now ensued more tortuous negotiations during which the mediators alternately encouraged and cajoled the recalcitrant negotiators.[24] Home conditions were so confused in both countries that in February, 1936, the peace commission adjourned for an indefinite period to find out where matters stood. Four days later the Paraguayan government was overthrown. A month later, March 17, the State Department announced that recognition was extended since the new administration seemed to rest on the consent of the governed. Not to be behind-hand, on May 17 a group of army officers overthrew the Bolivian government. In a couple of weeks this administration, too, was recognized. The next year a *coup d'état* took place in Paraguay, and again the same happened in Bolivia when Colonel German Busch seized power in La Paz. Though the last case had serious anti-Semitism features and a strong pro-Nazi

[22] David H. Zook, *The Conduct of the Chaco War*, pp. 240–241.
[23] *Survey of Int. Affs., 1936*, pp. 858 ff.
[24] See *The Chaco Peace Conference: Report of the Delegation of the United States.* . . .

flavor, both governmental changes were recognized by Washington.[25] Without governments there could be no peace; with one in charge of each capital there was at least a chance of it.

Correspondence printed in *Foreign Relations* as well as the report of the United States delegation to the Buenos Aires Conference bear ample evidence of the sheer endurance of the mediators.[26] The built-in difficulties of the negotiations were aggravated by the uncertain conduct of the Argentine presiding officer. Also involved were the rumors afloat that Argentine interests were dickering for petroleum concessions in the disputed area.[27] Fortunately, the belligerents were exhausted and at long last the mediators secured a treaty. It provided Bolivia with free transit rights to the Paraguay River system while war claims were reciprocally renounced. The Bolivian Congress ratified the convention by a vote of 102 to 7 and a plebiscite in Paraguay brought popular approval by a vote of 135,385 to 13,204. One item probably contributing to the agreement was the arrangement between Brazil and Bolivia for the construction of a railroad which would give Bolivian oil a better outlet to the Paraguay River and would do much to thwart Argentine efforts to control the product.[28]

West Coast Policies

General relations with west coast countries proceeded rather smoothly for the first year or so of the New Deal. One interesting item occurred in Ecuadorian relations. This was the recurring interest of strategists in the Ecuadorian-owned Galápagos Islands, which were located to the southwest of the Panama Canal. In early 1935 Assistant Secretary of State R. Walton Moore called the attention of the President to the fact that in case of threatened occupation of the Islands by a foreign power the United States could claim infringement of the Monroe Doctrine, but he advised that outright control by the United States was desirable. On February 4 Roosevelt responded that he feared even a confidential enquiry directed to Ecuador about a proposed cession would have un-

[25] *For. Rels., 1936,* V, 225 ff.; *1937,* V, 249 ff., 718 ff. Also *U.S. in World Affs., 1936,* pp. 194–195; articles by Herbert S. Klein in *Hisp. Amer. Hist. Rev.,* XLV, No. 1 (February, 1965), and XLVII, No. 2 (May, 1967).

[26] *For. Rels., 1935,* IV, 53 ff.; *1936,* V, 77 ff.; *1937,* V, 4 ff.; *1938,* V, 94 ff.

[27] Bryce Wood, *The Making of the Good Neighbor Policy,* pp. 170 ff.; Alberto Conil Paz and Gustavo Ferrari, *Argentina's Foreign Policy, 1930–1962,* various.

[28] Zook, *Conduct of the Chaco War,* pp. 253–254.

fortunate effects. He added that he was thinking of suggesting that the New World nations designate the Islands as a wildlife refuge and an international park. If the other American republics would "chip in" two or three millions the United States could put up the rest. This would forestall occupation by any other power. By September, Minister González in Ecuador reported that his suggestion along these lines to local authorities had been cordially received. Shortly thereafter, on April 15, 1935, an international treaty was signed by the twenty-one American republics to protect artistic and scientific institutions and historic monuments.[29] The terms were general and only the future could reveal what applications would be made of them.

When a revolution occurred in Ecuador in September, 1935, the United States minister in Quito extended *de facto* recognition. Hull at once informed him that he should not have used the term *de facto*. He instructed the minister to keep quiet, watch developments, and report. When no further disorders occurred, full recognition was extended by the middle of October. Shortly thereafter negotiations began for a trade agreement. This was consummated by the middle of 1936, though Ecuador refused to include the "unconditional" most-favored-nation provision. At the same time the small republic asked for the services of an American line officer and an engineering officer to serve as instructors in its Navy. This was agreed to. At the end of 1937 came a military *coup d'état*. Foreign nations at once enquired what Washington was going to do in the matter. Undersecretary of State Welles informed the Ecuadorian minister in Washington that the "sole considerations" of the United States would be based on the ability of the new administration to secure "substantial support" from the people of the country. Since conditions seemed stable, relations were maintained with the new authorities in Quito.[30]

The Leticia dispute strained relations with Peru when the State Department refused to let the Peruvian squadron secure provisions or use dry-dock facilities in the Canal Zone[31] and even asked other American republics to apply the same restrictions on similar facilities they might possess. A bill authorizing an arms embargo on Peru received support

[29] *For. Rels., 1935*, IV, 518 ff.; *British and Foreign State Papers, 1935*, pp. 316–317.

[30] This story is found in *For. Rels., 1935*, IV, 513 ff., 650, *1936*, V, 512 ff.; *1937*, V, 468 ff.

[31] Cooper, *Consultation in World Affairs*, pp. 311 ff.

in the House of Representatives, but the Senate first insisted that identical restrictions be placed on both belligerents and then finally refused to endorse any action at all. In addition, revelations of the Nye Committee further irritated Peruvian leaders in connection with the accusation that the United States Department State had forced them to resume diplomatic relations with Chile.[32]

Totalitarian forces in Peru were also a factor in relations. Ambassador Fred Morris Dearing wrote President Roosevelt that the French had relatively little influence in Peru and even the British were not too effective, but that "opinion in general . . . is veering towards Italy." "The Italian bank [which was loaning money to the Peruvian government], the Italian character of the Church, the numerous Italian colony, the wide ramifications of Italian business . . . and Latin and racial sympathies" all played a part.[33] The German share of Peruvian imports rose from 10.3 per cent to 19.7 per cent of the total between 1933 and 1937.[34] As for the Japanese, the ambassador reported that very few of them were in the country. They were mostly small shopkeepers and "only one owns a plantation of any size." He could see no signs whatever of military designs by the Japanese.[35] Similarly, he discounted the Communist influence, which, he stated, "was scotched opportunely and vigorously." He also understood that the Peruvian administration was continuing conversations "with Argentina, Chile, Bolivia, Uruguay and possibly with Brazil" to formulate plans to frustrate any future Comintern activities.[36]

In June, 1932, Chile had experienced a revolution with socialistic characteristics. The Hoover Administration watched the situation carefully. Then ensued four months of uncertainty, but by October power was transferred in regular fashion to the President of the Supreme Court, who proceeded with plans for regular elections. On October 21 the United States and British representatives extended recognition, it being undestood that Holland, Portugal, Belgium, and others would do

[32] See *U.S. in World Affs., 1936*, p. 115.

[33] Dearing to Roosevelt, December 2, 1935, "Personal and strictly confidential," p. 51, Roosevelt Papers, Hyde Park, P.S.F. Peru 1935–1936, 1939.

[34] N. P. Macdonald, *Hitler over Latin America*, p. 206.

[35] Dearing to Roosevelt, August 12, 1935, Roosevelt Papers, Hyde Park, P.S.F. Peru, 1935–1936.

[36] March 10, 1936, *ibid.*

the same.[37] This was the government in power when the New Deal took office.

United States commercial interests were concerned at the Chilean exchange control program,[38] especially since under it Germany had almost doubled its exports to Chile between 1933 and 1936. And these exports included chemicals, iron, steel, and motor cars. A key item in the trade situation was copper. The rapidly increasing output of South Africa, Canada, and the U.S.S.R. had driven down the United States' share of the world's market from 54 per cent in 1925 to a mere 17 per cent in 1933. In the same period the United States had reduced its domestic output below 20 per cent of what it had been, though the rest of the world continued to produce at the rate of 80 per cent.[39] In these adjustments Chilean production dropped severely as the new producers "dumped" their product on an already depressed market almost regardless of price. To make matters worse for Chile the copper collapse was more than duplicated when the nitrate fields could no longer compete with the new synthetic output pouring forth in the industrialized countries.

On the personal side, the New Deal kept Chilean sensibilities in mind. In March, 1935, Welles asked the President to receive a Chilean delegation headed by the rector of the University of Chile. Welles commented that one or two of the group had been noticeably anti-American but that their recent attitude had been more cordial. The interview was granted. Early in April, President Alessandri sent a personal emissary to invite President Roosevelt to visit the southern republic. The next day he was informed that the President hoped to make the trip a year later.[40] Toward the end of 1936 Secretary Hull commented that it was very desirable to be "in most cordial relations with Chile" because of "financial and commercial" questions involved when United States investments in Chile aggregated over half a billion dollars. He therefore, as a friendly gesture, asked the President to authorize sending a military team to a horse show in honor of the four-hundredth anniversary of the

[37] *For. Rels., 1932,* V, 431 ff.

[38] *Ibid., 1933,* V, 130.

[39] *Survey of Int. Affs., 1935,* I, 371 ff.; Macdonald, *Hitler over Latin America,* pp. 152–153.

[40] Alessandri to Roosevelt, April 1, 1937, and Roosevelt to Alessandri, April 24, 1937, Roosevelt Papers, Hyde Park, O.F. 429, 1933–1938.

founding of Valparaíso. In due course a memo of the War Department, dated February 2, 1937, indicated that "By personal direction" of the President five officers, five enlisted men, and ten horses had sailed for Chile on December 12, 1936.[41] This was the type of personal touch in which the President delighted and which the Latins much appreciated.

East Coast Policies

Argentina continued its lone-wolf policies in hemisphere affairs. One writer comments that in 1933 Argentina had ratified only four of fifty-six Pan-American conventions signed since 1890; and up to January 1, 1943, it had ratified only six out of ninety such agreements.[42] Secretary Hull reflected bitterly on the always uncertain Saavedra Lamas, whose conduct at the Montevideo and Buenos Aires Conferences he considered so contradictory. "This despite the fact that on the day before my arrival at Buenos Aires he had been awarded the Nobel Peace Prize, for which I unofficially had recommended him and virtually managed the movement in his behalf." For his part, the Argentine had recently presided over the League of Nations Assembly and was convinced that that organization was still vital and powerful. "His eyes would be more on the dying League than on the living Pan American idea."[43] In connection with Hull's strictures should be considered Welles' comment on his Chief's "violent antipathy to Argentina which was later to become an obsession."[44] Welles' opinion may have been affected by his own break with Hull but it was clear that a personality clash between the two heads of cabinets had complicated international suspicions.

A major sore spot in Argentine-United States relations had always been trade competition in Europe and the fact that so few Argentine products could find markets in the United States. The President's personal papers show that he was fully aware of the situation. On May 20, 1935, he wrote to the manager of the Union Credit Life Insurance Company in answer to a protest at importation of Argentine grain. He said that imports from Argentina had been largely due to the needs arising as a result of the drought of 1934. Less than a month later he wrote to

[41] Hull to Roosevelt, November 6, 1936, and Memorandum of War Department, February 2, 1937, *ibid.*, O.F. 429, Chile, Folder 429 and 429A, 1933–1941.

[42] Samuel F. Bemis, *Latin American Policy of the United States*, p. 261 n. Also Hull, *Memoirs*, I, 609.

[43] Hull, *Memoirs*, I, 497. Saavedra had recently led his country back into the League.

[44] Sumner Welles, *Seven Decisions That Shaped History*, p. 104.

Representative John L. McClellan to try to reassure farmers who were disturbed about the same question.[45] Before this, on August 19, 1933, he asked Secretary Hull to investigate the possibilities of increasing Argentine linseed, wine, and tinned beef imports.[46] Some progress may have been made in special fields, but over-all trade was little affected. United States authors received copyright protection in the southern republic[47] and services of United States officers were lent as technical experts to the Argentine Navy and as advisers at the War College, but trade remained static.

The Roca-Runciman agreements of 1933 and 1936 served notice that Argentina was going to buy from those who purchased supplies in Argentina. How then could it meet its unfavorable trade balance with the United States of between 150 million and 350 million pesos per year?[48] At the end of 1934 Ambassador Alexander W. Wedell in Buenos Aires notified the Secretary of State that local authorities were not much interested in facilitating trade with the United States but that they would of course aid in securing a more favorable trade treaty. Their protests were centered on the Smoot-Hawley Tariff of 1930, which imposed high rates on Argentine corn, beef, wheat, and hides. In addition, much Argentine beef was excluded by sanitary regulations because of alleged fear of hoof-and-mouth disease that was prevalent in certain parts of the southern republic.[49] Thus the impasse remained essentially unchanged until the outbreak of World War II. Argentina exercised exchange controls and bilateral balancing of trade; the United States maintained its tariff barriers and sanitary restrictions. A marked improvement in Argentine industrial production throughout the 1930's showed that both number of employees and output rose some 30 per cent,[50] but this was far from meeting existing needs of the great raw-materials producers.

[45] Roosevelt Papers, Hyde Park, O.F. 366 A-B, 1933–1936.

[46] Roosevelt to Hull, *ibid.*, O.F. 20, July–December, 1933.

[47] Phillips to Roosevelt, August 22, 1934, *ibid.*, O.F. 20, 1934; *For. Rels., 1934,* IV, 539 ff.

[48] Ysabel F. Rennie, *The Argentine Republic*, p. 245; *For. Pol. Assn. Reports,* XIII (1937–1938), No. 13, 163.

[49] *For. Rels., 1934,* IV, 538. Also *For. Rels., 1933,* IV, 654 ff.; *U.S. in World Affs., 1937,* 144 ff.

[50] *For. Pol. Assn. Reports,* XVII (1941–1942), No. 18, 213; Harold F. Peterson, *Argentina and the United States,* pp. 364–365; Frank E. Williams, "Economic Diversification in Latin America," *The Annals,* CCXI (September, 1940), 152.

The *Times* (London) might complain that Argentine news was controlled by an American press service but if so the news media had very little influence in forestalling deteriorating relations between Buenos Aires and Washington, even when Argentina was condemning the Runciman-Roca agreement and was placing severe restrictions on Communist agitators. Only Nazi agitators seemed relatively free from official restrictions.[51]

Uruguay continued its friendly relations with the United States. When the little republic broke relations with Argentina in July, 1932, it sought the good offices of Washington. Argentina declined the suggestion but did engage in direct negotiations which reopened contacts on September 12, 1932.[52] Now Brazilians protested that Uruguay, the only Latin American country to recognize the Soviet Union, served as a focus of Communist infections for the neighboring countries. In response Montevideo broke relations with the Soviets. Soviet representative Litvinoff in turn protested to the Council of the League of Nations and demanded that Uruguay submit proof of its allegations of illegal activity on the part of Soviet agents. Uruguay responded that it had acted on the basis of its internal rights. The League shelved the issue after both Argentina and Chile supported Uruguay in its contentions.[53] The United States played little part in this exchange.

The disastrous collapse of the coffee market reduced prices from 24.8 cents per pound in 1929 to 7.6 cents in October, 1931. In spite of reduced plantings and burning of excess stocks, a huge crop in 1934 further demoralized the market. The Brazilian national government, its states, and its counties all declared moratoria in efforts to avoid general bankruptcy.[54] Against this demoralized background Germany introduced its positive trade policy based on its blocked-mark program and barter exchange arrangements. "In 1929 Germany exported to Brazil only half as much as the United States, but in 1936 she exported more." Expressed another way, as early as 1932 the United States bought eighty-three dollars of Brazilian goods for every thirty-two-

[51] The *Times* (London), January 22, 1934, 13e; Macdonald, *Hitler over Latin America*, pp. 36–37.

[52] *For. Rels., 1932*, V, 316 ff.

[53] Royal Institute of International Affairs, *The Republics of South America*, p. 328; *New York Times*, December 28, 1935, 1.5; January 5, 1936, 37.4; January 24, 1936, 1.7.

[54] *For. Pol. Assn. Reports*, XI (1935–1936), No. 1, 9–10.

dollars worth sent in exchange. Brazilian exports of cotton to Germany rose from a token 59 tons in 1933 to an astonishing 30,000 tons in 1936; wool rose from 1,700 tons to 6,900 tons; rubber from 1,800 tons to three times that amount; and manganese ore from 45 to 10,000 tons. In 1936 the pressure was increased through a new trade treaty which allowed Brazil a 62,000-ton annual quota of cotton imports into Germany.[55]

Meanwhile the New Deal made its bid. Part of the answer was the Export-Import Bank. Military and naval missions were sent to serve as instructors in the armed forces.[56] Orders were issued for the construction of naval vessels in United States ship-yards, and aid was given to the southern republic to construct shipyards of its own.[57] To free frozen credits, arrangements were made for the United States to sell Brazil $60 million of gold to be held in the United States as collateral for a central reserve bank to be established in Brazil.[58] Coupled with the Export-Import Bank, these new credit arrangements opened the way for sales of raw materials on a cash basis. Next came a reciprocal trade agreement signed on February 2, 1935. The cumulative effects of these efforts made substantial inroads on the German barter-based trade.[59]

Of course German influence remained a factor for some time to come. Getulio Vargas had risen to power in 1930 on a popular social program but had rapidly tended to a totalitarian type control. Even so he had no intention of allowing German or any other foreign interest to undermine his power. Barter with Germany was not attractive in cases where Yankee gold was available; the new Brazilian money system was keyed to United States money centers; its military forces trained by United

[55] *For. Rels., 1933*, V, 47; Macdonald, *Hitler over Latin America*, pp. 106–107. Also *For. Rels., 1934*, IV, 588 ff.; *1936*, V, 257 ff.; *1937*, V, 323 ff.; *Survey of Int. Affs., 1934*, p. 52.

[56] *For. Rels., 1934*, IV, 623 ff.; *1935*, IV, 388; *1936*, V, 298.

[57] *Ibid., 1937*, V, 376–377.

In 1936 Brazil also asked the United States to sell it as many as ten naval cruisers at the rate or one or two per year. The first response was that the United States might be interested if all New World countries had the same opportunity and provided that vessels were available. Then, on July 6, President Roosevelt informed President Vargas of his regret that such sales were outlawed by the London Naval Conference (*For. Rels., 1937*, V, 299–300).

[58] The *Times* (London), July 17, 1937, 19f, and July 19, 1937, 22b; *U.S. in World Affs., 1937*, pp. 146 ff.

[59] *For. Rels., 1935*, IV, 300 ff.; *For. Pol. Assn. Reports* (1937–1938), No. 13, 158–159.

States advisers; and a favorable trade treaty had just been signed. All this added up to official support of democracy by a fascistic regime.[60]

Vargas' Green Shirts had early received support of the Communists. However, when Luís Carlos Prestes returned from Russia as a professed Communist in 1935 he was forthwith arrested and sentenced to seventeen years of penal servitude. Communism was driven underground.[61] Vargas would brook no rival.

By November, 1937, Vargas faced a critical electoral campaign, so he promulgated a new constitution under which he would continue in power for a new six-year term. When it was rumored that Germans had connived at his overthrow, he personally told Ambassador Caffrey that "it is laughable to think that Germans, Italians or Japanese had any connection whatever with the recent [revolutionary] movement; nor had integralists in any way."[62] The *Times* (London) informed its readers on November 15 that Vargas stated that his new constitution was neither Fascist nor Integralist but purely Brazilian. He also said that he was not interested in the anti-Comintern pact "because her [Brazil's] attentions are concentrated on a pan-American policy." Documenting this statement at least in part is the fact that anti-Integralist and anti-Nazi campaigns resulted in the emigration of an estimated ten thousand Germans in 1938.[63]

Cuba

Economic conditions in Cuba were alarming. The price of sugar had reached the abysmally low figure of .57 cent per pound in 1932 with a

[60] Macdonald, *Hitler over Latin America*, pp. 75 ff.; Ernest Hambloch, "The New Regime in Brazil," *For. Affs.*, XVI, No. 3 (April, 1938), 492.

An interesting side light, which may have been "planted," appeared in the report of Ambassador Gibson from Rio de Janeiro, December 27, 1935 (*For. Rels., 1935*, p. 387). He said the Brazilian ambassador in Tokyo had reported "rather alarming" Japanese preparations for eventual hostilities with the United States. Gibson continued that the Brazilian Foreign Minister told him that Vargas would "go as far as he liked" in assuring the United States of the fullest cooperation. If the United States desired Brazil to provide, or to secure, any further information along this line the latter would be pleased to do so.

[61] Germán Arciniegas, *The State of Latin America*, p. 210; Karl Lowenstein, *Brazil under Vargas*, pp. 30–31.

[62] *For. Rels., 1937*, V, 315. The State Department followed the suggestion of its legal adviser, Green H. Hackworth, who stated that no question of recognition was involved when a *coup d'état* was executed by a government itself (*ibid.*, p. 316).

[63] Macdonald, *Hitler over Latin America*, p. 101.

total crop value of less than $42 million, whereas the price ten years before had been 4.90 cents with a total value of over $400 million.[64] The collapse of the market brought a drop in national revenues from approximately $98 million in the middle 1920's to only slightly over $51 million in 1931–1932. Riding the storm was the dictator Gerardo Machado, who had riveted his grasp on the country in spite of steadily rising opposition.[65]

Strangely enough, the Hoover Administration seems to have been honestly unaware of the critical political unrest in Cuba. It was distraught with problems of domestic depression, with Japanese adventuring in the Far East, and with questions arising from defaults in payments of World War I debts. Under such circumstances the pleas of Cuban liberals and refugees received scant attention. Why be excited about a few malcontents when the whole world was suffering and unrest was rampant everywhere? Machado had obviously made himself a dictator and probably had disregarded the niceties of legal procedures, but he did appear to have a difficult situation in hand and he had observed most of his international obligations.

In answer to a series of increasingly alarming reports, the newly elected Roosevelt sent his trusted Latin American adviser and friend Sumner Welles to Cuba.[66] Nine days after arriving in the island, Welles reported on his early impressions. Conditions were worse than he had anticipated but he did not feel that either military or formal diplomatic intervention would justify the injury such action would inflict on the Latin American program of the Administration. He deplored Machado's unconstitutional election and his "pathological obsession" with methods of repression that at times included acts of "hideous cruelty," but he felt that the fundamental cause of Cuban unrest was the economic situation and that the dictator was not as bad as the reports indicated. Apparently somewhat reassured, Roosevelt responded more than a month later, June 24, that his delay in answering was due to his being "so taken up with the European situation" that he had merely read Welles reports and had dismissed them from his mind "for the very

---

[64] *U.S. in World Affs., 1933,* pp. 173 ff.; Chester Lloyd Jones, *The Caribbean since 1900,* p. 65.

[65] Raymond Leslie Buell *et al., Problems of the New Cuba; For. Rel., 1933,* V, 584 ff.; Jorge Mañach, "Revolution in Cuba," *For. Affs.,* XII, No. 1 (October 1933), 47

[66] For instructions to Welles see *For. Rels., 1933,* V, 283 ff.

good reason that you seemed to be getting the situation under control and to have the confidence of the people who count."[67]

Welles did his best to serve as mediator between Cuban factions but finally reached the conclusion that no progress could be made so long as Machado remained in power. In approaching the fundamental economic problem Welles reported, "I am, of course, keeping the negotiation of a commercial treaty as a leverage until I know definitely where I stand on the political situation." In Washington, Acting Secretary of State William Phillips tried to reassure the Cuban minister by saying that Welles had simply been so involved in other complications that he had not had time to take up the commercial matter. Phillips denied that the treaty was being held as a club over the head of Machado.[68]

Now Welles reached a third stage in his thinking and became convinced that "disaster would arise" if the dictator did not leave the country.[69] Whether Welles' decision was the determining factor may be debated, but on August 12 Machado fled. Still conditions failed to improve. Carlos Manuel de Céspedes tried to control affairs but failed. He was followed by Ramón Grau San Martín, a man in whom Washington, on the advice of Welles, developed little confidence. During this trying period Welles seemed to lose his nerve and on September 7 asked that troops be landed. Hull rushed to the President with a virorous dissent because of the "disastrous reaction which would follow throughout Latin America if we agreed to his [Welles] request." Some thirty naval vessels were assigned patrol duties on the Cuban coasts,[70] but no troops were landed in spite of Welles' desires.

Meanwhile Ambassador Daniels was reporting from Mexico that the Mexican government was doing all it could to secure Latin American

[67] Roosevelt Papers, Hyde Park, O.F. 470. Stimson records (Stimson Papers, Yale) in his diary for October 28, 1933, that he called on Roosevelt at the latter's invitation. The President told Stimson that Hoover had informed him before the inauguration that Cuba was "perfectly safe." Roosevelt now felt that the situation was bad but that Welles had made no mistakes.

[68] *For. Rels., 1933*, V, 325 ff.

[69] Wood, *Making of the Good Neighbor Policy*, pp. 62 ff.

[70] Hull, *Memoirs*, I, 315; *For. Rels., 1933*, V, 402; E. David Cronon, "Interpreting the God Neighbor Policy . . .," *Hisp. Amer. Rev.*, XXXIX, No. 4 (November, 1955), 550 ff.

In the Roosevelt Papers (Hyde Park, P.S.F. Cuba, 1933–1935) appear photostats of Hull to Roosevelt, August 13, on the Cuban crisis and of the original orders to the Navy of that date.

cooperation with United States policy. "They all feel that we will intervene unless order is restored in Cuba. . . . Unless you were in the atmosphere that fairly exudes opposition to intervention by us, you could not fully appreciate the intensity of the feeling," he wrote.[71] In response to such cautions, all the American republics as well as leading countries elsewhere were informed of the sending of the naval vessels but at the same time were assured that the step was taken "solely as a precautionary measure and there is [was] not the slightest intention of intervening or interfering with Cuba's domestic affairs."[72] Roosevelt's own recollection of these troubled days was expressed in an informal toast given in 1942:

The main point I want to make is that when these troubles occurred in Havana, an unprecedented meeting was called at the Executive Offices. At that meeting we had all the Ambassadors and Ministers of all the American Republics.

I said to them I thought it time to recognize "the practical exposition of the Good Neighbor policy." An old treaty of the United States with Cuba "permitted" and in a sense "compelled" the United States "to go into Cuba."

And I said, "Gentlemen, I am not going to do it. I am not going to apply the Platt Amendment. I am not going to send either the Army or the Navy to restore order in Cuba." There ensued a good deal of lifting of eyebrows among "a good many of these nineteen other envoys."[73]

Numerous memoranda in *Foreign Relations* indicate that frequent progress reports were given the several Latin American representatives, and that this gesture was much appreciated.

Welles failure to support Grau has been widely debated. "Intervention by inertia" it has been called. The fact is that, deprived of essential United States support, Grau resigned in January, 1934.[74] Welles wished to return to the United States but at the President's request remained at his post until replaced by Jefferson Caffrey at the end of the year.[75] By that date the Carlos Mendieta coalition, a puppet regime for the new

[71] Daniels to Roosevelt, September 9, 1933, *ibid.*, O.F. 237, Folder 1933.

[72] *For. Rels.. 1933*, V, 367 ff.

[73] Taken from transcript made at the time by Jack Romagna. Roosevelt Papers, Hyde Park, P.S.F. Cuba.

[74] Buell *et al.*, *Problems of the New Cuba*, pp. 13 ff.; *Survey of Int. Affs., 1933*, pp. 381 ff.

[75] Early to Hull, telegram of August 28, 1933. Roosevelt Papers, Hyde Park, O.F. 20, July–December, 1933; *For. Rels., 1934*, V, 96 ff.

strong man, Fulgencio Batista, came to power. Recognition was extended in five days.[76] Promptly negotiations began for a new treaty. As a preliminary, Congress enacted the Jones-Costigan Act providing for specific sugar import quotas. This gave Cuba a definite market in which tariffs on its products were reduced from 2 cents to 1.5 cents. Next came the new trade agreement act that further reduced the sugar tariff to .9 cent per pound and included special rates on other items.[77]

At the same time the old treaty of 1903, including the famous Platt Amendment, was cancelled.[78] Though some had qualms about the prominence of the military in the new Cuban government, the Senate promptly approved the treaty. A White House meeting was called with representatives from all the Latin American states except El Salvador, Cuba, and Uruguay to notify them that the United States was recognizing Mendieta.[79] A new loan was negotiated and shipments of arms to Cuba were restricted to those specifically indicated as desired and approved by the Cuban government.[80] Here was a well-intentioned new program under which there was to emerge another twenty-five-year dictatorship for the unfortunate island.

Other Islands

In 1928 Franklin D. Roosevelt had reviewed United States activities in the smaller republics of the hemisphere saying, "We have done a fine piece of material work, and the world ought to thank us. But does it? In these cases the world is really the Latin American world, for Europe cares little what goes on in Santo Domingo or Haiti or Nicaragua. The other republics of the Americas do not thank us, on the contrary

[76] Buell et al.. Problems of the New Cuba, p. 498. Also Raymond Leslie Buell, Isolated America, pp. 137 ff. Julius W. Pratt considers Welles' activities in Cuba as less than successful. He claims that Welles' resignation was arranged to save his face. If this is true it seems to have had little influence on Roosevelt's later opinion of Welles. Also "Cordell Hull," in Bemis, Amer. Secs. of St., XII, 145 ff.

[77] Buell et al., Problems of the New Cuba, p. 61; For. Rels., 1934, V, 136, 154 ff.; For. Pol. Assn. Reports, XI (1935–1936), No. 22, 272–273; Benjamin H. Williams, American Diplomacy. pp. 176–177.

[78] For. Rels., 1934, V, 183 ff.; Department of State Appropriations Bill for 1936, p. 8.

[79] New York Times, January 23, 1934, 1.2.

[80] For. Rels., 1934, V, 187–188. Also Buell et al., Problems of the New Cuba, p. 315.

they disapprove our intervention almost unanimously."[81] So far as Cuba was concerned, Hull and Roosevelt could claim that they had kept the faith and that even the Latin American world ought to thank them. What about the attitude to United States conduct in the other island republics?

The Virgin Islands remained a fiscal liabiliy, but in 1932 the governor of the Islands pointed out that from the date of their acquisition they had been a "defense investment" and that the appropriation for their support was "less than 25 per cent of the interest invested in a battle-ship."[82] New Deal relief measures now helped local conditions some-what, but since no international implications were involved, further discussion is out of place here.

Puerto Rico, under the Jones-Costigan Act, received similar treatment to that accorded Cuba. Proceeds from the processing tax levied on the American sugar consumer were used to carry out a land utilization pro-gram and rural reconstruction. About the same time the administration of the island was transferred from the War Department to the newly established Division of Territorial and Insular Possessions in the Depart-ment of Interior. Yet the islanders remained unhappy. Some talked of statehood but others called for outright independence. By 1932 some ardent nationalists turned to terrorist activities. These culminated in a fight with the police in which nineteen were killed and many times that number wounded. In response, a bill was rushed into the United States Senate in 1936 for a plebiscite on independence to be held in the island. Nothing came of this except that it apparently provoked some serious thinking among the islanders.[83] Properly the unrest should be considered the result of economic stresses of the day and so it is hardly a subject related to foreign policy except in the indirect effects it had on the attitude of neighboring republics.

Haiti still remained a difficult problem. In 1932 various features of the administration of Haiti had been turned over to the islanders, and Hull approved the expenditure of a small surplus in the local treasury for a needed irrigation project. Another step toward self-government took place when negotiations were completed on August 7, 1933, to provide for the replacement of United States officers of the Haitian

---

[81] *For. Affs.*, VI (1927–1928), 584.

[82] Quoted by Jones, *The Caribbean since 1900*, p. 199.

[83] Buell *et al.*, *Problems of the New Cuba*, p. 20; *U.S. in World Affairs.*, *1936*, pp. 196–197; *1937*, pp. 158–159; Stuart, *Latin America and the U.S.*, pp. 265–266.

garde by Haitians, and for the withdrawal of all marines by October 1, 1934. When complications arose over the approval of the treaty in the Haitian Senate, the convention was implemented by means of an executive agreement which did not entail approval by either the United States Senate or the Haitian National Assembly.[84]

The personal contacts of the new administration with Haiti were especially good. The tale in official circles of Roosevelt's interest in two lost casks of Haitian rum that he had once cached in the island, and of their partial replacement by five gallons of choice beverage secured by Ambassador Norman Armour, did the President no harm.[85] The final date for the evacuation of the last of the marines was set six weeks in advance of the date provided in the agreement and was personally ordered by the President when he dropped in on the island on his way to the Canal Zone.[86] Another personal touch.

When the marines left, arrangements were made to turn over to Haiti equipment, supplies, and material, including buildings and land leases, on the basis of a simple proviso that the local government would assume the obligations in the said leases and easements. This meant the gift of a complete radio station, a hangar, and substantial other materials.[87] When an American collector of customs at Port-au-Prince confessed to accepting bribes and to defrauding the local government, the State Department immediately notified Haitian authorities that the accused would be surrendered to the local courts for trial.[88]

A careful watch was still maintained on details of proposed foreign loans, especially in the case of a French loan, the predecessors of which had had various unhappy consequences on the island.[89] When the Haitian-Dominican boundary dispute presented trouble, the ensuing settlement was "unique because it was the only controversy [to that date] settled within the framework of the inter-American peace structure."[90]

---

[84] *For. Rels., 1932*, V, 692 ff.; *1933*, V, 734 ff.; *U.S. in World Affs., 1933*, pp. 186–187; *Report of the Secretary of the Navy, 1935*, p. 9; *Department of State Appropriation Bill for 1936*, p. 9.

[85] Taussig to Roosevelt. June 12, 1934, and Roosevelt to Armour, June 18, 1934, Roosevelt Papers, Hyde Park, O.F. 112, Norman Armour.

[86] *U.S. in World Affs., 1934–1935.* p. 127.

[87] *For. Rels., 1934*, V, 296 ff.

[88] *Ibid., 1933*, V, 789 ff.

[89] *Ibid., 1935*, IV, 661 ff.; *1936*, V, 600 ff.; *1937*, V, 547 ff.

[90] J. Lloyd Mecham, *The United States and Inter-American Security*, p. 174.

Diplomatic correspondence with the Dominican Republic featured questions of use of local funds in connection with debts already incurred. The general attitude toward additional expenditures was that the State Department had no interest in appropriations for any one fiscal year, but it insisted on the right to consider the details of appropriations that called for expenditures over an extended period or which might result in an increase of the public debt.[91]

In summary, it can be said that once more the flavor of the pudding of New Deal Latin American policy was held to be most appetizing from the Rio Grande to Tierra del Fuego.

The Panama Area

Panama protested that the payment of the annuity of 250,000 in devalued dollars was a violation of the intent of the original agreement of 1903. After considerable correspondence, the figure was adjusted to $430,000. Also it was agreed that the payment would be in balboas so that the actual cash transferred was increased by $7,500 at the existing exchange value of the day.[92]

A more complicated matter was the basic treaty between the United States and Panama, which had become further complicated by the abortive treaty of 1926. Conversations began soon after Roosevelt took office. Proposals and counterproposals canvased details until a completed document was ready for signature by March 2, 1936. The gold payment at the new rate was confirmed. The old guarantee of the independence of Panama disappeared, as did the automatic right of intervention by the United States and the right to acquire additional land for Canal purposes at the values of 1903 on mere notification of need. Ratifications were exchanged by the end of the year even though certain United States senators were unhappy when they thought of the implications for the Canal of the recent withdrawal of Japan from the London Naval Conference.[93] Military leaders too had misgivings over some of the proposed changes.[94] They were especially fearful that the new treaty

---

[91] *For. Rels., 1933,* V, 660; *1934,* V, 189 ff.; *1936,* V, 446.

[92] *Ibid., 1934,* V, 620; *Survey of Int. Affs., 1936,* p. 875.

[93] For the text of the treaty and notes see Department of State, *Treaties and Other International Acts of the United States,* No. 945. For comments see Sumner Welles, *The Time for Decision,* pp. 201–202; *U.S. in World Affs., 1936,* p. 203; *Survey of Int. Affs., 1936,* pp. 873 ff.

[94] Dean to Roosevelt, January 11, 1935, Roosevelt Papers, Hyde Park, O.F. 110, Panama.

would prevent prompt action by the United States to protect the area. Welles therefore arranged an exchange of notes to take place on February 1, 1939, providing in part that:

. . . in the event of an emergency so sudden as to make action of a preventive character imperative to safeguard the neutrality or security of the Panama Canal, and if by reason of such emergency it would be impossible to consult with the Government of Panama as provided in Article X of said treaty, the Government of the United States need not delay action to meet this emergency pending consultation. . . .[95]

Protests subsided to muted grumblings.

To the south of the Canal diplomatic relations remained relatively unchanged with both Colombia and Venezuela. Trade agreements were reached with both countries after normal negotiations. In 1937 a report did reach Washington that a Japanese mission visiting Bogotá had apparently established contacts with German settlers living along the coast. The President of Colombia was suspicious and suggested joint United States-Colombia surveillance of the area with especial reference to the coasts adjacent to Panama. Roosevelt promptly alerted Welles, saying: "I think we should meet this proposal more than half way." He added that the anticipated conversations "should include also the possibility of exchange of information in relation to certain other Nationals in the Republic of Colombia near the Panama border."[96]

North of Panama lay uncertain Central America. Substantial work was in progress on the Inter-American Highway. An early appropriation of $50,000 for joint reconnaissance surveys in 1929 had generated interest which soon involved Guatemala, Honduras, Nicaragua, Costa Rica, and Panama, while Mexico and El Salvador had indicated that they preferred to finance their own enterprises.[97] The Montevideo Conference endorsed the project and in 1935 Congress appropriated a million dollars to cooperate with interested governments in the survey and construction of the Central American part of the road.[98]

Foreign interests in the little republics were watched carefully. When

[95] William L. Langer and S. Everett Gleason, *The Challenge to Isolation*, p. 133.

[96] *For. Rels., 1937*, V, 439. Also *1933*, V, 249; *1935*, IV, 442; *1937*, V, 787–788.

[97] Warren Kelchner, "The Pan-American Highway," *For. Affs.*, XVI, No. 4 (July, 1938), 724–725.

[98] *Department of State Appropriation Bill for 1936*, pp. 9–10.

there was talk of a proposed treaty to grant Italians equality of treatment with Costa Ricans in potential canal rights via the Nicaraguan route, the United States minister was instructed to suggest "informally, orally and confidentially . . . the apparent inexpediency of placing in a treaty with another Government a provision whereby nationals of the latter would automatically enjoy the same rights as Costa Ricans in the use of canals." Apparently the treaty was actually consummated anyway; but it was to have little significance since it only provided for a five-year period,[99] and then World War II terminated the danger.

When word reached Washington of a proposed defense alliance in Central America against communism the Secretary of State sent word that he hoped no need for such would arise. Instead he anticipated the adjustment of international differences, asserting that the United States was in friendly relations with all nations on the continent and looked forward to even better relations in the future.[100]

The old *de jure* policy of recognition in Central America was clearly on the way out. Maximiliano Hernández Martínez had seized power in El Salvador in 1932. In accordance with the treaty of 1923 Hoover declined to extend recognition and Roosevelt confirmed his stand the next year. Meanwhile Costa Rica and El Salvador denounced the treaty of 1923. A short time later Guatemala, Honduras, and Nicaragua recognized the Martínez regime even though they still gave lip service to the treaty. Finally, on January 26, 1934, the United States fell in line. It instructed its chargé to "extend on behalf of the United States a formal and cordial recognition." Clearly this was the end of the treaty of 1923.[101] From Mexico City, Josephus Daniels sent this interesting commentary: "I have all along had a 'hunch' . . . that the Central American treaty as to recognition was inspired by Washington in order to secure co-operation with those countries to make revolution more difficult."[102]

Sporadic talk of Central American union continued. But the Secretary of State remained carefully aloof from it. In 1934 he wrote: "As regards the aspiration towards Central American Union, the United States conceives this to be fundamentally a Central American question, but is

[99] *For. Rels., 1933*, V, 266 ff.
[100] *Ibid., 1936*, V, 852–854.
[101] *Ibid.*, V, 349, 574 ff.; *1933*, V, 689 ff.; *1934*, V, 218 ff.; *1936*, V, 138 ff.
[102] Daniels to Roosevelt, January 29, 1934, Roosevelt Papers, Hyde Park, P.S.F. Mexico, 1933–1937.

not unsympathetic."[103] Wherever possible this same attitude was maintained in connection with the domestic problems of the small countries. In July, 1937, the United States minister in El Salvador asked if he could be authorized to give some sound advice to discourage revolutionary activities. Welles responded for the Secretary of State: "If this Government is not to become involved in the internal political situation in El Salvador, it is obvious that we must avoid expressing opinions or giving suggestions with reference to internal politics in that country."[104]

In April, 1935, came word that the President of Guatemala proposed to amend the local constitution so that he could remain in office. The American minister was instructed to inform the President that his Government did not approve illegal amendment of constitutions. The President expressed "surprise and pain" at the implied lack of appreciation for his previous cooperation. After careful instructions from Washington the minister reported that he had informed the Minister of Foreign Affairs that "the Government of the United States has no attitude, either of sympathy or lack of sympathy toward any movement such as the present movement to continue President [Jorge] Ubico in power and neither approves nor disapproves of whatever action may be contemplated, which it considers an internal matter in which it cannot intervene."[105]

On January 2, 1933, the American minister in long-troubled Nicaragua had reported that a new President had just been inaugurated. Following the inauguration, the command of the Guardia was turned over to Nicaraguan officers, and evacuation of American marines was completed the same day.[106] Soon a question arose about reorganization of the Guard. Acting Secretary of State Welles expressed an interest but stated that it was the view of the Department "that the proposed reorganization of the National Guard is not a subject on which it may appropriately express an opinion."[107] However, at the request of President Juan B. Sacasa the United States did maintain an embargo on all arms shipments except those approved by the Nicaraguan legation in Washington—this to discourage revolution.[108]

[103] *For. Rels., 1934,* IV, 441–442.
[104] *Ibid., 1937,* V, 525.
[105] *Ibid., 1935,* IV, 632.
[106] *Ibid., 1932,* V, 924.
[107] *Ibid., 1933,* V, 850.
[108] *Ibid., 1934,* V, 561 ff.; Wood, *Making of the Good Neighbor Policy,* p. 142.

Additional steps were taken to break up the detailed supervision of local affairs. When reports reached Washington from the collector general of customs in Nicaragua, the Administration stated that there was no reason for these to be submitted. To accept them would imply a responsibility which the United States did not have. The old Knox-Castrillo Convention, which had called for the reports, had never been ratified anyway.[109] When revolution broke out against Sacasa in the spring of 1936 the United States representatives were enjoined to observe strict neutrality. On June 9 the President resigned. Two days later Hull sent word that since legal forms had been observed there was no reason to refrain from friendly relations with the government that appeared to be in control.[110] Nicaragua was being extended the same treatment as faraway Paraguay and Bolivia.

In 1936 the President of Honduras went through the old performance of amending his nation's constitution to make himself eligible for re-election. During the uncertainty, the American minister on the ground suggested that a naval vessel cruise in the neighborhood for a couple of weeks. Washington declined the suggestion lest it relieve the local authorities of their proper feeling of responsibility for the maintenance of good order and the protection of life and property.[111]

Next to be noted was the faintly comic postage-stamp boundary controversy. An unidentified boundary between Nicaragua and Honduras had long existed but had been of little international significance. In 1937 the issue was aggravated when Nicaragua issued a postage stamp which designated the disputed territory as Nicaraguan. Honduras retorted with its own stamp showing the same territory as belonging to Honduras. Each country refused to accept mail for transport carrying the offensive stickers. This soon involved official mail addressed to foreign legations—more protests. Working behind the scenes, United States representatives restrained troop movements to the border and finally brought about a formal offer of good offices by three powers (Costa Rica, Venezuela, and the United States). Negotiations followed in accordance with the Declaration of Principles of Inter-American Solidarity and Cooperation approved at Buenos Aires. Six weeks later, on December 10, 1937, a Pact of Mutual Agreements for Preservation of

[109] *For. Rels., 1934,* V, 577 ff.
[110] *Ibid., 1936,* V, 841.
[111] *Ibid., 1936,* V, 683 ff.

Peace between the two countries was signed. The offending stamps were withdrawn, the mails went through and the crisis passed, though the boundary remained undelimited.[112]

Mexico

The central figure in international relations with Mexico was Woodrow Wilson's former Secretary of the Navy, Josephus Daniels. During his Cabinet service Daniels had also served as mentor to his then Assistant Secretary, Franklin D. Roosevelt. Now the latter, as President, selected his previous chief for the Mexican mission. In his own words, Roosevelt wished to place a man in Mexico "who would personify those qualities of neighborliness on which I have placed such emphasis."[113] As Secretary of the Navy Daniels had ordered the Veracruz occupation in 1914, hence was suspect by the Mexicans.[114] In addition, he was an ardent Prohibitionist, and such an idiosyncrasy was felt to be unsocial, to say the least, by most Mexicans. To counteract these factors was Daniels' genuine sincerity and undoubted integrity, coupled with an amazing knowledge of human nature and a reasonable dash of political guile. Once south of the border he was determined to do the "proper" thing. *El Excelsior*, the Mexican daily, noted that he called on Sra. Madero, to become "the first . . . American Ambassador [who] has shown such a courtesy to the widow of a Mexican President."[115] His unassuming attitude was well expressed in a letter to Roosevelt in which he commented that there were some army and navy officers "who constantly violate rule 6, which, as you know, reads: 'Thou shalt not take thyself too damn seriously'."[116]

As an old newspaperman Daniels promptly visited and talked shop in at least five newspaper plants of the City of Mexico.[117] Not a bad start. As early as April 28, 1933, he paid his respects by letter to former President Calles, who was in Lower California at the time. When Calles returned to the neighborhood of the capital, Daniels went down to visit

[112] *Ibid., 1937*, V, 56 ff.; Mecham, *U.S. and Inter-American Security*, p. 173.

[113] Roosevelt to Howell, May 14, 1934, Roosevelt Papers, Hyde Park, P.P.F. 86, 1933–1936.

[114] See Daniels to Roosevelt, April 19, 1933, with salutation "Dear Franklin (easy Boss)," *ibid.*

[115] Translation of article of June 10, 1933, *ibid.*, O.F. 237, Folder 1933.

[116] Daniels to Roosevelt. February 26, 1936, *ibid.*, P.P.F. 86, 1933–1936.

[117] May 12 and 13, 1933, Daniels Papers, LC, Diary, Box No. 6.

him at Cuernavaca. At once he confirmed Roosevelt's opinion that Calles was "really the big man of this country." Conversation between the two men ranged from the Mexican six-year development program, to the Montevideo Conference, international radio complications, and the matter of a possible *en bloc* settlement of international claims.[118] Meanwhile the seventy-year-old ambassador was engaged in a truly arduous visitation program to other parts of the republic, including distant Tabasco, Campeche, Yucatán, and Quintana Roo.[119] All the time he was keeping up a drumfire of advice in his correspondence with Washington. He urged Spanish as a cumpulsory language study at both West Point and Annapolis. He wrote freely on the Montevideo Conference, on Cuba and other matters.[120] He recognized the fact that Mexico was more "super-national" than most countries and advised that on such thorny matters as the religious question both Roman Catholics and Protestants in the United States should have nothing to say. Hull fully endorsed this advice.[121] In fact, a suggested presidential trip to Mexico was cancelled lest it be interpreted as implying an interest in some pending domestic problem of the southern republic.[122] It was all too easy for Mexicans to listen to the strictures of a José Vasconcelos, who rang the changes on those two American agencies, the Rotary Club and the Methodist missions, which he claimed were undermining Mexican independence.[123]

Mexico was striving manfully to find markets for its nationalized petroleum products. Eventually it organized a barter arrangement with Germany and Italy. Not surprisingly, the arrangement provided fertile soil from which could spring anti-Semitism and pro-Nazi propaganda.[124]

---

[118] Daniels to Calles, April 28 and August 14, 1933; and Calles to Daniels, May 6, 1933, *ibid.*, Diary, Box No. 6. Also Daniels to Roosevelt, August 15, 1933, Roosevelt Papers, Hyde Park, P.S.F. Mexico, 1933–1937.

[119] Daniels to Hull, undated but probably August, 1934, and March 28, 1936, Daniels Papers, LC, Diary, Box No. 9.

[120] Daniels to Roosevelt, September 9, 1933; June 19, 1939; July 6, 1937, *ibid.*, Correspondence with Roosevelt, Boxes 16 and 17. See also *ibid*, Diary, Box 6, entry for September 6, 1933; *For. Rels., 1933*, V, 394, 409.

[121] *For. Rels., 1936*, V, 775 ff.; Daniels to Roosevelt, November 18, 1935, Daniels Papers, LC, Correspondence with Roosevelt, Box 16.

[122] Daniels to Roosevelt, February 1, 1935, and February 19, 1935, *ibid.*

[123] José Vasconcelos, *Bolivarismo y Monroismo*, pp. 82–83.

[124] Ramón Bateta, "Mexico's Foreign Relations," *The Annals*, CCVIII (March, 1940), 179; Macdonald, *Hitler over Latin America*, pp. 198 ff.

But it should be noted that the Mexican foreign policy was its own, as seen in the fact that in spite of this pro-Nazi influence the administration pursued a consistent opposition to the Franco Administration in Spain. It even advised the diplomatic agents of Italy, Germany, Guatemala, and El Salvador not to attend a congressional celebration in honor of the Madero revolution since their governments had just recognized Franco.[125]

Mexico had long supported the Estrada Doctrine calling for automatic recognition of any government that actually held power in a country. Pursuing this line of thought, in October, 1933, J. M. Puíg Casauranc, Minister of Foreign Affairs, proposed to internationalize the Monroe Doctrine. He also urged that New World nations agree to "absolutely prohibit" an infringement of national autonomy, except in cases of obligatory arbitration agreed to by both parties. This stand gave Washington substantial misgivings.[126]

Meanwhile detailed negotiations on claims brought an agreement for payment by Mexico at the rate of $500,000 per year on the same basis as had been accepted by Belgium, France, Germany, Great Britain, Italy, and Spain.[127] Improved relations were also evident from the fact that Daniels forwarded a draft for a mutual defense commission which might be of service in case of war between the United States and Japan. Since conditions in the Pacific seemed to be improving, the suggestion was not acted upon[128] though it indicated a vastly different atmosphere in Mexico City to that which had obtained earlier.

On November 30, 1934, Lázaro Cárdenas was regularly inaugurated as Mexican President. The tone of the new administration was immediately noted by Daniels, who reported that "The Indian influence is pronounced in the Cárdenas Cabinet, probably more so than in any previous government." He added: "The future of Mexico rests upon giving the Indians, who constitute three-fourths of the population, a better chance than they have ever enjoyed."[129] Rumors soon began to spread

[125] Daniels Papers, LC, Diary, Box 9, November 24, 1936.

[126] Welles, *Time for Decision*, p. 199; Philip C. Jessup, "Generalization of the Monroe Doctrine," *Amer. Jour. of Internat. Law*, XXIX, No. 1 (January, 1935), 105–107; *For. Rels., 1933*, IV, 140–141.

[127] *For. Rels., 1934*, V, 467 ff.; E. David Cronon, *Josephus Daniels in Mexico*, pp. 77 ff.

[128] *For. Rels., 1933*, V, 830 ff.

[129] Daniels to Roosevelt, December 1, 1934, Daniels Papers, LC, Correspondence with Roosevelt, Box 16.

that the President was a Communist. This Daniels repeatedly and emphatically denied.[130]

True, the Mexican pendulum had swung back sharply in the direction of liberalism. The old, conservative strongman Calles was now pointedly ignored, and Daniels reported "Not a paper in Mexico will print any statement he makes . . . but he can do nothing about it."[131] The ambassador's sympathy for the new welfare programs was obvious, and he took transparent glee in reporting on his conservative fellow Americans in Mexico who represented the "big interests" with which he had little patience. He commented that on the eve of the 1916 election a ballot box in the American Club in Mexico City showed 99 votes for Hughes to one for Wilson. In November, 1936, a similar ballot box yielded 117 votes for Landon and 11 for Roosevelt. Progress, at any rate, he concluded.[132]

Routine international questions were disposed of in regular fashion. These included Chinese migration to the United States via Mexico; construction of the Pan-American Highway; control of hoof-and-mouth disease on western ranches of the two countries; and the application of new Mexican land laws in expropriation procedures against American owners, especially in the Yaqui Valley.[133] At this point new problems arose from the petroleum industry. The working arrangements established by Dwight Morrow (see above "Mexico," Chapter Six) were upset when an award by a Mexican labor board in an oil-field wage dispute was upheld by the Mexican Supreme Court. The Court had evidently been impressed by the argument that the companies paid far higher wages for work done in the United States than for identical work done in Mexico, hence could afford the increases demanded. In general Mexicans were convinced that the companies had long profiteered at the expense of Mexicans and that most companies had recovered their investment costs "ten years ago." In answer, the foreign corporations considered that this wage decision was simply the crowning act in progressive socialization. The British government protested the action so strongly that Mexico closed its Mexican legation in counterprotest.[134] Thus

[130] Daniels Papers, Diary, Box 9, entries for April 14, 1935; October 6, 1936; and April 15, 1937.

[131] *Ibid.*, Diary, Box 8, entry for February 8, 1936.

[132] *Ibid.*, Diary, Box 9, entry for November 7, 1936.

[133] *For. Rels., 1933*, V, 846; *1934*, V, 470 ff.; *1936*, V, 711 ff.; *1937*, V, 602 ff.

[134] Circular of Cordell Hull, dated April 1, 1938, Daniels Papers, LC, Box 800.

matters stood when the rapidly approaching World War II added new features to all international controversies. (See below, "Mexico and the Caribbean," Chapter Eleven.)

Canada

Even a casual investigation of the Franklin D. Roosevelt Papers shows the peculiarly informal and almost intimate relationship that existed between Prime Minister MacKenzie King and the President. Formal and informal letters, notes, occasional presents, and personal visits all bear out the statement. Yet both men were very careful to prevent their personal contacts from bearing evil fruit in international misinterpretations. On one occasion the President wrote: "In a sense [on the occasion of King's recent visit to the White House], we both took our political lives in our hands in a good cause and I am very happy to think that the result has proven so successful."[135] The historian is inclined to feel that the two made a substantial contribution to history through their mutual knowledge and efforts.

Canadian trade with Latin America remained negligible. The Latin republics took only about 2.89 per cent of Canadian exports in 1926, and this portion actually declined to 1.83 per cent a decade later. In the same period Canadian imports from Latin America declined from 3.82 percent to 2.89 per cent.[136] Trade treaties were periodically negotiated with the New World Latin republics[137] but they obviously secured limited results. Prior to the Montevideo and Buenos Aires Conferences there was considerable discussion of Canadian attendance on formal Pan-American meetings, and even of adherence to the Union. The instructions to the American delegates to the Sixth (Havana) Conference indicated that, though Hughes and Kellogg tended to favor Canadian adherence to the program, President Coolidge did not like the idea of this indirect admission of the British Empire into a New World organization. Again,

---

provides background of the oil expropriations. T. H. Reynolds, *The Progress of Pan-Americanism*, pp. 319–320, gives the Mexican point of view. Also see *U.S. in World Affs.*, *1937*, pp. 122 ff.; *1938*, pp. 237 ff.

[135] Roosevelt to Mackenzie King, April 16, 1936, Roosevelt Papers, Hyde Park, P.S.F. Canada, Mackenzie King.

[136] R. A. MacKay and E. B. Rogers. *Canada Looks Abroad*, p. 146. Also F. H. Soward, *Canada and the Americas*, p. 25.

[137] *British and Foreign State Papers, 1937*, pp. 567 ff.

just before the 1936 session at Buenos Aires, Welles reported that Brazil would object to Canadian membership and that President Roosevelt took the same position. If Canada were admitted why not Jamaica, or British, Dutch, or French Guiana?[138]

Yet Canadian orientation was increasingly American rather than European. It had of course endorsed the League of Nations, and on June 18, 1936, Mackenzie King told his Parliament that vacant chairs in the League sessions indicated broken links in the chain of collective security. Even so, Canada was reluctant to interfere in European affairs, which, if felt, should be settled by European nations and should not devolve obligations on non-European members of the League. Was not this logic also applicable to the New World? This was the very kind of regionalism that was a bit difficult to justify for a New World nation that remained conscious of its obligations to the British Empire.[139]

Canadian foreign policy was therefore frequently anomalous. One writer in 1907 commented that Canadians did not love the United States, they feared it; yet the Canadian provinces maintained closer relations with neighboring states south of the border than with the Mother Country or other Canadian provinces. They were loyal to the Crown but talked much more about the man in the White House. "The barrier between the two countries is [was] very frail."[140]

For its part, the United States might show its impatience periodically with Latin American republics, but it showed a consistent respect for its numerically weak northern neighbor.[141] On their part, Canadians were keenly conscious of the fact that their defense "in no way depends upon the British fleet, but rather upon the military power, or, if you prefer, on the immense potential power of the United States." The fact might be annoying to proud nationalists but it established a fundamental objective in Canadian foreign policy to maintain friendly relations with the southern neighbor, to keep Canada a white man's country (restrict

---

[138] *For. Rels., 1933*, IV, 127–128; *1936*, V, 11.

[139] MacKay and Rogers, *Canada Looks Abroad*, pp. 107–108; Charles G. Fenwick, "Question of Canadian Participation in Inter-American Conferences," *Amer. Jour. Internat. Law*, XXXI (1937), 473 ff.

[140] André Siegfried, *Canada*, p. 278. Also F. H. Soward, "Canada and the League of Nations," *International Conciliation Documents*, No. 283 (October, 1932), pp. 378–379.

[141] Arthur M. Lower, *Canada: Nation and Neighbor*, p. 177.

Orientals), and to foster an international trade already oriented south-ward in spite of temporarily demoralizing and arbitrary tariffs.[142] One Canadian commented that Canada was a daughter of Britain but was married to the United States—and there was no divorce law.[143]

When Roosevelt took office the State Department forwarded him a memorandum of questions pending in Canadian relations. Heading the list was the item of trade and tariffs. Then came questions of currency and exchange; the St. Lawrence Seaway project; war debts (the United States hoped Canada might serve as an intermediary here); and the need for high-calibre men on the International Joint Commission.[144] The depression had hurt Canada badly. Immigration had ranged up to 400,000 per year just before World War I but was down to less than 12,500 for each of the three years 1934, 1935, 1936.[145]

The reassuring note sounded in New Deal economic and social legis-lation for the United States rang loudly in Canadian ears. Devaluation of the dollar meant a splendid market for Canadian gold; pump-priming efforts for American industry affected Canadians too; and the repeal of American prohibition legitimized sales of Canadian brews and distil-lates.[146] Personal courtesies, the kind of thing Roosevelt loved, were not lacking. The *Times* (London) reported that the mace of the Upper Canada legislature, captured by United States forces on April 27, 1813, was returned in a appropriate ceremony with a guard of honor from the United States.[147]

While Canada was losing enthusiasm for collective force exerted through the League, and was even talking of neutrality legislation fully as drastic as that of the United States,[148] Roosevelt specifically author-ized the use of the term Good Neighbor in reference to Canadian rela-tions with this country. The State Department also had used the expres-

[142] Siegfried, *Canada*, p. 289; MacKay and Rogers, *Canada Looks Abroad*, p. 251.

[143] E. J. Tarr, "Canada in World Affairs," *International Affairs*, XVI, No. 5 (September–October, 1937), 688.

[144] Roosevelt Papers, Hyde Park, P.S.F. Canada, 1933–41.

[145] *For. Pol. Assn. Reports*, XIV (1938–1939), No. 8, 87 n.

[146] John Bartlet Brebner, *The North Atlantic Triangle*, pp. 307 ff.; Roger Shaw, "Canada Catches New Deal Fever," *Rev. of Revs.*, XCII, No. 6 (December, 1935), 18 ff.

[147] The *Times* (London), July 6, 1934, 13e.

[148] F. H. Soward *et al.*, *Canada in World Affairs: The Pre-War Years*, pp. 97 ff; *For. Pol. Assn. Reports*, XIV (1938–1939), No. 8, 93 ff.

sion in a press release in February, 1934.[149] But the immediate existing difficulties centered on trade restrictions. The juxtaposition of the Smoot-Hawley rates and the Ottawa Trade Agreements was a mean combination. On the other hand Canada was still interested in the old idea of reciprocal trade agreements. The Canadian minister in Washington complained to Stimson on October 28, 1934, that he had told the State Department "again and again" that Canada was ready to discuss the question but "they were bogged down in negotiations with a lot of two-penny South American countries."[150] As a matter of fact, it was about this time that the conversations actually began.

The details of the arrangements reached between 1935 and 1938 have been recorded so often that they need not be repeated here. They provided for a mutual lowering of rates which substantially canceled the Ottawa preferential agreements with Empire countries. At last seventy years of tariff controversy were closed. In the year following the 1935 agreement United States exports to Canada increased 24 percent in products whose rates had been reduced, but only 8 per cent in unaffected schedules.[151] The result received "almost equally approving support from Conservative, Liberal, and Labor members of the Canadian Parliament."[152] In his *Memoirs* Secretary Hull stated that no sector of his country's foreign policy during his twelve-year tenure as Secretary was more satisfactory than that with Canada.[153] Of course there remained some older Canadians who remembered Olney's bombast to the effect that three thousand miles of intervening ocean made any "permanent political union between an European and an American state unnatural and inexpedient." Also questions of separatism between French-speaking Canadians and English-speaking compatriots had some repercussions that might portend eventual absorption of all or part of Canada into the United States.[154] For the time, however, all were inclined to take full advantage of improved trade opportunities.

[149] Armour to McIntyre, November 12, 1936, and response of November 16, 1936, Roosevelt Papers, Hyde Park, O.F. 112. Also James Morton Callahan, *American Policy in Canadian Relations*, p. 557.

[150] Diary, October 29, 1934, Stimson Papers, Yale.

[151] Hugh L. Keenleyside, *Canada and the United States*, p. 296. Also O. J. Mc-Diarmid, "Canadian Tariff Policy," *The Annals*, CCLIII (September, 1947), 155.

[152] Keenleyside, *Canada and the U.S.*, p. 275.

[153] Hull, *Memoirs*, II, 1479–1480.

[154] John MacCormac, *Canada: America's Problem*, pp. 143, 207 ff.

In January, 1934, Roosevelt recommended approval of the St. Lawrence deep waterway treaty by the Senate. At once a bitter debate began. It included discussion of power distribution between the two countries, the use of lake waters, and trade controversies between rival commercial groups. The result was the defeat of the treaty by a vote of forty-six in favor to forty-two opposed—far from the two-thirds necessary. The Canadian Premier then announced to his House of Commons that due to the action of the United States Senate he would not submit the measure for their consideration.[155] This matter would have to await executive action on a national emergency basis in war time.

The relaxation of tension in Canadian relations was seen in Roosevelt's visit to Canada in July, 1936. He was welcomed as a good neighbor and as the first American President to visit Canada.[156] Businessmen could now pleasantly twit each other and smile together as in the case of an after-dinner speaker who pointed out the nuisance value of Canada in Anglo-American relations. He said an Englishman had expressed a typical attitude when he commented: "Now I know why Americans and Englishmen are not too friendly. You think we [Englishmen] are like these damn Canadians."[157] Roosevelt himself took keen delight in a cartoon which showed his flirtation with Canada atop the tariff wall while John Bull and Uncle Sam looked on in puzzled and quasi indignation.

Yes, the New Deal Good Neighbor policy pudding was palatable from Hudson's Bay to Tierra del Fuego.

---

[155] Callahan, *American Policy in Canadian Relations*, p. 554; *U.S. in World Affs., 1934–1935*, p. 342.

[156] Roosevelt Papers, Hyde Park, P.P.F 1710, contain twenty-nine pages of letter- and legal-size paper to which are attached clippings from Canadian papers hailing the visit.

[157] Harold A. Innis, *Essays in Canadian Economic History*, p. 237

CHAPTER XI

APPROACH TO WAR: POLITICAL

Personalities, Propaganda, and Problems

PERSONAL CONTACTS BETWEEN Washington and Ottawa remained close. Immediately following the President's Chicago address calling for a quarantine on aggressors, Lord Tweedsmuir, governor general of the Dominion, wrote personally to Roosevelt saying his statement was "the bravest and most important utterance of any public man for many a day."[1] Then as the year closed, Prime Minister Mackenzie King wrote again expressing his conviction that both United States and Canadian interests made frequent personal interviews essential.[2] Hull, too, continued his enthusiastic appreciation of Canadian relations. Some feared that Canada might drag the United States into war and even suggested that the northern nation had no right to go to war without the approval of its southern neighbor. Such suggestions, however, were relatively few.[3]

Annexationism in both countries declined; Americans were interested in other matters and though many Canadians still felt that for more than a century frontier adjustments "from Maine to the Alaska panhandle"

[1] October 8, 1937, Franklin D. Roosevelt Papers, Hyde Park, P.S.F., Canada, 1933–1941.
[2] December 30, 1937, *Ibid.*, Canada, Mackenzie King.
[3] P. E. Corbett, "Canada in the Western Hemisphere," *For. Affs.*, XIX (1940–1941), 786–787.

had been "made in the friendiest manner at our [Canadian] expense,"[4] serious thinkers felt that if the appalling European struggle ended in defeat for the Mother Country or in a stalemate, then Canada would logically turn isolationist with the United States. British observers commented that strategically and politically the Dominion was moving into the United States' sphere and considered the tendency "inevitable." The least that was expected was that after the war, Canada would demand a stronger voice in Empire affairs.[5]

For its part, the United States ceased to take Canada for granted, especially after Germany crushed France. One writer describes the relationship as that of big brother and small sister; "Ignore her as much as possible lest she get 'uppity', but be willing to stand up for her if any outsider presumed to molest her." This had long been true but now current cartoonists were inclined to represent the two countries in terms of Uncle Sam and Jack Canuck "in almost equal scale" as they worked together.[6]

Debate revived periodically over Canadian membership in the Pan-American Union. The implications of such a step were carefully explored. Yet the fact was that Canada had little interest in Latin America.[7] Even union with the British West Indies with their potentially supplementary trade commanded little consideration as Canadians shrank from facing the labor problem which would be posed by West Indians as laborers in their own industry.

Among the southern republics, latent fears and animosities could easily be revived against the United States. The old Brazilian lady returning across the Atlantic on her forty-fifth trip could disdainfully dismiss the question why she had never visited the United States with,

[4] Judith Robinson, "Canada's Split Personality," *ibid.*, XXII (1943–1944), 76.
[5] John MacCormac, *Canada: America's Problem*, pp. 122–123; *For. Pol. Assn. Reports*, XVI, No. 12 (1940–1941), 156; *Survey of Int. Aff., 1938*, I, 636.
[6] Bartlet Brebner, "The U.S.A., Canada's Problem," *Survey Graphic*, XXX (1941), 221.
[7] Among writers commenting on membership in the Pan-American Union and on Latin American contacts with Canada are: Corbett, *For. Affs.*, XIX (1940–1941), 783 ff.; John P. Humphrey, *The Inter-American System: A Canadian View*, pp. 1–6, 274; MacCormac, *Canada: America's Problem*, pp. 81–82; R. A. MacKay and. E. B. Rogers, *Canada Looks Abroad*, p. 152; Marcel Roussin, *Le Canada et le système interaméricain*, p. 7; F. H. Soward, *Canada and the Americas*, p. 27; *U.S. in World Affs., 1938*, pp. 216–217.

"Why should I? You are a race of dollar-chasing barbarians."[8] Now Europe in turmoil tended to verify the saying that external dangers brought about internal cohesion and tended to foster Pan-Americanism. The overmechanization of the United States; the totalitarianism of money; the race problems of the northern republic—all fostered southern suspicions.[9] Yet the Good Neighbor policy was most reassuring.

This moderating criticism was also supported by the personality cult which developed around the crippled President with his sparkling personality. The Colombian Senate passed a resolution in which he was referred to as "one of the greatest and most noble [men] of our epoch."[10] His re-inauguration in 1937 was greeted in usually critical Argentina with all but universal praise. His personal papers contain clippings in extravagant terms from *La Nación, Noticias Gráficas, El Mundo, La Fronda, La Razón, La Vanguardia,* and *La Crítica* under dates of January 20 to 22, 1937. In sending a similar set of reports in 1940, Ambassador Norman Armour reported that the only adverse comments that had come to the embassy's attention appeared in the German-subsidized papers *El Pampero* and *Crisól,* which were consistently anti-United States.[11] The *New York Times* commented on this Latin American tendency to personalize a movement and to refer to its leader simply as "El Hombre" (The Man). Accordingly, it characterized Roosevelt as El Hombre "to whom Latin Americans are looking for leadership more than to any of their own presidents."[12] The popularity of his utterances

[8] Charles A. Thompson, Department of State, *Inter-American Series,* No. 22 (1942), p. 15.

[9] Donald Marquand Dozer, *Are We Good Neighbors?,* pp. 68–69; Felipe Barreda Laos, *La segunda emancipación de América Hispana,* pp. 207 ff.; Erico Verissimo, *Un gato preso en la nieve,* pp. 84 ff.; T. H. Reynolds, ed. and trans., *The Progress of Pan-Americanism,* pp. 119 ff.

An interesting interpretation is found in Carleton Beals *et al., What the South Americans Think of Us,* p. 122. This relates that a minor official of the Brazilian Foreign Office commented: "I have often wondered . . . why such a great power as the United States has not just sent an army into Mexico to make certain that for always the Mexican conforms to the best interests of all." When the reporter seemed surprised the Brazilian added, "But just let 'em try it."

[10] *For. Rels., 1938,* V, 464–465.

[11] Welles to Roosevelt, February 17, 1937. Roosevelt Papers, Hyde Park, Argentina, 1933–1939; Armour to State Department July 23, 1940, *ibid.,* P.S.F. South America, 1939–1940.

[12] *New York Times,* September 5, 1939, 15.1.

was attested in the fact that an address by him to the Governing Board of the Pan-American Union used a continent-wide radio hookup, both for his own remarks and for follow-up translations in Portuguese and Spanish.[13] In addition, the activities of Hull at the Pan-American Conferences brought widespread approval.[14]

One factor to be watched in any New World policy was "The jittery tensions of . . . emotional nationalism." These were especially noticeable in Argentina, where nationalism was founded both on pride and on economic difficulties. Another illustration of this kind of pride came from Mexico on the occasion of a serious earthquake in Colima. The Foreign Affairs Committee of the United States House of Representatives introduced a unanimous resolution for an appropriation of $200,000 for the sufferers. Foreign Minister Ezequiel Padilla expressed great appreciation but stated that the aid would not be accepted. Mexico preferred to take care of its own unfortunate.[15]

Slowly it was becoming more and more true that numbers of the Latin American republics were "democracies in spite of our [their] governments."[16] For a dictator to acquire power, and often for him to remain in power, he was forced to give lip service to popular needs and rights. And even token observance of such statements established conditions favorable to the growth of democratic ideas.[17] Roosevelt was keenly aware of the effect of increasing the power of the people in any nation. Speaking to the Pan-American Scientific Conference on May 1, 1940, he said: "We feel that we are building human progress by conquering disease and poverty and discomfort, and by improving science and culture."[18]

The rapidly proliferating hemisphere activities brought a request from the President to coordinate the activities of various agencies of the na-

---

[13] Rowe to Roosevelt, March 3, 1940, Roosevelt Papers, Hyde Park, O.F. 480, Pan-American Union, 1939–1945.

[14] Arthur H. Kuhn, *Amer. Jour. of Internat. Law*, XXXII (January, 1938), 102. For a European view of Latin American misgivings see Ernest Hambloch in *Quar. Rev.*, CCLXXIV, No. 543 (January, 1940), 120–121, and *Survey of Int. Affs., 1938*, I, 664 ff.

[15] Josephus Daniels Papers, LC, Diary, Box 7, May 9, 1941. For similar feelings see Duncan Aikman, *The All-American Front*, p. 169, and George Pendle, *Argentina*, pp. 70 ff.

[16] Hambloch, *Quar. Rev.*, CCLXXIV, No. 543 (January, 1940), 128.

[17] Aikman, *All-American Front*, p. 208.

[18] Department of State, *Peace and War*, p. 524.

tional government in Latin American affairs. Thirteen different agencies cooperated in a series of detailed studies of social, economic, scientific, and cultural conditions in various areas. In July, 1941, Roosevelt gave his personal approval to four committees to advise the State Department on Latin America. These were:

1) A general advisory committee
2) A committee on agricultural education
3) A committee on foreign students in the United States
4) A committee on exchange fellowships and professorship.[19]

The last committee became concerned with the cultural-relations program of the United States. Other nations had long been active in using systematic propaganda methods to develop understanding. Of course cynics have said that "the political results of the great cultural campaign have been nil, and that it is extremely doubtful that its efforts have sold a single motor car or a single refrigerator."[20] Advocates of the program at once retorted that the criticism was irrelevant. The program was not intended to sell motor cars or refrigerators. This fact was illustrated in the presidential actions of September 2 and October 16, 1941, when Roosevelt personally approved nominations of ten members to serve on the Music Committee and nine to serve on the Art Committee to "Render Closer and More Effective the Relations between the American Republics."[21]

The Division of Cultural Relations of the Department of State was initiated by Departmental Order No. 367 of July 27, 1938, with a budget of $75,000. By 1944–1945 it commanded a budget of $4.5 million as a regular appropriation. Careful attention was paid to the personalities selected to work in the program.[22] Scholarships granted to Latin American students in 1938–1939 were only fifty-eight, though they were later

[19] Welles to Roosevelt, July 30, 1941, Roosevelt Papers, Hyde Park, O.F. 20, State Dept., 1940–1941. See also Laurence Duggan, *The Americas*, pp. 81–82; Philip Leonard Green, *Pan-American Progress*, pp. 104 ff.

[20] Nicholas John Spykman, *America's Strategy in World Politics*, p. 236.

[21] Roosevelt endorsement, October 16, 1941, to Welles, Roosevelt Papers, Hyde Park, O.F. 20, State Department, 1940–1941.

[22] Nina P. Collier and Marjorie Sachs, "Preliminary Survey of Inter-American Cultural Activities" (mimeographed copy of National Committee of U.S.A. on Intellectual Cooperation), pp. 7–8; George N. Shuster, "Nature and Development of Cultural Relations," in Robert Blum, ed., *Cultural Affairs and Foreign Relations*, pp. 10 ff. Charles A. Thompson and Walter H. C. Laves, *Cultural Relations and United States Foreign Policy*, give a good survey of this program to 1960.

increased. At the same time the number of Latin American students in American institutions rose to about 1,400 in 1940 and to over 2,600 in 1941. Travel grants were made to bring distinguished Latin Americans to the United States (about thirty of these trips were authorized in 1940) and leading Latin Americanists and literary men were assisted in traveling southward. In 1941 and 1942 grants were made to sixty-two persons from Latin America and to twelve from the United States. Medical men, engineers, dairymen, and physical-education experts were all included. On the academic level, a single press release listed thirty-five northern scholars available for exchange purposes and representatives of eleven southern republics seeking appointments in this country.[23]

To carry the work abroad in 1940, the Department sent 178 reels of motion pictures (113 to Latin America). Thirty-seven of these were from the Department of Agriculture and twenty from the Department of Interior. Others were sent by private industrial concerns, the National Tuberculosis Council, the American College of Surgeons, and the American Dental Association. A series of twenty-six radio programs were broadcast over more than one hundred stations, with over seventy thousand listeners writing to request a leaflet describing the series. Also two special culture centers were established in Argentina, four in Brazil, and one each in Chile, Colombia, Honduras, Peru, Uruguay, and Venezuela. Even during the war, the Division of Cultural Relations continued to maintain its cultural orientation[24] though war pressures inevitably affected both the objectives and volume of its output.

Efforts to counteract hostile cultural and propaganda activities also need to be noted. The general impression was that Communists were fighting merely a rear-guard action even in the three republics (Colombia, Chile and Mexico) where they had been reported most active.[25] This was probably true at the beginning of the war when the U.S.S.R. sided with Germany and victimized Poland and Finland. But when Germany attacked Russia the recently denounced "imperialist" was hailed for its

[23] *Inter-American Affairs, 1941*, p. 129; Department of State, "Program in Cultural Relations," *Inter-American Series*, No. 19 (1941); *Department of State Bulletin*, II, No. 41 (April 6, 1940), 357 ff.; the *New York Times*, April 6, 1940.

[24] See references in preceding two footnotes, also Department of State, *Inter-American Series*, No. 21 (1942), and Green, *Pan-American Progress*, pp. 86–87.

[25] McCulloch, "Influences from Overseas," *Survey Graphic*, XXX (1941), 114.

magnificent "war of liberation." Forthwith the Communist Party began to make substantial gains, and party membership in Latin America was reported as 330,000 by 1947. At the same time almost a million sympathetic votes were cast in various Latin American elections, more than half of them reported from Brazil.[26]

More popular, however, were such movements as Sinarquismo, especially in Mexico; the Hispanidad movement, which favored closer relations with Spain and Portugal; and that of the Integralistas, especially active in Peru. As a whole, these movements were strongly pro-Church, anti-United States, and extremely nationalistic. They generally repudiated "universal suffrage, parliamentary democracy, economic liberalism, the Marxists, the Jews and the influence of the United States." The leadership principle and political dictatorship as exemplified in Mussolini and Franco were held to point the way to salvation in the future.[27]

Here, ready to hand, were nuclei through which a victorious Nazi Germany could make an effective appeal. Periodically since Otto Richard Tannenberg's *Greater Germany: The Work of the Twentieth Century*, published in 1911, there had been suggestions of a new Germany in the Americas. On July 30, 1941, an editorial in the *New York Times* referred to a circular letter of Francisco Franco of Spain encouraging the formation of volunteer units in Latin America to fight for Germany against Russia. With Germany in control of France and the Low Countries, its airplanes raiding London, and its armies sweeping through Russia, did it not behoove sensible Latin Americans to take for granted a Germany-dominated Europe to which their goods would have to be sold? Germany did not neglect the opportunity. Propaganda by radio, films, and the like was supplemented by commercial contracts for goods to be delivered as soon as the Atlantic seaways were reopened. Sixty-three thousand Germans in the Argentine were said to be on the German payroll. Other reports referred to over two hundred German schools which catered to the children among over 235,000 resident Germans (of whom nearly 44,000 were reported to have been born in the old country). There were said to be "Five hundred thousand storm troopers . . . organ-

[26] Dorothy Dillon, "International Communism in Latin-America," *Latin American Monographs*, No. 19, pp. 11–12; John C. Campbell, "Political Extremes in South America," *For. Affs.*, XX (1941–1942), 519–520.

[27] Campbell, "Political Extremes," *For. Affs.*, XX (1941–1942), 524 ff.; *Inter-American Affairs, 1942*, pp. 26 ff.

ized and scattered strategically throughout Latin America."[28] Extreme statements of German nationalism were of course for home consumption in Germany and were seldom heard in the New World. Only occasionally did one creep out. One such was that of Friedrich Lange, *Reines Deutschtum*: "Decrepit nations like the republics of Argentina and Brazil, and more or less all those beggar South American countries, will be induced, by force or otherwise, to come to their senses."[29]

Pro-Communist and pro-Nazi sentiment fortunately tended to offset each other and increasingly the American republics became inclined to form their own opinions. Slowly the danger of pro-Nazi coups subsided.[30]

Mexico and the Caribbean

Strangely enough, Mexico, where there was so much pro-German sympathy in World War I, showed a very different attitude in the second world contest. German Minister Freiherr von Rudt reported to his Foreign Ministry in April, 1938, that as of that date little United States propaganda against Germany was to be noted in Mexico, though he admitted that the economic competition of the United States was very severe. He continued: ". . . the mood of a large and possibly decisive part of the population of Mexico . . . is so definitely oriented against authoritarian, or "fascist" countries, as they are called here, that in all probability even without pressure from the northern neighbor the Government would hardly be able to maintain a neutral attitude in case of armed conflict." He later reported that German business did not encounter any special difficulties and was held in high esteem; also "that the existence of the Party organization, the German community,

---

[28] *Documents on German Foreign Policy, 1918–1945*, Series D, XI, 753 ff.; Charles Wertenbaker, *A New Doctrine for the Americas*, pp. 42–43; *U.S. in World Affs., 1940*, pp. 135 ff.; Reynolds, *Progress of Pan-Americanism*, p. 109.

[29] Quoted by David Efron, "Latin America and the Fascist 'Holy Alliance'," *The Annals*, CCIV (July, 1939), 19.

[30] William L. Langer and S. Everett Gleason, *The Undeclared War, 1940–1941*, pp. 594–595.

The Roosevelt Papers, Hyde Park, P.S.F. Germany, Box 6, contain an interesting reproduction of a map published in Germany in 1911, and of another recently published in Germany, showing areas of hoped-for German control in Latin America. One or the other of these probably inspired the President's rash Navy Day charge on October 27, 1941, of the discovery of a Nazi plot to divide Latin America into vassal states. These maps appear to have reflected the ideas of enthusiasts, but not the ideas of German policy makers.

German schools, and other German institutions has not been threatened."[31]

At about the same time Ambassador Daniels reported that Mexico was steadily suppressing subversive activities.[32] Certainly there was Communist and Nazi propaganda, but Daniels, with the support of Roosevelt, consistently lent aid to the friendly Mexican administration. Disappointed candidates for office got scant sympathy and no support whatever for revolutionary activities.[33] Secretary of State Hull, however, was restless, and he commented in 1938: "Daniels is down there taking sides with the Mexican government, and I have to deal with these Communists down there and have to carry out international law."[34]

Formal relations with Mexico continued excellent. Recently that country had been exchanging surplus oil for oil-field equipment and heavy machinery from Germany, and for oil tankers and rayon from Italy. Yet in September, 1938, President Cárdenas suggested an inter-American boycott of aggressors, even at the probable cost of the loss of his new oil markets. A more severe test of his attitude came in the fall of 1940 when Washington imposed an embargo on shipments of scrap iron and military supplies to Japan. In short order Mexico did the same at the sacrifice of quick and easy profits.[35]

In Central America old boundary disputes still gave trouble. One between Gautemala and Belize (British Honduras) found the Guatemalans convinced that the British proposals for settlement were wholly unsatisfactory. United States efforts in 1940 to have Welles raise the question

[31] *Documents on German Foreign Policy*, Series D, V, 827–829, 880.

[32] Daniels to Roosevelt, June 28, 1940, May 2, 1941, and June 3, 1941, Daniels Papers, LC, Correspondence with Roosevelt, Boxes 16 and 17. Also Reynolds, *Progress of Pan-Americanism*, pp. 203 ff.

[33] E. David Cronon, *Josephus Daniels in Mexico*, p. 257; Bryce Wood, *The Making of the Good Neighbor Policy*, p. 155; Daniels to Roosevelt, telegram of December 2, 1940, Daniel Papers, LC, Correspondence with Roosevelt, Box 17.

[34] Wood, *Making of the Good Neighbor Policy*, p. 217.

[35] Cronon, *Daniels in Mexico*, pp. 233–234; Maurice Halperin, "Mexico Shifts her Foreign Policy," *For. Affs.*, XIX (1940–1941), 215.

The events of the period to 1941 bear testimony to the fact that Roosevelt really felt the kind words he sent to Daniels on his resignation and when he stated on October 31, 1941: ". . . it comes to me as a real shock that we have to face the situation that the country will have to do without the services of its Ambassador to Mexico, who perhaps, more than anyone else, has exemplified the true spirit of the good neighbor in the foreign field" (Daniels Papers, LC, Correspondence with Roosevelt, Box 19).

in London brought no results.[36] Another obstinate dispute existed between Nicaragua and Honduras. A special mediation commission under a United States chairman was so handicapped by local jealousies that it could not secure permission for an aerial survey to help obtain pertinent information. All efforts of Washington to serve as a *deus ex machina* were abortive. The one success along this line was a satisfactory delimitation in 1938 of the Panamanian-Colombian boundary.[37]

With the rise of war tensions increased attention centered on the Panama Canal. Nicaragua sought to prod the United States into conducting surveys of the potential Nicaraguan route so long discussed. The Secretary of State responded, after consulting with the Secretary of War, that Washington would not take the initiative, but if Nicaragua wished to undertake a survey the War Department would make available what pertinent data it had collected.[38] By early 1939 Costa Rica had also become interested because the Nicaraguan route would follow the boundary river between itself and Nicaragua. The United States thereupon informed all interested parties that it would be far cheaper to build a new set of locks in Panama, where the estimated cost would be $300 million, rather than undertake the Nicaraguan venture, whose costs were estimated at two and a half times that sum.[39]

Reports reached Washington that a Swedish firm was apparently acting as a cat's-paw for German acquisition of holdings in Pinas Bay in Panama and on two off-shore islands. Concerned, the Secretary of State, on July 1, 1938, sent word to Panama that the War Department had no desire to lease or purchase these points except "to prevent . . . acquisition by the German or Japanese Government." On September 26 a memo in the State Department reported that the Panama minister had left word that his government had decided to purchase the Pinas Bay property.[40]

---

[36] *For. Rels., 1939*, V, 175 ff.; *1940*, V, 416 ff.

[37] *Ibid., 1938*, V, 245 ff.; *1939*, V, 148 ff.; *British and Foreign State Papers, 1938*, pp. 494 ff.

[38] *For. Rels., 1938*, V, 796 ff.

[39] An editorial footnote in *For. Rels., 1939*, V, 747, indicates that new surveys were undertaken and completed by December of that year when the results were reported at a Cabinet meeting. The President, however, then said that he was no longer interested in the matter so it was allowed to lapse "apparently because of the excessive cost and lack of sufficient economic and political advantages."

[40] *Ibid., 1938*, V, 821 ff.

Though there is no indication of any connection whatever, this incident was fol-

On the occasion of pending elections in Panama the United States ambassador was instructed that his country was bound by policy and by treaty "not to interfere directly or indirectly" in the internal affairs of the southern republic. Accordingly, the ambassador was not to reply to suggestions or enquiries concerning forthcoming elections.[41] Unfortunately the recently elected President, Arnulfo Arias, launched a national program with strong pro-Nazi overtones. The resulting dissatisfaction soon forced him to leave "for medical treatment," much to the relief of Washington. Hull later commented: "I state categorically for the record, that the United States Government has had no connection, direct or indirect, with the recent Governmental changes in the Republic of Panama." A somewhat different view of the matter is seen in the Diary of Secretary of War Stimson, under date of January 9, 1941. Stimson commented that Arias had refused to let the United States have absolutely essential bases. "The President appreciated this fully—told me his troubles with Arias and told Hull to try some strong arm methods on him."[42] One may hazard a question, therefore, whether the Panamanian's need for medical treatment might have had a psychosomatic basis. Be that as it may, once Arias went out of the country the two governments became engrossed in working out details of arrangements for additional bases for Canal defense.

An interesting footnote to the incident appears in Roosevelt's personal papers. From exile in Mexico City, Arias wrote offering to see Roosevelt personally and assuring him that "I dream with you, and it was and is my desire to work with you to that great and ever increasing good-will and mutual respect." Roosevelt responded: ". . . I feel sure that you will appreciate that the very policies to which you refer in such laudatory terms prevent me from commenting upon questions relating to the internal affairs of Panama. The expressions of your interest in the constant development of cordial cooperation among the American republics were most heartening."[43] No invitation for an interview was included.

------

lowed in short order by raising both Panamanian and Colombian legations to embassy rank (Hull to Roosevelt, September 28, 1938, and February 27, 1939, Roosevelt Papers, Hyde Park. O.F. 313. 1936–38, and O.F. 110, Panama, 1939).

[41] *For. Rels., 1940*, V, 1091.

[42] See Langer and Gleason, *Undeclared War*, pp. 613 ff.; *Inter-American Affairs, 1941*, p. 57.

[43] Arias to Roosevelt, November 28, 1941, and Roosevelt to Arias, December 22, 1941, Roosevelt Papers, Hyde Park, O.F. 110, Panama.

In Guatemala there had been pro-German sympathies ever since pre-World War I days. These had been fostered by irritation over the sale of German holdings by the local enemy alien property custodian after the war. In 1939 the United States minister reported that the German minister had been involved in bolstering Guatemalan intransigence toward a settlement of the border dispute with British Honduras.[44] When the time came for the Havana Conference the German minister, riding the crest of Nazi victories, bluntly warned the Central American governments that it would be unwise for the Conference to take any action "which directly or indirectly might be directed against Germany." Repercussions were immediate and forceful. In response, Minister Otto Reinbeck withdrew with apologies his inopportune advice.[45]

Relations with Colombia remained cordial indeed. Just prior to a presidential election in 1938 the Liberal candidate—who was certain of election—visited Washington. To avoid the slightest appearance of trying to influence the election, United States officials, instead of giving a formal reception at the White House, merely received him privately at tea.[46] Through 1939 numbers of special agents rendered semiofficial services in Colombia. These included a technical assistant on road paving, a special agent to advise on methods of surveillance of alien activities, and two men to aid in development of agricultural resources.[47] By 1940 the increasing concern over German nationals working on airlines operating near the Canal resulted in a systematic policy of eliminating German personnel and of carefully supervising all sales of secondhand planes and parts to Colombian citizens.[48] In all these matters Colombia cooperated fully.

In the Caribbean islands the story was similar. Massacres on the Dominican-Haitian border were referred to a permanent commission for settlement. When the going became rough Undersecretary of State Welles was asked to lend his aid. Finally, a cash agreement was reached through the mediation of the papal nuncio.[49] As for Cuba, Hull informed

[44] *For. Rels., 1939*, V, 18.

[45] The *Times* (London), July 22, 1940, 4c; William L. Langer and S. Everett Gleason, *Challenge to Isolation, 1937–1940*, pp. 636–637.

[46] Welles to Roosevelt, March 5, 1938, Roosevelt Papers, Hyde Park, O. F. 313, 1936–1938.

[47] The presidential approval of each man may be found during the months of February, May, and October, 1939 (*ibid.*, 1939–1941).

[48] *For. Rels., 1940*, V, 724 ff.

[49] *Ibid., 1938*, V, 186 ff.

his chargé at Havana that since ratification of the treaty of May 29, 1934, the relations of Cuba with the United States were exactly the same as those of any other American republic and that " this Government would under no conditions give any indication of whether it would or would not recognize a future government of Cuba."[50]

The West Coast

On the west coast of South America, Ecuador and Peru were still quarreling over their boundary. The dispute was apparently settled at the Rio Conference in January, 1942, but during the war new complaints resulted in delays in applying the terms. Again Brazil took the lead in mediation and in February, 1945, finis was written to the oldest boundary dispute on the continent.[51]

Axis-Japanese propaganda on the west coast was carefully watched. Of special concern in Peru was the presence of 25,000 to 50,000 Japanese, mostly engaged in agriculture, small industry, and shopkeeping. Concentrated in five centers, they gave food for thought, especially after Pearl Harbor.[52] Fortunately, no disturbances occurred. At about the same time details were completed for Pan-American Grace Airways to acquire German airlines in Ecuador.[53] This eliminated another potential danger.

In Bolivia there were repeated alarms over German activity after 1939. In 1941 came the revelation of a German plot to seize control by means of a *coup d'état*. The German minister was at once expelled from La Paz.[54] This ended the immediate crisis, but conditions were obviously far from satisfactory.

In Chile, Pedro Aguirre Cerda had been elected President in October, 1938, by 221,000 votes to 214,000 for the opposition.[55] Already the German minister, on March 8, 1938, had reported that although there was still strong sympathy for Germany in Chile it should be realized that United States influence was materially stronger than it had been in 1917. Three months later he reported that Chile's position would depend upon

[50] *Ibid., 1940*, V, 741.

[51] *Ibid., 1938*, V, 225 ff.; *1941*, VI, 249; *1942*, V, 268; J. Lloyd Mecham, *The United States and Inter-American Security*, pp. 168 ff.

[52] Fernando de los Rios, "South American Perplexities," *For. Affs.*, XX (1941–1942), 654–655.

[53] *For. Rels., 1940*, V, 832 ff.

[54] *New York Times*, June 9, 1939; *Inter-American Affairs, 1941*, pp. 53–55.

[55] *New York Times*, October 26, 1938, 18.5, and October 27, 1938, 18.6.

the amount of pressure that could be brought to bear and would probably be determined by the price the United States would be willing to
pay. He commented on a rise of the idea of Pan-American solidarity
and noted the continued leadership of the United States.[56] By the end of
the year German agents in Chile asked for a German commodity credit
of from 150 to 200 million reichsmarks to foster trade relations. In this
process they planned payments of some 50,000 reichsmarks to the new
Socialist members and backers of the new Chilean Popular Front government. Then on December 27, 1938 (after the election), the embassy
proposed an immediate payment of 10,000 reichsmarks to place the principal wirepullers under obligation. On January 10 a telegram, presumably in answer to the above request, arrived saying, "Proposed payment
approved."[57]

Realists knew that the United States would continue to need Chilean
nitrates and copper regardless of whether that country declared war on
the Axis or remained neutral. Due to its location, Chile would encounter
little danger from a victorious Germany, but a victorious United States
might actually be more of a problem. Further, the scanty military resources of the country precluded effective military participation in the
war. Indeed there was serious question if it could protect its own territory—and this was as likely to be violated if Chile remained a nonbellig-
erent as if it joined in the conflict. Little could be gained by participation.
Therefore, play it safe and remain neutral.[58]

The new United States ambassador to Chile, Claude Bowers, reported
a cordial reception. He wrote to Roosevelt: "And something worth bearing in mind is that the present regime is wholly democratic, pro-Ameri-
can and pro-Roosevelt."[59] He assiduously cultivated the friendship he
encountered and early in January, 1941, was at work on a plan by which
each of nine American newspapers took a Chilean publisher on its staff
for two months. In each case the newspaper paid the transportation costs
and three hundred dollars expense money. The Grace interests reduced

[56] *Documents on German Foreign Policy*, Series D, V, 821–822, 836.

[57] *Ibid.*, pp. 889–891.

[58] Galvarino Gallardo Nieto, *Panamericanismo*, pp. 281 ff.

[59] Bowers to Roosevelt, November 15, 1940, Roosevelt Papers, Hyde Park, O.F.
303, Claude G. Bowers 1940–43, Chile.

In 1938 Chile and Argentina had agreed to submit the question of ownership of
islands in the Tierra del Fuego area to any one of three eminent United States
citizens as arbitrator. Attorney General Homer Cummings accepted the task (*For.
Rels., 1938*, V, 210 ff.).

travel rates by 50 per cent for the new tourists-employees, Roosevelt, much interested in the arrangement, received seven of the journalists at the White House for a brief interview.[60] Toward the end of 1941 *Time* magazine published an article that referred in slighting terms to the Chilean President. Roosevelt in person castigated the journal by referring to the "disgusting lie" for which his government had been forced to apologize. He added that the article was "being widely used by Nazi, Fascist and Falangist press."[61] Obviously all parties were watching all angles to make political propaganda wherever possible.

The East Coast

On the east coast of South America the pull and tug of propaganda and the maneuvering for international vantage took on an even sharper tone. An interesting side light with possible implications for the future was connected with Antarctic exploration and claims. The explorer Lincoln Ellsworth was instructed that his activities were to be conducted strictly as those of a private citizen. It was advisable for him not to explore, map, or photograph areas claimed by other countries, though he might reassert previous claims made by United States citizens. "It should be made clear to Ellsworth that he should not indicate or imply advance knowledge or approval of the Government of the United States but that he should leave it for this Government to adopt its own course of action."[62] This is reminiscent of instructions from London encouraging Canadian exploration of the Arctic. A year later the more ambitious Richard E. Byrd venture set out. Announced as a scientific expedition, it exchanged meteorological information with the Argentines and emphasized that it would not "prejudice in any way the rights and interests" of any other American republic. When Argentina and Chile asked to be allowed to attach experts to the expedition the answer was that space would not permit the courtesy but that one or two representatives of each government would be welcome as guests on the naval part of the trip.[63]

In Argentina there was a center of Nazi activity. Newspapers such as

---

[60] Bowers to Roosevelt, January 10, 1941, and January 25, 1943, Roosevelt Papers, Hyde Park, O.F. 303, Claude G. Bowers, 1940–43, Chile.

[61] *Ibid.*, O.F. 429, 1939–41 and 1941–45, contains several letters and a copy of a press release on this subject.

[62] *For. Rels.*, *1938*, VI, 972 ff.

[63] *Ibid.*, *1939*, II, 8 ff.

the *Deutsche La Plata Zeitung* were reported to be receiving subsidies through the German legation in Buenos Aires. To counteract this was the generally anti-German influence of the Jews, North American businessmen, and the Roman Catholic Church. A third type of sentiment and propaganda was that of the Italians, immigrants who were peculiarly free from restriction.[64] A possible explanation of the freedom lay in the similarity of Italian and Argentine mentality and cultural traits; in fact, Nazi agents suggested that the proud German might be able to take lessons from Italian experiences in cultural propaganda and in the Italian methods of organizing Fascist activities abroad.[65] Tours were arranged for Argentine teachers to visit Germany for three months, after which it was hoped they would return as missionaries to spread the gospel of Hitlerism. In response to Argentine suspicions caution was enjoined on all agents. The more blatant and pro-Nazi groups were to be restrained, and moneys heretofore contributed to them were transferred to such organizations as the German-Argentine Boy Scouts.[66]

Argentine officials became increasingly restless and early in 1939 started an investigation of Nazi maneuvers. The German embassy at Buenos Aires protested at once, denouncing the accusations as fraudulent and as injurious to good international relations.[67] Later the Blue Book of the United States Department of State was to refer to subsidies by both Italy and Germany for propaganda in the Argentine but was to conclude that in 1939 "the general sentiment in Argentina is [was] anti-German," and that early the next year there had been little change.[68] When local investigations showed the Nazi activities to be dangerous, the Chamber of Deputies passed a resolution, by a vote of seventy-eight to one, censuring the German ambassador for subversive conduct.[69] The extent of these activities may be inferred from the fact that the expenses of the German embassy in Buenos Aires increased from 850,000 pesos in 1938–1939 to 3,397,600 pesos and 5,983,100 pesos in the two following years. At the same time the shipments, presumably propaganda for

[64] *Documents on German Foreign Policy*, Series D, V, 819 ff., but especially pp. 857–858.
[65] *Ibid.*, pp. 852–853.
[66] *Ibid.*, pp. 869–871; N. P. Macdonald, *Hitler over Latin America*, pp. 39–41.
[67] *New York Times*, April 11, 1939, 6.1.
[68] Pages 34–35.
[69] *Inter-American Affairs, 1941*, p. 54.

the most part, by mail from German offices in the country reached the astonishing total of 502 packages weighing 4,394,850 kilograms (1 k. equals 2.2 lbs.). Those from British offices were only 127 packages weighing less than 730,000 kilograms.[70]

The friendly President, Roberto M. Ortiz was a sick man. He gave way to the determined neutralist Ramón S. Castillo in mid-1940. Undersecretary of State Welles considered Castillo "the tool of corrupt influences." Roosevelt found him so completely uninterested in international affairs that he characterized him as "really an Argentine Coolidge."[71]

Uruguay remained mistress of its own thinking. Public opinion was highly critical of the invasion of Finland by Russia[72] but voiced no objection to the opening of Comintern headquarters in Montevideo. "Anyhow, why should anybody 'give a damn'? They weren't going to invade Uruguay with an army, were they?"[73] The Axis menace was felt to be quite different. Large numbers of Axis citizens were present and their connivings were flagrant. Local sympathies and business connections were largely pro–Anglo-Saxon, but the choice between belligerency and neutrality in case of war would have to depend on developments and the amount of pressure the Anglo-Saxon powers might be able to bring to bear.[74]

In the summer of 1940 the British ambassador in Washington asked for an opinion as to the wisdom of landing British marines to protect British nationals in Uruguay. Welles responded that the effects would be "highly prejudicial." Soon thereafter Brazil sent Uruguay a million rounds of ammunition and the United States despatched two heavy cruisers to vist the coast.[75] When Nazi plotters were arrested in Uruguay, Berlin considered making reprisals but discarded the idea when it could find only fifty-three Uruguayans in German-controlled territory. All it could do was to provide the best possible legal talent to prove that its chief agent under arrest was insane.[76]

---

[70] Ysabel F. Rennie, *The Argentine Republic*, p. 276.

[71] Sumner Welles, *Where Are We Heading?*, p. 192.

[72] The *Times* (London), January 13, 1940, 5a.

[73] Carleton Beals *et al., What South Americans Think of Us*, p. 167.

[74] *Documents on German Foreign Policy*, Series D, V, 831 ff., 882 ff.

[75] *For. Rels.*, 1940, V, 1148 ff.; Langer and Gleason, *Challenge to Isolation*, pp. 611 ff.

[76] *Documents on German Foreign Policy*, Series D,, IX, 441 ff.

In June, 1941, Uruguay opened its ports to any American power (specifically to the United States) for the use of its naval vessels in case that power became involved in war with a non-American power. It next negotiated a $17 million loan from the United States with which to construct a large naval air base that would be available to the northern republic in case of war, but that, incidentally would, be excellent insurance against its powerful next-door neighbors.[77] Soon the badly damaged *Graf Spee* requested refuge in Montevideo harbor but the answer was a negative. Then after the vessel had been scuttled its sailors took refuge in Argentina. In short order, within a month after Pearl Harbor, Uruguay broke relations with the Axis.[78]

Brazil also received serious Nazi attention. As early as the end of 1937 the German ambassador in Rio de Janeiro was calling for anti-Comintern material. The next May an attempt was made on the life of President Vargas by Integralistas. This had followed hard on the heals of an executive "crackdown" on foreign organizations and propaganda agencies. Pro-Nazi sympathizers were suspected and Nazi Party members arrested. Now followed more recriminations and restrictions. The German ambassador returned home on leave—and Rio asked that he stay there. In retaliation Berlin asked the Brazilian ambassador to leave. After the lapse of some time feelings moderated. Vargas sent his son to Germany for an extended visit, and Brazilian air force officers and the Chief of Staff were invited to witness German military maneuvers. Diplomatic relations were resumed on June 1, 1939.[79]

Meanwhile Brazil was perturbed about local conditions. The powerful Argentine Navy endangered connections between Vargas' strategic and industrial centers, and his southern provinces; railway connections in the area were seriously inadequate.[80] Friendship with the United States therefore was doubly desirable. To protect his homeland, Vargas set aside frontier zones from 100 to 150 kilometers (sixty to ninety-five miles) wide in which only Brazilians could settle, while within thirty kilometers of the border free lands were to be assigned to army reservists. One reason for the limitation may have been fear of cross-border

[77] *Inter-American Affairs, 1941*, p. 46.

[78] George Pendle, *Uruguay*, p. 76.

[79] For this sequence of events see *Documents on German Foreign Policy*, Series D, V, 816 ff.; *For. Rels., 1938*, V, 413 ff.; *U.S. in World Affs., 1938*, pp. 265 ff.; Karl Lowenstein, *Brazil under Vargas*, pp. 167 ff.

[80] *Documents on German Foreign Policy*, Series D, V 825–826.

German activities.[81] On the other hand, Argentina and Uruguay were immediately fearful that the nationalized territories would be used as staging bases from which Brazilian armed forces might advance to the south and west.

Continued German military victories in Europe and the Italian entrance into the War had serious effects. Apparently trying to appease criticism, Vargas said in a public address, "The era of improvident liberalism, sterile demagoguery, useless individualism and the sowers of discord has passed." These repudiated undesirables were contrasted with "virile peoples." Although the remarks were made for home consumption and probably with scant consideration of possible foreign repercussions, the effects were felt in the United States at once.[82] Maybe Vargas was wavering in his sentiments, but if so popular feeling in his country was more stable. The German embassy had arranged the showing of a special film to the cadets of the Brazilian military academy to advertise the German military machine. All went well "until Hitler was flashed on the screen. Pandemonium then broke loose; catcalls and shouts of 'Take him away! Take him away!' " followed. The showing was suspended and the cadets sharply reprimanded, but their sentiments were clear.[83]

Conferences—Lima

Pan-American meetings were proliferating. Some of them represented little more than pious hopes but the total was impressive. In 1941 alone the following conferences took place:

Third Meeting of Ministers of Foreign Affairs
Inter-American Conference of Police and Judicial authorities
Second Inter-American Travel Conference
Second Inter-American Conference on Agriculture
First Meeting of Inter-American Defense Board
Eighth Pan-American Child Conference
Inter-American Conference on Systems of Economic and Financial Control.[84]

The position of the United States in these conferences was variously depicted as "wavering between the role of a law-giving Moses and that

[81] Lowenstein, *Brazil under Vargas*, pp. 189 ff.

[82] *For. Rels., 1940*, V, 616 ff.; Welles to Roosevelt, June 12, 1940, (Roosevelt Papers, Hyde Park, Welles, 1940, 1943).

[83] Welles to Roosevelt, October 16, 1940, *ibid.*

[84] Pan-American Union, *Bulletin*, LXXVI (1941).

of a benevolent school-master with a sheaf of edifying copybook texts for distribution."[85] The indirect effects in better acquaintance and understanding can be estimated only in general terms. In contrast to the above sessions an abortive meeting assembled at Port-au-Prince with representatives from thirteen members of the Inter-American Union of the Caribbean for its third session. Cuba and Mexico appeared to be the chief sponsors, with Sr. Isidro Fabela serving as the head of the Mexican delegation. The United States sent an observer, who threw the meeting into an uproar when he stated that his country could not accept the statutes proposed since they provided for activities overlapping those of the Pan-American Union.[86]

The first of the really important conferences of the period was the Eighth Inter-American Conference at Lima in December, 1938. Argentina was hesitant about approving a meeting at the time but acquiesced in the light of the Chaco situation and the unrest in Brazil. On August 2 the Peruvian Minister of Foreign Affairs issued the invitations and plans went forward.[87] A peculiarly significant appointment on the United States delegation (Secretary Hull headed the group) was that of the recently defeated Republican candiate for the Presidency, Alfred M. Landon. The appointment gave the kind of bipartisan support that was especially important in the eyes of Latin Americans, who all too seldom practiced bipartisanship in their politics. Instructions to the delegates specified that it was an established principle of American international policy that "among the foreign relations of the United States as they fall into categories, the Pan American policy takes first place in our diplomacy."[88] Landon emphasized the same idea in connection with defense of the New World against foreign aggressors, adding: "I know that in saying this I am speaking for Republicans as well as Democrats, because at home in this matter there is, and will not be, any party division."[89] And such assurances fell upon peculiarly attentive ears, for Latin America interpreted the recent Munich Agreement to mean that it now had scant hopes of British protection in case of need.[90]

[85] Hambloch, "South America and the War," *Quar. Rev.*, CCLXXIV, No. 543 (January, 1940), 131.

[86] *New York Times*, April 28, 1941, 6.5.

[87] *For. Rels., 1938*, V, 1 ff. Page 1 gives a bibliography of significant official publications on the Conference.

[88] *For. Rels., 1938*, V. 54.

[89] J. Wheeler Bennett, ed., *Documents on International Affairs, 1938*, I, 389.

[90] *U.S. in World Affs., 1938*, pp. 280 ff.

The Argentina delegation arrived at Callao on board the powerful *Almirante Brown*, the pride of the Argentine Navy. Immediate attention centered on proposals for a declaration of continental solidarity. An Argentine draft referred to danger from either a continental or a non-continental power. This was clearly unstatisfactory to both the United States and Brazil. As soon as he had presented his country's proposal, Sr. José María Cantilo, head of the Argentine delegation, left the Conference "because of his health." The delegates were stymied. Having thus demonstrated his importance, the Argentine reappeared and agreed to most of Hull's original proposals. It was commented that Cantilo secured attention but Hull secured a program. This provided:

1) An affirmation of continental solidarity

2) An expressed determination to maintain and defend the "absolute sovereignty" of the New World nations against all foreign intervention

3) The New World nations to proceed individually, with full recognition of their equality to make solidarity effective if any one of them were threatened

4) The ministers of foreign affairs of the American Republics to meet "when deemed desirable and at the initiative of any one of them" for consultation. [The resolution covering this proposal was to become known as the Declaration of Lima].[91]

The last provision had become a center of controversy. The United States wanted regular consultations at specified intervals; the Argentines wanted no such requirement. The wording agreed upon was in line with the Argentine desires but actually gave more freedom of action in meeting the emergencies of the approaching war. Professor Charles G. Fenwick commented that this Conference took the 115-year-old cornerstone of our foreign policy and converted it into a multilateral policy.[92] It was truly a landmark in the international history of the New World. The agreement for the meetings was in itself a weak and stumbling thing, but it was an accomplishment that had in it the makings of genuine cooperation. This fact became obvious a quarter of a century later in

[91] Department of State, *Peace and War*, pp. 440–441; *For. Rels., 1938*, V, 82 ff.; Charles G. Fenwick, "The Monroe Doctrine and the Declaration of Lima," *Amer. Jour. Internat. Law*, XXXIII, No. 2 (April, 1939), 264–265. For a general discussion of the Conference see *For. Rels., 1938*, V, 14 ff.; Beals *et al.*, *What South Americans Think of Us*, p. 256; Joseph Alsop and Robert Kintner, *American White Paper*, pp. 20–23.

[92] Charles G. Fenwick, "The Lima Conference in Relation to World Peace," *The Annals*, CCIV (July, 1939), 119–120.

the multilateral program applied to Cuba and again in 1965 in the multilateral intervention in Santo Domingo.

Numerous other resolutions and declarations were approved. These included substantial attention to the codification of international law and to the need for reasonable tariffs.[93] More important in view of European conditions was the common stand taken against any discrimination in the New World based on the grounds of race (the anti-Semitism program of Hitler was a latent danger that actually emerged in Bolivia and Argentina when Nazi victory appeared imminent in Europe), or on the basis of national origins (there was to be no Sudetenland in South Brazil).[94]

Foreign interest in the Conference was keen indeed. Germany and Italy engaged in active propaganda via newspapers and decorations displayed throughout the city.[95] Then, when the Conference was over, the German minister in Peru, putting the best face possible on the results of the Conference, reported to his home office:

> North America's plan of forming the entire continent into a military coalition under its own leadership has failed as completely as have its plans for establishing its economic hegemony by separating South America from Europe. On the other hand, the United States was successful in further inciting the continent against the authoritarian states, strengthening the democratic idea forming a united front against ideological influences and other external threats.
>
> Important resolutions of the Conference directed against us: Declaration of Lima, Declaration of American Principles, the resolutions denying minority character to foreign ethnic groups and opposing political group activities by foreigners. And especially the proposal on the racial question, which was adopted in considerably mitigated form after days of discussions.[96]

Conferences—Panama

On the heels of the Lima Conference the Second World War broke out. Here was a test of the significance of the Lima Declaration. As early as August 5 and 6 Welles and Roosevelt had drafted plans for a New World

---

[93] Spykman, *America's Strategy in World Politics*, p. 325; *Survey of Int. Affs., 1938*, pp. 684 ff.

[94] Charles A. Thompson, "Results of the Lima Conference," *For. Pol. Assn. Reports*, XV (1939–1940), No. 1, 3–4; *New York Times*, December 26, 1938, 22.1.

[95] *For. Rels., 1938*, V, 50–51.

[96] *Documents on German Foreign Policy*, Series D, V, 885–886.

meeting of Foreign Ministers if the European situation exploded.[97] On September 3, 1939. Secretary of State Hull asked eight Latin American governments if they thought a conference advisable. The next day favorable replies had been received from all, and on the fifth Panama issued invitations for the sessions to be held in that republic. Problems pending were legion. One question was what was to be done with sixty-six German vessels that were reported to be interned in ports of the American republics, plus sixteen more that were in Curaçao.[98] In addition there were questions of commerce raiding and of the rechanneling and protection of international trade.[99]

In advance of the meeting President Roosevelt, over the skepticism of Secretary Hull,[100] suggested naval patrol of neutral waters adjacent to the New World. When Welles was named to head the United States delegation to the Panama Conference he was entrusted with two primary objectives: the securing of the approval of the neutrality zone, a plan which had been suggested to the participating states in advance; and the establishment of a permanent economic commission to sit at Washington to help solve problems as they arose. By September 15 Welles was on his way. In a ten-day session (the final act was signed on October 3) attention was centered on the essential fact of continental neutrality. Three steps were taken to implement it: 1) A special neutrality committee was recommended; 2) An economic committee was approved; and 3) The neutrality zone was endorsed. On November 3 the Governing Board of the Pan-American Union announced that representatives of Argentina, Brazil, Chile, Costa Rica, Mexico, Venezuela, and the United States would constitute the Neutrality Committee, whose headquarters would be located at Buenos Aires.[101]

---

[97] Alsop and Kintner, *American White Paper*, pp. 51–52.

[98] By March, 1940, a total of ninety-three German vessels were reported as having been in New World ports since the opening of hostilities. Records were incomplete, but twenty-four were reported to have been scuttled, sunk, or captured. Apparently eleven made their way back to Europe and forty-nine remained interned. Of this last group a number were transferred to various South American flags and contributed no small amount to relieve trade pressures and to prepare for the new era (*For. Rels., 1940*, V, 409 ff., and *1941*, VII, 82 ff.).

[99] *Ibid., 1939*, V, 15 ff.

[100] Cordell Hull, *The Memoirs of Cordell Hull*, I, 690; Langer and Gleason, *Challenge to Isolation*, pp. 208 ff.

[101] "Report of the Delegate of the United States of America to the Meeting of the Foreign Ministers . . . held at Panama, September 23–October 3, 1939,"

The significance of immediate economic readjustments was obvious to all in the light of experience gained in World War I. Each country tended to send delegates in line with its own special problems. For instance, "the majority of the Cuban delegation was composed of sugar experts."[102] At the same time, Welles had the power to ruin or to succor a dozen or more of the countries whose trade with Germany had been destroyed. The United States was in the position of a man who "had suddenly become the only banker and grocer on his street."[103]

Of course Western Europe could do nothing but watch and wait. On October 5 Ambassador Joseph Kennedy in London sent word on a "Strictly personal for the President and Secretary" basis that Prime Minister Churchill gave sympathetic but restrained endorsement to the idea of the neutrality belt, asserting that if a commerce raider took refuge in the belt Great Britain would have to protect itself.[104] Publicly the British expressed fears that submarines out of Murmansk would take refuge in the prohibited area through the fogs off Scandanavia, Greenland, and Canada.[105] The hemisphere was a unit, as even the southern republics now began to realize.

Germany was especially interested. Its minister to Central America appeared in Panama with a considerable staff to "observe" the Conference. On hearing of the neutrality zone, his Foreign Office at once declared that the American governments had no right unilaterally to announce deviations from accepted rules of warfare. Further, they protested that the proposed zone partially surrounded and protected one of the belligerents, Canada.[106] The hemisphere again.

Conferences—Havana

The tempo of European events quickened. The Germans were everywhere victorious; Italy joined the apparent victor; and France fell on

---

Department of State Bulletin, I, No. 16 (October 14, 1939), 360, and No. 22 (November 25, 1939), 581; *For. Rels., 1939*, V, 47.

[102] Wood, *Making of the Good Neighbor Policy*, p. 311.

[103] Aikman, *All-American Front*, p. 10; *Department of State Bulletin*, I, No. 14 (September 30, 1939), 300 ff.

[104] *For. Rels., 1939*, V, 85.

[105] *Ibid., 1940*, I, 681 ff.

[106] *Documents on German Foreign Policy*, Series D, VIII, 86 ff., 347–348; *For. Rels., 1940*, I, 697–698; *New York Times*, September 20, 1939, 17.2.

June 17. That same day Secretary Hull advised his chiefs of mission in the American republics of developments and raised the question of another meeting. The meeting was agreed to and it assembled in mid-July. Of immediate concern was the fate of Danish, French, and even British possessions in the New World. Interestingly enough, the United States delegation to the Havana Conference included many economic experts but no military or naval men.[107] Apparently the hemisphere program was not primarily a military one.

The Latin American republics had now endorsed the cardinal principle of the Monroe Doctrine on a multilateral basis. Would they do the same for the no-transfer doctrine? Brazil was known to have ambitions for a mandate, or more, over the Guianas; Argentina longed for control of the Falkland Islands; and many of the Caribbean islands would form juicy morsels for acquisition by neighboring states, say Venezuela or Brazil. Also remembered was the fact that in World War I the United States had acquired the Danish West Indies for strategic purposes. Now Curaçao and its petroleum might be considered even more desirable. Cuba started talking about joint protectorates.[108] The ominous threat of a Nazi victory lent strength to pro-German activities in Argentina, Uruguay, and Brazil. To make matters worse, the illness of President Ortiz and the rise of a neutralist President in Argentina gave encouragement to German propaganda. The danger was that Latin America might decide either to get on the winning side, or at least "to walk with the devil" a bit. Argentina, certainly, appeared to be doing the latter.[109] Such were the pending problems.

At the opening of the Conference, Hull worked hard to secure endorsements for his proposals. As expected, there was little expressed opposition to the no-transfer idea. The rub came in defining procedures to implement the proposal. After prior warning to Great Britain, France, and the Netherlands, Secretary Hull launched his plan. It authorized any one country in case of pressing emergency to take preventive mili-

---

[107] *Second Meeting of the Foreign Ministers of the American Republics, Havana, Cuba,* July, 1940 (mimeographed by Pan-American Union, Washington, 1940). Also *Second Meeting of the Ministers of Foreign Affairs of the American Republics, Havana, Cuba, July, 1940. Report of the Secretary of State; For. Rels., 1940,* V, 180 ff.

[108] The *Times* (London), July 25, 1940, 4e; *U.S. in World Affs., 1940,* p. 141.

[109] Harold F. Peterson, *Argentina and the United States, 1810–1960,* pp. 401 ff.

tary action in a threatened colony, but hastened to add that provisional governments would be formed immediately.[110] These were to be composed of a commission of one member from each New World republic —multilateralism. President Roosevelt had been considering some such method of handling New World territories since December, 1938, and more definitely since early May, 1940.

Another resolution proclaimed that "any attempt on the part of a non-American state against the integrity or inviolability of the territory, the sovereignty or the political independence of an American state shall be considered an act of aggression against the states which sign this declaration." Reciprocal assistance was declared to be the duty of all American "States" in case such an act was committed. Not by accident was the term "States" used in place of the regular term "Republics." The door was open for Canadian inclusion—and Canadians were neither blind nor ungrateful.[111]

Germany again could only view the situation with concern. In spite of its European victories it could merely protest at what had been done in the Americas; even the blundering threat of its minister to Central America had backfired. The Foreign Office therefore sent a careful review of the actions of the Conference for the guidance of all its missions abroad.[112] Obviously its immediate concern was to try to forestall economic control of the Americas by the United States, and to prepare for future German trade with the area.[113] It bluntly rejected any suggestion

[110] This meant the United States might militarily occupy threatened French or Dutch islands. or that Venezuela or Brazil might interpose in such areas as Curaçao or the Guianas. Support of this proposal in the United States was widespread. When the Administration requested congressional approval the House of Representatives responded in the affirmative by a vote of 380 to 8 and the Senate acted unanimously (Langer and Gleason, *Challenge to Isolation*, pp. 624 ff., 695 ff.).

[111] Humphrey, *The Inter-American System*, pp. 263–264. Resolution XIV of the Conference recommended that the Governing Board of the Pan-American Union establish a committee of five (the United States, Mexico, Argentina, Brazil. and Cuba selected) to moderate disputes arising in the New World. This was duly established in Washington but did little or nothing until after the war, when it became quite active (see Gordon Connell-Smith, *The Inter-American System*, p. 115).

[112] *Documents on German Foreign Policy*, Series D, X, 449–450.

[113] *Ibid.*, pp. 229–230, 145–147. Also Reynolds, *Progress of Pan-Americanism*, p. 87.

of the pertinence of the no-transfer resolution to Germany,[114] but strove to direct attention to economics and trade.

[114] *Documents on German Foreign Policy,* Series D, IX, 603; X, 78. A recent study of the no-transfer idea at Havana may be secured in John A. Logan, *No Transfer: An American Security Principle,* pp. 287 ff. The regulations of the Conference are to be found on pp. 333–334.

CHAPTER XII

APPROACH TO WAR: ECONOMIC AND STRATEGIC

The Outlook

THE OUTBREAK OF WAR brought a realization that the solidarity of the hemisphere was not created of sentiment alone. Included in the conception were political, strategic, economic, and even cultural considerations. Canada quickly negotiated new trade agreements with Latin America —with Uruguay in 1937; Guatemala and Haiti in 1938; Santo Domingo in 1940; and Argentina, Brazil, and Chile in 1941—and sent missions to Ecuador and Peru, where they later secured trade conventions. Canadian export and import trade with Latin America increased from approximately $17.7 and $16.2 million in 1939 to over $60 and $86.6 million, respectively, in 1945.[1] The increase might have been only temporary but in a time of emergency it was a fact of significance.

Actual issues pending between the United States and Canada in 1938 included rivalry over air and mail routes between the United States and Alaska, the question of a Pacific coastal highway from the United States

[1] *Inter-American Affairs, 1945*, p. 91.

For trade agreements entered into see *British and Foreign State Papers, 1940–1942; Inter-American Affairs, 1941*, pp. 97 ff.; *Canada in World Affairs, 1941–1944*, pp. 137 ff.

On May 24, 1944, Canada and Brazil exchanged notes to provide for promotion of cultural relations by exchanging published materials, concerts, lectures, radio programs, and things artistic (*British and Foreign State Papers, 1943–1945*, pp. 539 ff.).

to Alaska, and the St. Lawrence Seaway. A fourth item, the negotiation of a trade agreement act was successfully accomplished in 1938.[2] The importance of the trade involved in the potential seaway was seldom appreciated. For instance, 111 million tons of freight passed through the Sault canals in 1941, while Panama was carrying only one-fourth that amount in 1939, and the Suez Canal only 30 million tons.[3] The total value and trends of Canadian international trade is seen from these figures:[4]

	Exports in thousands of Canadian Dollars		Imports in thousands of Canadian Dollars	
	To U.K.	To U.S.	From U.K.	From U.S.
1939	339,711	345,912	119,268	424,755
1945	963,238	1,196,977	140,517	1,202,418

A natural result was the contemplation of establishing an international commerce commission to consider such items as trade via the Panama Canal, the deepening of the Mississippi, a northern rail outlet between Hudson's Bay and the Great Lakes, and the St. Lawrence Seaway.[5] At the same time United States money was continuing to flow into Canada. Some four billion dollars invested north of the line at the beginning of the war had become approximately seven billion a decade later.[6] Economic solidarity, if not actual integration, of Canadian and United States business seemed to be in progress.

Similar developments took place toward the south. Welles informed delegates to the Panama Conference in September, 1939, that he was authorized to state that so long as the existing war situation continued, "the regular transportation facilities of the shipping lines between the United States and its American neighbors now in operation not only will not be curtailed, but will be strengthened and increased" as might be found desirable and feasible. He also pledged aid to curtail unwarranted fluctuations in inter-American exchange as well as efforts to meet essential needs for current and mill equipment, heavy goods, etc.,

[2] *Survey of Int. Affs., 1938,* I, 19 ff.; *U.S. in World Affs., 1938,* p. 204.

[3] John Bartlet Brebner, *North Atlantic Triangle,* p. 229. The seaway was opened in 1959, and traffic approximated 45,000,000 tons by 1965.

[4] *Inter-American Affairs, 1945,* pp. 94–95.

[5] William J. Wilgus, *Railway Interrelations of the United States and Canada,* pp. 233–234.

[6] Hugh L. Keenleyside, *Canada and the United States,* pp. 277 ff.

which would be financed by both long-term and short-term credit.[7] The Inter-American Financial and Economic Advisory Committee, with twenty-one representatives of the respective republics, met in Washington two months later. By the middle of May, 1940, plans were completed for an inter-American bank. Bolivia, Colombia, the Dominican Republic, Ecuador, Mexico, Nicaragua, Panama, Brazil, and the United States agreed to enter the project. Other ratifications were not forthcoming, however, and the proposal languished.[8] More successful were the efforts of the Financial and Economic Advisory Committee to establish an inter-American development commission for the exploitation of mineral, agricultural, and forest resources.[9] Likewise it sponsored an inter-American coffee-producers agreement signed at Washington on November 28, 1940. This assigned quotas to New World producers varying from 9,000,000 bags of sixty kilos each (about 130 lbs.) to Brazil down to 25,000 bags to Peru. Involved in the discussions with individual countries were projects varying from acquisition of strategic raw materials to purchase of the entire Cuban sugar crop for 1942.[10]

Prior to 1939 the Export-Import Bank had proceeded with extreme caution in extending produce loans to Latin America. Now the situation changed.[11] In September, 1941, congressional legislation authorized assistance "in the development of the resources, the stabilization of the economies, and the orderly marketing of the products of the countries of the Western Hemisphere by supplying funds, not to exceed $500 million outstanding at any one time." By the end of 1941 outstanding loans to Latin America exceeded $52 million, and total commitments had passed $262 million. A year later these figures had risen to $83 million and $349 million, respectively.

Axis trade with Latin America, which had burgeoned in the early 1930's, disappeared with the outbreak of the war. Also the Western and Southern European merchant marines were largely withdrawn for more vital services. At the same time intra-Latin American trade could do

---

[7] Sumner Welles, *The World of the Four Freedoms*, p. 5.

[8] *For. Rels., 1939*, V, 43–44; *1940*, V, 347 ff.; Eduardo Villaseñor, "The Inter-American Bank . . .," *For. Affs.*, XX (1941–1942), 166 ff.

[9] J. Lloyd Mecham, *The United States and Inter-American Security*, pp. 202 ff.

[10] *For. Rels., 1940*, V, 380 ff.; *1941*, VII, 237 ff.

[11] *U.S. in World Affs., 1939*, p. 241; *Inter-American Affairs, 1942*, p. 63; Raymond F. Mikesell, *United States Policy in International Relations*, pp. 207, 211.

little to take up the slack. Indeed, it amounted to only about 8 per cent of the area's entire world trade.[12] Also, strangely enough, per capita food production in Latin America in the 1930's had risen only about 2 per cent per year although population growth was in substantial excess of that figure.[13] Here was a matter of increasing concern for the few who realized that a major problem of the future was already emerging. The prognosis for postwar political health was not good.

Inevitably there appeared an intermingling of the economic and the strategic in United States relations with the southern republics. Some have said that the Good Neighbor policy ceased with the outbreak of war and that the Export-Import Bank illustrated the fact when it turned its attention to replacing German airline investments with United States control. Such statements are too simple. If single incidents are to be cited to prove a new "hard-nosed" dominance, single incidents of another type may be cited to indicate the contrary. At this time of fantastic national expenditure for war needs, the postage rates on books to New World countries were reduced to five cents per pound on packages up to twenty-two pounds. Also capable of mixed interpretations were purchases of huge amounts of unneeded products to relieve economic pressures in areas of over production: coffee was bought only to be stored in Brazil; and Nicaraguan, Haitian, and Peruvian cotton was purchased when huge reserves were already in United States warehouses.[14]

The reader should not forget that the financial foundation for new venture capital in Latin America became notoriously weak with the depression. In December, 1939, it was estimated that 77.1 per cent of Latin American dollar bonds were still in default, though direct investments had fared somewhat better with the trade revival that slowly followed the low point of the depression. Now, of some $7 billion in-

[12] David Efron, "Latin American Labor Comes of Age," *The Annals*, CCXL (July, 1945), 119. See Antonio Iraizoz, "Hacia un práctico Panamericanismo," *America*, VIII, 57–58.

[13] Simon G. Hanson, "Latin America and the Point Four Program," *The Annals*, CCLXVIII (March, 1950), 67; Laurence Duggan, *The Americas*, p. 27.

[14] Horace B. Davis, "Influences of the Second World War," in Latin American Economic Institute, *Economic Defense of the Western Hemisphere*, pp. 29–30; *Department of State Bulletin*, V, No. 106 (July 19, 1941), 66; Percy W. Bidwell, "Good Neighbors in the War, and After," *For. Affs.*, XXI (1942–1943), 526.

vested abroad, about $2,770 million were in Latin America, and of this, $1,550 million were estimated to be in South America.[15]

The British could be relied upon to keep an eye open to future trade possibilities. Even during the London blitz in 1940 Lord Willingdon was despatched to South America to mend trade fences.[16] For their part, the Germans insisted that Allied control of the seas was temporary. Western Europe would soon be conquered, then an all-out attack would be launched on British and United States dominance of Latin American trade. Reinforced economic missions were supplied with a complete arsenal of arguments with which to counter United States policy by stressing the inevitable victory of German might—hence Germany's value as a supplier and purchaser.[17] At the same time German agents in Latin America were instructed to negotiate contracts freely, even if they had to include clauses with provisions for 10 per cent to 20 per cent penalties for nondelivery of goods at specified dates. This practice was maintained in 1941 with Germany "scrupulously paying claims for nonperformance of contracts by means of Aski-mark credits."[18]

In a vain effort at self-help some regional trade meetings were called, as that of the River Plate countries and the Third Inter-American Conference of the Caribbean. These, however, so obviously lacked the essential component of a large buyer and had so little influence that other meetings proposed for the Amazon and Central American countries did not materialize.[19] For its part, the United States considered a variety of programs, even including the idea of a trade cartel to freeze trade into predetermined channels. Fortunately the idea never got beyond the planning stage. More conventional methods were to be employed.[20]

Mexico and the Caribbean

On April 2, 1938, came a major concession by the United States.

---

[15] *Inter-American Affs., 1942*, Appendix, pp. 200–201; Willy Feuerlein and Elizabeth Hannan, *Dollars in Latin America*, p. 15.

[16] Henry Albert Phillips, *Brazil, Bulwark of Inter-American Relations*, p. 212.

[17] *Documents on German Foreign Policy*, Series D, amply attests this. See X, 102–103, 172, 229–230, and 370.

[18] Donald Marquand Dozer, *Are We Good Neighbors?*, pp. 73–74.

[19] *Inter-American Affs., 1941*, pp. 58 ff.

[20] Dozer, *Are We Good Neighbors?*, pp. 72–73; William L. Langer and Everett S. Gleason, *The Challenge to Isolation*, pp. 633 ff.

Washington agreed that Mexico had the right to expropriate petroleum properties provided it reimbursed the concessionaires. Complicating the situation were questions of payment for agricultural lands expropriated. After extended negotiations Ambassador Daniels reported on May 31, 1939, that he had that day received a check for a million dollars as first payment on the sum agreed upon. The procedure followed for determining the value of lands involved was for each country to appoint a commissioner. When the two did not agree the question was referred to a sole arbiter, as provided in the Gondra Treaty of 1923.[21]

In approaching the petroleum settlement, each country held strong cards. Great Britain was so sure of its position that it stood flatly on its demand for arbitration under the Gondra Convention.[22] An additional trump card held by the United States was that its purchases of Mexican silver were a major prop to the southern economy. On the other hand, Mexico produced large quantities of raw materials essential to northern war industries. Various proposals, including arbitration which the British and Dutch consistently demanded, took up much of 1939.[23] Arbitrators notoriously tend to favor compromise, and Mexico felt it should pay far less than arbitrators were likely to award. It therefore proposed a two-man commission. Time passed and the tensions of war increased to reach a climax at Pearl Harbor at the end of 1941.

In 1939 Daniels had reported that the oil companies did not want to accept any settlement until after the elections of 1940, when they hoped an "apostle of the imperialist Big Stick" would come to power in Wash-

[21] *For. Rels., 1938*, V, 678 ff.; *1939*, V, 659 ff.; *U.S. in World Affs., 1938*, pp. 251 ff.

[22] "Correspondence with the Mexican Government . . . [concerning] Expropriation," *Accounts and Papers*, XXXI (1937–1938), 433 ff.

[23] For pressure on Mexico see the Josephus Daniels Papers, LC, Diary, Box 9, October, 1939. Also Daniels to Roosevelt, September 12, 1939, Franklin D. Roosevelt Papers, P.S.F. Mexico, 1938–1942; *For. Rels., 1939*, V, 697 ff.; *1940*, V, 946 ff.; Royal Institute of International Affairs, *Documents on International Affairs, 1938*, I, 427 ff.; *U.S. in World Affs., 1938*, pp. 257–258.

In response to nationalization of the oil fields by Mexico in 1938 Washington stopped the purchase of Mexican silver and boycotted oil imports from the expropriated fields. The Mexican peso fell 28 per cent. Daniels said that the termination of silver purchases was "like taking anaesthetics from a patient too soon" (Lloyd C. Gardner, *Economic Aspects of New Deal Diplomacy*, p. 115).

ington, and that a rightist successor of Cárdenas would inherit the halls of the Montezumas.[24] Instead, Roosevelt was re-elected and Manuel Ávila Camacho in Mexico continued the oil policy of his predecessor. Roosevelt and Daniels were viewing petroleum diplomacy in Mexico (as in the case of Bolivia) in the light of hemisphere needs in a time of world crisis. They might even sacrifice the best possible financial terms for private investors if by so doing national welfare could best be served. Hull, who really favored a sterner policy more in line with the British demands for arbitration, reluctantly went along with his Chief. The result was the acceptance of a Mexican proposal in the spring of 1942 which provided what the onetime owners of the properties considered little more than token payments.[25]

Mexico could breathe a sigh of relief. Sixty-seven per cent of its exports had been sent to the United States at the opening of 1938, and these had risen to 87 per cent in January, 1940. As one observer commented: "Mexico must export raw materials and has only one customer; she must have machinery and manufactured products but must buy in one country."[26] On the other hand, a memorandum of the State Department of May 12, 1942, summarized press opinion in the United States: ". . . newspapers from coast to coast had agreed three to one that the report of the experts [selected to determine the sum to be paid by Mexico] was 'hard on the companies' but of 'vital importance to maintain and strengthen friendly relations with Latin America' in war times."[27]

Farther south, highway surveys and construction proceeded steadily in the small republics, and the new trade agreement acts proved quite popular. Special attention was given to Panama, which cooperated by making bases throughout the republic available for defense purposes. The restless Roosevelt interest in anything dealing with the sea called

[24] Daniels to Roosevelt, January 31, 1939, Daniels Papers, LC, Correspondence with Roosevelt, Box 17.

[25] Robert H. Ferrell, *Amer. Secs. of St.*, XIII, 684 ff.; Bryce Wood, *Making of the Good Neighbor Policy*, pp. 205–206, 249.

[26] Maurice Halperin, "Mexico Shifts her Foreign Policy," *For. Affs.*, XIX (1940–1941), 220–221.

[27] Quoted by Wood, *Making of the Good Neighbor Policy*, p. 258. The same author notes the proposal by William Gibbs McAdoo for the United States to give Mexico $150 million, which that country would turn over to the oil companies at the same time that it ceded Lower California, including the mouth of the Colorado River, to the United States (p. 294).

for estimates on costs via alternate transit routes including a ten- to twelve-foot barge canal across Nicaragua, a ship-railway, and an ordinary steam railway across the Tehuantepec Isthmus in Mexico.[28] Also the War Department jealously watched interned vessels in the area, especially "a suspicious large liner of Italy" which it was feared might "be sunken so as to obstruct the [Canal] channel" in Panama.[29]

In the Caribbean islands there were similar situations. Cuba, flushed with war prosperity, negotiated a supplementary trade agreement but was discouraged from reckless negotiation of excessive loans.[30] A new convention was signed with Santo Domingo on September 24, 1940, to take the place of the treaty of December 27, 1924. This terminated the customs receivership that had been exercised since 1905. "The new convention provided for the establishment of a depository bank, to receive all Dominican revenues and funds, and to make no disbursement for the account of the Government until funds had been transmitted to pay interest and amortization charges on outstanding dollar bonds."[31]

In 1938 a cry of distress came from Haiti. The French were attempting to force payment of a pre-World War I loan in gold francs at some ten times the normal rate of exchange. The State Department advised ignoring the claim. France then cut off all coffee purchases from Haiti. To meet the resulting trade paralysis the Export-Import Bank extended a loan of $5.5 million. In addition, a joint development corporation was formed, similar to those recently established in Ecuador and Bolivia, to help stimulate trade and industry.[32] When the financial stringency continued, the interest rate on the loan was reduced to 4 per cent in

[28] Diary, November 27, 1948, December 12, 1940, and April 25, 1941, Henry L. Stimson Papers, Yale.

[29] *Ibid.*, March 7, 1941. Typical of the attention being paid to economic conditions was a survey or "educated guess" made by a State Department analyst of the Colombian debt. He reported that Americans owned $115 million out of a total debt of nearly $159 million. When a refunding loan for an additional $10 million was needed the Export-Import Bank announced the credit (Welles to Roosevelt, November 20, 1939, Roosevelt Papers, Hyde Park, Sumner Welles, 1939. Also *For. Rels., 1939*, V, 508 ff.; *1940*, V, 736; *1941*, V, 698 ff.).

[30] *Ibid., 1940*, V, 774 ff.

[31] *Inter-American Affairs, 1941*, p. 108. An interesting commentary, especially in view of later developments, was the report of Minister R. Henry Norweb on August 21, 1939, that treaty negotiations were dead and that no one would touch such a proposal until General Trujillo returned to the country (*For. Rels., 1939*, V, 587).

[32] *For. Rels., 1938*, V, 603 ff.; Duggan, *The Americas*, pp. 78–79.

1940. In September, 1941, came an executive agreement which terminated the offices of fiscal representative and deputy fiscal representative from the United States. Their duties were transferred to the reorganized Bank of Haiti, which was to supervise the accounting and disbursing systems, and the collecting of the internal revenue and customs of Haiti.[33]

The West Coast

Typical of the panmixia of conditions and actions of the time were relations with west coast countries of South America. Ecuador had signed a trade agreement, and when need arose in 1940 an Export-Import Bank loan authorized purchase of $900,000 of United States products and services for highway construction, $200,000 for purchase of locomotives and railway cars in the United States, and $50,000 for research on disease-resistant strains of cacao.[34] Throughout 1938 Peru proved unwilling to make payments on outstanding bonds in spite of general economic prosperity. Accordingly, the Export-Import Bank declined to authorize new loans. By the fall of 1939 came reports that Peru had lost the sale of 20 to 25 per cent of its cotton which theretofore had been sold to Germany, and of 35 per cent of the cotton it had regularly sold to Great Britain. The American chargé reported that the Peruvian President pounded his chair and complained that the United States helped only the east coast countries. The clamor for aid specified that $15 million was essential. Eventually two-thirds of that sum was authorized.[35]

In Bolivia the period from 1937 to 1940 saw more or less constant negotiation on the claims of Standard Oil of Bolivia. For the most part the State Department and its legation at La Paz restricted their services to good offices. No solution of the problem was reached until after the Japanese attack on Pearl Harbor. Immediately both nations realized that the situation might become urgent. When the Rio Conference met, the Bolivian Minister of Foreign Affairs suggested that his country might pay one million dollars to the company. New discussions then led to a settlement on April 22, 1942, by which the company received

[33] *For. Rels., 1940*, V, 922; *Inter-American Affairs, 1941*, p. 107.

[34] *For. Rels., 1940*, V, 875. For the trade treaty see Department of State, *Executive Agreement Series*, No. 133.

[35] For this Peruvian story see *For. Rels., 1938*, V, 874 ff.; *1939*, V, 773 ff.; *1940*, V, 1140 ff.

$1.5 million with accrued interest for a total sum of $1,729,375.[36] Now the way was cleared for the establishment of a new economic development program in Bolivia costing some $25 million.

Up to this date United States industry had largely used East Indian tin, but with the Japanese advance on Malaya a new $13 million plant was built to smelt Bolivian tin at Texas City on the Gulf of Mexico. In line with this, by October, 1940, Secretary of State Hull could report that the Metals Reserve Company, a subsidiary of the Reconstruction Finance Corporation, had signed a contract for 18,000 long tons of Bolivian fine tin per year. The contract was for a period of five years, at a price 1.5 cents below the company's buying price, or, if no such price existed at the moment, the figure would be 1.5 cents below the current New York price.[37]

When the army officer Germán Busch announced that he had assumed control of the government of Bolivia, the State Department, doubtless with considerable reluctance, took the position that a change from a totalitarian to a nontotalitarian form, or the reverse, did not in itself justify withdrawal of recognition. This of course had been the policy followed in the case of the accession of Hitler, Mussolini, and others to power. Soon the awkward situation was modified when Busch committed suicide and General Carlos Quintanilla became Provisional President with the old Busch Cabinet. On August 28, 1939, Hull again sent word to continue recognition.[38]

A good example of paternal and neighborly services rendered to Bolivia arose when that country received estimates of costs for construction of a railroad from Chile via Bolivia to Santos, Brazil. Only a part of the construction was estimated to cost from twenty-three to twenty-nine million dollars. Quietly an army engineer from the United States estimated that the cost of a six-meter (twenty-foot)-wide highway, covered with a 2.5 inch bituminous top, would cost less than seven million and would accommodate eight hundred vehicles daily.[39]

In Chile the accent was on copper. Long negotiation accompanied by substantial horse-trading had preceded a provisional trade agree-

[36] Wood, *Making of the Good Neighbor Policy*, p. 184. Also *For. Rels., 1937*, V, 296 ff.; *1938*, V, 323 ff.; *1939*, V, 328 ff.; *1940*, V, 513 ff.

[37] *Ibid., 1939*, V, 303 ff.; *1940*, V, 530 ff. Also Dozer, *Are We Good Neighbors*, p. 76; Feuerlein and Hannan, *Dollars in Latin America*, p. 74.

[38] *For. Rels., 1939*, V, 310.

[39] *Ibid., 1940*, V, 549 ff.

ments act that finally took effect January 5, 1940.[40] With the outbreak of war, Chilean copper, nitrate, iodine, and iron were in inexhaustible demand. Yet Chile complained that its trade entered a one-way street. Finally Ambassador Bowers wrote directly to President Roosevelt saying that Chile exported about 2,000,000 tons of iron ore per year to the United States, and asking why it could not get back the 80,000 tons of finished products so badly needed. When it sent 400,000 tons of copper north it could not understand why it could not get back some copper wire. When Chile's application for tin plate was declined it nevertheless found it could buy 10,000 tons of United States tin plate "which had been sent to Argentina."[41] Other complications arose from the fact that Chileans, having secured an authorization for Export-Import Bank credits up to $12 million, wished to use this as an "open" credit against which to make general purchases. The Bank, however, insisted that it had the right to approve individual items. In practice this was more of an irritation than a handicap, for of the first specific request for $656,000 of materials all but $6,489 worth were allowed.[42] To Washington, war-time control was a necessity; to Chile it was infuriating.

The East Coast

While German propaganda played no mean role in Argentine thinking,[43] the fact must be emphasized that trade was the cardinal factor in the republic's foreign policy. An especially awkward situation arose concerning corn (maize). The local 1940 crop was in excess of 10.5 million tons, or more than twice that of the previous year. Continental Europe had consumed more than half the Argentine crop but now was out of the market. Prices dropped to twenty-five cents a bushel, at which price the grain was being used for fuel. When the United States sold some of its government-subsidized stocks, Argentina was convinced that this was a deliberate effort to kick a man already down. Not surprisingly, all efforts to make a corn-marketing agreement between Argentina and the United

[40] *Ibid.*, *1937*, V, 391 ff.; *1939*, V, 429; *1940*, V, 681. For the personal interest of the President see Roosevelt Papers, Hyde Park, O.F. 303, Claude G. Bowers, including letter of Roosevelt to Bowers, January 4, 1940.

[41] Bowers to Welles, October 9, 1941, *ibid.*

[42] *For. Rels.*, *1940*, V, 686.

[43] Department of State, *Consultation Among the American Republics with Respect to the Argentine Situation*, pp. 49 ff.

States failed.[44] The slight improvement in the Argentine national economy arising from an increase in industrial employees from 462,00 in 1935 to 829,000 in 1941 was wholly inadequate to meet the needs,[45] and affected an entirely different group of people.

To save its meat trade with Great Britain and to crash the Empire trade controls set up by the Ottawa Agreement, Buenos Aires had made concessions to British capital invested in the meat industry. It also agreed to highway-building programs and railroad controls that gave substantial advantages to British-owned railways. The resulting "exploitation" by the "British owned octopus" was bitterly resented. Disgruntled with the United States and unhappy with its British connections, the Argentines were receptive to the siren call of German propaganda[46] even though trade connections were wholly disrupted—and the Allies were blamed for that also.

Levelheaded observers readily conceded the justice of the economic plaints of the Argentines,[47] and Roosevelt himself was alert to the situation. A file memorandum from Hyde Park in the President's handwriting under date of March 29, 1939, carries this notation:

HENRY WALLACE

I want State Department to go ahead with the Argentine Trade Agreement.

F.D.R.[48]

Negotiations continued through 1939 and 1940. Finally on October 14, 1941, the first trade agreement in ninety years between the United States and its southern neighbor was signed at Buenos Aires. This was supplemented by an Export-Import Bank loan of $60 million to foster trade,

[44] Percy W. Bidwell, *Economic Defense of Latin America*, p. 17; *For. Rels., 1940*, V, 484 ff.

[45] Ysabel F. Rennie, *The Argentine Republic*, pp. 328–329; Arthur P. Whitaker, *The United States and Argentina*, p. 35.

[46] *Documents on German Foreign Policy*, Series D, IX, 495, 531, 615; George Pendle, *Argentina*, p. 67; Ysabel Fisk, "Argentina: the Thirteen Year Crisis," *For. Affs.*, XXII (1943–1944), 259–260.

[47] Nicholas John Spykman, *America's Strategy in World Politics*, p. 328; Charles G. Fenwick, "The Lima Conference . . . [and] World Peace," *The Annals*, CCIV (July, 1949), 123.

[48] Roosevelt Papers, Hyde Park, O.F. 366 A-B, Folder 366A, 1937–1939.

and a Treasury Department credit of $50 million to help stabilize the Argentine peso.[49]

An amazing amount of heat was generated by the importation of Argentine corned beef into the United States. At the same time domestic producers protested vehemently the purchase of Argentine meat for the armed forces. On May 15, 1939, Sumner Welles reported to the President that the low bid of the Argentine Meat Producers Cooperative on forty-eight thousand pounds of corned beef for the use of the Navy had been 9.73 cents per pound and that the lowest bid from local packers had been 21.61 cents. He added that even when customs duties had been added the price of the southern product was only 15.73 cents, leaving a differential that amounted to more than 50 per cent.[50] The chief argument of the United States cattle raisers was danger of hoof-and-mouth disease, even though investigation showed that the infected Argentine areas were far from the regions from which the imports derived.

Investigation showed that substantial quantities of the meat were already coming into this country through regular trade channels. A telegram to the President from Sioux Falls, South Dakota, dated May 19, 1939, stated that the sender could find no United States corned beef in twenty-one local retail grocery stores in that meat-producing and beef-packing area. All of them seemed to be stocking South American products.[51] Another telegram from Pueblo, Colorado, on May 18, stated that if the local United States senator (who had been protesting the purchase of Argentine beef for the United States Navy) wanted to eat canned beef in his home community he would have to use a South American product. The reporter had found six brands for sale in Pueblo —but all were from South America, according to the labels.[52]

The Argentines were busy seeking local remedies. Captured German documents indicate that the Argentine ambassador in Berlin informed the German Foreign Office of plans for a customs union to include Uruguay, Paraguay, and Bolivia; and that his home government had also been exploring possibilities of such an arrangement with Brazil.

[49] *For. Rels., 1939,* V, 255, 293 ff.; *1940,* V, 460 ff. See Cordell Hull, *The Memoirs of Cordell Hull,* II, 1140.

[50] Welles to Roosevelt, May 15, 1939, Roosevelt Papers, Hyde Park, Sumner Welles, 1939.

[51] R. R. Benedict to Roosevelt, May 19, 1939, *ibid.,* O.F. 526, Government Contracts—Argentine Corned Beef Folder.

[52] *Ibid.*

Berlin was inclined to encourage the idea, feeling that it did not infringe on existing German trade treaties with Argentina. In any case there was little that Berlin could do about the proposal at the time though it did note that future complications might arise from ensuing industrialization. When a trade conference was held in Montevideo (actually of little significance) Berlin could merely express the hope that it might tend to make the area independent of the United States and thus help Germany indirectly.[53]

Uruguay itself faced the fact that the small states of Europe, dominated by Germany by mid-1940, had actually bought 46 per cent of Uruguayan exports while Britain had taken only 26 per cent. If Great Britain collapsed, Uruguay would inevitably fall under Nazi economic control unless the United States came to the rescue. Meanwhile Germany was reported to be promising delivery of goods for the following October. The response of the United States was made on December 12, when the Secretary of State sent word that the Export-Import Bank had extended $7.5 million in credits for various projects. In addition, requests for financing of arms purchases were under active consideration.[54]

Development Commissions, an outgrowth of the conference at Panama, opened in Uruguay, Paraguay, and Argentina. These included some of the best economic brains of the countries concerned. For instance, the one in Argentina had as its chairman the general manager of the Banco Central, who had just returned from Washington, where he had arranged details of the $110 million Argentine credits.[55] Paraguay, too, received small credits from the Export-Import Bank.[56]

In Brazil the German-United States rivalry was especially acute. Word was sent to the German embassy in Rio de Janeiro that Berlin stood ready to increase its average purchases of Brazilian produce from the prewar figure of 170 million reichsmarks to 300 million reichsmarks. Of the total, 30 per cent would be in coffee and the same amount in cotton. Payment would include 100 million reichsmarks of artillery equipment,

[53] *Documents on German Foreign Policy*, Series D, XI, 933 ff., 1177; *New York Times*, January 19, 1941, 21.1.

[54] *For. Rels., 1940*, V, 1168 ff.

[55] *Department of State Bulletin*, IV, No. 86 (February 15, 1941), 181–182. The *Bulletin* notes that twenty New World republics had established these commissions (VI, No. 134 [January 17, 1942], 68).

[56] *For. Rels., 1939*, V, 762 ff.

50 million of railway rolling stock, and a steel mill valued at 70 million.[57] Brazil, however, had asked the United States Steel Corporation to consider construction of a steel mill. After various proposals discussed over a number of months, it was agreed that Brazil would put up milreis equivalent in value to $25 million while the Export-Import Bank would provide as much as $20 million for equipment and the hiring of engineering and professional talent. The money was advanced at 4 per cent interest, and the necessary agreements were signed on September 26, 1940.[58] This placing of orders in the United States instead of in Germany had become "very noticeable" by the fall of 1939. It was the more easily accomplished once the Brazilian exchange situation improved and the blocked payments of arrears of profits and dividends were released.[59]

One harbinger of the future lay in cotton production and export. In 1933 cotton provided only two-tenths of one per cent of Brazilian exports, but by 1937 it accounted for 20 per cent of the country's exports. Increasingly this competition was brought home to the United States. Over the years sale of the fleecy staple to Canada was considered a natural monopoly of the United States and for the five years ending in 1940 annual sales to Canada had averaged 300,000 bales. But in the year ending July 31, 1941, sales had dropped to 194,000 bales, while Brazilian shipments to the Dominion reached some 450,000 bales. Efforts to secure a fifty-fifty division of the Canadian market found Brazil in no hurry to forego its new-found outlet.[60]

Argentine beef and Brazilian cotton sold at prices with which Yankee producers simply could not compete—one of the new facts of hemisphere trade.

Strategic—The Northern Zone

Strategic considerations for the hemisphere upon the outbreak of the war may be discussed for three geographical sections. First, there was the northern area including Canada with both its Atlantic and its Pacific approaches. The second region included the vital Panama Canal and its

[57] *Documents on German Foreign Policy*, Series D, IX, 598, 630, 659. Also Vol. X, various references, but especially pp. 177–178.

[58] *For. Rels., 1940*, V, 601 ff.

[59] *Ibid., 1939*, V, 400 ff.

[60] *Ibid., 1941*, III, 136 ff.; Pan-American Union, *Bulletin*, LXXII, No. 5 (May, 1938), 302.

outposts in the two oceans. Here were found both the Canal itself and raw materials of primary importance. The third was the lower part of the South American continent. This lay below the shoulder of Brazil, or south of about 10° to 15° south latitude. Defense of the first two were taken for granted; defense of the third was a question for debate.

The personal contacts between Roosevelt and his Canadian counterparts continued happy indeed. On October 5, 1939, the President frankly wrote Governor General Lord Tweedsmuir (John Buchan, the well-known historian) that it appeared unwise for the latter to visit Hyde Park at that time. He said that he had recently addressed Congress on modification of the neutrality laws; ". . . as you have probably sensed, I am almost literally walking on eggs." "I am at the moment saying nothing, seeing nothing and hearing nothing." As soon as the bill is through it would be "all to the good" for the visit to take place.[61] These personal contacts were widely praised. In the British Parliament the role of Canada as a connecting link with the United States was attributed "in no small measure to the personal friendship between the Canadian Prime Minister and the American President which rids contact between them, whether by telephone or in the flesh, of every vestige of formality."[62]

Over the years Roosevelt's feeling of responsibility for Canada had increased. As early as August 14, 1936, he had sent up a trial balloon at Chatauqua, New York, when he asserted that the United States would, if necessary, defend Canadian territory as it would its own. Little attention was paid to this. Two years later, August 18, 1938, on receiving an honorary degree from Queen's University (Kingston, Ontario) he said: "The Dominion of Canada is part of the sisterhood of the British Empire. I give you the assurance that the people of the United States will not stand idly by if Dominion of Canada soil is threatened by any other empire."[63]

Canadians applauded the recent billion-dollar appropriation for the United States Navy to the point that officials in Ottawa "were obliged to deny rumors that the two countries had reached an agreement on

---

[61] Roosevelt Papers, Hyde Park, P.S.F. Canada, 1933–1941.

[62] *Official Report of the Debates of the House of Commons of the Dominion of Canada* (2d Sess., 19th Par [1940]), I, 6.

[63] Royal Institute of International Affairs, *Documents on International Affairs, 1938,* I, 416.

defense plans."[64] Now they greeted the Roosevelt statement enthusiastically.[65] Officially Washington brushed off the pledge as merely a
natural application of the Monroe Doctrine. The *New York Times*, however, pertinently noted that the timing of the statement was more significant than its content. England, France, and Czechoslovakia cordially
applauded the statement; Berlin, Tokyo, and Rome received it cooly.[66]
A year later the President at a press conference reaffirmed his pledge to
Canada even after that country was in the war. He also calmly accepted
a comment of the British Information Ministry that this placed Canada
in a special position with regard to its defense.[67] Students of history
noted that in 1914–1915 Canada had asked for Japanese war vessels to
protect its Pacific coast when the British Navy was busy elsewhere; but
in 1938 when the Royal Navy could defend the Atlantic only the
United States became responsible for the Pacific coasts of Canada in
the face of Japan as a potential enemy.[68]

Representative of public opinion were the *Fortune* polls on whether
the United States should defend by force three selected countries. The
results showed affirmative answers as follows:

	January 1939	January 1940	August 1940
Canada	73.1%	74.2%	87.00%
Mexico	43.0	54.4	76.50
Brazil	27.0	36.8	54.17[69]

Very surely, and speedily at that, the public was absorbing something
of the sense of urgency with which the Roosevelt Administration viewed
events.

Lord Lothian presented his credentials as British ambassador at
Washington on August 31, 1939. He reported that he found "nothing
neutral" in the President's attitude. He gathered that if war broke out in
Europe the Neutrality Act would be applied in about five days but if the
hostilities were defined as a "police action" the act might not be invoked
at all. Even if the act were applied, the President, he felt, "would not

[64] *U.S. in World Affs., 1938*, p. 211.
[65] *Survey of Int. Affs., 1938*, I, 634–635.
[66] *New York Times*, August 20, 1938, 1, 3, 14.
[67] *Ibid.*, September 13, 1939, 1.6. Also Edward O. Guerrant, *Roosevelt's Good
Neighbor Policy*, pp. 138–139.
[68] *Survey of Int. Affs., 1938*, I, 636.
[69] Dexter Perkins, *Hands Off*, pp. 376–377.

declare aluminum sheets or engine blocks as aeroplane parts."[70] As a matter of fact, it later became known that as early as the spring of 1937 conversations between Mackenzie King and Roosevelt reached agreement for informal staff conversations between leading officers of the two countries. Rumors of these leaked out in 1938 only to be flatly denied, as noted above; yet the two leaders had discussed problems of defense at Kingston, Ontario, in 1938, at Washington that fall, and at Warm Springs in April of 1940.[71] Thus the ground for the later Ogdensburg Agreements was well broken.

Hostilities began in August, 1939. At the suggestion of Secretary of State Hull, Roosevelt telephoned to inform Mackenzie King that since Canada had not yet declared war it was not included in the neutrality proclamation being issued. When Canada formally entered war the proclamation was only applied as of September 10—another little courtesy that was greatly appreciated. In interpreting the neutrality laws, Canadians were given many privileges. Airplanes were pushed or towed across the boundary, hence not classed as finished military machines; port restrictions were waived; American oil was brought north by sea; and Canadians could trade via American ships with regions otherwise closed to them as belligerents.[72]

Now events moved fast. Canada was seriously short of munitions and asked Washington for an extended list of supplies. In spite of its own rapidly increasing needs, the answer was a promise of 80,000 Enfield rifles and 4,000,000 rounds of .30-calibre ammunition.[73] In mid-August, 1940, Roosevelt, Secretary of War Stimson, and the chairman of the House Committee on Military Affairs met Mackenzie King at Ogdens-

---

[70] *Documents on British Foreign Policy, 1919–1939*, Series 3, VII, 428.

On September 20, 1938, Sir Ronald Lindsay reported to Lord Halifax on a highly secret interview with Roosevelt, kept secret even from the State Department. In this the President was reported to have suggested a conference in some neutral area, which he might attend in person, to reorganize European boundaries. He advised that the British engage in a defensive war by blockade and resistance to attack only. The United States could aid in a blockade situation (Lindsay recalled Roosevelt's quarantine idea) (*ibid.*, pp. 627 ff.).

[71] Grant Dexter, "Canadian-American Relations in Defense," *Conference on Canadian-American Affairs, 1941*, p. 46; *U.S. in World Affs., 1940*, pp. 195 ff.

[72] Hull, *Memoirs*, I, 678–679; John MacCormac, *Canada: America's Problem*, pp. 43–44.

[73] Stetson Conn and Byron Fairchild, *The Framework of Hemisphere Defense*, p. 369.

burg, New York, near the Canadian border. On the eighteenth, announcement was made for a joint board for defense—and this was with a
country that was a part of the British Empire. Not a treaty, this agreement fit into the general defense program of the United States.[74] It was
restricted to a common study and report on mutual problems. As a
Canadian put it: "In so far as defense is concerned, Canada entered the
Pan American system through the back door," for now it was obligated
to study defense for a substantial portion of Latin America.[75]

Meanwhile the destroyer-for-bases deal had about jelled. In fact,
Roosevelt told Mackenzie King about it at Ogdensburg.[76] For this study
the significance of the arrangement rested in the question of bases,
rather than in that of aid to beleaguered Britain. On the same day,
August 16, that Roosevelt notified the press that negotiations were under
way with Canada for the defense of the continent, he also stated that
negotiations were in process with Britain on naval and air bases.[77] Six
of these were in the Caribbean area and were vital for protection of the
Canal. They were exchanged on a ninety-nine-year basis for overage
destroyers and arms. On the other hand, a base in the Bermuda Islands
and another in Newfoundland were outright gifts for the defense of
British interests in the hemisphere. This was implementing the new
interpretation of the Monroe Doctrine with a vengeance. No wonder
Count Chiano recounts in his diary that on receipt of this news there
was great excitement in Berlin.[78]

On September 3 Roosevelt notified Congress of the amazing executive
agreement he had consummated. He skillfully commented: "This is the
most important action in the reinforcement of our national defense that
has been taken since the Louisiana Purchase."[79] This delicately reminded Congress of another somewhat extracurricular move of another
strong President who found himself in circumstances in which reference
to expected, if not established, constitutional procedures was inadvisable. The President emphasized that the arrangement constituted ex-

[74] F. R. Scott, *Canada and the United States*, pp. 7, 58 ff.

[75] John P. Humphrey, *The Inter-American System*, pp. 16–17.

[76] Diary, August 17, 1940, Stimson Papers, Yale. Also Conn and Fairchild,
Framework of Hemisphere Defense, pp. 371–372.

[77] *Official Report of the Debates* (2d Sess., 19th Par. [1940]), I, 54.

[78] Samuel Eliot Morison, *History of United States Naval Operations in World
War II*, I, 34.

[79] Hull, *Memoirs*, I, 841–842; Department of State, *Peace and War*, pp. 564 ff.;
Langer and Gleason, *Challenge to Isolation*, pp. 760 ff.

change of vessels, relatively useless to the United States, for bases considered absolutely vital to continental defense. A press release of the Secretary of State on September 7 commented: "The resulting facilities at these bases will, of course, be made available alike to all American republics on the fullest cooperative basis for the common defense of the hemisphere and in entire harmony with the spirit of the pronouncements made and the understandings reached at the conferences of Lima, Panama, and Habana."[80]

Newfoundland had long been a strategic outpost of Canada; now it held the same significance for the United States. Inevitably, therefore, Canada was deeply interested in the negotiations. In fact, the first report of the new Permanent Joint Board on Defense raised the question of Canadian-United States cooperative action for the protection of Newfoundland.[81]

The conception of defense needs expanded steadily. In spite of the recent Senate defeat of the St. Lawrence Seaway project on October 5, 1940, the State Department now announced "preliminary and other engineering investigations" of the new waterway. Two days later the President notified Congress that he had allocated a million dollars from a special defense fund to the Army Engineering Corps and to the Federal Power Commission for the purpose. He commented that the seaway had once been an "opportunity" but that it had now become a "necessity" to provide access to a haven in which to build ships for ocean traffic. And only shipyards on the Great Lakes could be the answer when merchant shipping was being sunk by "tens of thousands of tons a month."[82]

---

[80] *Department of State Bulletin*, III, No. 63 (September 7, 1940), 196.

Stetson Conn, Rose C. Engelman, and Byron Fairchild, report that the actual cost of the installations at the eight bases was slightly more than $242,500,000. Most of the construction work was done by local labor, only some 7,400 Americans being engaged (*The United States Army in World War II*, pp. 378, 381).

[81] *Ibid.*, p. 364; *Canada in World Affairs, 1939–1941*, pp. 213 ff.

An interesting comment appears in the diary of E. M. House (Yale), July 20, 1914, concerning a talk of House with Lord Northcliffe in which the latter referred to the population of 230,000 Newfoundlanders as "an aggressive lot . . . [who] get more titles and have more government flummery than an ordinary empire. They tax imports enormously, and dislike Americans almost as much as they do Canadians. . . . the Newfoundland governmental machinery reminded one of an elephant trappings placed on a rat."

[82] *U.S. in World Affs., 1940*, p. 211.

An aroused interest in global maps and geography stimulated a new interest in Canada as the logical highway for cross-polar traffic, to say nothing of new thinking about both coasts of the two countries. Strategists began realizing that certain Alaskan bases were as close to the Panama Canal by air as those long-recognized ocean outposts of the Canal, the Hawaiian Islands. Also, in spite of its appalling climate, the potential value of Alaska as a springboard for penetration into the American continent could no longer be ignored. The treaty of Washington of 1922 had forbidden Japanese fortification of islands in the North Pacific and restricted the size of the Japanese Navy. This left Alaska relatively safe. But as soon as Japan withdrew from the naval limitation treaty, the Hepburn Board recommended (December, 1938) that Congress appropriate $19 million for defense installations by army and air corps in Alaska. Work began at Sitka and Zodiak within a year and by the middle of 1940 additional bases were authorized at Dutch Harbor. General Marshall first despatched a limited defense force, but the troops were steadily increased until by December, 1941, protective forces for the naval bases amounted to 21,500 men, plus an emergency garrison of 24,000.[83]

Still more problems arose in the North Atlantic. Greenland was a Danish colony; yet it was now an important outpost of the Americas. When Germany overran the Low Countries, Greenland was in imminent danger. Canada proposed the establishment of a "guard service" for the area but was informed on April 16, 1940, that Washington "was extremely anxious that no action of this kind be taken by the Canadian Government." Three days later Hull notified the Canadian minister, Mr. Norman Davis, that the chairman of the American Red Cross was going to look into the needs of the Greenlanders and "we would, of course, be able to look into any and all aspects of the situation there." The reason for such care was the danger that any action classed as "military" might be invoked as a precedent for Japanese expansion into the Netherlands' East Indies.[84]

[83] Conn, Engelman, and Fairchild, U.S. Army in World War II, pp. 223 ff. Alaska was also potentially valuable as one base for a pincer movement on Japan via the Kamchatka Peninsula or Siberia in advancing on Vladivostok (Diary, October 28, 1941, Stimson Papers, Yale).

[84] Hull to Roosevelt, undated but approximately April 22, 1940, Roosevelt Papers, Hyde Park, P.S.F. Canada, 1933–1941; Hull, Memoirs, I, 755–756. Also Langer and Gleason, Challenge to Isolation, pp. 429 ff.

On May 3 Greenland followed the lead of Iceland and declared independence of its German-occupied homeland, though it reaffirmed allegiance to its old sovereign. By April, 1941, the next step was in order. On the ninth an agreement was signed with a representative of the old Danish government giving the United States full rights to erect defense works and to protect the territorial integrity of Greenland. The resulting program included a dog-sledge patrol and an air and a naval patrol.[85] The day following the signature a White House press release announced inclusion of Greenland "in our system of cooperative hemisphere defense." This was clearly a bow in the direction of the Act of Havana of the previous July. The press release continued: ". . . we propose to make sure that when the German invasion of Denmark has ended, Greenland will remain a Danish colony."[86] As Stimson put it, the statement meant that if Germans landed in Greenland "we would put them out."[87]

Iceland presented an even more difficult decision. In July, September, and December, 1940, the island authorities had offered the United States air and naval bases. So long as it was defended by Great Britain it was a legitimate point of attack by the Nazis, hence occupation by the United States might be considered a direct provocation to Germany. Protection of the Azores was felt to be less of a provocation and could be better defended on the grounds of defense of the Western Hemisphere. Finally, in June, 1941, the decision was reached. By the time of the Japanese attack on the United States some ten thousand troops were located on this North Atlantic outpost.[88] Short of a major military effort, the fortification precluded use of the island for German bases from which to attack the west, though it must be admitted that protection of the convoy routes was the primary purpose of the occupation from the beginning.[89]

Strategic—The Central Zone

With the fall of France and the Low Countries, accentuated by the London blitz, the danger of Nazi occupation of New World possessions of

[85] Conn, Engelman, and Fairchild, *U.S. Army in World War II*, p. 457.

[86] *Department of State Bulletin*, IV, No. 94 (April 12, 1941), 443.

[87] Diary, April 10, 1941, Stimson Papers, Yale.

[88] Conn, Engleman, and Fairchild, *U.S. Army in World War II*, p. 533. The same authors state that by the end of 1942 the United States had up to 41,000 men in nearly three hundred posts scattered around the forty thousand square miles of Iceland (pp. 535–538).

[89] Conn and Fairchild, *Framework of Hemisphere Defense*, pp. 132–133.

the conquered countries was greatly feared. Could the no-transfer idea be made effective? The alternatives were either forced sales (as in the case of the Danish West Indies in World War I) or military occupation of threatened points.[90] Of immediate concern was Surinam (Dutch territory), whence came some 60 percent of the aluminum used by United States industry. Also Curaçao and Aruba were of untold value for petroleum supply. Great Britain hesitated to move into any of these islands for fear the action could be taken as justification for Japanese advance into the East Indies. Brazil sent troops to its northern frontier as a gesture of cooperation and the United States sent guards to help protect the bauxite mines.[91] For its part, "The Navy looked with covetous eyes on Fort de France [Martinique] as the best naval and air base between Puerto Rico and Trinidad." The French commanding officer was persuaded to accept a naval observer to help watch demobilized French warships in the port while the United States kept the island supplied with essentials no longer available from Europe. Admiral George Robert, of Martinique, carefully gave no occasion for further action though he needled the Allies by allowing broadcasts of the Nazi line. "So [as Morrison says] sleeping dogs, grounded planes and anchored ships were allowed to lie."[92]

As early as April, 1940, a proposal was sent to the President via his wife suggesting that the United States take over the British, Dutch, and French Guianas to produce tropical products in a "new American frontier." FDR responded that the Guiana coast had a "vile" lowland climate and that the interior was "unexplored and inaccessible." He was very doubtful "if the United States should undertake sovereignty or sole charge of development"; instead, he said he was thinking of some kind of Pan-American trusteeship for situations of this kind. The suggestion was referred to Welles, who commented: "I believe there is nothing that would more rapidly and completely destroy the relationship between the United States and the other American republics . . . than for the United States herself to acquire territory in South America." The trusteeship idea, he felt, was "the only possible solution."[93]

[90] As early as 1936 a thorough canvass had been made of the possibility of acquiring some of these European colonies in return for cancellation of European War Debts. For the time being the step was considered unwise (ibid., p. 11).

[91] Hull, Memoirs, I, 814 ff.; Department of State Bulletin, V, No. 127 (November 29, 1941), 425.

[92] Morison, U.S. Naval Operations, I, 33. Also Langer and Gleason, Challenge to Isolation, pp. 733–734; Hull, Memoirs, I, 818 ff.

[93] Hart to Mrs. Roosevelt, April 20, 1940, and Roosevelt to "E.R." May 4,

The cession of the British bases in the destroyer deal relieved the pressure substantially. The land screen of World War I was now reinforced with the new holdings in Bermuda, the Bahamas, Jamaica, Antigua, Saint Lucia, Trinidad, and British Guiana.

Periodically Honduras had laid claim to the uninhabited Swan Islands off its coast. They had been exploited by guano hunters from the United States since 1857, and a lighthouse had been established there by the United Fruit Company. Also a hurricane-season meteorological bureau was maintained by this country. Roosevelt felt debate concerning ownership was making "a mountain out of a molehill," but United States claims were maintained.[94]

In January, 1939, Major General David L. Stone again advised acquisition of the Galápagos Islands, owned by Ecuador, a thousand miles southwest of Balboa; and of the Cocos Islands, owned by Costa Rica, five hundred miles west of Balboa.[95] Still farther south, off the coast of Chile, was Easter Island. In 1921 the Navy Department had asserted: "The possibility of any foreign power gaining possession of the island [Easter] . . . would be attended with grave results to the power and prestige of the United States." By the late 1930's Chile was thought to be interested in a sale of the property to raise badly needed cash. The answer then, and again in March, 1939, was that the United States did not wish to acquire the Island but had a definite interest in any proposed sale to a non-American power. Roosevelt, realizing its possibilities as a stopping place for trans-Pacific airplane flights, suggested that it might be possible to "tie up Easter Island and the Galápagos in a Pan-American trusteeship." He also suggested including Cocos Islands in the arrangement.[96]

It will be recalled that a wildlife sanctuary for the Galápagos had been endorsed at the Lima Conference. In line with this, on May 6 Undersecretary Welles asked the President to authorize him to inform

---

1940; also Welles to Roosevelt, May 6, 1940. Roosevelt Papers, Hyde Park, Sumner Welles, 1940, 1943.

[94] Memorandum of Roosevelt, September 11, 1939, *ibid.*, Sumner Welles, 1939. Also *For. Rels., 1938*, V, 650 ff.; *1939*, V, 651–652; *1940*, V, 927 ff.

[95] Conn, Engelman, and Fairchild, *U.S. Army in World War II*, pp. 304–305.

[96] Welles to Roosevelt, March 14, 1939, and Roosevelt to Welles (memorandum), March 25, 1939, Roosevelt Papers, Hyde Park, Sumner Welles, 1939. Also *For. Rels., 1939*, V, 461 ff.

the Secretaries of the War and Navy Departments that the President "does not desire those two Departments at this time to recommend approval" of resolutions pending in Congress providing for their acquisition by the United States.[97] By July sulphur deposits of some value were reported to have been found on the Galápagos. Thereafter, with Ecuadorian approval, steps were taken for a wildlife refuge, for sulphur exploitation, for a meteorological station, and for permission to use the Islands for a naval patrol base. A military base followed Pearl Harbor.[98]

The lease of other bases was also under consideration. All offers to construct such in Mexico were declined. That country insisted on building its own bases and on making them available only on short-term leases—no ninety-nine-year idea to be entertained. And discussion of even short-term leases was declined until other pending matters were closed. On November 19, 1940, the agrarian claims were laid to rest with agreement on a gross sum of $40 million. Also a payment of $9 million was made on petroleum claims with commissioners appointed to determine the total amount due. A trade treaty was negotiated by which the United States agreed to help stabilize the peso, to take $25 million (6,000,000 ounces) of Mexican silver per year, and to loan $30 million for highway construction.[99] As the Mexican would put it, "Se marcha" ("The situation moves").

The acquisition of the British bases had essentially established a *mare clausum* in the Caribbean,[100] but small countries therein had their own hopes and plans. On the outbreak of war both Haiti and Santo Domingo had visions of partnership with the United States in bases which would attract millions in Yankee expenditures to enrich their own extremely limited incomes. By the end of May, 1940, Washington felt it wise to secure an over-all view of needs; so secret military and naval conversations were initiated through United States legations in the Latin American capitals.[101] Only Panama and Mexico were not included,

[97] Memorandum to Welles, May 6, 1939, Roosevelt Papers, Hyde Park, State Department 1939. Also *For. Rels., 1937*, V, 2; *1938*, V, 467 ff.; *1939*, V, 633; *1940*, V, 415.

[98] *Ibid., 1940*, V, 850 ff.; Conn, Engleman, and Fairchild, *U.S. Army in World War II*, pp. 342–343; *For. Rels., 1944*, VII, 1064–1078.

[99] E. David Cronon, *Josephus Daniels in Mexico*, p. 268. Also Daniels Papers, LC, Diary, Box 7, March 13, 1941; *For. Rels., 1941*, VII, 408–409.

[100] Conn, Engleman, and Fairchild, *U.S. Army in World War II*, p. 327.

[101] *For. Rels., 1939*, V, 638 ff.; Guerrant, *Roosevelt's Good Neighbor Policy*, p.

for special reasons having nothing to do with international disagreements on the subject. Responses were enthusiastic. Such continuing studies of defense costs for Latin America resulted in a staff memorandum of War and Navy Departments stating bluntly that expenses for defending the whole area would be excessively high and that needed supplies were not available. Priorities were accordingly established. By these Mexico and Brazil were given first place. Ecuador, Colombia, and Venezuela came next. Central America and the Caribbean republics ranked third. The rest of Latin America was in fourth place.[102]

Closely associated with the problems of defense plans and bases was the question of military missions in Latin America. When the war broke out, the United States had nine missions in six states—Argentina, Brazil, Colombia, Guatemala, Haiti, and Peru. By the end of 1939 additional missions had been sent to Bolivia, Chile, Costa Rica, Ecuador, El Salvador, Nicaragua, and Venezuela.[103] A glance shows that all but two of these (Argentina and Chile) were in the Central Zone.

The Army Judge Advocate General advised the President that his office held that an act of Congress of June 5, 1920, authorized the Secretary of War, with presidential approval, to dispose of surplus military equipment to foreign purchasers including foreign governments.[104] On June 16, 1940, the Pittman Act cleared all doubt and authorized manufacture of munitions and the direct purchase of munitions for Latin American republics. Once a sale was arranged the financing could be managed through the Export-Import Bank. On June 27, 1939, therefore, the State Department notified all its missions in Latin America that a joint resolution was pending in Congress to make available defense material (naval vessels, coastal defense artillery, antiaircraft guns, and ammunition) to those New World republics which wished to buy it. Within two weeks, seventeen enthusiastic responses (Mexico, Colombia, and Chile being the exceptions) had been received.[105] To make financing even more available, the Lend-Lease Act

---

155. Also *For. Rels., 1940,* V, 16 ff., 96 ff.; *1941,* VII, 607 ff.; Department of State, *Peace and War,* pp. 562–563.

[102] Langer and Gleason, *Challenge to Isolation,* pp. 733–734. Also *For. Rels., 1940,* V, 2 ff., for types of arms to be made available in individual cases.

[103] Mecham, *U.S. and Inter-American Security,* p. 201; *For. Rels., 1941,* VI, 493 ff.; Langer and Gleason, *Challenge to Isolation,* p. 273.

[104] Conn and Fairchild, *Framework of Hemisphere Defense,* pp. 207 ff.,

[105] *For. Rels., 1939,* V, 1 ff.

supplemented the Export-Import Bank, whose funds were somewhat limited.[106]

In addition to the highest priority items in the land-screened areas (defense of the Canal and protection of petroleum and bauxite supplies), was defense of the shoulder of Brazil. Brazilian military strength was normally concentrated well south of Recife—in other words, between Rio de Janeiro and the La Plata area. This left 2,500 miles of undefended coastline between available Brazilian military strength and the danger point. To make matters worse, no highways or railways existed that were adequate for strategic needs. Now the threatened attack would come from the sea or the air, and from the east or north, not from the south, where Brazilian reserves were available. On April 17, 1941, Brazil agreed for the United States to use selected ports for repair or overhaul of vessels, or for refueling purposes. But as of June 10 not a single United States naval vessel was within a thousand miles of the danger area, and Brazilian forces were twice as far away. The result was a clamor for air bases, planes, and men. Through an "almost providential occurrence" Germany turned eastward to attack Russia just at this time. This checked the momentum of its march southward via Spain and Dakar, thence westward via the Cape Verde Islands toward Natal.[107]

On July 10 Roosevelt asked Ambassador Jefferson Caffrey in Rio de Janeiro to deliver a personal message from him to President Vargas. In this he asked if Vargas would cooperate, in case of a westward advance by Germany, with the United States in emergency measures in Surinam, and also if necessary in the Azores. On August 22 Caffrey reported that Foreign Minister Oswaldo Aranha stated that his President would cooperate in Surinam, and that he was willing to approach the government of Portugal about the Azores "in an appropriate fashion at the appropriate time." The arrangements for Surinam provided that the United States could use Brazilian bases on the understanding that they would also be open to the use of all New World countries. On December 15, 1941, three fifty-men companies of marines sailed from Quantico for service in Natal, Recife and Belém. Once more, *se marcha*, but an all-too-familiar complaint now arose. Brazil felt that the northern

<hr />

[106] Edward R. Stettinius, *Lend-Lease: Weapon for Victory*, p. 39.
[107] Conn and Fairchild, *Framework for Hemisphere Defense*, pp. 119 ff., 138, 266.

republic was anxious "to get troops into northwestern Brazil but does not seem anxious to help Brazil defend the region."[108] The old problem: military efficiency versus political cooperation.

Throughout the Central Zone, however, it appears that pro-United States sentiment was at high tide. These countries were appalled at the Nazi conquests and apparently felt safer with the evil with which they were familiar (the United States) than with the militaristic and unknown Nazi.

Strategic—The Southern Zone

Quarter-sphere, hemisphere, or global strategy—which? Were the Arctic implications and complications more significant than those of the South Atlantic and South Pacific? Nicholas J. Spykman's *America's Strategy in World Politics* and Clarence K. Streit's *Union Now* as well as articles in leading periodicals such as *The Annals* and *Foreign Affairs* were only representative of the thinking of many who raised such questions. The Inter-American Defense Board was directly concerned with the discussions. Possibilities were regularly canvased by a standing liaison committee between the Chief of Staff, the Chief of Naval Operations, and the Secretary of State after April, 1938.[109] The uncertainties reflected, of course, had a keenly interested audience in South America.[110] Realists in the Southern Zone felt that they could not afford to overlook a probable future in which Germany would dominate European markets and become the logical source of their own military equipment.[111] In

---

[108] *For. Rels., 1941*, VI, 505 ff. Also Conn and Fairchild, *Framework for Hemisphere Defense*, pp. 305 ff.; Langer and Gleason, *Undeclared War*, pp. 602–604; *Documents on German Foreign Policy*, Series D, XI, 629–630; Stimson Papers, Yale, Diary, December 11, 1941.

Stimson's diary for December 17, 1941, also gives an excellent illustration of national pride in Brazil in conflict with the military man's impatience. Brazil disapproved of foreign troops appearing on its soil in foreign uniforms, Stimson insisted. Finally, a compromise was worked out for a reciprocal arrangement by which, Stimson commented, "we can let some of their soldiers come into the United States and prance around."

[109] Edwin Lieuwen, *Arms and Politics in Latin America*, pp. 188–189.

[110] Enrique Ruíz Guiñazú, *La Política Argentina y el futuro de América*, p. 95; Clarence K. Streit, "The North Atlantic Union and the Americas," *The Annals*, CCIV (July, 1939), 94; Arthur P. Whitaker, *The Western Hemisphere Idea*, p. 161 ff.

[111] Conn and Fairchild, *Framework of Hemisphere Defense*, p. 275.

In the early stages of the war the British allowed German arms to be shipped to

any case, would a victorious Germany be worse for them than a victorious United States? Would Roosevelt's noninterventionism bind a future executive?[112] The questions which had once been largely academic had become immediate and imperative.

The public statements of the President, even if at times he had personal qualms, never varied. Six weeks after the Munich settlement he stated that "the United States must be prepared to resist attack on the western hemisphere from the North Pole to the South Pole, including all of North America and South America." Even if resources were stretched exceedingly thin he was determined to protect the whole area and to supply countries with munitions in accordance with estimated needs. Even though the poorly protected areas felt exposed and protested when preferred shipments went elsewhere the policy was set.[113] As the popular Major General Frank R. McCoy put it: " 'Down to the bulge' sounds plausible, but would be catastrophic in its effect. It would void the Monroe Doctrine; tend to throw all of the most powerful countries of South America directly into the Axis camp; and certainly introduce into this hemisphere the same type of cultural, racial, and balance-of-power problems as those faced in Europe."[114]

With the advantage of hindsight, scholars have been surprised at the "fact that the United States Chiefs of Staff at the time regarded the Nazi threat to South American countries as perhaps the most immediate danger to national security." The Liaison Committee held approximately one hundred meetings, mostly in 1939 and 1940. In all but half a dozen of these top priority was assigned to questions of Latin America.[115] Later investigations have failed to reveal any actual German

---

Brazil via Italy. Even in the summer of 1941, at the urging of Washington, the British released a vessel loaded with arms for Brazil. Also in the summer of 1941 the British allowed a United States vessel to pick up a load of German arms in a Portuguese port to be brought to New York and then forwarded to Brazil. We seemed more successful in getting German arms into Brazil than in providing our own to them (*ibid.*, p. 271). Also N. P. Macdonald, *Hitler over Latin America*, p. 27.

[112] Spykman, *America's Strategy in World Politics*, p. 248.

[113] Conn and Fairchild, *Framework of Hemisphere Defense*, pp. 210 ff.; Langer and Gleason, *Challenge to Isolation*, pp. 615–617.

[114] Frank R. McCoy, "Our Common Defense," *Survey Graphic*, XXX (1941), 121.

[115] Langer and Gleason, *Challenge to Isolation*, p. 607; Ernest R. May, "The Alliance for Progress in . . . Perspective," *For. Affs.*, XLI (July, 1963), 759.

military plans for invasion of the New World, in spite of the writings of some politicians and businessmen.[116] Yet the concern of military leaders was logical, for German victories seemed to be self-sustaining and to be capable of expanding indefinitely in all directions. Once the Germans were victorious on the European continent and then in possession of the West Coast of Africa, the attraction of South America could be expected to prove almost irresistible. And South American German enthusiasts talked of a "Patagonian Anschluss" and circulated maps which showed "Antarctica Germanica" and sections of Brazil and Chile "which Germany considers its own colonies."[117] Secretary of State Hull commented in his *Memoirs*: "In general the Nazis in Latin America . . . were making no secret of their plans and were boasting openly that Germany could easily conquer South America."[118]

Probably it was fortunate for the United States that Vargas in Brazil was convinced that Germans had plotted his overthrow. He suppressed Nazi propaganda and eliminated German control of Brazilian airlines. German agents in Argentina also reported in the early days of the war that the government attitude was hostile. And this was true even though Hitler had been careful to state that his policy toward Latin America was definitely one of conciliation. As the war broke out, Argentina, Brazil, and Uruguay made plans for a joint naval patrol to protect their neutrality.[119] Meanwhile every effort was made to acquire merchant vessels to move Argentine foodstuffs. One such purchase was of sixteen Italian vessels aggregating more than 88,000 tons. On the military side, requests were sent to Washington for military instructions. The mere hint of such aid aroused an excited protest from Brazil. The logical answer of the United States was: "It would seem to be impossible for this Government to justify affording such facilities to the Brazilian Government and denying the same facilities to the governments of the other American republics." At later dates, in 1940 and 1941, aviation instructors were also sent to the Argentine. But this was as far as it went

[116] Conn and Fairchild, *Framework for Hemisphere Defense*, pp. 26, 81.

[117] David Efron, "Latin America and the Fascist 'Holy Alliance'," *The Annals*, CCIV (July, 1939), 19–24.

[118] Hull, *Memoirs*, I, 814.

[119] *For. Rels., 1940*, V, 659 ff.; *Documents on German Foreign Policy*, Series D, IX, 279 ff.; Welles to Roosevelt, July 24, 1939, enclosing clipping of July 17, Roosevelt Papers, Hyde Park, State Department, 1939, Box 21; *New York Times*, September 18, 1939, 8.5. The pro-United States Ortiz gave way to the critical, if not hostile, Castillo in mid-1940.

and Argentine requests for military equipment were given a low priority indeed.[120]

Uruguay had long been cast in the role of a buffer state. Argentine ambitions for the Banda Oriental were not dead and political refugees kept Uruguayan fears alive. The near-by menace was much more obvious and feared than that of the more powerful but much more distant United States. In spite of German propaganda,[121] Montevideo insisted on strict neutrality as the war began. In 1939 the German minister pleaded in vain for an extension of harbor rights for the *Graf Spee* beyond the allowed seventy-two hours. After the vessel had put to sea and was destroyed by its crew just outside the three-mile limit, Berlin instructed its legation to continue to insist that the action of Montevideo in refusing a time extension had been unjustified. Even so, Berlin admitted that current business should be attended to on a matter-of-fact basis and without breaking diplomatic relations.[122] When Nazi plotting became especially active twelve German leaders were arrested in June, 1940. Forthwith the U. S. cruiser *Quincy* and later the *Wichita* paid courtesy calls at Montevideo. At a dinner in honor of the captain of the *Quincy* the United States minister was authorized to state: "It is the intention and the avowed policy of my Government to cooperate fully, whenever such cooperation is desired, with all of the other American Governments in crushing all activities which arise from non-American sources and which imperil our political and economic freedom."[123]

The little country eagerly sought to purchase three destroyers from the United States. Critical shortages made the sale impossible but negotiations were undertaken to lend support by naval use of an Uruguayan base. At once Argentina protested that this violated Uruguayan sovereignty.[124] To such criticism Roosevelt responded in person: "I want to make it very clear that the United States Government has never sought directly or indirectly to obtain the lease or cession of air or naval

---

[120] *New York Times*, August 26, 1941, 4.8; *For. Rels., 1938*, V, 313 ff.; *1940*, V, 21 ff., 504; *1941*, VI, 402.

[121] Efron, "Latin America and the Fascist 'Holy Alliance'," *The Annals*, CCIV (July, 1939), 23; Guerrant, *Roosevelt's Good Neighbor Policy*, p. 150.

[122] *Documents on German Foreign Policy*, Series D, VIII, 541 ff.

[123] Hull, *Memoirs*, I, 821. For a demonstration of support against possible Argentine aggression see *For. Rels., 1944*, VII, 1591–1593.

[124] *For. Rels., 1940*, V, 162 ff.; *Documents on German Foreign Policy*, Series D, XI, 549–550.

bases in Uruguay." The Foreign Minister was soon stating that the two governments had reached an accord by which bases would be constructed in his country and "directed, maintained and controlled" by Uruguay. These would be at the service of any other American state on conditions to be announced.[125] This, of course, meant United States financing while periodic visits of naval units could be expected to have a sedative effect on the La Plata area. Local criticisms were largely suppressed when the Uruguayan Senate by a vote of fifty-three to twenty-one expressed confidence in the minister negotiating the accord.[126]

The strategic situation on the west coast of South America needs little further comment. The quarter-sphere idea would have left the long coastline of Chile unprotected. Could a one-ocean navy fight a two-ocean war (for most of the Pacific squadron rested on the bottom of Pearl Harbor or was laid up for repairs)? Long before this time the noted commentator Arthur Krock of the *New York Times* had said that defense of the whole hemisphere was practical only so long as the British fleet maintained its supremacy. This gone, the quarter-sphere defense policy was the only logical one.[127] In spite of the President's reassurance, therefore, Chile was fearful.

A military aviation mission was gladly received in Chile, but efforts by the United States to lease bases there were thwarted lest they lead to submission and colonialism.[128] Finally, late in 1941, an agreement was reached providing that United States war vessels might use the ports of Antofagasta and Valparaíso for refueling and supplies without previous notice. To forestall criticism, reciprocal privileges were granted to Chilean vessels in United States ports (which they never visited) and the refueling had to be done from on-shore tanks instead of directly from tankers.[129]

Another matter of considerable interest on the west coast was the fear that sudden incapacitation of the Panama Canal might route heavy traffic through the Straits of Magellan. By a treaty of 1881 between Chile and Argentina, Chile was not to fortify the straits. The United

[125] Guerrant, *Roosevelt's Good Neighbor Policy*, p. 158.

[126] Langer and Gleason, *Undeclared War*, pp. 155–156.

[127] *New York Times*, July 11, 1940, 18.5.

[128] *For. Rels., 1940*, V, 694; *New York Times*, November 9, 1940, 6.7, and November 17, 1940, 36.4.

[129] *For. Rels., 1941*, VI, 556–558.

States in 1879 had approved such a nonfortification proposal, but on the outbreak of World War II it endorsed the desire of Chile to establish defense works. Argentina gave consent in December, 1941, but then sought to establish such conditions that the matter was dropped.[130] It was increasingly obvious that the rivalries of the Big Three (Argentina, Brazil, and Chile) in South America remained almost as complicated as the relations of any one of them with the United States.

[130] Langer and Gleason, *Undeclared War*, pp. 618–619.

CHAPTER XIII

WORLD WAR II: PROBLEMS

The Northern Zone

HEMISPHERE DEFENSE HAD NOW become a joint effort to win the war. The extent of the effort may be judged from the multiple boards established:

The Permanent Board on Defense, August, 1940.
The Materials Coordinating Committee, May, 1941.
The Joint Economics Committee, June, 1941.
The Joint War Production Committee, November, 1941.
The Joint Agricultural Committee, March, 1943.
The Joint War Aid Committee, August, 1943.[1]

There is little question that the work of these committees was more effective on the military side with Canada than with Latin America. Stimson growled to his diary (March 30, 1942) that the Inter-American Defense Board gave him "grave doubts" but that Sumner Welles had had his way, so the committee had been set up. Now Stimson had to try to "make the best of it." A year later (April 17, 1943) he again was "rather leery" about a study by the Board of Inter-American Airfields, feeling that joint study of strategic installations might "let out secret weapons of our defense." He only hoped that with "special watchful-

[1] *Inter-American Affairs, 1943,* p. 57 n.

ness" the harm might be avoided and the good of cooperation might come.[2]

The extent of Canadian cooperation is easily forgotten and should be recorded. By the end of 1943 Canadian plants each week were turning out eighty fighting aircraft, six seagoing ships, 10,000 tons of chemicals and explosives, 4,000 military vehicles, and 450 armored cars and tanks. The sheer quantity of this production enabled Canada to furnish upward of a billion dollars of defense materials and services to its southern neighbor from 1942 to 1945. It operated the two largest blast furnaces in the British Empire and had become the fourth industrial producer in the United Nations.[3] No wonder the Canadian legation was raised to embassy rank.

Actual questions of military defense ramified extensively into the general commercial field. For instance, there was an initial agreement for the construction of the Canol pipeline for transportation of petroleum products across the western border. Next came arrangements for digging exploratory wells. Closely akin and also involved was the Alcan highway project that was approved in March, 1942, and rapidly pressed to completion. Subsidiary agreements, such as those for the construction of flight strips along the highway, followed in due course.[4] Another project was the development of the St. Lawrence Seaway, which affected the industrial life of the whole Great Lakes area on both sides of the boundary. The effects of these developments were also to be noted in the political sphere. For instance, Newfoundland found itself drawn steadily into the Canadian orbit, finally to become a province of the Dominion in 1949.

Of course there were Canadian misgivings concerning the influence

---

[2] Diary, March 30, 1942, and April 17, 1943, Henry L. Stimson Papers, Yale.

[3] Hugh L. Keenleyside, *Canada and the United States,* p. 371. Also Stetson Conn and Byron Fairchild, *The Framework of Hemisphere Defense,* p. 391.

[4] A report of Undersecretary of War Robert P. Patterson (copy in Stimson's diary at Yale following entry for December 9, 1943) shows that twenty-seven wells were producing 7,500 barrels of oil daily and that 20,000 barrels were available daily in proven areas. A pipeline, under construction at a cost estimated at $134 million, was due to start production on January 1, 1944. Canada had furnished rights of way and lands and had waived taxes and royalties. The United States owned the installations during the war and bought the oil at prices agreed upon. After the war Canada was to be entitled to buy the pipeline and refineries at arbitrated prices. See *For. Rels., 1942,* I, 589–591.

and the actual legal rights being acquired by its powerful southern neighbor.[5] On the other hand, as the war closed and the pressures of the new balance of power (the U.S.A. versus the U.S.S.R.) emerged, more cooperation became imperative.[6] Scientific research in the Arctic was coordinated. Recalcitrants and nationalists could declaim against dominance by the erratic United States,[7] but another point of view was also to be noted:

If we really cannot stomach having American troops on our soil, we had better give them some pieces of it [make a bargain with them if we can]. . . . But we do not need anything in return; there is no investment so valuable to us as a piece of land donated to an American who is willing to get killed on it in order to defend us from invasion. American defense installations in corners of our country constitute no real threat to our independence. If the United States wanted to use military invasion or infiltration to take over Canada we should have gone that way long ago.[8]

Then the writer cautioned that Canadian independence could be undermined by "customs union with U.S.A. Economic absorption is ten fold more likely than military absorption."

The actions of the American republics at Panama, looking to neutrality, and at Havana, still looking to neutrality but considering possible methods of administering European colonies in the Caribbean, were not reassuring to the Canadians. Even the Lima Conference struck a false note in some Canadian minds when it stated that "protection of ethnical, language or religious minorities" did not and should not exist in the Americas. Canadians demurred: "They do exist in Canada; we have a minority of this kind." The writer added that there was a lack of cultural

[5] B. K. Sandwell, "What Canadians Think of Post-War Reconstruction . . .," *For. Pol. Assn. Reports,* XVIII, No. 24 (March 1, 1943), 317.

[6] L. B. Pearson, "Canada Looks 'Down North'," *For. Affs.,* XXIV, No. 4 (July, 1946) 643, and "Canada's Northern Horizon," *For. Affs.,* XXXI, No. 4 (July, 1953), 582 ff.

[7] *New York Times,* February 16, 1947, 23.1.

[8] Wynne Plumptre, "Commonwealth or United States, Which . . .?," in *Life with Uncle Sam,* p. 11.

A contrasting point of view is that of the well-known Canadian writer Frank Hawkins, who violently inveighed against Great Britain in the 1920's, but who reversed his stand to support the Mother Country in the war. At the close of the war his admiration of the United States was seriously modified by fears lest it dominate Canada culturally, if not politically.

unity between his people and Latin Americans while talk of geographical unity of Canada and Latin America was farcical.[9]

When the Prime Minister was asked in the Canadian House of Commons about possible membership in the Pan-American Union, he replied cautiously that "there have been times quite recently when we might have expected invitations but were given reasons why it would not be advisable to have an invitation extended."[10] When plans were being made for the Rio de Janeiro Conference in 1942 the Dominican Republic suggested that Canada be invited to attend. Forthwith the telephones became busy between Washington and Ottawa to forestall any false hopes that might be aroused. Mr. Mackenzie King responded gallantly, asking merely "that the President be informed that he fully appreciated the validity of the reasons advanced by the President for believing that it was impossible, under existing inter-American agreements, for Canada to take part in that meeting." He continued that he greatly appreciated the "frankness and friendly nature" of the message that had discouraged the suggestion.[11] Again, at the Chapultepec Conference as the war was closing, a proposal to invite Canada to join the Pan-American Union was tabled.[12]

The Central Zone

The destruction of much of the United States Pacific Fleet at Pearl Harbor caused Latin America abruptly to face the fact that the United States, crippled though it was at the moment, was its only line of defense. This was especially the case for the west coast nations that faced Japan.

At the Rio de Janeiro meeting in 1942 the divergence of United States policy as advocated by Hull in contrast with that advocated by Welles became obvious to all. The Secretary was convinced that a breach in unanimity was preferable to compromise. "The Argentines must accept this situation or go their own way."[13] Welles found the situation more

[9] Vincent Massey, "Canada and the Inter-American System," *For. Affs.*, XXVI, No. 4 (July, 1948), 693 ff.

[10] *Inter-American Affairs, 1942*, p. 43.

[11] Memorandum of meeting of Canadian Chargé Wrong with Welles, December 18, 1941, Franklin D. Roosevelt Papers, Hyde Park, P.S.F., Canada, 1933–1941; *For. Rels., 1941*, VI, 129–131.

[12] Samuel Guy Inman, "An Inside View of the Inter-American Conference," *The South in World Affairs*, VII, Nos. 4–5 (April–May, 1945), 22.

[13] Cordell Hull, *The Memoirs of Cordell Hull*, II, 1144.

complicated than that: Argentina would not go its own way alone. The Chilean President had just died, and new elections could not be held for six months; hence immediate action by Santiago could not be expected. Uruguay would hesitate to act except in concert with at least one of its great neighbors, either Argentina or Brazil. And inaccessible Paraguay and Bolivia would not be likely to act unless their neighbors with sea coasts led the way. It was hoped that Brazil would be "safe," but even powerful Vargas was dependent on his Army, and his Army liked Fascism. Much more serious was the fact that President Roberto Ortiz of Argentina, a thorough cooperationist, had been forced to resign, and Axis-influenced Castillo had acceded to power.[14] Behind Castillo was a military clique that was pressing for a "greater Argentina" program which could only be brought into being at the expense of neighboring countries. It was one thing for Brazil to help the United States to fight the Axis; it was quite another for it to do so if Argentina was left in a position to take advantage of Brazilian preoccupation to run roughshod over the heart of the continent.

President Vargas told Welles frankly that he could not move unless he had the support of his Army, and it would only move if it felt that its back door was secured through Argentine cooperation.[15] Under these circumstances Welles agreed to the compromise to which Hull strenuously objected. Upon direct telephone appeal to Roosevelt, the President supported Welles. As a result, the Conference resolution as it was adopted did not call for the breaking of relations with the Axis as mandatory. Argentina accordingly insisted on its neutrality; Chile, fearing attack on its coasts, waited for its national election and then

[14] The type of feeling back of Argentine recalcitrance was that which sponsored rumors in Buenos Aires that books printed in the United States showed maps indicating future methods of conquest to be employed in the Argentine (Ysabel F. Rennie, *The Argentine Republic*, pp. 298–299).

The Argentine delegate to the Rio de Janeiro meeting and its Foreign Minister at the time was Dr. Ruíz Guiñazú, whom Sumner Welles characterized as "one of the stupidest men to hold office in that great nation's history" (*Seven Decisions that Shaped History*, p. 100). Ruíz feared that the United States would not protect the east coast below Rio de Janeiro. An additional fact was that Buenos Aires was at a safe seven thousand miles distance from Europe. Its position, insisted Ruíz, was that of fearing hegemony whatever the source, that is, whether from Brazil, the United States, or Europe (Ruíz Guiñazú, *La Política Argentina . . .*, pp. 187–188).

[15] Sumner Welles, *Seven Decisions that Shaped History*, p. 101.

moved so slowly that it did not break relations with the Axis until 1944.[16] When the Rio meeting adjourned all the rest of the New World republics had broken relations with Germany. Costa Rica, Cuba, the Dominican Republic, El Salvador, Guatemala, Honduras, Nicaragua, and Panama declared war; while Mexico, Brazil, Bolivia, and Colombia followed suit shortly.[17] The yeoman support given Welles by the Mexican delegate, Ezequiel Padilla, should be recorded. On one occasion he asked his fellow ministers:

How must we regard the United States? . . . . A nation with the highest living standards of all, a country whose people enjoy every comfort and convenience, how can we rightly estimate its action, as we see it cast into that fiery furnace the fantastic figure of its accumulated wealth, and divert into it the whole mighty stream of its prosperity, without thought of danger or of economy, to defend the heritage of its freedom and the untrammeled destinies of our continent? The answer may only be sought in the spirit of self-sacrifice shown by that nation on behalf of the loftiest incentives to the onward march of peoples.[18]

The rift between Hull and Welles grew steadily as Welles pressed for more consideration, or a "soft" approach, in dealing with Latin America. In part it appeared to be a personality clash. Welles' Ivy League associations and close friendship with the President irked Hull, who complained of the self-aggrandizement of his assistant who was "habitually" received by the President for discussion of foreign problems of which Hull was left in ignorance. Something of a climax was reached when Welles (but not Hull) went with his Chief to meet Churchill at the Atlantic Conference.[19] Hull, apparently fearing an attempt by Moscow to organize a regional program in Europe based on that of the Western Hemisphere organization, increasingly opposed Welles' proposals.[20] Welles continued to conciliate Latin American feelings, evidently with the approval of the President, while the Secretary made little secret of his anger that his subordinate "seemed to be operating a second State Department."[21] The friction became so serious that the President had

[16] J. Lloyd Mecham, *The United States and Inter-American Security*, p. 213.
[17] *Ibid.*
[18] Quoted by Samuel Flagg Bemis, *The Latin American Policy of the United States*, p. 393 n.
[19] Diary, August 19, September 20, 1941, Stimson Papers, Yale.
[20] Arthur P. Whitaker, *The Western Hemisphere Idea*, pp. 168–169.
[21] *For. Rels., Conferences at Malta and Yalta, 1945*, p. 136.

to choose between the two. All things considered the logical decision was a request for Welles to resign.

The financial heart of the war program was to be found in the Lend-Lease Act of March 11, 1941. Prior to Pearl Harbor $150 million had been set aside from these funds for Latin American purchases of military and naval supplies, and actual agreements had been signed with Bolivia, Brazil, Cuba, Santo Domingo, Haiti, Nicaragua, and Paraguay.[22] By the end of the war eighteen of the Latin American states had received Lend-Lease aid. This varied from about $160,000 for Costa Rica, to $18 million for Peru, over $22 million for Chile, nearly $39 million for Mexico, and almost $348 million for Brazil.[23]

Even more important in many ways than Lend-Lease were the purchases of Latin American commodities by the United States. These reached the astonishing figure of $2,500 million by October, 1945, or more than five times the amount of Lend-Lease.[24] The Export-Import Bank continued its credit program, which was increasingly channeled to semi-war actvities such as the stimulation of rubber production and highway construction (450 miles were constructed in Central America alone in 1943). General purchases ran the gamut from sugar (Cuba sold the United States over $700 million), to nitrates and copper from Chile (purchases valued at over $670 million), and to silver and other critically needed minerals from Mexico (purchases of more than $340 million).[25]

Latin America clamored for combat aircraft, anti-aircraft guns, coastal defense guns, and other munitions. Especially when these were critically needed on the fighting fronts Washington was reluctant to provide unstable governments with tactical weapons. Training planes only were sent in substantial numbers, and Chile and Brazil received a limited number of batteries of coastal defense guns. In all, before and just after the war, fifteen American republics received somewhat more

---

[22] Donald Marquand Dozer, *Are We Good Neighbors?*, p. 81.

[23] *Ibid.*, p. 124.

To begin with, Argentina had been included in prospective allotments of military equipment, but its failure to break international relations with the Axis blocked fulfillment of the assignments. Welles later commented that the Argentines never did understand that the United States' action was based on the conception of continental defense. See *For. Rels, 1941*, VI, 137–138, 332–333; *1942*, V, 307–308; Sumner Welles, *Time for Decision*, pp. 228–229.

[24] Mecham, *U.S. and Inter-American Security*, pp. 242–243.

[25] *Ibid.; Inter-American Affairs, 1943*, pp. 154, 219.

than two thousand planes, but only Brazil, Chile, Peru, and Mexico received tactical aircraft.[26]

At this point interest in inter-Americanism declined. The Ninth Conference, which was to have met in 1943, was postponed; and the Inter-American Juridical Committee at Rio de Janeiro frequently could not secure a quorum for meetings in spite of the fact that the third meeting of Foreign Ministers had referred significant questions to it. Also, after the three special sessions of the Foreign Ministers which assembled at the opening of the war, this important series lapsed until the contest was over.[27] Under the conditions this was not too surprising. United States attention was focused elsewhere, and the Latin Americans were increasingly concerned with domestic problems once the emergency adjustments had been made and the early dangers passed.

One of the more active inter-American organizations was the Committee for Political Defense, but its activities were largely restricted to war problems. Another feature of the waning enthusiasm for Pan-Americanism was a sober recognition of the fact that the theory and practices of democracy might vary widely. The Four Freedoms, if applied literally, would have outlawed many of the existing, and cooperating, Latin American governments that had acquired and retained power by procedures certainly not in harmony with the Four Freedoms. To displace the incumbents would have involved either revolutions—not to be considered in time of war—or intervention—equally unthinkable.[28] Result, enthusiasm for the United States as protector of Latin America by no means implied indiscriminate praise for all features of its society, its government, or its announced principles.

On the military side the power of the United States was everywhere evident. Nine South American republics (all but Uruguay) accepted either military, air, or naval advisers from the north and sent a steady parade of their own officers for special training in United States service academies or staff schools.[29] And Uruguay, the one exception, as already noted had constructed a substantial base that was available to the United States Navy and Air Force. Formal military bases were opened by the

[26] Conn and Fairchild, *Framework of Hemisphere Defense*, pp. 200–201, 227–228. Also *For. Rels., 1944*, VII, 673–691.

[27] *Inter-American Affairs, 1943*, pp. 36 ff.

[28] Frank Tannenbaum, "An American Commonwealth of Nations," *For. Affs.*, XXII, No. 4 (July, 1944), 587–588.

[29] Laurence Duggan, *The Americas*, pp. 178–179.

United States in Ecuador (including the long-debated Galápagos Islands), Cuba, Brazil, and Panama.[30] The Navy Department established a special Pan-American Division, which sought close military cooperation and advised on Lend-Lease grants and on the work of air and naval personnel engaged in Latin America.[31] Small service and meteorological detachments were stationed by the Army at various Latin American airfields, though these were nominally under local control. Coastal defense equipment sent to Chile was locally controlled and even in Panama it was agreed that if Canal Zone troops were employed on local missions they would operate under local command.[32] Only in Peru and Venezuela were coastal artillery batteries under the command of United State military attachés "on the theory that these detachments were engaged in training rather than a tactical mission." J. Lloyd Mecham notes that in one form or another, however, the United States had bases in sixteen of the southern republics.[33]

Brazil and Mexico were outstanding in their military cooperation. On the west coast of South America, Colombia and Peru shared with the United States in an antisubmarine patrol that was authorized to use Ecuadorian bases. Also Ecuador, Colombia, and Venezuela patrolled their own waters. These efforts reduced the load on the United States Navy, and Washington was pleased to pay the expenses involved for a total of approximately $50 million.[34] Thus the small nations were becoming something more than merely potential "potent allies," as Milton Eisenhower later expressed it.[35]

Local matters need some comments. Arrangements with Mexico reached the point that citizens of either country could serve in the armed forces of the other.[36] Panamanian cooperation was likewise noteworthy once the Arias Administration was eliminated.

With certain Caribbean countries and dependencies, however, relations were more complicated. Here a "very thick velvet glove" was at

---

[30] Stetson Conn, Rose C. Engelman, and Byron Fairchild, *The U. S. Army in World War II*, II, 340 ff.; Ferrell, *Amer. Secs. of St.*, XIII, 712.

[31] *Report of the Secretary of the Navy, 1942*, p. 16.

[32] Conn and Fairchild, *Framework of Hemisphere Defense*, pp. 202 ff.

[33] Mecham, *U.S. and Inter-American Security*, p. 218.

[34] Arthur P. Whitaker, *The United States and South America*, pp. 130–131.

[35] Milton S. Eisenhower, *United States-Latin American Relations: Report to the President*, p. 4. Hereinafter cited as Eisenhower, *Report to the President*.

[36] *British and Foreign State Papers, 1943–1945*, pp. 309 ff.

times needed to cover the realities of United States control. Giants were
struggling on the doorsteps of the island pygmies and the latter were
very conscious of their impotence. Vessels were sinking on all sides;
Great Britain had given up choice bases; trade was disrupted; and hunger itself threatened.[37] The Anglo-American Caribbean Commission
(later to become the Caribbean Commission when the Dutch and finally
the French joined) made significant plans. An emergency program of
transporting island produce to mainland markets, and of returning essential drugs, goods, and other supplies to the islands was undertaken.
The route was from Florida to Cuba (water); to Santiago de Cuba (railway); to Port-au-Prince, Haiti (water); to San Pedro de Macoris, Santo
Domingo (truck); to Mayagüez, Puerto Rico (water). Jamaica tapped
the supply line at Santiago, Cuba. The route eliminated eight hundred
miles of travel by submarine-infested water. On the surface this might
appear to be a relatively simple affair until one remembers that it
required the elimination of customs duties and called for special handling arrangements on the parts of sensitive small governments in Cuba,
Haiti, and the Dominican Republic, to say nothing of agreements with
three European countries whose colonies were involved. Nearly 29,000
tons of basic necessities were distributed from Santiago de Cuba; some
16,000 tons in Puerto Rico; and over 8,000 were sent to Jamaica.[38]
Another phase of the Commission's work was the channeling of surplus
Caribbean labor to the manpower-short mainland. In 1943 approximately 16,000 British West Indians were imported for labor in ten
states; the next year about 30,000 were in the country; and in 1945 some
46,000 had work in thirty-eight states of the Union.[39]

Brazil required special consideration on several counts. Here, as
elsewhere in South America, the problem of German and Italian airlines
was serious. To have closed abruptly Air France, German Condor, and
Italian lines in Brazil would have been economically disastrous for many
people and interests. The same was true in other countries. Stimson

[37] Nicholas John Spykman, *America's Strategy in World Politics*, p. 60.

Conn and Fairchild record losses in the twelve months of 1942 at 336 vessels
with a tonnage of 1,559,422. In 1943 the figures were down to 35 vessels with a
tonnage of less than 178,000, and in 1944 were only 3 ships with a tonnage of less
than 15,000 (*Framework of Hemisphere Defense*, p. 431).

[38] *Report of the Anglo-American Caribbean Commission . . . 1942–1943*, pp.
15 ff. The extra transportation costs of $80 to $90 per ton versus normal costs
of about $20 were gladly paid (*For. Rels., 1943*, V, 99–100).

[39] *Ibid.*, p. 19; *1944*, p. 31; *1945*, p. 13.

records (Diary, July 25, 1940) that Mr. J. E. Trippe, president of Pan-American Airways had told him a plan was already under way by which Pan-American would construct strategically located airfields which could be used by the United States for the defense of South America in case of need. On September 18, 1940, Stimson recorded that the money to be used by the airline was to come from the RFC (Reconstruction Finance Corporation) via Secretary Jesse Jones. Later entries show that the funds actually came from the President's Emergency Fund.[40] If Pan-American Airways became bankrupt, the United States held first lien on the bases which were to be open to the Air Corps.

Other items directly connected with Brazil included plans, completed by the end of 1942, for ten to fifteen airplane pilots from Brazil to enter training each month in the United States.[41] Airport construction by a Pan-American Airways subsidiary meant that Brazil furnished the land while construction was supervised by the United States Army Engineer Corps.[42] Thus suspect foreign airlines were replaced.

Brazil also experienced a significant impact from new industrial development that easily fit into its rising program of economic nationalism. One of the great needs of the country was for steel. An Export-Import Bank loan of $45 million launched the Volta Redonda project, which cost about $70 million, while housing and subsidiary facilities ran the total investment to approximately $100 milllion. Immediate effects were evident. In February, 1942, it was announced that medium-horsepower Wright aeronautical engines would be built in Brazil.[43] A railway building program was announced that would call for construction of 1,500 miles of road per year from 1944 to 1947.[44] Legislation envisioning petroleum development, an aluminum industry, and other types of manufacturing followed.

Less successful were the efforts to revive the Brazilian rubber output.

[40] Diary, July 25, 1940, September 18, 1940, and others, Stimson Papers, Yale.

[41] *For. Rels., 1942*, V, 671–672.

[42] Samuel Eliot Morison, *History of United States Naval Operations in World War II*, I, 378 ff. Also, *Inter-American Affairs, 1943*, pp. 152–153.

A memorandum from A. A. Berle to Roosevelt, October 29, 1943, notes that the United States had constructed airports and facilities costing $38 million in Brazil, using Pan-American Airways as its constructon agent (Roosevelt Papers, Yale, State Dept., 1941, 1943–1944, Box 22).

[43] Pan-American Union, *Bulletin*, LXXX, No. 5 (May, 1946), 250 ff.; *For. Pol. Assn. Reports*, XVII, No. 24 (March 1, 1942), 302.

[44] *Inter-American Affairs, 1944*, p. 111; *1943*, pp. 159 ff.

Henry Ford's efforts in the Amazon Valley became a well-known failure. In an area where population density was less than one person to the square mile labor was simply not available. As a result, by the end of 1943 "65,000 rubber trees remained untapped" on his plantation.[45]

In spite of such occasional misjudgments and failures, the industrialization of Latin America was under way. The First World War had given it a boost; the Second gave it a double stimulus. Favorable trade balances provided more local funds than ever before and new moneys poured in from United States bases and from loans and grants. In five years industrial development was consummated that normally would have taken decades. The large countries (Mexico, Colombia, and the ABC powers) led the way, but the smaller countries gleefully seized a share.

The Southern Zone

Argentina had long played the game of attending the Pan-American Conferences to have a voice in the proceedings without subsequently ratifying agreements that would carry obligations. Its unfortunate record in this respect makes the increasing restlessness of the State Department easily understood. Since unanimity at the conferences would not bring results from Argentina, strenuous efforts to secure it were often wholly fruitless. Thus argued Hull. Why not face the facts and proceed with a substantial majority? Frankly ignore the cantankerous La Plata republic, which in fact had refused to put into effect the very compromises on which it had insisted.

Throughout the course of the war Nazi activity in Argentina continued as long as possible. The State Department Blue Book documented the activities of German agents in aiding the election of pro-Castillo men in local elections,[46] and reported that Castillo had assured them that he believed in and hoped for the victory of the Axis powers, and that on this victory he "based his policy." After the military coup in Argentina in June, 1943, "The Ramírez régime immediately resumed . . . negotiations" for German military supplies including six submarines as well as aircraft. Germany was to ship the arms to Spain, which would act as middleman and forward them to Argentina. About the same time Argen-

[45] K. E. Knorr, "Rubber after the War," *War-Peace Pamphlets* (1944), No. 4, 41–42.

[46] Department of State, *Consultation . . . with Respect to the Argentine Situation*, pp. 29 ff.

tina was begging Germany and Japan to send submarines and coastal defense guns for use against its neighbors, especially Brazil.[47] An interesting explanation given by the German military adviser to the Argentine Army from 1937 to 1940 was:

Summarizing, it may be said that at present in Argentina they are making an attempt to build up the state internally on the nationalist viewpoints of the fascist trend whereas at the same time in foreign policy, in view of the complete isolation of Argentina and the failure thus far to form a bloc against the U.S.A., they are forced to protest constantly adherence to the democratic principle and the intention of cooperating within the framework of American solidarity.[48]

Washington did not know what to do. Stern measures might interrupt the flow of badly needed food to Great Britain. In view of this, Roosevelt sent "a fervent personal message" asking Churchill to recall his ambassador to the Argentine and to join the United States in bringing pressure on the uncooperative South Americans.[49] The Prime Minister "very reluctantly, and almost angrily" agreed to do so, stating that he only hoped "our war effort would not be adversely affected." "These Argentine rascals, he [Churchill] concluded, knew the hold they had over us for the time being, and had calculated very carefully."[50] In Washington, Adolph Berle and Carl Spaeth were reported to favor strong measures; while Nelson Rockefeller and Laurence Duggan merely advised reference of the whole matter to the inter-American community. To complicate matters further there was the split between Hull and Welles.[51]

An ever-present factor was the balance-of-power problem in the southern continent. Argentine military expenses were reported to have mounted as follows:[52]

1941	298,000,000 pesos
1942	424,000,000

[47] *Ibid.*, pp. 5–16.

[48] *Ibid.*, p. 65.

[49] Hull, *Memoirs*, II, 1415–1416.

[50] *Ibid.*, 1413. The official British point of view may be found in Sir David Kelly, *The Ruling Few; or, The Human Background to Diplomacy*. Sir David's memoirs of his service as British Ambassador in Buenos Aires during the war add little of information but are expressive of attitudes. Also *For. Rels. 1944*, VII, 327–377.

[51] Lottie M. Manross, *United States Policy toward Argentina*, p. 25. Also Welles, *Time for Decision*, pp. 236–237; Ferrell, *Amer. Secs. St.*, XIII, 713.

[52] Department of State, *Consultation with Respect to the Argentine Situation*, p. 85.

1943	535,000,000
1944	973,000,000
1945	1,428,000,000

The rise of the militarists brought increasing significance to such men as Juan Domingo Perón, who was convinced that "the victory of Germany is [was] assured, and it would be folly for us to be found in any other camp."[53] At the same time every effort was made to secure Lend-Lease aid equivalent to that extended to Brazil. Only this money, said Argentina, could preserve the balance of power. Hull replied:

I must point out emphatically that questions of military and naval equilibrium as between the American republics are surely inconsistent with the inter-American doctrine of peaceful settlement of international disputes. . . . To furnish arms and munitions for the purpose indicated . . . would appear to this Government to be clearly inconsistent with the juridical and moral foundations upon which existing inter-American understanding and agreements are based.[54]

At the same time Hull was convinced that the disorders in Bolivia were inspired from Nazi-influenced Argentina, and that it was only his own prompt cracking of the whip that had saved other neighboring countries from similar experiences.[55]

General Argentine imports from the United States had fallen off sharply and the reverse trade had barely held steady over the war period. Of the imports from the north none were of critical significance except newsprint, which did have to be rationed to meet the minimum needs of Argentine periodicals.[56]

Perón agreed that the day of the nation was being replaced by the

[53] Germán Arciniegas, *The State of Latin America*, p. 51.

[54] *For. Rels., 1943*, V, 458–459.

[55] Hull, *Memoirs*, II, 1378 ff., 1421. Also Ray Josephs, *Argentine Diary*, p. 354: *For. Rels., 1943*, V, 536 ff.

[56] *For. Rels., 1943*, V, 408.

Stimson records in his diary (Yale) on January 4, 1944, that Hull was concerned when the Army bought Argentine wheat. A week later Hull informed the Secretary of War that Argentine agents had overthrown the government of Bolivia and were seeking to do the same in Chile, Peru, and Uruguay. He asked the Army and Navy to help by "sprinkling" war supplies to stabilize the endangered administrations. Stimson at once ordered that wheat purchases from the Argentine be held up.

day of the continent, and that in South America only two states were to be considered as potential spokesmen (Brazil and Argentina). He added: "Our mission is to bring about our indisputable dominance."[57] According to a report that gained publicity through the Mexican weekly *El Tiempo*, the Argentine President insisted that his country stood alone:

The United States is our enemy.

Russia is our enemy.

The anti-Argentine circle will be broken by defeating the present Spanish speaking governments surrounding us, replacing them by governments supporting our own purposes.[58]

So matters worried along. The economic pressure of the increasingly powerful United States, the apparent stalemate or worse faced by the Axis in Europe, and a final serious threat to freeze Argentine funds in the United States finally forced action. On January 26, 1944, President Ramírez broke relations with both Germany and Japan and promised military cooperation with the Allies. Three weeks later Ramírez resigned in favor of his Vice President, General Edelmiro Farrell.[59] Once more the maneuvering set in as Perón, behind the scenes, cemented his power through the Colonels' League. Argentina now undertook a *démarche* of its own. On October 27, 1944, it asked that the Pan-American Union call a meeting to consider its relations with its sister republics. This was a peculiarly shrewd appeal to republics which had either faced or feared the heavy hand of the Yankee. It would impose on Washington the embarrassing task of justifying its position in an open hearing. The *Times* (London) characterized it as a "clever" move. The *New York Times* quickly pointed out that acquiescence in the meeting would in itself extend the formal recognition that had been withheld.[60]

The State Department countered the Buenos Aires move by announcing a meeting of the New World powers that had broken relations with the Axis. This meeting was also to consider the place of the inter-American system in the new world order that was being planned. Accordingly, the Pan-American Union postponed action on the Argentine request

[57] Arciniegas, *The State of Latin America*, p. 52.

[58] Quoted by Carleton Beals *et al.*, *What South Americans Think of Us*, p. 316.

[59] *Department of State Bulletin*, XI, No. 266 (July 30, 1944), 107 ff.; Rennie, *The Argentine Republic*, pp. 365 ff.; the *Times* (London), February 17, 1944, 4f.

[60] The *Times* (London), October 30, 1944, 4f.; *New York Times*, November 21, 1944, 8.4.

until the session called by the United States could be held.[61] Argentina retorted by instructing its member on the Governing Board of the Union to refrain from participating in future meetings. However, it was noticeable that it did not withdraw its membership in the Union. Instead, it accepted an invitation to attend the Inter-American Economic and Technical Conference in Washington on June 15.[62] Evidently the attention of all concerned was now being divided between war problems and postwar relationships that involved planning for the future.

Little Uruguay continued its friendly support of the United States. With good reason its people sympathized with the Allies while they kept a wary eye on their powerful neighbor across the La Plata. Professor Morison commented on the value of this in the joint war effort: "With Brazil as an ally, and Uruguay friendly, we only need French North Africa in the Allied camp to bring the Allied nations' influence down to the River Plate in America, and to Cape Agulhas in Africa. It would then be possible to establish a patrol across the 'Atlantic Narrows' to catch German and Japanese blockade runners."[63]

In the heart of the continent lay troubled Bolivia. Purchasing agreements had been entered into at guaranteed prices for Bolivian tin, and for all its tungsten, lead, and zinc mined for a period of three years. Also in the fall of 1941 a development loan of $25 million was extended to foster mining of other ores, for highway building and for agricultural expansion. In the process Bolivia settled the long-standing Standard Oil claims with one hand while with the other it received nearly four times as much to develop its own oil resources.[64] In answer to pleas for military equipment Roosevelt personally wrote President Enrique Peñaranda of Bolivia in August, 1942, pointing out that the latter as a military man could well appreciate the fact that the items requested were in short supply. He praised the trade agreements reached and thanked the President for Bolivia's "splendid cooperation" in matters related to "the defense of the New World and to the maintenance intact of the liberties of the peoples of the Americas."[65]

This was not enough. A miserable people remained unhappy, and just

[61] *Inter-American Affairs, 1944*, pp. 23–24.
[62] The *Times* (London), January 11, 1945, 3d, and February 10, 1945, 3d.
[63] Morison, *U.S. Naval Operations in W.W. II*, I, 376.
[64] *For. Pol. Assn. Reports*, XVIII, No. 5 (May 15, 1942), 61.
[65] Roosevelt to Peñaranda, August 13, 1942, Roosevelt Papers, Hyde Park, O.F. 659, Bolivia.

at the end of 1943 came another *coup d'état*. Reports out of Montevideo indicated that Nazi activities based on the home of Karl von Luxburg (who had also served as German minister in Buenos Aires in World War I) had provided the Bolivian rebels with "some millions of pesos." In addition the report stated that the by now ubiquitous Perón was thought to be the "strong man behind the military-revolution schemes."[66] At once Perón extended recognition to the victorious Bolivian rebels, but all the other nineteen American republics under the advice of the Committee for Political Defense refused to do so. Six months later the scene was evidently changing. The Bolivian administration was purged of Nazi sympathizers, Axis business firms were confiscated, and the most active Nazi agents were expelled. Next, the administration announced its sympathy for the Allied program and proceeded with arrangements to export strategic raw materials for Allied use. In response, on June 23 all nineteen of the hold-out republics extended recognition.[67]

The last country of the southern group to be noted is Chile. Naturally the Japanese made the most of their coup at Pearl Harbor to intimidate Chile and to hamstring United States supply lines.[68] On the other hand, Washington sought in every possible way to reassure Chileans. Ambassador Claude Bowers asked if he could assure them of United States aid in case of Japanese attack that might follow a rupture of Chilean relations with Japan. He was instructed to inform President Juan Antonio Ríos that he could "of course count on the support of the United States."[69] But in spite of this assurance, pleas for military equipment for coastal defense were met only after serious delays. Public opinion became stubbornly convinced, wrote the Ambassador, that relations with the Axis should not be broken until Germany attacked Chile or her ships. Bowers himself advised that if the vital Chilean military supplies were made available to the United States "I think we should go slow about too open reprisals [over the question of not breaking relations]" lest the effects "put us backward instead of forward."[70]

[66] *New York Times*, January 20, 1944, 11.2, and January 23, 1944, 25.3.

[67] Hull, *Memoirs*, II, 1398–1399; Mecham, *The U.S. and Inter-American Security*, pp. 230–231.

[68] *For. Rels., 1942*, VI, 14–15.

[69] *Ibid.*, p. 31. The Roosevelt Papers (Hyde Park, Claude Bowers) contain a number of significant letters on this subject between July 18 and August 11.

[70] Bowers to Roosevelt, *ibid.*, April 16, 1942; Hull to Roosevelt, January 24, 1942, *ibid.*, O.F. 429, Chile. Also *For. Rels., 1942*, VI, 2–13.

On October 8, 1942, Welles tried to stimulate Chilean action by a speech at Boston. He stated that he could not believe that Argentina and Chile "will continue long to permit their brothers and neighbors of the Americas, engaged as they are in a life and death struggle to preserve the liberties and integrity of the New World, to be stabbed in the back by Axis emissaries." The effect was to "put us backward." Embassies of both accused nations lodged protests in Washington, and the Chilean government announced the postponement of a visit already planned by its President to the United States. Early the next month the Committee for Political Defense made public a note it had just sent to Santiago on Nazi activities in Chile. In response a number of Nazi agents were arrested and President Ríos severed relations with the Axis on January 22, 1943.[71] Thereafter Chile's attitude and conduct settled into something of a pattern. It still felt dangerously exposed and begged for military supplies. Washington answered that the danger was lessening and merely sent enough supplies to keep Santiago from becoming too actively unhappy.

As fears of possible Japanese attack subsided, Chilean attention, like that of other Latin American peoples, turned increasingly to the postwar era. They wanted to avoid such a disastrous collapse as had followed World War I in their nitrate fields. In addition, they wanted to raise the seriously inadequate standards of living of their masses. Immediately thoughts turned to other sources of supply when it was known that European credits were completely unavailable. Among inducements offered were assurances that investors could withdraw their capital at will in five annual installments.[72] But this too was the beginning of another story as another country sought to speed up industrialization and longed for economic self-sufficiency.

[71] *For. Rels.*, 1942, 21 ff.; Edward O. Guerrant, *Roosevelt's Good Neighbor Policy*, p. 181.

[72] *Inter-American Affairs, 1945*, pp. 190–191.

CHAPTER XIV

WORLD WAR II: POLICIES FOR THE FUTURE

Defense Considerations

THE LONDON *Times* COMMENTED on May 29, 1941, that Roosevelt's proclamation of unlimited national emergency had expanded the Monroe Doctrine across the Atlantic to include the Azores, the Cape Verde Islands, and the "Atlantic fortress of Dakar." In short order the course of the war itself brought confirmation of the wide scope of United States policy in the hemisphere. The corners of the area included were the Iceland-Greenland-Labrador complex to the northeast; Alaska and the North Pacific to the northwest; the Galápagos, Juan Fernández Islands, and Chile to the southwest; and the region from Uruguay to the shoulder of Brazil to the southeast. Incidentally, the question of the Falkland Islands was never allowed to arise, though Argentina wished to make it an issue.

The new facts of global power forced Canadians to realize that their relatively small nation lay directly between the two great power centers, the U.S.S.R. and the U.S.A. The Canadian Arctic ice wastes were obviously no barrier to air thoroughfares in case of a struggle between the two.[1] The more the Soviets complained of encirclement, saying that "United States expansion in the Arctic was a step on the highway to

[1] George Ferguson, "The Only Way to Peace," *The Listener*, XXXIII, No. 837 (January 25 1945), 88.

world domination,"[2] the more Canadians realized that their only safety lay in active association with their southern neighbor.

By February, 1947, a considerable amount of water had passed over the dam. Canadians had been restless over United States occupation of bases in the Dominion. Now a number of adjustments became possible. Officially, however, the facts of the international scene were well known. On February 12 the Associated Press reported from Washington that "the United States and Canada announced today they will continue in peacetime their close wartime collaboration for the military security of North America." This was to be done "within the broader framework of the United Nations."[3] The permanent joint committees for the time de-emphasized their preoccupation with military affairs and turned attention to reconstruction in both countries. However, the machinery was left extant for use at a moment's notice. Also the D.E.W. (Distant Early Warning) system of radar outposts across the Canadian north and the regular use by United States military planes of such bases as that at Goose Bay, Labrador, had become facts of everyday existence.

Some complained that the Dumbarton Oaks report did not even use the word "justice" and that the term "international law" appeared only in a negative sense.[4] So far as Canada and its southern neighbor were concerned such omissions were a minor matter. They had long since established procedures to eliminate lesser international controversies; so the leaders of each nation were the more free to grapple with problems of the future. These centered on defense and economy. Involved in the economic problems were the facts that Canada's manpower supply was showing substantial growth, its industrial potential was astounding, and its mineral resources commanded consideration.

South of the United States also were military potentials coupled with certain liabilities. In 1953 Milton Eisenhower's careful analysis in his *Report to the President* asserted that Latin American manpower now had military significance, as had been shown in the cases of Mexico (Mexican troops had fought with distinction against the Germans in Italy) and Brazil in World War II, and in the case of Colombia in the Korean conflict. They could "help guard the lines of communication and shipment, including the Panama Canal." Then he added that perhaps

[2] *New York Times*, February 2, 1947, I, 13.1.

[3] *The State* (February 13, 1947), p. 1.

[4] Clyde Eagleton, "The Pacific Settlement of Disputes under the Charter," *The Annals*, CCXLVI (July, 1946), 24 ff.

the greatest military importance of Latin America was its rapidly growing potential; that in the near future some of these nations could become
"potent allies" indeed. Conversely, Latin American leaders had become
conscious of the fact that the United States was tremendously important
to their nations even though their own political pronouncements for
home consumption still belittled the fact. Their vaunted prosperity would
be frail indeed without the protection of the powerful and friendly northern navy. On the single day of February 17, 1942, seven tankers carrying
Venezuelan oil to neighboring states had been sunk.[5] Responsible leaders
knew this.

Inevitably there were irritations and disagreements in working out
details for the return of bases occupied during the war. Everything
considered, the arrangements were made with surprisingly little friction.
In addition to those in Canada, the two most significant groups of bases
were in Brazil and Panama. All the Brazilian posts were released by
April 15, 1947. In Panama 134 bases, areas, or sites had been occupied
by the United States under an arrangement dated May 18, 1942. By
early May, 1947, 98 of these had been returned. By the following December only 14 were still retained. A public clamor for their immediate
return was echoed by the National Assembly of the republic. In response,
the United States announced that it would retire from all of them at once.
This was more than some Panamanians bargained for, and people in the
localities affected raised an outcry against the loss of greatly enjoyed
Yankee dollars. But so it was. The bases were evacuated.[6] To settle the
accounts due, the United States Congress authorized a blanket reim-
bursement to Panama of $10 million for the bases that had been made
available at no expense to the United States originally.[7]

Latent or heretofore suppressed Latin American criticisms of the
United States now began to emerge increasingly. Why did United States
officials so often become "rowdy and drunk"? Why were American radio
broadcasts prepared for "12-year old morons" when only persons of
quality in Latin America had radio sets?[8] Why had newsprint shortages
due to shipping restrictions during the war limited their newspapers to
four pages while those of the United States had been printing twenty

[5] Milton Eisenhower, *United States Latin American Relations: Report to the President*, p. 4.
[6] J. Lloyd Mecham, *The United States and Inter-American Security*, pp. 295 ff.
[7] Roland Young, *Congressional Politics in the Second World War*, pp. 179–180.
[8] The *Times* (London), June 10, 1944, 3d.

pages daily? Officials began to complain that military missions exercised far more prerogatives than had been assigned to the original technical missions. They inspected forts, military academies, arsenals, airports, and other military, naval, or air facilities as though they were located in Texas, Ohio, or the Dakotas.[9]

Washington was not unaware of these criticisms. After a meeting in June, 1945, with the Secretaries of State and the Navy, Secretary of War Stimson noted in his sometimes outspoken diary that the heads of military missions frequently disagreed with a "number of American Ambassadors" on the use of Lend-Lease funds for military equipment. Secretary Stimson was inclined to attribute the disagreements to "arrogance" of the heads of military missions and the "absence of anything important to do on the part of the diplomats."[10]

For the United States the following, taken from the annual report of the Secretary of the Navy for 1946, was perfectly logical:

To provide full scale test of mobility and of the plans of an expeditionary force, a sizeable task force (TF 100) was activated on 29 April 1946. The force consisted of one cruiser, four destroyers, six high-speed transports, one attack cargo vessel, other amphibious craft, and the First Special Marine Brigade. Amphibious exercises, including landing on the beaches of Puerto Rico and Culebra, were conducted in the Caribbean area from 29 April to 20 May 1946.[11]

Logic might tell Latin Americans that this was a proper and routine action but even logical men could be afraid, and ardent nationalists seldom listened to logic. Defense of the Panama Canal was said to demand control of an arc with a thousand-mile radius from Florida to Trinidad, and from Guatemala to the Galápagos Islands. Included were all the Central American republics, Colombia, Ecuador, Peru, and parts of Mexico and Venezuela.

Latin American opinion varied. One faction was represented by Castillo Nájera of Mexico at the Chapultepec Conference in the spring of 1945. He proposed a permanent body to coordinate the military forces

[9] Ricardo A. Martínez, *De Bolívar a Dulles*, p. 176. Another irritating practice that gave trouble in some areas was for all officers on missions to outrank local officers of equal grade with themselves (see Juan José Arévalo, *Fábula del tiburón y las sardinas*, p. 111).

[10] Diary, June 26–30, 1945, Henry L. Stimson Papers, Yale.

[11] *Report of the Secretary of the Navy, 1946*, p. 3.

of the New World.[12] Others retorted that there was scant choice between the ideologies of the U.S.A. and the U.S.S.R., that any coordination of military forces would be dangerous in the extreme. Yet the choice was weighted when it was a case of acquisition of military equipment from the near-by and powerful Yankee, or from the distant European nation whose supplies could only be transported at the mercy of the world's most powerful navy, which belonged to the said Yankee. The United Nations would, at best, be a fragile house of refuge. Even if it did become an effective force it was likely to be heavily influenced by the nation within whose borders its headquarters were located. Another thought as expressed by a Mexican was in the form of a question: Might not the UN see fit to interpose in Latin America at some time or other and call upon Mexicans to aid in the enterprise?[13] The chances of Latin Americans in a hemisphere or regional program became more attractive the more they thought of the possibilities in the world organization. The logic was strangely similar to that of the French-speaking Canadians who quarreled with English-speaking fellow nationals but insisted that union with them was preferable to annexation to the United States. Would Latin American interests not be safer and Latin American relative strength greater in the hemisphere than in the world organization?

In the light of such reasoning the United States had a relatively easy time in standardizing the training, tactics, and methods adopted for military training in Latin America. This was chiefly developed through the mission system. The number of missions in operation varied from time to time, but as late as 1957 fourteen army, eleven navy, and fifteen air force missions were serving in the southern republics. They varied from a single officer in one case in Panama to eighty officers and men in Venezuela. Under the Mutual Defense Assistance Pacts with twelve of the republics, the United States provided the equipment and sent men to oversee its use. Also, all of the republics had become recipients of what was known as reimbursable military aid. In most cases the details were tailored to suit the needs of each recipient instead of all programs being modeled on one contract.[14]

---

[12] Samuel Guy Inman, "An Inside View of the Inter-American Conference," *The South in World Affairs*, VII, Nos. 4–5 (April–May, 1945), 20.

[13] Isidro Fabela, *Buena y mala vecindad*, pp. 61–63.

[14] Edwin Lieuwen, *Arms and Politics in Latin America*, pp. 205 ff.; *Report of the Secretary of the Navy, 1947*, p. 9; *1948*, p. 96. For a Latin American protest

Much heated debate took place in Latin America over collective intervention or collective security. The continued recalcitrance of Argentina and political unrest in other countries made the question immediately pertinent. On November 22, 1945, Uruguay, probably with the tacit approval of Washington, proposed a system of collective intervention in a note addressed to Secretary of State James F. Byrnes.[15] It suggested that the policy be invoked against a state guilty of flagrant and persistent violation of its international obligations or of "the essential rights of man." Argentina, Cuba, and Santo Domingo expressed approval of the proposal, while Mexico, Guatemala, and Venezuela proposed amendments. Obviously not many openly approved the suggestion, though it was at least a corollary of the "helping hands" suggestion made by Roosevelt back in 1928. Gallup polls might show that three-fourths of the people of Great Britain, the United States, and Canada wanted an international police force,[16] but Latins were less certain of the desire. They had never been fond of police of any kind, and foreign police as they knew them meant intervention. In 1948 the inter-American conference in session at Bogotá expressed this thinking when it wrote into the charter of the Organization of American States (the name just then adopted for the old Pan-American Union): "No State or group of States has the right to intervene, directly or indirectly, for any reason whatever, in the internal or external affairs of any other State. The foregoing principle prohibits not only armed force but also any other form of interference or attempted threat against the personality of the State or against its political, economic or cultural elements."[17] Another article did exempt application of this sweeping pronouncement to "measures adopted for the maintenance of peace and security in accordance with existing treaties." Thus the United Nations Charter and the Inter-American Treaty of Reciprocal Assistance were technically placed on a special footing,

---

see Manuel Medina Castro, *EE. UU. y la independencia de América Latina,* pp. 145 ff.

[15] This was consistent with Uruguayan policy at Havana (1928), Montevideo (1933), and Buenos Aires (1936) (*Department of State Bulletin,* XIII, No. 335 [November, 1945], 866, and No. 336 [December 2, 1945], which cite press release of November 27).

[16] *Inter-American Affairs, 1945,* pp. 30–31; W. W. Pierson, *The South in World Affairs,* VIII, No. 10 (December, 1945), 1–3. See Institute of Pacific Relations, *Security in the Pacific,* p. 118.

[17] Quoted by Laurence Duggan, *The Americas,* p. 207.

but evidently the ghost of intervention had not yet been exorcised.

In the United States the tide of public opinion was running high in favor of "the creation of appropriate international machinery with power adequate to establish and maintain a just and lasting peace among the nations of the world." A resolution to this effect passed the House of Representatives by a vote of 360 to 29 on September 21, 1943. Simultaneously a declaration came from Moscow to the effect that the United States, Great Britain, Russia, and China recognized "the necessity of establishing at the earliest practicable date a general international organization, based on the principle of the sovereign equality of all peace-loving States, large and small, for the maintenance of international peace and security." The Senate, accordingly, added this provision to the House resolution and approved the whole by a vote of eighty-five to five[18]—a far cry from the rejection of the League of Nations.

Latin American republics found themselves torn between two points of view. Should they rally to the United Nations as a protector against the United States or should they fear intervention from the United Nations itself either through its observers and peace-keeping forces or through the Court of International Justice?[19] In practice, the Security Council followed the lead of the old League of Nations and sought to avoid New World controversies. In the case of Guatemala in 1954 the Council, by a vote of five to four (two abstaining), left the matter to the OAS. In the controversies involving Cuba, Haiti, and Panama, only Cuba was able to secure a hearing before the Council; the other two problems were left to the OAS.[20]

For its part, the United States judiciously used the stick but kept the carrot in sight. Just before the sixth meeting of the foreign ministers at San José, Costa Rica, in August, 1960, Eisenhower asked Congress to appropriate $600 million for economic assistance for the Latin American republics. The implications were obvious. The conferees agreed to break diplomatic relations and to enforce a strict arms embargo on the Dominican Republic. When the major Cuban crisis erupted in 1962 the New

[18] Arthur Sweetser, "The League of Nations and Associated Agencies," *International Conciliation Documents*, No. 397 (February, 1944), pp. 142–143. Also *Inter-American Affairs, 1943*, pp. 45 ff.

[19] C. Neale Ronning, *Law and Politics in Inter-American Diplomacy*, p. 58. See also John H. Houston, *Latin America in the United Nations*, pp. 87 ff.

[20] Gordon Connell-Smith, *The Inter-American System*, pp. 234–314. See also Ronning, *Law and Politics in Inter-American Diplomacy*, pp. 77 ff.

World republics as a group supported the United States and, after some maneuvering by Washington, at the eighth meeting of consultation of the Ministers at Punta del Este, Uruguay, in January, 1962, seventeen states agreed that Cuba had placed itself "outside the American System." Then, when it became evident that Cuba was endeavoring to embroil Venezuela in revolution, all countries but Mexico agreed to break diplomatic and consular relations with Cuba.

Against this background of global internationalism and Western Hemisphere regionalism as desired by Latin America came the Rio Pact of 1947. The major provisions were carefully considered in Washington before the Rio de Janeiro Conference began. Senators Tom Connally and Arthur H. Vandenberg, representing the two major parties, agreed to support the general idea of mutual aid against aggression at the expense of an American state.[21] Once more Latin American fears emerged. Rather than describe the convention as a treaty of continental defense, one writer commented: "Perhaps it would be more exact to call it a Pact of Servitude or a Convention for Colonization of Latin America."[22] But the logic of events was powerful and a legal foundation was established that could be invoked later to secure cooperation in the Cuban and Dominican crises of the 1960's.

In Washington, too, there were some reservations about entering into multilateral military alliances for the defense of the Western Hemisphere if Argentina was to be a member. The objections were not merely the reflection of old suspicions; they also arose from the recent Buenos Aires repudiation of its pledge on signing the Chapultepec Pact. Slowly the atmosphere cleared and finally all was ready for the Conference to proceed.[23] Once the Rio Pact was signed it was referred to the Senate. Senator Vandenberg enthusiastically supported the measure with the statement that it constituted "the greatest advance ever made in the business of collective peace." The Senate approved twenty-seven to one. This Inter-American Treaty of Reciprocal Assistance provided: 1) joint political, economic, and military measures for defense against attack; 2) consultation on any threat of attack; 3) arbitration of differences arising between New World nations; 4) a defense zone extending from

[21] Arthur H. Vandenberg, Jr., and Joe Alex Morris, eds., *The Private Papers of Senator Vandenberg*, pp. 369–371.

[22] Medina Castro, *EE. UU. y la independencia de la América Latina*, p. 182.

[23] *New York Times*, October 4, 1945, 1.2; also editorials, October 6, 1945, and January 3, 1946.

Greenland (exclusive of Iceland) to the South Pole; and 5) an agreement not to resort to force of arms "in any manner inconsistent with the
provisions of the Charter of the United Nations." Coupled with the
military aid program and economic assistance, the pact gave the United
States a major part of its postwar hemisphere program.[24]

Political and Organizational Considerations

As the war closed, a significant change in personnel occurred in Washington. The adjustable Welles had retired in September, 1943. Now
Hull, who had been physically ailing for some time, followed him. Hull
had tended to pursue a "hard" line with Latin America, especially in
the case of Argentina. However, he was a known personality and his
earlier work at the Buenos Aires and Montevideo conferences had left
a heritage of respect. His successor, E. R. Stettinius, Jr., was unknown.
After a moderately "soft" performance at the Chapultepec Conference
the new Secretary seemed to lose his nerve at the San Francisco Conference of 1945, where he appeared ready to scrap the whole regional
system, the darling of the Latin American republics. At this point it was
Senators Vandenberg and Connally who did much to save the idea.[25]
Shortly after this James F. Byrnes took over the State Department until
the end of 1946. He was a master of domestic political management but
had had limited contact with foreign affairs of any kind, and practically
no contact at all with Latin America. He was inclined to follow the lead
of his Assistant Secretary Spruille Braden with regard to the southern
republics. Braden himself had had a "rough" experience as ambassador
to Argentina and could hardly be expected to be too conciliatory.[26]

The major change, however, was the sudden death of the overshadowing Franklin D. Roosevelt. "El Hombre," he was the very personaliza-

---

[24] *Ibid.*, December 14, 1947, E, 1–2. Also Kenneth Colegrove, *The American
Senate and World Peace*, pp. 150 ff.

[25] See Sumner Welles, *Where Are We Heading?*, pp. 214–217.

Latin American demands for recognition of absolute juridical equality of all
nations were rejected at San Francisco (Houston, *Latin America in the United
Nations*, p. 26), but the Latin American republics gave strong support and steady
pressure on behalf of what became Article 51 of the Charter guaranteeing the
"inherent right of individual or collective self-defense" prior to action by the Security Council of the United Nations (Connell-Smith, *The Inter-American System*,
pp. 140, 217).

[26] Lottie M. Manross, *United States Policy toward Argentina*, pp. 31 ff. Also
O. Edmund Smith, *Yankee Diplomacy*, various.

tion of the Good Neighbor, the one who had never quailed, in spite of skilled military advice to the contrary, in insisting on the defense of the whole continent. Mexico expressed the overwhelming Latin American sense of loss when it proclaimed three days of mourning throughout the republic on receipt of the news of his death. In happier days this feeling had been expressed in a clipping from *El Imparcial*, of Chile, now to be found in the Roosevelt Papers. It reported the answer of a seven-year-old girl to the question "Who is Roosevelt?" With all certainty she responded: "He is President of the world."[27]

A new tone of responsibility now became obvious in American foreign policy. By May 1, 1946, the Department of State had 303 embassies, legations, and consulates scattered throughout the world, and a staff of about eleven thousand for its activities.[28] Senators J. W. Fulbright and Vandenberg openly and enthusiastically advocated internationalism.[29] Ex-presidential candidate (Republican) Wendell L. Willkie wrote an article entitled "Our Sovereignty: Shall we Use It?" He noted that by joining the Universal Postal Union, and by agreeing to international sanitary regulations and to the international control of radio wave lengths, a nation gave up some of its vaunted sovereignty. He concluded that "in the world today no single state which wishes to have friendly relations with other states is able to exercise *all* its rights independently of other states." The best way to protect national sovereignty was to create an effective instrument of peace. "If this is called 'bartering,' I would say it is a profitable transaction, and I would rather see the United States enter into it than to pursue its own aloof way into a third world war."[30]

This new sense of responsibility and maturity was also seen in more systematic contacts between the State Department and Congress. The days when John Hay could deplore having a Congress on his hands were literally a thing of the past, for Congress was in session nearly all the time anyway. A Secretary of State simply had to learn to live with it. To help meet this need, the State Department in the reorganization of January, 1944, named an Assistant Secretary as liaison officer with

[27] Franklin D. Roosevelt Papers, Hyde Park, O.F. 429-A, 1942–1945.

[28] *Fortune*, XXXIV, No. 1 (July, 1946), 81; William P. Maddox, "The Foreign Service in Transition," *For. Affs.*, XXV, No. 2 (January, 1947), 304 ff.

[29] J. W. Fulbright to American Bar Association, August 26, 1943, *International Conciliation Documents*, No. 395 (1943), Sec. 1, pp. 606 ff.

[30] *For. Affs.*, XXII (1943–1944), 356, 360.

Congress. Bipartisanship was a major objective, and a series of meetings were scheduled by key men including four Democrats, three Republicans, and one Progressive to discuss collective security. During the campaign of 1944 Secretary Hull himself held a number of conferences with John Foster Dulles, foreign-policy adviser of the Republican candidate Thomas E. Dewey. In addition there were such sessions as that at Mackinac Island, Michigan, of leading Republicans. It fully endorsed international collaboration,[31] even though the program was likely to be applied as Democratic policy. Public sentiment was keeping pace. A July, 1942, Gallup poll showed that 59 per cent of the people of the United States favored some form of world organization; in December, 73 per cent gave their approval; and by June, 1943, 78 per cent favored United States participation in a postwar peace system, and only 13 per cent opposed.[32] True, this very emphasis on global internationalism did raise the question of whether regionalism on a hemisphere basis was outgrown. Had not Woodrow Wilson given up his Pan-American Pact for the League of Nations?

Canada was also growing up. Its old inferiority complex had largely disappeared. At San Francisco the Dominion played a substantial part among world nations and allied itself with a new group of middle-sized powers.[33] A few unreconstructed critics still argued that "American foreign policy has been a disgraceful illustration of the irresponsibility of a powerful nation which promises little for the future stability of the western world."[34] Most Canadians, however, found that their southern neighbor, as in the period between the world wars, was quite likely to express their own opinion when it came to specific action in any one case involving relations with third powers. Internally, too, the Dominion was facing an increasingly acute situation arising from vociferous French Canadians. Sitting astride the St. Lawrence Waterway the Québeçois demanded an increasing voice in national affairs. And periodically there arose the old question of annexation which the French Canadians did not want. A Gallup poll in the spring of 1943 showed that

---

[31] Arthur H. Vandenberg, *International Conciliation Documents*, No. 422 (1946), 305; Alistair Cook in *The Listener*, XXXII, No. 833 (December 28, 1944), 707; *For. Pol. Assn. Reports*, XX (1944–1945), No. 21, 272–273.

[32] Colegrove, *The Senate and World Peace*, pp. 117–118.

[33] Lionel Belber, "Canada's New Stature," *For. Affs.*, XXIV, No. 2 (January, 1946), 277 ff.: Hugh L. Keenleyside, *Canada and the United States*, p. 362.

[34] Harold A. Innis, *Great Britain, the United States and Canada*, p. 24.

only 49 per cent of the Canadian population wanted to remain in the British Empire, and that 21 per cent professed to want to join the United States. That same year the speaker of the Ontario legislature stated that 40 to 45 per cent of Canadians would vote for union with their southern neighbor.[35] This might well be dismissed as the effects of German victories and war tragedies, but another still more disconcerting report was to follow well after the close of the war. In June, 1964, a survey by *Maclean's Magazine* showed 29 per cent of all Canadians still favored political union with the United States, and 42 per cent wanted economic union only. Then followed the old complaint that the able young men were migrating southward, "an estimated 50,000 in 1963."[36] These figures carry the reader beyond the time limits of this study, but they reveal something of the atmosphere in which the people of the two countries faced the future as the war closed and each reconsidered its national policies.

International Conferences

The Atlantic Charter of August 14, 1941, was followed on January 1, 1942, by the joint declaration of the United Nations. The United States, Canada, and nine of the Latin American republics signed immediately. Others adhered later. On July 23, 1942, Secretary Hull stated in a radio address: "It is plain that some international agency must be created which can—by force, if necessary—keep the peace among nations of the future."[37] By December, 1943, active discussions were begun by military, political, and private leaders under the name of the Informal Political Agenda group. In the first half of 1944 they held fifty-two sessions. After some changes in name and organization their work culminated in plans for the Dumbarton Oaks conversations.[38]

In August, 1943, Churchill and Roosevelt met at Quebec. The Casablanca meeting and other conferences had been based on military problems. This session still had military questions at the head of the agenda, but it was also "concerned with a wide range of political and economic problems, and both Mr. Hull and Mr. Eden were present."[39] Canada was

[35] *Inter-American Affairs, 1943*, p. 65.
[36] Mordecai Richler, "Quebec Oui, Ottawa, Non!," *Encounter*, XXIII, No. 6 (December, 1964), 79.
[37] Department of State, *Postwar Foreign Policy Preparation, 1939–1945*, p. 94.
[38] *Ibid.*, pp. 247–249.
[39] *Ibid.*, p. 187.

proud to serve as host and was quick to endorse what was being done, but Latin Americans felt peculiarly ignored. At the very time of the Quebec Conference the Colombian Foreign Office called on six neighboring states (Venezuela, Ecuador, Peru, Chile, Uruguay, and Paraguay) to send delegates to a meeting to agree upon their "political position" as "associates of the United Nations." The delegates were to consider war emergencies "and define the multiple problems to be met after the war."[40] The proposal for the meeting was not antagonistic to the United States but reflected a feeling that it behooved Latin Americans to look after their own interests.

The by now sharply critical Welles complained that the Inter-American Judicial Committee, authorized at Panama in 1939, had been entrusted with consideration of postwar problems, yet it was not called on for advice in planning the Dumbarton Oaks sessions.[41] Hull logically argued that to bring in the Latin American republics would require admission of all other members of the United Nations, and that such a body would be completely unwieldy. In an effort to moderate the criticism, on June 26, on July 11, and on three other dates the Secretary held conferences with Latin American representatives in Washington to keep them informed of what was going on.[42] Once the Dumbarton proposals were drafted they were submitted to members of the United Nations for consideration. By the end of the year about half of the Latin American republics had made suggestions. As a group these recommendations were calculated to give Latin America more representation in general as well as formal representation on the Security Council.[43]

Section C of Chapter VIII of the Dumbarton draft endorsed the formation of regional systems "for dealing with such matters relating to the maintenance of international peace and security as are appropriate for regional action." Recognition of the Latin American republics on the Security Council, however, was left to their ability to secure votes for their representatives to the elective seats.[44] A quite different point of

[40] *New York Times,* August 20, 1943, 7.7.
[41] Welles, *Where Are We Heading?*, pp. 34–35. Also Charles G. Fenwick in *Department of State Bulletin*, XII, No. 294 (February 11, 1945), 194 ff.
[42] Cordell Hull, *The Memoirs of Cordell Hull*, II, 1709–1710.
[43] *New York Times,* December 31, 1944, 18.1.
[44] Walter R. Sharp, "The Inter-American System and the United Nations," *For. Affs.*, XXIII, No. 3 (April, 1945), 450. Also *International Conciliation Documents*, No. 405 (November, 1944), pp. 728–729.

view was expressed by the U.S.S.R. The Soviets were openly fearful of all these New World votes, which it considered the United States had in its "back pocket." Thus Washington was forced to try to pacify restless Latins on one hand while it reassured the Russians on the other.

The New World republics which had cooperated in the war (all but Argentina) sent representatives to the Chapultepec Conference in February and March, 1945. The able Mexican Foreign Minister, Ezequiel Padilla, presided. His keynote address called for continued support for the war effort but centered its main attention on the future and on postwar conditions. He endorsed plans for future peace and security but reserved his major emphasis for the economic needs of Latin America.[45] As he later viewed the Conference, Padilla felt that the two chief instruments adopted were the one dealing with the reorganization, consolidation, and strengthening of the Inter-American system; and the pledge of reciprocal assistance and of American solidarity.

The first of these provided that the members of the Governing Board of the Union would have the rank of ambassadors but would not necessarily represent their countries at Washington.[46] The board would have the power to call both consultative and extraordinary meetings. It was to be under the chairmanship of a director-general, elected for a ten-year term, not eligible for re-election, and not to be followed by a national of the same country. This ended the indefinite tenure of the United States Secretary of State as chairman. The inter-American conferences were to meet at four-year intervals, with consultative meetings yearly. An Economic and Social Council was to replace the old Financial and Economic Advisory Committee, with cultural relations to be stressed.

The Reciprocal Assistance and American Solidarity Agreement went beyond the provisions of the Buenos Aires, Lima, and Havana Conferences in that it outlawed all attacks from both without and within the continent. The enforcement measures were spelled out on an ascending scale as: "the withdrawal of the chiefs of mission and rupture of diplomatic relations, the imposition of economic sanctions, and the use of

[45] Inman, "Inside View," *The South in World Affairs*, VII, Nos. 4–5 (April–May, 1945), 10, 33. Also *Inter-American Affairs, 1945*, p. 2; Mecham, *U.S. and Inter-American Security*, pp. 259 ff.

[46] Between the Chapultepec and Bogotá Conferences only nine countries appointed special representatives on the Governing Board of the Union. Accordingly, the board, to keep its representation complete "voted to consider appointment of special delegates optional" (Duggan, *The Americas*, p. 197).

military force."[47] As a friendly gesture calculated to bring Argentina back into good standing a special provision authorized that republic's later subscription to the convention.

Any hope of Axis victory was gone, so Buenos Aires went through the gesture of a death-bed repentance. In spite of the disapproval of former Secretary Hull,[48] the United States sponsored admission of Argentina to the San Francisco Conference, which assembled in April, 1945. On May 1 the Executive Committee voted nine to three to admit Argentina. The opposition was composed of the U.S.S.R., Czechoslovakia, and Yugoslavia, which were bargaining for the admission of Poland. Nationalist China abstained. In the plenary session of the Conference the vote was thirty-one to four.[49]

The ineptitude of the U.S.S.R. in handling its Latin American relations cropped up once more. V. M. Molotov, the head of the Soviet delegation, made a "biting attack" on that outstanding Mexican, Padilla, claiming that he was a United States puppet. "The Latin Americans regarded the attack as an insult to all of them and as an expression of contempt for the belief in the dignity and independence of the smaller nations."[50] The paradox: a high tide of nationalism side by side with a high tide of internationalism. It was a case of power politics by the great powers with the rights of small nations safeguarded in the context of their great-power agreements.[51] Under such pressure it is not surprising that Stettinius began to weaken in his support of the regional pacts as demanded at Chapultepec. Another group giving the great powers concern was the Arab League, to say nothing of other incipient cliques. After considerable maneuvering, the conference decided to approve "collective" resistance to "armed attack" and to endorse peace efforts by regional groups. The endorsements did not go so far as the Chapultepec demands, which looked to preventive regional action as

[47] Ezequiel Padilla, "The American System and World Organization," *For. Affs.*, XXIV, No. 1 (October, 1945), 103.

[48] Hull, *Memoirs*, II, 1407–1408.

[49] *New York Times*, May 1, 1945, 1.1. This did not mean that Argentina gave up its "almost fanatic" demands for "freedom of action" and for the "protection of the last vestige of unadulterated sovereignty" (Houston, *Latin America in the United Nations*, p. 191). It simply acquiesced for the moment.

[50] Vandenberg, *Private Papers*, p. 179.

[51] Quintin Hogg, "British Policy, A Conservative View," *For. Affs.*, XXII, No. 1 (October, 1943), 30 ff.

well as mere defensive action, but the Latin American contention was at least partially accepted.[52] This was the point at which the Rio de Janeiro Pact of 1947 undertook to solidify the Act of Chapultepec into a positive regional defense pact.

A major difference between conditions in 1945 and those at the end of World War I had become obvious. At the earlier date the United States was striving to protect its own regional sphere of influence; now it was the smaller republics which sought regional autonomy as a group. As one writer has put it, the inter-American states were adapted to, and able to cope with, the problems of the Western Hemisphere and felt able "to run their own neighborhood affairs."[53]

Where did Canada fit into this hemisphere regionalism? Its trade was certainly increasing and it had established ministries in each of the ABC powers. Also, for the first time it had an unofficial observer at the Havana Conference in 1942.[54] It had agreed to take membership in all technical Pan-American Conferences and sent delegates to the Conference on Criminology at Santiago, Chile; to the Conference on Geography and Cartography at Rio de Janeiro, Brazil; and to the Conference of the Inter-American Bar Association in Mexico City—all in 1944. The same year it sent an observer to the meeting of the Inter-American Development Commission at New York.[55] Enthusiasts increasingly referred to the "twenty-two independent democracies" of the New World, instead of to the twenty-one New World republics. In April, 1947, Senator Vandenberg, chairman of the Senate Foreign Relations Committee, spoke to the fifty-seventh anniversary meeting of the Pan-American Union. He called vigorously for Canada to fill the twenty-second chair around the mahogany table of the Union board.[56] In spite of widespread support, the proposal was soon forgotten. Apparently Canada, recently anxious to join the Union, was tired of rebuffs and had lost its enthusiasm for the project. At San Francisco a tendency developed for the Latin American republics to vote as a bloc to prevent Canada

[52] Helen Dwight Reid, "Regionalism under the UN Charter," *International Conciliation Documents*, No. 419 (March, 1946), pp. 120 ff.; *Inter-American Affairs, 1945*, pp. 21–22.

[53] George H. Butler, Chairman Division of River Plate Affairs, *Department of State Bulletin*, XIII, No. 316 (July 15, 1945), 89.

[54] *New York Times*, June 1, 1942, 20.4.

[55] *Inter-American Affairs, 1944*, pp. 84 ff.

[56] *New York Times*, April 20, 1947, IV, 2.1, and April 15, 1947, 1.4, 24.3.

from serving on the UN Council, and to place both Brazil and Mexico ahead of the Dominion in questions of air transport. A Canadian writer dismissed the matter with the statement that the issue had lost its urgency. Canada was now in the United Nations and had made direct military arrangements with the United States for defense.[57]

Argentina[58]

Argentina continued to be a problem. After the Chapultepec Conference, Buenos Aires broke relations with the Axis, but a German agent could still report on August 30, 1944, that German societies, schools, churches, hospitals, and welfare institutions had not been interfered with, and that in some cases orders placed with German firms had actually been increased.[59] In spite of uncomfortable rumors, Stettinius and Nelson Rockefeller tried to look on the bright side.[60] Had not Argentina subscribed to the Act of Chapultepec and had not its Supreme Court declared three of the most unfortunate acts of the Colonel's government unconstitutional?[61] On the scene and observing what went on behind the façade, Ambassador Spruille Braden became disillusioned. At this point he was recalled to Washington to replace Rockefeller and to become the chief Latin American adviser for the new Secretary of State, James F. Byrnes.[62]

It was now evident that power in the southern republic lay in the hands of Juan Domingo Perón. He had long made obeisance at the shrine of Mussolini as the greatest man of the century. Claiming to be the Mussolini of the New World, he first acquired as his mistress, and later as his wife, the shrewd and glittering idol of the masses María Eva Duarte. Late in 1945 he announced his candidacy for the Presidency.

[57] Keenleyside, *Canada and the U.S.*, p. 396. Also *Inter-American Affairs, 1944*, pp. 77–78.

[58] General conditions in Argentina are reflected in *For. Rels.* and the *Department of State Bulletin*, IX, No. 225 (October 16, 1943), and XII, No. 289 (January, 1945). The *Times* (London) carried regular reports with a British accent. A keen American observer was Ray Josephs, *Argentine Diary*, while the Argentine point of view is found in Enrique Ruíz Guiñazú, *La Política Argentina*.

[59] Department of State, *Consultation Among the American Republics . . .*, pp. 42–43.

[60] Welles, *Where Are We Heading?*, p. 205; *New York Times*, January 6, 1945, 4.8, and January 12, 1945, 14.2.

[61] *New York Times*, April 6, 1945, 14.3.

[62] *Ibid.*, September 2, 1945, IV, 2.

He was supported chiefly by the city masses, the *descamisados* ("shirt-less ones," so named in contradistinction to Mussolini's Black Shirts).[63] By implication these poor fellows could not afford shirts at all. Be it remembered that the Axis was now visibly crumbling. Suddenly Washington tried to defeat Perón by releasing information that showed his complicity with the Axis cause. He loudly proclaimed that this was all a case of the "big lie" and was typical political dabbling of the hated Yankee in the internal affairs of a neighboring state. The result was a wave of nationalist feeling which helped instead of hindered his over-whelming election.

As soon as he was in office Perón showed that he was mindful of world events. At the time of the crisis over Iran between the U.S.A. and the U.S.S.R. he opened diplomatic relations with Russia. Simultaneously he asked his Congress to ratify the Act of Chapultepec and the United Nations Charter.[64] Obviously he was playing all sides of all international streets: first the Axis against the Allies; now the Soviets against the United States. At the same time he made a shrewd economic move. The *Times* (London) complained that the Russian economic mission in Buenos Aires had half a dozen ships in the harbor waiting to load the supplies that they were buying right and left from the glutted Argentine warehouses. The British found that they were priced out of the linseed market, and that the Russians were even promising delivery of Russian and German technicians, 10,000 motor lorries (trucks), 10,000 tractors and 2,000 aviation motors.[65] But soon the Russians were to get a lesson in Argentine procedures. Early in 1947 the *Times* reported that Buenos Aires police had raided a Russian fund-raising ball, and that the trade treaty remained unsigned[66]—still playing both sides of the street.

Once the Blue Book effort to defeat Perón failed, Washington turned to other matters, mostly economic. Its chief political gesture was to take an active part in the Rio de Janeiro Conference of 1947 in order to amplify and clarify the Act of Chapultepec for the defense of the New World. At the same conference Argentina sought to limit collective action to measures repelling aggression from outside the hemisphere,

---

[63] Welles, *Where Are We Heading?*, pp. 229–230. The *Times* (London) also re-ported the election on April 9, 1946, 3d.

[64] Arthur P. Whitaker, *The United States and Argentina*, pp. 217–218.

[65] The *Times* (London), May 29, 1946, 3e.

[66] *Ibid.*, February 17, 1947, 3d, and March 8, 1947, 4f.

and advised peaceful consultation only for intracontinental disputes. The proposal was rejected by a vote of fifteen to five in the Conference steering committee.[67]

Vague Enthusiasms

One emergent theme to be noted was Latin American sympathy for the U.S.S.R. The fact that during the war Russians had held at bay the German Army, recently thought invincible, commanded unstinted admiration. In addition, there was the recognized fact that the Communist revolution on behalf of the downtrodden masses had been a substantial success. Still further, there was the feeling that the Soviets had no territorial ambitions in the New World. Not a few agreed with Medina Castro when he said: "The United States and the Soviet Union polarize the international politics of our day. The Soviet Union defends peace as necessary to its existence and development. The monopolistic system resolves its difficulties through war."[68] A plausible appeal. Never reluctant to encourage world revolution, the Soviets dazzled the Latins with huge legation staffs of highly trained specialists. To Mexico they sent the famed Constantin Oumansky. Cuba also received special attention, and new or enlarged legations were opened in other capitals. When Oumansky was killed in an airplane accident his funeral obsequies found Sinarchists, Fascists, and other extremist groups vying with each other in paying homage.[69] Washington was alert to the situation and in December 1943 informed its foreign officers in a circular letter that good relations were desired with the Communists but "this does not mean we should pass over in silence . . . Soviet activities in the hemisphere which we consider inimical to the security of the hemisphere, to its political or economic stability, or to our own interests."[70]

In Canada the Communists had less success and the party was actually outlawed for subversive activity during the war. Going underground they then engaged in espionage. The sole Communist party member of Parliament was expelled, and the movement declined until only an

---

[67] *New York Times*, August 23, 1947, 1.4.

[68] Medina Castro, *EE. UU. y la independencia de América Latina*, p. 229

[69] See Robert J. Alexander, *Communism in Latin America*, p. 41; Inman, "Inside View," *The South in World Affairs*, VII, Nos. 4–5 (April–May, 1945), 23–24; *Inter-American Affairs, 1943*, pp. 43–44; The *Times* (London), December 23, 1948, 5c.

[70] Quoted by Gardner, *Economic Aspects of New Deal Diplomacy*, p. 215.

estimated twenty-five thousand hard-core fanatics remained as "adepts at fomenting industrial strife."[71]

All in all, in spite of the admiration for the Russian war effort, the Communists as a party were able to make only limited progress in the major Latin American states. Typical was the fact that both Brazil and Chile in 1947 imposed restrictions on party activity. Brazil broke relations with Russia, and Chile arrested two hundred Communist agitators.[72] The chief exception to this statement occurred in Guatemala, where the overthrow of dictatorship left a power vacuum. Skilled Communist leadership took quick advantage of the situation in 1945. But the rise and subsequent elimination of this regime becomes part of the postwar policy of the United States and so is omitted here.

The general decline of Communist popularity did not necessarily mean that United States stock was rising. Unfortunately, Washington was so busy in other parts of the world that it relaxed its efforts on behalf of Latin American needs. As early as 1945 Hull notified Roosevelt that the appropriation for the State Department carried only $3,450,000 for cooperation with the other American republics and this figure was over a million dollars below the budget estimates.[73] Secretary George C. Marshall tried to explain to the delegates at the Bogotá Conference in 1948 that much of the world was in a critical condition.[74] Since Latin

[71] John A. Stevenson, "The Political Situation in Canada," *Quar. Rev.* CCLXXXVII, No. 580 (April, 1949), 255.

After 1960 the Central American republics in particular seriously feared the rise of Communism among restless peoples and of subversive activities being actively stimulated from Cuba. At their insistence a conference of finance and commerce ministers was called to meet at Punta del Este, Uruguay, in August, 1961. The result was the launching of the Alliance for Progress and of the idea of a common market throughout Latin America. Even though such a market might militate against the trade interests of the United States, the program was cordially endorsed in Washington. Admittedly the movement got off to a slow start. However, in 1967 nineteen Presidents and Presidents-elect of New World republics saw fit to grace a second conference at the same place. Again, President Johnson lent full support to the common-market idea and it appears to have acquired a new lease on life (Adolf A. Berle, *Latin America—Diplomacy and Reality*, p. 56; Lincoln Gordon, "Punta del Este Revisited," *For. Affs.*, XLV, No. 4 [July 1967], 624–638).

[72] The *Times* (London), October 22, 1947, 4f, and October 23, 1947.

[73] Hull to Roosevelt, July 1, 1944, Roosevelt Papers, Hyde Park, O.F. 20, State Department, September–December, 1943, and January, 1944–April, 1945, folder for 1944.

[74] George Catlett Marshall, *Address by the Secretary of State . . .*, pp. 4–5.

America was not considered a critical area it could expect other areas to receive preference. Beset by its own reconstruction problems, its delegates were resentful. More and more even the friendly Latin Americans were inclined to feel with the Mexican ambasador: "We see the United States advancing as a giant, fighting nobly for our ideals, but in the degree that the giant grows, its shadow falls on us, and we are frightened."[75]

Observers remarked that relations reached the lowest ebb in a decade.[76] Even in Brazil the surest way to political oblivion was said to be to advocate collaboration with the United States. In Central America it was popular to blame all local ills on the northern republic whose policy was said to fluctuate between banana diplomacy and petroleum diplomacy. If some Latin Americans continued to recognize their own shortcomings, few indeed proposed remedies without at least blaming their northern neighbor in some way for their plight.

Now came kaleidoscopic changes in Latin American administrations as restless agitators succeeded each other in power. At times this was done legally; at times, extralegally; and often illegally.[77] By early 1947 the far-sighted Vandenberg was calling for a more positive program, saying it was "past time" to do something.[78] When the new Secretary of State Marshall took office he did try to do something for Argentina, but unfortunately his major attention, like that of his predecessors, was forced in other directions. Positive New World leadership from Washington had lapsed for the time being.

Economic and Cultural Conditions

The year 1944 had seen successful revolutions or forced changes of government in Ecuador, Guatemala, Argentina, and El Salvador; armed revolts fail in Bolivia and Colombia; and Cuba and Brazil forced to

[75] Quoted by Mecham, *U.S. and Inter-American Security*, p. 258.

[76] For Latin American criticism see Germán Arciniegas, *The State of Latin America*, pp. 20–21; Raúl Osegueda, *Operación Centroamericana*, pp. 227–228; Galo Plaza, *Problems of Democracy in Latin America*, p. 17. For some American reactions see Olive Holmes, "Latin Americans for Overhauling of Hemisphere Policies," *Foreign Policy Bulletin*, XXIV, No. 19 (December 15, 1944); 2–3; Donald Marquand Dozer, *Are We Good Neighbors?*, pp. 224–225. For a British view see Arthur F. Lovejoy, "Some South American Republics," *Quar. Rev.*, CCLXXXV, No. 574 (October, 1947), 562.

[77] *Inter-American Affairs, 1945*, pp. 55 ff.

[78] The *Times* (London), January 13, 1947, 4d.

make substantial changes in their administrations.[79] In 1945 army officers ousted the Brazilian President; in 1946 a coup eliminated the Nicaraguan President; and the Bolivian President was assassinated. The next year the President of Ecuador was removed by the military and in 1948 forced changes took place in the administrations of Costa Rica, Colombia, Paraguay, Peru, Venezuela, and El Salvador.[80]

These movements were variously attributed to extremist groups of the far Right or the far Left, but seldom did any movement derive from a single fundamental cause. A well-expressed protest might serve as a catalyst to express a people's unhappiness, but the causes lay deeper. Here were industrial developments that attracted large numbers of country folk to the cities where housing was tragically inadequate. At the same time the beginnings of modern farming methods were displacing increasing numbers of the 70 per cent of the Latin American population that was estimated to be engaged in agriculture. Apparently 10 per cent of the population of the United States can produce a surplus above the agricultural needs of the United States. If even moderate efficiency were introduced into the Latin American farm system approximately half of the total population of these countries would have to be retrained for industry and transferred to new homes. These actually displaced persons were being subjected to all the pressures of serious postwar trade adjustments complicated by runaway inflation. As yeast to disrupt the unhappy mass were the radio, moving pictures, and the propaganda of some of the world's most skillful agitators, who promised wealth and happiness to all who would follow some particular doctrine or leader. Panaceas offered were legion but had a common denominator in repudiation of those responsible and heretofore powerful. It is noteworthy that the criticism from both extremes usually included damnation of the disliked Yankee, who was consistently blamed for collusion with the hated local tyrant. This was the more plausible since the United States was so busy with world problems that its primary desire in New World affairs was that Latin American administrators would maintain peace in their communities. Accordingly it did supply military equipment to them, and thus indirectly helped them to become, or to

[79] *Inter-American Affairs, 1944*, p. 210. The volumes of this series catalogue the story of the unrest from 1943 onward.

[80] *New York Times*, November 27, 1949, printed an illustrative map with a chronology of the disturbances.

remain, tyrants. Would-be rebels, in turn, sought to attract support of the local military to gain access to the force it had at its disposal. The result was that militarism seemed to be on the ascendant. Actually, the general social upheaval was fundamental and in many ways similar to the one in Mexico during the Revolution of 1910–1920. It remained to be seen whether its tools (the military) would remain tools or become masters.

As early as 1942 discussions and periodic conferences took place among the major powers to consider postwar global economic reconstruction. In June, 1944, representatives of some fifteen major nations met at Atlantic City, and the next month forty-four nations sent representatives to the Bretton Woods Conference. The product of the expert thinking of the time was to establish two international organizations—the International Monetary Fund, and the International Bank. The one was to help stabilize exchange and the other to finance worthy projects for national and international development. Both of these became part of the United Nations machinery and began their work by 1946.[81] The board of governors of each institution included representatives of the five nations contributing the largest quotas to the capital stock, and seven elective members. Canada had elective representation on both boards, while Brazil and Mexico were elected to the Fund board, and Chile and Cuba to the Bank board.[82] Counting the United States representatives, the Western Hemisphere had four votes out of twelve on each board.

As the war closed, a large loan was negotiated by the United States to support British credit. It carried a provision that effectively terminated the Ottawa Agreements and ended most of the Empire trade controls. Strangely, this change had relatively little significance for Canada. Jack Canuck turned from the war to home development and economic progress. He was part of an important industrial and trading nation capable of producing large quantities of exports of both raw materials and

[81] Treasury Department, *Articles of Agreement. International Monetary Fund and International Bank. . . .* Also D. H. White, "The Monetary Fund: Some Criticisms Examined," *For. Affs.*, XXIII, No. 2 (January, 1945); Fred M. Vinson, "After the Savannah Conference," *ibid.*, XXIV, No. 4 (July, 1946); John H. Williams, "Currency Stabilization," *ibid.*, XXI, No. 4 (July, 1946), 645 ff.; Henry Morgenthau, "Bretton Woods and International Cooperation," *ibid.*, XXIII, No. 2 (January, 1945), 182 ff.

[82] *United Nations News*, April, 1946, p. 7.

finished products.[83] When any new arrangements were made in international finance and trade Canadians could confidently expect to be considered and to have their interests treated respectfully.[84] If United States economic and political policies in international affairs were somewhat uncertain, most of the uncertainties were those with which Canadians sympathized.

The opening of huge ore beds in Canada was simply another step in bringing the two economies closer together, for most of the ore was processed south of the line. No wonder some British scholars were again openly predicting that Canada would soon join its southern neighbor. Others, often deploring United States shortcomings, faced the economic facts of postwar life in the statement that "Canada moved from colony to nation to colony."[85] The two contradictory statements here presented are deliberately placed together. Canada, standing on its own feet, versus Canada, a subsidiary of the United States—these were the contradictions inherent in the conditions of the day.

Policy dealing with European colonies in the New World centered in the Caribbean Commission. The inspiration for the organization had arisen from war needs, yet the original statement of objectives carried the wording "for the purpose of encouraging and strengthening social and economic cooperation" by means of attention to problems of "labor, agriculture, housing, health, education, social welfare, finance, economics and related subjects."[86] Even at the time when the British home standard of living was steadily declining, Parliament, deeply concerned over the Caribbean, set up the Colonial Welfare and Development Fund to make one million pounds available per year for its colonial empire over a twenty-year period.[87] After the war closed, the work of the

[83] O. J. McDiarmid, "Canadian Tariff Policy," *The Annals*, CCLIII (September, 1947), 155 ff.

[84] Lester B. Pearson, "Good Neighborhood," *For. Affs.*, XLIII, No. 2 (January, 1965), 260 ff.

[85] Innis, *Great Britain, the U.S. and Canada*, p. 4; John A. Stevenson, "The Problem of French Canada," *Quar. Rev.*, CCLXXXVI, No. 575 (January, 1945), 113.

[86] *Report of the Anglo-American Caribbean Commission, 1942–1943*, p. 3. Also *Accounts and Papers*, XXIV (1946–1947), 71 ff. Bernard L. Poole, *The Caribbean Commission*, provides a careful study of the working of the early days of the Commission.

[87] Harold Mitchell, *Europe in the Caribbean*, p. 35.

Commission was found to be good, so it was reorganized on October 30, 1946, and reoriented toward peacetime reconstruction. It gave special attention to technical guidance and systematic research into problems peculiar to the region.

At the Chapultepec Conference, Assistant Secretary of State William L. Clayton took an approach similar to that of Padilla and urged the termination of economic nationalism in facing the future.[88] This sounded fine, but new economic conditions in Latin American republics enabled them for the first time to taste the fruits of economic nationalism as beneficiaries. Most of them were anxious to enjoy more of the same. Milton Eisenhower bluntly said: "Latin America is destined to be an economically powerful area of the globe." He added that "its firmest and most extensive relations can and should be with the United States."[89] True, but with their own mineral- and water-power resources Mexico, Colombia, Brazil, Chile, and others aspired to become self-sufficient. Then they would be in a position to trade surplus products for sought-after luxuries and special items. Where, because of local conditions, self-sufficiency was not immediately foreseeable there arose a demand for a local customs union with neighboring republics. This was true in Argentina in regard to Chile.[90]

For its part, Brazil, the newly conscious giant with a burgeoning population (already in 1945 nearly twice as large as that of the United States and the Confederacy combined at the time of the Civil War), was now seeking new markets. There were even suggestions that its "manifest destiny" called for an outlet on the Pacific. Had the United States not demanded this a century earlier? Also, why not trade some of Brazil's now exceedingly productive iron and steel output for Argentine wheat at a distance of five hundred miles, instead of for United States wheat at a distance of nearly five thousand miles?[91] The northern republic would always want Brazilian coffee, and so that source of "velvet" income was always safe. In his report for 1948 the United States Secre-

[88] *Inter-American Affairs, 1945*, pp. 12–13.

[89] Eisenhower, *Report to the President*, p. 23.

[90] *For. Rels., 1943*, V, 796; *Inter-American Affairs, 1943*, pp. 115 ff.; Lovejoy, "Some South American Republics," *Quar. Rev.*, CCLXXXV, No. 574 (October, 1947), 559.

[91] Bryce Oliver in Carleton Beals *et al., What South Americans Think of Us*, pp. 100–101.

tary of Commerce commented that it was obvious that the peak of Latin American imports from the United States had passed.[92] This was a new day.

Relations with Argentina improved. Special courtesies were extended to United States Ambassador George E. Messersmith in Buenos Aires. Also, belatedly, Argentina subscribed to the Rio Pact, and by 1950 the Export-Import Bank extended a credit of $125 million.[93]

Another factor was that the "have" nations no longer monopolized the merchant marine of the world. Hard behind the United States, Great Britain, and Norway in tonnage came Panama with approximately four hundred vessels, aggregating some 1,600,000 tons. This change was a result of war dangers when ships of various flags took refuge under the minimal controls of the isthmian republic (protected by the United States Navy) in governing wages, hours, crew selection, and taxation. But a new factor had appeared in the equation, and a new sense of self-reliance and of independence had appeared in another country.

As the war closed, there arose the problem of what to do with war-stimulated commodities (industrial, mineral, and agricultural). The failure of rubber exploitation in Brazil was paralleled by the experience of other smaller "war babies." The United States entered into at least fourteen rubber-production agreements with sixteen Latin American countries and colonies before the end of 1942.[94] These in most cases provided that the northern republic would take the total output for a term of years at established minimum prices. The output in volume was small in any one case yet the total was substantial. Even though the product could not compete with the new synthetic production in the United States for certain needs, nor with the East Indies with their cheap labor once the Oriental plantations were again accessible, the fact remained that more or less rubber latex had been made available for the world's markets. In the inevitable reorganizations many original investments were lost. The tendency was to sell out to local interests at a fraction of the original cost. With little capital on which to pay dividends the new owners made their product available at cheap prices

[92] *Report of the Secretary of Commerce, 1948*, p. 171.

[93] The *Times* (London), December 23, 1946, 3d; *U.S. in World Affs., 1950*, pp. 342–343.

[94] *Department of State Bulletin*, VII, Nos. 158–173, reports these as being signed by October 17, 1942.

for local manufacture. Another market for northern industry had been curtailed perceptibly.

More spectacular was the huge investment in such enterprises as the Volta Redonda steel works in Brazil, with smaller but similar plants in Chile, Colombia, Mexico, and elsewhere. As war needs for steel declined United States industry once more sought its old outlets in the south. But now the local product, just as had happened with rubber, was supplying no small part of local needs. To prevent dumping and the destruction of the new industries of which the small nations were so proud, high tariffs were imposed. And again the devil quoted scripture. This time it was the Latin American nations who repeated the old arguments used by the United States at the Santiago Conference (1923) and the Havana Conference (1928): Tariffs were an internal question to be determined by each nation for itself. To further protests came an answer in the form of a question: Which do you want—your money or your markets? If Latin American nations lowered their tariffs and bought United States products, the new local industry would perish and the money loaned thereon would be lost.

Of course it was easy in Latin America to repeat the old refrains and condemn the foreigner. In Bolivia, some publicists blamed Standard Oil even for the Chaco War.[95] United States tariffs were a favorite whipping boy.[96] Violent critics stated that 23 per cent of the United States population (Indians, Jews, Negroes, Latins, Irish, and Japanese) were subjected to segregation, discrimination, and violence.[97] A "smart" taxi driver in Lima informed his passenger that a given handsome building was the United States embassy; "but, do you know, asked the chauffer, with a sarcastic and bitter laugh, what they call it?" When the passenger professed ignorance, the answer was that it was called "the Palace of the Viceroy."[98] An intelligent British analyst commented on this anti-Americanism, saying that it was largely emotional and founded on a number of misconceptions, the main element of which was fear of economic, if not of cultural, dominance.[99]

[95] Beals, *What South Americans Think of Us*, p. 32.
[96] Eisenhower, *Report to the President*, p. 18.
[97] Osegueda, *Operación Centroamericana*, p. 155.
[98] Felipe Barreda Laos, *La segunda emancipación de América Hispana*, pp. 239–240. H. S. MacKintosh, "Politics and Economics in Latin America," *International Affairs*, XXI, No. 3 (July, 1945), 334.
[99] George C. Curry, "James F. Byrnes," in Robert H. Ferrell, *American Secre-*

Such was the mixture of conditions (fear, economic readjustment, and awakening peoples) that made up the international picture in the New World. The question left was whether a unifying procedure could be found to integrate it all. Obviously, a significant amount of the existing criticism was based on personality clashes and the lack of cultural understanding. To make matters worse, the State Department was so concerned about European and Far Eastern problems that it tended to neglect Latin America.

A New Approach

One writer has commented that after Pearl Harbor the United States began to realize that Latin America was its second line of defense. In view of the peculiar needs involved it extended its public-relations program, sent southward Walt Disney cartoons and films on United States life and customs, and greatly expanded its health and sanitation efforts.[100] The Foreign Ministers meeting at Rio de Janeiro in 1942 pledged joint efforts to improve health and raise the standards of living throughout the hemisphere. Soon all the republics except Cuba and Argentina entered agreements for projects jointly financed with the United States. By August, 1945, the northern republic had advanced $35 million (matched by $22 million in local funds), plus personnel, materials, and services. In 1942 alone some six hundred projects were launched for malaria control, vaccination, sewage disposal, water supply, and the like.[101] The tragic need for such was evidenced by a death rate of 10.5 per thousand in the United States; while Chile had a rate of 20.1; Mexico, 21.8; and Brazil, 25.8. Infant mortality in the United States was 45.3 per thousand; in progressive Uruguay it was 82; in

---

taries of State, XIV, 129, states that Byrnes, in the eighteen months of his Secretaryship, attended seven international conferences beyond the borders of the United States, and that one of these lasted nearly three months. Argentine affairs in that volume are disposed of in a paragraph and a half (in two entries); while Canada receives about the same amount of space. Ferrell in his own volume on Secretary Marshall in the same series (XV, 73) states that when the Secretary was preparing to go to the Ninth Conference of Inter-American States he "had so many things on his mind that he must have thought about Bogotá only on fleeting occasions anyway."

[100] Dozer, Are We Good Neighbors?, pp. 115–116.

[101] Duggan, The Americas, p. 163; Inter-American Affairs, 1942, pp. 132 ff., 153 ff.

Chile, 200; in Mexico, 126; and in Bolivia, 267.[102] The astonishing results of the program could be seen in Uruguay, where 300,000 were immunized against diphtheria. Between 1944 and 1946 the diphtheria rate dropped from 216 to 55.[103]

By 1947 the Inter-American Affairs Institute had centered attention on rural needs in Brazil, Costa Rica, El Salvador, Guatemala, Haiti, and Honduras. In Panama and Paraguay it had featured vocational agriculture and industrial education; Chilean activities centered in the secondary schools; while the program in Santo Domingo emphasized vocational education, physical education, and the teaching of English.[104] Even in critical Argentina was found the Instituto Cultural Argentino-Norte Americano, which owned its own building and had 4,000 students in attendance. As the war closed, the Institute was divided, and a new branch enrolled an additional 1,200 students. Brazil could boast seven such institutes, with one in São Paulo enrolling 2,500 students in English in 1945 and 7,000 in 1953. Even Asunción, Paraguay, reported 1,200 enrollees. American libraries were in great demand. One small one, with only 8,000 volumes reported 48,000 checkouts in 1952.[105]

Akin to this intellectual interest in the southern republics were the indirect and intangible influences arising from thousands of Caribbean laborers who came into the war-stimulated labor market of the mainland, and the migration of Mexican labor to the north. This latter migration reached as many as 110,000 at a time. The largest group of these laborers was in agriculture (they were said to have gathered 21 per cent of California's crops in 1943), but 50,000 were reported to be in railway maintenance and smaller numbers found their way into other activities.[106]

Another phase of cultural understanding came through student exchange. A special effort was made in 1942 to bring exchange graduate

[102] Duggan, *The Americas*, pp. 30–31.

[103] Luis J. Halle, Jr., *The Significance of the Institute of Inter-American Affairs . . .*, pp. 12–14.

[104] *Ibid.*, p. 19.

[105] Eisenhower, *Report to the President*, p. 9; G. N. Shuster, "Nature and Development of United States Cultural Relations," in Robert Blum, ed., *Cultural Affairs and Foreign Relations*, pp. 9 ff.; Herschel Brickel, "Cultural Relations in South America," *Department of State Bulletin*, XIII, No. 331 (October 28, 1945), 697–698.

[106] Marion Parks, in *Department of State Bulletin*, XI, No. 268 (August, 13, 1944), 160 ff.

students to American universities. Manpower demands caused suspension of grants to those who wished to go southward, but Latin Americans wishing to come to the United States were not restricted.[107] The special encouragement of graduate students merely served as pump-priming for the influx of undergraduate students who, at great expense and effort, made the journey northward. The year 1946–1947 found 3,813 of these prospective leaders of the southern nations in the northern republic. Only Paraguay (16 students), Uruguay (19), and the Dominican Republic and Haiti (46 each) had less than 75 enrollees on the list. The number from other nations ranged as high as 631 (Mexico). Indeed, Milton Eisenhower was to state in 1953 that 75 per cent of the South American students who studied abroad came to the United States.[108]

As at earlier dates, some of these students became unhappy and critical of their hosts. Others, more disconcerting to relate, merely became disenchanted with their old society and were to advocate smashing existing social and economic conditions in order to rebuild from the ground up. The Spanish writer Salvador Madariaga in the *Saturday Review* (March 25, 1961) pointed out that in Latin America the poet on Friday might well become the President or Minister of Foreign Relations the following Sunday.[109] And it was often the poetic nature that reacted to endorse the most violent procedures.

Conditions had changed and a new record had to be written for restless peoples and emergent nations. They could no longer enjoy essentially private revolutions of little more than academic interest to outsiders. Revolution in Peru menaced the vanadium supply of the United States steel industry, and interruption of Brazilian manganese and cotton exports was of immediate import to Canadian industry, to say nothing of its influence on United States industrial laborers and farmers.

For good or ill, the whole hemisphere had become a unit in United States industry and foreign policy. The program for the most part had originated in opportunism and self-interest in response to special incidents or special interests. At first quite different policies were adopted for the two different neighboring areas—Canada and the Caribbean. Then trade developed, industry demanded new products, and national power grew. Strategic defense involved both economic and military

[107] *Ibid.*, VI, No. 134 (January 17, 1942), 69, and VIII, No. 184 (January 2, 1943), 8.
[108] *Noticias*, April, 16–22, 1947; Eisenhower, *Report to the President*, p. 5.
[109] Cited in Blum, *Cultural Affairs and Foreign Relations*, p. 71.

factors on an ever broader scale until the whole hemisphere had to be considered in unity. In the nineteenth century cultural contacts were of interest to few except humanitarians and were subordinated to politics and economic need. By 1945, however, cultural policy as such began to emerge as a vital factor in its own right—a factor without which the political, strategic, and economic problems could not hope for solution.

Hemisphere thinking had come a long way in the nineteenth and first half of the twentieth centuries. Canadians, Latin Americans, and citizens of the United States had learned that they had become a part of an economic and strategic unit. Their political ideals were similar, and closer contacts had brought more cultural understanding. The major remaining problems were old ones become so intensified by world conditions that they became essentially new in their significance. These centered largely in social injustices and inequalities that all of the twenty-two democracies faced both intranationally and internationally. Unless the strong helped the weak to solve these problems the threat was omnipresent that embittered and frequently illiterate peoples would embrace extremist measures or alien ideologies in misguided and spasmodic efforts at self-improvement. Whether the approach was selfish or altruistic, and whether undertaken from Ottawa in connection with the French-Canadian question, from Washington on behalf of civil rights, or from Havana, Mexico City, or Buenos Aires in response to social needs or to fascistic or communistic agitation, the repercussions were felt throughout the hemisphere. Increasingly, national problems were international in significance, and national welfare depended on hemisphere thinking and welfare.

Bibliography

Abbreviations Used in Annotation

Amer. For. Rels.—Survey of American Foreign Relations
Amer. Hist. Rev.—American Historical Review
Amer. Jour. Internat. Law—American Journal of International Law
Amer. Secs. of St.—[Samuel Flagg Bemis, ed.; Robert H. Ferrell, ed.], *The American Secretaries of State and Their Diplomacy*
F. O.—Public Records Office, London, Foreign Office collection
For. Affs.—Foreign Affairs
For. Pol. Assn. Reports—Foreign Policy Association Information Service Reports
For. Rels.—Department of State, *Papers Relating to the Foreign Relations of the United States*
Hisp. Amer. Hist. Rev.—Hispanic American Historical Review
LC—Library of Congress, Washington, D.C.
North Amer. Rev.—The North American Review
Pol. Sc. Quar.—Political Science Quarterly
Quar. Rev.—The Quarterly Review
Rev. of Revs.—Review of Reviews
Survey of Int. Affs.—Survey of International Affairs
U.S. in World Affs.—The United States in World Affairs

Manuscript Collections

United States Repositories

Chandler Parsons Anderson Papers and Diary, Library of Congress, Washington, D.C.
William Jennings Bryan Papers, Library of Congress.
Philippe Bunau-Varilla Papers, Library of Congress.
Josephus Daniels Papers, Library of Congress.
James R. Garfield Papers and Diary, Library of Congress.
Walter Q. Gresham Papers, Library of Congress.
Edward M. House Papers and Diary, Historical Manuscripts and University Archives, Yale University Library, New Haven, Connecticut.
Philander Chase Knox Papers, Library of Congress.
Robert Lansing Papers, Library of Congress.
Richard Olney Papers, Library of Congress.

Franklin Delano Roosevelt Papers, Franklin D. Roosevelt Library, Hyde Park, New York.
Elihu Root Papers, Library of Congress.
Henry L. Stimson Papers and Diary, Yale University Library.
William Howard Taft Papers, Library of Congress.
Woodrow Wilson Papers, Library of Congress.

Public Records Office, London

F.O. 6, 1890–1905, Argentine Republic.
F.O. 371, 1905–1913, Argentine Republic.
F.O. 13, 1895–1904, Brazil.
F.O. 371, 1906–1913, Brazil.
F.O. 371, 1911–1913, Central America.
F.O. 55, 1900–1902, Colombia.
F.O. 135, 1903–1913, Colombia.
F.O. 371, 1906–1913, Colombia.
F.O. 5, 1890–1905, United States (America).
F.O. 371, 1906–1913, United States (America).
F.O. 371, 1906–1910, Venezuela.

Periodicals and Serials

America. Asociación de escritores y artistas americanos. Havana, Cuba, 1939–1958.
American Historical Review. New York: The Macmillan Company, 1895—.
American Journal of International Law. New York, 1907–1921; Concord, New Hampshire, 1922——.
The Annals. American Academy of Political and Social Science. Philadelphia, 1890——.
Atlantic Monthly. Scattered articles, 1890–1935. Boston and New York.
Canada in World Affairs. New York: Oxford University Press, 1941–1956.
Edinburgh Review. 1900–1930. London: Longmans, Green and Company.
English Historical Review. London.
Foreign Affairs. New York: Council on Foreign Relations, 1922——.
Foreign Policy Association Information Service Reports. New York: Foreign Policy Association, 1925–1944.
Hispanic American Historical Review. Baltimore, 1918–1922; Durham, North Carolina, 1926——.
Inter-American Affairs. New York: Columbia University Press, 1941–1944.
International Affairs, Journal of the Royal Institute of. 1931–1950. London.
International Conciliation Documents. Scattered documents of value. Endowment for International Peace.

The Listener. London: British Broadcasting Corporation, 1929——.

New York Times. 1894–1950.

The North American Review, Boston, 1815–1940.

Noticias: Weekly Digest of Hemisphere Reports. New York: Council for Inter-American Cooperation; National Foreign Trade Council, 1945——.

Pan-American Union *Bulletin.* 1907–1948. Washington, D.C.: The Pan-American Union.

Political Science Quarterly. 1886–1940. Lancaster, Pennsylvania, and New York.

The Quarterly Review. 1909–1950. London.

Review of Reviews. 1900–1937. New York.

Revue des Deux Mondes. 1891–1940. Paris.

The State. Columbia, South Carolina, 1940–1966.

Survey Graphic. Special articles in March and April, 1941. New York.

Survey of American Foreign Relations. Vols. 1–4. New Haven, Connecticut: Council on Foreign Relations.

Survey of International Affairs. New York: Oxford University Press, 1920–1955.

Times (London). 1896–1950.

United Nations News. New York: Woodrow Wilson Foundation, 1946–1949.

The United States in World Affairs. 1931–1941. New York: Harper and Brothers for Council on Foreign Relations.

War-Peace Pamphlets. Varying dates. Stanford, California: Stanford University.

Government Documents

United States

The Chaco Peace Conference: Report of the Delegation of the United States of America to the Peace Conference held at Buenos Aires, July 1, 1935–January 3, 1939. Washington, D.C., 1940.

Clark, Joshua Reuben. *Memorandum on the Monroe Doctrine.* Senate Document No. 114, 71st Cong., 2d Sess. Washington, D.C., 1930.

Correspondence Relating to Wrongs done to American Citizens by the Government of Venezuela. . . . Senate Document No. 413, 60th Cong., 1st Sess. Washington, D.C., 1908.

Department of State. *Consultation Among the American Republics with respect to the Argentine Situation.* Washington, D. C., 1946.

——. *Executive Agreement Series.* Washington, D.C., 1929——.

——. *Inter-American Series.* Washington, D.C., 1932–1943.

——. *Papers Relating to the Foreign Relations of the United States, 1890–1944.* Washington, D.C., 1891–1968.

————. *Papers Relating to the Foreign Relations of the United States. The Lansing Papers, 1940–1920.* 2 vols. Washington, D.C., 1940.

————. *Papers Relating to the Foreign Relations of the United States. The Paris Peace Conference.* Vols. I and XI. Washington, D.C., 1942, 1945.

————. *Peace and War. United States Foreign Policy, 1931–1941.* Washington, D.C., 1943.

————. *Postwar Foreign Policy Preparation, 1939–1945.* Washington, D.C., 1949.

————. *Press Releases.* Issued weekly. Washington, D.C.

————. *Report of the President's Commission for Study and Review of Conditions in Haiti.* Washington, D.C., 1930.

————. *Report of the United States Commission on Education in Haiti. October 1, 1930.* Washington, D.C., 1931.

————. *Response to resolution, correspondence between November 5, 1875 and date of pacification of Cuba in 1878 relating to intervention by United States in Affairs of Cuba.* Washington, D.C., 1896.

————. *The Right to Protect Citizens in Foreign Countries by Landing Forces. Memorandum of the Solicitor for the Department of State* [By J.R.C.]. Washington, D.C., 1929.

————. *Treaties and Other International Acts of the United States, 1776——.* Washington, D.C., 1931——.

————. *Treaty Information Bulletin.* Issued monthly. Washington, D.C.

————. *The United States and Nicaragua. A Survey of the Relations from 1909 to 1932.* Washington, D.C., 1932.

Department of State Appropriations Bill for 1936. Hearings before Subcommittee of House Committee on Appropriations, 1935. Washington, D.C., 1935.

Department of State Bulletin. July 1, 1939–December, 1945. Washington, D.C., 1939–1945.

Diplomatic Correspondence with Colombia in Connection with the Treaty of 1914, and Certain Oil Concessions. Senate Document No. 64, 68th Cong., 1st Sess. Washington, D.C., 1924.

Diplomatic History of the Panama Canal. Correspondence relating to the negotiation and application of certain treaties on the subject of the construction of an interoceanic canal, and accompanying papers. Senate Document No. 474, 63rd Cong., 2d Sess. Washington, D.C., 1914.

Eisenhower, Milton S., Special Ambassador. *United States Latin-American Relations: Report to the President. Inter-American Series* No. 47. Washington, D.C., 1953. (Cited as Eisenhower, *Report to the President.*)

Gries, Caroline G., and Dorothy M. Ellis. *Cotton. Selected Statistics Relating to Latin America and the United States, 1923–1940.* Mimeographed by Department of Agriculture. Washington, D.C., April, 1941.

Hearings Before a Special Committee on the Investigation of the Munitions Industry. 73rd Cong., 2d Sess., Pts. 1–17. Washington, D.C.

Hull, Cordell. *Addresses and Statements of the Honorable Cordell Hull . . . in connection with his trip . . . to attend the Inter-American Conference at Buenos Aires. . . .* Washington, D.C., 1937.

Inquiry into the Occupation and Administration of Haiti and Santo Domingo. Hearings before Select Committee. Senate, 67th Cong., 1st and 2d Sess. 2 vols. Washington, D. C., 1922.

Inquiry into the Occupation and Administration of Haiti and the Dominican Republic. . . . Senate Report No. 794, 67th Cong., 2d Sess. Washington, D.C., 1922.

Investigation of Mexican Affairs. Hearings before a sub-committee of the Committee on Foreign Relations, United States Senate, 66th Cong., 1st Sess., pursuant to Sen. Resolution 106 . . . to investigate . . . outrages on citizens of the U.S. . . . Senate Document 285, 66th Cong., 2d Sess. 3 vols. Washington, D.C.

Knox, Philander C. *Relations between the United States and the Republic of Colombia.* House Document No. 1444, 62d Cong., 3d Sess. Washington, D.C., 1913.

Knox, Philander Chase. *Speeches incident to visit of Philander Chase Knox . . . to the Countries of the Caribbean, February 23 to April 17, 1912.* Washington, D.C., 1913.

The Lansing Papers, 1914–1920. (Published as a supplement to Department of State, *Papers Relating to the Foreign Relations of the United States.*) 2 vols. Washington, D.C., 1940.

Manross, Lottie M. *United States Policy toward Argentina: A Survey of Past and Present Policy.* Washington, D.C.: Library of Congress Legislative Reference Service (mimeographed), February 26, 1947.

Marshall, George Catlett. *Address by the Secretary of State before the Second Plenary Session of the Ninth International Conference of American States.* Department of State Publication No. 3139. Washington, D.C., 1948.

Moore, John Bassett. *A Digest of International Law.* 8 vols. Washington, D.C., 1906.

Report of the Anglo-American Caribbean Commission to the Governments of the United States and Great Britain, 1942–1946. 4 vols. Washington, D.C., 1943–1946(?).

Report of the Delegates of the United States of America to the Seventh International Conference of American States. Washington, D.C., 1934.

Report of the Delegation of the United States of America to the Inter-American Conference for the Maintenance of Peace, Buenos Aires, Argentina, December 1–23, 1936. Washington, D.C., 1937.

Report of Special Committee on the Investigation of the Munitions Industry.

Senate Report No. 480, 75th Cong., 1st Sess. Washington, D.C., 1937. [See also *Hearings Before a Special Committee on the Investigation of the Munitions Industry.*]

Report of the Secretary of Commerce and Labor. 1905–1956. Washington, D.C.

Report of the Secretary of the Navy, 1907–1948. Washington, D.C.

Richardson, James D. *A Compilation of the Messages and Papers of the Presidents, 1789–1897.* 10 vols. and 2 supplements. Washington, D.C., 1896–1899.

Roosevelt, Theodore, Jr. *American Naval Policy as Outlined in Messages of the Presidents of the United States from 1790 to 1924.* Washington, D.C., 1924.

Sale of Foreign Bonds or Securities in the United States. Hearings before Senate Committee on Finance. 72d Cong., 1st Sess. 4 pts. Washington, D.C., 1931–1932.

Scott, James Brown, ed. *The International Conferences of American States, 1889–1928.* London: Oxford University Press, 1931.

Tariff Commission. *Latin America as a Source of Strategic and Other Essential Materials.* Washington, D.C., 1941.

———. *Reciprocity and Commercial Treaties.* Washington, D.C., 1919.

———. *Reciprocity with Canada. A Study of the Arrangement of 1911.* Washington, D.C., 1920.

Treasury Department. *Articles of Agreement. International Monetary Fund and International Bank for Reconstruction and Development. United Nations Monetary and Financial Conference* [Bretton Woods, New Hampshire, July 1–22, 1944]. Washington, D.C., 1944.

———. *Statistical Abstract of the United States, 1878–1959.* Washington, D.C., 1900–1957.

United States–Latin American Relations. Senate Document No. 125, 86th Cong., 2d Sess. Washington, D.C., 1960.

Use by the United States of a Military Force in the Internal Affairs of Colombia. . . . Senate Document No. 143, 58th Cong., 2d Sess. Washington, D.C., 1904.

The Venezuelan Arbitration before the Hague Tribunal, 1903. Proceedings of the Tribunal. . . . Senate Document No. 119, 58th Cong., 3d Sess. Washington, D.C., 1905.

Weitzel, George T. *American Policy in Nicaragua. Memorandum on the Convention . . . relative to an interoceanic canal and a naval station.* Senate Document 334, 64th Cong., 1st Sess. Washington, D.C., 1916.

Foreign

Accounts and Papers. [Twenty or more of these used for period from 1900 to 1941. Each identified in footnote as used.] London.

British and Foreign State Papers, 1891–1945. London, 1893–1953.

Calles, Plutarco Elías. *Informe . . . al H. Congreso . . . relativa al ramo de Educación Pública.* México: Secretaría de Educación Pública, Vol. XVII, No. 19, 1928.

Documents Diplomatiques Français (1871–1914). 2ᵉ Serie (1901–1911). Paris: Commission pour la publication des documents relatifs aux origines de la Guerre de 1914–1918, 1934–1937.

Documents on British Foreign Policy, 1919–1929 [First Series]; *1930–1938* [Second Series]; *1938 to Outbreak of World War II* [Third Series]. London, 1947——.

Documents on German Foreign Policy, 1918–1945. Washington, D.C.: Government Printing Office, 1949–1960.

Fabela, Isidro, ed. *Documentos históricos de la Revolución Mexicana.* 4 vols. México, D.F.: Fondo de Cultura Económica, 1960–1964.

Gooch, G. P., and Harold Temperly, eds. *British Documents on the Origins of the War, 1898–1914.* 11 vols. in 13 parts. London, 1926–1936.

Obregón, Álvaro. *Informes rendidos . . . ante el H. Congreso de la Union durante el periodo de 1921 a 1924 y contestaciones. . . .* México, 1924.

Official Report of the Debates of the House of Commons of the Dominion of Canada. Ottawa, various dates.

Royal Institute of International Affairs. *Documents on International Affairs, 1938.* London: Oxford University Press, 1942.

Published Memoirs and Letters

Adams, Charles Francis, ed. *Memoirs of John Quincy Adams, Comprising Portions of His Diary from 1795 to 1848.* 11 vols. Philadelphia: J. B. Lippincott, 1876.

Alvarado, Salvador, *Mi actuación revolucionario en Yucatán.* Librería de la Vᵈᵃ de Ch. Bouret: México, 1918.

Atkins, Edwin F. *Sixty Years in Cuba: Reminiscences of Edwin F. Atkins.* Cambridge, Massachusetts: Riverside Press, 1926.

Baker, Ray Stannard. *Woodrow Wilson: Life and Letters.* 8 vols. Garden City, New York: Doubleday, Page and Company, 1927–1939.

——. *Woodrow Wilson and World Settlement, Written from His Unpublished and Personal Material.* 3 vols. Garden City, New York: Doubleday, Page and Company, 1922.

Bernstorff, Count. *My Three Years in America*. New York: Charles Scribner's Sons, 1920.

Bigelow, John. *Retrospections of an Active Life*. 5 vols. Garden City, New York: Doubleday, Page and Company, 1909–1913.

Bryan, William Jennings, and Mary B. *The Memoirs of William Jennings Bryan*. Philadelphia: John C. Winston Co., 1925.

Bishop, Joseph Bucklin. *Theodore Roosevelt and His Time. Shown in His Own Letters*. 2 vols. New York: Charles Scribner's Sons, 1920.

Byrnes, James F. *Speaking Frankly*. New York: Harper and Brothers, 1947.

Cleveland, Grover. *Presidential Problems*. New York: Century Company, 1904.

———. *The Venezuela Boundary Controversy*. Princeton, New Jersey: Princeton University Press, 1913.

Dawes, Charles G. *Journal as Ambassador to Great Britain*. New York: The Macmillan Company, 1939.

Dennis, Alfred L. P. *Adventures in American Diplomacy, 1896–1906*. New York: E. P. Dutton and Company, 1928.

Dodd, William E., Jr., and Martha, eds. *Ambassador Dodd's Diary, 1933–1938*. New York: Harcourt, Brace and Company, 1941.

Foster, John Watson. *Diplomatic Memoirs*. 2 vols. Boston: Houghton Mifflin Company, 1909.

Grew, Joseph C. *Ten Years in Japan: A Contemporary Record Drawn from the Diaries and Private and Official Papers of Joseph C. Grew, United States Ambassador to Japan, 1932–1942*. New York: Simon and Schuster, 1944.

———. *Turbulent Era: A Diplomatic Record of Forty Years, 1904–1945*. Walter Johnson, ed. 2 vols. Boston: Houghton Mifflin Company, 1952.

Gwynn, Stephen, ed. *The Letters and Friendships of Sir Cecil Spring-Rice*. 2 vols. New York: Houghton Mifflin Company, 1929.

Hammond, John Hays. *The Autobiography of John Hays Hammond*. 2 vols. Murray Hill, New York: Farrar and Rinehart, 1935.

Hendrick, Burton J. *The Life and Letters of Walter Hines Page*. 3 vols. Garden City, New York: Doubleday, Page and Company, 1922–1925.

Hoover, Herbert. *The Memoirs of Herbert Hoover*. 3 vols. New York: The Macmillan Company, 1951–1952.

House, Edward Mandell, and Charles Seymour, eds. *What Really Happened at Paris: The Story of the Peace Conference*. New York: Charles Scribner's Sons, 1921.

Houston, David F. *Eight Years with Wilson's Cabinet*. 2 vols. Garden City, New York: Doubleday, Page and Company, 1926.

Hull, Cordell. *The Memoirs of Cordell Hull*. 2 vols. New York: The Macmillan Company, 1948.

Lloyd George, David. *Memoirs of the Peace Conference.* 2 vols. New Haven, Connecticut: Yale University Press, 1939.

Lodge, Henry Cabot, ed. *Selections from the Correspondence of Theodore Roosevelt and Henry Cabot Lodge, 1884–1918.* 2 vols. New York: Charles Scribner's Sons, 1925.

Millis, Walter, ed. *The Forrestal Diaries.* New York: The Viking Press, 1951.

Phillips, William. *Ventures in Diplomacy.* Boston: The Beacon Press, 1952.

Quaife, M. M., ed. *Diary of James K. Polk.* 4 vols. Chicago: McClurg, 1910.

Roosevelt, Theodore. *Fear God and Take Your Own Part.* New York: George H. Doran, 1916.

———. *Theodore Roosevelt: An Autobiography.* New York: The Macmillan Company, 1919.

Morison, Elting E., and Jno. M. Blum, eds. *The Letters of Theodore Roosevelt.* 8 vols. Cambridge, Massachusetts: Harvard University Press, 1951–1954.

Root, Elihu. *Addresses on International Subjects.* Robert Bacon and James Brown Scott, eds. Cambridge, Masscahusetts: Harvard University Press, 1916.

———. *Latin America and the United States: Addresses by Elihu Root.* Robert Bacon and James Brown Scott, eds. Cambridge, Massachusetts: Harvard Univerity Press, 1917.

———. *The Military and Colonial Policy of the United States: Addresses and Reports.* Robert Bacon and James Brown Scott, eds. Cambridge, Massachusetts: Harvard University Press, 1916.

Scott, James Brown, ed. *President Wilson's Foreign Policy: Messages, Addresses, Papers.* New York: Oxford University Press, 1918.

Seymour, Charles. *The Intimate Papers of Colonel House.* 4 vols. Boston: Houghton Mifflin and Company, 1926–1928.

Sutton, Eric, trans. *Memoirs of Count Bernstorff.* New York: Random House, 1936.

Trevelyan, George Macaulay. *Grey of Fallodon: The Life and Letters of Sir Edward Grey, afterward Viscount of Fallodon.* Boston: Houghton Mifflin Company, 1937.

Vandenberg, Arthur H., Jr., and Joe Alex Morris, eds. *The Private Papers of Senator Vandenberg.* Boston: Houghton Mifflin Company, 1952.

Volweiler, Albert T., ed. *The Correspondence between Benjamin Harrison and James G. Blaine.* Philadelphia: American Philosophical Society, 1940.

White, Andrew Dixon. *Autobiography of Andrew Dixon White.* With Portraits. 2 vols. New York: The Century Company, 1905.

Wilson, Henry Lane. *Diplomatic Episodes in Mexico, Belgium and Chile.* New York: Doubleday, Page and Company, 1927.

General References

Abernethy, Thomas Perkins. *The Burr Conspiracy*. New York: Oxford University Press, 1954.

Ackerman, Carl W. *Mexico's Dilemma*. New York: George H. Doran, 1918.

Adler, Selig. *The Uncertain Giant, 1921–1941: American Foreign Policy between the Wars*. New York: The Macmillan Company, 1965.

Aikman, Duncan. *The All-American Front*. New York: Doubleday, Doran and Company, 1940.

Aitken, Hugh G. J., *et al*. *The American Economic Impact on Canada*. Durham, North Carolina: Duke University Press, 1959.

Alexander, Robert J. *Communism in Latin America*. New Brunswick, New Jersey: Rutgers University Press, 1957.

Alsop, Joseph, and Robert Kintner. *American White Paper: The Story of American Diplomacy and the Second World War*. New York: Simon and Schuster, 1940.

Álvarez, Alejandro. *The Monroe Doctrine: Its Importance in the International Life of the New World*. New York: Oxford University Press, 1924.

Angell, James W. *Financial Foreign Policy of the United States. A Report to the Second International Studies Conference* ... (London, May 29–June 2, 1933). New York: The Council on Foreign Relations [1933].

Angus, H. F., *et al*. *Canada and Her Great Neighbor. Sociological Surveys of Opinions and Attitudes in Canada* . . . . Toronto: Ryerson Press, 1938.

Arciniegas, Germán. *Caribbean Sea of the New World*. Harriet de Onís, translator from the Spanish. New York: Alfred A. Knopf, 1946.

———. *The State of Latin America*. New York: Alfred A. Knopf, 1952.

Arévalo, Juan José. *Fábula del tiburón y las sardinas. América Latina Estrangulada*. Mexico and Santiago de Chile: Ediciones América Libre, 1956.

Arias, Harmodio. *The Panama Canal: A Study in International Law and Diplomacy*. London: P. S. King and Son, 1911.

Bacon, Robert. *For Better Relations with our Latin American Neighbors: A Journey to South America*. Washington, D.C.: Carnegie Endowment for International Peace, 1916.

Bailey, Thomas A. *The Policy of the United States toward Neutrals, 1917–1918*. Baltimore: The Johns Hopkins Press, 1942.

———. *Woodrow Wilson and the Great Betrayal*. New York: The Macmillan Company, 1945.

———. *Woodrow Wilson and the Lost Peace*. New York: The Macmillan Company, 1944.

Balch, Emily Green, ed. *Occupied Haiti, Being a Report of a Committee of*

. . . Americans, who . . . Favor the Restoration of the Independence of the Negro Republic. New York: Writers Publishing Company, 1927.

Balderrama, Luis C. *El clero y el gobierno de México. Apuntes para la historia de la crisis en 1926.* México: Editorial "Cuauhtemoc," 1927.

Baldwin, Hanson W. *Defense of the Western World.* London: Hutchinson and Company, 1941[?].

Barber, Joseph. *Good Fences Make Good Neighbors: Why the United States Provokes Canada.* Indianapolis and New York: Bobbs-Merrill, 1958.

Barreda Laos, Felipe. *La segunda emancipación de América Hispana.* Buenos Aires: Imps. Linari, 1947.

Beale, Howard K. *Theodore Roosevelt and the Rise of America to World Power.* Baltimore: The Johns Hopkins Press, 1956.

Beals, Carleton. *Banana Gold.* Philadelphia: J. B. Lippincott Company, 1932.

———. *The Crime of Cuba.* Philadelphia: J. B. Lippincott Company, 1933.

———, et al. *What the South Americans Think of Us: A Symposium.* New York: Robert M. McBride and Company, 1945.

Beard, Charles A. *American Foreign Policy in the Making, 1932–1940: A Study in Responsibilities.* New Haven, Connecticut: Yale University Press, 1946.

———. *The Idea of National Interest: An Analytical Study in American Foreign Policy.* New York: The Macmillan Company, 1934.

Bell, Edward I. *The Political Shame of Mexico.* New York: McBride, Nast and Company, 1914.

Beman, Lamar T., comp. *Selected Articles on Intervention in Latin America.* New York: H. W. Wilson Company, 1928.

Bemis, Samuel Flagg, ed. *The American Secretaries of State and Their Diplomacy.* 10 vols. New York: Alfred A. Knopf, 1927–1929. [See also, Ferrell.]

Bemis, Samuel Flagg. *John Quincy Adams and the Foundations of American Foreign Policy.* New York: Alfred A. Knopf, 1949.

———. *La política internacional de los Estados Unidos: Interpretaciones.* New York: Carnegie Endowment for International Peace, 1939.

———. *The Latin American Policy of the United States: An Historical Interpretation.* New York: Harcourt, Brace and Company, 1943.

Bendiner, Robert. *The Riddle of the State Department.* New York: Farrar and Rinehart, 1942.

Benes, Eduard, *et al. International Security.* Chicago: University of Chicago Press, 1939.

Benton, Elbert J. *International Law and Diplomacy of the Spanish-American War.* Baltimore: The Johns Hopkins Press, 1908.

Berle, Adolf A. *Latin America—Diplomacy and Reality.* New York: For Council on Foreign Relations by Harper and Row, 1962.

Bernstein, Marvin D., ed. *Foreign Investment in Latin America: Cases and Attitudes*. New York: Alfred A. Knopf, 1966.

Bidwell, Percy W. *Economic Defense of Latin America*. Boston: World Peace Foundation, 1941.

Bingham, Hiram. *The Monroe Doctrine, an Obsolete Shibboleth*. New Haven, Connecticut: Yale University Press, 1913.

Birdsall, Paul. *Versailles Twenty Years After*. New York: Reynal and Hitchcock, 1941.

Bishop Joseph Bucklin, and Farnham Bishop. *Goethals, Genius of the Panama Canal: A Biography*. New York: Harper and Brothers, 1930.

Blaine, James G. *The Foreign Policy of the Garfield Administration* (a reprint from *The Chicago Weekly Magazine* of September 16, 1882).

Blakeslee, George H., ed. *Mexico and the Caribbean* (Clark University addresses). New York: G. E. Stechert and Company, 1920.

Blakeslee, George H. *The Recent Foreign Policy of the United States*. New York: Abingdon Press, 1925.

Blanco-Fombona, Rufino. *Crímenes del imperialismo Norte-Americano*. México: Ediciones Churubusco, 1927.

———. *La evolución política y social de Hispano-América*. Madrid: B. Rodríguez, 1911.

———. *El hombre de hierro (Novelin)*. Paris and Caracas: Tipografía Americana, 1907.

———. *El Hombre de Oro*. Madrid: Editorial América, 1916 (?).

Blanksten, George I. *Perón's Argentina*. Chicago: University of Chicago Press, 1953.

Blanshard, Paul. *Democracy and Empire in the Caribbean*. New York: The Macmillan Company, 1947.

Blum, Robert, ed. *Cultural Affairs and Foreign Relations*. Englewood Cliffs, New Jersey: Prentice-Hall, Inc., 1963.

Bonsal, Stephen. *The American Mediterranean*. New York: Moffat Yard and Company, 1913.

Brandes, Joseph. *Herbert Hoover and Economic Diplomacy: Department of Commerce Policy, 1921–1928*. Pittsburg, Pennsylvania: University of Pittsburg Press, 1962.

Brebner, John Bartlet. *The North Atlantic Triangle: The Interplay of Canada, the United States and Great Britain*. New Haven, Connecticut: Yale University Press, 1946.

Brown, William Adams, and Redvers Opie. *American Foreign Assistance*. Washington, D.C.: The Brookings Institution, 1953.

Brum, Baltasar. *The Peace of America*. Montevideo: Imprenta Nacional, 1923.

Bryce, James. *The American Commonwealth.* 2 vols. New York: The Macmillan Company, 1910.

———. *South America: Observations and Impressions.* New York: The Macmillan Company, 1929.

Bryn-Jones, David. *Frank B. Kellogg: A Biography.* New York: G. P. Putnam's Sons, 1937.

Buehrig, Edward H., ed. *Wilson's Foreign Policy in Perspective.* Bloomington: University of Indiana Press, 1957.

Buell, Raymond Leslie. *Isolated America.* New York: Alfred A. Knopf, 1940.

———, et al. *Problems of the New Cuba: Report of the Commission on Cuban Affairs.* New York: Foreign Policy Association, 1935.

Bulnes, Francisco. *The Whole Truth About Mexico: President Wilson's Responsibility.* Dora Scott, trans. New York: M. Bulnes Company, 1916.

Bunau-Varilla, Philippe. *The Great Adventure of Panama.* Garden City, New Jersey: Doubleday, Page and Company, 1920.

———. *Panama: The Creation, Destruction and Resurrection.* London: Constable and Company, 1913.

Bundy, McGeorge, ed. *The Pattern of Responsibility.* Boston: Houghton Mifflin Company, 1952.

Burns, James MacGregor. *Roosevelt: The Lion and the Fox.* New York: Harcourt, Brace and Company, 1956.

Caicedo Castillo, José Joaquín. *El panamericanismo.* Buenos Aires: R. Depalma, 1961.

Callahan, James Morton. *American Foreign Policy in Mexican Relations.* New York: The Macmillan Company, 1932.

———. *American Policy in Canadian Relations.* New York: The Macmillan Company, 1937.

———. *Cuba and International Relations: A Historical Study in American Diplomacy.* Baltimore: The Johns Hopkins University Press, 1899.

———. *The Evolution of Seward's Mexican Policy.* Morgantown: West Virginia Studies in History, 1908.

Callcott, Wilfrid Hardy. *The Caribbean Policy of the United States, 1890–1920.* Baltimore: The Johns Hopkins University Press, 1942.

———. *Liberalism in Mexico, 1857–1929.* Stanford, California: Stanford University Press, 1931; Hamden, Connecticut: Archon Books, 1964.

Canada in World Affairs: The Pre-War Years, published 1941; *Two Years of War, 1939–1941,* published 1943; *September, 1941 to May, 1944,* published 1950. New York: Oxford University Press.

Capdevila, Arturo. *América. Nuestras naciones ante los Estados Unidos.* Buenos Aires: M. Gleiger, 1926.

Carr, E. H. *Britain: A Study of Foreign Policy from the Versailles Treaty to the Outbreak of War.* New York: Longmans Green, 1939.

Carter, John. *Conquest: America's Painless Imperialism.* New York: Harcourt, Brace and Company, 1928.

Chadwick, French Ensor. *The Relations of the United States and Spain: Diplomacy.* New York: Charles Scribner's Sons, 1909.

Chapman, Charles Edward. *A History of the Cuban Republic: A Study in Hispanic American Politics.* New York: The Macmillan Company, 1927.

Cecil, Lady Gwendolyn. *Life of Robert, Marquis of Salisbury.* 4 vols. London: Hodder and Stoughton, 1921–1932.

Childs, J. Rives. *American Foreign Service.* New York: Henry Holt and Company, 1948.

Clark, Champ. *My Quarter Century of American Politics.* 2 vols. New York: Harper and Brothers, 1920.

Clark, Victor S., and associates. *Porto Rico and Its Problems.* Washington, D.C.: The Brookings Institution, 1930.

Clemenceau, Georges. *South America To-Day: A Study of Conditions, Social, Political, and Commercial in Argentina, Uruguay and Brazil.* New York: G. P. Putnam's Sons, 1911.

Clendenen, Clarence C. *The United States and Pancho Villa: A Study in Unconventional Diplomacy.* Ithaca, New York: Cornell University Press, 1961.

Colegrove, Kenneth. *The American Senate and World Peace.* New York: Vanguard Press, 1944.

Collier, Nina P., and Marjorie Sachs. *Preliminary Survey of Inter-American Cultural Activities in the United States.* (Mimeographed.) New York: The National Committee of the U.S.A. on Intellectual Cooperation, 1939.

Condliffe, J. B. *The Reconstruction of World Trade: A Survey of International Economic Relations.* New York: W. W. Norton and Company, 1940.

Condliffe, John B., and others. *Problems of Hemisphere Defense.* Berkeley: University of California Press, 1942.

Conference on Canadian-American Affairs, 1935, 1937, 1939, 1941. Boston: Ginn and Company, 1936–1941.

Conil Paz, Alberto, and Gustavo Ferrari. *Argentina's Foreign Policy, 1930–1962.* John J. Kennedy, trans. Notre Dame, Indiana: University of Notre Dame Press, 1966.

Conn, Stetson, Rose C. Engelman, and Byron Fairchild. *The United States Army in World War II.* 2 vols. (vol. I, *The Framework of Hemisphere Defense*; vol. II, *Guarding the United States and its Outposts*). Washington, D.C.: Office of Military History, 1960–1964.

Connell-Smith, Gordon. *The Inter-American System.* New York: Oxford University Press, 1966.

Coolidge, Archibald Cary. *The United States as a World Power*. New York: The Macmillan Company, 1909.

Coolidge, Louis A. *An Old-Fashioned Senator: Orville H. Platt of Connecticut*. New York: G. P. Putnam's Sons, 1910.

Cooper, Russell M. *American Consultation in World Affairs for the Preservation of Peace*. New York: The Macmillan Company, 1934.

Corti, Egon Cesar. *Maximilian and Charlotte of Mexico*. 2 vols. New York: Alfred A. Knopf, 1928.

Corwin, Edward S. *The President's Control of Foreign Relations*. Princeton, New Jersey: Princeton University Press, 1917.

Cox, Isaac Joslin. *Nicaragua and the United States, 1909–1927*. Boston: World Peace Foundation, 1927.

Creel, George. *The People Next Door: An Interpretative History of Mexico and the Mexicans*. New York: The John Day Company, 1926.

Crichfield, George W. *American Supremacy: The Rise and Progress of the Latin American Republics and Their Relations to the United States under the Monroe Doctrine*. 2 vols. New York: Brentano's, 1908.

Croly, Herbert. *The Promise of American Life*. New York: The Macmillan Company, 1919.

Cronon, E. David. *Josephus Daniels in Mexico*. Madison: University of Wisconsin Press, 1960.

Crowther, Samuel. *The Romance and Rise of the American Tropics*. Garden City, New York: Doubleday, Doran and Company, 1929.

Current, Richard N. *Secretary Stimson: A Study in Statecraft*. New Brunswick, New Jersey: Rutger's University Press, 1954.

Dangerfield, George. *The Era of Good Feelings*. New York: Harcourt, Brace and Company, 1952.

Daniels, Josephus. *The Life of Woodrow Wilson, 1856–1924*. Chicago: John C. Winston Company, 1924.

———. *The Wilson Era: Years of Peace—1910–1917*. Chapel Hill: University of North Carolina Press, 1944.

Davies, Joseph E. *Mission to Moscow*. New York: Simon and Schuster, 1941.

Dávila, Carlos G. *North American Imperialism: Address of His Excellency Don Carlos G. Dávila . . . Ambassador of Chile in the United States*. New York, 1930.

Davis, Harold Palmer. *Black Democracy*. New York: Dial Press, 1928.

Davis, Harriet Eager, ed. *Pioneers in World Order: An American Appraisal of the League of Nations*. New York: Columbia University Press, 1944.

Dawes, Charles G., *et al. Report of the Dominican Economic Commission*. Chicago: The Lakeside Press, 1929.

Dawson, R. MacGregor. *William Lyon Mackenzie King. A Political Biography, 1874–1923*. Toronto: Toronto University Press, 1958.

Dealey, James Quayle. *Foreign Policies of the United States. Their Bases and Development.* Boston: Ginn and Company, 1926.

Dean, Vera Micheles. *Foreign Policy without Fear.* New York: McGraw-Hill Book Company, 1953.

————. *The Four Cornerstones of Peace.* New York. McGraw-Hill Book Company, 1946.

DeConde, Alexander. *Herbert Hoover's Latin American Policy.* Stanford, California: Stanford University Press, 1951.

Dennett, Tyler. *John Hay, from Poetry to Politics.* New York: Dodd, Mead and Company, 1934.

Dennison, Eleanor E. *The Senate Foreign Relations Committee.* Stanford, California: Stanford University Press, 1942.

Dillon, Dorothy. "International Communism and Latin America: Perspectives and Prospects" in *Latin American Monographs* (No. 19 [1962]). Gainesville: University of Florida Press, 1962.

Dillon, E. J. *Mexico on the Verge.* New York: George H. Doran, 1921.

Dozer, Donald Marquand. *Are We Good Neighbors? Three Decades of Inter-American Relations, 1930–1960.* Gainesville: University of Florida Press, 1959.

Drago, Luis M. *Al honorable Elihu Root, 17 de agosto de 1906.* Buenos Aires, Coni Hermanos, 1906.

Duffy, Herbert S. *William Howard Taft.* New York: Minton, Balch and Company, 1930.

Dugdale, Blanche E. C. *Arthur James Balfour, First Earl of Balfour . . . .* 2 vols. New York: G. P. Putnam's Sons, 1937.

Duggan, Laurence. *The Americas: The Search for Hemisphere Security.* New York: Henry Holt and Company, 1949.

Dulles, John W. F. *Yesterday in Mexico: A Chronicle of the Revolution, 1919–1936.* Austin: University of Texas Press, 1961.

Dunn, Frederick Sherwood. *The Diplomatic Protection of Americans in Mexico.* New York: Columbia University Press, 1933.

Dunning, William Archibald. *The British Empire and the United States: A Review of their Relations during the Century of Peace following the Treaty of Ghent.* New York: Charles Scribner's Sons, 1914.

Duroselle, Jean-Baptiste. *From Wilson to Roosevelt: Foreign Policy of the United States, 1913–1945.* Cambridge, Massachusetts: Harvard University Press, 1963.

DuVal, Miles P. *Cadiz to Cathay: The Story of the Long Struggle for a Waterway across the American Isthmus.* Stanford, California: Stanford University Press, 1940.

Echanove Trujillo, Carlos A. *La vida pasional y inquieta de Don Crecencio Rejón.* México: El Colegio de Méjico, 1941.

Ellis, L. Ethan. *Frank B. Kellogg and American Foreign Relations.* New Brunswick, New Jersey: Rutgers University Press, 1961.

Emerson, Edwin. *Hoover and His Times: Looking Back Through the Years.* Garden City, New York: Garden City Publishing Company, 1932.

Estrada, Genaro, ed. *La doctrina de Monroe y el fracasado de una conferencia panamericana en México.* México: Antigua libreria Robredo de J. Porrua e hijos, 1937.

Evans, Henry Clay. *Chile and Its Relations with the United States.* Durham, North Carolina: Duke University Press, 1927.

Everts, William P., *et al. Economic Defense of the Western Hemisphere: A Study in Conflicts.* Washington, D.C.: American Council on Public Affairs, 1941.

Fabela, Isidro. *Buena y mala vecindad. Prólogo de Vicente Sáenz.* México: Editorial América Nueva, 1958.

Falconi R., Gerardo. *Hispanoamérica para los hispanoamericanos. Tesis doctoral.* Quito, Ecuador: Imprenta de la Universidad Central, 1930.

Feis, Herbert. *The Changing Pattern of International Economic Affairs.* New York: Harper and Brothers, 1940.

——. *The Diplomacy of the Dollar: First Era, 1919–1932.* Baltimore: The Johns Hopkins Press, 1950.

——. *The Sinews of Peace.* New York: Harper and Brothers, 1944.

Ferrara, Orestes. *The Last Spanish War: Revelations in "Diplomacy".* William E. Shea, trans. New York: The Paisley Press, 1937.

——. *El panamericanismo y la opinión europea.* Paris: Editorial Le Livre Libre, 1930.

Ferrell, Robert H. *American Diplomacy in the Great Depression: Hoover-Stimson Foreign Policy, 1929–1933.* New Haven, Connecticut: Yale University Press, 1957.

——, ed. *The American Secretaries of State and Their Diplomacy.* Vols. XI–XIV. New York: Cooper Square Publishers, 1963–1965. [See also Bemis.]

Feuerlein, Willy, and Elizabeth Hannan. *Dollars in Latin America: An Old Problem in a New Setting.* New York: Council on Foreign Relations, 1961.

Fischer, Fritz, *Griff nach der Weltmacht—Die Kriegszielpolitik des kaiserlichen Deutschland 1914–1918.* Dusseldorff; Droste, 1961.

Fisher, H. A. L. *James Bryce (Viscount Bryce of Dechmont, O.M.).* New York: The Macmillan Company, 1927.

Fitzgibbon, Russell H. *Cuba and the United States, 1900–1935.* Menasha, Wisconsin: George Banta Publishing Company, 1935.

Flack, Horace Edgar. *Spanish-American Diplomatic Relations Preceding the War of 1898.* Baltimore: The Johns Hopkins Press, 1906.

Fleming, Denna Frank. *The United States and World Organization, 1920–1933.* New York: Columbia University Press, 1938.

Foster, John W. *A Century of American Diplomacy, Being a Brief Review of the Foreign Relations of the United States, 1776–1876.* Boston: Houghton Mifflin Company, 1900.

Frank, Waldo. *America Hispana: A Portrait and a Prospect.* New York: Charles Scribner's Sons, 1931.

Froude, James Anthony. *The English in the West Indies; or, The Bow of Ulysses.* New York: Charles Scribner's Sons, 1888.

Frye, Alton. *Nazi Germany and the American Hemisphere, 1933–1941.* New Haven, Connecticut: Yale University Press, 1967.

Fuess, Claude M. *Calvin Coolidge: The Man from Vermont.* Boston: Little, Brown and Company, 1940.

Gallardo Nieto, Galvarino. *Panamericanismo.* Santiago, Chile: Imprenta Nascimento, 1941.

Gantenbein, James W., ed. *The Evolution of Our Latin-American Policy: A Documentary Record.* New York: Columbia University Press, 1950.

García Calderón, Francisco. *Latin America: Its Rise and Progress.* London: T. Fisher Unwin, 1919.

Gardner, Lloyd C. *Economic Aspects of New Deal Diplomacy.* Madison: University of Wisconsin Press, 1964.

Garvin, J. L. *Life of Joseph Chamberlain.* 3 vols. London: The Macmillan Company, 1932–1934.

Gelber, Lionel M. *The Rise of Anglo-American Friendship: A Study in World Politics, 1898–1906.* London: Oxford University Press, 1938.

Gelfand, Lawrence E. *The Inquiry: American Preparations for Peace, 1917–1919.* New Haven, Connecticut: Yale University Press, 1963.

Gibb, George Sweet, and Evelyn H. Knowlton. *History of the Standard Oil Company of New Jersey: The Resurgent Years, 1911–1927.* New York: Harper and Brothers, 1956.

Gil, Enrique. *Evolución del panamericanismo. El credo de Wilson y el panamericanismo.* Buenos Aires: J. Menendez, 1933.

Glazebrook, G. P. de T. *A History of Canadian External Relations.* London: Oxford University Press, 1950.

Goebel, Julius L. *The Struggle for the Falkland Islands: A Study in Legal and Diplomatic History.* New Haven, Connecticut: Yale University Press, 1927.

Gómez Robledo, Antonio. *The Bucareli Agreements and International Law.* México: National University of Mexico Press, 1940.

Gonzales, N. G. *In Darkest Cuba.* Columbia, South Carolina: The State Company, 1922.

Gonzales, William E. "Concerning Dollar Diplomacy, Crooks and Grafters—

Incidents: Paper . . . relating Experiences while Minister to Cuba and Ambassador to Peru." Typescript. [Columbia, South Carolina, 1937].

González-Blanco, Pedro. *De Porfirio Díaz a Carranza. Conferencias dadas en el ateneo de Madrid en los meses de marzo y abril de 1916.* Madrid, 1916.

Gooch, G. P. *Studies in Diplomacy and Statecraft.* London: Longmans, Green and Company, 1943.

Goslin, Ryllis Alexander, and William T. Stone. *America Contradicts Herself: The Story of Our Foreign Policy.* New York: Foreign Policy Association, 1937.

Graebner, Norman A., ed. *An Uncertain Tradition: American Secretaries of State in the Twentieth Century.* New York: McGraw-Hill Book Company, 1961.

Gregg, Robert D. *The Influence of Border Troubles on Relations between the United States and Mexico, 1876–1910.* Baltimore: The Johns Hopkins Press, 1937.

Green, Philip Leonard. *Pan-American Progress.* New York: Hastings House, 1942.

Gresham, Matilda. *Life of Walter Quintin Gresham, 1832–1895.* 2 vols. Chicago: Rand, McNally and Company, 1919.

Grey of Fallodon, Viscount. *Twenty-five Years, 1892–1916.* 2 vols. New York: Frederick A. Stokes Company, 1925.

Griscom, Lloyd C. *Diplomatically Speaking.* Boston: Little, Brown and Company, 1940.

Gruening, Ernest. *Mexico and Its Heritage.* New York: The Century Company, 1928.

Guerrant, Edward O. *Roosevelt's Good Neighbor Policy.* Albuquerque: University of New Mexico Press, 1950.

Guggenheim, Harry F. *The United States and Cuba: A Study in International Relations.* New York: The Macmillan Company, 1934.

Guzmán, Martín Luis. *Memoirs of Pancho Villa.* Virginia H. Taylor, trans. Austin: University of Texas Press, 1965.

Hacker, Louis M. *American Problems of Today: A History of the United States since the World War.* New York: F. E. Crofts and Company, 1938.

Hackett, Charles Wilson. *The Mexican Revolution and the United States, 1910–1926.* Boston: The World Peace Foundation, 1926.

―――, in *Mexico: Lectures before the Inter-American Institute of Pomona College and Claremont Colleges and the Pacific Southwest Academy of Political and Social Science. February 9, 10, 11, 1928.* Claremont, California: 1929.

Hall, Arnold Bennett. *The Monroe Doctrine and the Great War.* Chicago: A. C. McClurg Company, 1920.

Halle, Luis J. *The Significance of the Institute of Inter-American Affairs in the Conduct of U.S. Foreign Policy* (Reprint from the *Department of State Bulletin*). Washington, D.C.: Government Printing Office, 1948.

Hamilton, J. Cleland. *The Monroe Doctrine: Its British Origin and American Development.* Toronto, n.d.; also in *Canadian Law Review*, II, No. 6 (March, 1903).

Hannan, Elizabeth, and Willy Feuerlein. *Dollars in Latin America: An Old Problem in a New Setting.* New York: Council on Foreign Relations, 1961.

Haring, Clarence H. *South America Looks at the United States.* New York: The Macmillan Company, 1928.

Harris, W. Eric. *Achates; or, the Future of Canada.* London: K. Paul, French, Trubner and Company, 1929.

Hart, Albert Bushnell. *The Monroe Doctrine: An Interpretation.* Boston: Little, Brown and Company, 1920.

Healy, David F. *The United States in Cuba, 1898–1902: Generals, Politicians, and the Search for Policy.* Madison: University of Wisconsin Press, 1963.

Heindel, Richard Heathcote. *The American Impact on Great Britain, 1898–1914: A Study of the United States in World History.* Philadelphia: The University of Pennsylvania Press, 1940.

Henao, Jesús María, and Gerardo Arrubla. *History of Colombia.* J. Fred Rippy, trans. Chapel Hill: The University of North Carolina Press, 1938.

Henríquez Ureña, Max. *La Liga de Naciones Americanas y la Conferencia de Buenos Aires.* New York: L. and S. Printing Company, 1937.

―――. *Los yanquis en Santo Domingo.* Madrid: M. Aguilar, 1929.

Hill, Howard C. *Roosevelt and the Caribbean.* Chicago: The University of Chicago Press, 1927.

Hill, Lawrence F. *Diplomatic Relations between the United States and Brazil.* Durham, North Carolina: Duke University Press, 1932.

Hill, Roscoe R. *Fiscal Intervention in Nicaragua.* New York: Paul Maisel Company, 1933.

Hinton, Harold B. *Cordell Hull: A Biography.* Garden City, New York: Doubleday, Doran and Company, 1942.

Hodgins, Thomas. *British and American Diplomacy Affecting Canada, 1782–1889: A Chapter of Canadian History.* Toronto: The Publishers Syndicate, 1900.

Holland, Henry F. *Objectives of United States Foreign Policy in Latin America.* Washington, D.C.: The Department of State, 1955.

Holmes, Olive, "Latin Americans for Overhauling of Hemisphere Policies," *Foreign Policy Bulletin,* XXIV, No. 9 (December 15, 1944) 2–3.

Holt, W. Stull. *Treaties Defeated by the Senate: A Study of the Struggle be-*

tween President and Senate over the Conduct of Foreign Relations. Baltimore: The Johns Hopkins Press, 1933.

Homberg, Octave. *L'Imperialisme Américain*. Paris: Plon, 1929.

Hoover, Herbert, and Hugh Gibson. *The Problems of Lasting Peace*. Garden City, New York: Doubleday, Doran and Company, 1943.

Houston, John A. *Latin America in the United Nations*. Foreword by Ricardo A. Alfaro. New York: Carnegie Endowment for International Peace, 1956.

Hudson, Manley O. *The Permanent Court of International Justice, 1920–1942: A Treatise*. New York: The Macmillan Company, 1943.

Huete Abella, Rodolfo. *Los banqueros y la intervención en Nicaragua*. Managua, Nicaragua: Tipografía Perez, 1931.

Hughes, Charles Evans. *Our Relations to the Nations of the Western Hemisphere*. Princeton, New Jersey: Princeton University Press, 1928.

———. *Pan-American Peace Plans*. New Haven, Connecticut: Yale University Press, 1929.

———. *The Pathway of Peace—Representative Addresses Delivered during His Term as Secretary of State (1921–1925)*. New York: Harper and Brothers, 1925.

Hull, Cordell. *The Foreign Policy of the United States*. [An address.] New York: Carnegie Endowment for International Peace, 1940.

Humphrey, John P. *The Inter-American System: A Canadian View*. Toronto: The Macmillan Company, 1942.

Hunt, Gaillard. *The Department of State of the United States: Its History and Functions*. New Haven, Connecticut: Yale University Press, 1914.

Hutchison, Bruce. *The Struggle for the Border*. New York: Longmans Green and Company, 1955.

Inman, Samuel Guy. "An Inside View of the Inter-American Conference, Mexico City, February 21–March 9, 1945," *The South in World Affairs*, Vol. VII, Nos. 4–5 (April–May, 1945). Chapel Hill, North Carolina.

Innis, Harold A. *Essays in Canadian Economic History*. Mary Q. Innis, ed. Toronto: University of Toronto Press, 1956.

———. *Great Britain, the United States and Canada*. Nottingham, England: John Clough and Son, 1948.

Institute of Pacific Relations. *Security in the Pacific: A Preliminary Report of the Ninth Conference of the Institute. . . .* New York: International Secretariat, Institute of Pacific Relations, 1945.

Ise, John. *The United States Oil Policy*. New Haven, Connecticut: Yale University Press, 1928.

James Henry. *Richard Olney and His Public Service. With Documents Including Unpublished Diplomatic Correspondence*. Boston: Houghton Mifflin Company, 1923.

James, R. Warren. *Wartime Economic Co-operation: A Study of Relations between Canada and the United States.* Toronto: The Ryerson Press, 1949.

Jenks, Leland H. *Our Cuban Colony: A Study in Sugar.* New York: Vanguard Press, 1928.

Jessup, Philip C. *Elihu Root.* 2 vols. New York: Dodd, Mead and Company, 1938.

Jones, Chester Lloyd. *Caribbean Backgrounds and Prospects.* New York: D. Appleton and Company, 1931.

————. *Caribbean Interests of the United States.* New York: D. Appleton and Company, 1916.

————. *The Caribbean since 1900.* New York: Prentice-Hall, 1936.

————. *Guatemala, Past and Present.* Minneapolis: University of Minnesota Press, 1940.

————, H. K. Norton, and Parker T. Moon. *The United States and the Caribbean.* Chicago: University of Chicago Press, 1929.

Josephs, Ray. *Argentine Diary.* New York: Random House, 1944.

Keasbey, Lindley Miller. *The Nicaragua Canal and the Monroe Doctrine: A Political History of Isthmus Transit. . . .* New York: G. P. Putnam's Sons, 1896.

Keenleyside, Hugh L. *Canada and the United States: Some Aspects of Their Historical Relations.* New York: Alfred A. Knopf, 1952.

————, et al. *The Growth of Canadian Policies in External Affairs.* Durham, North Carolina: The Duke University Press, 1960.

Kelchner, Warren H. *Latin American Relations with the League of Nations* (World Peace Foundation Pamphlets, XII, No. 6 [1929]). Boston: World Peace Foundation, 1929.

Kellogg, Frank B. *Foreign Relations.* Published by the Republican National Committee as Bulletin No. 5, 1928.

Kelly, Sir David. *The Ruling Few; or, The Human Background to Diplomacy.* London: Hollis and Carter, 1952.

Kelsey, Carl. *The American Intervention in Haiti and the Dominican Republic. (The Annals* [March, 1922]). Philadelphia.

Kennan, George F. *American Diplomacy, 1900–1950.* Chicago: The University of Chicago Press, 1951.

————. *Realities of American Foreign Policy.* Princeton, New Jersey: The Princeton University Press, 1954.

Kinnaird, Lawrence, ed. *Spain in the Mississippi Valley, 1765–1794. (Annual Report of the American Historical Association, 1945, Vols. II and III).* Washington, D.C., 1945.

Kirk, Grayson, *The Monroe Doctrine Today.* New York: Farrar and Rinehart, 1941.

Kirkpatrick, Frederick Alexander. *South America and the War . . . the Sub-*

stance . . . *of Lectures . . . in the University of London.* Cambridge: Cambridge University Press, 1918.

Knight, Melvin M. *The Americans in Santo Domingo.* New York: Vanguard Press, 1928.

Kurtz, Roberto. *La Argentina ante Estados Unidos.* Buenos Aires: Librería del Colégio, 1928.

LaFeber, Walter. *The New Empire: An Interpretation of American Expansion, 1860–1898.* Ithaca, New York: Cornell University Press, 1963.

Langer, William L. *The Diplomacy of Imperialism.* New York: Alfred A. Knopf, 1951.

————, and S. Everett Gleason. *The Challenge to Isolation, 1937–1940.* New York: Harper and Brothers, 1952.

————. *The Undeclared War, 1940–1941.* New York: Harper and Brothers, 1953.

Laski, Harold J. *The American Presidency: An Interpretation.* New York: Harper and Brothers, 1940.

Latané, John Holladay. *Diplomatic Relations of the United States and Latin America.* Baltimore: Johns Hopkins University Press, 1900.

————. *The United States and Latin America.* Garden City, New York: Doubleday, Page and Company, 1920.

Latin American Economic Institute. *The Economic Defense of the Western Hemisphere: A Study in Conflicts.* Washington, D.C.: American Council on Public Affairs, 1941.

Lewis, Cleona, and Karl T. Schlotterbeck. *America's Stake in International Investments.* Washington, D.C.: The Brookings Institution, 1938.

Lieuwen, Edwin. *Arms and Politics in Latin America.* New York: F. A. Praeger, 1960.

————. *Venezuela.* London: Oxford University Press for Royal Institute of International Affairs, 1961.

Link, Arthur S. *Wilson: Confusions and Crises, 1915–1916.* Princeton, New Jersey: Princeton University Press, 1964.

————. *Wilson: The New Freedom.* Princeton, New Jersey, Princeton University Press, 1956.

————. *Wilson: The Struggle for Neutrality, 1914–1915.* Princeton, New Jersey, Princeton University Press, 1960.

————. *Wilson the Diplomatist: A Look at His Major Policies.* Baltimore: Johns Hopkins University Press, 1957.

Lippmann, Walter. *U.S. Foreign Policy: Shield of the Republic.* Boston: Little, Brown and Company, 1943.

Lockey, Joseph Byrne. *Pan-Americanism: Its Beginnings.* New York: The Macmillan Company, 1926.

Lodge, Henry Cabot. *The Senate and the League of Nations.* New York: Charles Scribner's Sons, 1925.

Logan, John A., Jr. *No Transfer: An American Security Principle.* New Haven, Connecticut: Yale University Press, 1961.

Logan, Rayford W. *The Diplomatic Relations of the United States and Haiti, 1776–1891.* Chapel Hill: University of North Carolina Press, 1941.

Lowenstein, Karl. *Brazil under Vargas.* New York: The Macmillan Company, 1942.

Lowenthal, David, ed. *The West Indies Federation.* New York: Columbia University Press, 1961.

Lower, Arthur M. *Canada: Nation and Neighbor.* Toronto: The Ryerson Press, 1952.

Lower, Arthur R. M., *et al. The North American Assault on the Canadian Forest: A History of the Lumber Trade between Canada and the United States.* Toronto: The Ryerson Press, 1938.

MacCormac, John. *Canada: America's Problem.* New York: The Viking Press, 1940.

Macdonald, N. P. *Hitler over Latin America.* London: Jarrolds, 1940.

MacKay, R. A., and E. B. Rogers. *Canada Looks Abroad.* London: Oxford University Press, 1938.

Mahan, Alfred Thayer. *The Interest of America in Sea Power, Present and Future.* Boston: Little, Brown and Company, 1918.

Malin, James C. *The United States after the World War.* Boston: Ginn and Company, 1930.

Manning, W. R. "The Nootka Sound Controversy," in American Historical Association, *Annual Report, 1904.* Washington, D.C.: Government Printing Office, 1905.

Manross, Lottie M. *United States Policy toward Argentina: A Survey of Past and Present Policy.* Washington, D.C.: Library of Congress Legislative Reference Service (mimeographed), February 26, 1947.

Marett, R. H. K. *An Eye-Witness of Mexico.* New York: The Oxford University Press, 1939.

Marsh, Margaret Alexander. *The Bankers in Bolivia: A Study in American Foreign Investment.* New York: The Vanguard Press, 1928.

Márquez Sterling, M. *Los últimos días del Presidente Madero (Mi gestión diplomático en México).* Habana: Imprenta El Siglo XX, 1917.

Martin, Percy Alvin. *Latin America and the War.* Baltimore: The Johns Hopkins Press, 1925.

Martínez, Ricardo A. *De Bolívar a Dulles. El panamericanismo, Doctrina y Práctica Imperialista.* México: Editorial América Nueva, 1959.

McCain, William D. *The United States and the Republic of Panama.* Durham, North Carolina: The Duke University Press, 1937.

McElroy, Robert. *Grover Cleveland: The Man and Statesman.* 2 vols. New York: Harper and Brothers, 1923.

McGann, Thomas F. *Argentina and the United States, and the Inter-American System, 1880–1914.* Cambridge, Massachusetts: Harvard University Press, 1957.

McInnis, Edgar W. *The Unguarded Frontier: A History of American-Canadian Relations.* New York: Doubleday, Doran and Company, 1942.

Mecham, J. Lloyd. *The United States and Inter-American Security, 1889–1960.* Austin: University of Texas Press, 1961.

Medina Castro, Manuel. *EE. UU. y la independencia de América Latina. La soberanía nacional en la constitución Ecuatoriana.* Guayaquil, Ecuador: Artes Gráficas Senefelder, 1947.

Meikle, Louis S. *Confederation of the British West Indies versus Annexation to the United States of America.* London: S. Low, Marston and Company, 1912.

Mikesell, Raymond F. *United States Economic Policy and International Relations.* New York: McGraw-Hill Book Company, 1952.

Millis, Walter. *The Martial Spirit: A Study of Our War with Spain.* Boston: Houghton Mifflin Company, 1931.

Millspaugh, Arthur C. *Haiti under American Control, 1915–1930.* Boston: Peace Foundation, 1931.

Miner, Dwight Carroll. *The Fight for the Panama Route: The Story of the Spooner Act and the Hay-Herran Treaty.* New York: Columbia University Press, 1940.

Mitchell, Sir Harold. *Europe in the Caribbean: The Policies of Great Britain, France and the Netherlands towards Their West Indian Territories in the Twentieth Century.* Edinburgh and London: W. & R. Chambers, 1963.

Moffett, Samuel E. *The Americanization of Canada.* New York, 1907.

Moon, Parker Thomas. *Imperialism and World Politics.* New York: The Macmillan Company, 1926.

Moore, John Bassett. *Candor and Common Sense* (Address before Association of the Bar of the City of New York, December 4, 1930). N.p., n.d.

Morison, Elting E. *Turmoil and Tradition: A Study of the Life and Times of Henry L. Stimson.* Boston: Houghton Mifflin Company, 1960.

Morison, Samuel Eliot. *History of United States Naval Operations in World War II* (Vol. I: *The Battle of the Atlantic, September 1939–May 1943*). Boston: Little, Brown and Company, 1947.

Mowat, R. B. *The Diplomatic Relations of Great Britain and the United States.* London: Edward Arnold and Company, 1925.

———. *The Life of Lord Pauncefote: First Ambassador to the United States.* Boston: Houghton Mifflin and Company, 1929.

Munro, Dana G. *The Five Republics of Central America.* New York: Oxford University Press, 1918.

————. *Intervention and Dollar Diplomacy in the Caribbean, 1900–1921.* Princeton, New Jersey: Princeton University Press, 1964.

————. *The United States and the Caribbean Area.* Boston: World Peace Foundation, 1934.

Muzzey, David Saville. *James G. Blaine, A Political Idol of Other Days.* New York: Dodd, Mead and Company, 1934.

Myers, William Starr. *The Foreign Policies of Herbert Hoover, 1929–1933.* New York: Charles Scribner's Sons, 1940.

Nearing, Scott, and Joseph Freeman. *Dollar Diplomacy: A Study in American Imperialism.* New York: B. W. Huebsch and the Viking Press, 1925.

Nerval, Gastón [pseudonym for Raúl Díez de Medina]. *Autopsy of the Monroe Doctrine: The Strange Story of Inter-American Relations.* New York: The Macmillan Company, 1934.

New Cambridge Modern History. Vols. XI and XII. Cambridge: The Cambridge University Press, 1960–1962.

Nevins, Allan. *Grover Cleveland: A Study in Courage.* New York: Dodd, Mead and Company, 1932.

————. *Hamilton Fish: The Inner History of the Grant Administration.* With an Introduction by John Bassett Moore. New York: Dodd, Mead and Company, 1937.

————. *Henry White: Thirty Years of American Diplomacy.* New York: Harper and Brothers, 1930.

————, and Louis M. Hacker, eds. *The United States and Its Place in World Affairs, 1918–1943.* Boston: D. C. Heath and Company, 1943.

Nicholson, Harold. *Dwight Morrow.* New York: Harcourt, Brace and Company, 1935.

Nogales, Rafael de. *The Looting of Nicaragua.* New York: Robert M. McBride and Company, 1928.

Normano, J. F. *The Struggle for South America: Economy and Ideology.* Introduction by Clarence H. Haring. Boston: Houghton Mifflin Company, 1931.

Norton, Henry Kittredge. *The Coming of South America. El resurgimiento de Sud América.* New York: John Day Company, 1932.

Notter, Harley. *The Origins of the Foreign Policy of Woodrow Wilson.* Baltimore: The Johns Hopkins University Press, 1937.

Offutt, Milton. *The Protection of Citizens Abroad by the Armed Forces of the United States.* Baltimore: The Johns Hopkins University Press, 1928.

Oliveira Lima, M. de. *La evolución histórica de la América Latina. Bosquejo Comparativo.* Translated from Portuguese to Spanish by A. C. Rivas. Madrid: Editorial América, c. 1913.

Osegueda, Raúl. *Operación Centroamericana.* México: Editorial América Nueva, 1958.

Osgood, Robert Endicott. *Ideals and Self-Interest in America's Foreign Relations: The Great Transformation of the Twentieth Century.* Chicago: University of Chicago Press, 1953.

O'Shaughnessy, Edith. *A Diplomat's Wife in Mexico.* New York: Harper and Brothers, 1916.

Palmer, Thomas W., Jr. *Search for a Latin American Policy.* Gainesville: University of Florida Press, 1957.

Pargellis, Stanley. *The Quest for Political Unity in World History.* (Vol. III of *Annual Report of the American Historical Association,* 1942). Washington, D.C.: United States Printing Office, 1944.

Parks, Wallace Judson. *United States Administration of Its International Economic Affairs.* Baltimore: The Johns Hopkins University Press, 1951.

Paxson, Frederick L. *The Independence of the South American Republics: A Study in Recognition and Foreign Policy.* Philadelphia: Ferris and Leach, 1916.

Pearson, James Constantine. *The Reciprocal Trade Agreements Program: The Policy of the United States and Its Effectiveness.* Washington, D.C.: The Catholic University of America Press, 1942.

Pendle, George. *Argentina.* London: Royal Institute of International Affairs, 1955.

———. *Uruguay.* London: Oxford University Press, 1957.

Pereya, Carlos. *El mito de Monroe.* Madrid: Editorial América, 1914.

Perkins, Dexter. *Charles Evans Hughes and American Democratic Statesmanship.* Boston: Little, Brown and Company, 1956.

———. *Hands Off: A History of the Monroe Doctrine.* Boston: Little, Brown and Company, 1941.

———. *The Monroe Doctrine, 1823–1826.* Cambridge, Massachusetts: The Harvard University Press, 1927.

———. *The Monroe Doctrine, 1826–1867.* Baltimore: The Johns Hopkins University Press, 1933.

———. *The Monroe Doctrine, 1867–1907.* Baltimore: The Johns Hopkins University Press, 1937.

Peterson, Harold F. *Argentina and the United States, 1810–1960.* New York: State University of New York, 1964.

Phillips, Henry Albert. *Brazil, Bulwark of Inter-American Relations.* New York: Hastings House, 1945.

Pierson, W. W., in *The South in World Affairs,* VIII, No. 10 (December, 1945). Chapel Hill, North Carolina.

Pike, Frederick B. *Chile and the United States, 1880–1962: The Emergence of Chile's Social Crisis and the Challenge to United States Diplomacy.* Notre Dame, Indiana: University of Notre Dame Press, 1963.

Plaza, Galo. *Problems of Democracy in Latin America.* Chapel Hill: University of North Carolina Press, 1955.

Pletcher, David M. *Rails, Mines, and Progress: Seven American Promoters in Mexico.* Ithaca, New York: Cornell University Press, 1958.

Plumptre, Wynne. "Commonwealth or United States, Which . . .?" in *Life with Uncle Sam* (reprint of articles in *Saturday Night*), p. 11.

Poole, Bernard. *The Caribbean Commission: Background of Cooperation in the West Indies.* Columbia: University of South Carolina Press, 1951.

Portell Vilá, Herminio. *Historia de Cuba en sus relaciones con los Estados Unidos y España.* 3 vols. Havana: Jesús Montero, 1938–1939.

Pratt, Julius W. *Cordell Hull, 1933–1944.* (Vols. XII and XIII of Robert H. Ferrell, ed., *The American Secretaries of State and Their Diplomacy*). New York: Cooper Square Publishers, 1964.

———. *Expansionists of 1898: The Acquisition of Hawaii and the Spanish Islands.* Baltimore: The Johns Hopkins Press, 1936.

Pringle, Henry F. *The Life and Times of William Howard Taft.* 2 vols. New York: Farrar and Rinehart, 1939.

———. *Theodore Roosevelt: A Biography.* New York: Harcourt, Brace and Company, 1931.

Proudfoot, Mary. *Britain and the United States in the Caribbean.* New York: Praeger and Company, 1953.

Puleston, Captain W. D. *Mahan: The Life and Work of Captain Alfred Thayer Mahan, U.S.N.* New Haven, Connecticut: Yale University Press, 1939.

Pusey, Merlo J. *Charles Evans Hughes.* 2 vols. New York: The Macmillan Company, 1951.

Range, Willard. *Franklin D. Roosevelt's World Order.* Athens: The University of Georgia Press, 1959.

Rennie, Ysabel F. *The Argentine Republic.* New York: The Macmillan Company, 1945.

Reynolds, T. H., trans. and ed. *The Progress of Pan-Americanism: A Historical Survey of Latin-American Opinion.* Washington, D.C.: Public Affairs Press, 1942.

Richler, Mordecai. "Quebec Oui, Ottawa, Non!," *Encounter* (London), XXIII. No. 6 (December, 1964), 79.

Rippy, J. Fred. *The Capitalists and Colombia.* New York: The Vanguard Press, 1931.

———. *The Caribbean Danger Zone.* New York: G. P. Putnam's Sons, 1940.

———. *Latin America in World Politics: An Outline Survey.* New York: Alfred A. Knopf, 1928.

————. *The United States and Mexico.* New York: F. S. Crofts, 1931.

Robertson, William Spence. *Hispanic American Relations with the United States.* New York: Oxford University Press, 1923.

Robinson, Edgar Eugene, and Victor J. West. *The Foreign Policy of Woodrow Wilson.* New York: The Macmillan Company, 1918.

Rodó, José Enrique. *Ariel.* Boston: Houghton Mifflin and Company, 1922 (?) ; Montevideo, 1935.

Rodríguez, Mario. *A Palmerstonian Diplomat in Central America, Frederick Chatfield, Esq.* Tucson: University of Arizona Press, 1964.

Rojas, Luis Manuel. *La culpa de Henry Lane Wilson en el gran de sastre de Méjico.* México: Companía editorial La Verdad, 1928.

Romero Jones, Concha. *The Pan-American Union in the Field of Inter-American Cultural Relations* (mimeographed memorandum of chief of Division of Intellectual Cooperation, Pan-American Union, Washington, 1938).

Ronning, C. Neale. *Law and Politics in Inter-American Diplomacy.* New York: John Wiley and Sons, 1963.

Roussin, Marcel. *Le Canada et le système interaméricain.* Ottawa: University of Ottawa, 1959.

Royal Institute of International Affairs. *The Republics of South America: A Political, Economic and Cultural Survey.* London: Royal Institute of International Affairs, 1937.

Rubens, Horatio S. *Liberty: The Story of Cuba.* New York: Harcourt, Brace and Company, 1932.

Ruíz Guiñazú, Enrique. *La Política Argentina y el futuro de América.* Buenos Aires: Librería Huemul, 1944.

Salmon, C. S. *The Caribbean Confederation . . . A Plan for the Union of the Fifteen British West Indies Colonies . . . A Refutation of the Chief Statements made by Mr. Froude in . . . "The English in the West Indies."* New York and London: Cassel and Company [1888].

Sands, William Franklin. *Our Jungle Diplomacy.* Chapel Hill: University of North Carolina Press, 1944.

Sanso, Aro [pseudonym for Mjia Deras Ismael]. *Policarpo Bonilla: Algunos a puntes biográficos.* México: Imprenta Mundial. 1936.

Sayán Vidaurri, Alberto. *Por la cooperación interamericana.* Buenos Aires, 1936.

Schoenrich, Otto. *Santo Domingo: A Country with a Future.* New York: The Macmillan Company, 1918.

Scott, F. R. *Canada and the United States.* Boston: World Peace Foundation, 1940.

Senior, Clarence. *Land Reform and Democracy.* Gainesville: The University of Florida Press, 1958.

Seymour, Charles. *American Diplomacy During the War*. Baltimore: The Johns Hopkins University Press, 1934.

Shaw, Albert. *International Bearings of American Policy*. Baltimore: The Johns Hopkins University Press, 1943.

Sherwood, Robert E. *Roosevelt and Hopkins: An Intimate History*. New York: Harper and Brothers, 1948.

Shotwell, James T. *At the Paris Peace Conference*. New York: The Macmillan Company, 1937.

Sibelleau, Pierre. *Le Canada et la Doctrine de Monroe. Étude historique sur l'influence de l'imperialisme américain dans l'évolution de l'Empire Britannique*. Paris: Recueil Sirey, 1937.

Siegfried, André. *Canada*. H. H. and Doris Hemming, trans. London: J. Cape, 1937.

Smith, Arthur D. Howden. *Mr. House of Texas*. New York: Funk and Wagnalls Company, 1940.

Smith, O. Edmund. *Yankee Diplomacy: U.S. Intervention in Argentina*. Dallas, Texas: Southern Methodist University Press, 1953.

Smith, Robert F. *The United States and Cuba: Business and Diplomacy, 1917–1960*. New York: Bookman Associates, 1960.

Soward, F. H. *Canada and the Americas*. Toronto: University of Toronto Press, 1937.

————, et al. *Canada in World Affairs: The Pre-War Years*. New York: Council for Inter-American Cooperation; National Foreign Trade Council, 1945.

Speigel, Henry William. *The Brazilian Economy; Chronic Inflation and Sporadic Industrialization*. Philadelphia: Blakiston Company, 1949.

Spender, J. A. *Weetman Pearson, First Viscount Cowdray, 1856–1927*. London: Cassell and Company, 1930.

Spykman, Nicholas John. *America's Strategy in World Politics: The United States and the Balance of Power*. New York: Harcourt, Brace and Company, 1942.

Stern, Siegfried. *The United States in International Banking*. New York: Columbia University Press, 1951.

Stettinius, Edward R., Jr. *Lend-Lease: Weapon for Victory*. New York: The The Macmillan Company, 1944.

Stettinius, Edward R. *Roosevelt and the Russians: The Yalta Conference*. Walter Johnson, ed. Garden City, New York: Doubleday and Company, 1949.

Stevens, Guy. *Current Controversies with Mexico: Addresses and Writings*. N.p., n.d.

Stimson, Henry L., and McGeorge Bundy. *On Active Service in Peace and War*. New York: Harper and Brothers, 1948.

Stolberg-Wernigerode, Count Otto zu. *Germany and the United States during the Era of Bismarck.* Reading, Pennsylvania: The Henry Janssen Foundation [?1937].

Stovall, John A. *Canada in the World Economy.* Cambridge, Massachusetts: Harvard University Press, 1959.

Stuart, G. H. *Cuba and Its International Relations.* New York: Institute of International Relations, 1923.

Stuart, Graham H. *Latin America and the United States.* New York: D. Appleton Century Company, 1938.

Stuntz, A. Edward. *To Make the People Strong.* New York: The Macmillan Company, 1948.

Taft, William H. *The United States and Peace.* New York: Charles Scribner's Sons, 1914.

Tannenbaum, Frank. *The Mexican Agrarian Revolution.* New York: The Macmillan Company, 1929.

Tansill, Charles Callan. *Canadian-American Relations, 1875–1911.* New Haven, Connecticut: Yale University Press, 1943.

———. *The Foreign Policy of Thomas F. Bayard, 1885–1897.* New York: Fordham University Press, 1940.

———. *The Purchase of the Danish West Indies.* Baltimore: The Johns Hopkins University Press, 1932.

Temperly, H. W. V. *The Foreign Policy of Canning.* London: G. Bell and Sons, 1925.

Temperly, Harold, and Lillian Penson. *Foundations of British Foreign Policy from Pitt (1792) to Salisbury (1902).* . . . Cambridge: Cambridge University Press, 1938.

Thayer, William Roscoe. *The Life and Letters of John Hay.* 2 vols. Boston: Houghton Mifflin Company, 1915.

Thomas, D. Y. *One Hundred Years of the Monroe Doctrine.* New York: The Macmillan Company, 1927.

Thomas, Lowell. *Old Gimlet Eye: The Adventures of Smedley Butler. As told to Lowell Thomas.* New York: Farrar and Rinehart, 1933.

Thompson, Charles A., and Walter H. C. Laves. *Cultural Relations and United States Foreign Policy.* Bloomington: Indiana University Press, 1963.

Tischendorf, Alfred. *Great Britain and Mexico in the Era of Porfirio Díaz.* Durham, North Carolina: Duke University Press, 1961.

Tosca, Henry J. *The Reciprocal Trade Policy of the United States: A Study in Trade and Philosophy.* Philadelphia: University of Pennsylvania Press, 1938.

Tuchman, Barbara W. *The Zimmermann Telegram.* New York: The Viking Press, 1958.

Tumulty, Joseph P. *Woodrow Wilson as I Know Him.* Garden City, New York: The Garden City Publishing Company, 1921.

Tyler, Alice Felt. *The Foreign Policy of James G. Blaine.* Minneapolis: University of Minnesota Press, 1927.

Ugarte, Manuel. *El destino de un continente.* Madrid: Editorial Mundo Latino, 1923.

———. *The Destiny of a Continent.* Introduction and Bibliography by J. Fred Rippy. New York: Alfred A. Knopf, 1925.

Uribe, Antonio José. *Colombia y los Estados Unidos de América.* Bogotá, Colombia: Imprenta Nacional, 1926.

Usher, Roland G. *The Challenge of the Future: A Study in American Foreign Policy.* Boston: Houghton Mifflin Company, 1916.

Vagts, Alfred. *Deutschland und die Vereinigten Staaten in der Weltpolitik.* 2 vols. New York: The Macmillan Company, 1935.

Van Alstyne, Richard W. *American Crisis Diplomacy: The Quest for Collective Security, 1918–1952.* Stanford, California: Stanford University Press, 1952.

Vasconcelos, José. *Bolivarismo y Monroismo. Temas Iberamericanos.* Santiago de Chile: Editorial Ercilla, 1937.

———. *Ulises Criollo. La vida del autor escrita por él mismo.* México: Editorial Jus, 1958.

———. *La Tormenta: Segunda parte de Ulises Criollo.* México: Ediciones Botas, 1948.

Verissimo, Erico. *Un gato presa en la nieve.* Buenos Aires and Porto Alegre, Argentina: Livraria do Globo, 1942 and 1947.

Viallate, Achille. *Economic Imperialism and International Relations During the Last Fifty Years.* New York: The Macmillan Company, 1923.

Weinberg, Albert K. *Manifest Destiny: A Study of Nationalist Expansionism in American History.* Baltimore: The Johns Hopkins Press, 1935.

Welles, Sumner. *Naboth's Vineyard: The Dominican Republic, 1844–1924.* 2 vols. New York: Payson and Clarke, Ltd., 1928.

———. *Seven Decisions that Shaped History.* New York: Harper and Brothers, 1950.

———. *The Time for Decision.* New York: Harper and Brothers, 1944.

———. *Where Are We Heading?* New York: Harper and Brothers, 1946.

———. *The World of the Four Freedoms.* New York: Columbia University Press, 1943.

Wertenbaker, Charles. *A New Doctrine for the Americas.* New York: The Viking Press, 1941.

Whitaker, Arthur P. *Argentine Upheaval.* New York: Frederick A. Prager, 1956.

———. *The United States and Argentina*. Cambridge, Massachusetts: Harvard University Press, 1954.

———. *The United States and South America: The Northern Republics*. Cambridge, Massachusetts: Harvard University Press, 1948.

———. *The Western Hemisphere Idea: Its Rise and Decline*. Ithaca, New York: Cornell University Press, 1954.

White, T. R., and Charlemagne Tower. *Our Duty Concerning the Panama Canal Tolls*. Boston: World Peace Foundation, 1913.

Wilgus, A. Curtis, ed. *Argentina, Brazil and Chile since Independence*. Washington, D.C.: George Washington University Press, 1935.

Wilgus, William J. *The Railway Interrelations of the United States and Canada*. New Haven, Connecticut: Yale University Press, 1937.

Williams, Benjamin H. *American Diplomacy: Politics and Practice*. New York: McGraw-Hill Book Company, 1936.

———. *Economic Foreign Policy of the United States*. New York: McGraw-Hill Book Company, 1929.

Williams, Charles Richard. *The Life of Rutherford Birchard Hayes, Nineteenth President of the United States*. 2 vols. Boston: Houghton Mifflin Company, 1914.

Williams, Mary W. *Anglo-American Isthmian Diplomacy, 1815–1915*. Gloucester, Massachusetts: P. Smith, 1965.

Williams, William Appleman. *The Tragedy of American Diplomacy*. Cleveland and New York: World Publishing Company, 1959.

Wiltz, John E. *In Search of Peace: The Senate Munitions Inquiry, 1934–1936*. Baton Rouge: Louisiana State University Press, 1963.

Winkler, Max. *Investments of United States Capital in Latin America*. Boston: World Peace Foundation, 1929.

Wood, Bryce. *The Making of the Good Neighbor Policy*. New York: Columbia University Press, 1961.

———. *The United States and Latin American Wars, 1932–1942*. New York: Columbia University Press, 1966.

Wright, Theodore Paul. *American Support of Free Elections Abroad*. Washington, D.C.: Public Affairs Press, 1964.

Wriston, Henry Merritt. *Executive Agents in American Foreign Relations*. Baltimore: The Johns Hopkins University Press, 1929.

Ybarra, T. R. *America Faces South*. New York: Dodd, Mead and Company, 1940.

Young, Desmond. *Member for Mexico: A Biography of Weetman Pearson*. .... London: Cassell, 1966.

Zook, David H., Jr. *The Conduct of the Chaco War*. New York: Bookman Associates, 1960.

Index

ABC alliance: 140–141

Acre dispute: 100–101

Adams-Onís Treaty: 5–6, 15

Adee, Alvey A., Assistant Secretary of State: 9

Agassiz, Louis F., United States scientist: 29

Aguirre Cerda, Pedro, President of Chile: 353

airlines, Axis: in Latin America, 353, 410–411

Alabama claims: 24

Alaska: concern in Canada over purchase of, 24; boundary dispute, 81–83; and Clayton-Bulwer Treaty, 82; defense needs of, 388; and Alcan Highway and Canol pipeline, 402, 402 n. 4

Alessandri, Arturo, President of Chile: 227, 315

Allen brothers (Ethan, Ira, and Levi): interest of, in Canada, 10

Alliance for Progress: 438 n. 71

Alsop claim: 145–146

Alverstone, Lord Chief Justice of Great Britain: on Alaska boundary tribunal, 82

"America": name adopted officially, 90–91

American Club in Mexico City: opinion of, of Wilson and F. D. Roosevelt, 335

Anderson, Richard C., diplomat: 19

Anglo-American Caribbean Commission: 410, 410 n. 38, 442–443

anti-Semitism: 311, 333, 362

Apristas: 235

arbitration: decisions adverse to Hispanic America, 149–150

— by United States officials: Argentine-Paraguay boundary, 58; Argentine-Brazilian boundary, 58; Argentine-Chilean boundary, 58; Costa Rica-Panama boundary, 103, 205; Antarctic islands of Argentina and Chile, 354 n. 59

— of international disputes: accepted in principle, 93; commissions for, 243

— of justiciable disputes: agreed upon, 243

Argentina: first minister sent to, 16; efforts of, to acquire Falkland Islands, 28, 45, 55, 58, 365; poor control of provinces, 32; isolationism of, 43, 272; urges codification of international private law, 48; U.S. relations with, 48, 94–95, 229–230, 361, 379–380, 397 n. 119, 407 n. 23, 414, 435–436, 444; aspires to be spokesman of Latin America, 48, 139, 173, 361; arbitrations of, with Paraguay, Brazil, and Chile, 58; sympathy of, for U.S. policies, 91–92, 135; Root visit to, 94–95; military and naval problems of, 135, 175, 230, 317, 358–359, 397–398, 413–414; German propaganda and contacts in, 137, 172, 347–348, 355–357, 378, 412–413, 415, 435; cost of living in, 138; on Pan-American Pact, 142, 173; and non-ratification of international agreements, 139, 171–172, 316, 412; British relations with, 170, 172, 227, 271, 357, 365, 379; neutrality of, in WWI, 173; and Conference of Neutrals, 173; "Red scare" in, 173–174; decline of Golden Age in, 192–193, 270–271; petroleum production in, 193; Italian relations with, 229, 356; Hoover trip to, 230; and Runciman-Roca Agreement, 271; interest of, in Chaco area, 272, 310; industrial conditions in, 317; U.S. press service in, 318; emotional nationalism in, 344; interest of, in Straits of Magellan and Antarctic, 354 n. 59, 355, 399–400; Castillo as President of, 357; fears Brazil, 358–359; at Eighth (Lima) Inter-American Conference, 361; plans for customs union fail, 380–381; acquires Italian merchant vessels, 397; at 1942 Rio de Janeiro Conference, 404–405; not recipient of Lend-Lease, 407 n. 23, 414;